NAVAL LONG SERVICE MEDALS
1830–1990

NAVAL
LONG SERVICE
MEDALS

1830-1990

Kenneth Douglas-Morris

Contents

Illustrations

Medal Rolls

Foreword

Following the publication of *'Naval Medals 1793–1856,'* two years of further work has been spent on research for the companion volume *'Naval Medals 1856–1902.'* During the course of amassing the data for this second volume, it became evident that it would reach unmanageable proportions if all aspects of Naval Long Service and Good Conduct awards and campaign medals were both to be included. After much deliberation and discussion with medal collectors specialising in Long Service awards, it became clear that it would be sensible to separate these two distinctly different aspects of Naval Medals.

To this end the author has produced this specialist volume, devoted solely to Naval Long Service Medals awarded during the past 160 years (1830–1990). The coverage is extensive, covering not only the history behind the introduction of the Long Service and Good Conduct medal awarded to regular forces, but also the medallic awards available to the Reserve forces. Additionally the work covers long service medals to lesser known, but equally deserving organisations such as Board of Trade Rocket Apparatus Volunteers, The Hong Kong Dockyard Police, and the Royal Naval Auxiliary Service. For the specialist collector a number of hitherto unpublished medal rolls have been included. Additional information covers the official numbering systems as well as the history behind the issue of seaman's parchment certificates.

The author regrets that an unscheduled period of hospitalisation during the latter stages of preparation has resulted in a small delay in publishing. The many good wishes received during my various stays in hospital were greatly appreciated, and did much to provide the encouragement needed during the finalisation stages of this work.

Acknowledgements

The completion of this work owes much to the immense help and encouragement given to me by Lieutenant Commander (SCC) Allan V. Hall R.N.R. I am also indebted to Oliver Stirling-Lee for his welcome assistance in certain sections of this work. Unravelling the history of awards to Rocket Apparatus and Coast Watching personnel was aided by information provided by Laurie Manton, and from even more references provided by Paul Lane, Regional Controller of Clyde Search & Rescue Region.

Most of the source material has come from the archives held within the Public Record Office, Kew – Crown Copyright reserved, published by permission of the Controller of Her Majesty's Stationary Office. I record my gratitude to Spink and Son Ltd for allowing me to use part of my previously published material in *'Numismatic Circulars'* during 1972/1973, and also to Mr John B. Hayward for similar permission to reproduce material from an Article of mine published in *'Hayward's Gazette'* for March 1977.

Further assistance has been provided by Jim Balmer and Chris Buckland on matters pertaining to the production of the book, and my thanks also go to Bob Scarlett for his photographic skills in providing some of the illustrations.

PLATE 1

ANCHOR TYPE LONG SERVICE & GOOD CONDUCT MEDAL

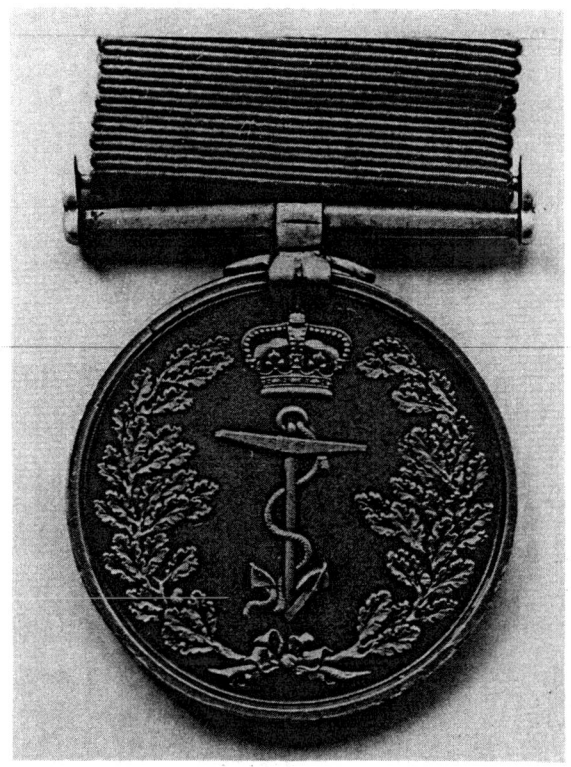

OBVERSE

REVERSE

INVERTED REVERSE ON ANCHOR TYPE LS & GC MEDAL AWARDED TO JOHN CAMELFORD

THE EXCEPTIONALLY RARE REFERENCE TO 'CUTTER' FOUND ON THE REVERSE OF THE ANCHOR TYPE LS & GC MEDAL AWARDED TO EDWARD EMBLING

PLATE 2

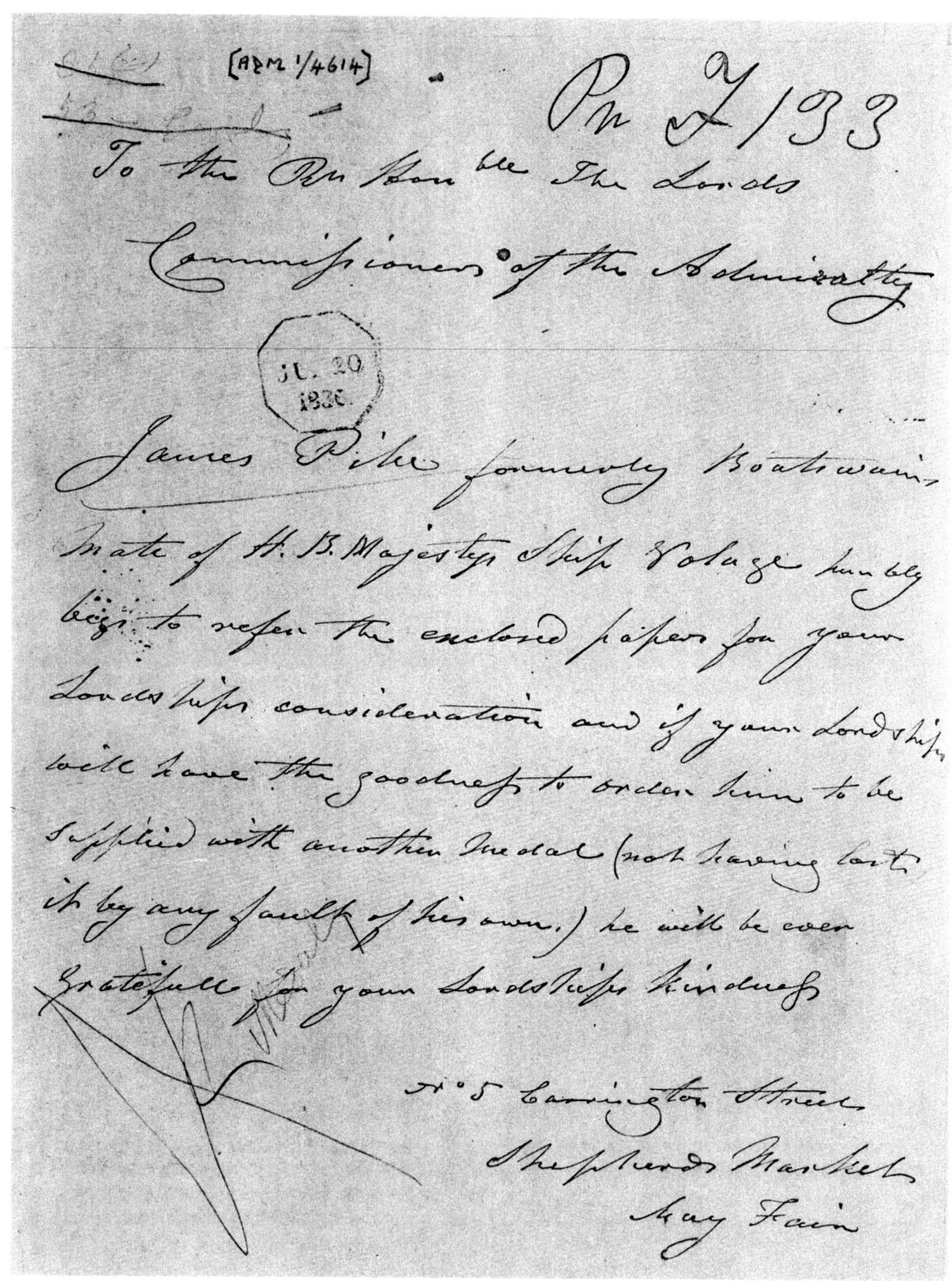

JAMES PIKE'S MISFILED LETTER TO THE ADMIRALTY REQUESTING REPLACEMENT LS & GC MEDAL
FOLLOWING ITS THEFT BY HIS GIRL FRIEND CATHERINE DICKSON

PLATE 3

UNADOPTED PATTERN OF VICTORIAN NAVAL LS & GC MEDAL AND
BOARD OF TRADE WRECK TOKEN

OBVERSE
SHOWING SMALLER QUEEN'S HEAD

REVERSE
WITH SAILING SHIP FACING LEFT

BOARD OF TRADE PROOF OF SERVICE AT
WRECK TOKEN – IDENTICAL SAILING SHIP

THE ENIGMATIC 'M' SYMBOL FOUND ON THE REVERSE OF TYPES C, E & F
(1865–1879) WIDE AND NARROW SUSPENSION LS & GC MEDALS

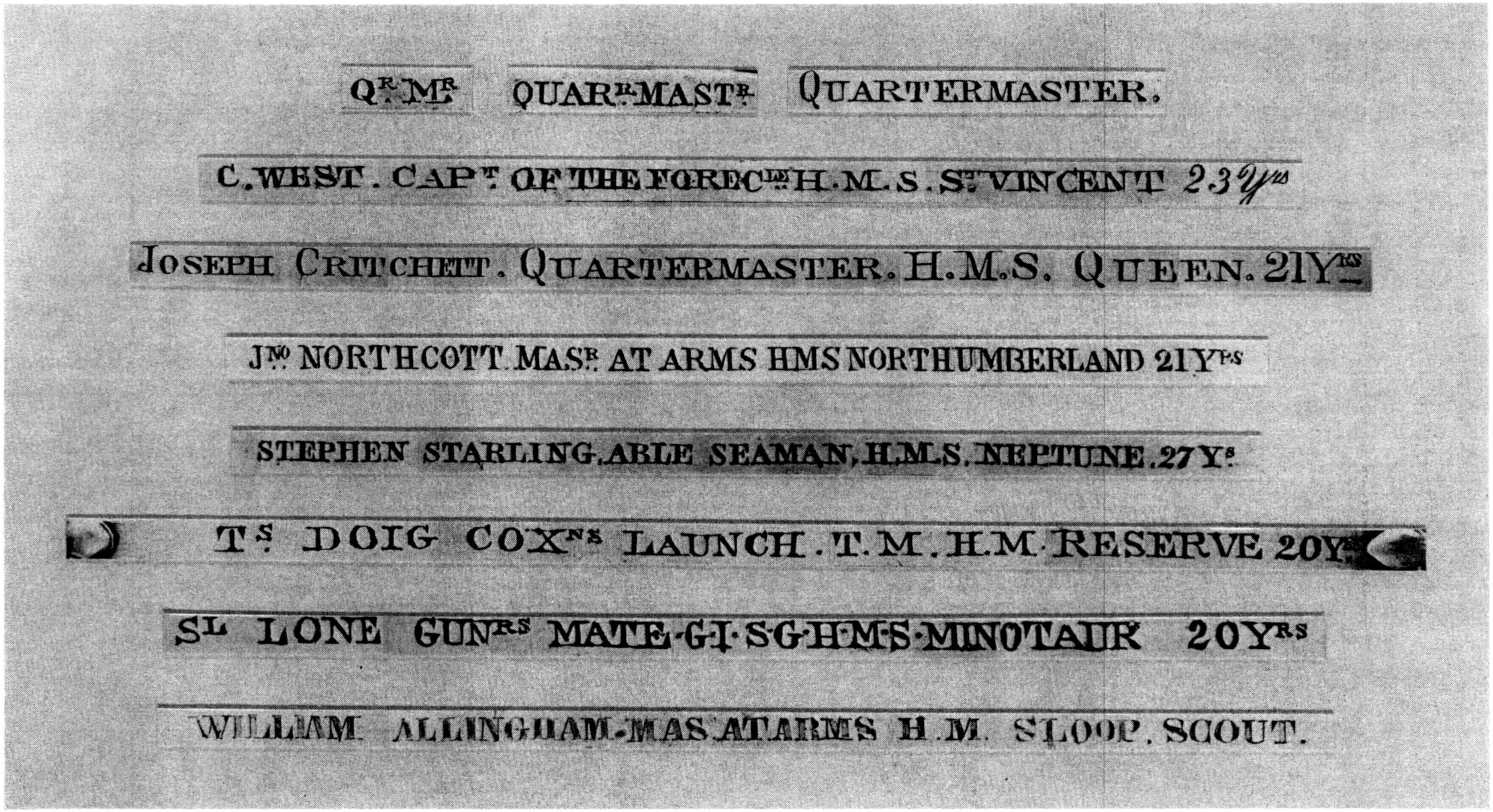

PLATE 4

EXAMPLES OF EDGE DETAILS WITH UPRIGHT AND SLOPING 'YRS' FOUND ON VICTORIAN WIDE SUSPENSION NAVAL LS & GC MEDALS, INCLUSIVE OF TM (TRAINED MAN), SG (SEAMAN GUNNER) AND GI (GUNNERY INSTRUCTOR)

PLATE 5

THE LOCATION AND PROGRESSION OF CRACKING FOUND ON THE
REVERSE DIE OF THE ANCHOR TYPE LS & GC MEDAL LEADING TO ITS
FINAL FAILURE IN 1847

PROOF SPECIMEN APRIL 1831

AWARDED 13 JULY 1841

AWARDED 7 NOVEMBER 1845

AWARDED 20 MAY 1847

PLATE 6

Victorian Wide Suspension LS & GC medal Reverse die varieties

Die Type A(i), B(1848) and A(ii) (1847–1862)

Die Type BB (1862–1864)

PLATE 7

VICTORIAN WIDE SUSPENSION LS & GC MEDAL REVERSE DIE VARIETY

DIE TYPE C (1865–1875)

THE RARE '1848' IN EXERGUE OF OBVERSE

PLATE 8

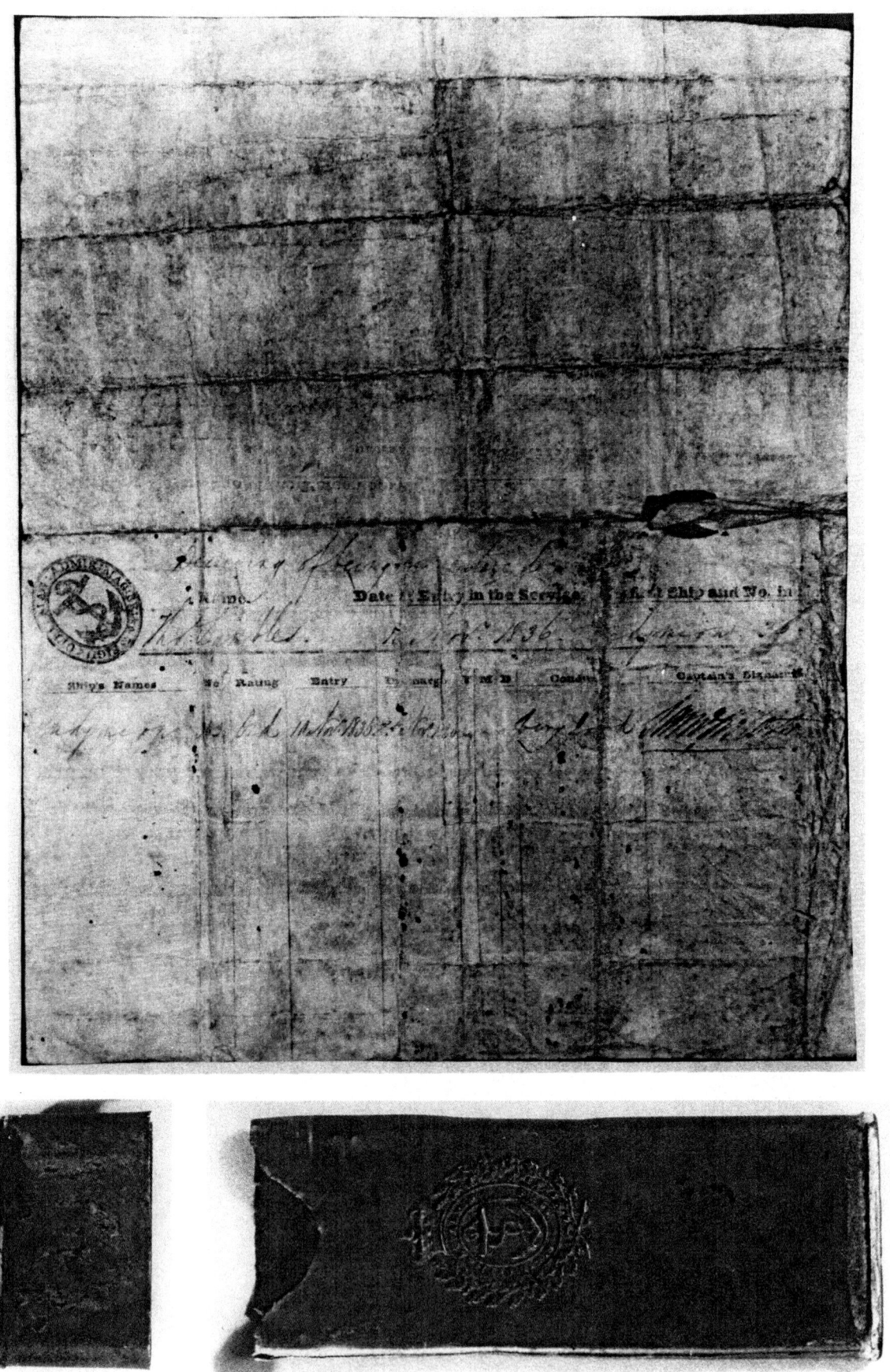

EMBOSSED TIN CARRYING CASE – OFFICIALLY ISSUED WITH 1ST TYPE (MODE A) OF
PARCHMENT SERVICE CERTIFICATE TO A.B. THOMAS SAMBLES

PLATE 9

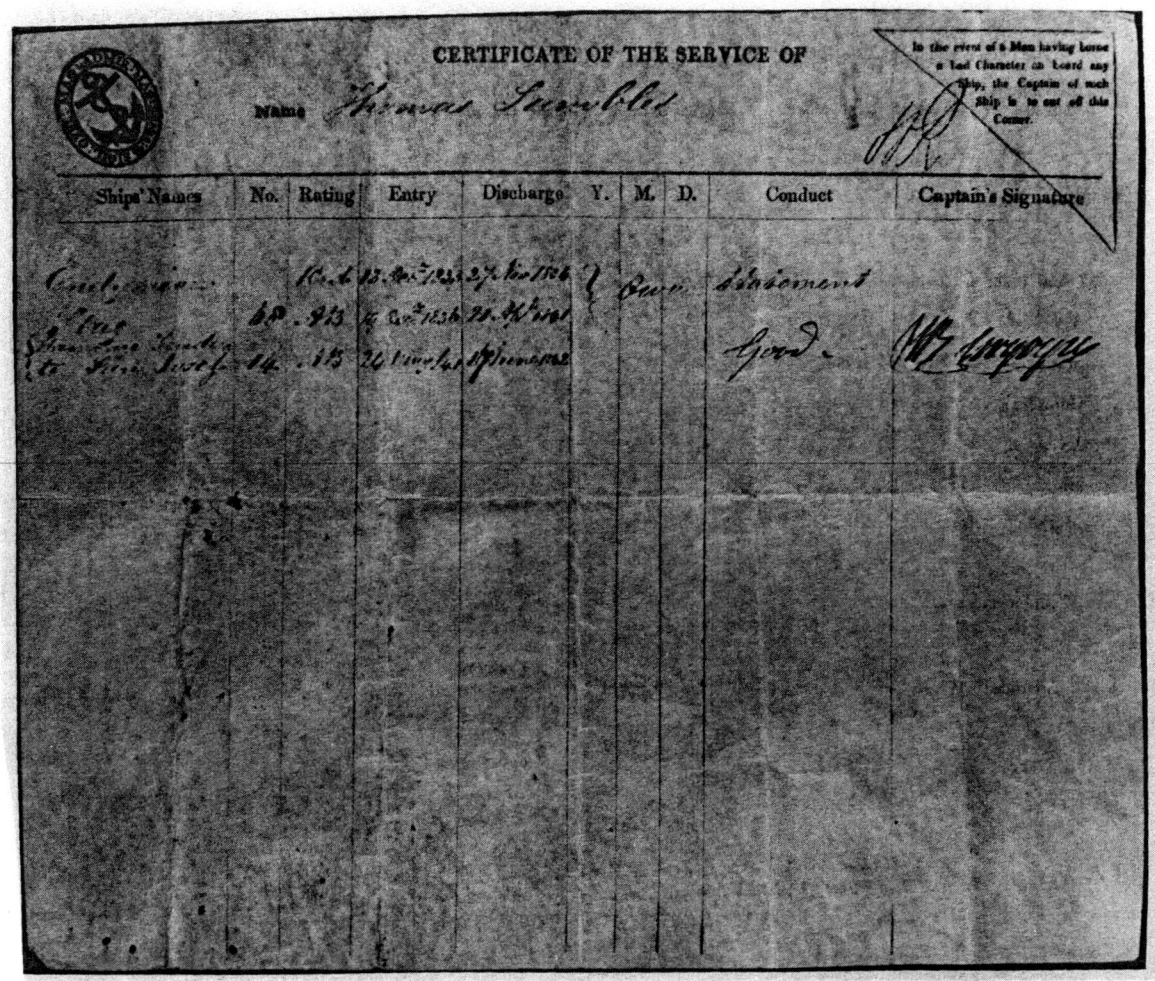

PARCHMENT CERTIFICATES 1ST TYPE (MODE B 1837–1840) TO HOLLAND AND 2ND
TYPE (1840–1848) TO THOMAS SAMBLES

PLATE 10

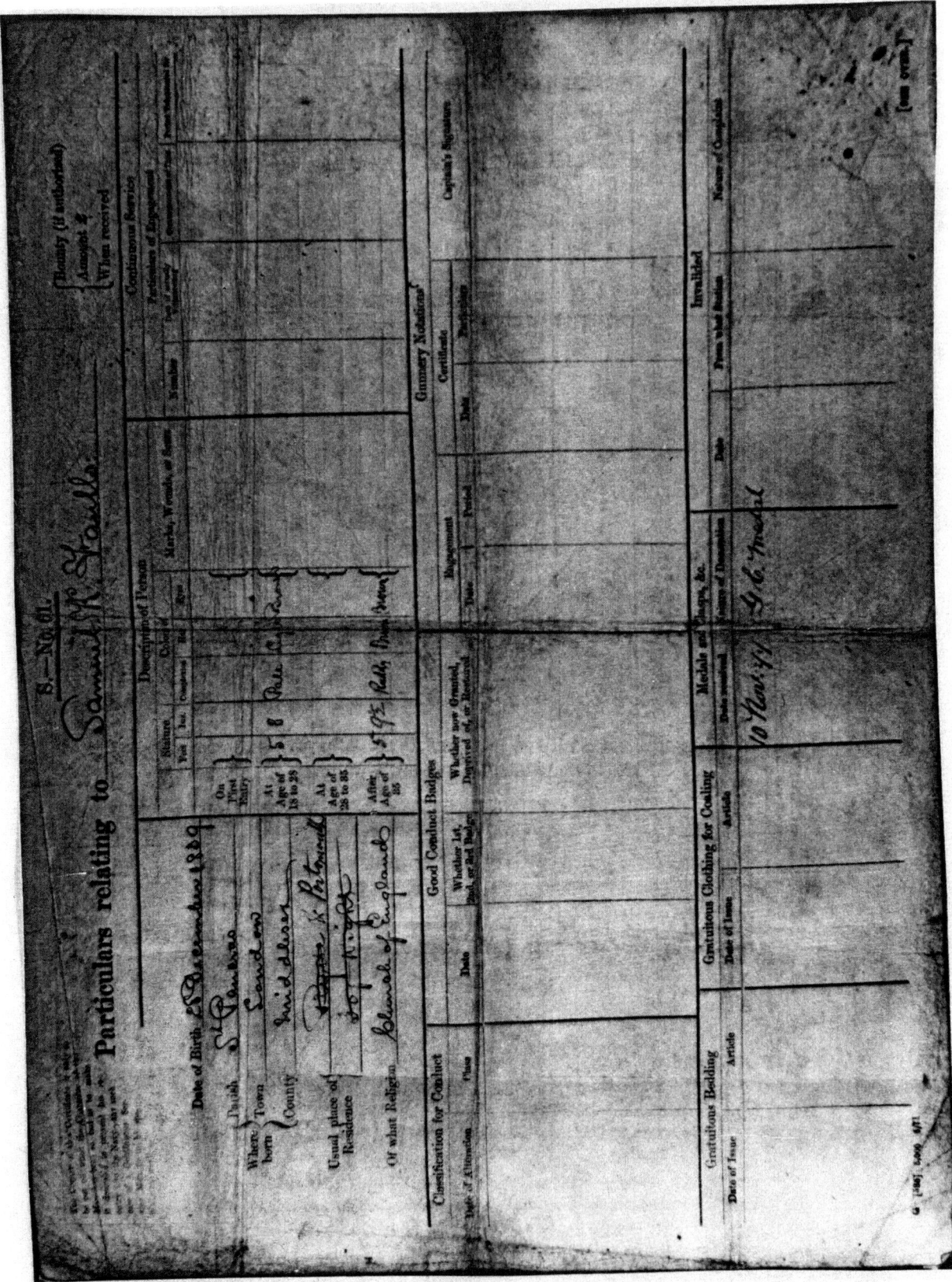

PARCHMENT CERTIFICATE 6TH TYPE (1866–1874) TO SAMUEL RD. FAULLS

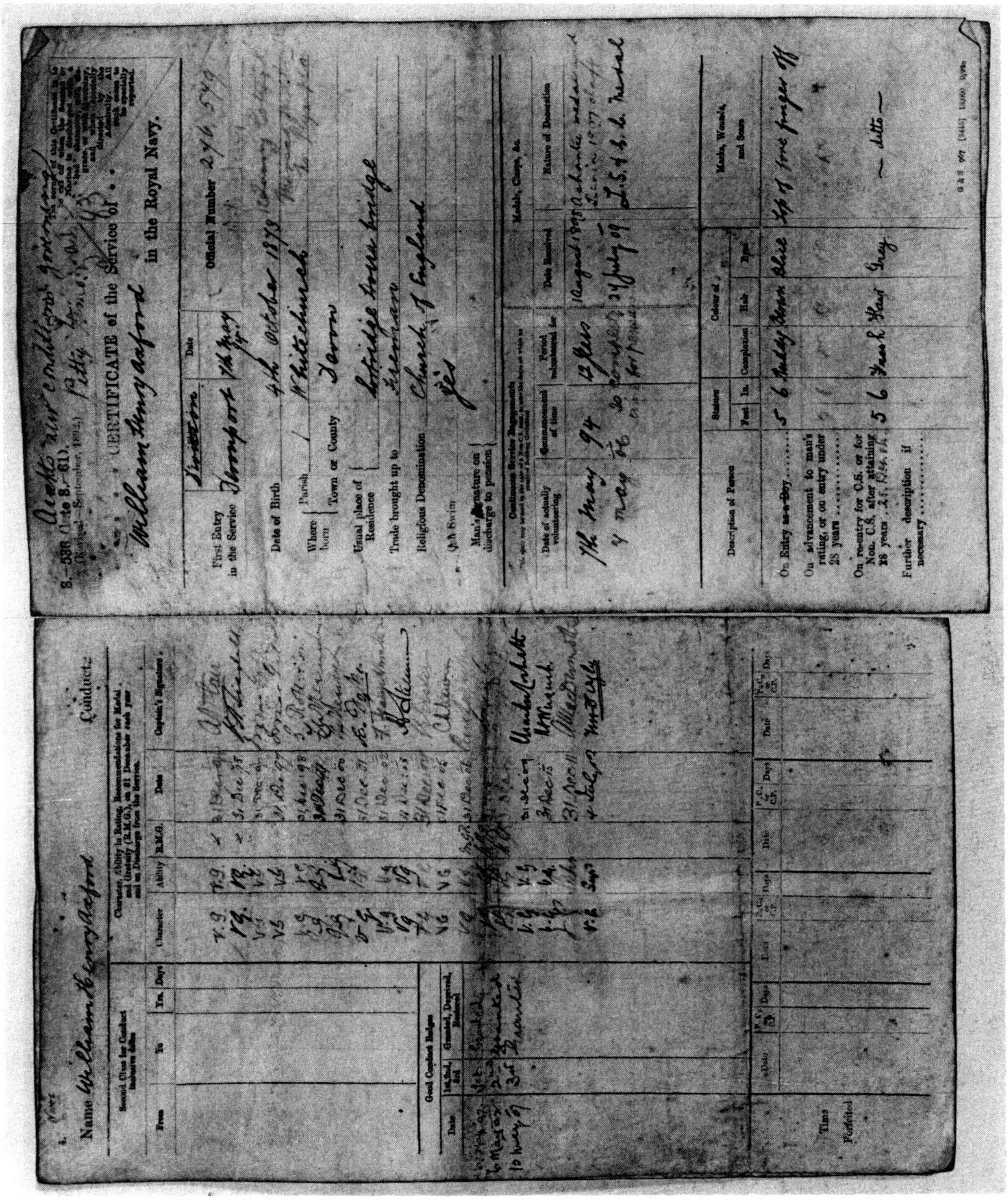

EARLY MODERN 4 PAGE SERVICE CERTIFICATE (1892) TO WILLIAM H. AXFORD. FRONT AND BACK PAGES

PLATE 11

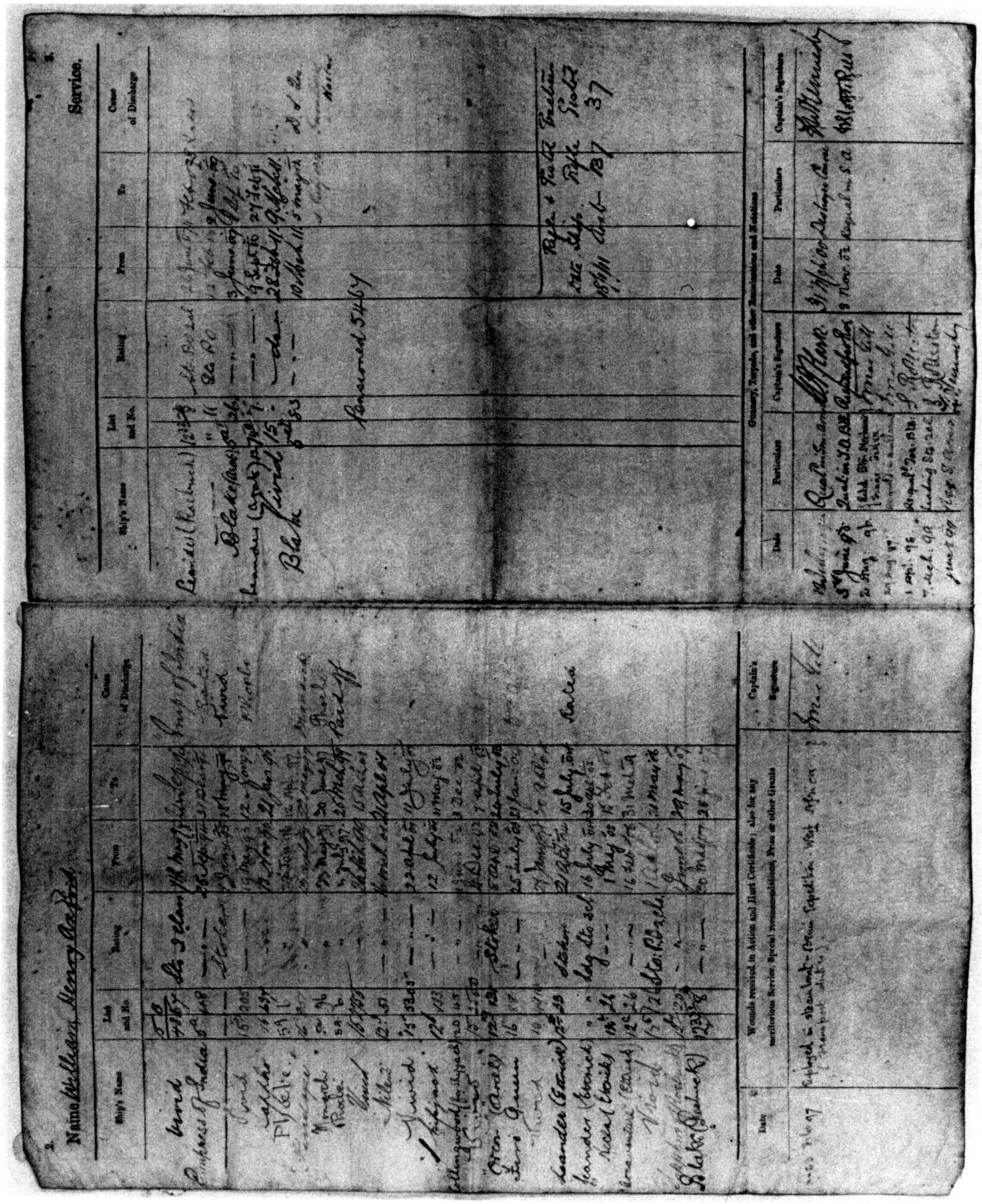

PLATE 12

EARLY MODERN 4 PAGE SERVICE CERTIFICATE (1892) TO WILLIAM H. AXFORD. CENTRE PAGES

PLATE 13

NOTIFICATION

OF

Good Conduct

OF

John Mc Elroy

a *Private* . . . . . of the Royal Marines, to whom the Honorary Medal, and a *Gratuity* of £ *5*, has been presented for " ~~Long Service and Good~~ *Gallant* Conduct," *before the Enemy ;* as a mark of Her Majesty's special approbation.

DESCRIPTION.

Age, *25* Years, *6 Months* — Eyes, *Hazel*.   Hair. *Dark*. *Fresh* Complexion.   Height, *5* Feet, *7* Inches.

PERIOD OF SERVICE.

7 Years, *6* Months, *15* Days.

DATE OF DISCHARGE. *Invalided, for Loss of Left Arm, 31st July, 1855.*

PENSION awarded for LIFE.

£ *18 . 4 . 0* Per annum.

By Command of the Lords Commissioners of the Admiralty.

~~WELLINGTON~~

Pursuant to the Provision of the *75* Section of the Marine Mutiny Act.

PARISH NOTICE ISSUED FOR GALLANT CONDUCT OF PRIVATE JOHN McELROY R.M. WHEN DISCHARGED 31 JULY 1855

PLATE 14

VICTORIAN NARROW SUSPENSION LS & GC MEDALS, TYPES E–J SHOWING DIE VARIATIONS IN MAINMAST HALYARDS, STERN ENSIGN AND PEAK PENNANT

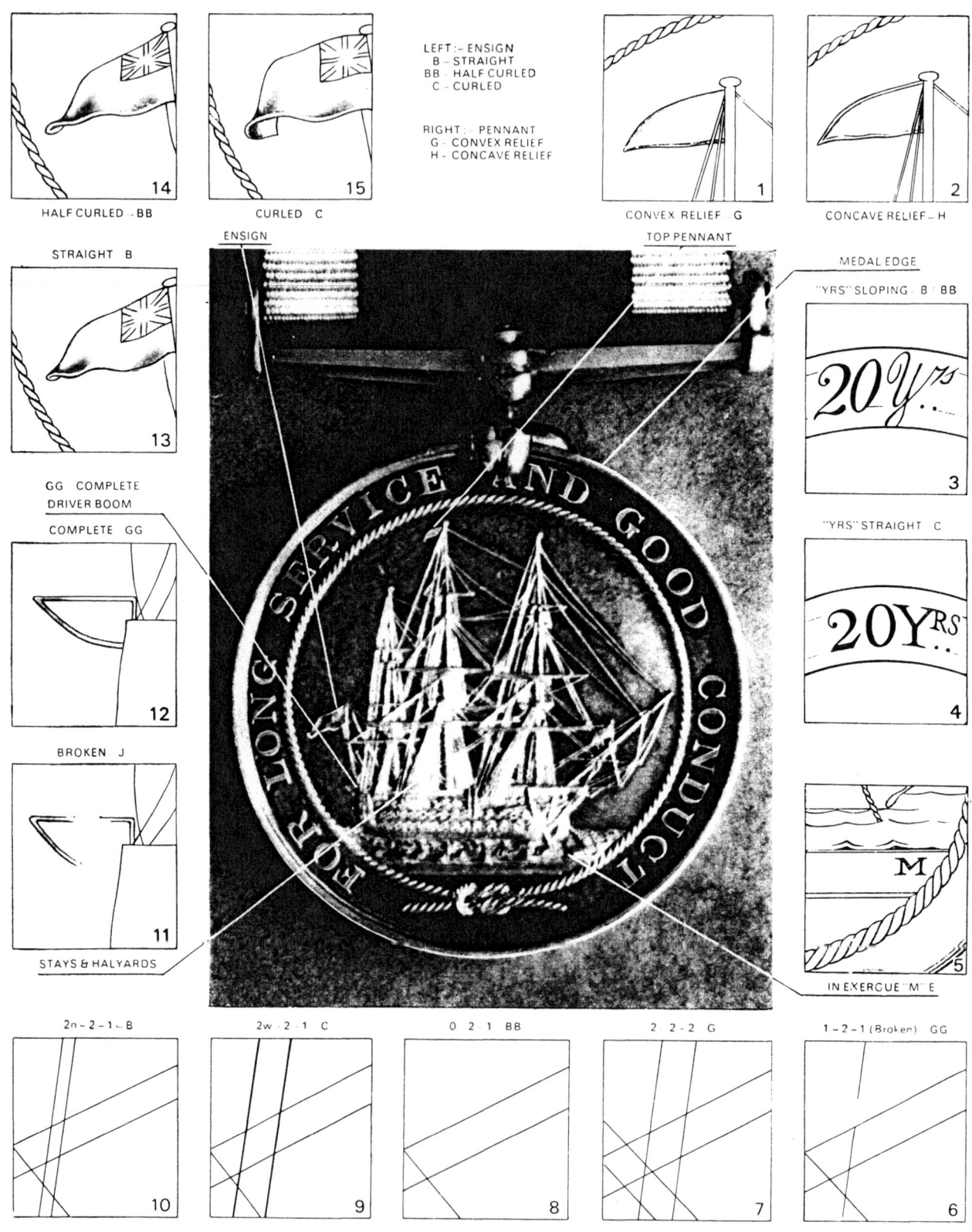

LEFT :– ENSIGN
B – STRAIGHT
BB – HALF CURLED
C – CURLED

RIGHT :– PENNANT
G – CONVEX RELIEF
H – CONCAVE RELIEF

HALF CURLED – BB   14

CURLED   C   15

CONVEX RELIEF – G   1

CONCAVE RELIEF – H   2

STRAIGHT   B   13

ENSIGN

TOP PENNANT

MEDAL EDGE

"YRS" SLOPING – B · BB   3

GG COMPLETE DRIVER BOOM

COMPLETE GG   12

"YRS" STRAIGHT   C   4

BROKEN   J   11

STAYS & HALYARDS

IN EXERGUE "M" E   5

2n – 2 – 1 – B   10

2w – 2 – 1   C   9

0 · 2 · 1   BB   8

2 · 2 · 2   G   7

1 – 2 – 1 (Broken)   GG   6

Reprinted from Spink's Numismatic Circular, April 1971

PLATE 15

ROYAL NAVY & ROYAL MARINE LS AND GC MEDALS, THEIR OBVERSES
AND REVERSES 1830–1990

 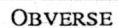 

OBVERSE	REVERSE

ANCHOR TYPE 1830–1847

REVERSE 1847 TO DATE	VICTORIA 1847–1902	EDWARD VII 1902–1911

   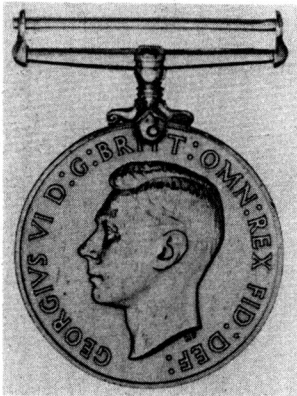

GEORGE V A OF F 1911–1931	GEORGE V COINAGE HEAD 1931–1937	GEORGE VI 1ST ISSUE 1937–1949	GEORGE VI 2ND ISSUE 1949–1952

ELIZABETH II 1ST ISSUE 1952–1953	ELIZABETH II 2ND ISSUE 1953 TO DATE

PLATE 16

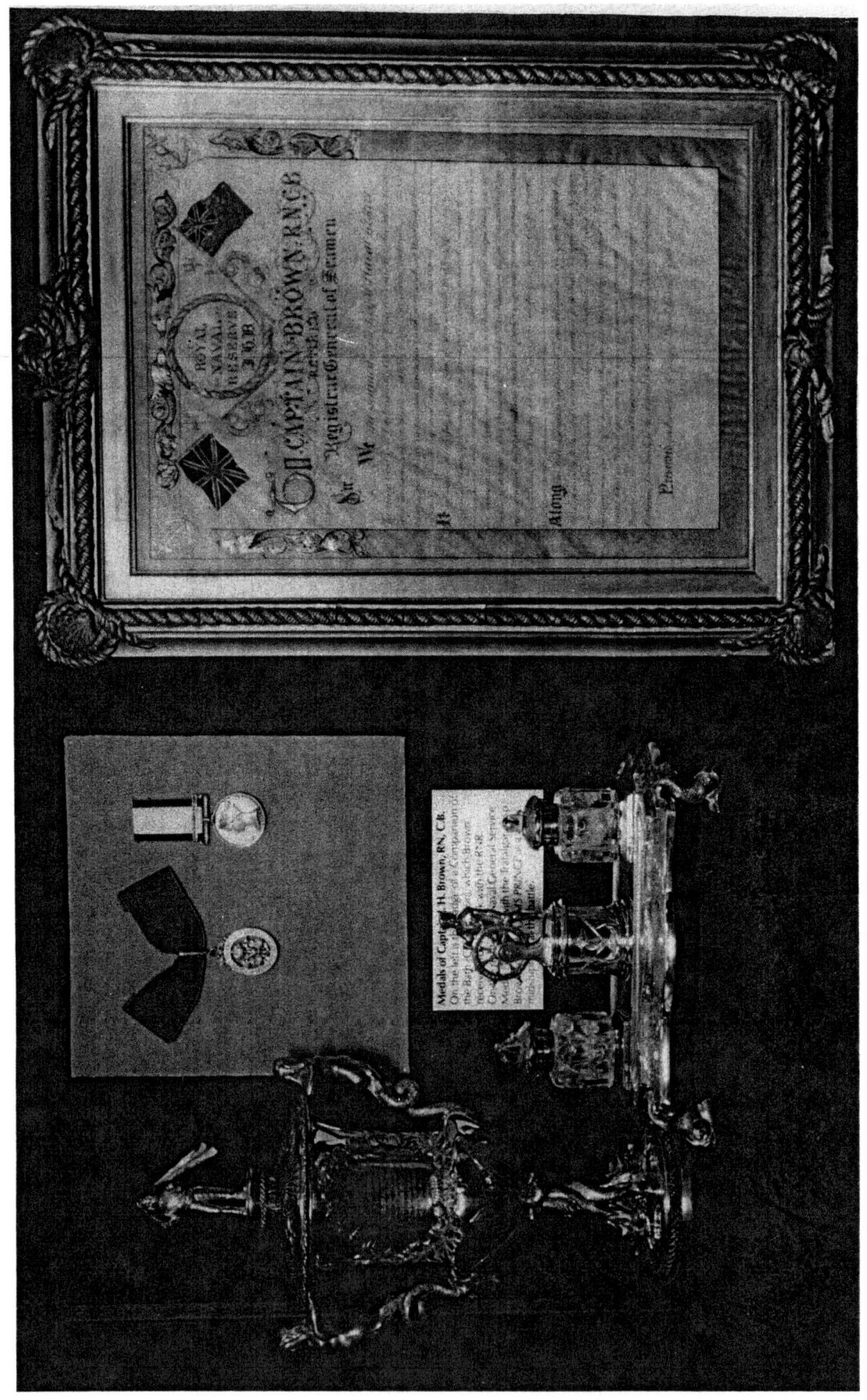

ILLUMINATED SCROLL AND SILVERWARE PRESENTED TO CAPTAIN J. H. BROWN, C.B. ON HIS RETIREMENT (1862) AS REGISTRAR GENERAL AND INSTIGATOR OF ROYAL NAVAL RESERVE

PLATE 17

DESIGN OF 'RESERVES' DECORATIONS AND MEDALS

EDWARD VII   GEORGE V

GEORGE VI   GEORGE VI   ELIZABETH II
1ST ISSUE   2ND ISSUE

REVERSE, RNR, RNVR,   REVERSE RFR   REVERSE RNXS
RNVWR, RNASBR   LS&GC MEDAL   LS&GC MEDAL
LS&GC MEDAL

PLATE 18

ROCKET APPARATUS VOLUNTEER LONG SERVICE MEDALS

ADDITIONAL 10 YEARS
SERVICE BAR

1ST TYPE INSTITUTED 1911

BOARD OF TRADE

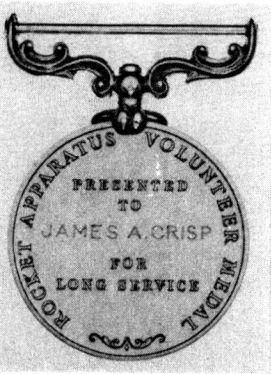

ROCKET APPARATUS
VOLUNTEER

THE COAST LIFE
SAVING CORPS

THE COAST GUARD
AUXILIARY SERVICE

ROYAL NAVAL DOCKYARD
POLICE HONG KONG

Introduction

For its first forty years, the Naval Long Service and Good Conduct Medal could only be earned by seamen and marine 'pensioners'. The early history of events leading to the institution of this visible emblem, as a special additional compliment to a few men already eligible for pecuniary benefit, must therefore be sought from the era when a monetary long service pension – by itself – first became available to all seamen and marines.

The year 1814 can be taken as the year when 'pensions' – as we would colloquially call them today – began. Prior to that year pensions were indeed awarded, but only to persons maimed in action or hurt whilst on service duty, and more relevantly to this story, only awarded after 'long service' to others who had been medically surveyed as 'worn out', and pronounced to be 'unserviceable' servants of the Crown. Thus, men who had kept themselves physically fit for 20, 30 or even 40 years in the Navy were ineligible to receive a pension – unless they were pronounced to be unfit for further service.

In 1814, with the end of the French Revolutionary and Napoleonic Wars ('The Great War') in sight, the British Government began to pay off hundreds of ships and tens of thousands of mainly physically fit men, many of whom had served sufficient time at sea to consider themselves worthy of some sort of annual monetary reward. The murmurings from disgruntled seamen, marines and concordant officers caused the Admiralty to issue a reminder to the Fleet of the law governing such existing awards :

> ' *Admiralty Office. 1st July 1814*. My Lords Commissioners of the Admiralty observing that many seamen, who have been discharged from His Majesty's Ships, from time to time attend at this Office, as Candidates for the Out-Pension of Greenwich Hospital, who, not being "worn out and become decrepit in the Service of their Country" are not entitled thereto; ... with a view to prevent the said Men being put to unnecessary trouble and expense, ... you are to acquaint such Men as may, from time to time, be discharged from the Ship you Command, that they cannot be allowed Pensions, unless they come within the description above mentioned.'

This Memorandum suitably amended, since its principles applied equally to marines, was despatched on 5 July 1814 to the Commandants of all Marine Divisions. It was not well received when read out at various parades in the four Divisional Headquarters, and within a week many copies of a printed 'broadsheet' – expressing dissatisfaction with the unchanged discharge arrangements – were being circulated throughout the R.M. Barracks at Woolwich and Chatham. Their Lordships at the Admiralty were distressed and disturbed by this external encitement of servicemen to question pension regulations and rules, over which the Admiralty stated that they had no power to change. Their swift response was to ask what efforts had been made to discover who the author and distributor of this printed paper might be?

On 15 July the Admiralty were informed that Mr William Pinn – a tailor in Chatham who was a discharged Sergeant of Marines – had avowed himself to be the author of the handbill. Ex-Sergeant Pinn was no ordinary man; literate and possessing a prior history of impeccable patriotic duty – as their Lordships were soon to appreciate. When interrogated by General Winter, Commandant of Chatham Headquarters, Pinn stated that he had no intention of circulating anything to the prejudice of the Service.

He also begged to state that he was the man who wrote an answer to the inflammatory handbill (unfortunately removed from the archives) which had been thrown into the Royal Marine Barracks at Chatham in 1797 – a missive inciting the Army and Marines to revolt in sympathy with the sailor mutineers. He went on to remind the General that not only had he received the thanks of their Lordships of the Admiralty, and the Duke of York, for his prompt and effective response at that earlier troubled time, but subsequently he had also been voted the considerable sum of sixty pounds by the Lloyds Patriotic Fund Committee. The quill pen of this particular marine turned tailor was thus a potential force and had commanded much respect formerly – a regard which might yet again be fulfilled – at this crucial juncture some seventeen years later.

Although no further problems came from the Medway area, the Admiralty were still meeting with clever resistance – elsewhere – to the contentious and imperfect 'worn out' pension restriction. The Port Admirals were informed in early September 1814 of the Admiralty Board members' observations that a great number of men had lately been invalided – adding that no doubt this was due to ships' Captains conceiving that the present political circumstances authorised them to be less strict in the assessment of the degree of physical disability of men than heretofore. The Admirals and Captains were told in blunt terms to see to it that no man was to be invalided who was not a bona-fide case of being unfit for further duty.

Perhaps the shades of the mutinies of 1797 loomed large, with Pinn's handbill touching upon a well founded ground swell for change. But as happens in the aftermath of most major wars, social consciences alter and new pressures and coalitions force a re-think of old and outworn customs. In 1814, there was to be a considerable difference to the former lower deck demands and insurrections at Spithead, The Nore and The Cape of Good Hope. The men of the lower-deck were not now alone in promoting their grievances; the officers of the Fleet, and senior ones at that, were consorting to act more in the breach of these unfair pension regulations rather than abiding loyally to their intended purpose. By deeds the Officers rather obviously displayed an empathy with the 'people's' dissatisfaction after twenty one tempestuous years of war and privations – a powerful sympathetic benevolence which did not apparently go unnoticed in high places.

Within three months this miasma of disaffection had evaporated, simply because the quests were found justified and acted upon by Parliament. The first step was now taken which would ultimately lead – sixteen years later – to the introduction of the first official Medal for long service and good conduct to any group of persons (military, para-military or civilian) providing 'Long Service' to the community at large – the Naval LS & GC award, closely followed by a similar benefit to the Army.

On 26 November 1814 a reforming Act of Parliament was passed entitled 'For the encouragement and Reward of Petty Officers, Seamen and Royal Marines for long and faithful service, and the consolidation of the Chest at Greenwich with the Royal Hospital there.' The first words of the opening paragraph of the text of this Act (55.George III. Cap.I.) effectively amount to the conceptual announcement of awards of LS & GC medals :—

> 'Whereas it is just, that Petty Officers, Seamen, and Marines, should be rewarded for long and faithful service : ...'

For the next sixteen years the benefits for all eligible long serving personnel were to be solely of a monetary nature (the pension) – a rather long gestation period prior to the announcement on 19 July 1830 of the institution of additional distinctions – a gratuity and 'Silver Medal' – which could also be earned by some specially selected 'Pensioners'.

By this (1814) Act of Parliament, the range of men eligible for pensions was specifically extended to include healthy long serving seamen and marines. The Act also provided the Commissioners and Governors of Greenwich Hospital with additional financial means to meet their increased obligations. The various monies in the 'Chatham Chest' were henceforth to be incorporated in the funds of Greenwich Hospital. These accumulations were to be continuously used to pay for all the expenses of 'In Pensioners' and the enlarged numbers of 'Out Pensioners', and provide 'Smart Money' (annuities or gratuities) to seamen and marines wounded or disabled as described on their 'Wounds and Hurts Certificates'. Henceforth the House of Commons ruled that the regulations concerning Naval pensions, by scale and proportion, were to be established from time to time by Orders in Council – unlike the Army, where Royal Warrants were the customary mode of effective alteration to former practices.

These broad principles were translated into more precise rules by an Order in Council dated 14 December 1814, in which the pecuniary awards for wounds, hurts and pensions were detailed. Pensions were to be divided into two classes of men discharged 'not for wounds, hurts, sickness or debility' – i.e. the healthy men formerly ineligible. Those with 14 to 20 years who had 'faithfully served' would be allowed pensions, provided they applied upon a reduction of the Fleet – as was the case obviously at this time. The other more important and ever-lasting 'Class' referred to similarly healthy men with 21 years or more servitude, who were now – at last – to be granted a long service pension. In the Army the rules stipulated a similar period of 21 years for the Infantry, but increasing to 22 years for the Artillery and 24 years for the Cavalry. The fourteen year minimum rule at this time might well have been chosen because of the engagement structure for Royal Marines, divided into three terms of seven years during which the marines progressed from 3rd to 1st Class for each seven year period served irrespective of 'Rank' – a not unhelpful designation when searching for attestation dates of marines in various 'Muster' (ADM 36/– & 37/– series) and 'Description' (ADM 158/– series) books.

This Order also covered a number of minor subsidiary points, such as pensioners being allowed to re-enter and so gain ultimately higher pensions, but there was no mention of an ensuing practice of dis-rating most of the ex-Petty Officers – who decided to serve longer as 'Pensioners' – to 'Able Seamen'. The rules also stated that any time served prior to desertion would not be allowed to count towards a pension for re-entered men – a regulation which was sometimes misinterpreted later to debar all men who had 'Run' placed against their names in muster books – irrespective of the time served after desertion. Article 4 of this Order in Council, whilst stating that the period necessary to gain a pension was to be '... twenty one years service ...' – did not state the age from which this computable 'service' time was allowed to be counted. In practice it was to be eighteen years of age for both seamen and marines. All these three points were to spill over into the period when the Medal and Gratuity were awarded (after 1830), and each facet is commented upon later in the 'Case Law' instances covering these additional rewards.

Of equal importance to 'Pensions', the subject of 'Naval Reservists' is referred to in this same Order in Council. Article 9 stipulated that a Register was to be kept of all healthy naval pensioners, and those not wholly incapable of service whose age did not exceed fifty years. These men were all to be liable to appear within a reasonable time after a Requisition to such effect in prospect, or in time of War at such port or place of assembly appointed. It does not seem that this 'Register' was used for Lord Exmouth's Expedition to Algiers in August 1816 when the shortage of crews caused considerable problems – for no reference to it was made at the time by the Admiralty or any Admiral – if indeed it was ever set up!

Nothing of historic note affecting the introduction of the LS & GC Medal was to occur until the year 1829, except one small – intervening – snippet concerning the ubiquitous ex-Sergeant William Pinn – tailor extraordinary! At the Court in Brighton on 2 January 1817, an Admiralty sponsored Memorial was read before the Prince Regent in Council singularly referring to William Pinn and his activities during the great mutinies in 1797. The Lords Commissioners of the Admiralty added that they were satisfied with his meritorious conduct on that occasion, and recommended him for a much enhanced pension of £30 per annum – obviously accepting that his other 'Handbill' written in 1814, unmentioned in the Memorial, had also been of similar benefit. When this special Order in Council was approved, Pinn was duly informed of '... this mark of Royal Bounty to a meritorious soldier ...'. Few persons of lowly birth can ever have been so regally honoured in those gracious and spacious days, when the 'common man' was kept firmly in his lowly place below the salt!

RULES FOR AWARD OF GRATUITY AND MEDAL FOR LONG SERVICE

By a Royal Warrant dated 14 November 1829, the Army consolidated and revised many rules and orders dealing with conditions of service, pensions, allowances and relief on discharge – formerly approved in ten Royal Warrants dating from 1806 to 1826 – which were now made void. It is the radical content of Article 50 of their new Warrant which sets in motion, by evolutionary process, official rather than regimental – medallic recognition for long service. Since this part of the Warrant is of such importance in historic terms, it is here quoted in full : —

' Article 50. With the view of *rewarding meritorious Soldiers* (*sic.* italics) when discharged, and of encouraging good conduct in others whilst serving, His Majesty has been pleased to direct that a Gratuity in addition to the Pension may in certain cases be given to one Sergeant, or Corporal, and one Private, annually in every Regiment of an Establishment of 700 Rank and File and upwards.

The men to be recommended must have completed 21 years of actual Service in the Infantry, or 24 in the Cavalry; have never been convicted by Court Martial, and must have borne an irreproachable Character, or have particularly distinguished themselves in the Service.

The Sergeants must have served ten years, and the Corporals seven years in their respective Ranks as Non Commissioned Officers, and must have been discharged as such. The Gratuity to the —

Sergeant, shall be .... £ 15
Corporal, shall be .... £ 7
Private, shall be .... £ 5

The names and Services of the Individuals receiving the Gratuity shall be published in Regimental Orders, and sent to the Parishes to which they belong, after the Commander-in-Chief shall have confirmed the Regimental Commanding Officer's recommendation, and after the Commissioners of Chelsea Hospital shall have notified to the Secretary-at-War that the Gratuities have been paid.

In Corps of a lower Establishment than 700 Rank and File, one individual may be recommended every Year for the above-mentioned Gratuity, to be selected by alternate Years; that is to say, one year a Sergeant or Corporal, the next year a Private.'

The perspicacious reader will already have noticed the incorrect use of the words 'Actual Service' in paragraph two of Article 50, which is fortunately contradicted by Article 36 of this same Warrant by establishing that 'No Soldier shall be allowed to reckon his Service under Eighteen Years of Age.' Misunderstandings by future Commanding Officers on the practical differences between these two forms of service – 'Actual' and 'Reckonable' – quite often occurred. Nevertheless, exceptions were sometimes to be made which allowed youthfully entered Drummers (or Boys in the Navy) some degree of advantage over adult enlisted personnel!

For some months the Admiralty deliberated upon the effect of the changes wrought by the Army's Royal Warrant dated 14 November 1829, and by 12 June 1830 had produced a draft Memorial proposing '... alterations necessary to bring the Pensions of Seamen and Marines as similar to those of the Army as circumstances will admit ...'. The latter remark emphasised the constitutional fact that the seamen were still not members of a 'Standing Navy', wherein men might be contracted for certain periods of service dictated by time, be it 5, 7 or 10 years initially with additional periods to complete time to pension – a secure form of enlistment which had been in force for a very long time in the Army and Royal Marines. Seamen (all as volunteers since 1815) were still being intermittently hired merely for the length of a Ship's Commission, usually of three years duration, and then beached (fired!) when that vessel was 'paid off'. A promised 'career' in the Royal Navy as a fighting arm was as yet unachievable. Continuous Service agreements for most 'sailors' (Domestics excluded) became available in 1853, but it was even then not compulsory. Naval personnel were not to become subject to enforceable terms of engagement for all men joining 'the Andrew' until January 1873, and then for the first time the R.N. (Domestics still excepted) became throughout its Lower Deck a 'Standing Navy' – nearly two centuries after the country had witnessed the commencement of a 'Standing Army.'

This Admiralty Memorial (12 June 1830) included not only amendments to various existing Articles in the printed *'Regulations for granting Out-Pensions from Greenwich Hospital to Warrant Officers, Petty Officers, Seamen and Royal Marines'* (dated 1825), but it introduced an additional Article in which the all important 'Silver Medal' was proposed as a decorative emblem to overtly dignify the covert award of the faithful service 'Gratuity'. This Article 12 read : –

' As a further encouragement to good Men to continue in the Service, and to behave with propriety, His Majesty has been pleased to command, that at the expiration of every three years any of His Majesty's Ships shall be in Commission, the Captain or Commander of such Ship may send to the Admiralty the name or names of any Petty Officer or Seaman, or Non-Commissioned Officer or Private of Marines (not exceeding in number one for every hundred of the Crew) who may be on board such Ship, having served *above twenty one years (sic.* italics), who shall have behaved invariably well in such Ship, and be in possession of Certificates of good conduct throughout his former service, and be in the Captain's opinion in every respect deserving to be so rewarded; when the person or persons so reported by the Captain or Commander shall be paid a gratuity, in addition to all other allowances, of Fifteen Pounds if a 1st Class Petty Officer, of Seven Pounds if a 2nd Class Petty Officer, and of Five Pounds if an Able Seaman; but to entitle the First Class Petty Officer to the Fifteen Pounds, he must have served as such Ten years, and to entitle the Second Class Petty Officer to the Seven Pounds, he must have served Seven years as such, otherwise they can only be paid as Able Seamen. And all men receiving the said Gratuity will be afterwards entitled to wear a Silver Medal the size of a half-crown, at the third button-hole of their jackets, having on one side of it the words "For Long Service and Good Conduct", and on the other "An Anchor and Crown".'

Here then is the very first specific mention of a medal – and its design – as a complementary award for long service to men of good behaviour, but not as the primary distinction for such conduct – only as a secondary adjunct to the 'Gratuity' granted for the same purpose. Found also for the first time within this Memorial (Article 4) is a definition of 'service time', whereby men with '... twenty one years service, or any greater length of service reckoning only from the age of eighteen shall receive a pension ...' – and thus also become eligible for the proposed additional distinctions.

The Commander-in-Chief of the Army, General H.Hills, received a copy of this draft Memorial from the Admiralty, on which his comments to the Secretary at War dated 15 June 1830 are well worth repeating in full :

' The Admiralty have generally speaking adopted the principle laid down for the Army, as far as was consistent with the different routine of the two Services, which must more or less defy a strict uniformity of system.

By the concluding paragraph [Article 12] a Seaman or Marine may, by good conduct, be entitled in addition to the Gratuities taken from 50th Article of the Army Regulations, to a Silver Medal after 21 years service, having on one side of it "For Long Service and Good Conduct", and on the other "An Anchor and Crown"

I beg to premise in what I am about to offer, that I am by no means inclined to recommend any extended system of Medals to be distributed to Soldiers whilst serving for individual good conduct. I conceive that Medals ought never to be conferred at the discretion or fancy of a Commanding Officer of a Regiment. They ought in my view of the subject only be issued when conferred for great and important Victories in which the interests of the Nation, the Honour of the Crown and the pride of the soldiers are clearly combined, as in the case of the Waterloo Medal.

When however an Old Soldier has returned to his friends, has been distinguished for good conduct for 21 years, and is in receipt of a liberal pension, it would in my opinion not only be extremely gratifying to him to be able to wear such an honourable testimonial of his character and services, but that it might tend to stimulate Men to steady conduct whilst serving, and when out of the Army inspire other men with respect for the Military Service.

Three men out of 700 could only receive a medal each year, and it should be strictly limited to the men awarded under the 50th Article. These men would in a few years be dispersed over a large part of the Country from which the Army is recruited. Any measure calculated in private life to uphold the Military Service must be useful to the Profession.

The wearers of these medals would be Men selected for irreproachable good conduct, and would prove in their own persons by an ample pension and good character, the benefits which are derived from the Military Profession. Even if it should have no effect, I consider the personal gratification it would afford to the most deserving Men of the Army when retired would be harmless gratification, and I therefore beg leave to propose for Your Lordships consideration – the question having risen out of consultation between the Admiralty and War Office on the Pensioner Regulations – that it may be convenient to confer this medal upon this class of Man in the Army as well as the Navy; …'

In the knowledge that the Army would also introduce a 'Silver Medal', the Admiralty's way was clear for their Memorial (12 June 1830) to be submitted to the Court at St James's, where it was subsequently approved by an Order in Council dated 19 July 1830. For some quite unknown and unusual reason this particular Order in Council was not published at that time, nor since, and thus it has never appeared in the printed Volumes containing all Orders in Council. The Fleet however, were sent copies of the content of this Order in Council, which naturally included all the revised Pension arrangements, and Article 12 instituting the Gratuity and 'Silver Medal' for Long Service and Good Conduct – but the heading of this printed Admiralty Instruction lacked any mention of its authorisation (the Order in Council) or its date of issue.

Eleven days after the Admiralty received assent to their Order in Council, the Army received approval for their Good Conduct Medal by a separate Order in Council dated 30 July 1830 stating:

' Discharged Soldiers receiving a Gratuity for meritorious conduct, shall be entitled to wear a Silver Medal, having on one side of it the words "For Long Service and Good Conduct"; and on the other side in relief the King's Arms, with the name and rank of the soldier, and the year, inscribed on the Medal. The Medal will be transmitted by the Adjutant General to the Officer Commanding the Regiment, who will deliver it to the Soldier on the parade, with the parchment certificate, on which the grant will be recorded, as well as in Regimental Orders, and in the Register of Soldiers' Services. If circumstances should prevent the discharged Soldier from receiving the Medal at the Regiment, it will be delivered to him through the Adjutant-General at the Board of Chelsea Commissioners.'

The first book of reference on this subject, published in 1842, *'History of Medals, Chains, Clasps and Crosses'* written by the distinguished historian Sir N. Harris Nicholas, included the statement that the introduction of the naval LS & GC Medal had been '… Pursuant to an Order in Council of the 24th August 1831 …' – a myth which was slavishly followed by others. In 1871 a prominent collector and student of medals, Surgeon Major J.W. Fleming, produced a book for private circulation in which he repeated this 1831 introductory date for the naval LS & GC medal, a date which also recurred in the erudite works of Tancred (1891) and Mayo (1897). These renowned authors placed a stamp of authenticity on the introductory date until the myth was expelled in 1972 by this researcher. The August 1831 Order in Council dealt with exactly the same pension and medal subjects as the July 1830 Order in

Council, and but for very few words and figures it contained exactly the same content as the original handwritten (but unpublished) Order in Council.

The 1831 edition of the Order in Council received very different treatment as regards dissemination of information. It was publicised in printed form as a Broadsheet, and also appeared continuously for many years in the *'Navy List'* commencing from September 1831. The most cogent reason for acceptance of the second Order in Council (1831), as the inaugural instrument for the LS & GC gratuity and medal, probably lies in the last part of its printed heading which stated – rather emphatically : 'Established by His Majesty's Order in Council of the 24th August 1831'. Whilst the new pension scales and the LS & GC Medal were not instituted by this Order (containing very few minor revisions of the former Order), it is quite understandable why its printed word 'Established' was taken to mean 'Instituted' in the absence of any officially printed version of the similar 1830 Order in Council.

Introduction of the Anchor Type Naval LS & GC Medal

It appears probable that the Fleet were informed of the institution of the new awards for long service in October 1830, and that at the same time (13 October) John Barrow, then Second Secretary to the Admiralty, asked the Chief Engraver at the Royal Mint, William Wyon, to call on him at the Admiralty to discuss designs for the LS & GC medal – concluding with Wyon being commissioned to carry out the work. On 13 November 1830 Barrow told a subordinate :

> ' ... to write to William Wyon of the Mint to say that having submitted to the Lords of the Admiralty his several designs for the medal appointed to be bestowed on Seamen, who by long service and good conduct may merit distinction – [that] – I am commanded to acquaint him they have chosen the designs herewith returned and he is to prepare the dies accordingly observing that there must be room to mount a ring by which the medal is to be suspended at the spot marked X on the designs. The legend round the reverse "FOR LONG SERVICE AND GOOD CONDUCT" commencing at the lower leftt hand side of the medal, and a blank space being left in the centre for the seaman's name and rating.' (*Vide* : Plate No. 1)

It is at this point in time (December 1830) that William Wyon displayed entrepreneural abilities in addition to his undoubted artistic flair. He managed to obtain permission from the Deputy Master of the Mint to strike private medals on the Great Press when not in official use. An arrangement he enlarged to include official medals, commencing with these Anchor Type LS & GC awards, and kept until his death, when aged 58 years, in Brighton on 29 October 1851 – a contract which his son was allowed to continue for a few years. On 25 March 1831 Wyon received an order to strike thirty 'fine silver' (LS & GC) medals, which were delivered to the Admiralty on 5 April 1831 '... from dies executed agreeable to Mr Barrow's order ...'. William Wyon's invoice for the manufacture of the (Anchor Type) dies amounting to £35-10-0 was paid on 12 April. By this time four men had already been granted the 'Gratuity' but its attendant medallic reward could not be despatched to them. Since one of these medals is known to have survived in Otago Museum, New Zealand (to Private Thomas Williams, R.M.), it is assumed that medals were issued retrospectively to all four men.

When the second order was given in early 1832 for the re-supply of these medals (60 in number), the significant request that they should be '... supplied with rings [for suspension] ...' suggests that the individual recipients of the first 30 medals issued had to obtain their own rings privately.

'CASE LAW' AS IT WAS APPLIED TO AWARDS OF THE NAVAL LS & GC MEDAL

Since the Rules for award of the Gratuity and Medal to sailors and marines in Article 12 of the Order in Council were of a somewhat generalised nature, their interpretation in many particular instances led to precedents being set on the opinions expressed by the responsible Naval Board Member. Such individual 'Case Law' rulings led eventually to much more complex Regulations for the award (or denial) of the LS & GC Gratuity and Medal – covering almost all eventualities to be found in Commanding Officers' submissions.

Whilst the point is clarified later, it should be remembered that approval had first to be given for the 'Gratuity' – when '... all men receiving the said Gratuity will be afterwards entitled to wear a Silver Medal the size of a half-crown ...'. Hence the early shortened expression to be found on men's service histories was 'G & M', which was reversed later to 'M & G' in August 1833 when priority was accorded to the 'Medal'.

Since virtually all relevant Port Admirals', Captains', Station and Promiscuous Letters – as well as most of the correspondence concerning Royal Marines – have survived within the archives held at the Public Record Office up to the year 1840, complete with the Admiralty decisions and remarks written thereon, it has been possible from these treasures to build up a history of the 'Case Law' as it was applied to this 'Silver Medal'. In contrast, however, not one letter from a Commanding Officer concerning a ship award has survived the drastic weeding of documents covering events from 1840 onwards. However, correspondence alluding to most shore awards to marines has survived up to 1885 (ADM 56/ & 191/– Series). For seamen after 1840 it then becomes the turn of the Admiralty Digest Books (ADM 12/– Series) to supply their fallow facts on the subject, albeit from only a few of the ships, and then only in shortened prose.

The first man to be recommended for the 'Gratuity and Medal' ('G & M') was a marine, and as a result of this submission the rules for awards to marines were promulgated to all Colonels Commandant of Divisions in this manner :—

' *Admiralty Circular.*   22nd November 1830

Colonel McCleverty, Commanding the Woolwich Division of Royal Marines having recommended a Color Sergeant [John Herring], lately discharged for long service from that Division, for a Gratuity and Medal under the 12th Article of the Regulations established for granting Pensions to seamen and marines of the Fleet.

I am commanded by my Lord's Commissioners of the Admiralty to acquaint you that they have, in the instance in question, granted the Gratuity and Medal. But I am at the same time to observe to you for your information and guidance that the 12th Article of the Navy Regulations referred to, is meant to apply only to the men in ships afloat, and that the gratuities to marines on shore, must be regulated by the 50th Article of the Army Regulations for granting a Gratuity fixed by that Article. A Medal will also be added by their Lordships, – you are therefore to understand that you are at liberty to recommend for this distinction, one non-commissioned officer and one private annually if the average strength of the Division on shore under your command exceeds 700 men, or if below that strength one of each rank in alternate years.

(signed) John Barrow'

The second award of the 'Gratuity & Medal' was a much more complicated affair. Sergeant William Osborne R.M. was highly commended for his conduct during an Action between H.M.S. *PRIMROSE* and a Spanish Slaver *VELOS PASSAGERA* in October 1830. Osborne had single-handedly overpowered a Spaniard hell-bent on setting fire to a magazine, and by such hand-to-hand meritorious activity thus saved '... both vessels from being blown up ...'. Furthermore, Commander Broughton stated that '... he [Osborne] was also instrumental in saving my life by shooting a man who was in the act of firing at me ...', and completed his report (20 December 1830) with the recommendation that Osborne be placed on the list for Colour Sergeant. His Commandant at Plymouth had most recently placed a man on this List, also for Gallantry, and proposed an alternative since vacancies for Colour Sergeants very seldom occurred.

Colonel Abernethie took leave to suggest to their Lordships that the '... Silver Medal without pension ...' might be extended to Sergeant Osborne in this instance of Gallantry, as it might prove beneficial to the service. The Admiralty conceded the principle of an award of the Medal upon completion (in four years time) of 21 years servitude *(sic)* for pension – and that he should be placed on the Colour Sergeant's List.

A precedent was thus set for a man to be guaranteed a 'Silver Medal' ahead of its more timely presentation at pensionable age, when its award was subject to the lottery of a very small quota allowance. In point of fact, Osborne did not receive his Gratuity and Medal until 1839, by which time he had served 26 years and was a Colour Sergeant. (*Vide* : 13 Oct 1831 on Anchor Type LS & GC Roll)

This apparent disregard for the Admiralty ruling that Osborne should receive the award after 21 years service was neither insubordinate nor due to forgetfulness. It had become common practice for awards to marines to be postponed until their final discharge from the service to pension – after 21 or many more years servitude. This less than gracious approach emerges in the response given to the first 'sea' recommendation for a 'G & M' to be awarded to a marine at the end of a ship's commission. Sergeant Thomas Hulme R.M. was recommended for the long service awards when H.M.S. *KENT* was paid off on 6 December 1831, having a total service exceeding twenty one years. His 'G & M' was approved on 30 December 1831 but with the proviso that application for the money and the medal was to await his final discharge. On 27 June 1832 – the day of Hulme's final discharge – his Commandant at Plymouth Division requested both the rewards, of which the medal was duly despatched two days later.

When the submission from the Commanding Officer of H.M.S. *DESPATCH* (4 February 1832) for Private Richard Walker to receive the 'G & M', an exception to former common practice occurred. The decision was taken for Private Walker '... to have the Medal and Gratuity, but the Gratuity was to be withheld until his final discharge from the service – to be observed in all similar circumstances ...'. However, this new rule was not promulgated as a Brigade Order – only the Commandant at Chatham heard of it at this time, and as matters turned out it did not become a precedent, with the former harsh regulation remaining in force until 1833. It was these sort of fickle announcements – thought to be precedents – being communicated to individual Divisions which were to lead to incorrect submissions being made unwittingly by the other Colonels Commandant – leading to their receipt of some rather unjustified rebukes from the Royal Marine Office!

ADULT SERVICE FOR SEAMEN TO COUNT FROM AGE 20 YEARS

By a printed Order in Council dated 24 August 1831 many subtle alterations were made to the (June 1830) 'Out-Pensions' rules, but the 12th Article (for the 'G & M') remained untouched. Of vital importance to the men – and students of the LS & GC medal – was a seemingly small change made to the 3rd Article (formerly Article 4 in the 1830 Order in Council) which was of considerable consequence. The length of time to be served which would count as 'adult reckonable service' for a Pension – and thus the Gratuity and Medal – was in future to be a minimum of twenty one years servitude counting from a man's twentieth birthday. This additional service of two years was to apply to seamen for the next twenty two years, but as will be shown immediately, the marines managed to avoid such distress.

This lengthened service time could have had a profound effect upon marines, since their entrants had always been contracted to serve (as adults) from the age of eighteen, and in effect it meant that all marines would now have to serve two years longer to receive their pension – and then only if they had 'signed on' for total of 23 years! For seamen there was no contractual problem. Their case was entirely different since they were in effect only employed under casual labour terms, as explained earlier in this text. The Royal Marine Office was to prove successful in its efforts to ameliorate their predicament for their serving personnel who had already attested/enlisted for their first seven years, and for others who had already 'signed on' to complete their time towards receipt of a pension. The R.M. modified rules were published in an Admiralty Circular dated 8th October 1831 :—

> ' My Lords Commissioners of the Admiralty are pleased to direct (with reference to the 3rd Article of the Regulations for granting Pensions from Greenwich Hospital) that the limitation of Twenty-one Years Service, reckoning from the age of Twenty, shall be considered

applicable, in the case of the Royal Marines, to such men only as shall have enlisted, instead of to such men as shall be discharged, subsequent to the promulgation of the said Regulations ...'

Thus, commencing from July 1830 and reaching forward to July 1853 there were to be differing 'adult reckonable service time' for pensions as between seamen and marines. Seamen's allowable time to count for pension would henceforth commence at the age of twenty years for 'old tars' and new recruits, whereas marines already enlisted could amass their time from the earlier age of eighteen years. This differential age rule led directly to an intriguing refusal of a 'M & G' in April 1836. A seaman had served 19 years in the Navy, to which he could add two years former service as a Royal Marine commencing from the age of eighteen years – a period which, had he remained in that Corps, he would have been allowed to count as adult reckonable service to pension. The Admiralty looked upon this two years as ineligible 'seaman boy's time'!

By a stroke of good fortune (or was it ?) the Admiralty introduced 'Continuous Service' agreements in 1853, and concurrently lowered the 'reckonable time' to earn a pension from 21 to 20 years, and the Board also reduced the age from which pensionable time could be amassed from 20 to 18 years for R.N. and R.M. personnel. Bold moves which provided cataclysmic beneficial effects.

The scene is now turned back to the earliest awards to seamen of the long service gratuity and consequential Anchor Type medal – to see how they fared.

The first recommendations for sailors were forwarded from H.M.S. *BLONDE* on 6 February 1831 quoting as their authority the '... Regulations established by His Majesty's Order in Council dated the 19th of July 1830 granting a gratuity etc etc ...'. Thus confirming previous remarks concerning the date of institution of the naval LS & GC awards by the 1830 Order in Council, and that its contents had been transmitted to Commanding Officers at sea. Of the three men recommended only one man – Henry Mitchell (Ropemaker) – received the rewards. The other two men were refused for reasons mentioned later in codified form in this monograph – one for his time in the Transport Service and the other who had previously 'Run'.

IMPRESSED MEN WHO RECEIVED LS & GC MEDALS

Quite often in these early submissions from Commanding Officers there are included some lengthy autobiographical 'Memorials' alluding to the service history of the recommended seamen. In one such case (February 1832) when H.M.S. *GALATEA* was 'paid off', Arthur Holding (Captain of the Hold) pointed out that he had been '... impressed and put on board the Tender *ENTERPRIZE* in January 1806 ...', thus proving in this instance that not every 'prest' man was a rogue or vagabond, nor a man dissatisfied with his lot whilst serving 24 years without blemish as a prime seaman in His Britannic Majesty's Navy. In similar vein, James Brown (Ropemaker) of H.M.S. *BELVIDERA*, who received his 'G & M' in December 1833 when aged 63 years, had been impressed into H.M.S. *LION* in the year 1806. Not unnaturally he returned to civil occupation after his discharge in 1813 – only to return voluntarily in 1819 to the harsh, but just regime of the Navy to complete his time for pension. Subsequently he fought at the Battle of Navarino aboard H.M.S. *ALBION*, and lived long enough to receive his Naval War Medal at the advanced age of 78 years in 1849.

Another seaman - 'impressed' into the service in 1805 – proved to be an exception to the general rule regarding 'prest' men. Some thirty three years later – of which he had served twelve years (1815-1826) unreckonable time 'In Ordinary' (Reserve Ships) at Portsmouth – he received the 'G & M' under unusual circumstances. George Stirling (Quarter Master) had been 'paid off' from H.M.S. *MALABAR* in December 1837, still unable to catch the selector's eye for the long service distinctions since he was a few months short of the 21 years servitude to be a pensioner. Still finding the disciplined naval life convivial, the old tar yet again sought another Commission at sea – aboard H.M.Sloop *ROVER* – but in June 1838 he was irrevocably invalided from the Navy because of 'age and rheumatism' prior to her being 'paid off' –

and thus not eligible for a Captain's recommendation for the 'G & M'. Now, as a 'worn out' naval pensioner ashore he solicited the Admiralty on his own behalf for the long service rewards by means of a testimonial describing his naval career, which included gallant service aboard the famous Fire-Ship *MEDIATOR* at the Basque Roads Action in April 1809 – but his name does not appear on the 'Naval War Medal' Roll for this Action.

As an exception to the Regulations, the Admiralty Board Member was moved to state that '... [he] can be granted the Medal & Gratuity if recommended by the late Captain of the *MALABAR*, Sir William A. Montagu ...'. This officer wrote to the Second Naval Lord (Sir Thomas Troubridge) stating – '... I return Stirling's Petition – had he served his time [21 years] on my paying off the *Malabar*, I should certainly have recommended him for a Medal, as it was I gave the best certificate I was authorised to do to Sailmaker's Mate Henry Clarke. I hope this declaration of my disposition towards this highly respectable old sailor may serve him ...'. George Stirling duly received his Anchor Type Medal and a £15 gratuity, but it is unknown if it is engraved to H.M.S. *MALABAR* where he was unqualified but recommended, or H.M.Sloop *ROVER* where he achieved 'pensioner' status thereby allowing '21 Yrs' to be engraved on his award.

SOME REASONS FOR REFUSAL OF AWARDS AND EXCEPTIONAL CASES OF AWARDS

A man's former Desertion unknown to Commanding Officers

The recommendations for six men from H.M.S. *THUNDERER*, when she was 'paid off' in January 1837, illustrate the problems facing the Captain in his choice of men most deserving the 'M & G'. He could only be guided by their conduct whilst under his command for the past three years, with all earlier service afloat and declaration of conduct being supplied by the man himself from the Certificates he held from his former Captains. It was not uncommon for these Certificates to have been lost by accident or at sea, which was a perfect excuse for the men who never received such a 'Reference' because they had deserted. The remark often seen on official documents of 'own statement' refers to those men not able (or willing!) to provide these all important certificates, which had also been needed to confirm payment of Prize Money during former war torn years.

Amongst the six names submitted from *THUNDERER* for the 'M & G', two seamen had deserted during their earlier days in the Navy – unknown to the Commanding Officer who was now recommending them for 'Good Conduct' during the past twenty one years. The Admiralty Clerk, on checking all the men's careers, found that one Able Seaman had previously deserted on two occasions, and furthermore had been disrated only three years earlier '... for taking spirits out of the grog tub ...'. Another man was found to have 'Run' some seventeen years earlier, but the Admiralty exercised their right in his favour '... to have his 'Run' removed ...', a statement not infrequently found for other seamen who conducted themselves properly during many subsequent years after that misdemeanour.

Other refusals resulting from the discovery of a man's former desertion can be cited. The recommendation for John Crews (Captain of the Hold) aboard H.M.S. *BLONDE* when she was paid off on 6 February 1831 was refused, because the clerk found that in 1806 he had deserted from H.M.S. *Conqueror* – after he had fought aboard her at the Battle of Trafalgar as an Ordinary Seaman. When H.M.S. *KENT* was paid off on 6 December 1831, a Captain of the Forecastle, William Spence, with fourteen years of his 22 years total adult servitude in the Rate of 1st Class Petty Officer, was refused the awards since much earlier in his career an Admiralty clerk 'traced' his desertion in one of the muster books.

Four men were recommended for the 'G & M' from H.M.S. *WINDSOR CASTLE* in June 1831 of whom three seamen eventually received their awards. The fourth man was discovered to have deserted in 1820 after a clerk '... had taken out his time ...' as normally requested in all these cases by the Admiralty Board Member. However, not all such checks were perfect, since one of the three LS & GC recipients

(James Curtis) aboard *WINDSOR CASTLE* had also deserted even earlier in 1811, but the clerks did not find this out [this Author did!], and thus Curtis was most fortunate to receive his 'Anchor Type' reward which he could be-sport later, paired with a Naval War Medal adorned by the clasp for 'Navarino'.

When Curtis received his LS & GC medal in August 1831 he shewed it to one of his old shipmates from *WINDSOR CASTLE,* who by now was also pensioned ashore. This as yet unsatisfied seaman, Robert Reeves lately a Quarter Master, wrote to his former Captain stating that '... You was pleased to recommend me for the Medal and Gratuity which I have not been informed their Lordships decisions ...' [sic]. There is evidence that Reeves eventually received his 'assigned' reward, as did John Thomas (Quarter Master) of *WINDSOR CASTLE* whose medal had been '... mislaid in a drawer ...' at the Admiralty – which was ultimately despatched to him a year late on 18 September 1832.

A more lenient attitude to a single former case of 'desertion' was taken in October 1831 when Joseph Rodgers (Caulker) of H.M.S. *CALCUTTA* had his 'G & M' approved. The Board member in this instance stated that the seaman was to have the medal since he had nearly 23 years good service since he had deserted. This less harsh ruling (than had been applied formerly to John Crews) was to survive for a very long time, and was in conformity with the spirit of the original intentions enshrined in the regulations ordained in 1814 for pensioners.

Transport Service

The submission for John Sait (Gunner's Mate) aboard H.M.S. *BLONDE* when she was paid off on 6 February 1831 was refused. This rebuttal was because his total servitude of 24 years included twelve years in the Transport Service which was not allowed to count towards '... time for a naval pension ...', and therefore he was ineligible for the 'G & M'.

Ship not in Commission for three years

In April 1831 Samuel Hamilton (Quarter Master) was invalided from H.M.S *PRINCE REGENT* as a pensioner with a recommendation for '... the bounty ...', but this submission was refused since the vessel had only been in commission for ten months '... whereas the regulations say that the Captain shall recommend the men for such indulgence at the expiration of every three years the ship has been in commission ...'. Whilst this rule was not always enforced during the next two years, a precedent for change took place in 1833.

On 2 February 1833 the Commanding Officer of H.M.S. *VICTORY* recommended two men for the '... gratuity for good conduct and long service ...' when his vessel was 'paid off' at Portsmouth – but only after a Commission lasting sixteen months, and not the full three years as required by the relevant Order in Council (24 August 1831) in force at this time. This particular submission led to another Order in Council receiving Royal approval on 6 March 1833, in which these statements are made :

'... and as it sometimes occurs that the exigences of Your Majesty's Service require that a ship should be put out of Commission before her crew can have completed in her a full Service of three years, whereby many deserving men who should otherwise have benefited by Your Majesty's gracious intention, have been deprived of their well earned rewards. We humbly beg ... that the medal and gratuity may be granted at the Admiralty's discretion to ... Ships and Vessels, being seagoing Ships, which may be paid off within three years of being put into Commission ...'

There was to be a variation on this same theme concerning eligibility of men not serving a full three year Commission in April 1833, when two men were recommended aboard H.M.S. *DONEGAL.* In this instance the vessel was not 'paid off', but an Admiralty Order had been issued to her Commanding Officer to discharge ratings who had served two and a half years aboard her. Both these seamen were granted their pecuniary and medallic rewards.

In May 1838, Patrick Gill (Quarter Master) was invalided to shore from H.M.S. *BARHAM* nine months before she was due to be 'paid off', but her Captain thought so highly of this man that he made a special plea for him to receive the 'M & G' – even though the three year rule aboard his vessel could not be complied with. Gill had been discharged to Sick Quarters in Malta due to an attack of chronic dysentry. In a manner as yet unknown, Gill managed to obtain a testimonial from a 'Mate' (Charles G. Phillips) aboard H.M.S. *EDINBURGH*, who told a chilling tale concerning an earlier act of gallantry by Gill when he was captured by pirates: -

> ' I feel the highest gratification in making known the following instance of gallantry and fidelity displayed many years ago by the bearer, Patrick Gill, now of H.M.Ship *BARHAM*. In the year 1822 I was Midshipman of H.M.S. *TYNE* (Captain William Godfrey – since deceased) and was employed in one of her Tenders for the suppression of Piracy, under the immediate command of Lieutenant William Hobson (now Captain of H.M. Ship *RATTLESNAKE*). Patrick Gill, then Boatswain's Mate of the *TYNE* was one of the Tender's crew.

> In September 1822 we were overpowered and taken by two heavy pirate schooners – great inducements were held out by the pirates towards Gill, to make him join them, but his fidelity was unshaken. He was equally unmoved by their frequent threats of death and ill usage. On the last day of our detention he was commanded by the pirate Commodore to assist in defending one of the vessels against an expected attack of the *TYNE's* boats upon pain of death if he refused. This he resolutely told them he would not do – he was then seized up in the rigging and cruelly beaten with a cutlass – he still continued true to his duty, and his heroic conduct at length made such an impression on the crew of one of the pirate vessels, that they turned their guns on their own Commander, whom they compelled to desist from his purpose, and finally to liberate Lieutenant Hobson, myself and the rest of the party.

> I shall offer no comment upon the above plain statement, further than to say that I was an eye witness of everything related above – that I firmly believe our liberation was in a great measure owing to Gill's intrepid conduct – and that I will vouch for Captain Hobson corroborating every sentence above written. It may not be superfluous to add that the two schooners in question were afterwards captured by our boats, and most of the crew condemned and executed as pirates.'

At the Admiralty Patrick Gill's total adult service time was verified to be in excess of 23 years, and the Board member made an exception in this case when granting his 'Medal and Gratuity' – thus following the precedent set for those early awards of this LS & GC medal for meritorious deeds.

Cases of men serving aboard Royal Yachts

In May 1832 the Commanding Officer of His Majesty's Yacht *ROYAL SOVEREIGN* recommended his coxswain, John Watkins, for the medal and gratuity. A worthy man with actual service of 24 years (mainly in the seagoing Fleet) since the year 1799, but now invalided with defective vision. The Admiralty Board decision was unexpectedly cruel when stating that '... this indulgence was not intended to be given to those who serve in H.M.Yachts ...' – thus denying all men, who ended their active duty in the Navy aboard such vessels, the chance to benefit from their former long and faithful service. It might prove to have been a doubly unfair decision since surely only the best Petty Officers should have been chosen for such Royal attendance.

This precedent was also quoted to deny the rewards to Owen Williams (Gunner's Mate), who received his recommendation for the 'G & M' when H.M.Yacht *ROYAL CHARLOTTE* was 'paid off' (September 1832). But the refusal was more justifiable in his case, since he had served continuously since 1811 in the Yachts *DORSET, WILLIAM and MARY*, and *ROYAL CHARLOTTE* – sometimes sailing the seas, but never beyond peaceful limits in home waters. From 1843 onwards this precedent was either forgotten, or the indulgence deliberately extended to personnel serving in Royal Yachts. An award of the 'M & G' was approved (July 1843) to Joseph Hill (Quarter Master) aboard *ROYAL GEORGE*, and then later in February 1846 and October 1847 approval was granted for men aboard H.M. Royal Yacht *WILLIAM and MARY* – the second group of men having only served for a Commission lasting twenty months – not three years as required in the Fleet, which might mean that Royal Yachts were now receiving preferential treatment.

At this stage in the sequence of events pertaining to the issue of the Naval Long Service and Good Conduct Medal, the opportunity is taken to describe the first of two fascinating and beautiful Anchor Type Medals (in this Collection), and their historical and numismatic background in a wider context than 'case law'. The first example is named to :

John BRIAN alias JOHN CAMELFORD Late Acting Sailmaker
H.M.S. ZEBRA 23 Years

(His Anchor Type Award is one of the rare 'Inverted Reverse' variety)
[LS & GC Medal awarded 10 May 1833]

A curious feature relating to the two initial different designs of the Army and Navy LS & GC medals (1830), was the total absence of the Sovereign's portrait. Whilst the soldier's reward respected regal patronage by portrayal of the Royal coat of arms, the lower-deckmen's medal was to recognise the King's benefice more simplistically with the motif of a single crowned anchor. Perhaps this naval design by William Wyon was intended to recognise, and honour, the country's friendly title accorded to William IV, their 'Sailor King'; an accidentally inappropriate gesture since this 'Anchor Type' (often referred to as 'William IV Type') continued to be distributed for the first ten years of Queen Victoria's reign (1837-1847).

However, it is not the obverse where the greatest interest lies – it is from the reverse of this Anchor Type LS & GC medal (1830-1847) that a number of fascinating facets occasionally emerge. The design of this side was of unusual format for medals, allowing the detailed personal description of the recipient to be engraved on the circular virgin area of the medal's face. Its design was not unlike some other medallic rewards – also designed and struck by William Wyon – presented as Prizes in certain scholastic establishments, and similarly named on this central empty space – not on the edge.

This circular area on the reverse of the Anchor Type reward thus accorded the 'naming' engraver considerable licence to exploit his artistic flair and skill of hand. A master craftsman's ability could thus lead to refreshingly appealing beauty as witnessed on many of these numismatic pieces, when embellishments brought elegance to bald personal details. It is perhaps superfluous to add that this facility to practice caligraphic niceties on virtually all subsequent military medals was inhibited by the narrow linear boundaries of the 'naming' edge.

The illustration of John Camelford's particular award (*Vide* : Plate No. 1) reveals more than aesthetic enjoyment. The content of the engraved details and the 'variety' of the striking of its reverse – combine to demonstrate some important historical features pertaining to the numismatic and naval-social history of that period.

A quick glance at photographic reproduction of this seaman's medal is surely sufficient for the reader to glean the classic reason for its choice as the foremost illustrative example of this 'Type' of award. Where else – for instance – has any medal collector seen a recipient's full name followed by the title of 'alias' and his former nomenclature? [Two 20th century naval LS & GC medals have recently been sighted with 'alias' indented on the medal's edge.]

The details also include the unusual additional word of 'Late' which is explained later, and the observant specialist may well have noticed that the encircling inscription – 'For Long Service and Good Conduct' – is inverted, commencing as it does here at one o'clock – not seven o'clock as shewn in the next illustration of Edward Embling's medal, which was the usual mode for this medal. Once the history of the man had been researched, an extra hidden peculiarity was to surface since the engraver had 'artfully' interchanged the recipient's two surnames – portraying his name to be Camelford alias Brian in lieu of his signature of Brian alias Camelford.

The administrative manner in which Brian's reward had been sought was also irregular. The application rules for this LS & GC award stipulated that recommendations for the 'silver medal and gratuity' were to be submitted by the Commanding Officer (through his Port Admiral) to the Admiralty, but in this instance the Commander of H.M.Sloop *ZEBRA* took the lazy approach. He only issued John Brian with a detailed personal certificate of recommendation on the day the ship 'paid off', thus inconsiderately leaving total responsibility squarely on the shoulders of this humble sailor to seek his hard earned money and medal – on his own.

Most untypically amongst seamen for this period, John Brian was literate and capable of writing a well reasoned and grammatically sound letter in his own well formed hand. His submission – which was signed 'John Brian alias Camelford' – contained details of his early career and referred to his late Commanding Officer's certificate '... recommending me to Your Lordships for the usual reward for faithful services [pension], and that you will be pleased to confer a Medal etc, similar to my other shipmates ...'. He stated that he had joined the Navy as John Camelford in 1809, but subsequently had lost all his ship certificates whilst serving under that particular former name. He did enclose some certificates on which his name was shewn as John Brian, but these were from his four most recent vessels.

At this time (May 1833) the Admiralty still had not attempted to keep any individual service records for their 'hire & fire' casual labour force of seamen, and were thus unable immediately to check the veracity of Brian's statements, except by the normal time consuming search of all relevant Muster Lists of the ships mentioned – just as researchers today must do at the Public Record Office. The practice of collectively documenting individual 'seaman's servitude' was to commence a year later in 1834 (ADM 29/– Series), but at first only selectively for those receiving a pension of some kind.

So, when John Brian said that he had joined the service in 1809 as John Camelford without any contemporary corroborative evidence, the Admiralty were alerted to a possible and not unusual trick – that of using another seaman's (similar) name to lengthen the applicant's service time for the purpose of gaining a pension, medal and gratuity. Brian was promptly informed that he '... must produce a certificate of identity as John Camelford before [his] claims can be considered ...'. As luck would have it, the Dockyard Superintendent at John Brian's port of Portsmouth was Rear Admiral Sir Frederick Maitland, K.C.B. (of earlier fame aboard H.M.S. *BELLEROPHON* accepting Napoleon's surrender), who had formerly been Brian's Commanding Officer in H.M.S. *GOLIATH* when this seaman had served with the name Camelford. This illustrious senior officer was sought out by the energetic sailmaker from H.M.S. *ZEBRA*, with the satisfactory result that he gained possession of the required signed document by the Admiral within two days. It declared that '... John Camelford served as one of the sailmaker's crew in H.M.Ship *GOLIATH* under my Command from July 1813 until June 1814 ...'.

Armed with this unchallengeable evidence, John Brian was awarded his pension, a gratuity of seven pounds and his 'Silver Medal' on 29 May 1833; only a fortnight after his original submission to the Admiralty – in those so called 'bad old days'!

The next step was that of indenting all his personal details – as supplied by the Admiralty to the engraver – on to the reverse face of his medal. In this particular instance, the sub-contracted craftsman was presented with the knotty problem of neatly fitting more information than usual into the restricted confines of the circular space. As the reader will have noticed from the former illustration of Camelford's award – the engraver succeeded. He transposed the surnames to arrive at a proportionally balanced arrangement of lettering – which also included that enigmatic word 'Late'.

USE OF THE WORD 'LATE' WITHIN THE RECIPIENT'S DETAILS

The knowledge gained from surviving Anchor Type medals shows that the word – 'Late' – appears on all six known awards issued between January and November 1833, with an exceptional medal (seventh) issued in May 1834 amongst others known to be lacking this prefix. It would be interesting to know if the extant medal – but only partially described – issued to Charles Beaumont of H.M.S. *SERINGAPATAM* on 6 September 1832, has the word 'Late' inscribed before 'Sgt R.M(s?)' upon its reverse face. Coincidentally in this series of awards, some medals were engraved with the title 'R.M.' in the singular, others can be found to have been originally engraved or altered later privately to the correct service style of 'R.Ms.'

Whilst no direct official reference to the use of this word 'Late' on these awards has yet come to light, the reasons for its appearance and demise most probably derives from two circumstantially relevant Admiralty directives which fit an empirically derived time scale. In August 1832 their Lordships altered the regulations for some obscure and unnecessary reason, which led to all recommendations for the 'silver medal' reaching the Admiralty after (repeat – after) the respective ships had been 'paid off', and the men consequently dispersed to another ship or beached to some shore abode. The medal with the laudably accurate inscription of 'Late' (in the sense of 'formerly' and not 'deceased') was received by recipients elsewhere than aboard the vessel named on the award.

A year later in August 1833 a new policy (described later) was adopted, whereby the medal had to be ready and available for presentation '... in the presence of the whole of the ship's company, the last thing prior to paying off ...', thus negating the need to continue use of the prefix – 'Late'.

The story of an eighth medal with 'Late' upon it (not known to have survived) might be of amusing interest. When H.M.S. *VOLAGE* was 'paid off', her Commanding Officer, Captain Lord Colchester, recommended his Chief Boatswain's Mate – James Pike – for the gratuity and Long Service Medal. It was duly despatched (26 January 1833) to this Trafalgar veteran (who had formerly served as a Boy aboard H.M.S. *COLOSSUS*) at his dwelling in Number 5 Carrington Street, Shepherds Market, London. After spending a well earned rest there with a girl friend, the pensioner Pike returned to the sea for his living, but this time with the Merchant Navy. He did not return to home shores until the middle of 1836, after serving aboard the *DUKE OF SUSSEX* operating out of Madras.

Pike was obviously a very meticulous man. Upon return to 'Number Five', he checked his inventory of personal effects left there in the care of his inamorata, Catherine Fickens. Two articles were missing, a shawl and his medal. On 11 June 1836 his former girl friend was charged (at Great Marlborough Street Crown Court) with stealing these two items. The Justice of the Peace heard the 'old salt' state that '... the medal had been presented to him by the Lords of the Admiralty bearing the inscription of James Pike *late* (Author's italics) Boatswain's Mate of his Majesty's Ship Volage for 27 Years Long Service and good Conduct ...'. A witness, James Potter of Newcastle Street, The Strand, stated that he had purchased '... a silver medal of the above description which he afterwards melted down'. Miss Fickens was found guilty and committed to Tothil Fields, Bridewell for the space of two months, and Pike received a duplicate award after writing to the Admiralty. The bureaucratic decision was minuted laconically as – 'Under the circumstances let him have another medal' – written on the reverse flyleaf of Pike's letter, which can be found today in ADM 1/4614, letter number 'Pro F 133'.

Normally the capital letter after 'Pro' – an abbreviation for 'Promiscuous' letters sent to the Admiralty of a demi-official or private nature – would represent the first letter of the surname of the person sending the submission. So, why 'Pro F' and not 'Pro P' for Pike? This letter is illustrated showing the name 'James Pike' underlined to tell the junior clerk to file the letter with a 'Pro P' suffix. What seems to have happened is that the clerk took no notice of the underlining, and mistook the address at the bottom, which indeed sloped to the right not unlike a normal 'end of letter' signing format. The clerk obviously assumed that the bottom two words were the names of the sender, but as the reader can see they describe the postal district of 'May Fair', and not a lady named Miss May Fair! Fortunately, another more wide awake clerk logged this 'Pro F' letter against Pike's name in the Admiralty Digest Book (ADM 12/– Series), otherwise this little story would never have come to light (*Vide* : Plate No. 2).

VARIETY OF THE 'INVERTED REVERSE' ON THE MEDAL

There is the final numismatic aspect of the 'inverted reverse' on Camelford's medal which merits some attention. The normal striking of the circumferential words 'FOR LONG SERVICE AND GOOD CONDUCT' commences at seven o'clock, but seven medals have been sighted with these descriptive words inverted 180 degrees and thus beginning at one o'clock. These seven medals were awarded between 15 May 1833 and 15 July 1835, and the inadvertent placement of this reverse die can be traced to three separate re-stocking batches of 'strikings' under William Wyon's jurisdiction at the Royal Mint – totalling some 96 medals. Another eight Anchor Type awards are also known to have survived for this same period, but their descriptions in various catalogues did not include reference to the 'Inverted Reverse'. The Author would welcome confirmation (or rebuttal) that awards to Emmanuel Jobblin, William Peters, Uriah King, William How, Richard Bond, George Layton, Thomas Levy and Thomas Davidson all bear the 'FOR...' at one o'clock on the reverse.

Turning now to the other fascinating and beautiful medal in this Collection, that awarded to Edward Embling (*Vide* ... Plate No. 1). Beyond its novel and beautiful representation of 'A.B.' in monogrammed form, as well as the words 'Her Majesty's' which are so stylishly engraved in full, there is an additional feature of exceptional interest lying innocently in the rare reference to the Class of Ship – CUTTER – in which Embling reaped his rewards. A vessel with this particular classification should have indicated the reason to refuse the submitted recommendation for this seaman's medal – but most fortunately it manifestly did not.

QUOTA ALLOWANCE OF ONE MAN TO BE ALLOWED THE MEDAL PER HUNDRED OF THE CREW

The rules for the award of the naval (LS & GC) 'silver medal' at its inception (Order in Council 19 July 1830) included a quota allowance, irrespective of the number of fully qualified seamen or marines aboard at the time when the vessel was 'paid off' after a Commission of not less that three years duration. Recommendations for award(s) of the 'Gratuity and Medal' forwarded by Commanding Officers could only be entertained on a numerical basis of '... one [name] for every hundred of the crew'.

Not only did this rule minimise awards in large ships to the point of being a 'lottery' amongst men of due worth, but it denied any awards at all to vessels with crews of less than one hundred personnel. Although the quota rule was slightly relaxed in February 1832 to allow 'Sloops' to become eligible vessels, the allowance still remained at 'one per hundred' of the ship's company, but its starting point was lowered to allow one medal for 50-149 of the crew, and a second for 150 to 249 etc of the vessel's official complement. But even this concession still debarred the Captains of the smallest vessels (Cutters, Bomb & Gun Boats) with crews of 49 men or less, commanded by Lieutenants or Masters, from forwarding recommendations for any awards.

The officially allowed complement of H.M.Cutter *SEAFLOWER* was 47 men, and Edward Embling could therefore count himself most fortunate to have received his medal and gratuity on 18 July 1842. As with virtually all Admiralty correspondence for the 'post 1840' period, his letter of recommendation from Lieutenant Nicholas Robillard to the Admiralty has been weeded, and all trace lost of any possible extenuating circumstances surrounding the approval of this award. The fact that Embling had served two successive Commissions aboard *SEAFLOWER*, totalling eight years, may have tipped the balance his way.

This vessel appears to have led a charmed life for pensioners deserving the long service rewards, since Thomas Elliott (Gunner's Mate) of *SEAFLOWER* also escaped the '50 man rule' when presented with his medal in March 1847. A marine (Jabey Drain), 'paid off' from H.M. Cutter *RAVEN* in September 1844, was similarly fortunate to escape the exclusive regulation. Quite a few other prospective recipients were less successful from H.M. Cutters – Petty Officer Josiah Rowe had been recommended in November 1833 for the medal from H.M.Steam Vessel *HERMES*, with a complement of 43 men. In this case the Board member at the Admiralty wrote the following decision on Lieutenant John Wright's submission; '... The complement of *HERMES* not amounting to 50 men, he is not entitled to recommend a man for the gratuity and medal ...'

Proof of the unfairness of the 'Ship' quota rules for the 'M & G' come poignantly to light in the recommendations from H.M.S. *WARSPITE* in September 1837. With a complement of 790 men the Captain stated that '... I have found considerable difficulty in making a selection for such as may be deserving the medal and gratuity ...'. Two lists were submitted – the first containing the eight men (maximum allowed) he had chosen for the rewards, and in the second another eight men fully eligible for conduct and time and almost equally deserving. Almost forty more years were to pass before the quota rule was abolished, thus allowing all men eligible by time and conduct to receive their justly earned distinctions – albeit sometimes because their wayward indiscretions were never revealed!

SEAMEN DISMISSED FROM THE SERVICE SUBSEQUENTLY EARNING THE LS & GC AWARDS

Amongst the five recipients of the 'G & M' aboard H.M.S. *WARSPITE* when she was 'paid off' in March 1833 there was one man with an unusual story. Robert Gibson (Quarter Master) received his award for 38 years servitude, of which time he had served fifteen years as a Warrant Officer (Gunner R.N.). In October 1828, whilst serving as the Gunner aboard H.M.S. *LEDA*, he absented himself for two days from his vessel and returned in a very drunken state – resulting in a Court Martial at which he was sentenced to be dismissed from the service. He re-entered the Navy shortly afterwards aboard H.M.S. *WARSPITE* as a rating with the Rate of Quarter Master, and later received a certificate from his Captain (Talbot) stating that '... his conduct in this Ship was most praiseworthy ...'. His recommendation from *WARSPITE* for the Long Service and Good Conduct 'Gratuity and Medal' received special treatment. There had been a precedent as the Senior Clerk noted to the Admiralty Board member in a Minute stating : 'In a case something similar to this, which occurred some time ago, it was decided that a man should not forfeit his servitude previous to his mis-conduct – but that it should only be counted as Able Seaman time '. Gibson's rewards of the 'Gratuity & Medal' were duly granted – a benevolent act of grace followed some decades later in 1867 under very similar circumstances for ex-Boatswain William Tipper R.N. whose fine group of medals are in this Collection. (*Vide : 'Naval Medals 1793-1856'*, First New Zealand War. H.M.S. *HAZARD*)

COMMANDING OFFICERS' RECOMMENDATIONS WHO LEFT THEIR VESSEL EARLY

Examples exist of Commanding Officers of Ships recommending men for the Long Service rewards when they themselves were relieved of their Command, and discharged to shore on Half Pay. As an example; in April 1833 the Admiralty response was '... The *VERNON* not having been paid off, the Captain is precluded by the Regulations from recommending a man for the Medal.'

When H.M.S. *SAN JOSEF* was 'paid off' in May 1833 as a Flag Ship, one seaman was to be the sad recipient of a 'green rub' rather than his just deserts. Francis Leonard was Admiral Sir Manley Dixon's Coxswain, and thus borne as part of the Admiral's Retinue – separate (as the Captain thought) from the Ship's Company under the jurisdiction (for awards) of the Commanding Officer who had recommended two of his own men – successfully. Coxswain Leonard wrote two long letters to the Admiralty pleading his worthy case, for he had served thirty three years of which his last twelve years had been as a First Class Petty Officer (Coxswain) to Captains and Admirals. He possessed 'Smart Certificates' for a broken limb suffered in his ordinary line of duty, and also for a wound received at the Battle of Algiers (1816) '... since nearly depriving him of the sight of one eye ...'. Earlier in his career he had served as a Boy at the Battle of Trafalgar – and was to live long enough to receive his Naval War Medal with two commemorative clasps (which has survived). He ended one of his submissions by stating that '... Your Memoralist begs to state the reason why he was not recommended at the time of his discharge, was on account of Admiral Sir Manley Dixon and his Secretary being both dangerously ill at the time, consequently I was not recommended at the time the *SAN JOSEF* was paid off when I was the Admiral's Coxswain ...'. The matter did not end there. A few days later the Commanding Officer of *SAN JOSEF* (Captain Richard Curry, C.B.) wrote to the Admiralty saying inter alia '... Great was my surprise and concern, yesterday, when it was intimated to me that the late Commander-in-Chief, Sir Manley Dixon was displeased at my not having recommended, as one [of the two allowed awards – complement 210 men] – Francis Leonard his Coxswain. But as this man certainly did not form part of the crew of *SAN JOSEF*, he being like the Domestics on the Admiral's Retinue [borne only for Victuals] but not employed on board, it did not occur to me that he [Leonard] came within the Regulations ...'.

Captain Curry concluded his letter by giving an insight into the mode he adopted for the award of the 'G & M'. He expected that '... such of them [my crew] as had the least pretension to the indulgence respectfully submitted their claims to me, as soon as they were aware that the ship was to be paid off, and the two named in my return [already rendered] were those I considered the most deserving ...'. He also noted that unlike his own crew aboard, Leonard had neglected to make his timely application – until three days previous, which was far too late. The Admiralty made no exception in their reply, stating that no more than two awards could be made to *SAN JOSEF* – so the combined efforts of Admiral Manley and Leonard proved fruitless.

There had been an Admiralty instruction issued circa 1832 stating that all Royal Marines were to be discharged after serving 21 years of adult time, but this order was not always adhered to. When it was strictly applied to a man who wished to stay in 'A Fighting Arm', such an ex-marine had recourse to acceptable alternative employment. He could volunteer for, and was often accepted as, a Ship's Corporal or Master at Arms in the Royal Navy – a 'Service' where this 21 years maximum time limit did not similarly apply. A study of the Anchor Type Medal Roll reveals a fair number of recipients with seaman 'Rates' (ex R.M.) who benefited from this change of environment. Other marines were clever enough to apply for a sea-commission when they had some 20 years service, and trusted (usually with success) that they would not be discharged from their vessel on attaining pensionable time. One such ex-marine pensioner was John Occleston who received even better treatment. In November 1833 John Occleston was awarded his 'G & M' as a Master at Arms aboard H.M.S. *BADGER* but only with the 2nd Class (seven pounds) gratuity. He continued to serve in the Navy for another commission as a M.A.A. aboard H.M.S. *TALBOT*, and was the only man aboard to be recommended for the 'M & G' when that vessel was 'paid off' in July 1837. The Admiralty rather naturally refused him a second medal, but they increased his gratuity since by now he had served sufficient time to earn the maximum sum allowable – and Occleston was paid the additional eight pounds in 1837 plus an increased pension because he had served 28 years. A very astute 'bootneck' indeed!

THE ABOLITION OF 'LATE' AWARDS

As already briefly stated in the treatise on 'John Brian alias John Camelford', the short-lived need to place the word 'Late' within the medal's inscription was to disappear in 1833. Since the revised regulations causing this cessation were to endure for forty years, the opportunity is taken here to publish the full text of the excellent submission which caused this change of heart – as submitted on 19 August 1833 to the Admiralty Board by Mr John H. Hay (Senior Clerk) : –

   ' I understand it is the practice in the Army when Medals for good conduct are awarded, to
   have them presented by the Colonel or Commanding Officer of the Regiment who does it,

with a suitable address, in the presence of the whole Corps. By this method the moral good intended is effected, or at least some publicity is given to the measure as to hold out an inducement to others to good conduct.

In the Navy the case is quite different – the recommendations do not reach the Admiralty until after the ship is paid off and the men consequently dispersed – the medals can therefore only be sent [Late] to their respective addresses, but sometimes they call for them here at the Admiralty.

As by this method the object intended is in a great measure, if not entirely defeated, I would respectfully submit that some proceeding similar to that adopted by the Army should be established and this, I apprehend, can be easily effected, if the Captain on being ordered to pay off were immediately to send up the names of such men whom they would recommend, together with a list of ships in which they have served, so that the Pension would be fixed and the medal prepared. The latter being sent down for delivery, the last thing prior to paying off – the gratuity attached could be afterwards remitted to the men.

As to Marines, as they are discharged from Head Quarters of their respective Divisions, the same course might be pursued.'

Mr Hay's scheme was accepted by the Admiralty Board, who promptly issued a Memorandum (21 August 1833) mirroring all his ideas, which were in fact to be the first set of regulatory details on the method of application for, and presentation of, what was soon to be titled the 'Naval Long Service and Good Conduct Medal' and its Gratuity to seagoing personnel – land based marines excepted.

The Royal Marine Office took longer to issue their complementary regulations for sea and shore recommendations, simply because the Adjutant General sought to redress the anomalous situation whereby their men – unlike seamen – were not allowed to receive either the gratuity or the medal until the final date of their discharge from the Corps at their respective Head Quarters. This constraint, if retained, would still preclude any presentations of the medal to marines earning the award whilst afloat – as envisaged in the new presentation arrangements.

The Admiralty Solicitor was approached to discover if the new Admiralty Memorandum inferred '... that these distinctions should not as heretofore be confined to men when discharged, but be equally open to, and available for, men continuing in the Service ...'. On this particular question the answer was in the affirmative, provided a new rule was introduced stating that '... such men shall forfeit and be deprived thereof of these distinctions, upon conviction by a Court Martial of subsequent misconduct ...'. On 2 September 1833 a Brigade Order was issued stating these changes for all marines, and substantiating the fact that those awarded medals in ships could receive them in conformity with the recent Admiralty Memorandum – which was also forwarded to all Colonel Commandants. This Brigade Order, whilst regularising the method of presentation of the medallic reward whereby '... the entitled individuals were henceforth to receive their medals on the general parade in front of the whole Division ...' – did nothing to alleviate the somewhat haphazard application procedure for shore awards to marines.

THE MEDAL GAINED PRECEDENCE OVER THE GRATUITY
'M & G' IN LIEU OF 'G & M'

In this reply to the Royal Marine Office, the Admiralty Solicitor also made some additional comments. Quite correctly, and amusingly with tongue in cheek no doubt, he begged to observe that in the original Order in Council the men receiving the Gratuity are 'entitled to wear' the reward – but that no provision was made therein for giving them the Medal! He then ventured to suggest that in any new Order issued, which should be as perfect as possible, that '... as the Medal is the Honor, whether it might not be more advisable that the acquisition of the Medal should confer the Gratuity, rather than (as in the existing regulation) the receipt of the Gratuity giving the right to the Medal ...'. This point was well taken, and from approximately this time onwards the cryptic letters of 'G & M' were reversed, and since the approval also usually included the Pension the abbreviation 'P, M & G' came into common usage on service documents.

REVISED RULES FOR THE ISSUE OF MEDALS TO ROYAL MARINES ON SHORE

The Royal Marine Office now bent its mind to the formulation of a more efficient system for the submissions from all R.M. Divisions for their recommendations of shore awards of the 'M & G'. By a Brigade Order dated 14 February 1834 a new system was introduced which remained in use for forty years, until the period when the RN and RM criteria for 'Long Service' was reduced to the almost farcically short period of only ten years of adult service time. Henceforth from the year 1834, except in very exceptional cases, submissions for the quota of shore awards for marines were to be rendered in December of each year, '... in order that all the cases which may arise within the [preceding] period which the medal is to cover, may be equally admitted to competition and consideration ...'

INTRODUCTION OF A PRINTED FORM FOR RECOMMENDATIONS FROM SEA

When the Commanding Officers of vessels recommended their quota of seamen, they were expected to gather the mens' Certificates for each ship in which they had served and include them with the submission. Some Captains also asked their men to write a Memorial on their service career, others gave a very brief chronological list of their mens' ships and the years in which they served aboard – in the margin of their letter. The more assiduous Commanding Officers made out a Table with various useful columns – similar to those to be found in the (then) recently introduced 'end of commission' Description Books – which included a 'Remarks' column on the personal assessment of the man which – if completed by the C.O. – are of superb use to a collector who may possess the man's medal. In order to standardise the 'M & G' submissions, and make the task of checking the validity of each man's claim (since many men had lost some or all of their Certificates), the Accountant General introduced (May 1834) a printed form for use at sea – very much along the lines of the best hand ruled Tabular Lists already received from Captains at sea.

It was also (coincidentally ?) in the year 1834 that centrally collated service histories of seamen were first commenced in the Admiralty, but only for pensioners of one sort or another at the outset. All these Volumes are available today at the Public Record Office in the ADM 29/– series, leaving an impression that the origination of these records of the 'Servitude of Seamen' was prompted in some measure by Mr Hay's extremely sensible submission already referred to.

Whilst all should have proceeded henceforth without a hitch in an administrative sense, cases still arose which caused the Admiralty Board to admonish Commanding Officers. Submissions were being sent direct to the Admiralty Board or Accountant General without passing through the offices of the Commanders in Chief. Some Captains took no notice at all of the age from which 'reckonable time' was allowed to commence, some took a degree of notice but assumed the '18 Year' rule for marines also applied to seamen (when it was from age 20 years). In a few cases the Admiralty did occasionally allow one or even two years of boy's time to count towards a man's Pension, Medal and Gratuity – but even this dispensation might occasionally have been made at the Admiralty by mistake. The Admiralty clerks also muddled up the 18 and 20 years of age rule – as they did in January 1835 for a seaman aboard H.M.S. *SAMARANG* when stating the award could not be granted to John Miggley '... until he can produce proof of having served 21 years subsequent to the age of 18 ...'

WERE COOKS INELIGIBLE OFFICERS OR ELIGIBLE RATINGS FOR THE LS & GC AWARDS?

In May 1834 the Admiralty failed to approve a recommendation for a Cook to receive the 'M & G' for a curious and interesting – if seemingly very unfair – reason. David Turlock of H.M.Sloop *RALEIGH* had joined the Service as an Able Seaman in March 1804, and was probably wounded at Calder's Action (1805) and made an Acting (Warranted) Cook. In his next vessel and all subsequent appointments he served as a Warranted 'Cook'.

By 1834 there were only a few Cooks who still received a Warrant – but most were First Class Petty Officer 'Ship's Cooks' (ratings) – with one exceptional 'perk'. Until the early 1830s, Cooks were not beached when a ship was 'paid off', they were retained along with the Warrant Officers to serve with pay and provisions aboard (or on the books of) their same (paid off) vessel when she was placed 'in Ordinary' (in Reserve). In this instance in 1834, Turlock was 'paid off' from H.M.S. *RALEIGH*, but under recent regulations re-admitted immediately to the Service when signed on the books of the Clerk of the Cheque to receive his pay and provisions – not being placed 'In Ordinary'. The final decision by the Board in his case was minuted as ; 'Their Lordships do not consider Cooks entitled to Medals as they are retained in the Service when the ship is paid off'. This precedent did not apply to Acting Warranted Cooks, nor to Ship's Cooks as witnessed when approval was granted a year later (26 May 1835) for a 'M & G' to Acting Ship's Cook Thomas Davidson of H.M.S. *ARACHNE*, but refused yet again to Warranted Cook John Ledan 'paid off' at the end of H.M.S. *ASTRAEA's* Commission in June 1835.

Even though the Regulations for these awards were more explicit at this time, there was a problem since they were not consolidated in one book – in later years these separate rules and regulations became enshrined in the 'Queens Regulations and Admiralty Instructions'. Prior to the introduction of this all embracing tome, each Captain would hopefully have aboard with him – to exercise his responsibilities and functions efficiently – all the Admiralty Letters, Circulars and Memoranda, in addition to the printed 'Instructions relating to His Majesty's Service at Sea'. Often, one or more of these essential tools of management might be missing – as seems to have been the case for the revised 'Quota Rules' for awards of the 'G & M' issued in 1832, which altered the rules from one medal per 100 men aboard, to one award per 50 – 149 borne of the ship's company. Many Captains referred in their submissions to a phrase '... The Regulations say, one for every hundred ...' from the old regulations some years after the easement of this Quota rule, often to the detriment of one less award being granted to a worthwhile seaman or marine in the ship.

INTRODUCTION OF SEA-TIME NECESSITY·FOR ROYAL MARINE APPLICANTS

In December 1835 the Royal Marine Office refused a submission for a 'M & G' to a Sergeant, who upon investigation, was found never once to have been on Active Service, neither had he ever embarked in a Ship during his thirty one years as an N.C.O.! This case led to a new regulation being made. Applications would only be approved in future if men recommended whilst on shore had '... performed a reasonable and competent share of general service in addition to their office time ...'. The Royal Marine 'Statement of Services' Tabular Form was amended at this time whereby the column for 'Total Service' was sub-divided to cover time spent 'Afloat' and 'On Shore' – remaining effective for many decades. The first marine to be shown on this revised form had only served one commission of three years at sea and he too was refused the 'M & G'.

In late December 1835 yet another case was presented to the Royal Marine Office in which it transpired that the Sergeant had only served eighteen months at sea during his 28 years total service, but what appeared even more exasperating to the Deputy Adjutant General was the revelation that the man – Joseph Woolley – after being enlisted in 1805 had somehow or other been promoted to Corporal only twelve days later, and made a Sergeant after only an additional two months. His 'M & G' was not surprisingly refused by Sir James Cockburn, but not without added proposals to their Lordships based on this case concerning 'sea service', and a somewhat whimsical idea he proposed for those consistently tied to desk duty ashore.

The Admiralty gave approval to the General's new rule that every applicant must have served at least six years afloat and eleven years with a Battalion or on Military service, plus a maximum of four years on extraneous duties. Private John Spratt was later (February 1836) refused a medal even with his six years afloat, but his next nineteen years as a Shoemaker flawed his eligibility. By a Brigade Order dated 22 July 1837, the 'sea service' rules were altered yet again. From this date marines newly joining their Corps would have to serve '... ten years actually at sea or on foreign service ...' within a total of twenty one years service to become eligible for their 'P, M & G' under the quota rules already in force. The inference was that men already enlisted prior to July 1837 could receive the awards with only six years 'sea service' – that is if the administrators fully comprehended the complicated rules. Of some historical interest – a marine was refused the 'M & G' (November 1837) since his Commandant had included his Sea Fencible time, which type of duty was '... disallowed in calculating the services of seamen or marines for medal and gratuity or Greenwich Pension ...'

It was also the General's view that a second sort of LS & GC medal should be introduced for marines mainly engaged on administrative work ashore. This award for 'Office Duties' service was suggested as '... a medal of a somewhat different stamp, suspended by a ribband varied by a red stripe down the centre, together with a gratuity of two thirds of that for general service ...'. The Admiralty agreed with Cockburn's concept for the 'Office LS & GC Medal' – but never did anything about it.

For those collectors who possess an Anchor Type medal awarded to a marine for this and later periods, they might well approve of the Royal Marine Office clerk who, whilst recording the out-letter approving the award – drew a circle representing the reverse face of the medal in the margin of the 'Letter Book' (ADM 56/– Series) into which was placed the Rank, Name and Years service as seen engraved on the medal when it was sent out. This nicely aided the work involved in the construction of the Anchor Type LS & GC Medal Roll, even to the extent of revealing that the medal to Drummer John Brown (30 December 1835) '... is stamped 'Private', but which error in the rank of this man is not considered of any consequence ...'

WHAT WAS THE MOST SENIOR 'RATE' ENTITLING AWARD OF THE MEDAL?

Whilst the Rank of Sergeant Major was the most senior one to be found amongst those marines presented with the Anchor Type Medal, few people (including the Author) would have guessed the correct answer to the question ; 'What was the most senior seaman's Rate indented on an Anchor Type?' Most would say the Master at Arms – a Warrant Officer in that Rate's earlier days prior to 1830.

The answer lies in the award made to George Sturgess (so nearly an ineligible officer!) whilst holding the Rank of 'Acting Second Master' when recommended. In March 1836 the Admiralty approved the award since they found out that he could not be pensioned as an Officer under Article One of the Greenwich Pension Regulations, but that his pension in such a Rank was considered equivalent to that of a First Class Petty Officer – thus designating his status as a 'Rating' eligible to receive his Medal and Gratuity. This award has survived – in a most worthy Collection where it has been sighted with glistening eyes and much admiration.

TIME SPENT AS A PRISONER-OF-WAR TOWARDS A MAN'S PENSION AND MEDAL

The case of whether the lost years spent as a Prisoner-of-War was allowable towards a pension was tested when Charles Coleman (Quarter Master) was recommended for his medal in May 1836. One month after this man entered the service in November 1806 his vessel was wrecked on the French coast, and he remained a prisoner of the French until July 1814. Their Lordships' decision allowed all of this time in the hands of the enemy to count towards this man's Pension, Medal and Gratuity – even though he was younger than 20 years at the commencement of his incarceration.

BONUS TIME

Unlike the Army, where soldiers who were present at the Battle of Waterloo were allowed to add two (bonus) years to their actual time served for their 'P, M & G', and those soldiers enlisted prior to 1829 who were allowed to reckon two years for each year served after the age of eighteen in the East or West Indies (in other than West-India Regiments) – the seamen and marines were never accorded bonus time for Battles or climatic conditions (not until the Indian Mutiny). However a marine (Thomas Crowson) who earned the Anchor Type medal (held in this Collection) in September 1841, had previously been awarded not only the Waterloo medal whilst in the Army – during his seven years with the 73rd Regiment of Foot – prior to enlisting as a marine, but he had also received the Naval War Medal with Syria clasp. This man's singleton Anchor Type LS & GC, accompanied by two specimens of his missing campaign medals, are in this Collection on display at the Royal Navy Museum, Portsmouth. Another marine who had served in the Peninsular War and at Waterloo was Colour Sergeant Thomas Griffiths, who received his 'M & G' in December 1838. He had served for seven years (1811-1818) in the 95th Regiment – The Rifle Brigade – prior to joining as a Private R.M. at Chatham in April 1819. Both marines received two years bonus time for Waterloo.

Additional bonus time did become available to those seamen who passed their 'Seaman Gunner's' (S.G) examination aboard the gunnery training vessel H.M.S. *EXCELLENT*, instituted in 1830, who were also the first group of men in the Navy to be allowed to 'sign on' for continuous service – years before continuous service engagements were introduced generally in 1853. These 'S.G.' men were allowed one fifth of the time they served in a 'Seaman Gunner' billet as bonus time, which was allowed to count towards their 'P, M & G'. This type of bonus service time is described on the mens' service histories (ADM 29/– and 139/– Series) by the cryptic note of '1/5th Addl' followed by the number of days or weeks allowed as additions to their period of actual service afloat.

PETTY OFFICERS RATED ABLE SEAMEN UPON BECOMING PENSIONERS

There was discussion concerning the eligibility of one of a group of men recommended for the long service rewards when H.M.S. *THUNDERER* was 'paid off' in January 1837. The rating had served as a Purser's Steward for 34 years, but the problem arose because he was not a 'seaman'. His rewards were refused but with an illuminating piece of administrative history. The Board Member ruled that '... Purser's Stewards are to be pensioned as Able Seamen in future ...', a philosophy noted many times by the Author during other searches – for which no regulation has yet been found – applying apparently equally to most Petty Officers who were disrated to Able Seamen upon becoming Pensioners. Thus many LS & GC medals with the rate 'A.B.' engraved upon them with more than 21 years service may well be for men who had served a very long time earlier as Petty Officers (Captains of Tops etc). Not all Petty Officers were disrated when pensioned, and those found to have retained their higher status could well have been especially excellent professionals in sturdy health.

TIME SPENT ASSISTING WITH THE BUILDING OF
PLYMOUTH BREAKWATER INELIGIBLE

When William P. Manley (Captain of After Guard) was recommended from H.M.S. *RACEHORSE* in July 1837 for the 'M & G', he was noted as consistently showing '... alacrity, sobriety, cleanliness and respect, and being on all points a perfect seaman ...'. He had twenty one years servitude, but for fourteen of these years '... he had been in Government employ on the Works at the [Plymouth] Breakwater, ... the individual [Manley] states that the Secretary (Mr Orchard) asked him to enter that service, he was informed that his [naval reckonable] time should go on – without which understanding he [Manley] would not entered it ...'. Manley submitted his naval type service certificate, signed by a Master R.N., which covered his duties during this period stating that : '... William Payne Manley was employed on the service of the Breakwater from 20 February 1816 to 13 April 1830. Eleven years of this time he was coxswain of one of the gigs, and for three years a Mate of Government Store Vessels. He conducted himself the whole time with the greatest propriety as a sober, steady and attentive man, and gave general satisfaction ...'

Unlike the benefits of time sometimes allowed by the Admiralty for periods when seamen served ashore as riggers in Dockyards, the Board member minuted that Manley '... cannot be granted the Medal and Gratuity – service on the Breakwater not being allowed to reckon as sea time ...'. Since Manley had joined the Navy in 1803, and subsequently served 19 years as an adult in the Fleet, this refusal might be considered a trifle heartless – as precedents already existed to allow the rules to be marginally bent in his favour.

ADMINISTRATIVE ERRORS LEADING TO REFUSAL OF AWARDS

In July 1838 James Morgan (Master at Arms) joined the fraternity who were wrongfully refused the medal through no fault of their own. When the clerk at the Admiralty '... took out his time ...' from his individual certificates of service, he accidentally excluded one covering the period 1824-1827. Morgan's recommendation was not approved since he thus appeared to have served only for 18 years. A few months later he was pensioned from the service by a document showing his correct servitude – in excess of 21 years.

Since there has been robust 'weeding' of all naval correspondence written after 1840, no other 'case laws' or interesting facts concerning individual sailors – destined to earn or be refused Medals and Gratuities – can be unearthed today. However this is not true of correspondence which refers to rewards to marines which can be found in ADM 56/– and 191/– Series up to 1885.

As a tail-piece to this monograph on the Anchor Type LS & GC medal, the chance is taken to record a few rare vignettes of sailors' social habits, and the attitudes of two officers towards them – which emerged whilst searching the correspondence concerning this reward.

Amongst the papers attached to the submissions from H.M.S. *GALATEA* there is a private letter (February 1832) inserted by a Captain James Pinhorn. He had been asked to substantiate part of the service record for a seaman, and completed his letter by stating that : –

' It appears to me that some regulation is wanting to guide the individuals (when paid off) in the mode of obtaining this mark of merit [G & M]. Sailors in general are so helpless in what concerns their own interest, they are obliged to be looked after like children ...'.

A few years later an Admiral was to take a very different stance – viewing the humble seaman as a pretty shrewd individual. In May 1838 the Commander-in- Chief, Plymouth, complained to the Admiralty that whilst H.M.S. *TALBOT* was in all material respects ready for sea, with the exception of a chain messenger, she could not proceed to the Sound since there was not sufficient men '... to take care of her ...'. Fortunately for posterity, Admiral Beauclerk gave the reason for the lack of volunteers when he reported that :

'... From the disinclination men have to enter [H.M.S. *TALBOT*], she may be a full month longer before being manned – as those seamen who are paid off husband their money, and by paying an advance to Boarding Houses, secure an asylum which enables them to remain a long time on shore. The *WEAZLE* is so little advanced with her manning, that I cannot speak respecting her time [before proceeding to sea]. Both vessels enter men very slowly ...'

This respectful comment is at variance with many tales told about sailors of that period, proving that not all of them squandered their pay received at the end of a three year commission, or had their pockets picked when so drunk on their first night's leave ashore.

The Admiral would also have been aware that this need for a lengthy 'sailor's rest' between Commissions was occasioned just as much for physical rejuvenation, as it was to ensure the seamen obtaining as good a 'billet at sea' as was possible in the future. Prior to the forthcoming days of a 'Standing Navy' (1853) when sailors were drafted to specific ships – not necessarily of their choice – this was a era when they themselves could choose their next vessel. The sensible sailor therefore needed time ashore to avoid, say, a vessel with a Commanding Officer who had a reputation for being a 'flogging Captain', or perhaps those ships destined to proceed on anti-slavery patrols off the dreaded disease ridden West Coast of Africa – 'White man's grave'.

It would be nice to think that the sentiments expressed by one old salt, when seeking this distinction from his Captain in 1834, was shared by all sailors and marines similarly honoured :—

' Should it be my good fortune to wear the medal for long servitude and good conduct, I shall not only wear it as an Honorary Gift of my Country, but with a lasting gratitude to you for your kindness ...'

The epilogue to this narrative comes from a passage in '*A Farewell to my old Shipmates and Messmates*' by the Old Quarter Master [Gunner John Bechervaise R.N.] published in 1847.

' Among the various changes introduced since the Peace, for the benefit of the seamen of the Royal Navy, there is not one that has been so useful, or tended to so much good, as the medal and gratuity money, given for long service and good conduct. If a medal of treble value, and three times the money given in any other cause, it would be as gratifying to the old seamen; and the manner in which it was given (that has been neglected of late) makes it doubly pleasing.

He is selected from among a large body of men, placed in front on the quarter-deck, pointed at, and recommended to the younger branches of the naval tree, as a bright example to follow. The medal is then handed to him as a token of the approbation of those who are placed high over him, and endowed with more than kingly power. It seems a bond of amity between himself and his superiors, an assurance of friendship and protection; it goes beyond that, it gives to his children a claim on the service in which the father faithfully served.'

Anchor Type LS & GC Medal Roll. 1830-1847 – Chronological Sequence

It was only at the beginning of the 20th Century that the Admiralty began to keep correlated records on the issue of Long Service and Good Conduct Medals to sailors and marines, and only recently have they been released for public appraisal.

Since no naval LS & GC Medal Roll for the 19th Century was ever thought to be an administrative necessity within the Admiralty – and thus never initiated – its creation for any particular period is left to the efforts of modern day researchers. Compilation has perforce to come from the extant records dealing with each individual's recommendation – and approval – for the awards of the Long Service medal and its gratuity.

The Anchor Type LS & GC Medal Roll published here is the result of nearly twenty years work. It has been the intermittent scanning of countless number of pages for scraps of information, from numerous archival sources, which in total has led to the creation of this, and other – Naval LS & GC Rolls. A challenging task which also faces other researchers on similarly chosen projects. Against each name on the following Medal Roll the source is quoted from which the details have been derived.

From its inception this list of accumulated information from various archives was intentionally placed in strict chronological order, for only in this manner could the evolutionary history of the award be charted – an alphabetical list of recipients was (and still remains) of secondary consideration. Since much was missing from archival material of interest to numismatically minded collectors, the only place where these finer details could be found were on the medal itself. The history which was locked uniquely in the medal – either in its type of striking or engraved details on its face – needed to be recorded in its known chronological sequence to establish or ascertain if any primary source material could be found to account for the change.

NAVAL ANCHOR TYPE LS & GC MEDAL ROLL. 1830 – 1847

Date Approved/ despatched	Name	Rate/Rank PRO reference	Ship/R.M.Division	Years Served. Medal known (*)
		1830		
20 Nov	HERRING, John	C/Sgt R.M. ADM 201/21	Woolwich Div	25
		Medal despatched 9 June 1831 upon his request. NGS/Algiers		

20 Dec	OSBORNE, William	Sgt R.M. ADM 1/3285, 56/5/223 & 56/13/198	(PRIMROSE) Plymouth Div	(17) 26

Recommended for his gallantry during a fight with a slaving vessel, but he did not receive his award (LSGC) until 20 March 1839.

1831

23 Feb	MONGER, Edward	C/Sgt R.M. ADM 1/3285	Plymouth Div	21
16 Mar	ALLEN, James	Sgt R.M. (Arty Coys) ADM 1/3357 NGS/Guadaloupe	Portsmouth Div	27
25 Mar	WILLIAMS, Thomas	Pte R.M. (Arty Coys) ADM 1/3285 In Otago Museum. N.Z.	Plymouth Div	22 *
25 Apr	MITCHELL, Henry	Ropemaker ADM 1/454, N.124	BLONDE	24
25 Apr	WHITE, William	Sgt Mjr R.M. ADM 56/2/6 Presentation Silver Snuff Box with medal	Portsmouth Div	22 *
(9 June)	HERRING, John	(*Vide* : 20 Novr 1830)		
18 June	REEVES, Robert	Q.M. ADM 1/1579, B.109	WINDSOR CASTLE	21
18 June	CURTIS, James	Bosun's Mate NGS/Navarino	WINDSOR CASTLE	23
18 June	THOMAS, John	Q.M.	WINDSOR CASTLE	26
14 July	ARMSTRONG, Francis	M.A.A. ADM 1/863-B.350 *Vide* : 9- 9-1835 when granted second medal	SEMIRAMIS	23
29 Sept	ROBERTS, William	Q.M. ADM 1/1366	MELVILLE	23 *
(13 Oct)	SEYMOUR, Richard	Sgt Mjr R.M. ADM 1/3302	Portsmouth Div	24 (*)

Recommended for an award for conduct during a riot in U.K. *Vide* : 14 Feb 1832 when gratuity and medal were despatched.

28 Oct	RODGERS, Joseph *alias* HARRIS	Caulker ADM 1/865, B.660	CALCUTTA	22
2 Dec	BELLMAN, Joseph	Q.M. ADM 1/1367, A.1404	MADAGASCAR	21
6 Dec	SMITH, James	M.A.A. ADM 1/2368, P.188	KENT	26 *

NGS/Basque Roads 1809, Algiers & Navarino. (Not paired with NGS)

(6 Dec)	HULME, Thomas	Sgt R.M. ADM 1/2368, P.188	(KENT – not on medal – 21) Plymouth Div	 24

Awards of 'Gratuity & Medal' approved at end of KENT's commission, but both were witheld until his final discharge – *vide:* 2 July 1834.

14 Dec	ALDIS, Smithers	Sgt Mjr R.M. ADM 191/1 (ex W. Yorkshire Militia 2 Yrs)	Chatham Div	26

16 Dec	SHAPCOTT, Thomas	Q.M.	TRIBUNE	22
		ADM 1/1748, D.93		
16 Dec	POLLARD, Richard E.	Sgt R.M.	TRIBUNE	22
		ADM 1/1748, D.93		
		(Argyleshire Fencibles 3 Yrs)		
(20 Dec)	LACEY, Joseph	Sgt R.M.	(SHANNON – not on	
		ADM 1/1688, C.3	medal – 21)	
			Portsmouth Div	22
		Awards of 'Gratuity & Medal' approved at end of SHANNON's commission, but both to be witheld until his final discharge – *vide :* 18 Feb 1832		
21 Dec	WEAVER, Thomas	Pte R.M.	Portsmouth Div	21
		ADM 1/3302 (One year of R.M.Boy's time counted)		

1832

2 Jan	WOLFINDALE, James	C/Sgt R.M.	Plymouth Div	21
2 Jan	BISHOP, William	Pte R.M.	Plymouth Div	21
		ADM 1/3286		
4 Feb	WALKER, Richard	Pte R.M.	DISPATCH	21
		ADM 1/1818		
		Under a new policy the medal was despatched immediately, but the 'Gratuity' was to be witheld until a recipient's final discharge. (Discharged 14 Dec 1832)		
14 Feb	SEYMOUR, Richard	Sgt Mjr R.M.	Portsmouth Div	24 *
		(*Vide :* 13 Oct 1831)		
17 Feb	WALKER, William	M.A.A.	GALATEA	25 *
17 Feb	KNIGHT, John	Captain Forecastle	GALATEA	23 *
17 Feb	HOLDING, Arthur	Captain of Hold	GALATEA	24
		ADM 1/1370, A.505		
		NGS/Algiers		
18 Feb	LACEY, Joseph	Sgt R.M.		
		(*Vide* : 20 Dec 1831)		
28 Apr	MALCOLM, James	C/Sgt R.M.	Chatham Div	21 *
		ADM 56/3/121		
		NGS/Algiers		
29 June	BARRETT, James	Pte R.M.	Chatham Div	21
		ADM 56/3/121		
24 Augt	ROBINSON, James	Bosun's Mate	PROCRIS	30
		ADM 1/2621, T.48		
3 Sept	HARRINGTON, John	Gunner's Mate	MAIDSTONE	23
		ADM 1/2559, S.63		
3 Sept	FLEMING, Michael	Captain Forecastle	MAIDSTONE	22
		ADM 1/2559, S.66		
6 Sept	VALE, Richard	Chief Bosun's Mate	SERINGAPATAM	23
6 Sept	BEAUMONT, Charles	Sgt R.M.	SERINGAPATAM	21 *
		ADM 1/2728, W.66		
		NGS/Algiers		
12 Oct	BROOKS, James	Bosun's Mate	JASEUR	21
		ADM 1/774, C.731		
17 Oct	TAYLOR, Robert	Gunner's Mate	CROCODILE	24
		ADM 1/2208, M.75		
		(Medal lost in 1833. Duplicate issued 23-1-1836)		

1833

16 Jan	McCARTHY, James	Sgt R.M. ADM 1/3286 & 1/4948	Plymouth Div	27
16 Jan	NICOL, James	Pte R.M. ADM 1/3286	Plymouth Div	21
24 Jan	PIKE, James	'Late' Chief Bosun's Mate ADM 1/1372 ADM 1/4614 Duplicate June 1836. Original stolen and melted down. *Vide* : text under 'Case Law' and reference to prefix 'Late'.	VOLAGE	27
1 Feb	HUTT, James	Q.M.	SOUTHAMPTON	24
1 Feb	JENKINS, William	Q.M. ADM 1/2087, L.20 NGS/Navarino	SOUTHAMPTON	21
18 Feb	BENTLEY, John	Pte R.M. ADM 56/4	Chatham Div	21
28 Feb	WALSH, Dennis	M.A.A. ADM 1/2208, M.17 37/7895	BRITON	24
5 Mar	BROWN, Anthony	'Late' Admiral's Coxswain ADM 1/2622, T.12	WARSPITE	25 *
5 Mar	McPHERSON, Michael	Q.M. 29/26/96	WARSPITE	23
5 Mar	GIBSON, Robert	Q.M. (Acting Gunner RN for 15 years, but never confirmed as a Warrant Officer)	WARSPITE	38
5 Mar	MARTINBURY, Abraham	Captain After Guard	WARSPITE	21
5 Mar	WHITE, John	Captain of Mast ADM 1/2622, T.12	WARSPITE	23
13 Mar	WOOLLEY, Henry	M.A.A. (ex R.M.)	VICTORY	29
13 Mar	HARDING, William	Coxswain of Launch ADM 1/1372, A.193	VICTORY	21
27 Mar	SMILIE, Alexander	'Late Royal Marine' (a Pte) ADM 158/66 Normal Reverse	Woolwich Div	24 *
18 Apr	FENNING, John	Captain Forecastle	DONEGAL	?
18 Apr	DWYER, Edward	Captain of Mast ADM 1/1819, F.36	DONEGAL	?
5 May	FRAZIER, David	Captain's Coxswain	SAN JOSEF	28
5 May	COOK, Samuel	M.A.A. ADM 1/1688, C.44	SAN JOSEF	25
15 May	HANKS, Thomas	'Late' Pte Marine Inverted Reverse ADM 56/4/213	Portsmouth Div	21 *
18 May	KELLY, Patrick	Q.M.	CALEDONIA	22
18 May	WILLIAMS, William	A.B.	CALEDONIA	25
18 May	SIMMONDS, John	Bosun's Mate	CALEDONIA	26
18 May	BARNES, William	Yeoman of Signals ADM 1/1967, H.73	CALEDONIA	22

Date	Name	Rank/Details	Ship	No.
29 May	BRIAN, John *alias* CAMELFORD, John	'Late' Acting Sailmaker ADM 1/4488, Pro C.390. Inverted Reverse. *Vide* : Text under 'Case Law' & illustration.	ZEBRA	23 *
3 June	BROWN, Joseph	Bosun's Mate ADM 1/2914, AG.36 ('Prest' in 1811)	CALEDONIA	22
6 July	KENBY, William	Q.M. & Gnr's Mate ADM 1/1819, F.67	CHALLENGER	23
(6 July)	YOUNG, Thomas	Sgt R.M. Medal and gratuity withheld until discharged, *vide* 15 December 1834.	CHALLENGER	(21)
6 Sept	PENNY, Samuel	Sgt R.M. ADM 56/5/113. Joined aged 10 yrs in 1804	Woolwich Div	21
12 Sept	ODGERS, John	Q.M. ADM 1/1374, W.721	AETNA	24
28 Oct	JOBBLIN, Emmanuel	'Late' Gunner's Yeoman ADM 1/1375, A.861 Inverted Reverse	BLANCHE	28 *
8 Nov	SHACKLES, William	Pte. R.M. ADM 56/5/199	BLANCHE	22
23 Nov	OCCLESTON, John	M.A.A. (ex R.M.) 29/16/63.	BADGER (on medal)	25
		M.A.A. (ADM 1/888) 'Gratuity' increased on 2nd recommendation, but not awarded a second medal. NGS/Algiers	TALBOT	28
10 Dec	PETERS, William	Gunner's Crew	BELVIDERA	21 *
10 Dec	BROWN, James	Ropemaker NGS/Navarino Prest 6-5-1806 to LION. Aged 63 years when receiving this medal!	BELVIDERA	21
10 Dec	BAILEY, William	Coxswain of Launch ADM 1/1375, A.997	BELVIDERA	22

1834

Date	Name	Rank/Details	Ship	No.
9 Jan	SCHUYLER, William *alias* SKYLEN	Sailmaker 29/9/10	RACEHORSE	23
16 Jan	KING, Uriah	Sgt Mjr R.M. ADM 56/5/307	Plymouth Div	28 *
18 Jan	CLAYTON, James	Captain Forecastle 29/9/19	TYNE	22
6 Feb	HUNT, Thomas	C/Sgt R.M. ADM 56/5/343-5	Portsmouth Div	21
25 Feb	CAKEBREAD, David	Pte R.M. ADM 1/3271	GANNET (Chatham Div)	21
12 Mar	COLLINS, Michael	Ship's Corporal 29/9/82	REVENGE	22
7 May	HILL, Richard	M.A.A. (ex R.M.) 29/9/153	PALLAS (RM-Plymouth Div)	21
7 May	ROBSON, Thomas	Ship's Cook 29/9/154	PALLAS	23
7 May	MELDRUM, Robert	Captain After Guard 29/9/155 & 29/16/211	PALLAS	23
17 May	SPARROW, Charles	Pte R.M.	TALBOT (Po Div)	24

17 May	PLANT, William	Pte R.M. ADM 1/875, B.294	TALBOT (Po Div)	21
23 May	MARTIN, John	Caulker 29/9/171	ST VINCENT	25
23 May	TAYLOR, William	Q.M. 29/9/173 NGS/Algiers	ST VINCENT	21
23 May	JOHNSTONE, Samuel	Q.M. 29/9/174	ST VINCENT	22
23 May	GERRARD, George	Q.M. 29/9/176	ST VINCENT	26?
26 May	NEAL, Samuel	Q.M. 29/9/195	ST VINCENT	23
26 May	EARNEST, John	Seaman (ex R.M.) 29/9/196	St VINCENT	24?
26 May	PEARCE, James	'Late' Seaman (ex RM & RMA) Inverted Reverse	ST VINCENT	22 *
26 May	WILLIS, Joseph	Gunner's Crew 29/9/198	ST VINCENT (ex RM & RMA)	?
20 June	MAHONEY, Dennis	Bosun's Mate 29/9/268	PYLADES	23
26 June	JACOBS, Robert	Captain of Mast 29/9/272	DONEGAL	21
2 July	HULME, Thomas	Sgt R.M. (*Vide* : 6 Dec 1831)		
5 July	ROBSON, Edward	A.B. 29/9/289	DONEGAL	22
15 July	CAMERON, James	Q.M. 29/9/296	ASTRAEA	23
18 July	POULTER, James	Sgt Mjr R.M.A. Coys ADM 191/2/232 & 238	Portsmouth Div	29
21 July	WATKINS, Richard	Sailmaker's Crew 29/9/312. No 'Late'. Inverted Reverse	ASIA	21 *
22 July	HOW, William	Bosun's Mate 29/9/313	ASIA	21 *
22 July	DREW, John	Bosun's Mate 29/9/314 NGS/Algiers	ASIA	24
22 July	SULLIVAN, William	Gunner's Mate 29/9/315	ASIA	24
22 July	ROBINSON, James	Captain of Hold 29/9/316	ASIA	21
22 July	YARWOOD, Matthew	Ship's Corporal 29/9/317	ASIA	24
26 July	PLEDGER, John	A.B. (ex R.M.A.) 29/9/318 NGS/Algiers	ALFRED	26(?)
26 July	HUMPHREYS, Thomas	M.A.A. (ex R.M.) ADM 1/779, C.361	ALFRED	24(?)
26 July	OLIVER, George	Sgt R.M. ADM 1/779, C.361	ALFRED (Chatham Div)	21

26 July	WELSH, John	Sgt R.M. ADM 56/6/212 ADM 1/876, B.477 NGS/Algiers. P.O.W. ex HMS JAVA 4-1813	MALABAR (Ply Div)	21
2 Augt	WATERS, William WALTERS *or* BOWEN	Q.M. 29/9/310	ALFRED	22
20 Augt	DAVIS, Francis	Armourer 29/9/384	ROMNEY	21
7 Sept	MONDAY, John	Captain After Guard 29/9/399	ACTAEON	21
23 Sept	WINNETT, Clement	Gunner's Crew 29/9/442 NGS/Algiers	DUBLIN	22
23 Sept	DUCKHAM, George	Gunner's Mate 29/9/443	DUBLIN	21
23 Sept	PETTARD, John	Pte R.M. ADM 1/877, B.640	DUBLIN (Plymouth Div)	21
27 Sept	KNOWLES, Richard	Pte R.M. ADM 56/6/373	Woolwich Div	21
22 Oct	BASTARD, Theodore	Captain of Mast 29/9/492	DUBLIN	21
10 Dec	DAVIS, John	Sgt Mjr R.M. ADM 56/6/521	Chatham Div	27
11 Dec	BOND, Richard	M.A.A. 29/10/73	ISIS	25 *
11 Dec	LAYTON, George	Sgt R.M. ADM 1/2370-153 Inverted Reverse	ISIS (Plymouth Div)	22 *
15 Dec	YOUNG, Thomas	C/Sgt R.M. (*Vide* : 6 July 1833)	Portsmouth Div	22
16 Dec	LEVY, Thomas	Drummer R.M. ADM 56/6/540	Chatham Div	28 *
17 Dec	SMEE, Charles	Captain of Mast 29/10/88	BUFFALO	25
20 Dec	WEBB, William	Sgt R.M. ADM 56/6/548 & ADM 191/2/385	Woolwich Div Inverted Reverse	28 *

1835

14 Jan	TEAGUE, John	Pte R.M. ADM 1/1381/32	MADAGASCAR (Chatham Div)	21
19 Jan	ISUM, Henry	M.A.A. (ex R.M.) 29/10/135	SAMARANG (ex Ply Div)	?
22 Jan	FALLON, Henry	Pte R.M. ADM 56/7/103	Portsmouth Div	22
29 Jan	WRIGHTON, Edward	Armourer 29/10/146	TALAVERA	22
29 Jan	SAXTON, John	Q.M. 29/10/147	TALAVERA	22
29 Jan	PAYNE, William	Gunner's Mate 29/10/149 Inverted Reverse	TALAVERA	23 *

10 Feb	CONNOLLY, Michael	Q.M. 29/10/169 NGS/Algiers	BRITANNIA	21
12 Feb	MONTPELLIER, Alexander	Captain of Mast 29/10/170	BRITANNIA	26
12 Feb	GRIBBLE, Robert	A.B. 29/10/171	BRITANNIA	21
12 Feb	REDDING, Owen	A.B. 29/10/172 NGS/St Sebastian	BRITANNIA	22
12 Feb	CHRISTIAN, Peter	Q.M. 29/10/173 NGS/Algiers	BRITANNIA	21
12 Feb	CASSIAN, Silvester	Yeoman of Signals 29/10/174	BRITANNIA	22
16 Mar	APPLEBY, Henry	1st Drill & C/Sgt RM ADM 1/4375/64 & 86 Personal application. Medal only, no Gratuity.	Chatham Div	21
15 May	PICKFORD, James	C/Sgt R.M.A. Coys ADM 56/7/328 Inverted Reverse. NGS/Algiers	Portsmouth Div	21 *
16 May	HARRIS, George	Cpl R.M. ADM 1/879, B.298	NIMROD (Plymouth Div)	21
26 May	DAVIDSON, Thomas	Acting Ship's Cook 29/11/4	ARACHNE	22
4 July	WHITE, William	C/Sgt R.M. ADM 56/7/417 & 191/2/528. Discharged in 1832. Award part of 1834 allocation of 'Ms & Gs'	Plymouth Div	26
11 July	THOMAS, Richard	Gunner's Mate 29/11/94 NGS/Navarino	HARRIER	25
15 July	BUTLAND, Thomas	A.B. 29/11/100	MELVILLE	25
15 July	CRACKER, Henry	Gunner's Mate 29/11/101	MELVILLE	23
15 July	EDNEY, Thomas	Q.M. 29/11/102 Inverted Reverse. P.O.W.	MELVILLE	22 *
23 July	FITZGERALD, Michael	Q.M. 29/11/113	CURACOA	22
31 July	OWENS, David	Q.M. 29/11/126	IMOGENE	29
31 July	ADLAM, James	M.A.A. (ex RM & RMA) 29/11/127	IMOGENE (ex Portsmouth Div)	26
7 Augt	HOARE, Edward	Q.M. (ex R.M.) 29/11/114	CURACOA	21
31 Augt	BAKER, Thomas	M.A.A. (ex R.M.) 29/11/205	OCEAN	?
31 Augt	CRISP, John	Captain Forecastle 29/11/206	OCEAN	22 *
31 Augt	MOORE, Thomas	Sailmaker 29/11/207	OCEAN	22

31 Augt	SHEAN, Alexander *or* SHEEN	Gunner's Crew 29/11/208	VICTORY	21
31 Augt	CAVENAGH, Patrick	Q.M. 29/11/209	VICTORY	22 *
7 Sept	BUMBY, William	Gunner's Mate 29/11/236	SPARTIATE	21
7 Sept	ARMSTRONG, Francis	M.A.A. 29/11/237	SPARTIATE	26
		Vide : 14- 7-1831 for award of LSGC medal		
7 Sept	BAINE, William	Gunner's Mate 29/11/240	SPARTIATE	23
19 Sept	RICKARDS, William *alias* RICKETTS	Yeoman of Signals 29/11/220 & 279	OCEAN	23
6 Oct	GEE, Thomas	A.B. 29/11/304	SAN JOSEF	21
16 Oct	DAVIDGE, Joseph	Armourer 29/11/335	ASTRAEA	22
26 Oct	TROKE, James	M.A.A. 29/11/359	CONWAY	24
26 Oct	FARRELL, Richard	Gunner's Mate 29/11/360	CONWAY	23
31 Oct	BACON, James	A.B. 29/11/370	PIQUE	21
3 Dec	CHAPMAN, George	Sgt Mjr R.M. ADM 56/8/117	Woolwich Div	21
11 Dec	CARTLEDGE, Joseph	Pte R.M. ADM 56/8/131 NGS/Navarino	Woolwich Div	26
11 Dec	PLUNKET, Luke *alias* BOLAND, John	Bosun's Mate 29/12/62	STAG	22
11 Dec	CAMPBELL, Benjamin *or* CAMMELL	Bosun's Mate 29/12/63	STAG	23
11 Dec	HOLLAND, William	Sgt R.M. 29/12/64 ('Reverse' details unknown)	STAG	21 *
19 Dec	PERCY, James	C/Sgt R.M. ADM 56/8/133	Portsmouth Div	30
30 Dec	GOODFELLOW, Peter	Sgt R.M. ADM 56/8/165 'Reverse' not inverted	Plymouth Div	34 *
30 Dec	BROWN, John	Drummer R.M. ADM 56/8/165 *Vide* : text. 'Pte' engraved	Plymouth Div	

1836

4 Jan	CHALMERS, William	Q.M. Sgt R.M. ADM 191/3/559 Normal Reverse	Chatham Div	30 *
1 Feb	ANSTEAD, Joseph	Pte R.M. ADM 191/3/577	Chatham Div	22
10 Feb	BRYANT, George	Pte R.M. ADM 191/3/584	Portsmouth Div	23

11 Mar	STURGESS, George	Actg 2nd Master 29/12/218	HOWE	24 *
		Inverted Reverse. Most senior 'Rate' awarded a LSGC medal – not (quite) an Officer. 'Inverted' reverse, probably from mislaid old stock. *Vide* : Text.		
7 Apr	PERREY, John	Yeoman of Signals 29/12/262	BRITANNIA	21
7 Apr	LEE, James *alias* JOHNSON, J.J.	Gunner's Crew 29/12/268	BRITANNIA	22
7 Apr	GIBBONS, Edward	A.B. 29/12/269	BRITANNIA	22
7 Apr	NORRIS, George *alias* WOODS, Geo & RUSSELL, Edwd	Q.M. 29/12/270	BRITANNIA	23
		NGS/4 Clasps Copenhagen 1801, …		
26 Apr	BURRIDGE, Henry *or* POURRIDGE	A.B. 29/12/316	ROYAL ADELAIDE	21
28 Apr	SUMNER, Jonas	Sgt 1st Arty Coy ADM 1/1971, H.78	EXCELLENT	21
30 May	COLEMAN, Charles	Q.M. 29/12/363	TRINCULO	23
		P.O.W. 1806-1814		
13 June	CHARLSTON, Charles	Q.M. 29/12/386	LARNE	25
16 June	NOYES, James	Bosun's Mate 29/12/394	PRESIDENT	22
24 June	CAMPBELL, Peter	Gunner's Crew 29/12/410	PRESIDENT	22 *
		Awarded for 'Gallantry'		
11 July	MIGGLEY, John	Sailmaker 29/10/136 & 29/13/23	DUBLIN	21 *
		In Group with 2nd LSGC medal		
21 Oct	CLYNE, David	Captain of Mast 29/13/231	NORTH STAR	24
22 Oct	HENDERSON. Thomas	Captain's Coxswain 29/13/235	BEAGLE	22
14 Nov	KENNEDY, John	Acting Cook 29/13/280	ENDYMION	27
9 Dec	BANFIELD, Henry	Sgt R.M. 12/314	Plymouth Div	23 *
		NGS/Trafalgar, BS 7-7-09		

1837

12 Jan	BOSWELL, James	Purser's Steward 29/13/572	THUNDERER	34 *
12 Jan	JAMES, Edward	Q.M. 29/13/573	THUNDERER	21
12 Jan	LACEY, Andrew	Gunner's Crew 29/13/574 & 29/20/136	THUNDERER	23
12 Jan	McKEDDIE, Donald	Q.M. 29/13/575	THUNDERER	22
12 Jan	FORT, Thomas *alias* PARRY	Q.M. 29/13/576	THUNDERER	26

20 Jan	LEE, William	Sgt R.M.A. Coys ADM 191/4/104	Portsmouth Div	29 *

Pair. RM MSM, dated 1848 Type '16 Jan 1849'

25 Jan	BROWN, Richard	A.B. 29/13/582	EDINBURGH	25
25 Jan	DAFTY, William	Captain of Mast 29/13/589	EDINBURGH	27
28 Jan	WINGETT, John	Bosun's Mate 29/13/600	CASTOR	25
28 Jan	KING, George	Sgt R.M. ADM 1/2436, R.16	CASTOR (Woolwich Div)	24
30 Jan	BARRETT, Thomas	C/Sgt R.M. ADM 1/1390, A.72	EDINBURGH (Plymouth Div)	23
11 Feb	HIGGINS, Henry	Bosun's Mate 29/14/31	CORNWALLIS	21
11 Feb	WADDLE, Henry	Bosun's Mate 29/14/34	CORNWALLIS	21
16 Feb	THORNHILL, Richard	Bosun's Mate 29/14/41	CANOPUS	21 *
21 Mar	BRIDGER, William *alias* PEARCE, James	Bosun's Mate 29/14/166	VERNON	21
8 Apr	BROWN, Francis	Pte R.M. ADM 191/4/167	Woolwich Div	21
8 Apr	POINTER, Samuel	C/Sgt R.M. ADM 191/4/167	Plymouth Div	22
18 Apr	DIBBINS, Samuel	Color Serjeant R.Ms. ADM 1/887, B.230	RINGDOVE (Plymouth Div)	22 *
6 May	BASS, William *alias* EVANS	Carpenter's Mate 29/14/110 & 198	SCORPION	22
11 May	VICK, Richard	Bosun's Mate 29/14/417 & 473	BRITANNIA	24
17 June	JENKINS, David	Q.M. 29/14/487	REVENGE	22
17 June	TRIGGER, Philip	A.B. 29/14/489	REVENGE	23
17 June	RICHARDSON, Henry E.	Captain of Mast 29/14/490	REVENGE	26 *
29 June	CROWLEY, William *or* COWLEY	A.B. 29/14/491	REVENGE	22
25 July	LARK, John	Q.M. 29/16/113	VOLAGE	21
31 July	FRANCE, William F.	C/Sgt R.M. ADM 191/4/315	R.Marine Office (Woolwich Div)	23 *

Group R.M.Museum with NGS/Algiers and RM MSM, dated 1848 Type.

8 Augt	GARDNER, John	Sgt R.M. ADM 12/327, 85a	[No Ship or Div] (Portsmouth Div)	21 *
28 Augt	WILMSHURST, George	Q.M. 29/11/143	MELVILLE	21
28 Augt	WILLIAMS, William	Cpl R.M. ADM 1/1751, A.733	MELVILLE	25 *
12 Sept	METHERELL, Edward	Q.M. 29/16/220	CALEDONIA	23
12 Sept	COX, Charles	Pte R.M. ADM 1/888, B.549	CALEDONIA	26

12 Sept	MANNING, Michael	Bosun's Yeoman 29/16/221	CALEDONIA	24 *
		In Group with NGS/BS 14 Dec 1814 & Algiers, and China 1842.		
12 Sept	BARRETT, Edward	Captain of Mast 29/16/222	CALEDONIA	23
12 Sept	REILLY, Charles *or* RILEY	Q.M. 29/16/223	CALEDONIA	22
12 Sept	CALLAGHAN, John	Q.M. 29/16/226	CALEDONIA	22 *
12 Sept	CARBY, James *or* McCARTHY	Gunner's Mate 29/16/228 Joined Navy in 1795	CALEDONIA	23
21 Sept	PEARCE, Thomas	Captain Forecastle 29/16/251	ANDROMACHE	21
21 Sept	CRESSEY, William	M.A.A. 29/16/252	ANDROMACHE	29 *
21 Sept	EDWARDS, John	Seaman Gunner 29/16/254	ANDROMACHE	23
10 Nov	GIBBS, William	Q.M. 29/16/346	BLONDE	21
10 Nov	PATCHET, William	Pte R.M. ADM 1/2213, M.194	BLONDE	22 *
11 Nov	HENDERSON, William	Q.M. 29/16/348	BELVIDERA	22
11 Nov	LINTON, Robert	Carpenter's Crew 29/16/349	BELVIDERA	23
30 Nov	THORPE, John	Captain Forecastle 29/18/30	ROYAL GEORGE	22
4 Dec	MURPHY, James	Sgt R.M. ADM 56/11/149 Pair. NGS/Bsq Rds 1809	Portsmouth Div	34 *
27 Dec	HEANY, William *alias* MACOUN	Sailmaker's Mate 29/18/97	MALABAR	22
28 Dec	CLARKE, Henry	Captain Forecastle 29/18/106	FAIRY	23

1838

1 Jan	ROGERSON, George *alias* ROGERS	Bosun's Mate 29/18/100	MALABAR	22
2 Jan	JOHNSTON, John	M.A.A. (ex R.M.) 29/9/142 & 29/18/112	HASTINGS	?
2 Jan	HARCOURT, William *alias* URQUHART, John	Ship's Corporal 29/18/113	HASTINGS	22
19 Feb	WOOD, Andrew	Sgt R.M. ADM 1/789, C.122	GANNET (Chatham Div)	24 *
3 Mar	HUDSON, William	Caulker 29/18/204	TRIBUNE	21
19 Mar	STRANGE, Lot	Captain of Mast 29/18/225 NGS/Navarino	ACTAEON	22 *
16 Apr	LEONARD, William *alias* LENNARD	Captain Forecastle 29/18/255 NGS/Java & Navarino	ORESTES	24 *

1 May	GILL, Patrick	Q.M. 29/18/279	BARHAM	23
		For gallantry against pirates		
7 May	GILL, William *alias* MARTEN	Bosun's Mate ADM 1/891, B.293	PORTLAND	21
7 May	WARDELL, Thomas D.	Captain's Coxswain 29/18/294	PORTLAND	22 *
7 May	MARTIN, William	Bosun's Mate 29/18/293	PORTLAND	21
10 May	WILLIAMS, James *or* John	Bosun's Mate 29/17/286	PORTLAND	24
16 May	WILSON, William	Bosun's Mate 29/18/302	PORTLAND	21
25 May	RIVET, William	Bosun's Mate 29/18/335	CHILDERS	23
28 May	LEGGETT, William	Q.M. 29/18/336	DUBLIN	22
28 May	ARNOLD, John	Sailmaker 29/18/338	DUBLIN	23
		(*Vide* : 'Smuggler's Medals')		
28 May	FRY, Charles	Ship's Corporal 29/18/339	DUBLIN (ex RM)	27?
29 May	SCOATES, William *or* SCOATS	Q.M. 29/9/20	RAINBOW	24
30 May	KERSHAW, Thomas	Sgt Mjr R.M. ADM 56/11/548	Woolwich Div	22
2 June	WINTERMAN, Thomas	Sailmaker 29/18/350	THALIA	24
2 June	WOOD, John	Coxswain of Launch 29/18/351	THALIA	21 *
		NGS/Navarino		
2 June	McNISH, William	A.B. 29/18/352	THALIA	21
8 June	PHILLIPS, William	Captain After Guard 29/20/17	WINCHESTER	22
8 June	WEBSTER, John *alias* NAUGHTY, Eleazor	Captain After Guard 29/20/18	WINCHESTER	22
8 June	BELLINGER, Edward	Sailmaker's Mate 29/20/19	WINCHESTER	23
12 June	STIRLING, George	A.B. 29/20/30	MALABAR or ROVER	21
		At Basque Roads 1809		
30 Sept	THOMPSON, William	Ship's Corporal 29/10/214	CLIO	23
24 Oct	McGILL, Alexander	C/Sgt R.M. (ex Army) ADM 1/791, C.628	ZEBRA	23 *
		Ryl Arty 1812-17, USA 1813		
26 Oct	COX, John	M.A.A. (ex R.M.) 29/20/266	HOWE	24
26 Oct	BURRELL, Henry	Q.M. 29/17/8 & 29/20/265	HOWE	24
13 Nov	GILLETT, Charles	Sgt R.M. ADM 56/12/394	Woolwich Div	22 *
		North Coast Spain 1837 & Arctic 1823 – GRIPER.		

17 Nov	GOLDING, Joseph *or* GOULDING	Ropemaker 29/20/299	CLEOPATRA	24
24 Nov	THOMAS, James	Ship's Cook 29/20/306	PHOENIX	21
27 Dec	GRIFFITHS, Thomas	Clr Sgt R.M. ADM 1/791, C.770	PEARL	27
		Ex Army, 95th Regt 1811-1818, Peninsular War & Waterloo		

1839

10 Jan	DRAKE, Robert	Sgt R.M. ADM 191/5/277	Chatham Div	27
14 Jan	KIRK, John *alias* QUICK	Q.M. 29/21/7	RUSSELL	25
14 Jan	STROPERS, Jacob	A.B. 29/21/6	RUSSELL	28
13 Feb	LEWIS, William	Pte R.M. ADM 56/13/111	Portsmouth Div	21
16 Feb	SHANNON, John	Pte R.M. ADM 56/13/198	Woolwich Div	21
20 Mar	OSBORNE, William	C/Sgt R.M. 56/13/198	Plymouth Div	25
		Medal previously approved 22 Dec 1830 for gallantry in HMS PRIMROSE		
28 Mar	WILSON, John	Bosun's Mate 29/21/101	BARHAM	21
28 Mar	LEEF, William H.	Ropemaker 29/21/102	BARHAM	21 *
16 Apr	GULLICK, William	C/Sgt R.M. ADM 1/84, R.33	Ascension Island (Portsmouth Div)	23 *
16 Apr	WADE, William	Gunner's Mate 29/12/278	BRITANNIA	23
18 Apr	CARTER, Aaron	Captain Fore Top 29/21/142	BRITANNIA	22
18 Apr	CARR, George	Captain Forecastle 29/21/143	BRITANNIA	21 *
25 Apr	GREEN William	Captain Forecastle 29/21/163	PELICAN	22
25 Apr	PAUL, Thomas	Sailmaker 29/19/59	PELICAN	22 *
27 Apr	MARTELL, Moses	Captain Fore Top 29/11/334	ROYAL ADELAIDE	22
27 Apr	TARSWELL, John *or* TAZEWELL	Captain's Coxswain 29/21/165	ROYAL ADELAIDE	21
27 Apr	WEBB, Richard	Pte R.M. ADM 1/895, B.242	ROYAL ADELAIDE (Plymouth Div)	21
11 June	FARLAM, Thomas	Q.M. 29/21/241	PYLADES	22
25 June	SHAW, Felix	Pte R.M. ADM 56/13/407	Plymouth Div	21 *
19 Augt	PEED, James	M.A.A. 29/21/241	NIMROD	21
6 Sept	ROBERTS, William	Captain of Hold 29/22/9	MADAGASCAR	23

13 Nov	SULLIVAN, Patrick	A.B. 29/16/246	HERCULES	24
13 Nov	DOUGLAS, John	Q.M. 29/22/67 & 83	HERCULES	23
13 Nov	KILLBURY, John	Bosun's Mate 29/22/68	HERCULES	22
11 Dec	WAINWRIGHT, John	Sgt Mjr R.M.A Coys ADM 56/14/222	Portsmouth Div	27
19 Dec	BOLEY, Benjamin	C/Sgt R.M. ADM 56/14/246	Plymouth Div	34 *
21 Dec	PARKER, John	Coxswain of Launch 29/12/31	TALAVERA	21
21 Dec	VERCOE, John *or* VERCOLE	Sailmaker 29/22/114	TALAVERA	21
21 Dec	BRADEN, James	M.A.A. 29/9/426	TALAVERA	27
21 Dec	HOUSE, Thomas	Q.M. 29/22/115	TALAVERA	22
21 Dec	ANDREWS, William	Pte R.M. ADM 1/2214, M.120	TALAVERA	21 *

1840

17 Jan	PRIM, Philip *or* BRIM	Q.M. 29/22/158	MASTIFF	22
25 Jan	WALKER, Thomas	Ship's Corporal 29/22/166 (ex R.M.)	PEMBROKE	27
25 Jan	BORE, George	Gunner's Crew 29/22/167	PEMBROKE	24
25 Jan	BLEACH, Thomas	Gunner's Mate 29/22/170 Paired with NGS/Algiers, Navarino & Syria	PEMBROKE	21 *
12 Feb	CURRAN, John *or* CORRIN	Bosun's Mate 29/22/195	MINDEN	26
26 Mar	MASON, William	Coxswain of Pinnace 29/10/326	VANGUARD	22
26 Mar	CROSS, John	M.A.A. (ex R.M.A.) 29/10/144	VANGUARD	26
26 Mar	THOMAS, John	Captain After Guard 29/12/408	VANGUARD	23
4 Apr	ELKINS, John	Pte R.M. ADM 56/14/461	VANGUARD (Portsmouth Div)	26
21 Apr	HARRIS, William	C/Sgt R.M. ADM 56/14/482	BEACON (Portsmouth Div)	21
7 May	RENWICK, Thomas	Q.M. 29/26/16	RODNEY	21 *
7 May	REEVES, James	Sailmaker 29/26/17	RODNEY	21
7 May	BEAN, James	Q.M. 29/26/19 & 25	RODNEY	21
7 May	RILEY, John	A.B. 29/26/20	RODNEY	21
7 May	COBB, John *alias* COTT, James	Carpenter's Mate 29/26/24	RODNEY	21
7 July	ROSS, Rolla	Ship's Corporal 29/26/144	BLAZER	21

30 July	DUNN, John	Q.M. 29/26/276	FLY	21
23 Sept	REID, John	Bosun's Mate 29/26/276	SAN ROSAMOND	22
23 Oct	BEE, Richard	C/Sgt R.M. ADM 191/6/288	Portsmouth Div	28
12 Dec	RITCHIE, John	Q.M. 29/26/415	SERPENT	21

1841

4 Jan	WITCHER, Thomas	Ward Room Steward 29/18/291	POWERFUL	25
8 Jan	TAYLOR, Thomas	Sgt Mjr R.M. ADM 56/16/277	Woolwich Div	22
8 Jan	HENNIKER, William	Sgt R.M. ADM 56/16/278	Chatham Div Pair known.	22 *
		First award of dated (1848) R.M. M.S.M.		
19 Jan	BEACH, William	Cpl R.M.A. Coys ADM 56/16/300	Portsmouth Div	21
19 Feb	DAILEY, John	Pte R.M. ADM 191/6/388	Plymouth Div	21
11 Mar	WATSON, Richard	Q.M. 29/9/331	SALAMANDER	24 *
7 Apr	ANDERSON, George	Q.M. 29/27/72	ASIA	21
7 Apr	FEIGHLY, Roderick *alias* FALEY	Bosun's Mate 29/27/73	ASIA	25
7 Apr	HAYES, John *alias* WILSON, Joseph	Carpenter's Crew 29/27/75	ASIA	22
		NGS/Algiers. At Syria but not on Roll.		
16 Apr	BELL, John	Q.M. 29/27/94	STAG	24
16 Apr	MAY, John	Coxswain of Launch 29/27/95	STAG	24
16 Apr	DODDS, Alexander	Captain of Mast 29/27/96	STAG	22
31 May	MAGNESS, Peter	Cooper 29/27/185	TRINCULO	22
31 May	WINBURN, Gabriel	Ship's Corporal 29/27/186	TRINCULO	26
1 June	MERCHANT, William	Q.M. 29/27/188	BELLEROPHON	21 *
1 June	BREWER, Josh *or* Jethro *or* John	Captain of Hold 29/27/189 & 349	BELLEROPHON	29
1 June	CLANSEY, William	Bosun's Mate 29/27/187	BELLEROPHON	26
1 June	LONG, William	Q.M. 29/27/190	BELLEROPHON	21 *
3 June	CLEVERLY, James	Ship's Corporal 29/27/218 (ex R.M.) NGS/Syria	BELLEROPHON	?
16 June	LENHAM, Joseph	C/Sgt R.M. ADM 56/17/154	TRINCULO	22 *

6 July	RUSTON, William	Sgt Mjr R.M. ADM 56/17/210	NORTH STAR	22 *
		Pair. Cross of Maria Isabella. *Vide* : 'Carlist War' (North Coast Spain)		
8 July	VENNER, William *or* VANNAR *or* WENNER	Bosun's Mate 29/18/333	THUNDER	22
8 July	HOSLE, Joseph	Gunner's Mate 29/27/297	THUNDER	21
12 July	THOMPSON, William	Q.M. 29/27/298	EDINBURGH	22
12 July	FLEETWOOD, Thomas	Ship's Corporal 29/27/300	EDINBURGH	22
13 July	PYE, William	Gunner's Mate 29/27/303 (ex R.M.)	EDINBURGH	30 *
15 July	HUGHES, George	Q.M. 29/27/288	ZEBRA	21 *
21 July	WHITE, James	Bosun's Mate 29/27/340	EDINBURGH	21 *
23 July	POLKINGHORNE, William	Q.M. 29/11/217 NGS/Syria	PRINCESS CHARLOTTE	22
23 July	DOUGLAS, William	Q.M. 29/27/343	PRINCESS CHARLOTTE	25
23 July	HARRIS, Thomas	Admiral's Coxswain 29/27/345 NGS/Navarino & Syria	PRINCESS CHARLOTTE	22
23 July	POWELL, Thomas	Captain of Hold 29/27/346 NGS/Syria	PRINCESS CHARLOTTE	21
23 July	ANDERSON, Thomas	Q.M. 29/27/347	PRINCESS CHARLOTTE	24
29 July	FOSTER, William	Carpenter's Mate 29/27/352	CASTOR	21

30 July	PAYNE, Samuel	Coxswain of Pinnace
		29/27/375
		  NGS/Syria
			PRINCESS
			    CHARLOTTE
				22 *

30 July	FLINN, Patrick *or* John	A.B. 29/27/376	PRINCESS CHARLOTTE	22
16 Augt	McCORMICK, Richard	Captain of Mast 29/11/345	MELVILLE	23 *
16 Augt	EDWARDS, James	Q.M. 29/27/433	MELVILLE	22
16 Augt	GARRETT, William	Captain of Mast 29/27/434	MELVILLE	24
20 Augt	BAILEY, Thomas	Pte R.M. ADM 56/17/351	Woolwich Div	22
25 Augt	SLIGHT, Will	Q.M. 29/13/332	DIDO	24 *
		Medal set in Church plate. OMRS Journal Decr 1972. NGS/Syria		
26 Augt	ABBOTT, William	Carpenter's Mate 29/27/462	SAMARANG	24
26 Augt	RANDALL, William	Armourer 29/27/463 as Blacksmith	SAMARANG	22 *

28 Augt	BRADLEY, John	A.B. 29/27/224	PIQUE	24 *
		NGS/Algiers, Navarino & Syria		
26 Sept	CROWSON, Thomas	C/Sgt R.M. (ex Army) ADM 157/360	HAZARD	27 *
		Entitled Waterloo & NGS/Syria 9 yrs 73rd Regt Foot. (*Vide* : Collection)		
28 Oct	ELLIS, John	M.A.A. 29/28/88	CARYSFORT	23
		NGS/Syria		
9 Nov	SMITH, James	Captain of Mast 29/28/115	ORESTES	22
12 Nov	GREEN, William	Bosun's Mate 29/28/119	BRITANNIA	22
12 Nov	LOBB, William	Q.M. 29/16/18	BRITANNIA	23
12 Nov	LOBB, John	Caulker 29/28/126	BRITANNIA	22
12 Nov	MANLEY, William P.	Captain After Guard 29/28/127	BRITANNIA	23
12 Nov	LANE, John	Ship's Corporal 29/28/128	BRITANNIA	27
12 Nov	CLARKE, James	Captain Forecastle 29/16/158	BRITANNIA	23 *
17 Nov	MOONEY, John	Captain of Hold 29/14/492	SERINGPATAM	24
18 Nov	PORTER, John *or* Thomas	Gunner's Crew 29/28/150	SERINGPATAM	29
30 Nov	DICKS, James	Bosun's Mate 29/28/179	TYNE	21
18 Dec	AYLMER, William	C/Sgt R.M. ADM 191/7/226	Woolwich Div	29 *
22 Dec	ALFORD, William	Captain Forecastle 29/28/227	ROYAL GEORGE	22
31 Dec	DOUGLAS, Peter *alias* FOSTER	A.B. 29/28/248	POWERFUL	21
		NGS/Syria		
31 Dec	LYONS, James	Captain After Guard 29/28/250	POWERFUL	22

1842

12 Jan	CAREY, William	C/Sgt R.M.	Plymouth Div	21 *
12 Jan	JOHNSON, William	Sgt Mjr R.M. ADM 56/18/310	Portsmouth Div	21
12 Jan	GOLSNEY, William	Cpl R.M. ADM 56/18/307	Chatham Div	21
24 Jan	HOLMES, William	A.B. 29/28/307	IMPLACABLE	22
		NGS/Syria		
24 Jan	BEAN, William	Bosun's Mate 29/28/308a	IMPLACABLE	23
		NGS/Syria		
24 Jan	CORNELIUS, Henry	Ropemaker 29/28/306	IMPLACABLE	22 *
		NGS/Syria		

24 Jan	RICHARDS, James	Coxswain of Launch 29/28/309 NGS/Syria	IMPLACABLE	22 *
31 Jan	McCONNELL, James *alias* TAYLOR	A.B. 29/20/2 NGS/Syria	HASTINGS	28
31 Jan	WALKER, Thomas	A.B. 29/28/321	HASTINGS	22
31 Jan	WILLIAMS, John	A.B. 29/18/160 NGS/Syria	HASTINGS	28
31 Jan	MORRIS, Joseph	A.B. 29/28/322 NGS/Syria	HASTINGS	23 *
31 Jan	JOHNS, Simon	Carpenter's Crew 29/28/323 NGS/Syria	HASTINGS	22
31 Jan	RILEY, Joshua	C/Sgt R.M. 56/18/366	Woolwich Div	23
16 Feb	TREGASKING, John	Sailmaker 29/21/103 NGS/Algiers, Navarino & Syria	REVENGE	23
16 Feb	DAVIDGE, John	M.A.A. 29/20/175 NGS/Syria	REVENGE	22
16 Feb	BURNETT, John	Pte R.M. 158/37	REVENGE (Woolwich Div)	22 *
16 Feb	LOVATT, William	Pte R.M. ADM 158/55	REVENGE (Woolwich Div)	21 *
29 Mar	LLOYD, Richard *alias* SMITH, John	M.A.A. 29/28/438	ATHOLL	22
8 Apr	WILLCOX, William	M.A.A. 29/18/292	TALBOT	23
12 Apr	DALY, James	M.A.A. (ex R.M.) 29/20/117 NGS/Guadaloupe & Syria	GANGES	25
12 Apr	PARKER, Peter	Q.M. 29/28/474	GANGES	22
12 Apr	WILLIAMS, Benjamin	A.B. (ex R.M.) 29/28/476	GANGES	?
20 Apr	DAVIS, Robert	Bosun's Mate 29/20/257	CALEDONIA	22
21 Apr	BODLEY, William *or* BODDILLY	Q.M. 29/29/7	CALEDONIA	29
9 May	YOUNG, William	Carpenter's Crew 29/9/117	PRESIDENT	24
11 May	CLARK, John	Color Sergeant R.M. ADM 12/389	COMUS	22 *
12 May	WINDSOR, Henry	Blacksmith 29/29/1434	DAPHNE	21
14 May	BINSTEAD, Stephen	Ropemaker 29/29/55	PRESIDENT	23
14 May	NEWSON, Thomas	Blacksmith 29/29/57	PRESIDENT	22

16 May	ROBINSON, William *alias* WALL, John	Q.M. 29/29/70 NGS Navarino & Syria	BENBOW	23
18 May	PASCOE, William	Ship's Corporal 29/21/160 NGS/Syria	BENBOW	26 *
18 May	SNELL, Richard	Bosun's Mate 29/29/96	FIREFLY	22
7 June	WILCOX, Lewis	Ship's Corporal 29/27/222 NGS/Syria	PIQUE	21
7 June	CULVERHOUSE, James	Captain Forecastle 29/29/147 Allowed to count 3 years of 'Boys' time. NGS/Navarino & Syria	PIQUE	21 *
13 July	SPARLING, Richard	Sgt R.M. ADM 12/393	VESTAL	22 *
16 July	CHAPMAN, George	Carpenter's Mate 29/15/237	ACTAEON	21
16 July	BRAY, William	Q.M. 29/29/242	ACTAEON	24
18 July	WITTERN, William	Captain After Guard 29/29/144 NGS/Navarino & Syria	BENBOW	21 *
18 July	EMBLING, Edward	A.B. 29/29/250	SEAFLOWER H.M.Cutter	22 *
19 July	ALLCOCK, John	Pte R.M. ADM 191/7/471	LARNE (Portsmouth Div)	21
26 July	MORTIMER, John	Sailmaker 29/14/233 NGS/Alg-Nav & Ch 1842	WELLESLEY	25 *
26 July	WHITMARSH, Thomas	Yeoman of Storerooms 29/29/265	WELLESLEY	24
6 Aug	REYNOLDS, Joseph	Pte R.M. ADM 56/19/394	Ascension Island (Chatham Div)	29
10 Aug	TRAILL, James	Q.M. 29/29/307	St VINCENT	22 *
10 Aug	YEARWORTH, Thomas	Q.M. 29/29/303	St VINCENT	28
10 Aug	RUDD, Richard	Captain Forecastle 29/29/304	St VINCENT	21
10 Aug	LANAWAY, John	Bosun's Mate 29/29/305	St VINCENT	22
16 Aug	SLADE, Henry	Armourer's Mate 29/29/339	BRISK	26
27 Sept	AIRY, Christopher	A.B. 29/29/448	JUPITER	22
16 Nov	HARRIS, Richard	A.B. 29/29/593	CALCUTTA	22
16 Nov	WILSON, Charles	Captain of Mast 29/29/595	CALCUTTA	31
16 Nov	SEAWARD, Edward	Q.M. 29/29/596	CALCUTTA	22 *

16 Nov	ROBINSON, Samuel	Captain of Mast 29/29/597	CALCUTTA	25
16 Nov	BROWN, John	A.B. 29/29/598	CALCUTTA	24
16 Nov	FENTON, Joseph	Ship's Corporal 29/29/599 (ex R.M.)	CALCUTTA	23 *
18 Nov	HARDY, William	C/Sgt R.M. ADM 191/8/42	RACEHORSE (Plymouth Div)	21 *
25 Nov	HUGHES, Thomas	Admiral's Coxswain 29/29/630	SOUTHAMPTON	25
30 Nov	HUTTINGDON, George	S.B.A. (ex R.M.) 29/29/630	CURACOA	?
26 Dec	BILLETT, James	Pte R.M. ADM 56/20/157	NIAGARA (Chatham Div)	21

1843

6 Jan	PLUMMER, John	Sgt R.M. (Carlist War. 'Gallant conduct')	Portsmouth Div	21
6 Jan	RICE, William	Pte R.M. ADM 56/20/188	Portsmouth Div	21 *
6 Jan	THOMPSON, William	Pte R.M.	Plymouth Div	21 *
6 Jan	MARSHALL, Henry	Pte R.M. ADM 56/20/189	Woolwich Div	21
9 Jan	KELLY, Jeremiah	C/Sgt R.M. ADM 56/20/194	Chatham Div	21 *
9 Jan	MOSTON, Joseph	C/Sgt R.M. ADM 191/8/94	Ship? (Portsmouth Div ?)	?
10 Jan	YOUNG, William	Cpl R.M. ADM 191/8/95	Ship? (Div ?)	?
17 Jan	FRAZER, Daniel	Ship's Cook 29/30/92	ROVER	21
24 Jan	BAINE, Robert	A.B. 29/30/108	CHARYBDIS	27 *
25 Jan	CRANN, Thomas	A.B. 29/30/3 NGS/Syria	CAMBRIDGE	22 *
25 Jan	JOHNSON, Abraham	Captain of Mast 29/30/5	CAMBRIDGE	31
25 Jan	BOURKE, William	Purser's Steward 29/30/7 NGS/Syria	CAMBRIDGE	21 *
25 Jan	WOODROW, Frederick	M.A.A. (ex R.M.) 29/30/112 NGS/Syria	CAMBRIDGE	?
25 Jan	DUNDAS, Thomas *alias* SAYES, Manuel	A.B. 29/22/325 NGS/Syria	CAMBRIDGE	21
26 Jan	MARTIN, John	Captain After Guard 29/21/129	CAMBRIDGE	26
1 Mar	SHIELDS, Henry	Captain After Guard 29/30/177	ANDROMACHE	24 *
1 Mar	HILL, Daniel	Bosun's Mate 29/30/178	ANDROMACHE	22

17 Mar	ROBINSON, Alexander	Bosun's Mate 29/30/217 China 1842 medal	BLONDE	24
23 Mar	JONES, James	Ship's Cook 29/30/238 China 1842 medal	BLONDE	21
27 Mar	ENDICOTT, James	Sgt R.M. ADM 56/21/64	INCONSTANT (Plymouth Div)	22 *
27 Mar	BELL, John	Pte R.M. ADM 56/21/64 & 97	INCONSTANT (Plymouth Div)	21
3 Apr	HUDSON, William	Pte R.M. ADM 56/21/79	Chatham Div	22
7 Apr	NICHOLAS, John	C/Sgt R.M. ADM 191/8/168	Ship? (Chatham Div)	23
13 Apr	RYAN, John	Captain After Guard 29/30/293 China 1842 medal	DRUID	28 *
13 Apr	DELANY, Mark	Q.M. 29/30/294 China 1842 medal	DRUID	29
13 Apr	DREW, John	Ropemaker 29/30/295 China 1842 medal	DRUID	22
13 Apr	HAMMOND, Simon	Q.M. 29/30/296 China 1842 medal	DRUID	22 *
1 May	ROBERTS, James	Bosun's Mate 29/30/318	HERALD	24
8 May	VENNING, Richard	Caulker 29/30/353	PILOT	22
12 May	PAGE, William *alias* DAWSON	Q.M. 29/17/337	CYCLOPS	24 *
17 May	SPARROW, George	Sgt R.M. ADM 56/21/154	MODESTE (Chatham Div)	22 *
2 June	MOSELY, David	Q.M. 29/30/407	IMPREGNABLE	24 *
12 June	FAULKNER, James	Q.M. 29/30/426	FAVOURITE	27
22 July	HILL, Joseph	Q.M. 29/30/521	ROYAL GEORGE H.M.Yacht	21 *
24 July	BATES, Henry	Ropemaker 29/21/314	HOWE	24
2 Aug	FORDHAM, Wm/John	Pte R.M. ADM 191/8/276	Ship? (Chatham Div)	21
8 Aug	MEARS, William	Pte R.M. ADM 191/8/296	Chatham Div	21
11 Aug	GORMAN, Hugh	Blacksmith 29/29/648	VANGUARD	21
11 Aug	BLACKMORE, William	Ship's Cook 29/29/649 NGS/Syria	VANGUARD	23
11 Aug	BRADY, Robert	Ship's Corporal 29/29/651 NGS/Syria	VANGUARD	22 *

11 Augt	BARRY, William	Cooper 29/29/650 NGS/Syria	VANGUARD	22 *
11 Augt	PALMER, John	Captain of Hold 29/22/333	VANGUARD	22
11 Augt	ELLIOTT, William	Q.M. 29/26/22	VANGUARD	23 *
18 Aug	HOPCRAFT, Edward	Cpl R.M. ADM 56/21/361	Chatham Div	22
19 Aug	LAWLOR, Edward	Q.M. 29/30/8	VANGUARD	22 *
19 Aug	ROSKILLY, Thomas	Gnr R.M.A. Coys ADM 191/8/312	HECATE	?
15 Sept	WOODWARD, James	Bosun's Mate 29/31/84	EREBUS	21
21 Sept	SHOWL, Daniel	Pte R.M. ADM 191/8/333 China 1842 Medal	BELLEISLE (Plymouth Div)	21 *
29 Sept	PORTE, Henry	M.A.A. 29/31/129	GRECIAN	23
6 Oct	ARMSTRONG, Richard	Ship's Corporal 29/29/368	THUNDERER	21
6 Oct	SAVAGE, Samuel	Captain Forecastle 29/30/199 NGS/Syria	THUNDERER	23
6 Oct	JOHNSON, Thomas	A.B. 29/11/271 (Awarded 21 Nov 1839)	THUNDERER	30
6 Oct	DONOUGHE, Dennis	Bosun's Mate 29/25/165 NGS/Syria	THUNDERER	21 *
6 Oct	PALMER, Edward	C/Sgt R.M. 12/407 only NGS/Syria	THUNDERER	22 *
9 Oct	NORMAN, George	Acting Cook 29/31/155	ACORN	24
10 Oct	SPURR, Stephen	Ship's Corporal 29/31/158	RODNEY	21
10 Oct	BLACKMAN, William	Ward Room Steward 29/29/71 NGS/Syrla	RODNEY	23
10 Oct	BRAY, William	Captain of Mast 29/29/488	RODNEY	24
10 Oct	JACKSON, Mark	Q.M. 29/29/491 NGS/Syria	RODNEY	24
10 Oct	FERNADEZ, Richard *alias* PETERSON, Jn	Q.M. 29/31/162 NGS/Syria	RODNEY	28
17 Oct	YELF, Thomas	Bosun's Mate 29/31/174 China 1842 medal	CLIO	23
17 Oct	BEVIS, James	Captain Forecastle 29/31/176	CLIO	24

17 Oct	RICKETTS, John	Bosun's Mate 29/20/144 China 1842 medal	ENDYMION	21
17 Oct	WILLIAMS, John	Q.M. 29/26/437 China 1842 medal	ENDYMION	26
19 Oct	COX, Matthew *or* Mathias	Sailmaker 29/27/74	MONARCH	25
31 Oct	MORRISON, Thomas	Carpenter's Mate 29/30/195	TWEED	22
15 Nov	SMITH, William	Ship's Cook 29/30/86	TARTARUS	21
25 Nov	MILLS, James *alias* HARRISON	Q.M. 29/31/275 NGS/Syria	MAGICIENNE	21
25 Nov	GANNIMORE, Lawrence	Ship's Cook 29/11/108 NGS/Syria	MAGICIENNE	30
2 Dec	MILLS, George	Captain Forecastle 29/20/36	CAMELEON	26

1844

1 Jan	ROGERS, Michael	C/Sgt R.M. ADM 56/22/227	Chatham Div	22
10 Jan	DUMPHEY, Samuel	Ship's Cook (ex RM) 29/31/357,359-360	BONETTA	29
17 Jan	CHURCH, John	Admiral's Coxswain 29/31/372	CAMPERDOWN	22 *
23 Jan	MILNER, R.	Pte R.M.	Chatham Div	27
23 Jan	SALTER, William	Sgt R.M.	Portsmouth Div	21
23 Jan	MACKEY, John	C/Sgt R.M.	Plymouth Div	24
23 Jan	McCORMICK, John	Pte R.M. ADM 56/22/281	Woolwich Div	23
31 Jan	MILLER, Frederick	Musician 29/29/79 NGS/Syria	CAMPERDOWN	21
31 Jan	BOWIE, Hugh	Yeoman of Signals 29/29/120	CAMPERDOWN	23 *
3 Feb	HOOPER, Richard	Pte R.M. ADM 56/22/308	Plymouth Div	21
28 Mar	HOLLOWAY, James	Q.M. 29/31/474	AETNA	21 *
29 Mar	HULBERT, John	Cpl R.M. ADM 56/22/425	Portsmouth Div	21
21 Apr	MAYO, John	A.B. 29/16/250 NGS/Syria	FORMIDABLE	29
24 May	BROWN, Henry	Gunner's Mate 29/32/39	RATTLESNAKE	25
29 May	NELDER, Peter	Carpenter's Crew 29/20/37	MALABAR	24 *
29 May	KENNEDY, Patrick	Ord (ex R.M.) 29/31/54	MALABAR	25

29 May	HODGKISS, Samuel	A.B. 29/30/6 NGS/Syria	MALABAR	22 *
11 June	SALWAY, Walter	Blacksmith 29/32/86	INDUS	22
11 June	DENHAM, John	M.A.A. (ex R.M.) 29/32/89 NGS/St Domingo & Algiers	INDUS	29 *
10 July	FOWELL, John	Q.M. 29/32/157 NGS/Syria	QUEEN	25 *
10 July	GRANT, James	Q.M. 29/32/157 NGS/Syria	QUEEN	21
10 July	ABBOTT, Joseph	Captain After Guard 29/32/163	QUEEN	21
12 July	ROBINSON, Francis	A.B. 29/16/309	QUEEN	25
12 July	DAVIS, George	A.B. 29/28/180	QUEEN	23
17 July	WIRE, Daniel	Pte R.M. ADM 56/23/73	QUEEN (Chatham Div)	21
31 July	RADFORD, George	Blacksmith 29/32/197	VINDICTIVE	22 *
8 Aug	STEWART, William	Q.M. 29/32/213	IMAUM	21 *
19 Augt	BARSBY, William	Sgt R.M. ADM 191/9/111	MAGAGASCAR (Portsmouth Div)	21
22 Aug	PEEK, Chamberlain	Pte R.M. ADM 191/9/113	POICTIERS (Chatham Div)	21
13 Sept	DRAIN, Jabey	Pte R.M. ADM 191/9/132	H.M.Cutter RAVEN (Chatham Div)	21 *
17 Sept	SPENCE, George	Bosun's Mate 29/25/115	VICTORY	21 *
17 Sept	DRUDGE, James	Ship's Cook 29/27/298 NGS/Syria	VICTORY	22
17 Sept	BOOTH, William	A.B. (ex R.M.) 29/32/300	VICTORY	25
17 Sept	TOMS, William	Captain's Coxswain 29/29/427 'Gallant conduct before the enemy during late operations on the coast of China.'	VICTORY	30 *
30 Sept	FAIRWEATHER, William	Sgt R.M. ADM 56/23/232 China 1842 medal	Chatham Div	21 *
12 Nov	WHITE, Benjamin	Ship's Cook 29/20/249 China 1842 medal	CORNWALLIS	21
13 Nov	COX, Joseph	Sailmaker 29/32/430 China 1842 medal	CORNWALLIS	22 *
13 Nov	NEIL, Peter	Cooper 29/32/431 China 1842 medal	CORNWALLIS	23 *

14 Nov	SNEDWELL, John	Sgt Mjr R.M. ADM 191/9/179	Portsmouth Div	31
14 Nov	LAYTON, Francis	Gunner's Mate 29/32/438	NIMROD	21
2 Dec	KERKING, Edward	Sgt R.M. ADM 56/23/355	CRESCENT (Plymouth Div)	21

1845

18 Jan	PEECH, Thomas	Pte R.M.	Chatham Div Spike Island Bn	21
18 Jan	McCREA, John	Cpl R.M. ADM 56/23/466	Chatham Div Spike Island Bn	22
18 Jan	DIBBEN, George	Sgt Mjr	Portsmouth Div	21
18 Jan	LEWIS, James	Pte R.M.	Portsmouth Div	21 *
18 Jan	CANTER, Robert P.	C/Sgt R.M.	Plymouth Div	21 *
18 Jan	MORGAN, George	Cpl R.M.	Plymouth Div	22
18 Jan	SUTTON, Edward	C/Sgt R.M.	Woolwich Div	21
18 Jan	DONKIN, Andrew	Pte R.M. ADM 56/23/467	Woolwich Div	21
21 Jan	RILEY, William *alias* STRUTT, John	Captain's Coxswain 29/27/365 & 446	ISIS	22 *
21 Jan	WARREN, John	Carpenter's Mate 29/35/20	ISIS	21
21 Jan	MALISON, Robert	Captain of Mast 29/35/21	ISIS	22
21 Jan	HUTSON, James	Captain's Cook 29/35/22	ISIS	23
21 Jan	DEMPSTER, Thomas	Carpenter's Mate 29/14/150	MASTIFF	21
27 Jan	OSWALD, James *alias* OSWELL	M.A.A. 29/27/9	PELICAN	23
28 Jan	BROWN, Richard	Q.M. 29/35/34	VOLAGE	21
29 Jan	GODMAN, William	C/Sgt R.M. ADM 56/24/24	HARLEQUIN (Chatham Div)	22
14 Feb	COLEMAN, Richard	Pte R.M. ADM 56/24/78 Inverted 'Reverse' – old medal stock?	Portsmouth Div (Spike Island Bn)	21 *
1 Mar	MASON, Benjamin	Ship's Corporal 29/35/122	BELVIDERA	21
1 Mar	COLLINS, William	Blacksmith 29/21/146	BELVIDERA	25
15 Mar	COX, Francis	Pte R.M. ADM 191/9/289	BELVIDERA (Portsmouth Div)	23
9 Apr	HEATHCOTT, Thomas	Q.M. 29/35/198 NGS/Syria	DUBLIN	23 *
9 Apr	THOMPSON, John	Sailmaker 29/35/200	DUBLIN	21
14 Apr	ROWE, William	Blacksmith 29/29/5	CALEDONIA	23
15 Apr	REMFRY, John	Bosun's Mate 29/35/909	CALEDONIA	22 *
18 Apr	WOODBRIDGE, George	Q.M. 29/31/157	BEACON	22

21 Apr	KING, William	M.A.A. (ex R.M.) 29/35/931	CALEDONIA	?
6 May	DUFFIELD, John	Sgt R.M. 158/20	POICTIERS (Chatham Div)	21 *
		Carlist War. Order of Maria Isabella.		
3 June	STRICKLAND, Joseph	Q.M. 29/30/187	ILLUSTRIOUS	24
3 June	DYE, Martin	Q.M. 29/31/28	ILLUSTRIOUS	23
3 June	ROSS, James	Ropemaker 29/35/1013	ILLUSTRIOUS	24
3 June	ROGERS, Samuel	Carpenter's Mate 29/35/1014	ILLUSTRIOUS	22
6 June	PARRIS, William	Bosun's Mate 29/31/502 & 549	ELECTRA	24 *
6 June	RAVENHALL, Richard	Sgt R.M. ADM 191/9/338	H.M.Stm Ship MEDEA (Portsmouth Div)	21
26 June	ADAMSON, Thomas	Carpenter's Mate 29/35/1065	CARYSFORT	22
26 June	CARSE, John	Sailmaker's Mate 29/35/1066	CARYSFORT	23
5 July	NOBLE, William	Sgt R.M. ADM 191/9/366	CARYSFORT (Portsmouth Div)	21

15 July	PEARSON, Andrew	M.A.A.
		29/30/518 & 572
		   NGS/Navarino &
		   Syria
			BITTERN	22 *

1 Augt	MARTIN, Thomas	Q.M. 29/35/1162 & 1262	FERRET	21
1 Augt	FURNACE, Robert	Bosun's Mate 29/35/1166 NGS/Navarino.	CAMBRIAN	21 *
19 Augt	FRASER, Simon	C/Sgt R.M. ADM 191/9/408	SCOUT (Chatham Div)	22
26 Augt	HAKE, John	Ropemaker 29/35/1230 NGS/Syria	AIGLE	21
26 Augt	SAVAGE, Henry	Captain After Guard 29/35/1231	AIGLE	21
27 Augt	NASH, David *or* Levi	Q.M. 29/32/79	SPARTAN	21
28 Augt	HORGAN, William	Captain's Coxswain 29/32/522	EXCELLENT	21
28 Augt	WHITE, Weeks	M.A.A. (ex R.M.) 29/35/58	EXCELLENT	21
1 Sept	GODBY, William	M.A.A. (ex R.M.) 29/35/1245	SPARTAN	?
6 Sept	WELSH, Richard	Pte. R.M. ADM 191/9/421	ALFRED (Woolwich Div)	21
23 Sept	BROWN, George	M.A.A. 29/28/118 & 132	SNAKE	26 *
8 Oct	WHITMARSH, Stephen	Cook 29/36/48	FORMIDABLE	21
8 Oct	SMITH, David	Captain of Hold 29/36/49	FORMIDABLE	23

8 Oct	BUTTON, Sylvester	Carpenter's Mate 29/36/50	FORMIDABLE	22
8 Oct	BROWN, George	A.B. 29/28/4	DEVASTATION	24
11 Oct	FORD, John	Sgt R.M. ADM 56/25/182	EXCELLENT (Portsmouth Div)	21
11 Oct	WYLIE, William	Bosun's Mate 29/36/57	FORMIDABLE	22
11 Oct	FURZE, James	Sailmaker's Mate 29/36/59 NGS/Syria	FORMIDABLE	23
11 Oct	HURLEY, Timothy *or* HENLEY	M.A.A. 29/30/262 A of I/Ava & NGS/Syria	FORMIDABLE	23
14 Oct	HOSKINS, William	Sailmaker 29/35/13	GROWLER	22
31 Oct	WILLETTS, Charles	M.A.A. 29/36/105	St VINCENT	27 *
31 Oct	REYNOLDS, James	Ship's Corporal 29/36/106 (ex R.M.)	St VINCENT	?
31 Oct	RICKETTS, John	Cpl R.M. ADM 191/10/7	DEVASTATION (Portsmouth Div)	24
31 Oct	HUNT, Robert	Pte R.M. ADM 191/10/7	FORMIDABLE (Chatham Div)	22
17 Oct	NEWPORT, William	Sgt R.M. Pro.N.191 for Pension only.	Chatham Div	21 *
7 Nov	THORPE, Thomas *alias* JONES	Coxswain of Launch 29/22/291	St VINCENT	26
7 Nov	TURNBULL, William C.	Bosun's Mate 29/30/541	St VINCENT	23 *
7 Nov	ARMSTRONG, Thomas	Sailmaker 29/32/105	St VINCENT	22
7 Nov	FLYNN, John	Captain Forecastle 29/36/127 NGS/Syria	St VINCENT	22
26 Dec	ROBINSON, John	Sgt R.M. ADM 56/25/460	THALIA (Woolwich Div)	21

1846

9 Jan	BURNS, Edward	C/Sgt R.M. ADM 56/25/414	Ship? (Woolwich Div)	22
21 Jan	AUSTIN, Norton	Sgt Mjr R.M.	Chatham Div	21 *
21 Jan	HOGBIN, John	Pte R.M.	Chatham Div	21
21 Jan	MORGAN, Henry	C/Sgt R.M.	Chatham Div	24
21 Jan	WILSON, Alexander	Sgt R.M.	R.M.A. Companies	25 *
21 Jan	DAVENPORT, Thomas	Pte R.M.	Plymouth Div	21
21 Jan	COOPER, Thomas	Sgt Mjr R.M. Paired NGS/Syria	Woolwich Div	23 *
21 Jan	JONES, Peter	Pte R.M. ADM 56/25/444	Woolwich Div	21
5 Feb	HOBBS, Joseph	Sgt R.M. ADM 56/26/7	Portsmouth Div (Spike Island Bn)	21
5 Feb	HERN, Jacob	Pte R.M. ADM 56/26/7	Plymouth Div (Spike Island Bn)	21 *

10 Feb	MARTIN, Richard	Pte R.M. ADM 191/10/116	WILLIAM & MARY H.M.Yacht (Woolwich Div)	21
18 Feb	BALL, Richard *or* BULL	Armourer's Mate 29/36/326 NGS/Syria	POICTIERS	24 *
10 Mar	ALDRIDGE, John	Sgt R.M. ADM 191/10/138	ROMNEY (Portsmouth Div)	22
9 Apr	HILL, Benjamin	Gun Room Cook 29/20/164	VICTORY	26
13 Apr	JAGO, William	Carpenter's Mate 29/36/19 Also 'M & G August 1852'	VICTORY	21 *
13 Apr	DEVEREUX, Michael	Gunner's Mate 29/29/612	VICTORY	26
13 Apr	TAYLOR, Edward	Gunner's Mate 29/31/298 NGS/Syria	VICTORY	24
13 Apr	MATTHEWS, Henry	A.B. 29/32/538	VICTORY	22
13 Apr	RAWLINGS, Henry	M.A.A. 29/35/1260	VICTORY	22
14 Apr	BAWDEN, Henry	A.B. 29/29/114	EURYDICE	21 *
16 Apr	MAHONEY, Cornelius	Ship's Cook 29/36/422	EURYDICE	21 *
18 Apr	JONES, Thomas	Ship's Cook 29/29/394	WARSPITE	25 *
18 Apr	GILL, Samuel B.	Bosun's Mate 29/36/431	WARSPITE	21
18 Apr	WYBORN, John	Ship's Corporal 29/36/432 NGS/Syria	WARSPITE	22
18 Apr	THURSTON, Edward	Gunner's Mate 29/36/433 (ex R.M.) NGS/Syria	WARSPITE	?
27 Apr	GARDNER, William *or* GARDINER	Q.M. 29/31/140	WINCHESTER	24
27 Apr	DON, John	Q.M. 29/36/455	WINCHESTER	21
1 May	LUNT, Luke	Pte R.M. ADM 56/26/252	Portsmouth Div	22
4 May	BROOKS, Henry	Q.M. 29/36/471 (3 yrs of boys time counted)	SERPENT	23
5 June	BUTTON, William	C/Sgt R.M. ADM 56/26/353	SERPENT (Chatham Div)	21 *
18 June	RAYMOND, James	Captain Forecastle 29/35/1001	PHILOMEL	23 *
7 July	HARDMAN, John	C/Sgt R.M. Capt.G.54 China 1842 medal. Carlist War. Order of Maria Isabella	H.M.Steam Vessel VIXEN (Woolwich Div)	22 *
8 July	TUCKER, John	Caulker 29/37/113	ALBATROSS	21 *

8 July	TALBOT, John	Q.M. 29/37/113	ALBATROSS	21 *
15 July	NEWMAN, Robert	Q.M. 29/36/104	St VINCENT	21 *
28 July	CARLTON, Stephen	Q.M. 29/36/512	PENELOPE	23
13 Augt	BLACKBURN, James	Pte R.M. ADM 191/10/326	FLY (Plymouth Div)	21
20 Augt	MASON, Joseph	C/Sgt R.M. ADM 56/27/51	PENELOPE H.M.Stm Ship	21 *
5 Sept	CROW, David *or* CROWS	Q.M. 29/28/129 China 1842 medal	NORTH STAR	25
8 Sept	ARMSON, William	Ship's Corporal 29/37/254 (ex R.M.)	POICTIERS	24 *
24 Oct	CARR, George	Bosun's Mate 29/37/357	WASP	22
28 Nov	WOOLRET, Samuel	Bosun's Mate 29/37/406 A of I/Ava	GORGON	24 *
12 Dec	HUTCHINSON, William *or* HUTCHESON	Q.M. 29/29/90 NGS/Navarino & Syria	OCEAN	26 *
24 Dec	BELL, William	Captain Forecastle 29/36/33	OCEAN	22 *
28 Dec	HODGE, Edward	Bosun's Mate 29/35/1156	CYCLOPS	22

1847

6 Jan	MURPHY, John	M.A.A. 29/37/519 Group 5. China 1842, Baltic, Crimea & Tu Cr.	TYNE	21 *
12 Jan	KEEMER, George	Captain Forecastle 29/21/104	SAMARANG	23
26 Jan	BARKER, Edward	Gunner's Mate 29/37/47	VICTORY	23
28 Jan	ASHDOWN, Thomas	Pte R.M.	Woolwich Div	21
28 Jan	BALDWIN, Thomas	Sgt R.M.	Woolwich Div	23
28 Jan	DADE, Jonathan	Sgt R.M.	Chatham Div	23 *
28 Jan	GROVES, George	Pte R.M.	Portsmouth Div	21 *
28 Jan	SAMSON, Richard	Q.M. Sgt R.M.	Plymouth Div	21
28 Jan	WOODMAN, Daniel	Cpl R.M. ADM 56/28/95	Portsmouth	23
24 Feb	HEMSWELL, Joseph	Bosun's Mate 29/36/25 Group 4. Baltic, Cr/Seb & Azoff, and Tu Cr	OCEAN	23 *
2 Mar	WHITE, James	C/Sgt R.M. ADM 191/11/78	Portsmouth Div	21
9 Mar	ELLIOTT, Thomas	Gunner's Mate 29/38/96	SEAFLOWER H.M.Cutter	21 *
21 Mar	FAULKNER, Thomas *or* FALCONER	M.A.A. 29/38/151 A of I/Ava & NGS/Syria	TALBOT	21 *

22 Mar	DEDAMESS, George	Gunner's Mate 29/38/130	CLEOPATRA	22
22 Mar	WILSON, William	Yeoman of Storerooms 29/38/131	CLEOPATRA	25 *
31 Mar	STRONG, James	Captain Fore Top 29/37/68 NGS/Syria	OCEAN	21 *
5 Apr	CABLE, William *alias* James	Q.M. 29/36/340	SALAMANDER	23
5 Apr	HAYWARD, George	Gunner's Mate 29/38/170	SALAMANDER	21
14 Apr	BARTLETT, John	Q.M. 29/38/189	INCONSTANT	22 *
14 Apr	WALKER, William	Sailmaker 29/38/190	INCONSTANT	21
14 Apr	LLOYD, Charles	Q.M. 29/38/192	INCONSTANT	23
14 Apr	HOLLAND, William	Captain of Hold 29/38/193	INCONSTANT	23
16 Apr	AYLEY, Thomas	M.A.A. 29/38/206 NGS/Syria	HYDRA	21 *
21 Apr	MARTIN, James *or* William	A.B. 29/38/215	INCONSTANT	21
4 May	WALL, George	Ship's Cook 29/38/253	THUNDERBOLT	24
8 May	CURRY, Edward	Ropemaker 29/38/274	STAR	21
11 May	FREATHY, James	Ship's Cook 29/38/272	WOLVERENE	26
20 May	CHIVERS, Thomas	C/Sgt R.M. ADM 191/11/165 NGS/Syria. LSGC medal of abnormal thickness	THUNDERBOLT (Portsmouth Div)	22 *
24 May	BAKER, Richard	Q.M. 29/38/335	FLYING FISH	21
3 June	WALKER, Robert	Seaman 29/19/39	VICTORY	28 *
7 June	JELLY, Robert	Sgt R.M. ADM 12/469 only China 1842 medal	HAZARD	22 *
24 June	FABER, John	Bosun's Mate 29/36/543	EXCELLENT	21
26 June	DUFFILL, John	A.B. 29/35/1147 A of I/Ava & NGS/Syria	EXCELLENT	27 *
26 June	SMITH, George	Ship's Cook 29/32/440 NGS/Syria	EXCELLENT	26 *
26 June	BETTIS, William	Gunner's Mate 29/38/413	EXCELLENT	21 *

29 June	HOCKERSTONE,
	Nathaniel
		Seaman's Schoolmaster
		29/29/169 & ADM
		  1/1372, A.67. 21 Jan
		  1833
		(ex R.M.A. 21 yrs, then 27 yrs in R.N.)
			EXCELLENT	32 *

1 July	VINCENT, George	Pte R.M. ADM 191/11/195	FROLIC (Portsmouth Div)	22 *
6 July	KING, Joseph	Ship's Cook 29/37/210	LARNE	22
10 July	BRADFORD, John	Sailmaker 29/37/75	VESTAL	23 *
13 July	BLENHEIM, John	Bosun's Mate 29/38/476 China 1842	CONWAY	21 *
15 July	PUGH, Thomas	Carpenter's Mate 29/38/493	CONWAY	23
17 July	RANDALL, William	Captain of Mast 29/38/477	CONWAY	21
30 July	BONE, Hugh	Ropemaker 29/38/519	SPITEFUL	23
21 Augt	PETERS, Edward	Sailmaker 29/39/35	EXPRESS	23
21 Augt	TREVERTON, Henry	Bosun's Mate 29/39/36	EXPRESS	23
30 Augt	WALL, Edward	Captain of Mast 29/39/44 NGS/Syria	AGINCOURT	23
30 Augt	WOOD, John	Captain Forecastle 29/36/466 NGS/Syria	AGINCOURT	24
30 Augt	GASKELL, John	Pte R.M. 158/46	AGINCOURT (Woolwich Div)	21 *
31 Augt	HODGES, William *alias* COOMBES	Bosun's Mate 29/31/146	PLUTO	21
1 Sept	HODGE, Thomas	Sailmaker 29/39/57	CURACOA	21
1 Sept	BOWLEY, Edward [Edwin on medal]	Coxswain of Launch 29/39/58 China 1842 as Edward	CURACOA	21 *
9 Sept	CUMMINS, Richard	A.B. 29/28/147 & 173	VICTORY	28
21 Sept	BALLINGTON, Joseph	Q.M. 29/39/114	BELVIDERA	23
22 Sept	BUTTON, William	Captain Fore Top 29/39/112 NGS/Syria	PILOT	21 *
22 Sept	GRAY, Thomas	A.B. 29/39/113	PILOT	21
28 Sept	RIDLEY, Thomas	Ship's Cook 29/35/189 NGS/Syria	SEALARK	23 *
30 Sept	ELLIS, William	Bosun's Mate 29/35/23	FISGARD	23
7 Oct	SIMPSON, William	A.B. 29/39/115	FISGARD	23
8 Oct	DAY, Robert	A.B. 29/18/345	VICTORY	26
8 Oct	LOVE, Henry	A.B. 29/29/326 & 342	VICTORY	25
8 Oct	BARTON, Edward	Gunner's Mate 29/37/47	VICTORY	24

13 Oct	ANDERSON, John	Q.M. 29/35/7	FIREFLY	23
16 Oct	DAWE, Thomas	Q.M. 29/29/485	AMERICA	26 *
17 Oct	MITCHELL, Henry	Bosun's Mate 29/38/75	AMERICA	22 *
20 Oct	MACKETT, John	Gunner's Mate 29/39/204	BLAZER	21
23 Oct	TODD, George	Captain's Coxswain 29/39/214	WILLIAM & MARY H.M.Yacht	34 *
23 Oct	NIELD, Mark	Pte R.M. 158/59	WILLIAM & MARY H.M.Yacht (Woolwich Div)	21 *
28 Oct	TERRELL, John	Bosun's Mate 29/39/245	SHEARWATER	21
5 Nov	ROUND, Joseph	Pte R.M. 158/262	FISGARD (Plymouth Div)	22 *
8 Nov	SIMMONDS, Henry	Ship's Cook 29/32/130	STROMBOLI	23
12 Nov	JAMIESON, William	Blacksmith 29/30/171	VIRAGO	24
16 Nov	JENKINS, Richard	C/Sgt R.M. ADM 56/30/345	AGINCOURT	22
16 Nov	MAY, Henry	Captain After Guard 29/39/272	CASTOR	21
16 Nov	PRIDEAUX, John	Q.M. 29/25/447	CASTOR	23 *

Group known in 1881 included NGS/Navarino (in this collection), China 1842 and 2nd Vic Wide LSGC (27 March 1856). All these medals had become separated by the turn of this century.

16 Nov	HUGHES, Charles	Bosun's Mate 29/39/270	CASTOR	21 *
16 Nov	BUCHANAN, William	Gunner's Mate 29/34/266	CASTOR	22 *
17 Nov	MURRAY, William	M.A.A. (ex R.M.) 29/39/276	CASTOR	25
19 Nov	McCOY, Jeremiah	Gunner's Mate 29/25/440	RACER	24 *
27 Nov	TURNBULL, John	Carpenter's Crew 29/29/308	VICTORY	27 *
27 Nov	BONE, William	A.B. 29/36/449 & 467	VICTORY	22 *

Abbreviations.

ADM	Admiralty Series of papers at Public Record Office
ADM 1/–	Admiralty In Letters from all sources.
ADM 12/–	Admiralty Index & Digest Books.
29/39/325	The ADM series 29/-. Records of sailors' servitude. Volume 39, page 325.
ADM 56/– & 191/–	Royal Marine Office correspondence.
ADM 158/–	Royal Marine Description Books for their four Divisions.
*	Placed after the years of service denotes medal once known.

The 'Anchor Type Reverse' die became unuseable during the striking of a normal batch of replenishment supplies in October 1846. The stock of 'Anchor Type' medals was finally exhausted with the issue of William Bone's award on 27 November 1847. This medal which has survived in a private collection of naval LS & GC awards of all 'Types' awarded to men who earned this distinction whilst serving aboard H.M.S. *VICTORY*.

Eleven days later the first of the newly designed LS & GC medals was issued. The design of this replacement 'Type' broke new ground with its uniquely wide riband, which was to grace men's chests for thirty years. Its 'Reverse' depicted the starboard side of a fully rigged man-of-war which has remained unchanged for the past 140 years, and the 'Obverse' now portrayed the Monarch's head whereby the naming was henceforth indented on the edge of the medal. (*Vide* : Plate No. 3 for illustration of an unadopted Pattern with a smaller Young Queen's head on the 'Obverse,' with a fully rigged ship facing left (its port side) on its 'Reverse' – similar to that used on the Board of Trade, Rocket Apparatus proof of service at wreck token.)

By a piece of good fortune not only has the last of the 'old' but also the first of the 'new' forms of these Naval LS & GC awards survived.

VICTORIAN WIDE SUSPENSION LS & GC MEDAL

Medals in the Collection

First recipient to receive this LSGC 'Type' of award.

8 Dec 1847	NORRIS, Henry	Bosun's Mate	CORMORANT	23 Yrs

Paired with a China 1842 medal with indented details of 'P.O.' (Bosun's Mate) who served aboard H.M.S.BLENHEIM. (ADM 29/39/325)

Anchor Type LS & GC Medal Roll. 1830-1847
– Alphabetical Index

ABBOTT, Joseph	10-7-1844	BEACH, William	19-1-1841	BROWN, Henry	24-5-1844
ABBOTT, William	26-8-1841	BEAN, James	7-5-1840	BROWN, James	10-12-1833
ADAMSON, Thomas	26-6-1845	BEAN, William	24-1-1842	BROWN, John (RM)	30-12-1835
ADLAM, James	31-7-1835	BEAUMONT, Charles	6-9-1832	BROWN, John (RN)	16-11-1842
AIRY, Christopher	27-9-1842	BEE, Richard	23-10-1840	BROWN, Joseph	3-6-1833
ALDIS, Smithers	14-12-1831	BELL, John (RM)	27-3-1843	BROWN, Rchd (A.B.)	25-1-1837
ALDRIDGE, John	10-3-1846	BELL, John (RN)	16-4-1841	BROWN, Rchd (QM)	28-1-1845
ALFORD, William	22-12-1841	BELL, William	24-12-1846	BRYANT, George	10-2-1836
ALLCOCK, John	19-7-1842	BELLINGER, Edward	8-6-1838	BUCHANAN, William	16-11-1847
ALLEN, James	16-3-1831	BELLMAN, Joseph	2-12-1831	BULL, Richard	18-2-1846
ANDERSON, George	7-4-1841	BENTLEY, John	18-2-1833	BUMBY, William	7-9-1835
ANDERSON, John	13-10-1847	BETTIS, William	26-6-1847	BURNETT, John	16-2-1842
ANDERSON, Thomas	23-7-1841	BEVIS, James	17-10-1843	BURNS, Edward	9-1-1846
ANDREWS, William	21-12-1839	BILLETT, James	26-12-1842	BURRELL, Henry	26-10-1838
ANSTEAD, Joseph	1-2-1836	BINSTEAD, Stephen	14-5-1842	BURRIDGE, Henry	26-4-1836
APPLEBY, Henry	16-3-1835	BISHOP, William	2-1-1832	BUTLAND, Thomas	15-7-1835
ARMSON, William	8-9-1846	BLACKBURN, James	13-8-1846	BUTTON, Sylvester	8-10-1845
ARMSTRONG, Francis	14-7-1831	BLACKMAN, William	10-10-1843	BUTTON, William (RM)	5-6-1846
ARMSTRONG, Richard	6-10-1843	BLACKMORE, William	11-8-1843	BUTTON, William (RN)	22-9-1847
ARMSTRONG, Thomas	7-11-1845	BLEACH, Thomas	25-1-1840		
ARNOLD, John	28-5-1838	BLENHEIM, John	13-7-1847	CABLE, William/James	5-4-1847
ASHDOWN, Thomas	28-1-1847	BODLEY, William	21-4-1842	CAKEBREAD, David	25-2-1834
AUSTIN, Norton	21-1-1846	BOLAND, John	11-12-1835	CALLAGHAN, John	12-9-1837
AYLEY, Thomas	16-4-1847	BOLEY, Benjamin	19-12-1839	CAMELFORD, John	29-5-1833
AYLMER, William	18-12-1841	BOND, Richard	11-12-1834	CAMERON, James	15-7-1834
		BONE, Hugh	30-7-1847	CAMMELL, Benjamin	11-12-1835
BACON, James	31-10-1835	BONE, William	27-11-1847	CAMPBELL, Benjamin	11-12-1835
BAILEY, Thomas	20-8-1841	BOOTH, William	17-9-1844	CAMPBELL, Peter	24-6-1836
BAILEY, William	10-12-1833	BORE, George	25-1-1840	CANTER, Robert P.	18-1-1845
BAINE, Robert	24-1-1843	BOSWELL, James	12-1-1837	CARBY, James	12-9-1837
BAINE, William	7-9-1835	BOURKE, William	25-1-1843	CAREY, William	12-1-1842
BAKER, Richard	24-5-1847	BOWEN, William	2-8-1834	CARLTON, Stephen	28-7-1846
BAKER, Thomas	31-8-1835	BOWIE, Hugh	31-1-1844	CARR, Geo (Capt Fxle)	18-4-1839
BALDWIN, Thomas	28-1-1847	BOWLEY, Edward	1-9-1847	CARR, George (B.Mate)	24-10-1846
BALL, Richard	18-2-1846	BRADEN, James	21-12-1839	CARSE, John	26-6-1845
BALLINGTON, Joseph	21-9-1847	BRADFORD, John	10-7-1847	CARTER, Aaron	18-4-1839
BANFIELD, Henry	9-12-1836	BRADLEY, John	28-8-1841	CARTLEDGE, Joseph	11-12-1835
BARKER, Edward	26-1-1847	BRADY, Robert	11-8-1843	CASSIAN, Silvester	12-2-1835
BARNES, William	18-5-1833	BRAY, Wm (C.Mast)	10-10-1843	CAVENAGH, Patrick	31-8-1835
BARRETT, Edward	12-9-1837	BRAY, Wm (Q.M.)	16-7-1842	CHALMERS, William	4-1-1836
BARRETT, James	29-6-1832	BREWER, Jsh/Jn/Jethro	1-6-1841	CHAPMAN, George (RM)	3-12-1835
BARRETT, Thomas	30-1-1837	BRIAN, John	29-5-1833	CHAPMAN, George (RN)	16-7-1842
BARRY, William	11-8-1843	BRIDGER, William	21-3-1837	CHARLSTON, Charles	13-6-1836
BARSBY, William	19-8-1844	BRIM, Philip	17-1-1840	CHIVERS, Thomas	20-5-1847
BARTLETT, John	14-4-1847	BROOKS, Henry	4-5-1846	CHRISTIAN, Peter	12-2-1835
BARTON, Edward	8-10-1847	BROOKS, James	12-10-1832	CHURCH, John	17-1-1844
BASS, William	6-5-1837	BROWN, Anthony	5-3-1833	CLANSEY, William	1-6-1841
BASTARD, Theodore	22-10-1834	BROWN, Francis	8-4-1837	CLARK, John	11-5-1842
BATES, Henry	24-7-1843	BROWN, Geo (A.B.)	8-10-1845	CLARKE, Henry	28-12-1837
BAWDEN, Henry	14-4-1846	BROWN, Geo (M.A.A.)	23-9-1845	CLARKE, James	12-11-1841

CLAYTON, James	18-1-1834	DREW, John (R'pmkr)	13-4-1843	GILL, Samuel B.	18-4-1846
CLEVERLY, James	3-6-1841	DRUDGE, James	17-9-1844	GILL, William	7-5-1838
CLYNE, David	21-10-1836	DUCKHAM, George	23-9-1834	GILLETT, Charles	13-11-1838
COBB, John	7-5-1840	DUFFIELD, John	6-5-1845	GODBY, William	1-9-1845
COLEMAN, Charles	30-5-1836	DUFFILL, John	26-6-1847	GODMAN, William	29-1-1845
COLEMAN, Richard	14-2-1845	DUMPHEY, Samuel	10-1-1844	GOLDING, Joseph	17-11-1838
COLLINS, Michael	12-3-1834	DUNDAS, Thomas	25-1-1843	GOLSNEY, William	12-1-1842
COLLINS, William	1-3-1845	DUNN, John	30-7-1840	GOODFELLOW, Peter	30-12-1835
CONNOLLY, Michael	10-2-1835	DWYER, Edward	18-4-1833	GORMAN, Hugh	11-8-1843
COOK, Samuel	5-5-1833	DYE, Martin	3-6-1845	GOULDING, Joseph	17-11-1838
COOMBES, William	31-8-1847			GRANT, James	10-7-1844
COOPER, Thomas	21-1-1846	EARNEST, John	26-5-1834	GRAY, Thomas	22-9-1847
CORNELIUS, Henry	24-1-1842	EDNEY, Thomas	15-7-1835	GREEN, Wm (Bsn's Mte)	12-11-1841
CORRIN, John	12-2-1840	EDWARDS, James	16-8-1841	GREEN, Wm (Capt Fxle)	25-4-1839
COTT, James	7-5-1840	EDWARDS, John	21-9-1837	GRIBBLE, Robert	12-2-1835
COWLEY, William	29-6-1837	ELKINS, John	4-4-1840	GRIFFITHS, Thomas	27-12-1838
COX, Francis	15-3-1845	ELLIOTT, Thomas	9-3-1847	GROVES, George	28-1-1847
COX, John	26-10-1838	ELLIOTT, William	11-8-1843	GULLICK, William	16-4-1839
COX, Joseph	13-11-1844	ELLIS, John	28-10-1841		
COX, Matthew	19-10-1843	ELLIS, William	30-9-1847	HAKE, John	26-8-1845
CRACKER, Henry	15-7-1835	EMBLING, Edward	18-7-1842	HAMMOND, Simon	13-4-1843
CRANN, Thomas	25-1-1843	ENDICOTT, James	27-3-1843	HANKS, Thomas	15-5-1833
CRESSEY, William	21-9-1837	EVANS, William	6-5-1837	HARCOURT, William	2-1-1838
CRISP, John	31-8-1835			HARDING, William	13-3-1833
CROSS, John	26-3-1840	FABER, John	24-6-1847	HARDMAN, John	7-7-1846
CROW, David	5-9-1846	FAIRWEATHER, William	30-9-1844	HARDY, William	18-11-1842
CROWLEY, William	29-6-1837	FALEY, Roderick	7-4-1841	HARRINGTON, John	3-9-1832
CROWSON, Thomas	26-9-1841	FALLON, Henry	22-1-1835	HARRIS, George	16-5-1835
CULVERHOUSE, James	7-6-1842	FARLAM, Thomas	11-6-1839	HARRIS, Joseph	28-10-1831
CUMMINS, Richard	9-9-1847	FARRELL, Richard	26-10-1835	HARRIS, Richard	16-11-1842
CURRAN, John	12-2-1840	FAULKNER, James	12-6-1843	HARRIS, Thomas	23-7-1841
CURRY, Edward	8-5-1847	FAULKNER, Thomas	21-3-1847	HARRIS, William	21-4-1840
CURTIS, James	18-6-1831	FEIGHLY, Roderick	7-4-1841	HARRISON, James	25-11-1843
		FENNING, John	18-4-1833	HAYES, John	7-4-1841
DADE, Jonathan	28-1-1847	FENTON, Joseph	16-11-1842	HAYWARD, George	5-4-1847
DAFTY, William	25-1-1837	FERNANDEZ, Richard	10-10-1843	HEANY, William	27-12-1837
DAILEY, John	19-2-1841	FITZGERALD, Michael	23-7-1835	HEATHCOTT, Thomas	9-4-1845
DALY, James	12-4-1842	FLEETWOOD, Thomas	12-7-1841	HEMSWELL, Joseph	24-2-1847
DAVENPORT, Thomas	21-1-1846	FLEMING, Michael	3-9-1832	HENDERSON, Thomas	22-10-1836
DAVIDGE, John	16-2-1842	FLINN, Patrick/John	30-7-1841	HENDERSON, William	11-11-1837
DAVIDGE, Joseph	16-10-1835	FLYNN, John	7-11-1845	HENLEY, Timothy	11-10-1845
DAVIDSON, Thomas	26-5-1835	FORD, John	11-10-1845	HENNIKER, William	8-1-1841
DAVIS, Francis	20-8-1834	FORDHAM, John/Wm	2-8-1843	HERN, Jacob	5-2-1846
DAVIS, George	12-7-1844	FORT, Thomas	12-1-1837	HERRING, John	20-11-1830
DAVIS, John	10-12-1834	FOSTER, Peter	31-12-1841	HIGGINS, Henry	11-2-1837
DAVIS, Robert	20-4-1842	FOSTER, William	29-7-1841	HILL, Benjamin	9-4-1846
DAWE, Thomas	16-10-1847	FOWELL, John	10-7-1844	HILL, Daniel	1-3-1843
DAWSON, William	12-5-1843	FRANCE, William F	31-7-1837	HILL, Joseph	22-7-1843
DAY, Robert	8-10-1847	FRASER, Simon	19-8-1845	HILL, Richard	7-5-1834
DEDAMESS, George	22-3-1847	FRAZER, Daniel	17-1-1843	HOARE, Edward	7-8-1835
DELANEY, Mark	13-4-1843	FRAZIER, David	5-5-1833	HOBBS, Joseph	5-2-1846
DEMPSTER, Thomas	21-1-1845	FREATHY, James	11-5-1847	HOCKERSTONE,	29-6-1847
DENHAM, John	11-6-1844	FRY, Charles	28-5-1838	HODGE, Edward	28-12-1846
DEVEREUX, Michael	13-4-1846	FURNACE, Robert	1-8-1845	HODGE, Thomas	1-9-1847
DIBBEN, George	18-1-1845	FURZE, James	11-10-1845	HODGES, William	31-8-1847
DIBBINS, Samuel	18-4-1837			HODGKISS, Samuel	29-5-1844
DICKS, James	30-11-1841	GANNIMORE, Lawrence	25-11-1843	HOGBIN, John	21-1-1846
DODDS, Alexander	16-4-1841	GARDNER, John	8-8-1837	HOLDING, Arthur	17-2-1832
DON, John	27-4-1846	GARDNER, William	27-4-1846	HOLLAND, Wm (RM)	11-12-1835
DONKIN, Andrew	18-1-1845	GARRETT, William Nathaniel	16-8-1841	HOLLAND, Wm (RN)	14-4-1847
DONOUGHE, Dennis	6-10-1843	GASKELL, John	30-8-1847	HOLLOWAY, James	28-3-1844
DOUGLAS, John	13-11-1839	GEE, Thomas	6-10-1835	HOLMES, William	24-1-1842
DOUGLAS, Peter	31-12-1841	GERRARD, George	23-5-1834	HOOPER, Richard	3-2-1844
DOUGLAS, William	23-7-1841	GIBBONS, Edward	7-4-1836	HOPCRAFT, Edward	18-8-1843
DRAIN, Jabey	13-9-1844	GIBBS, William	10-11-1837	HORGAN, William	28-8-1845
DRAKE, Robert	10-1-1839	GIBSON, Robert	5-3-1833	HOSKINS, William	14-10-1845
DREW, John (B.Mate)	22-7-1834	GILL, Patrick	1-5-1838	HOSLE, Joseph	8-7-1841

HOUSE, Thomas	21-12-1839	LEE, William	20-1-1837	MITCHELL, Hy (B.Mte)	17-10-1847
HOW, William	22-7-1834	LEEF, William H.	28-3-1839	MITCHELL, Hy (Rpmkr)	25-4-1831
HUDSON, William (RM)	3-4-1843	LEGGETT, William	28-5-1838	MONDAY, John	7-9-1834
HUDSON, William (RN)	3-3-1838	LENHAM, Joseph	16-6-1841	MONGER, Edward	23-2-1831
HUGHES, Charles	16-11-1847	LENNARD, William	16-4-1838	MONTPELLIER, Alxnder	12-2-1835
HUGHES, George	15-7-1841	LEONARD, William	16-4-1838	MOONEY, John	17-11-1841
HUGHES, Thomas	25-11-1842	LEVY, Thomas	16-12-1834	MOORE, Thomas	31-8-1835
HULBERT, John	29-3-1844	LEWIS, James	18-1-1845	MORGAN, George	18-1-1845
HULME, Thomas	6-12-1831	LEWIS, William	13-2-1839	MORGAN, Henry	21-1-1846
HUMPHREYS, Thomas	26-7-1834	LINTON, Robert	11-11-1837	MORRIS, Joseph	31-1-1842
HUNT, Robert	31-10-1845	LLOYD, Charles	14-4-1847	MORRISON, Thomas	31-10-1843
HUNT, Thomas	6-2-1834	LLOYD, Richard	29-3-1842	MORTIMER, John	26-7-1842
HURLEY, Timothy	11-10-1845	LOBB, John (Caulker)	12-11-1841	MOSELY, David	2-6-1843
HUTCHINSON, William	12-12-1846	LOBB, William (Q.M.)	12-11-1841	MOSTON, Joseph	9-1-1843
HUTSON, James	21-1-1845	LONG, William	1-6-1841	MURPHY, James	4-12-1837
HUTT, James	1-2-1833	LOVATT, William	16-2-1842	MURPHY, John	6-1-1847
HUTTINGDON, George	30-11-1842	LOVE, Henry	8-10-1847	MURRAY, William	17-11-1847
		LUNT, Luke	1-5-1846		
ISUM, Henry	19-1-1835	LYONS, James	31-12-1841	NASH, David/Levi	27-8-1845
				NAUGHTY, Eleazor	8-6-1838
JACKSON, Mark	10-10-1843	MACKETT, John	20-10-1847	NEAL, Samuel	26-5-1834
JACOBS, Robert	26-6-1834	MACKEY, John	23-1-1844	NEIL, Peter	13-11-1844
JAGO, William	13-4-1846	MACOUN, William	27-12-1837	NELDER, Peter	29-5-1844
JAMES, Edward	12-1-1837	MAGNESS, Peter	31-5-1841	NEWMAN, Robert	15-7-1846
JAMIESON, William	12-11-1847	MAHONEY, Cornelius	16-4-1846	NEWPORT, William	17-10-1845
JELLY, Robert	7-6-1847	MAHONEY, Dennis	20-6-1834	NEWSON, Thomas	14-5-1842
JENKINS, David	17-6-1837	MALCOLM, James	28-4-1832	NICHOLAS, John	7-4-1843
JENKINS, Richard	16-11-1847	MALISON, Robert	21-1-1845	NICOL, James	16-1-1833
JENKINS, William	1-2-1833	MANLEY, William P.	12-11-1841	NIELD, Mark	23-10-1847
JOBBLIN, Emmanuel	28-10-1833	MANNING, Michael	12-9-1837	NOBLE, William	5-7-1845
JOHNS, Simon	31-1-1842	MARSHALL, Henry	6-1-1843	NORMAN, George	9-10-1843
JOHNSON, Abraham	25-1-1843	MARTELL, Moses	27-4-1839	NORRIS, George	7-4-1836
JOHNSON, John J.	7-4-1836	MARTEN, William	7-5-1838	NOYES, James	16-6-1836
JOHNSON, Thomas	27-11-1839	MARTIN, James	21-4-1847		
JOHNSON, William	12-1-1842	MARTIN, John (Aft Gd)	26-1-1843	OCCLESTON, John	23-11-1833
JOHNSTON, John	2-1-1838	MARTIN, John (Clker)	23-5-1834	ODGERS, John	12-9-1833
JOHNSTONE, Samuel	23-5-1834	MARTIN, Richard	10-2-1846	OLIVER, George	26-7-1834
JONES, James	23-3-1843	MARTIN, Thomas	1-8-1845	OSBORNE, William	9-10-1830
JONES, Peter	21-1-1846	MARTIN, William	7-5-1838	OSWALD, James	27-1-1845
JONES, Thos (C of L)	7-11-1845	MARTINBURY, Abraham	5-3-1833	OWENS, David	31-7-1835
JONES, Thos (Cook)	18-4-1846	MASON, Benjamin	1-3-1845		
		MASON, Joseph	20-8-1846	PAGE, William	12-5-1843
KEEMER, George	12-1-1847	MASON, William	26-3-1840	PALMER, Edward	6-10-1843
KELLY, Jeremiah	9-1-1843	MATTHEWS, Henry	13-4-1846	PALMER, John	11-8-1843
KELLY, Patrick	18-5-1833	MAY, Henry	16-11-1847	PARKER, John	21-12-1839
KENBY, William	6-7-1833	MAY, John	16-4-1841	PARKER, Peter	12-4-1842
KENNEDY, John	14-11-1836	MAYO, John	21-4-1844	PARRIS, William	6-6-1845
KENNEDY, Patrick	29-5-1844	McCARTHY, Jas (RM)	16-1-1833	PARRY, Thomas	12-1-1837
KERKING, Edward	2-12-1844	McCARTHY, Jas (RN)	12-9-1837	PASCOE, William	18-5-1842
KERSHAW, Thomas	30-5-1838	McCONNELL, James	31-1-1842	PATCHET, William	10-11-1837
KILLBURY, John	13-11-1839	McCORMICK, John	23-1-1844	PAUL, Thomas	25-4-1839
KING, George	28-1-1837	McCORMICK, Richard	16-8-1841	PAYNE, Samuel	30-7-1841
KING, Uriah	16-1-1834	McCOY, Jeremiah	19-11-1847	PAYNE, William	29-1-1835
KING, William	21-4-1845	McCREA, John	18-1-1845	PEARCE, James (B.Mte)	21-3-1837
KIRK, John	14-1-1839	McGILL, Alexander	24-10-1838	PEARCE, James (Late)	26-5-1834
KNIGHT, John	17-2-1832	McKEDDIE, Donald	12-1-1837	PEARCE, Thomas	21-9-1837
KNOWLES, Richard	27-9-1834	McNISH, William	2-6-1838	PEARSON, Andrew	15-7-1845
		McPHERSON, Michael	5-3-1833	PEECH, Thomas	18-1-1845
LACEY, Andrew	12-1-1837	MEARS, William	8-8-1843	PEED, James	19-8-1839
LACEY, Joseph	20-12-1831	MELDRUM. Robert	7-5-1834	PEEK, Chamberlain	22-8-1844
LANAWAY, John	10-8-1842	MERCHANT, William	1-6-1841	PENNY, Samuel	6-9-1833
LANE, John	12-11-1841	METHERELL, Edward	12-9-1837	PERCY, James	19-12-1835
LARK, John	25-7-1837	MIGGLEY, John	11-7-1836	PERREY, John	7-4-1836
LAWLOR, Edward	19-8-1843	MILLER, Frederick	31-1-1844	PETERS, Edward	21-8-1847
LAYTON, Francis	14-11-1844	MILLS, George	2-12-1843	PETERS, William	10-12-1833
LAYTON, George	11-12-1834	MILLS, James	25-11-1843	PETERSON, John	10-10-1843
LEE, James	7-4-1836	MILNER, R.	23-1-1844	PETTARD, John	23-9-1834

PHILLIPS, William	8-6-1838	ROGERSON, George	1-1-1838	TAYLOR, Robert	17-10-1832
PICKFORD, James	15-5-1835	ROSKILLY, Thomas	19-8-1843	TAYLOR, Thomas	8-1-1841
PIKE, James	24-1-1833	ROSS, James	3-6-1845	TAYLOR, William	23-5-1834
PLANT, William	17-5-1834	ROSS, Rolla	7-7-1840	TAZEWELL, John	27-4-1839
PLEDGER, John	26-7-1834	ROUND, Joseph	5-11-1847	TEAGUE, John	14-1-1835
PLUMMER, John	6-1-1843	ROWE, William	14-4-1845	TERRELL, John	28-10-1847
PLUNKET, Luke	11-12-1835	RUDD, Richard	10-8-1842	THOMAS, James	24-11-1838
POINTER, Samuel	8-4-1837	RUSSELL, Edward	7-4-1836	THOMAS, John (C.A'Gd)	26-3-1840
POLKINGHORNE, Wm	23-7-1841	RUSTON, William	6-7-1841	THOMAS, John (Q.M.)	18-6-1831
POLLARD, Richard E.	16-12-1831	RYAN, John	13-4-1843	THOMAS, Richard	11-7-1835
PORTE, Henry	29-9-1843			THOMPSON, John	9-4-1845
PORTER, John/Thomas	18-11-1841	SALTER, William	23-1-1844	THOMPSON, Wm (Q.M.)	12-7-1841
POULTER, James	18-7-1834	SALWAY, Walter	11-6-1844	THOMPSON, Wm (R.M.)	6-1-1843
POURRIDGE, Henry	26-4-1836	SAMSON, Richard	28-1-1847	THOMPSON, Wm (Sh Cpl)	30-9-1838
POWELL, Thomas	23-7-1841	SAVAGE, Henry	26-8-1845	THORNHILL, Richard	16-2-1837
PRIDEAUX, John	16-11-1847	SAVAGE, Samuel	6-10-1843	THORPE, John	30-11-1837
PRIM, Philip	17-1-1840	SAXTON, John	29-1-1835	THORPE, Thomas	7-11-1845
PUGH, Thomas	15-7-1847	SAYES, Manuel	25-1-1843	THURSTON, Edward	18-4-1846
PYE, William	13-7-1841	SCHUYLER, William	9-1-1834	TODD, George	23-10-1847
		SCOATES, William	29-5-1838	TOMS, William	17-9-1844
QUICK, John	14-1-1839	SEAWARD, Edward	16-11-1842	TRAILL, James	10-8-1842
		SEYMOUR, Richard	13-10-1831	TREGASKING, John	16-2-1842
RADFORD, George	31-7-1844	SHACKLES, William	8-11-1833	TREVERTON, Henry	21-8-1847
RANDALL, Wm (Armr)	26-8-1841	SHANNON, John	16-2-1839	TRIGGER, Philip	17-6-1837
RANDALL, Wm (C.Mast)	17-7-1847	SHAPCOTT, Thomas	16-12-1831	TROKE, James	26-10-1835
RAVENHALL, Richard	6-6-1845	SHAW, Felix	25-6-1839	TUCKER, John	8-7-1846
RAWLINGS, Henry	13-4-1846	SHEEN, Alexander	31-8-1835	TURNBULL, John	27-11-1847
RAYMOND, James	18-6-1846	SHIELDS, Henry	1-3-1843	TURNBULL, William C.	7-11-1845
REDDING, Owen	12-2-1835	SHOWL, Daniel	21-9-1843		
REEVES, James	7-5-1840	SIMMONDS, Henry	8-11-1847	URQUHART, John	2-1-1838
REEVES, Robert	18-6-1831	SIMMONDS, John	18-5-1833		
REID, John	23-9-1840	SIMPSON, William	7-10-1847	VALE, Richard	6-9-1832
REILLY, Charles	12-9-1837	SKYLEN, William	9-1-1834	VENNER, William	8-7-1841
REMFRY, John	15-4-1845	SLADE, Henry	16-8-1842	VENNING, Richard	8-5-1843
RENWICK, Thomas	7-5-1840	SLIGHT, Will	25-8-1841	VERCOE, John	21-12-1839
REYNOLDS, James	31-10-1845	SMEE, Charles	17-12-1834	VICK, Richard	11-5-1837
REYNOLDS, Joseph	6-8-1842	SMILIE, Alexander	27-3-1833	VINCENT, George	1-7-1847
RICE, William	6-1-1843	SMITH, David	8-10-1845		
RICHARDS, James	24-1-1842	SMITH, George	26-6-1847	WADDLE, Henry	11-2-1837
RICHARDSON, Henry E.	17-6-1837	SMITH, James (C.Mast)	9-11-1841	WADE, William	16-4-1839
RICKARDS, William	19-9-1835	SMITH, James (M.A.A.)	6-12-1831	WAINWRIGHT, John	11-12-1839
RICKETTS, John (RM)	31-10-1845	SMITH, John	29-3-1842	WALKER, Richard	4-2-1832
RICKETTS, John (RN)	17-10-1843	SMITH, William	15-11-1843	WALKER, Robert	3-6-1847
RICKETTS, William	19-9-1835	SNEDWELL, John	14-11-1844	WALKER, Thomas (A.B.)	31-1-1842
RIDLEY, Thomas	28-9-1847	SNELL, Richard	18-5-1842	WALKER, Thos (Sh Cpl)	25-1-1840
RILEY, Charles	12-9-1837	SPARLING, Richard	13-7-1842	WALKER, Wm (M.A.A.)	17-2-1832
RILEY, John	7-5-1840	SPARROW, Charles	17-5-1834	WALKER, Wm (Slmker)	14-4-1847
RILEY, Joshua	31-1-1842	SPARROW, George	17-5-1843	WALL, Edward	30-8-1847
RILEY, William	21-1-1845	SPENCE, George	17-9-1844	WALL, George	4-5-1847
RITCHIE, John	12-12-1840	SPURR, Stephen	10-10-1843	WALL, John	16-5-1842
RIVET, William	25-5-1838	STEWART, William	8-8-1844	WALSH, Dennis	28-2-1833
ROBERTS, James	1-5-1843	STIRLING, George	12-6-1838	WALTERS, William	2-8-1834
ROBERTS, Wm (C.Hold)	6-9-1839	STRANGE, Lot	19-3-1838	WARDELL, Thomas D.	7-5-1838
ROBERTS, Wm (Q.M.)	29-9-1831	STRICKLAND, Joseph	3-6-1845	WARREN, John	21-1-1845
ROBINSON, Alexander	17-3-1843	STRONG, James	31-3-1847	WATERS, William	2-8-1834
ROBINSON, Francis	12-7-1844	STROPERS, Jacob	14-1-1839	WATKINS, Richard	21-7-1834
ROBINSON, Jas (B.Mte)	24-8-1832	STRUTT, John	21-1-1845	WATSON, Richard	11-3-1841
ROBINSON, Jas (C.Hld)	22-7-1834	STURGESS, George	11-3-1836	WEAVER, Thomas	21-12-1831
ROBINSON, John	26-12-1845	SULLIVAN, Patrick	13-11-1839	WEBB, Richard	27-4-1839
ROBINSON, Samuel	16-11-1842	SULLIVAN, William	22-7-1834	WEBB, William	20-12-1834
ROBINSON, William	16-5-1842	SUMNER, Jonas	28-4-1836	WEBSTER, John	8-6-1838
ROBSON, Edward	5-7-1834	SUTTON, Edward	18-1-1845	WELSH, John	26-7-1834
ROBSON, Thomas	7-5-1834			WELSH, Richard	6-9-1845
RODGERS, Joseph	28-10-1831	TALBOT, John	8-7-1846	WENNER, William	8-7-1841
ROGERS, George	1-1-1838	TARSWELL, John	27-4-1839	WHITE, Benjamin	12-11-1844
ROGERS, Michael	1-1-1844	TAYLOR, Edward	13-4-1846	WHITE, James (R.M.)	2-3-1847
ROGERS, Samuel	3-6-1845	TAYLOR, James	31-1-1842	WHITE, James (R.N.)	21-7-1841

WHITE, John	5-3-1833	WILSON, Alexander	21-1-1846	WOODBRIDGE, George	18-4-1845
WHITE, Weeks	28-8-1845	WILSON, Charles	16-11-1842	WOODMAN, Daniel	28-1-1847
WHITE, Wm (Ply Div)	4-7-1835	WILSON, John	28-3-1839	WOODROW, Frederick	25-1-1843
WHITE, Wm (Po Div)	25-4-1831	WILSON, Joseph	7-4-1841	WOODS, George	7-4-1836
WHITMARSH, Stephen	8-10-1845	WILSON, Wm (Bsn's Mte)	16-5-1838	WOODWARD, James	15-9-1843
WHITMARSH, Thomas	26-7-1842	WILSON, Wm (Yeo St Rm)	22-3-1847	WOOLLEY, Henry	13-3-1833
WILCOX, Lewis	7-6-1842	WINBURN, Gabriel	31-5-1841	WOOLRET, Samuel	28-11-1846
WILLCOX, William	8-4-1842	WINDSOR, Henry	12-5-1842	WRIGHTON, Edward	29-1-1835
WILLETTS, Charles	31-10-1845	WINGETT, John	28-1-1837	WYBORN, John	18-4-1846
WILLIAMS, Benjamin	12-4-1842	WINNETT, Clement	23-9-1834	WYLIE, William	11-10-1845
WILLIAMS, James/John	10-5-1838	WINTERMAN, Thomas	2-6-1838		
WILLIAMS, John (A.B.)	31-1-1842	WIRE, Daniel	17-7-1844	YARWOOD, Matthew	22-7-1834
WILLIAMS, John (Q.M.)	17-10-1843	WITCHER, Thomas	4-1-1841	YEARWORTH, Thomas	10-8-1842
WILLIAMS, Thomas	25-3-1831	WITTERN, William	18-7-1842	YELF, Thomas	17-10-1843
WILLIAMS, Wm (RM)	28-8-1837	WOLFINDALE, James	2-1-1832	YOUNG, Thomas	6-7-1833
WILLIAMS, Wm (RN)	18-5-1833	WOOD, Andrew	19-2-1838	YOUNG, William (R.M.)	10-1-1843
WILLIS, Joseph	26-5-1834	WOOD, Jn (Capt Fxle)	30-8-1847	YOUNG, William (R.N.)	9-5-1842
WILMSHURST, George	28-8-1837	WOOD, Jn (Cox Launch)	2-6-1838		

Medals in the Collection

Award Date	Recipient's name	Rate/Rank	Ship/Unit	Yrs
1830 die	Un-named Pattern	Claw mounted narrow suspender		—
29- 9-1831	ROBERTS, William	Quarter Master	MELVILLE	23

Born 1776, Anglesea. In 1818 he had received a pension of £14/Year for serving in the Navy since 1803. Rejoined the service in June 1823 to complete time for a full pension of £21/Year. His 'Great War' history remains unknown.

6-12-1831	SMITH, James	Master at Arms	KENT	26

Born 1784, Quebec. His 3 clasp NGS medal for Basque Roads 1809 (Ord – *REVENGE*), Algiers (M.A.A. – *SUPERB*) and Navarino (M.A.A. – *ALBION*) does not appear to have survived.

17- 2-1832	KNIGHT, John	Captain Forecastle	GALATEA	23

Born 1792, Guernsey. He had been a First Class Petty Officer for ten years, but beyond this fact nothing has yet been uncovered concerning his former career.

6- 9-1832	BEAUMONT, Charles	Sergeant.	Royal Marines ('s' originally engraved)	21

His NGS medal with clasp for Algiers (Pte R.M. – *ALBION*) does not appear to have survived.

He had been a baker prior to enlisting as a Royal Marine on 13 December 1810 and sent to Chatham Division when aged 19 years born Shoreditch, London. Promoted to Corporal in August 1822, and to Sergeant on 18 April 1827. Records shew that he served relatively short periods aboard 14 different Ships, prior to being recommended for the 'Silver Medal' aboard H.M.S. *SERINGPATAM* in August 1832. Since the prevailing Rules prevented physical award of the medal until Beaumont was pensioned on 10

September 1832, the name of the Ship in which it was earned does not appear on the medal. (ADM 1/2728 – Capt W.66 & ADM 158/18)

27- 3-1833   SMILIE, Alexander   Late Royal Marine   Woolwich Division   24

Enlisted on 13 October 1808 in No 179 Coy, which became No 52 Coy after 1815 – both belonging to Woolwich Division. He was aged 18 years born Edinburgh when he joined, and completed his 21 years service as a Private R.M. Since no details of the submission for this LS & GC medal have to date been found, its date of award has been given as that on which he was pensioned. (ADM 158/66)

29- 5-1833   CAMELFORD, John   Late Acting Sailmaker   ZEBRA   23

An 'Inverted Reverse' Type medal. Naming also includes his 'alias John Brian' (*Vide* : 'Anchor Type – Case Law' for details and Plate No. 1)

Joined the service as a Boy 2nd Class aboard H.M.S. *DRUID* on 4 February 1808, aged 18 years born Waterford, Ireland.

Having completed a Commission aboard H.M.S. *ZEBRA*, he chose to re-join her when she was re-commissioned at Plymouth on 25 January 1829, remaining aboard until she was 'paid off' on 10 May 1833 – when he gained his Long Service awards of a gratuity and medal on being pensioned to shore.

26- 5-1834   PEARCE, James   'Late Seaman'   ST VINCENT   22

An 'Inverted Reverse' Type medal. The rate of 'Seaman' on his medal masks his former career as a Private R.M., enlisting in March 1811 aged 18 years born London. He later sought transfer to the Royal Marine Artillery in March 1817, and served in that Corps until he was unexpeectedly discharged – made redundant – in January 1831 when the R.M.A. was reduced from eight companies to four. It was reduced further to only two companies in 1832. His opportunity to complete the time necessary to claim a pension soon arrived. On 10 March 1831, he and 43 other ex-R.M.A men were allowed to join H.M.S. *ST VINCENT* as seamen in the rate of Able Seamen. Pearce remained there until she was 'paid off' on 23 May 1834, by which time he had completed an adequate number of years to allow his request to be pensioned. He was amongst eight men who were recommended for the LS & GC medal and gratuity when *ST VINCENT* was 'paid off'.

(*Vide* : Portsmouth letter A.411 – ADM 1/1378)

29- 1-1835   PAYNE, William   Gunner's Mate   TALAVERA   23

An 'Inverted Reverse' Type medal. He joined the Navy as a 'prest' man, taken from a merchant ship lying at Port Royal, Jamaica on 8 January 1808 to serve as an 'Ord' aboard H.M.S. *MUROS* – aged 20 years born Stroud, Kent. Was rated a Petty Officer in 1813, a status he retained until finally pensioned – except for the two years (1816-1818) when he earned his living in the Merchant Fleet. (ADM 29/10/149)

4- 1-1836   CHALMERS, William   Q.M. Sergeant   Royal Marines   30
                                                                ('s' added after issue)

This medal has a normal 'Reverse'. Enlisted on 30 April 1805 aged 20 years born Stirling, Scotland – having served the previous two years in the Stirling Militia. Promoted to Corporal on 3 November 1809, and four days later received his Sergeant's stripes – which suggests the possibility of special advancement for some gallant deed. His status did not end there, he was made a Colour Sergeant in September 1814, Sergeant Major in

December 1831 and a Q.M. Sergeant in July 1832. He was finally discharged in February 1842 – having served a total of more than 36 years with the Corps.   (ADM 158/17 & 18)

| 25-.1-1840 | BLEACH, Thomas | Gunner's Mate | PEMBROKE | 21 |

An 'Inverted Reverse' Type medal.

Group 3.

NGS. 3 Clasps.	Algiers	Ord	QUEEN CHARLOTTE
	Navarino	Captain Main Top	TALBOT
	Syria	Gunner's Mate	VANGUARD
	Turkish Acre.		

Joined the service as Henry Beach a month before the Battle of Algiers as an 'Ord' aboard H.M.S. *QUEEN CHARLOTTE* on 13 July 1816, aged 24 years born Shoreham – changing his name in 1819 to Thomas Bleach. After receiving his Pension, Medal and Gratuity in January 1840, he continued to serve as a pensioner without losing his Petty Officer status until he had completed 28 years servitude in April 1846 – when finally discharged aged 63 years!   (ADM 29/22/170)

| 6-7-1841 | RUSTON, William | Sgt Mjr R.M. | NORTH STAR | 22 |

Pair. Cross of Isabella Louisa. Original buckles & ribbons.

Enlisted in 1807 as a Drummer before his sixth birthday, a marginally lower age than the dispensation allowed to the sons of serving members of the Corps. He subsequently served as the Sergeant Major with the R.M. Battalion on the North Coast of Spain in the Carlist War – being finally pensioned as a Captain R.M. in 1857.

(*Vide* : '*Naval Medals 1793-1856*' – 'Carlist War' for his career and 'Naval Activities' for colour illustration)

| 13-7-1841 | PYE, William | Gunner's Mate | EDINBURGH | 30 |

Entitled to the Naval War Medal, clasp Syria, for services aboard H.M.S. *EDINBURGH* during her Commission ending in July 1841. The Roll names him as W.H. (& Wm) Pye, incorrectly shewing his Rate by ditto marks under the man on the list above him, noted as a 'Boy 2nd Class?' *(sic)*. This medal to Pye does not appear to have survived.

His career is an exceptional case. Enlisted as a Royal Marine at Woolwich on 17 April 1810 aged 18 years born Elsenham, Norfolk – he served for 21 years as a Private R.M. until pensioned on 4 May 1831. He then chose to commence a new career as a seaman – joining H.M.S. *BARHAM* as an 'Ord' at the age of 39 years in October 1831. Within four months he was rated Able Seaman, reaching Petty Officer status as a Gunner's Mate at the end of his gunnery course aboard H.M.S. *EXCELLENT* – on 15 July 1835. He was invalided in November 1843 with a total combined service (RM & RN) of 33 years.

(ADM 158/62 & 29/27/303)

26- 9-1841	CROWSON, Thomas	Color Sgt R.M.	HAZARD	27

	Group 3.	Waterloo.	Pte	73rd Regt of Foot
		NGS/Syria.	Clr Sgt	HAZARD

(This group is displayed at the Royal Naval Museum, Portsmouth, but the Waterloo and Syria medals were acquired as specimens of his entitlement – since his original rewards had become separated from his Anchor Type LS & GC Medal)

Enlisted in Nottingham on 30 January 1824, a brass founder by trade and literate – born 1795 in Birmingham. Previously served 7 years in the 73rd Regiment of Foot, earning not only the Waterloo Medal but also the bonus of two years service time for his presence at that Battle. Promoted to Corporal R.M. in May 1826, and Sergeant in February in 1828. He was invalided because of giddiness and loss of memory on 10 August 1844. (ADM 157/360)

18- 7-1842	EMBLING, Edward	A.B.	H.M.Cutter SEAFLOWER	22

Joined the service as a 'Landsman' aboard *ROCHFORT* on 30 September 1818 aged 20 years born Plymouth. Advanced to Coxswain aboard H.M.S. *PROCRIS* in 1825, prior to being promoted to Acting Gunner R.N. – a rank he did not retain for more than a few months. Ultimately served two successive Commissions aboard H.M.Cutter *SEAFLOWER*, as Gunner's Crew in the first and Able Seaman for his final Commission afloat. (ADM 29/29/250)

(*Vide* : 'Anchor Type – Case Law' and Plate No. 1)

26- 7-1842	MORTIMER, John	Sailmaker	WELLESLEY	25

	Group 3.	NGS/Algiers, Navarino	Sailmaker	SUPERB/TALBOT
		1st China War.	Sailmaker	WELLESLEY

Joined the service on 26 October 1815 aboard H.M.S. *TONNANT* as a Sailmaker, a 'Rate' he held for his active service career of more than twenty five years. Born St Andrews, Plymouth in 1793.

Large numbers of seamen were transferred from *TONNANT*, whilst she was being refitted, so as to complete the crews of the vessels sailing under Admiral Lord Exmouth's command for Algiers. Mortimer found himself a supernumerary aboard H.M.S. *SUPERB* from July until October 1816, participating in the Battle of Algiers on 27 August 1816 – subsequently being returned to his 'proper ship' *TONNANT*.

After serving for two consecutive Commissions aboard H.M.S. *PANDORA* (1819-1825) he was drafted to H.M.S. *TALBOT* in September 1825, taking part in that last sea battle fought under sail at Navarino on 20 October 1827 before being paid off in December 1828.

His next Commissions were aboard H.M.S. *KENT* (1829-1831), H.M.S. *CANOPUS* (1833-1837) and H.M.S. *WELLESLEY* (1837-1842) in which latter vessel he saw action during the 1st China War and from which he was pensioned and awarded his medal and gratuity after 25 years service in July 1842.

On the 'Reverse' of his Anchor Type LS & GC award, the die crack stretches faintly across the whole of the face of the medal from lower right to upper left edge.

| 16-11-1842 | SEAWARD, Edward | Quarter Master | CALCUTTA | 22 |

Pair.　　Baltic.　　A.B.　　ROYAL WILLIAM

Joined the service as a Landsman aboard H.M.S. *SUPERB* on 16 July 1819, aged 19 years born Plymouth. His advancement to the status of Petty Officer – Captain of the Fore Top – took place on board H.M.S. *DRUID* in December 1829. After receiving his pension, medal and gratuity he continued to serve for a further ten years – in the reduced Rate of Able Seaman, being finally discharged from H.M.S. *ROYAL WILLIAM* in May 1856 after earning his Baltic Medal.　　(ADM 29/29/596)

| 11- 8-1843 | ELLIOTT, William | Quarter Master | VANGUARD | 23 |

Joined the service as a Landsman aged 19 years, born Gosport, aboard H.M.S. *HYPERION* on 5 October 1818. Was advanced to Captain of Main Top ten years later aboard *SPARTIATE*. He retained this status as a Petty Officer until receiving his 'P,M & G'. He earned entitlement to the NGS Medal with clasp 'Syria' whilst aboard H.M.S. *VANGUARD*, but his name does appear on the clasp roll.　　(ADM 29/26/22)

| 6-10-1843 | PALMER, Edward | Color Sgt R.M. | THUNDERER | 22 |

Awarded NGS medal, clasp 'Syria', whilst serving as a Sergeant aboard H.M.S. *THUNDERER*, but this award – known to have survived – has over the years become separated from the recipient's Anchor Type LS & GC medal.

Enlisted as 'First substitute for Private James Massey, 67th Company' Royal Marines on 26 March 1831, aged 18 years born Dean Prior, Devon. His service papers in ADM 157/141 have been weeded. Discharged on 18 December 1843.

| 10- 7-1844 | FOWELL, John | Quarter Master | QUEEN | 21 |

Awarded NGS medal, clasp 'Syria', when serving as Captain of the Mast, H.M.S. *PRINCESS CHARLOTTE* – which does not appear to have survived.

His entered the Royal Navy rather late in his seafaring career, joining H.M.S. *HASTY* on 13 April 1822, aged 28 years born Chatham. His past experience with the trade of the sea allowed immediate advancement to Able Seaman. Within three years he was a Captain of the Fore Top, serving later in this Rate aboard H.M.S. *RATTLESNAKE* in the Action against Greek pirate vessels at Grabusa on 31 January 1828 – when H.M.S. *CAMBRIAN* was wrecked. After being pensioned, he served a further three years as a Seaman Rigger in Woolwich Yard – enhancing his naval pension.

| 13-11-1844 | COX, Joseph | Sailmaker | CORNWALLIS | 22 |

Awarded the 1st China War Medal as a Quarter Master aboard H.M.S. *CORNWALLIS*, which does not appear to have survived. Also entitled to the Baltic Medal as a Sailmaker aboard H.M.S. *ST GEORGE*.

He joined the service as a Boy 2nd Class aboard H.M.S. *DOTEREL* on 1st November 1819, aged 18 years born Plymouth. After being pensioned he continued to serve for a further eight years as an A.B., except for his time aboard H.M.S. *ST GEORGE* during the Baltic Campaign when he was rated as a 'Sailmaker'. Finally discharged to shore on 15 May 1856.　　(ADM 29/32/430)

| 7-11-1845 | TURNBULL, Wm C. | Bosun's Mate | St VINCENT | 23 |

Awarded NGS medal, clasp 'Navarino', whilst serving as Captain of the Fore Top, TALBOT – which does not appear to have survived.

First entered the Navy as a Boy 2nd Class aboard H.M.S. *TIBER* on 20 November 1815, aged 18 years born Greenwich – with the name William J. Matthews. Advanced to Landsman on 1st July 1817 and 'paid off' in October 1818. He re-joined the service (as William C. Turnbull) three years later as an A.B. aboard H.M.S. *VIGO*, and gained Petty Officer status – Captain of the Fore Top – aboard H.M.S. *NAIAD* in December 1824. Whilst aboard H.M.S. *GANNET* he was promoted to Acting Boatswain R.N., but after a year was reverted to Bosun's Mate in January 1833 – being pensioned and discharged to shore in November 1845.   (ADM 29/30/541)

| 18- 6-1846 | RAYMOND, James | Captain Forecastle | PHILOMEL | 23 |

With the forename Joseph he first entered the service as a prime seaman aboard H.M.S. *TARTAR* on 7 November 1822, and was rated 'Able Seaman' – aged 26 years born Norfolk.

He joined H.M.S. *BEAGLE* in March 1826 for her four year Commission as Captain of the Forecastle, but not before 1844 did he consistently hold Petty Officer status. His service record (ADM 29/35/1001) makes no reference to the award of this LS & GC medal when H.M.S. *PHILOMEL* was 'paid off'. It was such oversights by the clerks – excluding mention of 'M & G' – which caused difficulties in the construction of the Anchor Type Medal Roll. He served for a further three years – intermittently – after the award, before being invalided from the service in March 1852.

| 28-11-1846 | WOOLVET, Samuel | Bosun's Mate | GORGON | 24 |
| | (Woolret on medal) | | | |

His Army of India medal, earned as an Ordinary Seaman, H.M.S. *LIFFEY* – was once sold with this LS & GC award, but has since been separated.

Joined the service as a Boy 2nd Class on 19 October 1821 aboard H.M.S. *LIFFEY*, aged 19 years born at Chatham. Gained advancement to Captain of the After Guard (Quarter Deck) in September 1830 whilst aboard one of the earliest of H.M. Steam Vessels to be Commissioned – H.M.S. *LIGHTNING*. For a year he changed his 'Branch' and served as a 'Stoker', but reverted to supervisory seamanship duties.

Many of the vicissitudes met during his four year Commission aboard the H.M. Steam Frigate *GORGON* are recorded in *'Memoirs of Sir Astley Cooper Key'* by Vice Admiral P.H. Colomb (1898), pp 99-116. These include the stranding of GORGON in the Bay of Monte Video from 10 May until 15 July 1844, and the forcing of the chain boom on the River Parana under the guns of the Forts at Obligado in November 1845. He continued to serve for a further 15 years after receiving his long service award as an 'Able Seaman', which included five years aboard H.M.S. *ROYAL WILLIAM* and the time she served in the 1854 Baltic Campaign. He was discharged to shore after 39 years servitude in November 1861.   (ADM 29/37/406)

| 6- 1-1847 | MURPHY, John | Master at Arms | TYNE | 21 |

Group 5.	China 1842.	P.O. (Q.M.)	BLENHEIM
	Baltic.	A.B. (Pensioner)	ST GEORGE
	Crimea/Seb.	A.B. (Pensioner)	HANNIBAL
	Turkish Crimea.		

Joined the service as a Boy 2nd Class aboard H.M.S. *SEMIRAMIS*, aged 16 years born Cove, Cork. Achieved Petty Officer status aboard H.M.S. *BLENHEIM* in March 1841 as a 'Quarter Master'. The clerk neglected to make any notation of the award of his 'P, M & G' on his service records in ADM 29/37/519. He returned to serve in the R.N. three years after his awards – in the reduced Rate of A.B – completing 25 years servitude in March 1856.

| 24- 2-1847 | HEMSWELL, Joseph | Bosun's Mate | OCEAN | 23 |

	Group 4.	Baltic.	Bosun's Mate	MIRANDA
		Crimea/Seb & Azoff.	Bosun's Mate	MIRANDA
		Turkish Crimea.		

As an experienced seafarer he joined the service as an A.B. aboard H.M.S. *SYBILLE*, aged 25 years born Newport, Lincolnshire. He had to wait 16 years before he attained Petty Officer status as a Bosun's Mate aboard H.M.S. *DEE* in July 1839. The clerk neglected to make any notation of the award of his 'P, M & G' on his service records in ADM 29/36/25. Returned to serve a further 5 years after receiving his rewards, at first as an A.B., but later when joining H.M.S. *MIRANDA* in April 1854 he was advanced to Bosun's Mate – with his final discharge occurring on 31 March 1857.

| 14- 4-1847 | BARTLETT, John | Quarter Master | INCONSTANT | 22 |

Joined the service as a Landsman on 9 May 1824 aboard H.M.S. *WELLESLEY*, aged 21 years born Portsmouth. Attained Petty Officer status as Captain of the Hold twelve years later aboard H.M.S. *PEMBROKE*. Notation of 'M & G' was not made on his service records in ADM 29/38/189. He was re-employed as a Seaman Rigger in Portsmouth Yard for a year during the Crimean War.

| 20- 5-1847 | CHIVERS, Thomas | Color Sgt R.M. *(sic)* | THUNDERBOLT | 22 |

| | Pair. | NGS/Syria. | Colour Sgt R.M. | PRINCESS CHARLOTTE |

His Anchor Type medal was struck on the only known extra thick flan. This measure was taken by the Mint to ease the stresses upon a badly cracked die – but since it is the only one (so far) known, might it not have also had the opposite effect? Causing the die to become quite unuseable during the last striking of these medals in October 1846.

He enlisted on 5 October 1824 aged 18 years born Shoreham, Sussex. Promoted to Corporal in April 1829, to Sergeant in February 1835 and gained his Colours in June 1839. His papers shew that '... he produced a certificate of a musquet ball wound received at the storming of Sidon on 26 September 1840 ...'. He was pensioned from Portsmouth Division on 11 May 1847.   (ADM 157/371 & ADM 191/11/165)

| 17-10-1847 | MITCHELL, Henry | Bosun's Mate | AMERICA | 22 |

| | Pair. | Baltic. | Bosun's Mate | NILE |

Joined the service as a Boy 2nd Class aboard H.M.S. *VALOROUS* on 21 March 1821, aged 16 years born Plymouth. On 6 May 1828 he 'Ran' (deserted) as an A.B. from H.M.S. *RINALDO*, a stigma which was no longer to affect his career – pension and medal prospects – when his 'R' ['Ran' or 'Run'] was officially removed from his records on 14 October 1846. He achieved Petty Officer status as a Bosun's Mate in December 1831 aboard H.M.S. *REVENGE*. No notation was made on his records of 'M & G' for his awards in October 1847. He returned to serve aboard H.M.S. *NILE* as a Bosun's Mate for two years commencing February 1854, and yet again for three years as a Ship's Cook aboard H.M.S. *CAESAR* before being finally discharged in January 1862 – when he was once more recommended for a second (?) 'Medal & Gratuity' after serving a total of 28 years – which might have been issued judging by the standards allowed to Prideaux mentioned below.

The N.G.S. Medal, clasp 'Navarino' awarded John Prideaux (A.B. – *TALBOT*) is held in this Collection. Prideaux's Group of four medals – sold in 1881 – consisted of this NGS award, a China 1842 medal, an Anchor Type LS & GC Medal (November 1847 – Q.M./*CASTOR*/23 years) and a Victorian Wide Suspension LS & GC award (March 1856). The latter medal issued as a 'Bar' for an additional period of service – similar to the present practice which did not commence for practical purposes until 1951. Prideaux's exciting and historic Group was split up and all awards sold separately circa 1900.

ANCHOR TYPE NAVAL LS & GC MEDAL MINTING & NAMING DETAILS

(*Vide* ; Plate No. 5)

The 'Reverse' die used for striking all Anchor Type medals (1830-1846) must have become damaged whilst being hardened during its initial manufacture. The earliest known example of this medal – awarded to Private Thomas Williams Royal Marines (Artillery Companies) on 25 March 1831 – exists in the Otago Museum, New Zealand. The die cracks on the 'Reverse' of that medal exactly match those found on a 'Proof' specimen held in this collection – and other known early awards.

As an illustration of this proof specimen reveals, there is a circumferential crack from the lower part of 'F' of 'FOR' to the left hand edge of 'L' of 'LONG', and an axial crack from the edge of the medal running inwardly between the 'E' and 'R' of 'SERVICE'. During the first ten years this LS & GC medal was issued – after delivery to the Admiralty of the first stock on 5 April 1831 – every medal sighted by the Author possesses signs of these precise cracks, which did not extend further until the awards presented in late 1841. A list of the dates when all these batches of medals were struck for stock, and their quantities, is provided later.

During this decade (1830-1841), those awards issued during 1833-1835 display a rare numismatic variety of this medal. When the 2nd and 3rd strikings of this Anchor Type took place, the 'Reverse' die was accidentally inverted relative to the 'Obverse' on the stamping machine. This lapse caused the first word 'FOR' of the circumferentially named title of the medal to appear abnormally at one o'clock and not seven o'clock – the latter position appearing on other strikings. Although one medal with an inverted reverse is known to have been issued in 1836, it is probable that this piece was old stock intermingled in a drawer with more recently struck medals.

From late 1841 onwards, a faint crack curving upwards across part of the medal face from 5 o'clock can be discerned on the 'Reverse', which in later years becomes more pronounced and finishes at the edge at 9 o'clock. At about this same period two further cracks appear, one stretching axially – but not too far – towards the centre of the medal from the 'R' of 'FOR', and the other commencing on the original crack between the 'F' of 'FOR' to the 'L' of 'LONG' – and extending at right angles from it to the outer edge. The illustrations shew how all these cracks increased dimensionally – as the further strikings continued with the deteriorating die.

The final crack to appear occurs from the outer rim at the 6 o'clock position, just to the left of the rose motif – and this flaw is found on medals awarded from late 1844. In even later strikings this vertical lower crack can be seen to pass – for a small distance – through the circumferential set of raised dots – until the die became unuseable for striking large numbers in 1846. However, this die may well have been re-used in period of 1854-1856 for striking very small quantities of this medal on a number of occasions (*Vide* : '*Naval Medals 1793-1856*' – 'Arctic Meritorious Service Medals'). Of the medals in the last batch delivered for issue during 1846-1847, one Anchor Type medal is known which was struck on an extra thick blank – despatched to Colour Sergeant Thomas Chivers, R.M. on 20 May 1847 – which is in the author's Collection. This would have been an intentional practice in an attempt to make the distressed die last longer – but on this occasion the palliative might not have succeeded – hence, perhaps, the unusual number of 84 medals delivered by the Royal Mint to the Admiralty in 1846. The style and positioning of the engraved naming hardly varies during the time this award was issued.

The following statistical Table has been constructed from information gleaned over the past two decades on matters to do with the Anchor Type LS & GC Medal – an award which has proved irresistibly attractive to the Author.

Year	Medals struck	Names on roll	Stock at end year	Number of Medals	Yearly %age survived	Running %age survived
1830/31	30	16	14	4	25	25
1832	87	17	84	5	29	27
1833	24	36	72	6	17	22
1834	(30)	50	52	8	16	19
1835	(30)	47	35	7	15	18
1836	Nil	20	15	5	25	19
1837	60	47	28	13	28	21
1838	50	34	44	7	21	21
1839	50	31	63	7	23	21
1840	48	20	91	2	10	20
1841	50	60	81	17	28	21
1842	48	59	70	17	27	22
1843	98	70	98	21	30	23
1844	50	41	107	15	37	24
1845	Nil	68	39	14	21	24
1846	84	45	78	20	44	25
1847	Nil	80	Nil	35	44	27
	739	741		203	27%	

The numbers minted ( ) for the years 1834 & 1835 are estimated.

Whilst the absolute accuracy of this Table may be improved marginally over the coming years, such minor changes will not impair generalisations of a relative nature which can be drawn from it.

A SOCIAL SURVEY ON THE SURVIVAL RATE OF MEDALS

The figures in the 'Anchor Type Statistical Table' above are spread – year by year – across the period when the award of medals for campaigns to RN & RM personnel passed from being a novelty – to a quite normal mode of reward. The chance is thus offered of studying the earliest pre-history concerning the complex factors affecting the availability of medals to heritage bodies and collectors – from the time the hobby commenced to the present day.

The point of special significance in this Table is the marked 'sea change' in the survival rate from 1841 onwards. The contrast is even more dramatically demonstrated by the average figures for the two periods 1830-1840 (19%) and 1841-1847 (38%) with significantly higher percentages (44%) for the last two years 1846 & 1847. These differences are due entirely to the 'supply' side of these particular artefacts, unaffected by the 'demand' of collectors which commenced in earnest some 40 years later – by which time proof for this part of the thesis has lain until now hidden in the number of extant medals.

To explore the reason for the changing attitude of sailors and marines towards these medallic emblems during that former period 1830 to 1847, the conditions of day need to be summarised. This LS & GC award could only be given to men who had served sufficient time to earn a pension, and in the main most recipients then left the service with little reason to view the emblem with respect or pride, since there were few occasions when they might wear it. Some men might have viewed the award as a 'silver coin' rather than 'The Silver Medal' – as it was officially described by the Admiralty – and sold it for its bullion value and consequential desecration in the melting pot.

In 1843 there occurred the most evolutionary event in numismatic terms for sailors and marines. Now, for the first time since the Battles of the Nile and Trafalgar, entire ships' companies – from Admiral to Boy 3rd Class – were to receive a medal for participating in a campaign, albeit the un-named reward was an almost worthless (in monetary terms) foreign trinket, the Jean d'Acre Medal (*Vide* : '*Naval Medals 1793-1856*' – 'Syrian Campaign 1840. Turkish Awards'). Nevertheless, the subject of medals would have become a talking point never previously voiced on the lower deck or in the marine barracks, with some men no doubt mindful of a family relative who still proudly shewed off – or even wore – his illustrious medal commemorating the Battle of Waterloo. The question of pride and vanity may well have entered more minds than previously, especially since some fortunate pensioners could be possessors of a second award to complement their long service medal – not forgetting the greater esteem and lasting effect this may have had in family circles.

Only one year previously, another campaign involving thousands of sailors, marines and soldiers had been concluded in far eastern waters, and on land in China. During that 'First Opium War' conversations aboard those vessels which gave passage to soldiers could well have dwelt on the the subject of medals, especially concerning those worn proudly by some of the veteran soldiers from India. The examples seen might well have nurtured latent acquistive thoughts in the minds of many sailors aboard.

Commencing in 1846, Royal Naval personnel inclusive of Royal Marines were to receive the first official Campaign Medal available to military and naval forces sanctioned by the Queen. Seven thousand awards of this First China War Medal – aesthetic, named and fabricated in silver – were distributed to sailors and marines more ready to accept it for reasons beyond its bullion value. Pride of possession would have been taking an upward trend amongst a large proportion of recipients still serving afloat, with many years yet to serve in their chosen career.

Whilst this distribution of China medals was proceeding, the institution (in 1847) of the 'Naval War Medal' was announced not only for elderly beached 'salts' who had served in the late 'Great War', but also (in 1848) for more youthful sailors who had seen action only eight years earlier off the coast of Syria. Of the deluge of 21,000 'Naval War Medals' issued with its 231 commemorative clasps, some 7,000 awards were despatched during 1849 & 1850 for the Syrian Campaign in 1840, a large proportion of which would have been received by sailors and marines still on the books of ships, or in barracks. Medals were no longer a novelty, and there is little doubt that – at the time – most were retained by the recipient. The fact, today, that only a small fraction (from 8% to 12%) of the China and Syria medals are extant is a different story, to be discussed later.

Returning briefly to the 'Anchor Type Statistical Table', it is reasonable to ask if the retention by the recipients of their medal(s) – increasing from the low figure of about 20% to that of more than 44% – persisted, or were the figures for 1846 and 1847 shewn in this Table freakish examples? An answer to this question can be seen in the following Table, constructed from research carried out on the medals awarded for the First New Zealand War (1845-1847), which were not sanctioned or issued until the period 1870-1871.

75

1st New Zealand War. 1845-1847. Table showing survival of Medals

Ship	Reverse Date	No. of medals On Roll	No. of medals Survived	Percentage Survived
CASTOR	1845-46	62	31	50%
ELPHINSTONE	1845-46	6	2	33%
HAZARD	1845-46	35	21	60%
NORTH STAR	1845-46	41	24	59%
OSPREY	1845-46	11	6	55%
DRIVER	1846	10	6	60%
CALLIOPE	1846-47	69	30	43%
RACEHORSE	1845-47	36	22	61%
INFLEXIBLE	1847	20	12	60%
Totals		290	154	53%

With an overall survival rate of this order of magnitude (53%), there is sufficient proof that by 1870, the majority of medal recipients proudly coveted their rewards – retaining them for posterity – in contrast to a minority who had taken a less respectful view some thirty years earlier. It thus appears fair to state that any lack of medal availability – in the 20th century – cannot be attributed to the uncaring attitude of the recipients in the 19th century.

Having absolved the man who earned the reward from causing shortages of available medals, one passes to the attitude of next generation to whom these artefact(s) were bequeathed – and also to the commencement of medal acquisition by the founders of this hobby.

By 1860, most of the recipients of the 'Naval War Medal' for the 'Great War' had died, with the awards now in the hands of relatives and friends – some who cared deeply for the heirlooms and others who simply saw them as a means to acquire cash for some hedonistic purpose. The degree to which sales occurred is unknown, but many additional N.G.S. medals became available from this first generation of new ownership, even more from the second and third – the latter knowing very little of their great-grandfather. In the 1980s, the position with the seventh or eighth generations is completely reversed – it is not uncommon to find that they are attempting to re-purchase family heirlooms, either previously sold in the open market or gifted to museums by their forebears!

The forming of cabinets of war medals commenced circa 1855. Mr Washington of Liverpool had a collection by 1861, and the provenance of a four clasp 'Naval War Medal' (to James Sedeway) listed in the Whalley Collection catalogue (1877) dates back to purchase by Mr William Jackson of St Bees in 1857 – 'for a few shillings'! By the early 1880s there would appear to have been about twenty to thirty collectors, sufficient for the occasional but worthwhile auction sale of medals.

By the turn of this century the hobby was firmly established, the excellent reference books by George Tancred (1891) and John Horsley Mayo (1897) had been published, stocks of medals were held by a few London dealers who issued 'Lists', and at least four Auction houses held regular sales. There was, however, one fatal flaw for the future enthusiastic collector – the flow of medals available to the market (from descendants of the recipient of the awards) far outstripped the growth in the number of collectors, who by 1910 would appear to have numbered less than a hundred.

Not unnaturally the commonest medals were sold for their intrinsic worth – their bullion value – and consigned in their tens of thousands (army awards included) to the melting pot. Whereas Anchor Type LS & GC Medals (26% survived) always sold for three times their worth in silver, those medals awarded in their thousands to seamen and marines like the N.G.S. with Syria clasp (less than 15% survived), First China (8%) and Crimea (impressed) medals (7%) just melted away! The First New Zealand Campaign Medals (53% survived) fall into a slightly different category, since they were collected just as much by army and general collectors, as by naval specialists – most probably because they possessed 'Dated Reverses'.

It is the ten-fold explosion in the number of medal collectors in the past thirty/forty years which has high-lighted the apparent rarity of some almost commonplace awards which, a hundred years ago were to be found in abundance in the market place – only to be almost immediately destroyed.

Victorian LS & GC Wide Suspension Medal
1847-1875

Although this was a new 'Type' of naval Long Service and Good Conduct medal, it was initially awarded under identical regulations and restrictions as its worn out predecessor – the 'Anchor Type'. The new design relegated details of the recipient from the face of a medal, where artistic licence was possible, to the constraints encountered in the narrow confines of its 'edge'.

The opportunity to represent naval service on the new medal's 'Reverse' was grasped in masterful fashion. The chosen composition, a fully rigged sailing vessel, has survived many changes to the royal effigies on its 'Obverse' – and in essence, other than important retouching, continues to display the same 1st Rate sailing ship-of-the-line some 143 years after its original introduction in December 1847. Long may it remain so, as a well deserved compliment to the illustrious past endeavours of tars and jollies, untarnished by the developments of steam, steelhulled ships, breech loading guns, missiles, nuclear powered submarines and 'stone frigates'.

The numismatic niceties of medals are usually less important than the careers of the men who earned them, but in the case of Long Service medals which lack any obvious year of award – unlike campaign medals – their die differences can be used to date the latter end of a recipient's career. Just as the die cracks on the 'Anchor Type' awards, already mentioned, provide useful time scales, so too can this satisfactory approach be applied to 'Wide Suspension' (WS) Long Service and Good Conduct (LS & GC) medals.

'REVERSE' DIE VARIETIES.

Four basic and recognisably different 'Reverses' are discernible on WS LS & GC medals which, when classified, can be used to reduce the overall time span of this 'Type' from 28 years (1847-1875) to separate periods of shorter durations – a boon when researching a recipient who has a common name or whose ship had been in commission throughout the 28 year period – i.e. H.M.S. *EXCELLENT*. Even these narrower periods of issue can be reduced further – to no more than six years – when account is taken of the alternative of 'Yrs' found within the edge lettering ('Upright' or 'Sloping') – explained later in the 'Type Table'.

Quite the most distinctive of the four 'Reverse' varieties is the enigmatic 'M' in raised form at 5 o'clock, just within the surrounding rope border – on Type C (1865-1875). The precise positioning of this symbol 'M' – photographed at an angle to accentuate it – is illustrated on Plate No. 3 This 'M' mark also appears on the first Types of the Narrow Suspension (NS) LS & GC medal – on engraved edge named awards (1875-1877) and the subsequent impressed edge named medals (1877-1879).

The earliest 'Reverse Types' of the WS medal (1847-1865) can be discerned if scrutiny is directed to such areas as the ship's ensign, main mast pendant, driver boom, various cross trees, the knot on the encircling rope – and in particular the rigging lines within the triangular section abaft the base of the main mast – all of which can be seen on Plates Nos. 6 & 7, and described in detail on Plate No. 14.

'OBVERSE' DIE VARIETY DATED '1848'.

This is not only the most obvious identifiable 'Type', it also the rarest of the WS awards – of which only twenty one specimens are so far known to have survived from the 100 struck. Its 'Reverse' die is similar to the first Type of WS struck. The history and medal roll of this variety appears in a subsequent part of this Section.

ENGRAVED STYLE OF 'Yrs' IN MEDAL EDGE DETAILS.

The configuration of 'Yrs' engraved of the edge of the medal – representing total adult service (including Army, Royal Marine and Revenue Cruizer Service time for R.N. personnel) at the time of its award – appears in two obvious and differing styles. These modes referred to as either 'upright' or 'sloping' (*Vide* : Plate No. 4), allow the bracket for dates of award to be further sub-divided into no more than six year groups within the total of 28 years during which this particular award was distributed. This far narrower span of time can be put to good use by those wishing to research for the careers of recipients – and thus lead to revelations concerning campaign medals which they may also have earned.

WIDE SUSPENSION 'TYPE TABLE'.

The following Table includes the numbers of medals struck for each designated type, and their date of delivery to the Admiralty within the bounds of incomplete information provided in Royal Mint records. The various gaps between the earliest and latest known dates of award, for each 'Type' and sub-grouping by mode of 'Yrs', has been narrowed since this information was first published in 1977.

VICTORIAN LS & GC WIDE SUSPENSION MEDAL 'TYPE TABLE'

(*Vide* : Plate Nos. 6 & 7)

Die Type	Edge 'YRs'	Medals Minted Date	Number	Earliest/Latest Dates Known awards	Known edge 'YRs'	Type Totals
A (i)	Upright	24 August 1847	63	8 December 1847		247
		February 1848	24		All 'upright'	
		6 April 1848	160	15 May 1849		
B (1848)	Upright	25 April 1849	100	14 June 1849	All 'upright'	100
				25 November 1850		
A (ii)	Upright then Sloping	12 December 1850	100	17 May 1851		
		January 1852	100			
		August 1853	100		'upright' ends	
		May 1855	200	6 December 1856		
		January 1857	200			1,330
		December 1857	200		'sloping' begins	
		June 1858	200	27 March 1857		
		May 1861	200			
		26 May 1862	30	November 1862		
BB	Sloping	18 June 1862	270	July 1862	All sloping	270
				November 1864		

C	Sloping then Upright	15 February 1865 No details in Mint records for 5 years. Assume 200/year	300	March 1865	'sloping' ends June 187	
		1866-1869	1,000			2,200
		May 1870	300		'upright' begins	
		November 1872	300		August 1870	
		30 January 1874	300	23 February 1875		
					Total 'Wide' Minted	4,147
(Narrow Suspension)		(15 January 1875	300)	(22 February 1875)		

NOTES.

A 'latest known award date' may overlap an 'earliest known award date' of the next Type, due to an amalgam of the two 'Types' in stock awaiting issue. The issue of a duplicate medal – unrecorded on a man's papers – may also be a reason for discrepancy when its award date differs from Type Table above.

Types A (i) and A (ii) are the same but issued in two separate periods – before and after the '1848 Dated Type '

Type BB. On 27 February 1862 the Admiralty ordered 300 LS & GC medals for stock, of which the Mint delivered only 30 specimens on 26 May 1862. Since two Type A (ii) medals awarded in November 1862 (overlapping stock) are known with a die crack across the lower side of the 'O' in 'CONDUCT' – it is assumed that this Reverse Die became unusable after striking 30 medals of this batch. The remaining 270 medals of the original order were struck with a new Die (Type BB) – becoming available for distribution from 18 June 1862. This Type BB Die appears to have been used for only one striking, since there is no entry in the Mint records of an Admiralty restocking order for the period June 1862 to February 1865 (commencement of Type C).

'OBVERSE DIE VARIETY – DATED '1848' TYPE.

In 1849, whilst the Royal Mint were in the midst of striking thousands of Naval General Service Medals (1793-1840), a request was received from the Admiralty for one hundred Naval Long Service and Good Conduct medals. This small re-stocking order was soon met, but by mistake the Naval General Service Medal 'Obverse' die – with its date of '1848' in exergue (beneath the Young Queen's head) – had been used by a 'moneyer' in the stamping press (*Vide* : Plate No 7). The normal 'Obverse' die used for these Victorian LS & GC medals (both Wide and Narrow suspension Types) – previously and later – depicted the Queen's effigy without any date beneath it.

Thus quite unwittingly this minor error led to the striking of a batch of one hundred 'dated' medals which are amongst the rarest of any issued 'Type' of naval LS & GC award known today – if 'Pattern' or 'Proof' medals are excluded.

Similar mistakes, at differing times during this period, produced a few Army Meritorious Service Medals (MSMs) which were struck with the '1848' date. The error also occurred in the minting of the initial batch of fifty MSMs ordered by the Admiralty, for subsequent distribution to the earliest Royal Marine 'Sergeants' who received this 'Annuity Medal'. Because of an administrative whim, the issue of these fifty '1848' dated RM MSMs was not wholly confined to men meeting the medal's intended 'Meritorious' purpose. A number of these fifty RM MSMs with the '1848' dated 'Obverses' were usurped and adapted – by mutilation of the wording on the 'Reverse' – to become the official 'Type' of reward known as the 'Conspicuous Gallantry Medal (1855)'.

Whilst the Army authorities kept a Register (in effect a Medal Roll) of awards of their LS & GC Medals, the Admiralty did not commence this sort of book-keeping until early in the twentieth century.

To overcome this naval deficiency, the production of any 19th century Naval LS & GC Medal Roll can only be achieved by somewhat tedious means from differing groups of archival records. Such a 'Roll' for all these rare dated '1848' Victorian LS & GC Medals has been constructed for this Section – which also appears suitably annotated – within the overall 'Victorian Wide Suspension' Roll published later in this work.

The method adopted to produce this special 'Dated 1848 Roll' (1849-1850) might be of general interest to some collectors. The bulk of the names were extracted from the Wide Suspension Roll (1847-1875) already under construction by the author. However, it had already emerged that this main Roll would be incomplete since the clerks had failed to insert annotations regarding the award of the LS & GC medals in the 96 volumes of ADM 29/- Series (Records of seamen's servitude 1834-1873) in approximately three out of ten cases. The challenge thus set was one of attempting to find the names of the missing men who ought to have been annotated as recipients of this rare reward.

Firstly, a list was made of every ship which had been 'paid off' – after a three year commission – during 1849-1850, assumed to be the probable period of issue of this 'dated' medal. Then each 'description book' (ADM 37/- & 38/- Series) for all these vessels was perused, and the names of the men extracted who had served 21 years or longer by the end the ship's three year commission. This exercise produced a list of candidates who were eligible for the usual lottery of awards. The next step involved the use of the Alphabetical Index Volumes to the Admiralty Digest Books (ADM 12/- Series) for 1849 and 1850, since entries and notations were still being made therein of the names of those men recommended by the Commanding Officers of ships, and Colonels Commandant R.M. – for the award of the 'M & G' (Medal and Gratuity). These two exercises led to the production of a Medal Roll for most of naval and marine recipients of the LS & GC Medals (dated '1848' or undated) awarded during 1849 and 1850.

However, there was still one further question to be investigated before a finite and acceptable Roll could be completed. When were the first and last awards of this (1848) dated medal despatched ? Since bureaucratic records could not possibly contain such disclosures for use by future numismatists, it was obvious that the problem could only be solved by extracting such vital information from its locked position in the edge details on all known Wide Suspension medals – both dated and undated 'Types'.

Fortuitously the author had for many years compiled a list of 'Wide Suspension Medals' (dated and undated) which have appeared in auction catalogues and dealer's lists, aided also by the kindness of many friends who have passed on their sightings. The career of every one of these 'Wide Suspension Medal' recipients has been researched to reveal the date on which each award was approved, which in turn provided a coarse bracket of dates (June 1849 to June 1850) during which the '1848' dated medal was issued. A study was then made to find the closest dates of issue which externally abutted either side of these boundary dates – from amongst the data held on known 'undated Type' Wide Suspension Medals.

The outcome revealed that three known 'Wide Suspension' medals which lacked the date '1848' had been approved for men 'paid off' from H.M.S. *QUEEN* on 15 May 1849. These three recipients, Joseph Crichett (whose medal is in this Collection), John Edwards and William Stewart are amongst a total of seven men from *QUEEN* who were recommended to receive LS & GC awards that same day. Some, or maybe none, of the other four awards approved to this vessel (listed below) might materialise as dated '1848' LS & GC medals.

CRITCHETT, Joseph	Quarter Master	QUEEN	21 Yrs	15- 5-1849
CRUYS, William	M.A.A. (ex R.M.)	QUEEN	27 Yrs	15- 5-1849
DANIELL, John	Sailmaker	QUEEN	22 Yrs	15- 5-1849
EDWARDS, John	Bosun's Mate	QUEEN	22 Yrs	15- 5-1849
LEAN, Nathaniel	Ropemaker	QUEEN	23 Yrs	15- 5-1849
PHILLIPS, Alexander	Bosun's Mate	QUEEN	22 Yrs	15- 5-1849
STEWART, William	Sailmaker's Mate	QUEEN	22 Yrs	15- 5-1849

The next batch of LS & GC awards was approved a month later on 14 June 1849, of which one is known – as a dated '1848' variety – awarded to Samuel Johns (Quarter Master) aboard H.M.S.

HIBERNIA. This award has been used to set the earliest 'boundary' date of these dated medals in the constructed Roll.

To achieve the finalising boundary date, use has been made of a known 'undated' medal received by Edward Eastcott, an Able Seaman aboard H.M.S. *EXPRESS* who had served 22 years – which had been approved on 7 December 1850. The award to Frederick Woodrow, a Seaman's Schoolmaster aboard H.M.S. *VOLAGE*, approved one day earlier – on 6 December 1850 – has accordingly been assumed to be the last 'dated' variety issued.

The compilation of the '1848' dated LS & GC Roll has therefore been restricted to those recommendations for award of an LS & GC medal found to lie within these boundary dates. A total figure of 98 awards (which nearly matches the 100 medals struck at the Mint) have been identified – albeit some names may well have been missed in the complicated process of re-constituting the '1848' dated Medal Roll, and perhaps some men known to have been recommended (and included on this Roll) may not ultimately have had their submissions approved.

CONSTRUCTED ROLL OF DATED '1848' TYPE

Name	Rate/Rank	Ship/Div	Yrs	Date approved	
ABBOTT, William	Ship's Corporal	BOSCAWEN	24	9- 4-1850	
ALLINGHAM, William	M.A.A.	SCOUT	23	18- 9-1849	*
ATTRIDGE, Richard	A.B.	HIBERNIA	24	14- 6-1849	
BARTLETT, Robert	Pte R.M.	Chatham Div	21	14- 3-1850	
BAZELEY, John	Bosun's Mate	MEDEA	21	25- 7-1850	
BERETTO, Peter	Gun Room Cook	MELAMPUS	21	8- 8-1849	
BOREHAM, Edward	Pte R.M. (Cha)	RALEIGH	22	14- 3-1850	+
BRIGGS, John J.	Capt of Mast	HOWE	22	5- 7-1850	
BURNETT, Josh/Rchd	Ship's Corporal	CAMBRIAN	22	2-11-1850	
BUSSELL, Henry	M.A.A. (ex R.M.)	AMPHITRITE	?	24- 7-1850	
BUTLER, Thomas	Gunner's Mate	ROSAMOND	21	12- 4-1850	
BYFIELD, Thomas	Pte R.M. (Cha)	BULLDOG	21	5- 6-1850	*
CADDY, John	Ship's Cook	WELLINGTON	29	25-11-1850	
CADOGAN, Cornelius	Sick Berth Attdt	CROCODILE	25	29- 4-1850	
CAMPBELL, John	Clr/Sgt R.M.	Chatham Div	22	6- 9-1850	
CANN, Henry	Capt Forecastle	PANDORA	23	23-11-1849	
CARSE, John	Sailmaker	RALEIGH	26	11- 2-1850	+
CHRISTIE, Thomas	Bosun's Mate	VENGEANCE	21	4- 7-1850	
COATES, Robert	M.A.A. (ex R.M.)	RATTLESNAKE	36	11-11-1850	
COLE, Walter	Pte R.M.	Plymouth Div	21	6- 9-1850	
CONNOR, Michael	Bandsman (R.N.)	HIBERNIA	21	24- 6-1849	
CONSTINE, Jeremiah	Capt of Mast	TRINCOLMALEE	25	14- 8-1850	
CREW(E?)S, William	Gunner's Mate	TERRIBLE	25	25- 9-1849	
DAVIS, James	Quarter Master	DRAGON	22	8- 6-1850	
DOEG, James	Ship's Corporal	HIBERNIA	22	14- 6-1849	*
DOOR, Robert	Bosun's Mate	EURYDICE	24	4-12-1849	*
DUNN, John	Quarter Master	ALERT	24	16- 4-1850	
EARL, John	Coxswain Launch	SPARTAN	23	15- 6-1849	
EDWARDS, William	Bosun's Mate	HOWE	26	10- 7-1850	
EMBLETON, Thomas	Quarter Master	HOWE	22	5- 7-1850	
EUSTACE, John	A.B.	HARPY	25	5- 2-1850	
FORWARD, James	Clr/Sgt R.M.	Portsmouth Div	21	6- 9-1850	
GEDDS, George	Pte R.M.	Woolwich Div	21	14- 3-1850	
GRANT, Robert	M.A.A. (ex R.M.)	BELLEROPHON	23	2-11-1850	
GRAY, James	Quarter Master	AMPHITRITE	23	24- 7-1850	

GROVES, William	Quarter Master	HOWE	21	5- 7-1850 *
HALL, Walter	Quarter Master	PHILOMEL	22	17-10-1849
HANCOCK, John	A.B.	BELLEROPHON	25	4-11-1850
HARDIMAN, Thomas	Bosun's Mate	COLUMBINE	23	13- 4-1850 *
HARFLETT, Richard	Sgt R.M.	Chatham Div	21	6- 9-1850
HAWKE, Samuel	M.A.A.	HYDRA	23	14- 2-1850
HAYES, John	Capt Forecastle	INFLEXIBLE	23	22- 9-1849
HAYNES, Joseph	Clr/Sgt R.M.	Portsmouth Div	21	6- 3-1850 *
HEWETT, Thomas	Ship's Corporal	CHILDERS	21	26- 7-1849
HIGGS, John	Pte R.M.	Plymouth Div	21	15-10-1849
HOLLAND, James	Pte R.M.	Plymouth Div	21	6- 3-1850 *
HOLMES, William	Pay' & Pur' Stwd	HOWE	21	5- 7-1850 *
HONEY, James	Clr/Sgt R.M. (Ply)	NIMROD	22	14- 8-1849 *
HOWELL, William	M.A.A. (ex R.M.)	SPARTAN	?	15- 6-1849
JASPER, William	Quarter Master	SCOUT	22	21- 9-1849
JOHNS, Samuel	Quarter Master	HIBERNIA	22	14- 6-1849 *
(Entitled to NGS/Navarino. Not paired)				
KENDEL, John	A.B.	HIBERNIA	21	14- 6-1849
KNIGHT, Jonathan	M.A.A. (ex R.M.)	INCONSTANT	21	2-12-1850
LUCAS, William	Capt Mast	HOWE	21	5- 7-1850
MARTIN, George B.	Gunner's Mate	SPARTAN	22	15- 6-1849 *
MATTHIAS, James	Ship's Cook	ATHOLL	23	13- 4-1850 *
McCARTHY, John	M.A.A.	CHILDERS	22	26- 7-1849 *
McKENZIE, Jonathan	A.B.	CONSTANCE	21	1-12-1849
MILTON, William	Ship's Cook	HIBERNIA	22	14- 6-1849
MOFFETT, Robert	Capt's Steward	BELLEROPHON	22	4-11-1850
MOORE, John	Quarter Master	INCONSTANT	23	2-12-1850
MORRISON, Thomas	Carp's Mate	LIGHTNING	25	22-11-1850
NEWMAN, John	Quarter Master	BULLDOG	22	9- 4-1850 *
NORMAN, Richard	Ship's Cook	BELLEROPHON	23	1-11-1850
OWEN, John	Quarter Master	INFLEXIBLE	22	22- 9-1849 *
Group 4. NGS/Syria, Baltic & Jean D'Acre				
PARKINSON, John	Bosun's Mate	HIBERNIA	23	14- 6-1849
PARSONS, Robert	A.B.	CONSTANCE	21	1-12-1849
PARTRIDGE, William	Quarter Master	HIBERNIA	23	14- 6-1849
PAUL, John	Ship's Cook	INCONSTANT	24	3-12-1850
PAYNE, John	Pte R.M. (Ply)	TRINCOMALEE	22	14- 8-1850 *
PENNY, Charles	Quarter Master	HIBERNIA	23	14- 6-1849
PIPER, William	Carp's Mate	WELLINGTON	22	26-11-1850
PLUM, John	Pte R.M.	Plymouth Div	21	6- 3-1850
PURCHASE, William	Cabin Steward	FISGARD	43	22-11-1850
ADM 29/42/224	(6 Yrs boy's time included)			
QUIRK, David	Pte R.M.	Portsmouth	21	17-12-1849
RADFORD, William	Capt Forecastle	CONSTANCE	21	1-12-1849
RATTENBURY, John	Carp's Mate	PHILOMEL	24	17-10-1849
ROOK, William	Shp's Cpl (ex RM)	RATTLESNAKE	24	11-11-1850
SAYER, George	Pte R.M.	HASTINGS	21	17- 8-1850
(Later deserted – medal returned ?)				
SCALE, John	Quarter Master	BELLEROPHON	23	2-11-1850
SEAL, Daniel	Capt Forecastle	FURY	21	29-11-1850
SMITH, George	Quarter Master	BELLEROPHON	21	2-11-1850
SMITH, James	Bosun's Mate	VENGEANCE	23	4- 7-1850
SPENCE, John	Capt Forecastle	VENGEANCE	23	4- 7-1850
SPENCE, John	Ship's Corporal	ALECTO	21	26- 6-1849
SPURWAY, Robert	Pte R.M.	Plymouth Div	21	6- 3-1850
STABB, John D.	Coxswain Launch	HOWE	21	5- 7-1850

SULLIVAN, Cornelius	A.B.	WELLINGTON	25	25-11-1850	*
SUMMERFIELD, James	Clr/Sgt R.M.	Woolwich Div	21	6- 3-1850	
TOWLE, William	Pte R.M.	Woolwich Div	21	14- 3-1850	
URSELL, Frederick	Sgt R.M.	Woolwich	21	6- 3-1850	
VINCENT, John	Bosun's Mate	PHILOMEL	22	10- 9-1849	
WANSTALL, George	Quarter Master	CAMBRIAN	21	2-11-1850	
WEBB, Joseph	Ropemaker	TERRIBLE	24	23- 9-1849	
WEBB, Philip	Coxswain Launch	BELLEROPHON	21	2-11-1850	*
WOLFENDEN, George	Pte R.M.	Woolwich Div	21	14- 3-1850	*
WOODROW, Frederick	Seaman's Schoolmaster	VOLAGE	28	6-12-1850	
WOTTLEY, Thomas	Pte R.M. (Po)	TRINCOMALEE	21	14- 8-1850	
WRIGHT, John D.	Purser's Steward	ALARM	21	14- 5-1849	

Notes :   * = Medal known to have survived
           + = Only one of these two medals (for HMS *RALEIGH*) has survived.

DATED '1848' MEDALS KNOWN TO HAVE SURVIVED

Name	Rate/Rank	Ship/Div	Yrs	Date approved	
ALLINGHAM, William	M.A.A.	SCOUT	23	18- 9-1849	#
BOREHAM, Edward	Pte R.M. (Cha)	RALEIGH	22	14- 3-1850	+
BYFIELD, Thomas	Pte R.M. (Cha)	BULLDOG	21	5- 6-1850	
CARSE, John	Sailmaker	RALEIGH	26	11- 2-1850	+
DOEG, James	Ship's Corporal	HIBERNIA	22	14- 6-1849	
DOOR, Robert	Bosun's Mate	EURYDICE	24	4-12-1849	
GROVES, William	Quarter Master	HOWE	21	5- 7-1850	
HARDIMAN, Thomas	Bosun's Mate	COLUMBINE	23	13- 4-1850	
HAYNES, Joseph	Clr/Sgt R.M.	Portsmouth Div	21	6- 3-1850	
HOLLAND, James	Pte R.M.	Plymouth Div	21	6- 3-1850	
HOLMES, William	Paymaster and Purser's Steward	HOWE	21	5- 7-1850	
HONEY, James	Clr Sgt R.M. (Ply)	NIMROD	22	14- 8-1849	
JOHNS, Samuel (Entitled to NGS/Navarino. Not paired)	Quarter Master	HIBERNIA	22	14- 6-1849	
MARTIN, George B.	Gunner's Mate	SPARTAN	22	15- 6-1849	
MATTHIAS, James	Ship's Cook	ATHOLL	23	13- 4-1850	
McCARTHY, John	M.A.A.	CHILDERS	22	26- 7-1849	
NEWMAN, John	Quarter Master	BULLDOG	22	9- 4-1850	
OWEN, John Group 4. NGS/Syria, Baltic & Jean D'Acre	Quarter Master	INFLEXIBLE	22	22- 9-1849	
PAYNE, John	Pte R.M. (Ply)	TRINCOMALEE	22	8-1850	
SULLIVAN, Cornelius	A.B.	WELLINGTON	25	25-11-1850	
WEBB, Philip	Coxswain Launch	BELLEROPHON	21	2-11-1850	
WOLFENDEN, George	Pte R.M.	Woolwich Div	21	14- 3-1850	

+ = Only one of these two medals (for HMS *RALEIGH*) has survived. The description in Glendining's auction catalogue (5 Feby 1902, Lot 388) only included mention of the dated type of LS & GC medal and the ship's name – 'HMS *RALEIGH*'.
# = Medal edge details, most unusually, exclude his '23 Yrs' of service.

From these extant (21) medals – which show a survival rate of 21% – it might not be too unreasonable to assume that (say) about 13% (520 medals) of the more ordinary 'undated' Wide Suspension types (yet still as majestic) might be collectable today.

Medals in the Collection

ALLINGHAM, William   Master at Arms   SCOUT   (23 Yrs) 18- 9-1849
Engraved edge details lack mention of '23 Yrs'.

Joined the Navy as a Boy 2nd Class aboard H.M.S. *SURLY* on 1st October 1824 aged 16 years. Advanced to Petty Officer (Sailmaker's Mate) aboard *ACHERON* in April 1839. After receiving his Pension, Medal and Gratuity in September 1849 aboard *SCOUT* and seeking civilian employment, he returned two years later to continue service as a pensioner in the R.N. In July 1853 he was rated 'Admiral's Coxswain', serving a number of different Flag Officers aboard *AJAX*, *CONWAY* and *HOGUE* during the subsequent four years – prior to taking his time ashore in March 1857. A year later he sought service yet again in the R.N., and was accepted – somewhat normally for ageing re-employed pensioners – in the rate of 'Able Seaman' aboard *WELLESLEY*. He was finally discharged in November 1861 with 32 years servitude.

WEBB, Philip   Coxswain of Launch   BELLEROPHON   21 Yrs 2-11-1850

Also received China 1842 medal as an Able Seaman serving aboard H.M.S. *DRUID*. This medal is known to have survived separately.

Joined the service as a Landsman aboard H.M.S. *JASEUR* on 2 September 1828 aged 19 years. Advanced to Petty Officer (Coxswain of Launch) aboard *BELLEROPHON* in October 1847. He retained his P.O. status whilst continuing to serve as a pensioner, joining H.M.S. *SANS PAREIL* as Captain of the Mast when she arrived home from Crimean Waters in July 1855. He was finally discharged from the service on 10 August 1861 after serving for 29 years.

ELIGIBILITY AND RULES FOR AWARD 1847-1875

There was no change to the regulations regarding the award of the naval LS & GC medal when the 'Anchor Type' was replaced by the Victorian Wide Suspension medal in 1847. The old rules applied until 1853 whereby all prospective recipients (RN & RM) had to be in a position to satisfy authority on three basic factors and additionally blessed with luck : —

1. They had to be eligible for (or be in receipt of) a naval pension. Since August 1831 seamen were required to prove servitude of 21 years whilst above the age of 20 years. All marines enlisted prior to 8 October 1831 qualified for pension after serving 21 years above the lesser age of 18 years, whilst those attesting after that date came under the same rules as existed for seamen.

2. Approval for the award was only allowable when a ship was 'paid off' after a Commission of three or more years duration. Royal Marines stationed ashore were regulated by modified Army rules.

3. All ratings and marines had to prove from their various certificates that they had served their 21 years with 'Very Good' character assessments, had not been found guilty at a Court Martial, nor had 'Run' noted against their name.

4. Since the number of awards for seamen and marines were rigidly restricted without regard to the number of men who met the qualifications already mentioned, approval for the medal was a matter of 'catching the selector's eye' in the lottery of allowable number of quota rewards per ship or marine Division.

Bonus Time.

.Although the criteria for a pension until 1853 was proof of servitude of 21 years above a minimum age – this statement was not quite so straight forward as it appears at first sight, due to 'bonus time' which could be added to 'actual service' time. Those seamen who had qualified as 'Seaman Gunners' from the gunnery training ship H.M.S. *EXCELLENT* were granted additional time allowed to count as 'actual time' towards their pension – but only for the period they were in billets classified as requiring this qualification – at the rate of one fifth of such time, often noted on the man's service papers as '1/5th SG'.

In some cases part of time served by sailors or marines under the age of 20 or 18 years was wrongly allowed to count towards a pension, and in a few instances the whole of this pre-adult time was counted as 'Adult Service'.

Sailors were to receive another form of bonus in 1845. By an Order in Council dated 30 June 1845 the civil employment as a labourer or rigger in a naval dockyard – often taken up by 'paid off' seamen who wished to spend some time ashore – was allowed to count for the first time as reckonable naval service time towards the seamens' Pension, Medal and Gratuity – in their capacity as 'Reservists'. As one seaman rigger said later in evidence to an Admiralty Committee – 'the inducements are being with my family for a time, and my sea-time going on'.

Bonus time of one year was also granted for service during the Indian Mutiny, which was allowed to count towards the men's pension, medal and gratuity. However, this gift of the Crown was only given initially to certain Army personnel and marines. The benefit of this 'bonus' was not extended to seamen of the Naval Brigade until 14 January 1874 (Circular No 4.N), by which time most eligible old salts had been pensioned.

Quota allowances of medals.

Seamen and marines who passed the hurdles of service time and standard of conduct never had a 'right' to the award since it had been introduced in 1830, nor would they reap such equitable treatment until March 1875. The number of medals which could be awarded were rationed – dependent on the size of a ship's complement or Royal Marine Division ashore.

Originally one gratuity and medal was available for every hundred men in a ship's complement when she was 'paid off'. This rule debarred all types of vessels with less than one hundred men borne. In February 1832 the rule was changed so as to include the numerous 'Sloops' in Commission with complements of about 90 men. Henceforth one 'G & M' was allowed for 51-150 men borne, and two awards for 151-250 in complement and so on. Those ships (e.g. Cutters) with fifty or less men (a Lieutenant's or Master's command) were ineligible to submit an application for the long service rewards. In the fullness of time this 'one per hundred' rule, commencing from 51 men was ignored (or perhaps not even understood !) – and changed officially to one medal per 'the first and each' hundred in complement.

Marines at sea could earn the long service awards within the quotas already mentioned, but when ashore in their Divisional Head Quarters their allocation of awards were at first restricted by a quota dependent on the average numbers borne in the Divisional strength. To complicate matters further for them, the quota was altered from a certain number of medals to a specified sum of 'Gratuity' money, which in effect meant that more gratuities and medals could be given if Privates (£5) were chosen, and many less if the honours fell upon 'Sergeants'(£10) – still irrespective, as with seamen, of the number of fully eligible and deserving pensioner candidates. More detailed information concerning marines is mentioned in the introduction to the Section : 'Royal Marine Wide Suspension Medal Roll'.

In the same manner as innumerable suitably qualified seamen were denied the award because they were pensioned from a vessel which was not at the point of being 'paid off', so too were similarly situated shore based marines denied because the allocation of awards were only made at the end of each calendar year – with men becoming pensioners throughout every month of the year. Those really were the bad 'old days'.

From 1853, after the introduction of 'Continuous Service Engagements' for sailors, pensions were to be awarded to seamen and marines who had served 20 years (in lieu of 21 years) of adult service, but who now were also allowed to count their adult service from the age of 18 years (20 years formerly). This generous gesture was not lost upon sailors who could now earn a very reasonable pension three years earlier at the age of 38 years. It is noticeable from the Wide Suspension medal rolls that very few receipients gained their long service rewards at the lowered limit of 20 years prior to 1872, possibly because discretionary rules applied to men already in the service as to whether they could now (after 1853) earn a pension at the earlier age of 38 years in lieu of 41 years.

In 1860 some relaxation of the rules for awards of the LS & GC medal came into force (Circular No 440 dated 12 July 1860). Henceforth, additional LS & GC medals 'without gratuity' could be awarded on a one for one basis allowed under the old 'quota' regulations which allowed one medal and gratuity per 51-150 etc number of crew borne. But there was a slightly contradictory paragraph which stated that the medal without gratuity was to be allowed in the proportions of 'One for every hundred of the Crews of Her Majesty's Ships when paid off; three for each Division of Royal Marines annually' – the pre-1832 rule for seamen which excluded Sloops !

During 1870 further amelioration of the former unfair practices came into force (Circular No 13 dated 5 February 1870) – due to a recent Admiralty directive that all men on completing their time for pension were henceforth to be immediately discharged from the service. It was recognised that this new rule would effect the chances of men obtaining the their LS & GC medals – since it could still only be awarded when ships 'paid off'. From the date of this Circular commanding officers could recommend men for medals '.. during the period of a ship's commission, provided no more are recommended in the course of three years than would be allowed on the paying off of the ship, according to the scale laid down in Article 5, page 247 of the Queen's Regulations ..' Commanding officers were enjoined to spread their recommendations evenly, if possible, over the three year period – and thus apply quota restrictions at each recommendation should there be too many aboard who qualified.

These 'quota rules' governed by the size of ship's companies or R.M. Divisions remained in force until 16 December 1874, when unrestricted numbers of rewards became possible when the Admiralty stated '... it being their intention that there should not be any bar, except a man's own conduct, to his obtaining those distinguishing marks of their Lordships approbation.' The story of this dramatic departure from the old unfair rules, which coincided with the introduction of a new Type of award is told in the next Section on 'Narrow Suspension LS & GC Medals'. It should perhaps be mentioned here that 'Wide Suspension' medals were awarded under the old rules until the stock ran out on 25 February 1875, when issue of 'Narrow Suspension' awards commenced under the new '10 Year's Service' rules brought in during December 1874.

End of Commission 'Gratuities' in lieu of Naval M.S.MS

In January 1849 the Royal Marines introduced their own Meritorious Service Medal (MSM), following somewhat similar regulations to those applicable to the Army MSM (Sergeant's Medal) instituted in December 1845. The Admiralty chose a different course for use of the money made available for what could have been a Naval MSM (Petty Officer's Medal). To mark their approbation and the high sense their Lordships entertained of the Petty Officers of the Fleet, the Admiralty were pleased to direct that on a ship being 'paid off' in future, after the usual three years, Gratuities could '.. be awarded to the most deserving and well conducted Petty Officers, provided they are 'not' recommended for the Long Service Medal and Gratuity. Sergeants and Corporals of Marines are to be considered as eligible ..' There was a quota restriction of awards from seven awards (of the £7 or £5 gratuities to 1st or 2nd Class P.Os) in 1st or 2nd Rate Ships down to two awards in 3rd Class Steamers and Sloops. Thus 'failed LS & GC Petty Officers' at least had a chance to earn a gratuity if not a medal – in contrast to circumstances eleven years later (1860), when the Admiralty doubled the quota of LS & GC medals, albeit these additional medals were not to be accompanied by gratuities !

Verification of a man's previous service.

During the earliest years of awards of the 'Gratuity and Silver Medal' (1830-1840), Commanding Officers could only rely on the man himself producing proof from all his 'Captain's Certificates' (discharge tickets) that he had served for 21 years with high character assessments. Upon recommendation for the awards the clerks at the Admiralty would check these statements made by each man, verifying them from the various ship's Muster books- especially where the man's 'verbal/own statements' had been given because of his inability to provide such 'Captain's Certificates'.

In 1834, for the first time, the Admiralty created centralised records for 'sailors' in a series of books titled 'Servitude Records of men' (ADM 29/- Series), in which the career of each man claiming a pension was written up. Annotations of G & M, PM & G, M & G or M were also made on these records, but only in approximately seven out of ten cases of men receiving recommendations for the gratuity and long service rewards. Awards of campaign medals to sailors never appear in this ADM 29/- series.

Shortly afterwards in 1836 the Admiralty introduced the concept of 'Parchment Certificates'. These were single documents to be held by sailors on which their former and continuing career was to be recorded (*Vide* : separate Section 'Parchment Certificates'), thus eliminating the need for issue of 'Captain's Discharge Certificates'. The information on a man's 'Parchment Certificate' was to be copied into the newly created 'Description Books' (1836) made up for each Commission of a ship (ADM 37/- & 38/- Series). Information concerning the award of campaign medals was not called for on 'Parchment Certificates' until the 'Sixth Type' introduced in 1866.

Unfortunately not all Commanding Officers caused 'Parchment Certificates' to be made out initially, nor did they deal effectively with men who said they had lost them. In more than a few cases a man's former service remained unknown to his Commanding Officer – especially since previous desertion did not come to light when the man stated that his former 'Captain's/Parchment Certificates' had been lost. The worst of these cases so far met by the author applies to a George Clarke who joined the service in April 1820 as a prime seaman (Able Seaman) aged twenty years. At the end of a three year commission aboard H.M.S. *BITTERN* in January 1849 his Commanding Officer recommended him as a Boatswain's Mate for the good conduct Medal and Gratuity. When the clerk at the Admiralty took out his service details (ADM 29/42/321), he discovered that George Clarke had deserted on thirteen different occasions between 1827 and 1845 !

PARCHMENT CERTIFICATES

On rare occasions trusteeship of a lower-deck man's medallic rewards also extends to possession of his 'Parchment Certificate'. A document which immediately illuminates the recipient's personal details and provides an exhaustive chronological story of the 'sailor's' career. There is an added bonus on this certificate of a collection of signatures (autographs) from each of his Commanding Officers, some of whom might be found to bear household names for illustrious deeds or rising to the highest ranks in the Navy. The inquisitive collector might wonder when service certificates were initiated and how they were developed to present day standards ? The following treatise attempts to answer such questions.

Although long service pensions for healthy lower deck personnel came into force in 1814, no records dedicated to an individual's service history were introduced at the Admiralty to meet the enlarged number of claimants. The only documentation held by sailors were the series of Captain's discharge tickets supplied when either he or his Commanding Officer left his ship – in the main these tickets had been of use to verify claims to Prize Money rather than Pensions. In any case, even with these tickets and also for men who made verbal claims – having lost their documentation by accident, shipwreck or on purpose ! –

the clerks at the Admiralty were called upon to 'trace' a man's career from the muster books at times of pecuniary disbursement such as a pension – a search similar to that carried out by researchers today.

It is as well to remember that at this time 'sailors' were only hired for the period of a ship's commission and then beached, unlike the marines who were enlisted for a certain period of time in a Standing Force – everyone one of whom was logged in Description Books kept by their Port Divisions. Even when the initial concept of 'Continuous Service Engagements' was introduced in 1830 for men trained as Seaman Gunners aboard H.M.S. *EXCELLENT*, the records of these seamen failed to be recorded centrally at the Admiralty – nor did the introduction of Long Service Gratuities and attendant Good Conduct medals in 1830 lead to the creation of central service records. In 1834 moves were made within the Admiralty to provide better knowledge of 'seamen's careers', and additional attention given to their retention in His Britannic Majesty's Navy. Records of servitude were introduced (ADM 29/- Series) and the age old 'hire and fire' philosophy broached by allowing men '.. on being paid off, to re-enter before they have had time to spend their money ..', thus ensuring their right to an hitherto unheard of privilege of paid leave for up to one month.

But there was another side to these sensible improvements – that of combating fraudulent practices carried out by some 'tars'. Under the heading of 'Improvement in official checks and arrangements' a Memorandum was issued dated 16 June 1835 stating that : —

' Representations having been frequently made to their Lordships, that, notwithstanding the 10th Article of the Regulations for Pensions from Greenwich Hospital, seamen are being permitted to re-enter the Service who are unfit, and who have been previously invalided. Also that the men conceal the fact of such invaliding as well as their discharge tickets until it suits their purpose to produce them in order to quit a ship or station, or to complete a period of service, and that these documents are then used as a foundation for another discharge and further claims upon the Government.

It is their Lordships' intention that in order to prevent such irregularities, all men who re-enter the service shall be strictly questioned as to their previous servitude, and their discharge tickets examined, and that no man shall be received who is not in all respects fit for His Majesty's Navy.'

A note written beneath this Memorandum by an unknown hand states that : 'The Seaman's Parchment Certificate now proposed is a complete check to all these irregularities.' A proof of this 'Parchment Certificate' (known also as a 'Certificate of Servitude and Conduct') became available on 2 November 1835, with the regulations for its introduction communicated to all Commanding Officers by a Memorandum dated 24 December 1835 as follows : —

' The Lords Commissioners of the Admiralty deeming it desirable, for the interest of His Majesty's Service, as well as for the benefit of the Seamen of His Majesty's Fleet, that a Certificate of Servitude and Conduct for such Seamen, should be prepared upon parchment bearing the Seal of the Admiralty Office .... to be brought into use from 1st January 1836 .... and that the following instructions respecting it be strictly attended to.

For each Seaman of good conduct at present in the service, a copy is to be filled up of the Certificate so far as it can be, from any Official Documents in his own possession, or from any satisfactory information from himself, with great care as to neatness, legibility and correctness; and this is to be done for any man hereafter entered, who may have already served in the Navy.

.... [most] of the columns of it to be left blank until his discharge from the ship. Although the man may have several Ratings in the Ship's Books, only his last Rating is to be noted, and it is only on his discharge that this Certificate is to be signed, and not on the Captain or Commander leaving the ship.

The term 'fair', 'good' or 'very good' or 'indifferent' will be quite sufficient for insertion in the column for Conduct. .... As the loss of a Certificate must sometimes happen .... a copy of the Certificate is to be entered into the newly formed Description Book, in order that a man's conduct throughout his servitude in the Navy may be easily traced. .... [strict instructions concerning replacement of lost Certificates] ....

The men are to be particularly cautioned to preserve their Certificates from being in the least degree defaced, and to keep them folded in the tin cases provided for them. The copies of the Certificate marked with a red star are to be filled up for such men as have served 15 years and upwards, until the stock of that form is expended – when the ordinary form without the star will be used.

These Certificates and Tin Cases must be carefully accounted for by the Captain, in his General Stationary Account, until further instructions on the subject.'

'First Type' of Certificate (1836-1840).

Easily identifiable since this (7″ X 9″) form, when folded once, reveals a blank unprinted page on its reverse. After the first printing(s) some minor modifications were made to produce two 'modes' of this earliest 'Type' of Parchment Certificate. The first of these 'modes' (Mode A) can be distinguished by the style of lettering used and the lack of three additional columns – when compared with 'Mode B' certificates.

Mode A (1836-1837). The front page (of 4) of the form when folded bears the seal of the Admiralty Office in the top left hand corner – with either a blank right hand top corner or a red star there, the latter form to be used only for men who had served 15 years or more. The heading for this part of the Parchment Certificate reads : – 'Name. Date of Entry in the Service. His First Ship and No. in her'. Columns underneath call for entries covering Ship's Names, Ship Book Number, Rating, Entry & Discharge dates, Conduct and Captain's Signature, with similar column headings overleaf (page 2 when folded) – with the column headings printed in running sloping script on both pages 1 & 2. All other print style on the form is in upright Roman characters. Page 3 has the heading 'Description of the Person etc of ..... ' with three columns for completion beneath, beginning in the 1st column with sub-heading 'On his first Entry in the Service' seeking information (similar to that found in ADM 38/- Series Description Books) on ; Where born, Parish, Town, County, Usual place of residence, Age, Stature, Complexion, Eyes, Hair, Marks on Person, Wounds or Scars. The next two columns seek similar details 'On his discharge at the Age of 30 to 35' and 'After the age of 35'. Details are also sought at the bottom of this page 3 on such questions as 'If invalided : When', 'For what complaint' and 'From what Station' – questions which influenced the need to introduce this 'Parchment Certificate' in the first place.

Mode B (1837-1840). This form is very similar to 'Mode A' with the following exceptions. It appears likely that it was never produced with the red star in the top right hand corner on page one. The headings to the columns on pages 2 & 3 are in upright Roman characters, and three narrow columns are added on both these pages between those for 'Discharge' and 'Conduct' headed 'Y', 'M' and 'W' (Years, Months and Weeks) – which incidentally are hardly ever found to have been used by the clerk/officer completing the information on the form [*Vide* : Plate No. 9].

Unlike later editions of 'Parchment Certificates', neither the 'First Type' (Modes A or B) or the 'Second Type' shew the date of printing nor the numbers of forms printed. An example of 'Mode A' of 'Parchment Certificate' to Able Seaman Thomas Sambles complete with its embossed Tin Case, reside in the Author's Collection at the Royal Naval Museum, Portsmouth [*Vide* : Plate No. 8].

'Second Type' of Certificate (1840-1848).

An Admiralty Memorandum dated 14 October 1840 stated that a new form of Seaman's Certificate was forthwith to replace the existing one, and that Commanding Officers attention was to be particularly directed to : '.. the Note in Red Ink on the upper corner at the right hand, which is to be cut off in all cases in which the men's character shall not have been good, in order to prevent fraud by erasure' – thus establishing a precedent followed to the present day on all Parchment Certificates. On this 1840 'Type' form at the top right hand corner – within an outlining triangle – are the words printed in red : 'In the event of a Man having borne a bad Character on board any ship, the Captain of such Ship is to cut off this corner'.

This slightly larger Certificate (9" by 8") utilised the whole of the form – front and back – as a two page document, with folding only necessary to insert it into the tin case supplied for safe keeping. The front page with the Admiralty Seal now had the heading : 'Certificate of Service Of .... Name' – with exactly similar information sought to that already mentioned for pages 1 and 2 on the 'First Type' folded four page form – with the additional 'cut off' triangle in the top right hand corner already mentioned. The whole of the back page is devoted to similar questions on the 'Description of the Person, etc of ..' as those on page 3 of the 'First Type', but with a Note added at the bottom of the page : – 'If a Man who volunteers for a Ship should have lost his Certificate of Service the Captain of such a Ship is on no account to supply him with another, but is to apply for one to the Accountant General of the Navy'.

This second 'Type' of form remained in force until March 1848, but by late 1847 it had been given an official number – 'No. 155' – printed at the top of the front page [*Vide* : Plate No. 9].

'Third Type' of Certificate (1848-1853).

This was a slightly wider type of Certificate (10" by 8"), accommodating two extra columns. The first additional column set to the right of 'Conduct' was headed; 'Ability as Seaman' – sometimes found divided into three columns by the compiler in ink covering 'Seamanship', 'Gunnery' and 'Small Arms Drill'. This amendment to the old forms still in use was retrospectively directed when new regulations were introduced in June 1860. The second additional column was set immediately prior to 'Captain's Signature' was headed 'G.C. Badge' intended for Good Conduct Badges awarded or deprived. Other than the insertion of these two extra columns the information sought was similar to previous forms on both its sides, with a note on its reverse printed in red ink stating; 'Take notice that if you have been invalided and wish to re-enter the service and do not produce this document, or state to the officer that you have been invalided, you will not be allowed to reckon subsequent service for Pension or other advantage.'

This 'Third Type' of certificate (No. 155) was the first to shew the number of copies produced and the date they were printed, a practice which was repeated on all future printings of Parchment Certificates irrespective of 'Type'.

In 1853 a 'Standing Navy' was instituted, whereby most entrants were now allowed to 'sign on' for periods of time counting from the age of 18 years, and to re-engage to complete their time for pension. The former rules of 'signing on' for one ship's Commission at a time still applied for those men who did not wish to sign the new 'Continuous Service Engagement' – who were now referred to as NCS (non continuous service) men. Minor changes to the heading of the old Certificate 'No. 155' therefore followed in 1853.

'Fourth Type' of 'CS' & 'NCS' Certificates (1853-1861).

Whilst the size, format of and information required on the previous 'No. 155' forms remained the same, the headings on the front page were altered. The 'CS' certificate was renumbered 'No. 93A' with a heading of 'Continuous Service – Certificate of ... ', with questions beneath of ; 'Date of Entry for such Service', 'Age at that time', 'No of Registered Ticket', 'When and Where Registered'. A quite extraordinary omission was the directive to record the man's 'CS' number. Since the introduction of 'Registered Tickets' for British seamen of all types (naval, merchant and fishery service) in 1844, this was the only 'number' which a naval seaman might possess until the introduction of 'Continuous Service' numbers – and it was this Registered Ticket number which was supposed to be entered on all official references to the man, inclusive of muster and description books.

The heading on the top of the 'NCS' form reads ; '(Not for Continuous Service Men)', with the form 'No. 93' below followed beneath by 'Certificate of the Service of ....' with only one other question of 'Name'. However, it is not uncommon to find this form 'No. 93' used for CS men with the heading 'Not for etc etc' crossed out, and the man's details filled in as if it were the CS form (No. 93A).

A Note printed in red ink was added at the bottom of the front page of both certificates 'No. 93A' and 'No. 93' ; 'The conduct of a seaman being his Passport for future Service, the character of the party is to be impartially stated after most careful enquiry, and with reference to his whole period of service in the Ship'. The printed Note on the back page concerning invaliding remained the same as that found on the 'No. 155' form. These two types of Parchment Certificates were the last to feature the Admiralty Seal, which was never reinstated on any subsequent type of Parchment Certificate.

'Fifth Type' of Certificate (1861-1866).

Admiralty Circular No.428 dated 15 June 1860 not only established the introduction of a 'Record of Conduct' book for the crews of Her Majesty's Ships, with somewhat complicated instructions, but also made reference to the directive that 'Larger parchment certificates will in future be issued, which will have columns to shew the men's ability in Gunnery and Small Arm Drills as well as in Seamanship, and notations on these points are to be made on the certificates now in use.'

This new 'Type' of form was introduced in March 1861 measuring 14″ by 10″ which was intended to cover both 'CS' and 'NCS' men. The front page was headed with its form number – 'No. 93' – with the usual triangular 'cut off' instructions printed at the top right hand corner.

Part of the 'Description of the Person' details are now to be found placed as sub-headings in the uppermost part at the top of the front page – where the personal details sought included : – 'Date of Birth', 'Where Born. Parish/Town County', 'Age on first Entry. Years/Months', 'Date of Entry for Continuous Service' and 'Age at that time'. Yet again there was no directive to record the man's 'CS' number, which the compiler usually inserted in a blank area of the certificate.

The increased width of the form accommodated three additional columns for 'Seamanship', 'Gunnery' and 'Small Arm Drills' under the single heading 'Ability in', as well as a 'Remarks' column immediately prior to the 'Captain's Signature'. All other columns covered by this 'Certificate of Service' part of the man's form remained the same as on earlier types, with one minor exception whereby the three columns of 'Y', 'M' & 'D' were reduced to two columns headed 'Years' and 'Days' (still usually found uncompleted by the compiler) . Unlike earlier certificates, these details of service were continued for the top two thirds of the back page – the lower third accommodating all former details of 'Description of the Person' on earlier forms, except those now transferred to the top of the new form's front page.

By February 1862 minor modifications were made to this form. Its headed number became 'No. 61'. The single heading 'Conduct' now had three separate columns beneath it to permit differing assessments during a ship's commission, sub-headed 'End of 1st Year', 'End of 2nd Year' and 'On Discharge'. By

March 1863 the group heading 'Conduct' was amended to read 'Character' with the same three sub-headings beneath – compilers usually only filled in one assessment (Good or Very Good etc) written across the three columns.

'Sixth Type' of 'CS' & 'NCS' Certificates (1866-1874).

Whilst this two page Parchment Certificate remained the same size as the 'Fifth Type', it is the first certificate to be recognisable as the forerunner to the present day 'Type' of 'Certificate of Service' where its information is formulated in 'boxes' [*Vide* : Plate No. 10].

This form remained numbered – 'No. 61' – with the heading 'Particulars relating to . . . [name of rating]' – with the triangular 'cut off' printed part placed in the top left hand corner, counterbalanced on the top right hand side by 'Bounty (if authorised)', 'Amount £' and 'When received'.

The 'boxes' with their additional columns on the front page possessed headings of ; 'Description of Person', 'Continuous Service', 'Classification for Conduct', 'Good Conduct Badges', 'Gunnery Notations', 'Gratuitous Bedding', 'Gratuitous Clothing for Coaling', 'Invalided' and of special interest to readership of this work – 'Medals and Clasps etc'. The back page is devoted solely to chronological entries of the man's service time – under the general heading of : – 'Certificate of Service of ...... in the Royal Navy' printed sideways on the form. The columns beneath called for entries under these heading/sub-headings : – 'Ship's Name', 'Ship's Books/List – No', 'Rating', 'Entry', 'Discharge', 'Cause of Discharge', 'Character/End of 1st Year (31 Dec) – 2nd year – 3rd year – On Discharge', 'Ability as Seaman' and 'Captain's Signature'.

By August 1869 additional 'Boxes' and columns were added at the bottom of the back page relating to sickness and time spent in hospital. By May 1871 the Certificate was renumbered 'S. 61' – to conform with the recently introduced series of 'S' numbered forms which have now thus lasted for more than a century.

On 1st January 1873 every man in the navy of all branches was for the very first time to be given an 'Official Number' (O.No). Previously there were certain categories – such a Domestics (but not all of them) – who were not allowed to sign a continuous service engagement, but who now had an 'O.No' despite the fact that they were still unable to be 'CS' men, nor eligible incidentally for the Long Service and Good Conduct Medal.

'Seventh Type' of 'O.No' Certificate (1874-1883).

Still numbered 'S. 61', the content of its two pages (slightly larger in size at 14″ by 11″) are reversed from those printed on the 'Sixth Type'. The front page now has the 'cut off' triangle (top left side) alongside the heading 'Certificate of the Service of ...... in the Royal Navy', with '.... Official Number' beneath. The columns reverted to being printed lengthways on the form with similar headings (to 'Sixth Type' form) up to and including 'Cause of Discharge'. The next set of six columns are placed under the general heading of : – 'Character on 31st December in each year', with sub-headings of 'End of 1st Year', 'Captain's Initials' – same for 2nd year & 3rd year. Thereafter three additional columns appear with the general heading : – 'On Discharge', with sub-headings of 'Character', 'Class for Leave' and 'Ability as Seaman' – prior to the final column for 'Captain's Signature'.

The back page also printed lengthways covers 'Particulars relating to ... ' with a revised set of 'boxes'. Those previously referring to 'Gratuitous bedding' and 'Clothing for coaling' being deleted, with additional boxes for 'Vaccination' and 'Medical History'. The heading in the box 'Medals, Clasps, etc' remained with sub-headings : – 'Date Received' and 'Nature of Decoration'.

Institution of the modern four page 'Type' of Parchment Certificate (1884).

In 1882, Captain Harry Rawson (later Admiral Sir Harry Rawson, GCB, GCMG) – whilst Flag-Captain aboard H.M.S. *ALEXANDRA* – was directed by their Lordships to investigate thoroughly the whole question of awards of character to seamen and marines, together with advice on the most convenient form of Service certificates to be adopted, and other cognate matters such as good conduct badges as well as long service medals. After two years work he sought comment from many senior officers on his draft schemes before submitting his final report to a Committee set up to examine his proposals. With only a few minor exceptions his reforms were officially endorsed and approved in November 1884 – ultimately receiving almost universal approbation of every naval officer.

However, irrespective of approval being finally given for Rawson's proposals, a completely restyled Parchment Certificate was introduced in October 1884 with its size increased to produce in folded form four pages, each measuring 8″ by 13″. Its two inside centre pages were devoted solely to the man's service details, but they had to be entered (and viewed) 'sideways' in chronological order under one set of headings covering both centre pages, with the 'cut off' triangle inappropriately placed at the top left hand side of the 'Headings', thus placing it at the bottom left hand corner of page two when viewed in the upright position.

In March 1885 this four page format was revised to that closely resembling the 'Certificate of Service' found today – and containing most of the changes recommended by Rawson. The 'cut off' triangle now appeared on the top right hand corner of the front page, with the man's service details reading upright on page 2 with continuation columns on page 3. An additional 'box' was placed at the bottom of page 2 for wounds or hurt certificate(s) received, additionally covering meritorious service, special recommendations, prize or other grants. Whilst the back page now contained 'Conduct' as part of the main heading as Rawson wished – a word he proposed for use in lieu of 'Character' – the columns below retained (as they still do) classifications for 'Character' and 'Ability'. Assessments for both attributes were to be graded as Very Good, Good, Fair, Indifferent and Bad – thus excluding the former highest classification of 'Exemplary' which had been '.. admitted on all sides to have proved a failure ..' and replaced retrospectively by the older term 'Very Good'. It was to be some time before the assessments for 'Ability' were to be changed to Superior, Satisfactory, Moderate and Inferior.

On this 'Conduct' page an extra column headed 'RMG' (Recommended for Medal and Gratuity) was introduced, which also stemmed from Rawson's proposals. In future a man had to have received recommendations for his long service medal and gratuity from his 12th to his 15th year of adult service, recorded annually on his papers signed by his Commanding officer as 'RMG' in the appropriate column. Although the 1885 regulations directed that the heading and written insertion should read 'MGR' (Medal and Gratuity Recommended), the heading from its onset until it was annulled in April 1955 has always read 'RMG'. Nevertheless, on some 19th century certificates the compiler of the annual insertion can be found to have used the regulation (!) symbol 'MGR'.

It is perhaps of complementary interest that it was Rawson who obtained agreement to increase the time served for award of the LS & GC medal from 10 years – with a statement '... which at present is awarded too early and is too easily obtained ...'. However, his proposal that a man should have served 17 years before becoming eligible for the award – was reduced by their Lordships to 15 years of continuous 'Very Good' character time since the age of 18 years. All boys under training who were already in the service under the age of 18 years on 31 December 1884, and all new recruits joining after that date – were to be subject to this new rule of serving 15 years. All such similarly placed boys and new recruits also found that from this same date they had now to serve 22 years of adult service to gain a naval pension, whilst men joining prior to this date could still gain their LS & GC medal after 10 years and pension after 20 years.

In September 1892 the Parchment Certificate was revised slightly and given a new number, shewn as 'S.-536 (late S.-61)' which by September 1894 became 'S.-536'. The minor changes to the 1887 'Type' of form consisted of the removal of the column 'Time for Pension/Yrs-days' from pages 2 and 3, and an additional column inserted on page 4 for entries denoting 'Time Forfeited' headed 'P.,C.,C.P., or W.T.' (prison or cells) [*Vide* : Plate Nos. 11 & 12].

In December 1912 the Parchment Certificate was yet again given a new number, shewn initially as 'S.-459 (late S.-536)' which subsequently became 'S.-459'. An additional 'box' was placed in the upper right part of page 1 headed : – 'Nearest known relative or friend (Relationship, Name and Address)', more often than not entered by a compiler on earlier forms in any available space. On page 3 in the bottom 'box' the heading was altered from : – 'Gunnery, Torpedo, and other Examinations and Notations' to 'Examinations passed and Notations other than those entered on History Sheets'. The type of 'Time Forfeited' was changed to : – 'P, C. or C.P.'.

There were only a few differences between this 1912 form and the revised 'S.-459' certificate dated November 1956. On the front page the 'cut off' triangle still existed albeit in smaller format with horizontal lines printed within it and a Note at the bottom of the page stating : 'The top right corner of this certificate is to be cut off if the man is discharged with a 'bad' character or with disgrace, or if specially directed by the Admiralty' – the former words '.. or discharged with ignominy..' and '.. so as to make it desirable to prevent his re-entry into the Navy ..' being deleted.

The front page gave details of the man's personal description, his engagements and personal particulars which now included his 'Selected Depot', 'National Insurance No' and 'National Health Service No'. The lowest 'boxes' possessed space to record 'Swimming Qualification' and 'Medals, Clasps etc, Mentions in Despatches and Commendations' (space for award, deprivation, restoration or forfeiture of the man's LS & GC medal now appearing in a 'box' on page 4). The centre pages remained almost unchanged from the 1885 Certificate, recording horizontally the man's total career in precise chronological form whenever he changed ship or his 'rating', with two lower 'boxes' for 'Qualification and Examinations passed for Advancement' and 'Wounds received in Action, Hurt Certificates, Special Recommendations, Gratuities and other Grants'.

The back page was mainly devoted to the man's annual 'Assessment of Naval Character and Efficiency', with sub-headings for 'Naval Character', 'Efficiency in Rating', 'Rating held at time of assessment', 'Date' and 'Captain's Signature' – noticeably lacking the 'RMG' column. To aid the compiler there were Notes on the method of assessing Naval Character, in the order 'V.G.', 'V.G.*', 'Good', 'Fair', 'Indifferent' and 'Bad' – the 'V.G.*' could be awarded once to a man whose past assessments had been 'V.G.' but for that year had only been 'Good', thus allowing him to remain eligible for award of the LS & GC medal. The 'Efficiency' assessment was to be made without regard to the man's fitness for advancement measured in these four grades : – 'Sup' (Superior), above average efficiency, 'Sat' (Satisfactory), average efficiency, 'Mod' (Moderate), below average efficiency, and 'Inf' (Inferior), inefficient.

RESEARCH INFORMATION

Finding the Careers of Men awarded LS & GC Medals(1847-1875).

Unlike the Army, no medal rolls were ever compiled by the Admiralty for the Naval LS & GC medals awarded during the 19th Century. The author has constructed a partial roll for the Wide Suspension series comprising 1,430 seamen and 787 marines, a total of 2,217 out of the 4,147 known to have been issued and these rolls are printed later in this Section. Most of the missing names will be seamen as the Royal Marine roll appears to be almost complete.

The researcher who either owns a medal or has been able to examine one carefully is at a distinct advantage when it comes to researching the medal, for not only is that person privy to the details engraved on the edge, but is also able to narrow down the time-scale for the date of the award to a bracket of no more than six years by means of the 'Type Table' and illustrations already described.

The only places in Admiralty archives where notations can be found relating to the award of the LS & GC medals to 'sailors' occur in the volumes containing the mens' service records (ADM 29/-, ADM 139/- & ADM 188/- Series); the Admiralty Index & Digest Books (ADM 12/- Series) also contain such notes but only prove useful if the year of the award is known or guessed at (*Vide* : Section headed 'Victorian Wide Suspension LS & GC Medal – Dated 1848').

Only one of the 'Series' – ADM 29/- is accompanied by indexes, *viz* 'Name Indexes A – Z', ADM 29/97-100 (1802-1868) and ADM 29/101-104 (1868-1994) which will lead the researcher to all (or part) of a man's service career and/or supply reference to his Continuous Service Number (ADM 139/- Series). The career details for men earning the award after 1st January 1873 in the ADM 188/- (Official Number) Series are never written up prior to this date of introduction of 'O.Nos' – and have therefore to be read in conjunction with records found in the earlier 'Series' (ADM 29/ &/or ADM 139 Series); the Continuous Service ('C.S.') Number generally being noted at the top left hand part of the ADM 188/- sheet, or sometimes the ADM 29/- reference can be found written cryptically (such as 49/102 = Volume/Piece Number)) on the bottom left hand side for 'Non C.S.' personnel.

The A – Z Indexes of thr ADM 29/- Series can be a pitfall as experience has shown that relatively few of the men's forename and surname combinations prove to be unique in the Indexes, in fact it is not uncommon to find from five to twenty similar to that on the medal's edge. To avoid time consuming and frustrating failures the author has adopted a pet research procedure which has proved on average to lead to answers with a minimum of delay. The procedure involves the use of the ship's name on the medal taken in conjunction with the rule that from 1847-1870 the Wide Suspension medal could only be awarded to Pensioners at the unique time when a ship was 'paid off' at the end of a three year commission. The indexes (ADM 38/- Series) for the Muster Lists of ships for this period provide the clue, since they include 'Description Books' annotated with the boundary dates of each Commission to which each 'piece' refers – the latter date being the day when the vessel was 'paid off'. The dates on which the particular ship was 'paid off' can be thus logged as the only periods when the long service medal could be awarded – thus providing a series of years in which the recipient probably received his pension, as long as the years on the medal edge do not exceed pensionable time (21 or 20 years).

The general index to all 96 volumes of the ADM 29/- Series includes the dates covered within each volume ('piece') – which in most cases will refer to the date when a man's career was first compiled at the time his pension was awarded. These years/volume numbers can then be logged alongside the corresponding individual years already found when 'your' ship was 'paid off'. This pre-research data collection will automatically reduce the areas of search in the 'Name Index' volumes for the ADM 29/- Series, and takes very little extra time to produce since all the information is contained within books on open shelves in the reference room of the Public Record Office, Kew.

Researchers should remain mindful that some sailors received their long service awards some years after they received their pensions, which in turn means that their first entry into the ADM 29/- Series – by which they will be indexed in that series – will occur in Volumes covering the difference between pensionable time (21 or 20 years) and the years engraved on the edge of the medal, i.e. for a man with 25 years in the edge details, his volume will be 4/5 years prior to the date the ship was shewn to be 'paid off'.

Generally speaking, men with 22 years or more will be found to have received their awards before 1865. Although pensionable time was reduced to 20 years from 1853, it is most unlikely that any medal with 20 years on its edge will have been issued before 1860. Furthermore, since about 40% of all medals issued with 20 years on the edge were approved during the period 1873-1875, all such men will appear in the 'Official Number' indexes (ADM 188/- Series), where an additional column reveals their former CS numbers. If your medal was issued in the period 1870-1872 then none of these aforementioned 'tricks' work, added to which it is unfortunate that 'Description Books' for periods after 1870 were destroyed by enemy action during World War Two.

Quickly – or eventually ! – the page is found in a Volume where your man's name, rate, ship and number of years served are found which correspond with the indented details on the medal's edge. Only in about seven out of ten cases will the cryptic letters 'P M & G' (Pension, Medal and Gratuity) 'M & G', 'M' or 'Medal' be found in the ADM 29/- and 139/- Series on the man's service record, with an accompanying date when approval was given for the award. In the remaining instances – where the information in the career record matches the recipient's medallic details – the letter 'W' appears with a date which coincides with the time when the ship was 'paid off', or (after 1870) the date when the man received his pension, medal and gratuity. After 1860, when medals without gratuity could be awarded in equal numbers to those approved 'with gratuity' – the single letter 'M' or word 'Medal' is used as the notation of approval for the long service medal without gratuity.

If the matching details – career/edge of medal details – are found the ADM 188/- Series, it is unlikely that any reference to the award of the WS long service medal (1873-1875) will be found in the remarks column. The annotation of 'Traced M' in the ADM 188/- Series – invariably referring to the LS & GC award and not a campaign medal – will usually only be found in later years if the man did not have a CS Number.

To find the precise date of award in cases where there is no 'Traced M', the man's formerly written up career in the ADM 139/- series has to be sought which may well exclude part of his subsequent career, but will end either with the 'PM & G', 'M', 'Medal' or 'W' notation alongside details matching those on the edge of the medal. This procedure is sometimes lengthened because it was quite normal for men serving with 'O.Nos' at this time to have two (or even three) former C.S. Numbers, one without a suffix letter followed by one with either suffix 'A' or 'B' (or both).

The researcher should remember that it was never obligatory for ratings to sign a C.S. engagement from its inception in 1853, nor were certain ratings such as 'Domestics' allowed to 'sign on' for continuous service. In a few cases reference to where a man's former career (his CS No) may be found is not logged on the man's ADM 188/- career sheet – for such personnel who served as Domestics or Kroomen. For the more regular 'sailors' who never had a CS No, the clerk sometimes enters a cryptic notation (say) '45/145' at the bottom left hand side of the ADM 188/- career page – referring to ADM 29/- Series, Volume No 45, page 145 – where details of the man's earlier career and an annotation of 'PM & G', 'M & G', 'M', 'Medal' or 'W' will usually be found.

EARLIEST L.S. & G.C. AWARDS TO COAST GUARD
FLEETMEN

Although the Admiralty gained full control of the Coastguard in 1856, manned almost exclusively by former active service seamen from the Royal Navy since 1831 – these 'Boatmen' of all classes did not become eligible for any form of Long Service award until 1873 – when they were officially referred to as 'Coast Guard Fleetmen'. This rarely used title accurately describes their civil function as an anti-smuggling force composed of previously trained naval seamen upon whom the Admiralty could call in time of war as 'Reservists'. Their Long Service medal – albeit the same as that earned by active service ratings in the Royal Navy – can be said to be the progenitor of the 'Royal Fleet Reserve' Long Service award introduced 35 years later.

Amongst the normally urbane and usually much scorned Long Service and Good Conduct medals indented to Coast Guard personnel, there is at least one glittering 'Type' of this award which could enhance the cabinet of the most ardent specialist collector. It is only within recent times that a few of these earliest awards to Coast Guard Men have come to light in the form of the majestic Victorian Wide Suspension (1 1/2″ ribbon) LS & GC medal.

Due to robust 'weeding' of source material by the Treasury and Admiralty, no letters have survived which describe the detailed reasons leading to the precedent of honouring Coast Guard personnel in this manner. Nevertheless a few scraps of tantalising information have been gleaned. In February 1873 a Chief

Boatman in Charge wrote a private letter to the Admiralty, in which he sought approval for the award of a Long Service medal and gratuity. Although this request had to be refused, it was neither brusquely rejected nor disregarded.

Their Lordships' conscience had been pricked. Seemingly it caused an immediate approach to be made to the Treasury, with the aim of receiving financial approval for extension of the LS & GC rules to encompass 'Fleetmen serving in the Coast Guard on shore'. The Admiralty, in their submission, gave their reasons '.. why these medals have not been granted hitherto, and why these men should be equally eligible with those men serving in the Royal Navy ..', concluding with the remark that '.. the Coast Guard being now a Naval Force and of annual estimated cost.' This latter comment was a trifle naughty, since it had been true for more than sixteen years !

(Historical note: The Coast Guard and Revenue Services had been placed under Admiralty control on 1st October 1856, mainly due to criticisms concerning the numbers and competence of the Coast Guard 'Reserves' available to the Navy in that recent War with Russia. Some thousands of these 'old salts' had been embarked for the Baltic campaign, where their reported steadfastness was somewhat nullified by degrees of infirmity manifested overtly when the order 'off caps' at Church Service revealed so many bald pates !)

The Admiralty's proposal met with speedy approval by the Treasury, and a few days later an Admiralty Circular (No 15.P.) dated 10 March 1873 was published. This document set forth the regulations for future awards of LS & GC medals and gratuities to 'Fleetmen in the Coast Guard'. A man's service time over the age of eighteen years, whether in the Royal Navy, Revenue Service or Coast Guard could be aggregated towards the minimum qualifying period of 20 years for award of the LS & GC medal, but such a rule was only of academic interest to prospective recipients because of Governmental parsimony.

In exactly the same way as these awards were rationed on a quota basis per ship for seamen in the R.N., so too was an even tighter scale of awards to apply annually to 'Districts' in the Coast Guard – irrespective of the number of men in all respects eligible to receive the reward. All awards were to be 'With Gratuity'; the equal number of additional awards of the medal without pecuniary attachment allowed to R.N. seamen since 1860 was not to apply to this new class of recipient.

The restrictive allowance of 'medals & gratuities' for each Coast Guard 'District' was announced in the following manner : —

| Annually | FALMOUTH & WEYMOUTH (4) | KINGSTOWN (4) | NEWHAVEN (4) |
| | HARWICH (3)   HULL (2) | LIMERICK (2) | LIVERPOOL (1) |

| Every two Years | LEITH (1) |

| Every three Years | CLYDE (1) |

Since recommendations for these awards were to be transmitted annually on 1st April by the District Captains, only two such sets of lists could have been submitted prior to the introduction (February 1875) of the Victorian Narrow (1 1/4″) Suspension medal. Computing the total number of possible recommendations for this period, based on the aforementioned scales, leads to a maximum of forty two awards of Wide Suspension LS & GC medals to Coast Guard personnel.

Eligibility for consideration of this medal at this time (1873/74) required a minimum servitude of pensionable reckonable time, namely 20 years service over the age of 18 years, with '.. conduct and character rendering the man as deserving of this distinguished mark of approbation of the Admiralty.' With many hundreds of eligible candidates, it is hardly surprising that the first awards were made to men who had served considerably longer than 20 years. The attached Roll shows that most recipients had served 30 years or more, the exception being the Divisional Carpenter (Samuel Frost) with only 20 years.

Since no naval LS & GC medal roll for the nineteenth century has come to light, a reconstruction of any part of such a list involves the laborious task of checking all possibly relevant service histories. In the main, the clerks did note the award in cryptic fashion by use of the acronyms 'P.M & G','M & G' or 'M', but experience has proved that in about a quarter of cases the clerk forgot to annotate so specifically, beyond the use of the normal letter 'W'. This means that it is almost impossible to create a roll which can be more than 75% complete, even if the time to check more than a 1,000 volumes – each containing 100 service histories (ADM 139/ Series) – could ever be found.

By a stroke of good fortune, whilst researching another subject, it was noticed that the *'Naval and Military Gazette'* published the names of some naval LS & GC recipients during the year 1874. This source caused five extra names to be added to the Coast Guard Roll, which otherwise would have been excluded due to a lack of notation of 'M & G' on their papers.

Out of interest, a check has been made to see how many of these Wide Suspension Coast Guard recipients had previously received campaign medals, and also from which background all these LS & GC personnel came – Royal Navy or Revenue Cruizer Service. The findings of both these exercises are included in the following Roll.

ROLL OF WIDE SUSPENSION LS & GC MEDALS TO COAST GUARD PERSONNEL

(Maximum of 42 awards. 37 names so far found.)

Name	Rate	Yrs	Awd Date	Medal	ADM 29/—	
ALCOCK, Henry C.	Chief Btmn i/c	36	7- 4-1874	B1 (RN)	83/195	M&G
BERRY, David	Cmmd Btmn	23	31-10-1874	C1SI (RN)	83/255	PMG
BRADY, Thomas *	Boatman	35	8- 4-1874	B2 (RN)	83/197	M&G
COUGHLAN, Michael	Chief Btmn i/c	30	22- 7-1873	B3 (RN)	83/114	PMG
DICKER, William	Cmmd Btmn	34	23- 4-1873	(RN)	CS 1871	PMG
DRIVER, Abraham	Cmmd Btmn	34	17- 4-1873	B4 (RC)	84/65	M&G
FARROW, George *	Chief Btmn i/c	32	23- 4-1873	B5 (RN)	82/240	PMG
FORWARD, Thomas	Chief Btmn	32	24- 2-1874	(RN)	84/188	W
FROST, Samuel *	Div Carpenter	20	24-11-1874	B6 (RN)	22,229	PMG
HANCOCK, John	Chief Btmn i/c	29	2- 4-1874	B7 (RN)	83/194	M&G
				China 1842 VIXEN & C2S		
HARRISON, William	Chief Btmn i/c	37	14- 4-1874	B8 (RC)	83/202	M&G
HERRAGHTY, William	Chief Btmn i/c	34	14- 4-1874	B9 (RC)	83/201	M&G
				Crimea/S ROYAL ALBERT		
HOWE, Robert	Chief Btmn i/c	36	22- 7-1873	(RC)	84/91	M&G
KELLY, William	Cmmd Btmn	31	31-10-1874	B1 (RN)	83/254	W
LINDRIP, Thomas	Chief Btmn i/c	34	21- 4-1874	B3 (RN)	78/456	M&G
MARTIN, Samuel	Chief Btmn i/c	31	15- 4-1873	B6 (RN)	84/61	PMG
				NZ 1846-47 CALLIOPE & C2S		
MAYES, George	Chief Btmn i/c	29	15- 4-1873	C3- (RN)	CS 2638	M&G
McCREADY, John	Chief Btmn i/c	34	5- 5-1873	(RC)	84/77	M&G
McFARLANE, Donald	Div Carpenter	31	22- 7-1873	(RC)	84/92	PMG
MILLER, Joseph	Chief Btmn	29	25- 4-1873	B10 (RN)	83/87	W
				IGS/Pegu CONTEST		
MOFFETT, John	Chief Btmn i/c	32	20- 2-1874	B2 (RN)	70/217	W
				NGS/Syria CASTOR		
MURROW, Thomas	Chief Btmn i/c	31	17- 4-1873	B10 (RC)	84/64	M&G
PITT, William	Cmmd Btmn	34	8- 4-1874	B4 (RC)	83/198	M&G

REDDITT, Charles	Chief Btmn	32	9- 3/1874	B10 (RN)	82/285	W	
				China 1842 BELLEISLE			
RIDGE, William	Chief Btmn i/c	38	17- 4-1873	(RC)	84/66	M&G	
RULE, Billy	Chief Btmn i/c	41	18- 2/1874	(RN)	59/425	W	
SIMPSON, Henry	Cmmd Btmn	29	31-10-1874	B9 (RN)	83/253	W	
				Crimea/S ROYAL ALBERT			
SPRAGGS, James	Cmmd Btmn	33	8- 4-1874	B4 (RC)	83/199	M&G	
STEVENS, Henry *	Chief Btmn	32	11- 3-1874	B2 (RN)	82/204	W	
TANSLEY, Thomas	Chief Btmn i/c	38	5- 5-1873	(RC)	84/78	M&G	
THOMAS, Robert	Cmmd Btmn	33	17- 4-1873	B11 (RC)	84/63	M&G	
TIDRAY, Charles	Cmmd Btmn	28	11- 3-1874	(RN)	82/288	W	
				2nd China/- WINCHESTER			
TURNER, Joseph	Chief Btmn i/c	32	21- 4-1874	(RN)	CS 2586	M&G	
WADE, James	Chief Btmn	33	23- 4-1873	B2 (RN)	83/86	PMG	
				China 1842 DRUID			
WARREN, Henry C.	Chief Btmn i/c	33	8- 4-1874	B4 (RC)	83/196	M&G	
WHITER, Arthur	Div Carpenter	33	17- 3-1874	B4 (RN)	66/3	W	
WILLEY, William	Cmmd Btmn	32	9- 4-1874 ?	(RN)	O.No 78,692		

Abbreviations. Medal column.

Baltic Medal.	B1 = CRESSY B2 = DUKE OF WELLINGTON B3 = EXMOUTH
	B4 = CAESAR B5 = EDINBURGH B6 = AJAX B7 = PRINCESS ROYAL
	B8 = CALCUTTA B9 = PRINCE REGENT B10 = ROYAL GEORGE
	B11 = JAMES WATT
Crimea Medal.	C1 = BELLEROPHON C2 = PRINCESS ROYAL C3 = ARETHUSA
	S = Sebastopol I = Inkermann – = no clasp
Cmmd = Commissioned	Div = Divisional RN = Ex Royal Naval service
Btmn = Boatman	i/c = In Charge RC = Ex Revenue Cruizer service

*	= Medal known to have survived.
ADM 29/-	= P.R.O. Series for service histories.
83/196	= ADM Series 29, Volume 83, page 196.
CS	= Continuous Service numbers. (ADM 139/-)
O.No	= Official Number (ADM 188/-)
Final column.	P = Pension M = Medal G = Gratuity
W	= No notation on papers except 'W' with date, not unexceptional for issue of 'P, M & G'
	– *Vide* : known medal to Henry Stevens on Roll.

Notes. The hierarchical rating structure of the Coast Guard Service, *vis à vis* Royal Naval rates was as follows ; —

Chief Boatman in Charge	Chief Petty Officer
Chief Boatman	1st Class Petty Officer
Divisional Carpenter	1st Class Petty Officer
Commissioned Boatman	2nd Class Petty Officer
Boatman	Able Seaman

There was an outlet to Officer rank/status (who did not qualify for the LS & GC medal) as follows ; —

	Corresponding R.N. rank. With, but junior to : —
Chief Officer of Revenue Cruizer	Navigating Lieutenant
Senior Mate of Revenue Cruizer	Navigating Sub Lieutenant
Chief Officer of Station	Warrant Officer
Second Mate of Revenue Cruizer	Navigating Midshipman

(The specialist 'Navigating Branch' had been instituted in 1867, whose officers performed the duties formerly performed by Second Masters and Masters [the latter as 'Staff Commanders' since 1864]. Entry to the 'Navigating Branch' ceased in 1883.)

Medals in the Collection

Name	Rate	Yrs	Awd Date	Medal	ADM 29/—	
BRADY, Thomas	Boatman	35	8- 4-1874	B2 (RN)	83/197	M&G
FARROW, George	Chief Btmn i/c	32	23- 4-1873	B5 (RN)	82/240	PMG
FROST, Samuel	Div Carpenter	20	24-11-1874	B6 (RN)	22,229	PMG
STEVENS, Henry	Chief Boatman	32	11- 3-1874	B2 (RN)	82/204	W

VICTORIA. WIDE SUSPENSION. 1847-1875

Medals in the Collection listed in Type and award date sequence

Engraved abbreviations noted for many rates & ranks

Type A.(i). (upright 'Yrs')

Date awarded	Name	Rate ' ' on edge	Remarks
8-12-1847	NORRIS, Henry	Bosun's Mate Earliest WS LSGC known	23 Yrs. Pr. CH42/BLENHEIM
1-1848	LOCK, Charles	'BO : MATE'	24 Yrs. Gr NGS/Sy/THUNDERER
1-1848	FRYER, William	'BO : MATE'	22 Yrs. HMS ALBION
1-1849	DYER, Joseph	'SERJT'	HMS CALLIOPE
3-1849	HEMMINGS, William	'CAP AFT GD'	HM Sloop ELECTRA
15- 5-1849	CRITCHETT, Joseph	'QUARTERMASTER' Latest date pre 1848 Type	QM in full on edge

Type B. Dated 1848. (upright 'Yrs')

10- 9-1849	ALLINGHAM, William	'MAS : AT ARMS'	'23 Yrs' not on edge
2-11-1850	WEBB, Philip	'C of L'	Coxswain of Launch

Type A.(ii). (upright 'Yrs')

17- 5-1851	RADMORE, John	'ADs COX'	22 Yrs. Admiral Hornby
12-1851	LAKE, Robert	Ship's Cook	24 Yrs. Gr. CH42/BELLEISLE Carlist War Spanish award
1-1853	MOORE, Burton	'QUAr MASTr'	Edge abbreviation
1-1853	STARES, Thomas	Quartermaster	25 Yrs Gr. A of I/CHAMPION, NGS/Sy/PIQUE, SA53 /CASTOR, Baltic/ST VINCENT
4-1853	JOLLIFFE, John	'GUNrs MATE'	26 Yrs. HMS SCORPION
12-1853	HARVEY, John	'BNs MATE'	24 Yrs. No HMS. FISGARD
1-1854	LEARY, John	'BO : MATE'	23 Yrs. 'HMS Yacht' V & A

3-1854	STARLING, Stephen	'ABLE SEAMAN'	27 Yrs very neatly engraved
1-1855	BARRETT, Henry	'BOATSns MATE'	31 Yrs. HMS SPITEFUL
1-1856	TOLFREE, Charles	'CHf GUNs MATE'	Gr. Ch42/HERALD, Baltic /CALCUTTA
5-1856	CLEMENTS, Henry	Bosun's Mate	25 Yrs. Gr. NGS/Nav-Syria /DARTMOUTH – CAMBRIDGE
7-1856	SHEA, James	'Qr Mr'	25 Yrs. HMS PRINCESS ROYAL
8-1856	GOODYEAR, Robert	'Bo MATE'	30 Yrs (Entitled CH42)
3-12-1856	MITCHELL, George	'CAPT COXn'	Gr. NGS/Sy/CARYSFORT

Type A.(ii). (sloping 'Yrs')

27- 3-1857	COURT, William	'ADMLs COXn'	22 Yrs. Admiral Dundas
8-1857	ROLF, Jeremiah (ROLFF on medal)	'SERJt R.M.A.'	Edge 'Years' in full. Gr. NGS/Sy/VESUVIUS, 2nd CH/— BARRACOUTA
11-1857	STREET, Joseph	'Qr Mr'	Named SHEET on medal
11-1857	WRIGHT, John	Quarter Master	23 Yrs Pr. NZ 1846/CALLIOPE Entitled NGS/Sy & 2nd Ch
1-1858	MORRISON, John	'SERJt MAJOR'	Entitled RM MSM 1866
11-1859	ALPE, Aquila	'BOATSns MATE'	Entld CH42 & NZ/DRIVER
2-1860	GOOGE, George	'GUNrs MATE'	'VESUVIUS' edge correct Gr. NGS/Sy/GANGES, Cr/Seb & Azoff/VESUVIUS
2-1860	GOOJE, C.	'GUNrs MATE'	'VESUVISUS' & initial C & 'GOOJE' incorrect on edge
2-1860	PARTRIDGE, James	'COLOR SERJt'	No RM on edge. HMS ARACHNE. 22 Yrs. At Obligado
1-1861	JEFFERIES, William	'SERJt 5th Coy RM'	26 Yrs. Pr. RM MSM 1857
1-1861	JOHNS, William	'BOATSns MATE'	With his Bosun's Call
6-1861	MUSSELL, George	'CAPt M.T.'	22 Yrs Pr. IGS/Pegu/SERPENT
6-1861	DUKE, John (DUKES on medal)	'Qr Mr'	Entitled SA53, Baltic & 2nd China.
7-1861	HOOPER, John	'CAPt F CASLe'	23 Yrs. HMS SANS PAREIL
12-1861	PROUT, Thomas	'CARPrs MATE'	25 Yrs. HMS WELLESLEY
2-1862	HARRIS, William	'CHf GUNrs MATE'	21 Yrs. HMS CAMBRIDGE
3-1862	MADGE, John	'Pte. R.M.'	Gr. NGS/Sy/PIQUE, Cr/S & Ba
11-1862	HOULT, John	'Pte. R.M.'	22 Yrs. HMS HERO
21-11-1862	PLUMLEY, Charles	'Qr Mr'	22 Yrs. Gr. CH42/MELVILLE & bars, CH42/TF60 – URGENT, Cr/-/FURY

Type BB. (sloping 'Yrs')

20- 8-1862	RICH, Charles	'Qr Mr'	22 Yrs. Late issue ?
11- 2-1863	MORTIMORE, Thomas	'Cr SERGt 27th COy RM'	Lengthy edge details
1-1864	LUCAS, William	'SERGt 17th Coy RM'	27 Yrs. Gr. CH42/COLUMBINE, RM MSM circa 1890
2-1864	SNOOK, Elijah	'SERGt.48th Coy'	22 Yrs
24-11-1864	PRETTIEJOHNS, Edwd	'TAILOR'	Rare Rate

Type C.(i). (sloping 'Yrs')

2- 3-1865	BILLING, William	'Pte. 15th Co R.M.'	
12-1865	BLACK, John (Edge initial 'I')	'A.B.'	24 Yrs. Gr. CH42/NIMROD, 1st NZ/RACEHORSE
1-1866	BARFOOT, John	'CAPt FORE TOP'	'20 Yrs' not on edge.
2-1866	CROSSMAN, Joseph	'SHps COOK'	Edge HMS MEANCE for MEANEE. 23 Yrs Pr. Baltic/DESPERATE
12-1866	WEST, Charles	'CAPt OF THE FORELe'	23 Yrs. HMS ST VINCENT
12-1866	WALTON, Joseph	'CAPt OF THE HOLD'	HMS VICTORY
7-1867	TIPPER, William	Bosun's Mate	Gr 6. Cased. Photos. *Vide* NM Vol 1, pp 286-9
8-1867	CHITTENDEN, George	'ADMls COXn'	Admiral Lord Clarence Paget Gr. Late issue impressed Baltic, Crimea & Tu Crimea LSGC WS engraved.
12-1867	YOUNG, Charles G.	'CAPns COXn'	25 Yrs. Entitled Baltic
12-1867	JEFFERY, James	'1st CLASS STEWARD'	24 Yrs. Chief Petty Officer
2-1868	HANDCOCK, James	'Qr Mr'	23 Yrs. HMS PENGUIN
4-1868	ADAMS, William	'CARPrs Mte'	Gr. Cr/Ink-Seb/WASP
6-1868	BURGESS, Daniel	Color Sgt R.M.	Gr. Cr/Seb/AGAMEMNON and RM MSM 1895.
10-1868	LEPPARD, Richard	'COLr SERGt. 7th COy.R.M.A. HMS WIVERN'	Lengthy edge details Pr. Baltic/JAMES WATT
1-1869	BENSON, James	'Pte. 51st Co R.M.'	At Simoneseki
1-1870	MAXWELL, James	'SERGt. 76th Co.R.M.'	
21- 2-1870	SPARGO, John	Gunner's Mate	Pr. Cr/Seb/BRITANNIA

Type C.(ii). (upright 'Yrs')

28-12-1870	OLIVER, Charles T.	'NAVl SCHOOLmr'	22 Yrs. Pr. Baltic/VULTURE
5-1871	BROWN, Joseph A.	'CAPt OF THE MIZEN TOP'	Gr. Baltic/NEPTUNE, 2nd Ch /CA57/CALCUTTA
6-1871	MILLS, William	'GUNrs MATE. S.G.'	Seaman Gunner on edge
8-1871	PRESTON, Stephen	'Cf Grs MATE'	25 Yrs. Gr.Cr/Seb/AGAMEMNON
3-1872	NORTHCOTT, John	'MASr AT ARMS'	Nicely engraved Entld Ba, Cr & 2nd China
4-1872	BROWN, George	'SHIPS STEWd'	Chief Petty Officer Gr. Ba & Cr/Seb – ALGIERS
7-1872	PIZZEY, Thomas	Blacksmith	Gr. 2nd Ch & 2nd NZ – NIGER
10-1872	BARNES, Thomas	'SAILMKr'	Gr. Cr/Seb/LONDON, 2nd Ch/— /ROEBUCK
10-1872	CASTLE, John	'CHf YEOn of SIGNLs'	Rare Rate
12-1872	DOIG, Thomas	'COXns LAUNCH.	HM RESERVE. *Vide* Cooper T.M.' Key Memoirs page 300 Trained Man on edge
3-1873	FREELOVE, Joseph	'LEADg STO'	HM RESERVE. Entld Baltic
4-1873	SHEEHAN, Douglas	'ROPEMAKr'	Rare Rate

4-1873	FARROW, George	'CHf Btmn in	32 Yrs Rare WS LSGC to C.Gd CHARGE' Baltic/ EDINBURGH
4-1873	SPENCE, Charles H.	Ch Yeoman Signals	Gr. Ba & Cr/Seb – ST JEAN D'ACRE, 2nd NZ/IRIS and Abyssinia/OCTAVIA
4-1873	JOHNS, William	'CHf BO.MATE'	20 Yrs. Gr. Ba & Cr/Seb VALOROUS, 2nd Ch/3 clasps Canada GS/Fn Rd/AURORA
5-1873	LONE, Samuel	'GUNrs MATE G.I. S.G.'	Gunnery Instructor & Seaman Gunner on edge
6-1873	COTMAN, Charles E.	'GUN ROOM STEd'	22 Yrs. Domestic 2nd Class, not eligible for LSGC ! Entitled Baltic & Crimea
8-1873	PEPPERELL, John	'LEADg STOKr'	A Petty Officer rate
11-1873	GROSSMITH, William	'Mr at ARMS'	'at' in italics on edge
2-1874	TAYLOR, Thomas	'SHIPS COOK'	28 Yrs. HMS ANTELOPE
3-1874	STEVENS, Henry	'CHf BOATn'	32 Yrs Rare WS LSGC to C.Gd Baltic/DUKE OF WELLINGTON
4-1874	BRADY, Thomas	'BOATmn'	35 Yrs Rare WS LSGC to C.Gd Baltic/DUKE OF WELLINGTON
5-1874	ROACH, James	'COLr SERGt 47th Co RMLI'	21 Yrs. Pr. RM MSM 1904
9-1874	HART, Harry	'SAILMr'	Rare Rate. Entitled Crimea
10-1874	BROMLEY, Edward	'Qr Mr'	'ROYAL NAVAL BARRACKS'
11-1874	FROST, Samuel	'DIVISnl CARPtr'	Rare WS LSGC & rate to C.Gd. Baltic/AJAX
12-1874	NIXON, Robert	'YEOn STOREROOMS'	Rare rate. Gr. Cr/Seb /CURACOA
29- 1-1875	SCOBLE, Thomas	'BOs MATE'	With his Bosun's Call

VICTORIAN WIDE SUSPENSION 1847-1875

Medals in the Collection listed in alphabetical order of 'Rates'

RATE	SHIP	RECIPIENT	Yrs	Awarded	
Able Seaman	EXCELLENT	BLACK, John	24	12/1865	G
	NEPTUNE	STARLING, Stephen	27	3/1854	G
Admiral's Coxswain	CALEDONIA	CHITTENDEN, George	20	8/1867	G
	DUKE OF WELLINGTON				
		COURT, William	22	3/1857	S
	ASIA	RADMORE, John	22	5/1851	S
Blacksmith	AGINCOURT	PIZZEY, Thomas	20	7/1872	G
Boatswain's Mate	PRINCESS ROYAL	ALPE, Aquila	21	11/1859	S
	SPITEFUL	BARRETT, Henry	31	1/1855	S
	BLENHEIM	CLEMENTS, Henry	25	5/1856	G
	ALBION	FRYER, William	22	1/1848	S
	QUEEN	GOODYEAR, Robert	30	8/1856	S
	FISGARD (No HMS)	HARVEY, John	24	12/1853	S

	SATELLITE	JOHNS; William	20	1/1861	S
	VICTORIA & ALBERT	LEARY, John	23	1/1854	S
	ALBION	LOCK, Charles	24	1/1848	G
	CORMORANT	NORRIS, Henry	23	12/1847	P
	IRON DUKE	SCOBLE, Thomas	20	1/1875	S
	VICTORY	TIPPER, William	20	7/1867	G
Captain's Coxswain	WATERLOO	MITCHELL, George	21	12/1856	G
	FISGARD	YOUNG, Charles G.	25	12/1867	S
Capt' After Guard	ELECTRA. HM.Sloop	HEMMINGS, William	21	3/1849	S
Captain Forecastle	SANS PAREIL	HOOPER, John	23	7/1861	S
	ST VINCENT	WEST, Charles	23	12/1866	S
Captain Fore Top	RATTLESNAKE	BARFOOT, John	(20)	1/1866	S
Capt' of the Hold	VICTORY	WALTON, Joseph	20	12/1866	S
Captain Main Top	MAJESTIC	MUSSELL, George	22	6/1861	P
Capt' Mizzen Top	EUPHRATES	BROWN, Joseph A.	20	5/1871	G
Carpenter's Mate	PEMBROKE	ADAMS, William	20	4/1868	G
	WELLESLEY	PROUT, Thomas	25	12/1861	S
Chief Bosun's Mate	CAMBRIDGE	JOHNS, William	20	4/1873	G
Chief Gunner's Mate	CAMBRIDGE	HARRIS, William	21	2/1862	S
	PRESIDENT	PRESTON, Stephen	25	8/1871	G
	CALCUTTA	TOLFREE, Charles	21	1/1856	G
Chief Yeoman Signals	ROYAL ADELAIDE	CASTLE, John	20	10/1872	S
	ZEALOUS	SPENCE, Charles H.	20	4/1873	G
Coxswain of Launch	BELLEROPHON	WEBB, Philip	21	11/1850 ‡	S
Coxswn of Launch TM	H.M.RESERVE	DOIG, Thomas	20	12/1872	S
Gunner's Mate GI SG	MINOTAUR	LONE, Samuel	20	5/1873	S
Gunner's Mate SG	PENELOPE	MILLS, William	21	6/1871	S
Gunner's Mate	SCORPION	JOLLIFFE, John	26	4/1853	S
	RESISTANCE	SPARGO, John	20	2/1870	P
	VESUVIUS	GOOGE, George	21	2/1860	G
	VESUVISUS (sic)	GOOJE, C. (sic)	21	2/1860	S
Gun Room Steward	JUNO	COTMAN, Charles E.	22	6/1873	S
Leading Stoker	H.M.RESERVE	FREELOVE, John	20	3/1873	S
	(vide : HMS PEMBROKE 1873 Navy List)				
	AGINCOURT	PEPPERELL, John	20	8/1873	S
Master at Arms	SCOUT. HM.Sloop	ALLINGHAM, William	(23)	9/1849‡	S
	NORTHUMBERLAND	NORTHCOTT, John	21	3/1872	S
	MALABAR	GROSSMITH, William	21	11/1873	S
Naval Schoolmaster	CAMBRIDGE	OLIVER, Charles T.	22	12/1870	S
Quarter Master	ROYAL NAVAL BARRACKS	BROMLEY, Edward	20	10/1874	S
	QUEEN	CRITCHETT, Joseph	21	5/1849	S
	ESK	DUKE, John	20	6/1861	S
	PENGUIN	HANDCOCK, James	23	2/1868	S
	PLUMPER	MOORE, Burton	21	1/1853	S
	URGENT	PLUMLEY, Charles	22	11/1862	G
	HYDRA	RICH, Charles	22	8/1862	S
	PRINCESS ROYAL	SHEA, James	25	7/1856	S
	BRILLIANT	STREET, Joseph	21	11/1857	S
	CASTOR	STARES, Thomas	25	1/1853	G
	SPARTAN	WRIGHT, John	23	11/1857	P
Ropemaker	VALOROUS	SHEEHAN, Douglas	20	4/1873	S

Sailmaker	HECTOR	BARNES, Thomas	20	10/1872	G
	ASIA	HART, Harry	20	9/1874	S
Ship's Cook	MEANCE (MEANEE)	CROSSMAN, Joseph	23	2/1866	P
	HAVANNAH	LAKE, Robert	24	12/1851	G
	ANTELOPE	TAYLOR, Thomas	28	2/1874	S
Ship's Steward	PEMBROKE	BROWN, George	21	4/1872	G
1st Class Steward	ROYAL OAK	JEFFERY, James	24	12/1867	S
Tailor	MARLBOROUGH	PRETTIEJOHNS, Edwd.	21	11/1864	S
Yeoman Storerooms	BASILISK	NIXON, Robert	20	12/1874	G
Sergeant Major RM	25 Coy RM	MORRISON, John	21	1/1858	S
Colour Sergeant RM	CADMUS	BURGESS, Daniel	21	6/1868	G
	27th Coy RM	MORTIMORE, Thomas	21	2/1863	S
	ARACHNE	PARTRIDGE, James	22	2/1860	S
	47th Coy RMLI	ROACH, James	21	5/1874	P
Colour Sergeant RMA	WIVERN 7th Coy RMA	LEPPARD, Richard	21	10/1868	P
Sergeant RM	CALLIOPE	DYER, Joseph	21	1/1849	S
	5th Coy RM	JEFFERIES, William	26	1/1861	P
	17th Coy RM	LUCAS, William	27	1/1864	G
	76th Coy RM	MAXWELL, James	21	1/1870	S
	48th Coy RM	SNOOK, Elijah	22	2/1864	S
Sergeant RMA	BARRACOUTA	ROLF, Jeremiah	21	8/1857	G
Private RM	51st Coy RM	BENSON, James	21	1/1869	S
	15th Coy RM	BILLING, William	21	3/1865	S
	HERO	HOULT. John	22	11/1862	S
	ROYAL ADELAIDE	MADGE, John	21	3/1862	G
Boatman	H.M.COAST GUARD	BRADY, Thomas	35	4/1874	P
Chief Boatman	H.M.COAST GUARD	STEVENS, Henry	32	3/1874	P
Chief Boatman in Charge	H.M.COAST GUARD	FARROW, George	32	4/1873	P
Divisional Carpenter	H.M.COAST GUARD	FROST, Samuel	20	11/1874	P

Notes.   ‡ = Dated 1848 Type   ( ) = Number of years not engraved on edge
GI = Gunnery Instructor   SG = Seaman Gunner   TM = Trained Man
G = Group   P = Pair   S = Singleton

VICTORIAN WIDE SUSPENSION LS & GC MEDAL ROLL – ROYAL NAVY 1847 – 1875

Since the Admiralty did not compile any 'Rolls' for the award of naval Long Service and Good Conduct (LS & GC) medals until the beginning of the 20th century, it is left to the modern day researcher to attempt the construction of such 'Rolls' from extant records dealing – in the case of sailors – with each individual's recommendation for the award.

The following Wide Suspension (WS) 'Roll' is far from complete. Such an ambition will always prove to be an impossibility due to the failure of some latter-day clerks to register the recommendation for the award ('PMG' or 'Medal' etc) on a man's papers – in approximately three out of ten cases. Its other shortcoming to the author has been the lack of research time to evaluate facts from 800 volumes, each containing 100 service histories.

Of the total number of 4,147 WS LS & GC medals struck, it is probable that 3,187 were earned by 'sailors' and 960 by marines. Since the 'shore' awards part of the Royal Marine Roll is thought to be almost complete, of which 126 medals (17%) are known to have survived, it is not unreasonable to assume that a similar proportion of 'sailors' awards have survived – amounting to 540 medals.

The following incomplete 'sailors' Wide Suspension LS & GC Roll (1,430 names) has been compiled inclusive of 300 WS medals which are known to have survived. The remaining 1,130 have been compiled from sight of thousands of service histories of 'sailors'. In the first instance from the records of every 'sailor' written up in the ADM 29/- Series (96 volumes) – whose service history contains a cryptic annotation referring to the award of a long service medal. Latterly, the records of every 'sailor' in some 200 volumes of the ADM 139/- Series have been similarly treated – but over 800 volumes of this Series still need to be searched, wherein from experience it is likely that only one or two men will be noted to have received the LS & GC reward out of the 100 service histories contained in each volume. The names of at least 800 other recipients remaining hidden under the uninformative notation 'W' on men's service histories – in lieu of 'PMG' or 'Medal' etc.

As a matter of general interest, the earliest and latest known awards of the Wide Suspension LS & GC Medal, which have coincidentally survived are : —

Bosun's Mate   Henry Norris   HMS CORMORANT   23 Years   8 December 1847

Corporal RM   Henry Mullins   38 Coy Po Div   21 Years   23 February 1875

VICTORIAN WIDE SUSPENSION LS & GC MEDAL ROLL – ROYAL NAVY

Name	'No'	Rate	Ship	Awarded	Yrs	
ABBOTT, George	37,797	Gunner's Mate	ST VINCENT	30- 4-1873	20	*
ABBOTT, John	41/226	Ship's Corporal	LEANDER	12-10-1852	27	
ABBOTT, William	44/421	Ship's Corporal	BOSCAWEN (ex RM)	9- 4-1850	24	‡
ACKERMAN, Robert	18,171	Ropemaker	DEFENCE	29- 5-1866	20	
ADAMS, Nicholas	32,364A	Q.M.	IMPLACABLE	5- 2-1875	20	
ADAMS, William	4,496	Carpenter's Mate	PEMBROKE	27- 4-1868	20	*
ADDKOTT, ?	?	Admiral's Coxn	IMPREGNABLE	?	?	*
ADDICOCK, James	10,754	Q.M.	ROYAL ADELAIDE	17- 3-1874	22	*
AILLS, Henry	3,322	Caulker	CLIO	20- 8-1863	20	
ALCOCK, Henry	83/195	Chief Boatman i/c	H.M.Coast Guard	7- 4-1874	36	
ALDERSON, John	27,852	Bosun's Mate	BLENHEIM	1- 5-1863	20	
ALDRED, William	221	Ch Gunner's Mate	DUKE OF WELLINGTON	21- 5-1873	20	
ALFORD, Edward	38,094	Ship's Cook	LEANDER	9-10-1866	20	
ALFORD, William	13,062	Q.M.	CHARYBDIS	10- 6-1865	20	
ALLEN, Edward	33,213	Chief Boatman	H.M.Coast Guard	30-10-1873	25	
ALLINGHAM, William	36/171	M.A.A.	SCOUT (No Yrs edge)	10- 9-1849	23	* ‡
ALLMAN, Thomas	4,796A	Armourer	PEMBROKE	9- 5-1867	20	
ALPE, Aquila	15,693	Bosun's Mate	PRINCESS ROYAL	18-11-1859	21	*
ALRIDGE, Benjamin	5,314	A.B.	LAPWING	18- 1-1862	22	
AMIES, William T.	50/440	Bandsman	PRINCESS ROYAL	6- 8-1867	21	*
ANDERSON, James	35/1	A.B.	LEANDER	12-10-1852	28	
ANGUS, John	37/41	Q.M.	SIMOOM	6- 9-1856	29	
ANTHONY, John	41/293	Sailmaker's Mate	CALEDONIA	14- 6-1851	22	
ARTHUR, John	15,324	M.A.A.	CENTURION	6-12-1859	21	
ASH, Frederick	28,711	Ch Gunner's Mate	EXCELLENT	17- 7-1871	20	
ASHTON, Charles	47/160	Q.M.	DEE	5- 1-1852	21	
ATKINS, Robert	5,332	Q.M.	INDUSTRY	22- 4-1861	22	
ATKINS, William	10,600	Q.M.	NIGER	6- 9-1861	22	*
ATTRIDGE, Richard	35/1040	A.B.	HIBERNIA	14- 6-1849	24	‡
AUNGER, Robert	63/280	M.A.A. (ex RM)	RUSSELL	11- 4-1862	24	

AUSTEN, William	9,767B	M.A.A.	SIMOOM	26- 2-1874	20
AUTRILL, Charles	8,821	A.B.	VICTORY	27-11-1861	21
AYLING. Edward	2,149	Chief Q.M.	DUKE OF WELLINGTON	18-11-1873	20
BACON, Joseph	48/7	Ship's Cook	JACKAL	5- 2-1864	21	*
BAGEL, Robert	40/152	Captn Forecastle	SAPPHO	26-10-1852	23
BAGGS, Daniel	72/195	M.A.A. (ex RM)	TRIBUNE	12- 5-1866	25
BAILEY, George	44/50	Q.M.	LILY	11- 5-1855	25
BAILEY, Henry	3,310	Q.M.	MERSEY	7- 8-1862	22
BAILEY, John	8,091	Ship's Corporal	EXMOUTH	7-10-1862	25	*
BAILEY, Thomas	14,257	Q.M.	TOPAZE	28-12-1863	26
BALLARD, Matthew	32,086A	Carp's Mate	RINALDO	24- 4-1874	20
BAKER, Charles	2,670	Ship's Cook	CARADOC	1- 2-1861	20
BAKER, Daniel	5,092	Q.M.	NILE	24- 2-1860	22
BAKER, George	46/299	Captn Forecastle	HERALD	11- 6-1851	21
BAKER, George	65/440	Ward Room Steward	NARCISSUS	29- 7-1864	22
BAKER, George	16,544A	Carpenter's Mate	JASON	28- 3-1870	23	*
BAKER, Henry	29,025A	Chief Q.M.	R.N.Barracks	8- 4-1874	20
BAKER, James	36/450	Capt's Coxswain	SOUTHAMPTON	7- 1-1852	22
BAKER, Thomas	60/199	Ship's Cook	GANNET	5- 1-1863	23
BAKER, William	31/22	Ship's Cpl (ex RM)	BELLEROPHON	4- 4-1855	32
BALDWIN, George	4,051	Ch Gunner's Mate	EXCELLENT	23-12-1862	23
BALLARD, Stephen	284	Ch Carp's Mate	IRRESISTIBLE	9- 5-1867	22
BAMPTON, Thomas	6,169	Capt Forecastle	CYCLOPS	14- 5-1861	20
BARBER, James	47/237	Bosun's Mate	CORMORANT	23- 2-1852	21	*
BAKER, George	16,544A	Carpenter's Mate	JASON	28- 3-1870	23	*
BARBER, Samuel	52/117	Ship's Cook	WELLESLEY	27-12-1861	28
BARFOOT, John	30,635	Captn Fore Top	RATTLESNAKE	25- 1-1866	20	*
BARKER, Abraham	45/521	A.B.	CALEDONIA	14- 6-1851	22
BARLOW, George	33,771	Captn Forecastle	SCOUT	29- 4-1869	21
BARNARD, Henry	21,822	Q.M.	BRISTOL	27- 1-1871	23
BARNES, Edward	24,574	Ship's Cook	URGENT	16- 8-1869	25
BARNES, John	42/216	Bosun's Mate	SERPENT	13- 1-1854	24
BARNES, John	62/132	Ward Room Steward	EXCELLENT	23-12-1862	23
BARNES, Thomas	31,776	Sailmaker	NORTHUMBERLAND	30- 1-1875	20	*
BARNES, Thomas	19,042A	Sailmaker	HECTOR	30-10-1872	20	*
BARNES, William	30,704A	Q.M.	DUKE OF WELLINGTON	7- 1-187 1	20	*
BARNETT, George	61,339	Asst S.B.Attdt	RANGER	21- 1-1868	26
BARNETT, Jsh/Rchd	45/279	Ship's Corporal	CAMBRIAN	2-11-1850	22
BARNS, Francis	59	Q.M.	BRISK	19- 8-1863	29
BARRETT, Henry	29/409	Bosun's Mate	SPITEFUL	4-12-1852	31
BARRETT, James	2,056	Q.M.	BUZZARD	23- 2-1871	22
BARRY, Edward	4,499	M.A.A.	ROYAL ALBERT	26- 1-1861	20
BARRETT, Henry	26/220	Bosun's Mate	SPITEFUL	? 1-1852	31	*
BARRETT, Richard	2,373	Leading Stoker	MAGICIENNE	24- 4-1861	21	*
BARTLETT, George	29,026A	Q.M.	EXCELLENT	26- 1-1872	20
BARTLETT, Henry	45/248	Captain of Mast	RUSSELL	16- 5-1856	25
BARTON, Henry	3,168	M.A.A.	CONQUEROR	15- 3-1862	21
BATCHELOR, Henry	411	Leading Seaman	DIADEM	4- 4-1862	22	*
BATH, Cyrus	30,385A	Leading Stoker	JUMNA	25- 4-1874	20
BATH, James	45/435	Gunner's Mate	EXCELLENT	23- 6-1851	21
BATH, John	51/356	Blacksmith	VENGEANCE	24- 4-1855	22
BATT, Joseph	49/58	Ship's Cpl (ex RM)	PROMETHEUS	16- 2-1853	?

BATTEN, Richard	51/543	Ship's Cook	NEPTUNE	31-12-1855	23	
BAXTER, George	40/161	Ship's Cook	AVON	3- 4-1849	22	
BAZELEY, John	45/114	Bosun's Mate	MEDEA	25- 7-1850	21	‡
BEACHAM, John	2,082	Captn Fore Top	DONEGAL	26- 1-1866	20	
BEARD, Benjamin	2,668	Q.M.	EDINBURGH	2- 5-1863	24	*
BEAVIS, Joshua	7,567	Q.M.	DUKE OF WELLINGTON	23- 8-1874	20	
BEDDELL, Daniel	1,187	Gunner's Mate	CAESAR	18- 1-1862	23	
BEDLAM, John	36/153	Q.M.	FORMIDABLE	15- 9-1856	26	
BEEDING, Robert	30/161	Admiral's Coxswain	VICTORY	2-10-1848	21	*
BEER, Ebenezer	4,308	Q.M.	R.N.Barracks	4- 2-1874	20	
BEHENNA, John	11,372	Blacksmith	CENTURION	25-11-1861	22	
BELL, Thomas	637	A.B.	CUMBERLAND	31- 7-1867	27	
BELLMAIN, James	53/207	Q.M.	ODIN	2- 8-1856	22	*
BENNETT, Andrew	3,317	Ch Bosun's Mate	LYRA	9- 4-1868	26	*
BENNETT, James	52/476	M.A.A. (ex RM)	BRITANNIA	1- 3-1855	24	
BENNETT, John	47/459	Gunner's Mate	PHAETON	20- 1-1853	21	
BENNETT, Joseph	81/111	Leading Stoker	INDUSTRY	5-11-1870	21	
BENNETT, Mark	4,004	Captn After Guard	TRIBUNE	3- 8-1860	22	
BENNY, Richard	48/381	Q.M.	DIDO	16- 9-1856	25	
BENSON, William	5,565	Captn Forecastle	EDINBURGH	16- 7-1855	20	
BENWELL, Henry	397	Ch Gunner's Mate	WATERLOO	26- 2-1859	21	
BERETTO, Peter	41/455	Gun Room Cook	MELAMPUS	8- 8-1849	21	‡
BERRY, David	83/255	Cmmd Boatman	H.M.Coast Guard	23-10-1874	23	
BESPEDNICK, Wm.	6,350A	Q.M.	MARLBOROUGH	24-11-1864	21	
BESSER, William	5,474	Leading Stoker	TRIBUNE	12- 5-1866	21	
BETSWORTH, Geo.G.	4,629	Coxswain Launch	ACHILLES	4- 8-1874	20	*
BETSWORTH, Wm.	68/383	Leading Stoker	RINGDOVE	3-11-1864	23	*
BETTESWORTH, T.W.	33,586	Q.M.	VICTORIA & ALBERT	15-12-1873	21	*
BEVIS, Thomas	9,179	Chief Q.M.	AGAMEMNON	10-10-1862	23	
BEW, Jesse	33,859	Chief Q.M.	VICTORIA	27- 7-1867	23	*
BEW, William	36/70	A.B.	VICTORIA & ALBERT	24-12-1847	21	*
BIDDLECOME, Wm.	2,692	Bosun's Mate	FALCON	1-10-1862	22	
BILLING, William	49/174	Bosun's Mate	IMPREGNABLE	12-12-1856	24	
BINNEY, James	36,318	Ch Bosun's Mate	ROYAL ADELAIDE	11- 7-1874	20	
BIRCH, William	1,509	Bosun's Mate	VICTOR EMMANUEL	6- 5-1862	22	
BIRMINGHAM, Thos	45/301	Ship's Cook	ASIA	21- 5-1851	23	
BISHOP, Samuel	30,962A	Leading Stoker	AVON	23-10-1874	20	*
BLACK, John	60/375	A.B.	EXCELLENT	29-12-1865	24	*
BLACKETT, Henry	8,899	A.B.	IMPREGNABLE	3-12-1861	24	
BLYTH, Richard	41/310	Ship's Cook	ASIA	21- 5-1851	23	
BODDY, George	31/52	Gunner's Mate	BELLEISLE	2- 9-1848	26	
BODMIN, Benjamin	48/298	Ship's Cpl (ex RM)	LEANDER	12-10-1852	24	
BOGGELIN, John	36/413	Q.M.	VINDICTIVE	13- 6-1848	23	
BOGGURST, John	83/100	Blacksmith	PRINCESS CHARLOTTE	7- 6-1873	21	
BOLAND, Archibald	(*Vide* : BOWLAND)					
BOLE, James	3,862B	Leading Stoker	ASIA	5- 4-1874	20	
BOND, Richard	49/100	Capt's Coxswain	VICTORY	17-12-1853	23	
BOND, Samuel	32,582	Captn After Guard	AURORA	18-12-1867	20	
BORLASE, John	46/239	Q.M.	GANGES	14- 1-1852	22	
BOSWORTHICK, Rd.	49,502	Sailmaker	BRITANNIA	1- 3-1855	22	
BOUCHIER, Richard	55/210	A.B.	HANNIBAL	21-12-1861	26	
BOURKE, Michael	46/481	Q.M.	SANS PAREIL	11- 4-1855	25	*

BOWEN, Edward	23,914	Coxswain of Launch	NORTHUMBERLAND	15- 6-1870	20	*
BOWEN, Edward	(*Vide* : BREWER, Edward)					
BOWLAND, Archibald	51/520	M.A.A.	ARROGANT	4-12-1862	23	*
BOYCE, Thomas E.	9,027	Carpenter's Crew	DUNCAN	20- 3-1874	20	*
BRADDICK, John	6,315A	Leading Stoker	SCOUT	24- 4-1869	22	*
BRADLEY, John	48/443	Bosun's Mate	BLENHEIM	21- 5-1856	23	*
BRADY, Thomas	83/197	Boatman	H.M.Coast Guard	8- 4-1874	37	
BRAGG, John	46/325	Bosun's Mate	ARROGANT	18- 9-1852	22	
BRAKE, Thomas	11,537	Ch Gunner's Mate	VIGILANT	9- 1-1860	20	
BRAND, Joseph	47/446	Q.M.	WATERLOO	6-12-1856	25	*
BRAY, George	19,927A	Q.M.	LIFFEY	23-10-1865	20	*
BRAZIL, John	51/538	Q.M.	BELLEROPHON	4- 4-1855	21	
BRENCHLEY, Richard	45/458	Coxswain of Launch	ARROGANT	18- 9-1852	23	*
BRENCHLY, William	2,484	Gunner's Mate	MAJESTIC	2- 4-1864	20	
BRENT, Edward	72/338	Q.M.	LEE/RATTLESNAKE	10- 7-1866	22	
BREWER, Edward	39/86	Bosun's Mate	COLLINGWOOD	10- 7-1848	21	
BRICE, George	18,720	Q.M.	URGENT	21-11-1862	23	
BRIDLE, Simeon	60/326	Ship's Cpl (ex RM)	PIQUE	7- 2-1859	26	
BRIDLE, William	7,241	Ship's Cook	EXCELLENT	23-12-1862	21	
BRIGGS, John J.	46/7	Captn of Mast	HOWE	5- 7-1850	22	‡
BRINSON, James	4,402	Bosun's Mate	DAUNTLESS	2- 5-1863	20	*
BRITTON, R.J.	21,585	Gunner's Mate	CLIO	13- 7-1868	21	
BRITTON, Thomas H.	35	Armourer	VANGUARD	16- 9-1872	21	
BROAD, William	34,420	Q.M.	ROYAL ADELAIDE	18-12-1866	23	
BROKENSHAW, Wm.	30,261A	Gunner's Mate	CALEDONIA	28- 5-1874	21	*
BROCKWAY, Thomas	12,216	Blacksmith	NORTHUMBERLAND	14- 5-1874	20	
BROMLEY, Edward	33,994A	Q.M.	R.N. Barracks	12-1874	20	*
BROOKS, William	13,971	Yeoman of Signals	FAVORITE	19- 1-1875	20	
BROUGHTON, John	17,242	Captn After Guard	JASON	26-11-1864	24	*
BROWN, Alexander	26,937A	E.R.A.	GANGES	11- 3-1874	20	
BROWN, George	80/42	Ship's Steward	PEMBROKE	18- 4-1872	21	*
BROWN, John	372	Ship's Cook	'RESERVE'	5- 6-1873	25	
BROWN, John	58/289	Bosun's Mate	SIDON	18- 2-1862	23	
BROWN, John	19,725A	Sailmaker	ASIA	16- 1-1875	20	
BROWN, Joseph A.	935	Captn Mizzen Top	EUPHRATES	29- 5-1871	20	*
BROWN, Richard	13,755	Blacksmith	ABOUKIR	6- 6-1867	20	
BROWN, Thomas	47/248	Q.M.	CUMBERLAND	6- 4-1854	23	
BROWN, William	20,084	Q.M.	GLADIATOR	30- 5-1868	25	
BROWNING, William	42/258	Leading Seaman	BLENHEIM	21- 5-1856	30	
BRUNKARD, James	51/106	Ship's Cook	ALBION	28-12-1855	23	
BRYAN, Edward	51/265	Bosun's Mate	PRINCESS ROYAL	18-11-1859	25	
BUCHANAN, William	34/266	Gunner's Mate	CASTOR	16-11-1847	22	*
BUCKETT, Nimrod	6,689	Ropemaker	PEMBROKE	3- 4-1869	21	
BUCKINGHAM, George	13,632	Admiral's Coxswain	LEOPARD	13- 7-1861	22	
BUCKINGHAM, Wm.	45/118	Captain's Coxswain	FISGARD	7-12-1850	21	
BUCKINGHAM, Wm.	62/49	Captn After Guard	INDUS	18- 4-1860	21	

BUNKER, John	8,090	Coxswain of Launch	BOSCAWEN	11- 9-1860	21	
BUNSTER, William	3,012	Chief Q.M.	TRAFALGAR	22- 2-1864	22	
BURCH, William	2,508	Sailmaker	SAMPSON	3- 5-1861	23	
BURCH, William	52/316	Bosun's Mate	CRESSY	24- 5-1861	26	
BURCH, William H.	39,600	Captain of Mast	ROYAL ADELAIDE	3- 2-1875	20	
BURGESS, William	27,664	A.B.	INDUS	30-12-1868	22	
BURKE, Daniel	16,635	Capt's Coxswain	PIQUE	7- 2-1859	21	
BURLEIGH, James	12,962	Q.M.	SEVERN	2- 6-1866	24	
BURNETT, Josh/Rchd	45/279	Ship's Corporal	CAMBRIAN	2-11-1850	22	‡
BURNS, John	4,769	Caulker	RACOON	29-10-1866	20	*
BURNS, Thomas	2,218	Bosun's Mate	IMPLACABLE	19-12-1864	20	*
BURR, Michael	18,499	Chief Q.M.	FORMIDABLE	14-12-1864	24	
BURRIDGE, John	37/397	Chief Q.M.	HANNIBAL	21-12-1861	20	
BURRIDGE, Matthew	33,539	Ship's Cook	ZEBRA	1- 2-1871	26	
BURROUGHS, Alfred	3,852	Ch Carp's Mate	HANNIBAL	21-12-1861	23	
BURROWS, Joseph	247	Ropemaker	AUDACIOUS	26-11-1872	20	
BURT, Edward	55/291	Ship's Cook	LEOPARD	13- 7-1861	23	
BURT, William J.	59/218	Ship's Cook	CONSTANCE	16-12-1868	23	
BURTON, Thomas	11,736	Captn of Hold	VICTOR EMMANUEL	6- 5-1862	24	
BURTON, William	5,034	Leading Stoker	INDUS	24-10-1865	20	
BUSH, William	38,846	Coxswain Launch	PEMBROKE	8- 5-1862	21	
BUSHELL, Thomas	5,810	Blacksmith	AUDACIOUS	22- 2-1873	20	
BUSSELL, Henry	46/20	M.A.A. (ex RM)	AMPHITRITE	24- 7-1850	?	‡
BUTCHER, Edward	58/8	Ship's Cpl (ex RM)	CAESAR	2- 2-1861	28	
BUTCHER, William	28,266	Gunner's Mate	VICTORY	15- 2-1869	22	
BUTLER, John	32,267A	Bosun's Mate	PALLAS	3- 2-1875	20	
BUTLER, Thomas	44/426	Gunner's Mate	ROSAMOND	12- 4-1850	21	‡
BUTT, Joseph	36,466	Gunner's Mate	IMPREGNABLE	12- 9-1872	20	
BUTTERMORE, Robert	3,731	Ropemaker	SCOUT	24- 4-1869	21	
BYRNE, James	6,330A	Gunner's Mate	EXCELLENT	11- 4-1874	22	*
CADDY, John	31/414	Ship's Cook	WELLINGTON	24-11-1850	29	‡
CADOGAN, Cornelius	36/62	Sick Berth Attdnt	CROCODILE	29- 4-1850	25	‡
CAIN, Thomas	22,986	Gunner's Mate	ST GEORGE	22- 4-1865	24	
CALLAGHAN, James	10,444	Captain of Mast	HANNIBAL	21-12-1861	22	
CAMPBELL, Robert	951	Gunner's Mate	NEPTUNE	31-12-1855	22	
CANAWAY, Joseph	49/139	Sailmaker	VENGEANCE	24- 4-1855	23	
CANN, Henry	44/143	Captn Forecastle	PANDORA	23-11-1849	23	‡
CANNON, David	47/530	Bosun's Mate	TORTOISE	16- 7-1852	21	
CANNON, William	58/107	Captn After Guard	INDUS	18- 4-1860	24	
CARPENTER, William	13,163	Captn Forecastle	CORNWALLIS	1- 5-1863	21	
CARRICK, Thomas	39/93	Captain of Mast	COLLINGWOOD	10- 7-1848	22	
CARSE, John	35/1066	Sailmaker	RALEIGH	11- 2-1850	26	* ‡
CARTER, Edmund	12,009	Bosun's Mate	RACER	5-12-1862	20	
CARTER, James	8,462	Leading Stoker	HERCULES	10- 8-1871	20	
CARTER, John	36,935	Q.M.	STYX	23-10-1865	21	
CARTER, Robert H.	32,602	Seaman's Schoolmaster	ALGIERS	9-12-1862	22	
CARTER, William	47/460	A.B.	PHAETON	20- 1-1853	21	
CASELICK, John	37/284	Blacksmith	EXCELLENT	23- 6-1851	22	
CASHMAN, William	30,187	Q.M.	DANAE	4- 7-1874	20	*
CASS, Henry	4,880	Q.M.	VIXEN	22- 4-1861	21	

CASTLE, John	26,535	Ch Yeoman Signals	ROYAL ADELAIDE	14-11-1873	20	*
CAUNTER, Charles	2,816	Ship's Cook	LION	19-10-1869	23	
CHAMBERS, Francis	47/238	Ship's Cpl (ex RM)	SOUTHAMPTON	17- 7-1861	33	
CHANDLER, James	952	Ropemaker	DIADEM	4- 4-1862	23	
CHAPLA(I)N, Thos.	84/62	Ship's Stwd 1st Cl	INDUS	10- 4-1873	24	
CHAPMAN, George	11,965	Chief Q.M.	PELORUS	5-12-1862	22	
CHAPMAN, John	5,477	Bosun's Mate	RACOON	14- 1-1862	21	*
CHAPMAN, John	24,314	Q.M.	ZEALOUS	17- 3-1870	23	
CHAPMAN, Joseph	61/413	Ship's Cook	NILE	24- 2-1860	27	
CHAPMAN, Richard	40/170	Q.M.	CANOPUS	20- 5-1848	22	
CHARD, Francis	9,389	Ship's Cook	RUSSELL	13- 5-1861	21	
CHARTERS, William	49/248	Carpenter's Mate	AMPHITRITE	24- 5-1856	24	
CHILDS, George	1,771	A/Ch Carp's Mate	MAJESTIC	15- 6-1861	22	
CHILDS, James	8,094	Bosun's Mate	ASIA	26- 3-1872	20	
CHITTENDEN, Chas.	9,607A	Ship's Cook	RESISTANCE	13- 6-1867	21	
CHITTENDEN, Geo.	29,445	Admiral's Coxswain	CALEDONIA	2- 8-1867	20	*
CHITTENDEN, Wm.	65/334	Q.M.	TARTAR	11- 5-1865	22	
CHRISTIE, Thomas	45/56	Bosun's Mate	VENGEANCE	4- 7-1850	21	‡
CHUBB, Henry	10,607	Carpenter's Mate	ESK	25- 6-1861	20	*
CHURCH, John	45/510	Bosun's Mate	POWERFUL	4- 3-1851	21	
CLARK, George	12,376	Leading Stoker	MONARCH	20- 8-1874	20	
CLARKE, George	42/328	Gunner's Mate	ESPEIGLE	26- 1-1849	23	
CLARKE, Henry	19,420A	Q.M.	ROYAL ADELAIDE	14-12-1866	21	*
CLARKE, James	21,830	Actg E.R.A.	RESISTANCE	5- 7-1872	20	
CLARKE, John	3,439	Q.M.	PEARL	15- 6-1859	22	
CLARKE, William	60/14	Ship's Cook	TRIBUNE	12- 5-1866	28	
CLATWORTHY, Thomas	48/26	Cooper	GORGON	29- 1-1852	23	
CLAY, William	11,596	Gunner's Mate	MINOTAUR	28- 3-1872	20	
CLEMENTS, Henry	46/280	Bosun's Mate	BLENHEIM	21- 5-1856	25	*
CLEMENTS, Wm.	67/79	2nd Captn Aft Gd	HERO	12-11-1862	22	*
CLEVERLY, John	17,862	Gunner's Mate	EXCELLENT	23-12-1862	21	
CLIFT, Enoch	46/437	Q.M.	FIREBRAND	27-11-1852	22	
CLINICK, George	4,588	Admiral's Coxswain	ASIA	12-12-1866	22	
COATES, James	3,072	Q.M.	ARIADNE	22- 8-1873	20	*
COATES, Robert	21/312	M.A.A. (ex RM)	RATTLESNAKE	11-11-1850	36	‡
COCK, Richard	895	Q.M.	PENELOPE	2- 7-1858	22	
COCK, Richard	5,638	Blacksmith	NEPTUNE	11-12-1862	20	
CODDINGTON, George	1,221	Leading Stoker	INDUS	30-12-1868	20	
COKER, James	47/116	Q.M.	CLEOPATRA	20- 9-1853	23	*
COLE, Daniel	8,557	Captn Forecastle	CENTURION	6-12-1859	23	
COLE, Daniel C.	641	Q.M.	ORLANDO	23-12-1865	21	
COLEMAN, John	5,150	Gunner's Mate	CONWAY/WIZARD	4- 7-1856	21	
COLEMAN, Thomas	52/290	Ship's Corporal	EXCELLENT	14-12-1859	29	
COLEMAN, William	30/239	Bosun's Mate	ALBION	15- 1-1848	24	*
COLGAN, Patck.M.	48/3	Ship's Corporal	GROWLER	22- 9-1852	23	
COLLINS, George	33,564	Armourer	FORMIDABLE	14-12-1864	22	
COLLINS, Henry	404B	Coxswain of Launch	ROYAL GEORGE	27- 8-1869	28	
COLLINS, James	6,225	Chief P.O.	CAMBRIDGE	10-10-1873	21	
COLLINS, John W.	5,138	M.A.A.	ROYAL ADELAIDE	11-11-1873	20	

COLLINS, Robert	55/278	Ship's Cook	FERRET	2- 2-1856	25	*
COLLINS, Timothy	42/319	Q.M.	BITTERN	24- 1-1849	23	
COLLINS, William	1,904	Leading Seaman	NEWCASTLE	19- 6-1874	20	
COMPTON, James	1,104	Q.M.	PEMBROKE	2- 1-1861	21	*
CONNELL, Jeremiah	45/284	A.B.	CUMBERLAND	6- 4-1854	24	
CONNOR, Edward	48/254	Ship's Corporal	MAJESTIC	15- 6-1861	20	
CONNOR, Michael	42/484	Bandsman R.N.	HIBERNIA	24- 6-1849	21	‡
CONNOR, William	2,193	Q.M.	REVENGE	17- 6-1873	20	
CONROY, Henry	11,863	Leading Stoker	PEMBROKE	22-11-1873	20	
CONSTINE, Jeremiah	37/14	Captain of Mast	TRINCOMALEE	14- 8-1850	25	‡
COOK, James S.	10,604	Q.M.	MALACCA	4- 9-1869	23	
COOK, William	4,955	Q.M.	BUZZARD	6-12-1870	20	
COOKE, Henry	5,127	Q.M.	ORION	9-11-1861	22	*
COOTE, Thomas	30,844	Bosun's Mate	PRINCESS ROYAL	6- 8-1867	20	*
COPELAND, Henry	52/170	M.A.A.	WELLESLEY	27-12-1861	31	*
CORNELIUS, William	41/553	Q.M.	WELLESLEY	13- 6-1851	26	*
CORNISH, John	12,350	Carpenter's Crew	SUPPLY	15-11-1865	20	
COSGROVE, John	23,082	Chief Q.M.	JUMNA	9- 6-1870	23	
COTMAN, Charles E.	78/230	Gun Room Steward	JUNO	9- 6-1873	22	*
COTTER, Francis	10,346	Gunner's Mate	DONEGAL	3- 8-1868	21	
COTTER, Peter	21,832	Bosun's Mate	ZEALOUS	17- 3-1870	22	
COUGHLAN, Michael	83/114	Chief Boatman i/c	H.M.Coast Guard	22- 7-1873	30	
COURT, William	871	Admiral's Coxswain	DUKE OF WELLINGTON	27- 3-1857	22	*
COX, Frederick	13,407	Gunner's Mate	ROYAL ADELAIDE	23- 6-1874	20	
COX, Henry	36,236	Captn Forecastle	CURACOA	29- 5-1862	20	
COX, James	55/344	Captain of Hold	SIDON	23- 7-1856	24	
COX, William	13,577	Gunner's Mate	PEMBROKE	1- 5-1863	21	
COX, William	46/435	Captn Forecastle	QUEEN	22- 6-1852	23	
CRABB, Samuel	19,367	Ch Yeoman Signals	INDUS	5- 3-1870	24	
CRAGG, William	4,699	Q.M.	VULTURE	21- 6-1856	21	
2nd M&G ?		A.B.	INDUS	29-12-1863	26	
CREED, William	7,056	Captn After Guard	PYLADES	23- 7-1861	22	
CREW(E?)S, William	24/73	Gunner's Mate	TERRIBLE	25- 9-1849	25	‡
CRITCHETT, Joseph	41/237	Q.M.	QUEEN	13- 5-1849	21	*
CROAD, William	2,038	Ch Carp's Mate	PRINCESS ROYAL	18-11-1859	27	
CRONIN, Cornelius	2,096	Stoker	TAMAR	3- 8-1868	21	*
CROSSMAN, Joseph	1,429	Ship's Cook	MEEANEE	19- 2-1866	23	*
CROUCHER, James H.	3,106	Captain of Hold	AGAMEMNON	10-10-1862	23	
CRUYS, William	41/239	M.A.A. (ex RM)	QUEEN	15- 5-1849	27	*
CUMMINS, John	56/156	Seaman's Schoolmaster	VICTORY	27-12-1861	24	
CUMMINGS, Edward	32/469	Q.M.	HOGUE	15- 5-1856	26	
CUMMINS, Joseph	45/473	Leading Seaman	IMPREGNABLE	3-12-1861	30	
CUMMINS, Richard	28/147	A.B.	NEPTUNE	7- 3-1854	34	*
CURRY, Thomas	4,268	Captn Main Top	St VINCENT	25-10-1865	20	
CURTIS, Henry	3,632	Leading Stoker	DAUNTLESS	2- 5-1863	20	
DAILY/DALEY, Peter	9,166	Q.M.	COSSACK	20- 8-1862	20	
DALGLEISH, Archbld.	60/340	Ship's Cpl (ex RM)	NANKIN	17- 2-1859	24	
DAMERELL, John	47/484	Ship's Cpl (ex RM)	QUEEN	22- 6-1852	?	
DANIELL, John	41/236	Sailmaker	QUEEN	13- 5-1849	22	

DANN, George	8,790	Leading Stoker	ASIA	2- 6-1874	20	
DARLEY, Henry	4,170A	Ch Bosun's Mate	ROYAL ALFRED	10- 1-1874	20	
DARLEY, Richard	109	Q.M.	IMPREGNABLE	3-12-1861	22	
DARTON, Thomas	15,845	Ch Bosun's Mate	NILE	15- 4-1864	23	
DAVEY, John	29,423	Ship's Cook	PHOEBE	22- 6-1866	22	
DAVIDSON, John	70,860	Carpenter's Mate	ASIA	24- 6-1874	21	
DAVIS, James	45/8	Q.M.	DRAGON	8- 6-1850	22	‡
DAVIS, James	30/225	Q.M.	FIREBRAND	14- 6-1848	22	
DAVIS, John	53/68	Captn After Guard	SANS PAREIL	12- 4-1855	29	
DAVIS, John	33,518	Leading Seaman	BARROSA	7- 7-1873	21	
DAVIS, Robert	30/370	Ship's Cook	DAPHNE	9- 8-1852	30	
DAWE, Philip	3,991	Ship's Cpl 1st Cl	IMPREGNABLE	30- 1-1869	23	
DAYWELL, John	68/485	Bosun's Mate	BACCHANTE	27- 7-1864	23	
DEE, William	45/298	Captn Forecastle	FLYING FISH	8-12-1851	22	
DENNETT, Henry H.	1,708	Gunner's Mate	EXCELLENT	6- 6-1874	20	
DENNICK, Richard	2,524	Bosun's Mate	BRISK	15- 8-1863	22	
DERRETT, William	7,211	Ch Carp's Mate	INDUS	8- 7-1874	20	
DERRICK, James	30,487	Ch Gunner's Mate	REVENGE	21- 4-1874	20	
DEVONPORT, Joseph	51/274	Capt's Coxswain	BELLEROPHON	4- 4-1855	21	
DEW, William	42/356	Gunner's Mate	JUNO	7- 2-1849	22	*
DEWLAND, George	13,954	Coxswain Cutter	PALLAS	3- 2-1875	20	
DICKENS, Uriah	10,608	Ship's Cook	CUMBERLAND	5-12-1868	25	
DICKER, William	1,871	Cmmd Boatman	H.M.Coast Guard	23- 4-1873	?	
DIGBY, James	5,648	Gunner's Mate	BOSCAWEN	14- 3-1864	21	
DILNOT, George	4,079	Captain of Hold	QUEEN	5-12-1863	21	
DINGLE, William	4,557	Q.M.	RETRIBUTION	19-12-1860	20	
DINGYDERRY, G.T.	6,781	Sailmaker	BELLEROPHON	9- 2-1874	20	
DOEG, James	35/17	Ship's Corporal	HIBERNIA	14- 6-1849	23	* ‡
DOIG, Thomas T.M. on edge	30,817	Coxswain Launch	RESERVE	21-12-1872	20	*
DOMINY, Joseph	57/252	Gunner's Mate	CRESSY	24- 5-1861	21	
DOLE, Joseph	42/523	Ship's Cpl (ex RM)	ST VINCENT	13- 4-1849	25	
DOMINICK, Charles	60/347	Q.M.	HAVANNAH	16-11-1859	21	
DONAVAN, Morgan	37/76	Bosun's Mate	NERBUDDA/JUMNA	17-10-1848	23	
DONNELL, James	48/373	Blacksmith	PENGUIN	16- 7-1855	23	
DOOLAN, John	63/96	Captain of Hold	LIFFEY	10- 7-1862	23	
DOOR, Robert	44/166	Bosun's Mate	EURYDICE	4-12-1849	24	* ‡
DORAN, James	56/210	Ship's Cook	LIFFEY	10- 7-1862	24	
DORE, John	65/39	Bosun's Mate	CAESAR	18- 1-1862	21	
DORE, Richard	1,204	Leading Stoker	HECTOR	7- 5-1872	20	*
DORWOOD, David	42/469	Bosun's Mate	VANGUARD	24- 3-1849	??	
DOUGHTY, George	57/360	Ship's Cook	TERRIBLE	27- 1-1862	25	
DOUGLAS, Hugh	21/123	Captain of Mast	SIDON	28- 3-1849	21	
DOWLING, Paul	21,605A	Leading Stoker	CHANTICLEER	16- 2-1866	20	
DOWRICK, George	39/34	A.B.	LINNET	13- 2-1851	25	*
DRAKE, Thomas	64/373	Ship's Cook	INDUS	30-12-1868	20	
DRAVER, James	37/447	Q.M.	TRAFALGAR	26- 6-1848	22	
DREW, William	16,811	Ship's Corporal	HECTOR	29-11-1870	20	
DRISCOLL, John	8,431	Captn After Guard	CAMBRIDGE	17-12-1866	26	
DRISCOLL, Patrick	37,254	Stoker	ANTELOPE	26- 2-1874	21	
DRIVER, Abraham	84/65	Cmmd Boatman	H.M.Coast Guard	17- 4-1873	34	
DUCK, John	65/305	Capt's Coxswain	CUMBERLAND	23-12-1863	23	*
DUDLEY, Guildford	38,268	Q.M.	ROYAL ADELAIDE	19- 5-1874	20	
DUKE, John (DUKES edge)	64/9	Q.M.	ESK	25- 6-1861	20	*

DUKES, Thomas	10,157	Captn Forecastle	CHESAPEAKE	8-10-1861	20	*
DUMPHEY, Samuel	31/357	Ship's Cook (ex RM 26 Yrs)	LEOPARD	2- 8-1856	40	*
DUNCAN, George	12,102	Q.M.	NILE	15- 4-1864	21	
DUNLOP, James W.	2,578A	Ch Bosun's Mate	DUKE OF WELLINGTON	4- 2-1875	20	*
DUNN, John	39/253	Q.M.	ALERT	11- 4-1850	24	‡
DUNN, Richard	68/81	Q.M.	CORNWALLIS	16- 4-1864	23	
DUNN, William	57,353	Ship's Cook	FISGARD	16-12-1857	21	*
DUNNING, John S.	62/167	Q.M.	SCOURGE	5- 2-1862	23	
DUPE, Henry	26,193	Ch Gnr's Mate	EXCELLENT	29-12-1865	22	*
DURANT, Samuel	42/355	Blacksmith	JUNO	7- 2-1849	22	
DURRELL, Robert	(*Vide* : WILSON, George H.)					
DYER, T.	?	Cook	CENTAUR	?	?	*
DYMOND, John	63/135	Bosun's Mate	EURYALUS	16-11-1860	20	
EADES, James	3,153	Ch Bosun's Mate	COQUETTE	16- 1-1867	25	
EARL, John	40/277	Coxswain Launch	SPARTAN	15- 6-1849	23	‡
EARLE, George	42/357	A.B.	WELLESLEY	13- 6-1861	23	
EASTCOTT, Edward & M&G	40/460	A.B. Captain Hold	EXPRESS TOPAZE	7-12-1850 28-12-1863	22 34	*
EDDY, Richard	49/426	Ship's Cook	DAEDALUS	2- 9-1853	23	
EDGECOMBE, Joseph	58/505	A.B.	ROYAL WILLIAM	23- 3-1859	22	
EDGECOMBE, Joseph	32/283	A.B./Capt Aft Gd	VANGUARD	23- 3-1849	23	
EDWARDS, John	39/331	Bosun's Mate	QUEEN	15- 5-1849	22	*
EDWARDS, John	67/7	Q.M.	ALGIERS	9-12-1862	22	*
EDWARDS, Robert	57/383	Q.M.	CONQUEROR	6-12-1859	23	
EDWARDS, Thomas	61,338	A.B.	INDUS	29-12-1863	25	
EDWARDS, Thomas	36,474	A.B.	SCOUT	29- 4-1869	20	
EDWARDS, William	46/9	Bosun's Mate	HOWE	10- 7-1850	26	‡
ELLIOTT, James	37/54	Captn Forecastle	GANGES	14- 1-1852	23	
ELLIOTT, Thomas	38/96	Gunner's Mate	SEAFLOWER	31-12-1847	21	*
ELLIOTT, William	?	Leading Stoker	STAR	?	20	*
ELLIOTT, William H.	8,970	Carpenter's Mate	INDUS	28-12-1863	20	
ELLIS, Jacob	71/514	Ch Gunner's Mate	RIFLEMAN	31- 5-1866	20	
ELLIS, James	63/214	Ch Captn Forecastle	ORION	2-11-1861	21	
ELLIS, James	7,245	Gunner's Mate	DONEGAL	22 -4-1865	22	
ELLIS, William	33,137	Leading Stoker	PEMBROKE	2- 3-1867	20	
ELLIS, William	51/514	Captn After Guard	AMPHITRITE	24- 5-1856	22	
ELLIS, William	63/433	Ship's Steward	EDINBURGH	10- 4-1862	21	*
ELLIS, William	63/521	Gunner's Mate	CURACOA	29- 5-1862	20	
EMBLETON, Thomas	46/10	Q.M.	HOWE	5- 7-1850	22	‡
EMMETT, John	65/219	Bosun's Mate	CENTAUR	7- 6-1864	21	*
ENGLISH, Francis	32,331	Q.M.	LIVERPOOL	31- 7-1867	20	
ESSAM, Sendall	61/119	Ch Gunner's Mate	EXCELLENT	23-12-1862	25	
ESSARY, Robert	69/307	Ch Gunner's Mate	CAMBRIDGE	17-12-1866	23	*
EUSTACE, John	29/607	A.B.	HARPY	5- 2-1850	25	‡
EVANS, David	71/309	Captn Forecastle	DONEGAL	2- 5-1866	20	
EVANS, James	64/52	Gunner's Mate	HOGUE	11- 4-1862	22	
EVERSON, William	4,054	Ship's Cook	DRAGON	10- 2-1857	22	
EVES, Samuel	46/426	A.B.	QUEEN	22- 6-1852	21	
EWENS, John	57/74	Bosun's Mate	CAMBRIDGE	26- 2-1862	22	
EYNON, William	57/418	Captn Forecastle	ENCOUNTER	20- 2-1858	21	*
FANCY, James	68/360	Q.M.	VICTORY	14-12-1866	24	*
FARLING, George alias FARLOW	67/256	A.B.	EXCELLENT	1- 1-1866	23	
FARMER, Thomas	29,644A	Gunner's Mate		4-12-1871	20	*

FARRELL, Cornelius	51/60	Bosun's Mate	ARCHER	11-11-1853	22	
FARRELL, James	19,642A	Q.M.	INDUS	28-12-1863	21	
FARRELL, William	45/11	Bosun's Mate	BRITANNIA	16- 1-1852	22	
FARROW, George	82/240	Chief Boatman i/c	H.M.Coast Guard	23- 4-1873	32	*
FARROW, James	3,757A	Bosun's Mate	CROCODILE	30- 6-1871	20	
FATTY, Edward	37/45	Gunner's Mate	COLLINGWOOD	10- 7-1848	24	
FAULKNER, George	52/436	Bosun's Mate	NEPTUNE	31-12-1855	22	
FAULKNER, James	7,353	Ship's Cook	GRAPPLER	14- 5-1863	20	
FAVEN, Charles	81/356	Ship's Cook	NARCISSUS	11- 8-1871	21	*
FEARNLEY, Joseph H.	31,634A	Bosun's Mate	RATTLESNAKE	14- 3-1874	22	*
FEENY, James	53,1449	Yeoman Store Rooms	NILE	24- 2-1860	25	
FELTHAM, Thomas	57/315	Q.M.	MERSEY	7- 8-1861	24	
FERRIS, Thomas	9,443	Q.M.	ROYAL ADELAIDE	20- 2-1874	22	
FERRIS, William	720	Captain of Mast	ROYAL ADELAIDE	14-12-1866	22	
FIELDING, James	3,982	Captn Fore Top	RUSSELL	8- 4-1864	20	
FIRMAN, Elias	42/223	Ship's Cpl (ex RM)	SUPERB	24-11-1848	25	
FLASHMAN, William	44/459	Ship's Cook	ROSARIO	4-10-1866	21	
FLEMING, John	62/122	Sailmaker	OBERON	28-10-1862	23	
FLOYD, William	22,804	2nd Captain Quarter Deck Men	ROYAL ADELAIDE	21- 5-1874	20	
FOAL, Robert	794	Caulker	ROYAL ALFRED	10- 1-1874	20	
FOLLOWS, William	30,574A	Chief Captain of Forecastle	VICTORIA	27- 7-1867	20	
FORD, George	64/459	Ship's Cpl (ex RM)	CURACOA	29- 5-1862	24	
FORD, William	49/22	M.A.A. (ex RM)	INDEFATIGABLE	15-11-1852	24?	
FOREMAN, Edward	35/1005	M.A.A.	HELENA	29-11-1851	27	
FORSTER, Edward or FOSTER	65/374	Q.M.	BLENHEIM	2- 5-1863	21	
FORSTER, Thomas	46/450	Bandsman RN	WATERLOO	9- 3-1860	24	
FORWARD, Thomas	84/188	Chief Boatman	H.M.Coast Guard	24- 2-1874	32	
FOSS, George	61/168	Yeoman Store Rooms	BOSCAWEN	12- 9-1860	22	
FOWELL, John	72/162	Seaman's Schoolmaster	TRAFALGAR	2- 5-1866	20	
FOWELS, James	68/484	Ship's Cook	BACCHANTE	27- 7-1864	32	
FOWLING, Charles	36/506	Capt's Coxswain	CALEDONIA	10- 1-1848	23	*
FOX, William	54/137	M.A.A.	CAMBRIDGE	18- 2-1862	25	
FRANCIS, John	4,901	Q.M.	CAMBRIDGE	13- 5-1873	20	
FRANKS, John	27,715	Blacksmith	SATELLITE	23-11-1870	20	*
FREELOVE, Joseph	548	Leading Stoker	RESERVE	27- 3-1873	20	*
FREEMAN, Henry	48/416	Ch Bosun's Mate	CUMBERLAND	6- 4-1854	22	*
FRIEND, George	35,492	Bosun's Mate	WARRIOR	28- 1-1871	20	*
FRIEND, John	65/526	Q.M.	PEARL	6- 6-1854	21	
FRIEND, John	14,142	Q.M.	IMPREGNABLE	23- 2-1870	21	
FRIENDLY, J.H.	(*Vide* : FEARNLEY, Joseph H.)					
FRIENDSHIP, James	940	Chief Q.M.	INDUS	28-12-1863	21	
FROST, Samuel	22,229	Divisional Carpenter	H.M.Coast Guard	24-11-1874	20	*
FROST, William	1,427	Sailmaker	IRIS	30- 7-1861	21	
FRYER, William	39/434	Bosun's Mate	ALBION	15- 1-1848	22	*
FUDGE, William	16,080	Gunner's Mate	EXCELLENT	23-12-1862	25	
FUGE, Samuel	68/151	Captain Main Top	MEGAERA	2- 3-1864	21	*

FULLERTON, Charles	13,572A	Q.M.	R.N. Barracks	18- 8-1874	20	*
FUNNELL, Robert	71/417	Captn Fore Top	ST VINCENT	14-12-1866	22	
FURLONG, John	63/134	Chief Q.M.	DONEGAL	7- 6-1862	20	
GAINSFORD, Henry	18,174	Bosun's Mate	ROYAL OAK	5-12-1867	20	
GALLIENNE, T.H.	14,790	Carpenter's Crew	IMMORTALITE	22- 7-1874	20	*
GAMBLIN, Francis	40/329	Gunner's Mate	CALLIOPE	8- 1-1849	22	
GARD, William	32,123	Cooper	CORDELIA	4- 7-1868	20	*
GARDINER, Andrew	31.659	Carpenter's Mate	FORMIDABLE	6-11-1868	20	
GAR(DI)NER, John	39/445	A.B.	ALBION	28-12-1855	29	
GARLAND, Peter	49/168	A.B.	HASTINGS	29- 4-1853	22	*
GARRETT, William	27/434	Captn Mast/Q.M.	IMPREGNABLE	18-12-1851	24	
GARRETT, William	10,372	Leading Stoker	EXCELLENT	11- 4-1874	20	
GATER, William	38/470	Captain of Hold	VINDICTIVE	13- 6-1848	23	
GATTY, Edward	37/45	Gunner's Mate	COLLINGWOOD	10- 7-1848	24	
GAYDEN, Alexander	33,013	Gunner's Mate	ROYAL ADELAIDE	19- 5-1874	20	
GAZE, Benjamin	72/361	Ship's Cook	ECLIPSE	23-11-1872	25	
GIBBS, George	22,918	Blacksmith	REPULSE	10- 2-1871	20	*
GILBERT, Samuel	47/201	Carp's Mate	MAGICIENNE	24- 4-1861	22	
GILLIS, William	5,989	Bosun's Mate	COSSACK	20- 8-1862	22	
GLADMAN, George	10,724	Captain of Hold	EXCELLENT	14- 5-1874	20	
GLADWELL, Henry	42/339	Sailmaker	DIDO	29- 1-1849	21	
GLADWIN, Samuel	65/291	Cadet's Cook (ex RM)	EXCELLENT	23-12-1862	24	
GLANVILLE, George	33,155	Bosun's Mate	RATTLESNAKE	6- 5-1870	20	
GLANVILLE, John	63/529	Ropemaker	ALERT	27- 9-1861	21	
GLANVILLE, Richard	60/511	Q.M.	SCYLLA	26-12-1862	24	
GLANVILLE, Thomas	39/10	Bosun's Mate	SUPERB	24-11-1848	22	
GLEN, William	7,043A	Chief Q.M.	CROCODILE	24- 4-1874	20	
GLYNN, Joseph	33,793	Bosun's Mate	ST GEORGE	1- 5-1866	20	
GODBER, Thomas	41/195	Ship's Cpl (ex RM)	POWERFUL	4- 3-1851	22	
GODDARD, David	2,087	Ch Gunner's Mate	MAJESTIC	5- 5-1857	21	*
GODMAN, John H.	81/526	M.A.A. (ex RM)	BRILLIANT	29- 6-1872	21	
GOLDING, Luke	38,023	Capt's Coxswain	PEMBROKE	27- 4-1868	23	
GOLDSMITH, John	8,388	Q.M.	PHAETON	11- 3-1865	21	
GOODFELLOW, John	29,338	Ship's Cook	ADVENTURE	7- 8-1867	20	
GOODMAN, John	42/471	Bosun's Mate	VANGUARD	24- 3-1849	22	
GOODMAN, William	18,571A	Q.M.	GANGES	15- 5-1871	20	*
GOODYEAR, Robert	38/9	Bosun's Mate	QUEEN	6- 8-1856	30	*
GOOGE, George	1,572	Gunner's Mate	VESUVIUS	10- 2-1860	21	*
GORMAN, Dennis	41,211	Q.M.	FAVOURITE	7- 5-1849	23	
GOSLINGTON, John	42/522	M.A.A. (ex RM)	ST VINCENT	13- 4-1849	?	
GOULD, Edward	47/169	Q.M.	TWEED	9- 1-1852	21	
GOULD, Robert	61/468	Q.M.	RETRIBUTION	14-12-1860	21	
GOULDING, Christopher	41/275	Captn After Guard	PHAETON	20- 1-1853	21	
GOWING, Thomas J.	27,010	Bosun's Mate	SULTAN	31- 8-1872	20	
GRANT, Andrew	22,376	Yeoman of Stores	SPITEFUL	17- 9-1869	23	*
GRANT, James	58,370	Bosun's Mate	RETRIBUTION	14-12-1860	24	
GRANT, John	40/455	Q.M.	SALAMANDER	25-11-1854	25	
GRANT, Robert	41/211	M.A.A. (ex RM)	BELLEROPHON	4-11-1850	25	‡
GRANVILLE, William	17,252	Admiral's Coxswain	NILE	15- 4-1864	20	
GRAVES, James	53/455	Leading Seaman	HOGUE	15- 5-1856	22	
GRAVES, John	47/545	Bosun's Mate	VENGEANCE	24- 4-1855	24	
GRAY, James	38/452	Q.M.	AMPHITRITE	24- 7-1850	23	‡

117

GREEN, Joseph	69/490	Bosun's Mate	NARCISSUS	29- 7-1864	21
GREEN, William	39,505	2nd Captain After Guard	CALEDONIA	14- 6-1851	23
GREEN, William	18,076	Caulker	MARLBOROUGH	24-11-1864	21
GREENAWAY, James	47/534	Carpenter's Mate	ST VINCENT	5- 4-1859	27 *
GREENFIELD, Henry	2,951	Ship's Cook	PEMBROKE	3- 1-1861	21
GREGORY, Charles	47/126	Gunner's Mate	VICTORY	27-12-1861	33 *
GREY, John	31/345	Ship's Cook	APOLLO	12- 8-1851	22
GRIFFITHS, John	47/296	Q.M.	RACER	24- 3-1852	21
GRIFFITH(S), Wm.	60/357	Q.M.	HERMES	4- 6-1860	24
GRIBBLE, William	34,875A	Capt's Coxswain	TRAFALGAR	10-11-1869	22
GRINGER, Thomas	26,321	Q.M.	TORCH	17-10-1867	20
GROGAN, Denis	54/717	Captn Forecastle	ROYAL GEORGE	11- 5-1868	24 *
GROOMBRIDGE, Wm.	1,166	Gunner's Mate	CAESAR	10- 2-1862	20
GROSSMITH, William	8,565B	M.A.A. Ex Musician/S.B.A.	MALABAR	12-11-1873	21 *
GROVES, William	46/11	Q.M.	HOWE	5- 7-1850	21 * ‡
GRUNDY, Richard	69/540	Carpenter's Mate	CONQUEROR	10- 2-1866	21
GUNDRY, George	4,446	Ch Gunner's Mate	EXCELLENT	18-12-1868	21
GUNDRY, John	72/161	Leading Stoker	IRRESISTIBLE	2- 5-1866	21 *
GUTTERIDGE, James	29,265	Leading Stoker	LEANDER	9-10-1866	21
GUY, Henry	27,092	Gunner's Mate	DASHER	4-11-1873	20 *
GWILLIAM, W.L.	?	Captn Fore Top	IMPREGNABLE	?	? *
HAINES, Samuel	75/81	Q.M.	TAMAR	3- 8-1868	20
HALL, Walter	44/25	Q.M.	PHILOMEL	17-10-1849	22 ‡
HALL, William	60/523	Q.M.	ARIEL	30- 6-1859	20 *
HAMLIN, Henry	62/204	Ship's Cpl (ex RM)	CAESAR	2- 2-1861	24
HAMMERSLEY, Wm.	14,934A	Yeoman of Signals	RESISTANCE	21- 2-1870	20
HAMMOND, James	46/130	Sailmaker	TRIDENT	27- 3-1851	22
HAMMOND, Joseph	73/416	Ship's Cook (ex RM)	BASILISK	5- 4-1869	21
HANCOCK, John	45/286	A.B.	BELLEROPHON	4-11-1850	25 ‡
HANCOCK, John	83/194	Chief Boatman i/c	H.M.Coast Guard	2- 4-1874	29
HANCOCK, William	68/32	Ship's Cook	DESPERATE	3-11-1863	20
HANDCOCK, James	25,531A	Bosun's Mate	PENGUIN	25- 2-1868	22 *
HANDFORD, Richard	41/1	Captn Forecastle	RACEHORSE	21- 8-1848	21 *
HANNAFORD, Arthur	28,793	Captn Main Top	ROYAL ADELAIDE	20- 2-1874	20
HANNEY, Alexander	33,628	Captn Forecastle	FAWN	5- 6-1868	21
HANNING, John	35/179	Captain of Mast	ALBION	28-12-1855	33
HARBAN, William	53/466	Cooper	VIXEN	31- 8-1855	25
HARDIMAN, Thomas	31/11	Bosun's Mate	COLUMBINE	13- 4-1850	23 * ‡
HARDING, James	21,798	Gunner's Mate	DUKE OF WELLINGTON	26- 4-1871	21
HARDING, Robert	933A	Ch Bosun's Mate	SEVERN	2- 6-1866	21
HARDING, Thomas	40/390	Q.M.	CENTAUR	26- 6-1851	22 *
HARDY, Philip	60/386	Ship's Steward	ROYAL WILLIAM	23- 3-1859	22 *
HARDYWAY, William	63/335	Ship's Corporal	CONQUEROR	11- 3-1862	20
HARGAN, Timothy	(*Vide* : MILLS, John)				
HARMAN, William	64/481	Q.M.	ARROGANT	16- 4-1862	20
HARPER, George	61/432	Captn After Guard	ROYAL ALBERT	26- 1-1861	21
HARPER, Henry	52/413	P.O. 1st Class	SERINGPATAM	26- 4-1867	33
HARPER, John	64/480	Gunner's Mate	HOGUE	12- 4-1864	21

HARRIS, James	60/221	Admiral's Coxswain	INDUS	18- 4-1860	21	
HARRIS, John	43	Ship's Cook	CURLEW	13- 5-1865	25	
HARRIS, John	2,835	Gunner's Mate	ADVENTURE	17- 5-1861	23	
HARRIS, Joseph	60/330	M.A.A. (ex RM)	SANS PAREIL	9- 2-1859	24	
HARRIS, Peter	47/293	Bosun's Mate	ALARM	27-10-1852	21	
HARRIS, William	10,484	Captn After Guard	IRIS	30- 7-1861	21	
HARRIS, William	613	Ch Gunner's Mate	CAMBRIDGE	26- 2-1862	21	*
HARRIS, William	5,875	Q.M.	CONQUEROR	10- 2-1866	23	
HARRISON, William	83/202	Ch Boatman i/c	H.M.Coast Guard	14- 4-1874	37	
HART, Harry	39,201	Sailmaker	ASIA	22- 9-1874	20	*
HARTFIELD, James	36/116	Bosun's Mate	ST VINCENT	13- 4-1849	22	
HARTNELL, Thos.G.	16,826	Sailmaker	GREYHOUND	29-10-1861	21	*
HARVEY, John	41/131	Bosun's Mate	FISGARD	28-12-1853	24	*
HARVEY, William	48/479	Bosun's Mate	CASTOR	29- 1-1853	21	
HARVEY, William	631	Bosun's Mate	ORLANDO	12-12-1865	20	
HASSELL, George	68/458	Bosun's Mate	IMMORTALITE	9- 7-1864	22	*
HATCHER, Henry	19,959	Blacksmith	RENOWN	17- 9-1861	23	*
HATHERLY, Joseph W.	32,566	Ch Gunner's Mate	OCEAN	16- 8-1870	20	*
HAWKE, Eneder	67/518	Caulker	BACCHANTE	27- 7-1864	22	
HAWKE, Samuel	39/275	M.A.A.	HYDRA	14- 2-1850	23	‡
HAWKINS, Thomas	61/1	A.B.	INDUS	29-12-1863	25	
HAWKSWORTH, James	2,320	Capt's Coxswain	CHANTICLEER	16- 2-1866	20	
HAWTON, James	8,424	Coxswain of Launch	PEARL	9- 6-1864	20	
HAYDEN, Thomas	31,905A	Carpenter's Mate	MINOTAUR	30- 1-1871	20	
HAYES, John	41/551	Captn Forecastle	INFLEXIBLE	22- 9-1849	23	‡
HAYNES, John	54/287	Ship's Cook	VESUVIUS	8-11-1856	21	
HEAD, Robert	67/313	Q.M.	NIMBLE	19- 5-1868	23	
HEARNDEN, George	34,674	Q.M.	DAUNTLESS	3- 5-1869	20	
HEATH, Edward	63/304	Chief Stoker	CUMBERLAND	8-11-1866	20	
HEATHCOTT, Robert	46/397	Bosun's Mate	SEALARK	20- 7-1852	22	
HEAVERS, George	7,478	Leading Stoker	FAVOURABLE	26- 2-1874	20	
HEELAS, Robert	40/125	Ship's Cook	CUMBERLAND	6- 4-1854	26	
HEFFORD, John	3,551	Captn Main Top	CAMBRIDGE	17-12-1866	24	
HEMBRY, John	63/52	Ship's Cpl (ex RM)	BOSCAWEN	12- 9-1860	21	
HEMMINGS, William	42/410	Captn After Guard	ELECTRA	6- 3-1849	21	*
HENDERSON, John	(*Vide* : ANGUS, John)					
HENSON, William	40/351	A.B.	VINDICTIVE	13- 6-1848	22	
HERBERT, Edwin J.	14,143	Cooper	PRINCESS ROYAL	6- 8-1867	22	
HERRAGHTY, William	83/201	Chief Boatman i/c	H.M.Coast Guard	14- 4-1874	34	
HEWETT, Thomas	41/420	Ships' Corporal	CHILDERS	26- 7-1849	21	‡
HEWITT, Isaac	1,164	Ch Gunner's Mate	REVENGE	21- 4-1865	22	*
HEWITT, James	58/487	Carpenter's Crew	SIDON	18- 2-1862	24	
HEWITT, John	6,258	Ch Gunner's Mate	SUTLEJ	29- 7-1867	22	
HEWITT, William J.	68/215	Sailmaker	EURYALUS	13- 9-1865	23	
HEWSON, Thomas	62/5	Carpenter's Mate	MOHAWK	28-10-1861	22	
HIBBERD, Henry	20,070A	Q.M.	DUKE OF WELLINGTON	4- 3-1872	22	*
HICKLEY, Peter	62/513	Q.M.	ASSURANCE	2-11-1861	22	
HICKMAN, Edward A.	2,479	Q.M.	CHESAPEAKE	9-10-1861	20	
HICKS, George	57/465	Ch Gunner's Mate	EXCELLENT	23-12-1862	27	

HICKS, Richard	68/78	Ship's Cook	VICTORIA	27- 7-1867	22	
HIGGINS, William	5,966A	Captn After Guard	PYLADES	20- 7-1870	24	*
HIGH, Henry	65/181	Bosun's Mate	HERO	12-11-1862	20	
HIGHTON, William	52/348	Q.M.	DEVASTATION	23- 6-1855	24	
HILL, William	54/618	M.A.A. (ex RM)	MEANDER	4-11-1856	23	
HINAGAN, Patrick	7,497	Bosun's Mate	PYLADES	17- 8-1871	20	*
HIPPER, George	30/520	Ship's Cook	ALARM	22-10-1852	28	
HOARE, Thomas	62/393	Sick Berth Attdnt	HANNIBAL	21-12-1861	22	
HOBBS, Thomas	57/503	Leading Stoker	EXCELLENT	14-12-1859	22	*
HODGE, Edward	29,802	Gunner's Mate	ORONTES	25- 4-1873	21	
HODGE, Henry H.	61/532	Sailmaker	SANS PAREIL	4- 7-1861	21	
HODGE, James	49/232	Captn After Guard	CUMBERLAND	6- 4-1854	22	
HODGE, John	31,210	Capt's Coxswain	HIMALAYA	18-10-1865	20	
HODGES, Daniel	33,138	M.A.A.	VICTORY	15- 2-1869	20	
HODGES, James D.	37,035A	Ch Gunner's Mate	EXCELLENT	9- 9-1873	20	*
HOLBROOK, Henry	5,123	Stoker	SUTLEJ	29- 7-1867	20	
HOLDAWAY, John	156	Q.M.	OCTAVIA	19- 7-1869	21	
HOLLINSHEAD, Wm.J.	26,205	Bosun's Mate	CAMBRIDGE	15-12-1866	24	
HOLLOWAY, Geo.D.	10,588	Ship's Cook	CHALLEMGER	18- 6-1874	20	
HOLMAN, John P.	66/407	Q.M.	ROYAL OAK	5-12-1867	20	
HOLMAN, Robert W.	29,539A	Carpenter's Mate	ACHILLES	18-9-1873	20	
HOLMES, William	46/8	Paymaster & Purser's Steward	HOWE	5- 7-1850	21	* ‡
HOLMES, William	49/38	Q.M.	BRISK	19- 8-1863	34	*
HOLT, Edward	68/125	Tailor	TRAFALGAR	22- 2-1864	20	
HOMEWOOD, Richard	52/180	Q.M.	NANKIN	17- 2-1859	26	*
HOOK, David (John?)	62/530	Q.M.	PIONEER	16- 9-1863	21	*
HOOPER, John	7,667	Captn Forecastle	SANS PAREIL	15- 7-1861	23	*
HOOPER, John	32,596	Q.M.	IMPREGNABLE	14-12-1866	21	
HOOPER, John	3,899	Gunner's Mate	NORTHUMBERLAND	12- 3-1872	20	
HOOPER, William	3,798	Bosun's Mate	GALATEA	11- 5-1871	21	*
HOPKINS, Charles	45/122	Bosun's Mate	CALEDONIA	14- 6-1851	23	
HOPPINGS, James	61/155	Ship's Cpl (ex RM)	ST GEORGE	2- 5-1866	21	
HOPSON, Christopher	64/24	A.B. (Cadet's Servant ex RM)	EXCELLENT	23-12-1862	25	
HOSIE, Thomas	69/56	Leading Stoker	TRIDENT	14-12-1864	23	
HOSKIN, John	24,511	Captn Main Top	DEFENCE	29- 5-1866	23	
HOSKINGS, William	28,095	Leading Stoker	INDUS	30- 3-1874	20	
HOSKINS, James	34/419	Captn After Guard	HASTINGS	12- 5-1856	26	*
HOSKINS, William	21,251	Q.M.	PRINCESS ROYAL	6- 8-1867	20	
HOUGH, James	18,394	Captn Forecastle	EXCELLENT	21- 1-1874	20	*
HOWARD, William	41/212	Captn Forecastle	SCOURGE	9- 5-1849	22	
HOWE, Richard	47/486	Q.M.	BRITANNIA	24- 2-1855	23	
HOWE, Robert	84/91	Chief Boatman i/c	H.M.Coast Guard	22- 7-1873	36	
HOWELL, William	41/323	M.A.A. (ex RM)	SPARTAN	15- 6-1849	?	‡
HUGHES, Stephen	54/189	Bosun's Mate	PEMBROKE	28- 7-1856	21	
HUGHES, William	31/485	Q.M.	LONDON	23- 1-1856	23	
HUMPHREYS, William	69/539	Chief Captn Fcsle	CONQUEROR	10- 2-1866	20	*
HUNT, James	48/198	Bosun's Mate	TRAFALGAR	9- 4-1855	23	*
HUNT, Thomas	32/160	Q.M.	RODNEY	26- 2-1849	23	
HUNT, Thomas	44/425	Sailmaker	PANTALOON	25- 2-1852	23	*
HUNT, William	35/912	Captn Forecastle	PHOENIX	11- 8-1851	22	

HUNT, William	609	Q.M.	PALLAS	2-10-1869	21	*
HUNTER, Richard	65/224	Captain of Mast	EXMOUTH	7-10-1862	21	
HUSER, John/Wilson	55/195	Q.M.	NEPTUNE	31-12-1855	22	
HUSSEY, Joshua	3,461	Leading Stoker	SPITEFUL	18- 9-1869	20	
HUTCHINGS, Samuel	61/284	Chief Q.M.	CONQUEROR	6-12-1859	22	
HUTCHINGS, William	27,384	Q.M.	DEFENCE	29- 5-1866	23	
INKSTER, John	5,547	Q.M.	ABOUKIR	7-10-1862	20	
IRVIN, James	60/507	Q.M.	PEARL	14- 6-1859	21	
ISUM, John	60/192	Chief Captn Fcsle	ILLUSTRIOUS	23-12-1858	21	
JACKMAN, Frank	29,669	Ch Gunner's Mate	EUPHRATES	20- 4-1874	20	
JACKSON, James	42/465	Q.M.	WATERWITCH	14-12-1850	22	
JACKSON, John	41/99	Yeoman Store Rooms	SUPERB	7- 6-1852	22	
JACOBS, John	54/112	Ship's Cook	FIREFLY	19- 2-1866	31	
JAGO, Charles	3,521	Sailmaker	PRINCESS ROYAL	6- 8-1867	20	
JAGO, George	2,434	Gunner's Mate	EXCELLENT	11- 5-1874	20	
JAGO, James	63/156	Ch Bosun's Mate	EDGAR	5- 7-1862	21	
JAMES, George	53/480	Ch Gunner's Mate	EXCELLENT	19-12-1856	22	
JAMES, George	1,424	Bosun's Mate	JASON	29- 5-1870	23	
JAMES, George	3,212	Captn After Guard	LEOPARD	18- 7-1861	22	
JAMES, James	46/391	Q.M.	MEANDER	29- 7-1851	22	
JAMES, John	344	Gunner's Mate	CURACOA	15- 2-1867	21	
JAMES, John	60/325	Captn After Guard	PIQUE	7- 2-1859	22	
JAMES, John	2,199B	Captain's Coxswain	HERCULES	2- 4-1874	20	
JAMES, Richard	33,177	Coxswain of Launch	RUSSELL	20- 5-1863	21	
JAMES, Thomas	61/461	Captn After Guard	HIGHFLYER	30- 5-1861	24	
JAMES, William	67/262	Blacksmith	COLOSSUS	2- 5-1863	21	
JAMESON, John	58/522	Carpenter's Crew	SANS PAREIL	4- 7-1861	23	
JARMAN, Samuel	71/320	Sick Berth Steward	HIMALAYA	19-10-1865	21	
JASPER, William	41/550	Q.M.	SCOUT	21- 9-1849	22	‡
JEFFERY, James	74/202	Ship's Steward 1st Class	ROYAL OAK	5-12-1867	24	*
JEFFERY, Richard	10,831	Captn Forecastle	HERCULES	9- 8-1872	20	
JEFFERY, Robert	5,057A	Captain of Hold	NORTHUMBERLAND	23- 6-1874	20	
JEFFREY, Peter	8,436	Bosun's Mate	CHARYBDIS	10- 6-1865	23	
JENKINS, James	47/418	Capt's Coxswain	EDINBURGH	30- 5-1856	25	
JENKINS, John	573	Bosun's Mate	GALATEA	13- 1-1866	21	
JOB, William	13,207	Chief Q.M.	NILE	15- 4-1864	20	
JOHNS, Henry	46/383	Captn Forecastle	CENTAUR	12- 8-1852	22	
JOHNS, James	25,063	Gunner's Mate	SNIPE	24- 7-1867	22	
JOHNS, Samuel	40/41	Q.M.	HIBERNIA	14- 6-1849	22	* ‡
JOHNS, William	8,563	Bosun's Mate	SATELLITE	21- 1-1861	20	*
JOHNS, William	32,254	Chief Bosun's Mate	CAMBRIDGE	23- 4-1873	20	*
JOHNSON, Abraham	2,762	Ship's Cook	OCEAN	20- 3-1871	22	
JOHNSON, Henry M.	5,595A	Ch Bosun's Mate	VICTORIA & ALBERT	17- 8-1870	20	
JOHNSON, William	12,380	Leading Stoker	HERCULES	16- 3-1874	20	
JOHNSON, William	62/334	Ship's Cook	FOX	21-12-1865	26	*
JOHNSTON, Thomas	50/151	Ship's Cook	BRITANNIA	1- 3-1855	20	
JOLLIFFE, John	40/86	Gunner's Mate	SCORPION	12- 4-1853	26	*
JOLLY, George	33,590	Leading Stoker	ARIADNE	15- 3-1864	20	
JONES, Henry	39,701	Carpenter's Mate	SALAMANDER	23-12-1873	20	
JONES, John	31/83	A.B.	BRITANNIA	16- 1-1852	26	

JONES, John	45/316	A.B.	HANNIBAL	21-12-1861	31	*
JONES, M.L.	2,156	Ch Gunner's Mate	EXCELLENT	14- 5-1874	20	
JONES, Richard	42/298	Captn After Guard	ROSAMOND	2- 2-1856	28	
JONES, Thomas	4,654	Gunner's Mate	VALIANT	16- 1-1871	20	
JONES, Thomas	25,064	Ch Gunner's Mate	CAMBRIDGE	26- 2-1862	21	
JONES, William	45/231	Coxswain of Launch	HOGUE	25- 8-1852	23	
JORDAN, William	29,816	M.A.A.	EXMOUTH	7-10-1862	22	
JUPP, Charles	2,037	Armourer	HANNIBAL	21-12-1861	21	
KAHOON, John	11,880	Captain of Mast	LORD WARDEN	1- 4-1873	21	*
KEEP, Charles	67/242	Ship's Cook	CUMBERLAND	23-12-1863	23	
KELSO, Humphrey	32/507	Sailmaker	CARYSFORT	25- 3-1848	23	*
KELTY, Dennis	12,122	Q.M.	LEOPARD	22- 9-1866	20	
KEMP, George	32/288	Caulker	VINDICTIVE	13- 6-1848	23	*
KEMP, Henry	62/322	Ship's Cook	VICTOR EMMANUEL	6- 5-1862	22	
KEMPSTER, James W.	62/279	Ch Gunner's Mate	DIADEM	4- 4-1862	22	
KENDALL, Henry	1,433	Q.M.	WARRIOR	15-12-1866	23	
KENDALL, James/Wm.	58/518	Painter	INFLEXIBLE	26- 4-1861	23	
KENDEL, John	42/482	A.B.	HIBERNIA	14- 6-1849	21	‡
KENT, William	72/337	M.A.A.	PYLADES	2-11-1866	21	
KEYFORD, Thomas	44/269	Q.M.	REYNARD	1- 3-1852	23	
KEYS, George	69/277	Ch Bosun's Mate	PANTALOON	28- 2-1867	22	*
KIDGER, Charles	58/513	2nd Capt Aft Guard	CALCUTTA	1- 3-1860	22	
KILBY, William	14,876	Chief Q.M.	DEVASTATION	1- 9-1874	20	*
KING, James	32,734	Bosun's Mate	VALIANT	17- 1-1874	21	*
KING, John	4,369	Ch Captn Forecastle	MINOTAUR	14- 9-1872	20	
KING, Richard	40/91	Bosun's Mate	HASTINGS	29- 4-1853	24	
KINGCOMBE, Wm.H.	31,922A	Bosun's Mate	CAMBRIDGE	3-12-1872	20	
KNEEBONE, George	10,783	Armourer	CAMBRIDGE	10- 3-1874	20	
KNIGHT, Jonathan	45/342	M.A.A. (ex RM)	INCONSTANT	2-12-1850	21	‡
KNOTT, James	67/208	Ship's Cook	MELPOMENE	14- 3-1863	20	
KRIEBEL, Robert	13,067	Q.M.	SUTLEJ	29- 7-1867	22	
LABETT, Louis T.	22,419	Yeoman Signals	ENDYMION	6- 3-1874	20	*
LAKE, Robert	44,297	Ship's Cook	HAVANNAH	8-12-1851	24	*
LAMBERT, Alfred	64/478	Ship's Cook	RHADAMANTHUS	24-12-1862	22	
LAMPEY, Henry	38/363	Bosun's Mate	SUPERB	7- 6-1852	25	*
LAMPEY, John	40/214	Capt's Coxswain	IMPREGNABLE	2- 5-1851	21	
LAMPIER, John	26,842	M.A.A.	HIBERNIA	11- 4-1867	22	
LAMPORT, Alfred	(*Vide* : HARDING, James)					
LANCASTER, James	7,079	M.A.A.	URGENT	11- 8-1869	21	
LANE, James	64,257	Ship's Cook (ex RM)	ZEALOUS	6- 4-1872	26	
LANE, Joseph	47/465	Q.M.	AGAMEMNON	4- 7-1856	25	*
LANE, Peter	(*Vide* : SYMONDS, Edward)					
LANE, William	45/221	Bosun's Mate	EXMOUTH	13- 5-1859	29	
LANGDON, William	42/520	Q.M.	QUEEN	22- 6-1852	24	
LARKE, John H.	256	Chief Q.M.	MEGAERA	18- 1-1862	20	
LASKEY, John	40/280	Ward Room Steward	RODNEY	26- 2-1849	22	
LASSETER, Richard	40/138	Carpenter's Mate	EXCELLENT	23- 6-1851	22	
LATTIMER, George	49/391	Gunner's Mate	EXCELLENT	19-12-1856	25	

LAURENCE, Edward	62/363	Caulker	ESK	25- 6-1861	21	
LAWRENCE, John	12,394	Q.M.	R.N. Barracks	7- 2-1874	20	
LAWS, George	6,324	Captn Forecastle	EDGAR	5-12-1865	20	
LAWSON, Abel	65/280	A.B.	EXCELLENT	1- 1-1861	21	
LAWTON, George	62/452	Ch Captn Fcsle	MARS	31- 1-1863	21	
LAZARUS, Eleazer	33,750A	Leading Stoker	TERROR	26- 5-1874	20	
LEACH, Thomas	60/143	M.A.A.	VICTORIA & ALBERT	6- 3-1860	22	*
LEAN, Nathaniel	38/108	Ropemaker	QUEEN	15- 5-1849	23	
LEARY, John	42/244	Bosun's Mate	VICTORIA & ALBERT	18- 1-1854	26	*
LEE, Richard	39/339	Q.M.	FIREFLY	21- 7-1853	27	
LEE, Richard	61/162	Captn Forecastle	RETRIBUTION	14-12-1860	24	
LEE, Robert H.	52/474	Gunner's Mate	EXCELLENT	1-12-1856	24	
LEE, Thomas	61/122	Bosun's Mate	CENTURION	6-12-1859	21	*
LEEMUX, Samuel	4,572A	Capt's Coxswain	MUTINE	27- 3-1869	24	
LEGGE, Samuel J.	6,120	Ch Gunner's Mate	EXCELLENT	18-12-1868	21	
LEGGETT, Geo/Edwd	55/279	Gunner's Mate	PORCUPINE	16- 5-1856	23	
LEMMON, Sydney	56/487	Chief Q.M.	EXCELLENT	14-12-1859	21	
LEVER, John	40/108	A.B.	OCEAN	3- 2-1851	25	
LEVERS, Benjamin	28,448	Leading Stoker	BELLEROPHON	17- 3-1870	20	
LEVETT, Henry	2,883	Ship's Cook	HECTOR	15- 3-1869	20	
LEVETT, William J.	67/404	A.B.	EXCELLENT	1- 1-1866	23	
LEWARNE, Richard	34,508	Leading Stoker	PALLAS	4- 2-1875	20	
LEWIS, Isaac	61/250	Chief Q.M.	CRESSY	24- 5-1861	22	
LEWIS, John	51/59	Q.M.	ARCHER	11-11-1853	21	
LEWIS, Robert	72/337	Q.M.	PYLADES	2-11-1866	21	
LEWIS, William	25,307	Ship's Cook	PHAETON	11- 3-1865	22	
LIDDLE, William	55/115	Q.M.	APOLLO	11- 7-1856	21	*
LIFTON, George H.	28,275	Gunner's Mate	EXCELLENT	1- 1-1866	21	
LIGHT, William	37/501	Bandsman RN	POWERFUL	4- 3-1851	25	
2nd medal		A.B.	HANNIBAL	21-12-1861	35	
LINDRIP, Thomas	78/456	Chief Boatman i/c	H.M.Coast Guard	21- 4-1874	34	
LITTLEJOHNS, Geo.	62/373	Q.M.	MAGICIENNE	24- 4-1861	20	
LLOYD, Thomas	45/383	Q.M.	PANDORA	3- 6-1856	25	
LLUELLEN, James	63/500	Q.M.	NIGER	11- 9-1861	20	
LOCK, Charles	39/431	Bosun's Mate	ALBION	15- 1-1848	24	*
LOCKYER, George	30,968A	Leading Stoker	PIGMY	8- 6-1874	20	
LOFT, Robert	42/515	Captain of Mast	PENELOPE	10- 4-1849	21	
LOGAN, Robert	46/245	Captn After Guard	MONARCH	22-12-1853	22	*
LOMER, William	27,500	Capt's Coxswain	IRRESISTIBLE	26- 5-1865	20	*
LONE, Samuel	28,858	Gunner's Mate	MINOTAUR	21- 5-1873	20	*
LONG, John	55/202	Bosun's Mate	HAWKE	9- 5-1856	22	*
LONG, Samuel	46/324	Capt After Guard	ARROGANT	18- 9-1852	22	
LONGHURST, Thomas	40/47	Coxswain of Launch	TRAFALGAR	24- 2-1848	21	*
LONGLEY, Joseph	37/131	Bosun's Mate	ST VINCENT	13- 4-1849	24	
LOOKER, William	40/242	A.B.	NEPTUNE	31-12-1855	28	
LORAM, Gorge	35,817	Admiral's Coxswain	HIBERNIA	10-10-1873	20	
LORD, James	21,395	Leading Stoker	JACKAL	18- 4-1865	21	
LORING, John	62/324	Ship's Cook	SCOURGE	5- 2-1862	22	
LOVELESS, John	37/424	M.A.A.	HOGUE	25- 8-1852	21	
LOWE, William	48/376	Bosun's Mate	VENGEANCE	24- 4-1855	23	
LUCAS, William	46/12	Captain of Mast	HOWE	5- 7-1850	21	‡
LUCKETT, Thomas	33,747	Gunner's Mate	R.N. Barracks	2- 2-1874	21	
LUNDY, George	2,093	Q.M.	CYCLOPS	13- 8-1860	21	*
LUPTON, James	46/456	Cooper	HERCULES	10- 9-1851	21	

LYNE, William	42/219	Captn Forecastle	SUPERB	24-11-1848	21	*
LYNN, Simon	14,117	Bosun's Mate	SHANNON	5- 4-1865	20	
LYNSON, John R.	118	Ship's Cook	JUNO or ROYAL ADELAIDE	22-10-1868	23	
LYONS, William	48/175	Q.M.	MAGICIENNE	19- 5-1856	29	
MABERLY, Samuel	20,411	Capt's Coxswain	ROYAL ADELAIDE	1- 2-1873	20	
MAGNESS, Edward	81/476	Leading Stoker	GLADIATOR	23- 2-1872	20	
MAHONEY, Peter	28,277	Q.M.	AURORA	18-12-1867	21	
MALE, James S.G. on edge	38,781	Chief Q.M.	EXCELLENT	1- 6-1872	20	*
MANLY, John	(*Vide* : MAY, James)					
MANN, John A.	10,823	Carpenter's Crew	ROYAL ADELAIDE	18- 6-1874	20	*
MANNING, John	24,478	Q.M.	PELORUS	13- 4-1868	21	
MANNING, Joseph	42/327	Ship's Corporal	PRESIDENT	26- 1-1849	21	
MANSCOWEN, F.H.	21,267A	Carpenter's Mate	INDUS	21- 2-1872	21	*
MANSELL, George	61,231	Captain Main Top	MAJESTIC	15- 6-1861	22	
MANT, George	4,140A	Bosun's Mate	DUKE OF WELLINGTON	1- 9-1874	20	
MANT, Henry W.	6,851A	Ch Gunner's Mate	PRESIDENT	5- 6-1873	20	
MARCER, William	68/126	Barber	TRAFALGAR	22- 2-1864	20	
MARCOMBE, John	46/265	Ropemaker	PORTLAND	2- 5-1854	24	
MARKS, John	72/402	Ship's Cook	GIBRALTAR	3- 1-1867	21	
MARKS, Thomas	49,369	Ship's Cpl (ex RM)	LONDON	23- 1-1856	29	*
MARKS, William	5,396	Q.M.	INCONSTANT	29-12-1870	20	
MARSHALL, Benjamin	63/267	Ch Gunner's Mate	EXCELLENT	23-12-1862	22	*
MARSHALL, John	62/13	M.A.A.	VALOROUS	10- 8-1861	21	
MARSHALL, Joseph	47/73	Q.M.	VICTORY	11-12-1857	27	*
MARSHALL, William	12,172	Q.M.	CRUIZER	11-12-1873	20	
MARTIN, George	29,857	Bosun's Mate	ESK	8-10-1867	24	*
MARTIN, George B.	40/467	Gunner's Mate	SPARTAN	15- 6-1849	22	* ‡
MARTIN, John	3,399A	Bosun's Mate	DUKE OF WELLINGTON	13- 8-1874	20	*
MARTIN, John	64/98	Ch Gunner's Mate	HANNIBAL	21-12-1861	20	
MARTIN, Thomas	83/248	Ship's Cook	DUKE OF WELLINGTON	25- 9-1874	21	
MARTIN, Thomas	49/167	Q.M.	HASTINGS	29- 4-1853	21	
MARTIN, Thomas	61/176	Q.M.	INDUS	18- 4-1860	23	
MARTIN, William	5,129	Captn After Guard	SHANNON	5- 4-1865	20	
MASON, George	31,758A	Cooper	CALEDONIA	9- 2-1870	20	*
MASON, James	39/386	M.A.A.	PENELOPE	10- 4-1849	22	
MASON, Thomas	48/510	Sailmaker	BLENHEIM	21- 5-1856	24	
MATTHEWS, John W.	61/321	Gúnner's Mate	FORMIDABLE	14-12-1862	25	
MATTHEWS, Thomas	40/3	Capt's Coxswain	ST VINCENT	13- 4-1849	22	
MATTHIAS, James	40/374	Ship's Cook	ATHOLL	13- 4-1850	23	* ‡
MAY, James	39,610	Coxswain of Cutter	TOPAZE	20- 8-1869	20	
MAY, James	40/172	Bosun's Mate	TRAFALGAR	26- 6-1848	21	
MAY, John	73/5	Ship's Cook	SUPPLY	6-10-1866	20	
MAY, Stephen	68/132	Q.M.	PRINCESS CHARLOTTE	3- 6-1867	27	
MAYES, George	2,638	Chief Boatman i/c	H.M.Coast Guard	15- 4-1873	29	
McARTHUR, James	73/183	Ship's Cook	BARROSA	19- 1-1867	24	
McCARTHY, George	647	Q.M.	ORONTES	21-12-1866	20	*
McCARTHY, John	41/419	M.A.A.	CHILDERS	26- 7-1849	22	* ‡
McCARTHY, William	6,642	Ch Gunner's Mate	EXCELLENT	1- 1-1866	22	
McCLEOD, Henry	34,383	Captn Forecastle	ORLANDO	23-12-1865	21	
McCLOUD, Alexander	61/480	Bosun's Mate	SANS PAREIL	7- 6-1862	20	

Name	Number	Rank/Role	Ship	Date	Age	Mark
McCOLLEY, Wm.H.	5,465	Leading Stoker	SUPPLY	7-12-1858	21	
McCREADY, George	62/180	Captain of Mast	ABOUKIR	7-10-1862	21	
McCREADY, John	84/77	Chief Boatman i/c	H.M.Coast Guard	5- 5-1873	34	
McCUE, Thomas	36/133	Ship's Cook (ex RM)	SAMPSON	2-12-1848	25	
McDONALD, James	13,317A	Ch Bosun's Mate	EXCELLENT	11- 3-1874	20	
McDONALD, John	28/358	A.B.	CALEDONIA	14- 6-1851	27	
McDONALD, John	65/231	Ch Captn Fcsle	AGAMEMNON	10-10-1862	22	
McDONALD, John	1,970	Q.M.	ARROGANT	12- 2-1857	21	
McGHEE, James	48/77	Sailmaker's Mate	PHILOMEL	22- 5-1852	21	
McGUCKIN, Michael	5,371	2nd Captn Aft Gd	CAMELEON	21- 4-1866	24	*
McGOWAN, William	72/175	Stoker	HASTINGS	9- 5-1866	21	
McKEE, William	66/25	Ship's Steward	FORMIDABLE	14-12-1864	22	
McKENZIE, Jonathan	44/162	A.B.	CONSTANCE	1-12-1849	21	‡
McLAUGHLIN, James	31/248	A.B.	BELLEISLE	2-9-1848	37	
McLEAN, John	29,414	Coxswain of Launch	VANGUARD	23- 3-1849	22	
McFARLANE, Donald	84/92	Cmmd Boatman & Divnsl Carpenter	H.M.Coast Guard	22- 7-1873	31	
McMULLEN, John	13,350A	Capt's Coxswain	LYRA	13- 4-1868	20	
MEEK, John	61/93	Ship's Cook	TERMAGANT	8- 1-1863	26	
MENNEAR, Joseph	54/139	Q.M.	SIDON	23- 7-1856	23	
MEREDITH, Robert	65/465	Q.M.	ROYAL OAK	5-12-1867	22	
MERRIMAN, Alexander	61/130	Q.M.	HOGUE	10- 4-1861	25	*
MEW, Richard	64/455	M.A.A. (ex RM)	URGENT	21-11-1862	27	*
MIDDLETON, John	68/281	Q.M.	HORNET	10- 9-1864	21	
MIDDLETON, John	24,260A	Stoker	PENELOPE	23- 4-1874	20	
MILDRED, Hiram	74/419	Carpenter's Mate	PELORUS	13- 4-1868	21	*
MILDREN, James	31,570	Leading Stoker	INDUS	3- 5-1869	21	
MILDREN, Samuel	38,304	Bosun's Mate	IMPLACABLE	8- 5-1873	20	
MILLETT, John	53/275	A.B.	HASTINGS	3- 5-1856	22	
MILLER, David	12,534	Gunner's Mate	ROYAL ADELAIDE	21- 5-1874	22	
MILLER, James	33,488A	Ch Carptr's Mate	HART	5- 3-1874	20	
MILLER, John	39/9	A.B.	SUPERB	24-11-1848	22	
MILLER, John F.	36,688	Q.M.	BOSCAWEN	16- 8-1872	20	*
MILLER, Thomas	27,312	Bosun's Mate	FREDERICK WILLIAM	22- 4-1865	20	
MILLETT, John	53/275	A.B.	HASTINGS	3- 5-1856	22	
MILLS, Henry	55/42	2nd Captn Aft Gd	MERSEY	7- 8-1862	27	
MILLS, John	932	Bosun's Mate	VICTOR EMMANUEL	6- 5-1862	20	*
MILLS, William (S.G. on edge)	11,773	Gunner's Mate	PENELOPE	15- 6-1871	20	*
MILLS, William G.	57/251	Captn After Guard	HANNIBAL	21-12-1861	29	
MILTON, William	40/285	Ship's Cook	HIBERNIA	14- 6-1849	22	‡
MITCHELL, George	C.1551	Capt's Coxswain	WATERLOO	3-12-1856	21	*
MITCHELL, James	48/377	Captain of Hold	RUSSELL	16- 5-1856	26	
MITCHELL, John	72/163	Captn After Guard	VICTORIA	27- 7-1867	23	*
MITCHELL, William	1,672	Gunner's Mate	CAESAR	18- 1-1862	20	
MOFFETT, John	70/217	Chief Boatman i/c	H.M.Coast Guard	20- 2-1874	32	
MOFFETT, Robert	45/281	Capt's Steward	BELLEROPHON	4-11-1850	22	‡
MOGG, William	62/115	Butcher	BOSCAWEN	11- 9-1860	21	
MONK, Thomas	10,849	Gunner's Mate	ST VINCENT	27-12-1861	20	
MOON, Charles	49/25	Q.M.	DASHER	9-12-1856	23	
MOORE, Burton	48/431	Q.M.	PLUMPER	4- 1-1853	21	*
MOORE, H.	?	Leading Stoker	AGINCOURT	?	?	*

MOORE, James	48/364	Ldg Stoker (ex RM)	MAGICIENNE	19- 5-1856	27	
MOORE, James	20,412	Actg Ch Bsn's Mte	AGINCOURT	4-10-1873	20	
MOORE, John	40/196	Q.M.	INCONSTANT	2-12-1850	23	‡
MOORE, Thomas	30/22	Sailmaker's Mate	PRINCE REGENT	24- 2-1851	30	
MOREY, William	1,153	Ch Gunner's Mate	EXCELLENT	13- 9-1856	22	*
MORGAN, John	10,487	Ship's Cook	WIZARD	13- 8-1870	21	
MORGAN, Thomas	65/181	Sailmaker	HERO	12-11-1862	21	
MORLEY, James	4,097	Leading Stoker	NORTHUMBERLAND	15- 6-1870	20	
MORLEY, Windham	60/540	Carpenter's Mate	VICTORY	27-12-1861	22	
MORRISH, John	7,518B	Ship's Corporal	INDUS	11- 1-1875	21	
MORRISON, Thomas	30/195	Carpenter's Mate	LIGHTNING	22-11-1850	25	‡
MORTIMER, Thomas H.	84/83	Armourer	EXCELLENT	9- 6-1873	21	
MORTIMER, William	47/143	A.B.	SUPERB	7- 6-1852	22	
MOTT, Samuel	11,386B	Ropemaker	WOLVERENE	13- 5-1874	20	*
MULCAHY, James	36,589	Blacksmith	INDUS	30-11-1871	21	
MUNDEN, William	5,013	Leading Stoker	HECTOR	29-11-1873	20	*
MUNRO, Alexander	67/117	Bosun's Mate	JASON	26-11-1864	22	
MUNRO, James	22,953	Bosun's Mate	BARROSA	19- 1-1867	21	
MURPHY, Charles	8,151A	Q.M.	ST GEORGE	3- 5-1869	22	
MURPHY, Jeremiah	32,786	Cooper	BARROSA	19- 1-1867	21	
MURROW, Thomas	84/64	Chief Boatman i/c	H.M.Coast Guard	17- 4-1873	31	
MUSSELL, George	61/231	Captn Main Top	MAJESTIC	15- 6-1861	22	*
MYERS, James	49/408	Captn Forecastle	RODNEY	23- 1-1856	22	
NAIL, James	67/400	Ship's Cook	ALACRITY	3- 8-1863	22	
NAPIER, Thomas	61/153	Coxswain of Launch	CRESSY	24- 5-1861	22	
NATHAN, Michael	2,416	Leading Stoker	ABOUKIR	22-11-1869	20	
NETTING, Robert	3,770A	Bosun's Mate	MALACCA	4- 9-1869	24	
NEVILLE, Thomas	46/392	Coxswain of Pinnace	MEANDER	29- 7-1851	23	*
NEWMAN, John	44/422	Q.M.	BULLDOG	9- 4-1850	22	* ‡
NEWMAN, John	29,342	Captn After Guard	IMPERIEUSE	13-11-1862	23	*
NEWMAN, Michael	3,299	A.B.	PRINCESS ROYAL	6- 8-1867	22	
NEWMAN, Robert	36/104	Coxswain	ST VINCENT	13- 4-1849	23	
NEWMAN, Wm.H.	66/269	Ch Yeoman Signals	VICTORY	14-12-1866	21	*
NEWNMAN, Robert	5,935	Ship's Cook	SIRIUS	26-11-1873	24	
NICHOLLS, John	46/303	M.A.A. (ex RM)	RETRIBUTION	2- 6-1856	28	
NICHOLLS, William	4,521	Q.M.	WANDERER	18- 8-1865	24	*
NICHOLS, Thomas	62/179	Q.M.	CAESAR	18- 1-1862	22	
NICHOLSON, John	4,859	Blacksmith	MAGICIENNE	6-12-1865	20	
NICHOLSON, John	36,457	Caulker	ASIA	17- 4-1874	20	
NIXON, Robert	8,898B	Yeoman Store Rooms	BASILISK	5-12-1874	20	*
NOBES, John	51/12	Q.M.	MODESTE	15- 7-1856	25	
NORGATE, John C.	48/325	Ship's Corporal	INDEFATIGABLE	15-11-1852	21	
NORMAN, Richard	41/66	Ship's Cook	BELLEROPHON	1-11-1850	23	‡
NORRIS, Henry Earliest known award date of 'Wide'	39/325	Bosun's Mate	CORMORANT	8-12-1847	23	*
NORTHCOTT, John	7,143B	M.A.A.	NORTHUMBERLAND	3-1872	21	*
O'CONNELL, Edward	12,305	Ship's Corporal	MAJESTIC	8- 5-1861	20	*
OLDEN, Thomas	31,726	Ship's Cook	QUEEN	5-12-1863	20	
OLDING, George	48/425	Armourer	PRINCESS ROYAL	8- 7-1856	26	*

OLIVER, Charles T.	1,843	Naval Schoolmaster	CAMBRIDGE	28-12-1870	22	*
OLVAR, James	44/333	Q.M.	GANGES	14- 1-1852	23	
ORFORD, John	15,762A	Q.M.	INCONSTANT	9-10-1872	20	*
OUTFIN, Henry	64/163	Q.M.	INDUS	30- 6-1862	20	
OVERING, Richard	67/317	Bosun's Mate	BACCHANTE	27- 7-1864	22	*
OWEN, John	41/552	Q.M.	INFLEXIBLE	22- 9-1849	22	* ‡
OWENS, John	49/374	Q.M.	SANS PAREIL	4- 7-1861	29	
OXENHAM, William	49/472	Chief Q.M.	AGAMEMNON	4- 7-1866	24	
PAINE, Peter	40,275	Q.M.	RANGER	3- 4-1849	21	
PALMER, Charles	69/34	Bosun's Mate	HORNET	10- 9-1864	23	
PALMER, Charles	11,898	Carpenter's Crew	CHARYBDIS	26- 8-1871	20	
PALMER, Edward	42/477	M.A.A. (ex RM)	VANGUARD	27- 3-1849	?	
PALMER, James	20,097	Bosun's Mate	ROYAL ALFRED	25- 9-1869	20	
PALMER, Thomas	55/207	Carpenter's Mate	FIREFLY	16- 5-1856	21	*
PARKER, George	44/264	Bosun's Mate	EXCELLENT	23- 6-1851	21	*
PARKER, Thomas	62/316	Gunner's Mate	DASHER	1- 1-1863	23	
PARKER, William	8,295	Q.M.	JAMES WATT	14- 6-1862	21	
PARKIN, Richard	8,978	Gunner's Mate	CAMBRIDGE	15-12-1866	21	
PARKINS, George	68/490	Ch Bosun's Mate	NARCISSUS	29- 7-1864	22	
PARKINSON, John	41/322	Bosun's Mate	HIBERNIA	14- 6-1849	23	‡
PARKS, Thomas	62/525	M.A.A.	PYLADES	23- 7-1861	23	
PARNELL, Francis	42/218	Carpenter's Crew	QUEEN	22- 6-1852	21	
PARSONS, Robert	44/160	A.B.	CONSTANCE	1-12-1849	21	‡
PASCOE, Edwin	39,845A	Bosun's Mate	VICTORY	4- 3-1869	21	
PATISSON, Nimrod	69/534	Caulker	CAMBRIDGE	17-12-1866	21	
PATTERSON, James	55/262	Q.M.	PIQUE	7- 2-1859	23	
PATTERSON, John	7,533	Gunner's Mate	ALACRITY	3- 8-1863	20	
PAUL, John	37/317	Ship's Cook	INCONSTANT	3-12-1850	24	‡
PAUL, William	67/533	Q.M.	INDUS	29-12-1863	21	*
PAY, George	51/247	Bosun's Mate	ALBION	28-12-1855	23	
PAYNE, Joseph	79/46	Ship's Stwd 1st Cl	ASIA/ DUKE OF WELLINGTON	2-12-1871	21	
PEACHY, Uriah	6,574	Bosun's Mate	SALAMANDER	22-11-1873	20	
PEACHY, William	55/196	Chief Q.M.	NEPTUNE	31-12-1855	24	
PEARCE, Charles	39,996	Q.M.	CLYDE	12- 5-1874	21	
PEARCE, George	70/387	Ship's Steward	FISGARD	11- 1-1872	22	
PEARCE, John	78/423	Ship's Stwd 1st Cl	CROCODILE	17- 8-1870	21	
PEARCE, William	82/44	Captain's Cook	CHANTICLEER	6- 3-1872	22	
PEARSE, George	68/438	A.B.	EXCELLENT	1- 1-1866	21	
PEARSE, James	63/518	Bosun's Mate	DASHER	12-12-1866	26	
PEARSON, Chas.R/E.	71/277	Lamptrimmer	TRAFALGAR	11-11-1869	21	
PEARSON, John	48/360	M.A.A.	ST GEORGE	22-10-1853	21	
PENNICOTT, George	53/111	Bosun's Mate	IMPERIEUSE	27- 1-1857	22	*
PENNY, Charles	37/477	Q.M.	HIBERNIA	14- 6-1849	23	‡
PENVITT, George	47/395	Capt's Coxswain	MONARCH	22-12-1853	22	
PEPPERELL, John	31,640	Leading Stoker	AGINCOURT	12- 8-1873	20	*
PERCIVAL, William	30,224A	Ch Captn Fcsle	WARRIOR	12-11-1864	21	
PERDEW, Thomas	47/439	Captn After Guard	VULTURE	16- 5-1856	24	
PERKINS, James R.	51/88	Captn After Guard	MEGAERA	6- 5-1856	23	
PERKINS, William	5,549	Q.M.	PRINCESS ROYAL	6- 8-1867	23	*
PERRY, James	44/276	Q.M.	CALYPSO	2- 7-1855	25	
PETERS, George A.	27,731A	Armourer	ROYAL ADELAIDE	16- 3-1874	20	
PETERS, Thomas	353	Ch Gunner's Mate	EXCELLENT	1- 1-1866	21	
PETHICK, Abraham	4,104	Armourer's Crew	AGINCOURT	12- 8-1873	20	*
PETT, Richard	(*Vide* : HIGGINS, William)					

PHILLIPS, Alexander	40/344	Bosun's Mate	QUEEN	15- 5-1849	22	
PHILLIPS, Richard	60/369	Captain of Hold	IMPREGNABLE	3-12-1861	23	*
PHILLIPS, William	53/453	Painter	HIGHFLYER	27- 5-1856	22	
PHIPPS, James	47/550	Bosun's Mate	CRESSY	25- 5-1861	24	
PICOT, John	9,480	Q.M.	ICARUS	18- 5-1864	21	
PIDGEN, Henry	57/538	Ship's Cook	CONQUEROR	6-12-1859	22	
PIDGEON, James	64/172	Ch Captn Fcsle	CONQUEROR	15- 3-1861	21	
PIDGEON, William	36/199	M.A.A. (ex RM)	PHAETON	20- 1-1853	23	
PIERREPOINT, Josh.	44/406	Ship's Cook	AMAZON	3- 5-1852	23	*
PIKE, Phillip	61/545	Ship's Cook	MEGAERA	3- 3-1864	22	
PINHORN, James	33,934A	Q.M.	ROSARIO	21- 9-1871	21	*
PINK, James	54/171	Captn Main Top	FURIOUS	28- 7-1856	20	
PIPER, William	42/525	Carpenter's Mate	WELLINGTON	26-11-1850	22	‡
PITMAN, William	6,155	Carpenter's Mate	ROEBUCK	16- 7-1861	20	
PITT, Philip	67/301	Gunner's Mate	SNAKE	30- 5-1863	21	
PITT, William	83/198	Cmmd Boatman	H.M.Coast Guard	8- 4-1874	34	
PIZZEY, Thomas	8,021	Blacksmith	AGINCOURT	11- 7-1872	20	*
PLUMLEY, Charles	3,960	Q.M.	URGENT	21-11-1862	22	*
POAT, Richard	31,709A	Q.M.	ACHILLES	7-12-1874	20	*
POE, Leonard	33,325	Captain of Hold	ARIADNE	5- 8-1872	20	
POOR, Charles	12,455	M.A.A.	CADMUS	2- 1-1874	20	
POTTER, John	48/204	Q.M.	HOUND	27- 8-1852	22	
POPE, William	55/287	Stoker (ex RM)	EDINBURGH	31- 5-1856	24	
POUNDS, Henry	47/479	Ship's Cook	DAUNTLESS	10- 5-1853	21	
POWELL, Samuel	62/275	Ropemaker	BOSCAWEN	12- 9-1860	20	
POWERS, Charles	61/42	Gunner's Mate	RACOON	14- 1-1862	22	
PRATT, James	63/350	Captn After Guard	ARCHER	2-10-1861	22	*
PRATT, John	8,317	Bosun's Mate	INDUS	28-12-1863	21	
PRATT, William	21,254	Coxswain of Launch	RUSSELL	8- 4-1864	21	
PREATER, Thomas	36/185	A.B.	TRAFALGAR	26- 6-1848	23	
PRESLEY, John	5,763	Q.M.	MIRANDA	17- 4-1857	25	*
PRESSLEY, Francis	33,527	Bosun's Mate	PEARL	25-11-1870	22	
PRESTOE, William	8,541B	M.A.A.	LION	19-10-1869	21	
PRESTON, James	13,334	Bosun's Mate	TRIUMPH	14- 7-1874	21	
PRESTON, Stephen	4,895	Ch Gunner's Mate	PRESIDENT	20- 8-1871	25	*
PRETTIEJOHNS, Edwd.	69/29	Tailor	MARLBOROUGH	24-11-1864	21	*
PRIMMER, William A.	42/331	Bosun's Mate	HOGUE	25- 8-1852	23	*
PRIDEAUX, John (Anchor Type LSGC.	25/447	A.B. (2nd LSGC) Q.M.	ST GEORGE CASTOR	27- 3-1856 16-11-1847	31 23	* *
PRITCHARD, John	61/161	Gunner's Mate	NIGER	6- 9-1861	22	
PRIVETT, James	63/26	Chief Q.M.	CURACOA	29- 5-1862	21	*
PROUT, Thomas	54/723	Carpenter's Mate	WELLESLEY	27-12-1861	25	*
PUCKEY, Richard	34,181	Bosun's Mate	GALATEA	24- 6-1870	20	*
PUDIFOOT, James	35/938	Captain of Hold	ROYAL WILLIAM	23- 3-1859	34	
PURCHASE, William	42/224	Cabin Steward	FISGARD	22-11-1850	43	‡
PURDY, Joseph	61/262	Chief Bosun's Mate	VIGILANT	8- 1-1860	20	
PURSELL, Patrick	40/446	Bosun's Mate	TRAFALGAR	8- 7-1848	21	
PURVER, Richard	47/107	Bosun's Mate	TORTOISE	11-12-1851	21	
PYBURN, William	31,400A	Bosun's Mate	LANDRAIL	6- 2-1868	20	
PYE, William H.	69/260	Bosun's Mate	ST VINCENT	14-12-1866	22	
QUINTON, George	30/291	Ship's Cook A.B.	INDEFATIGABLE or ROYAL WILLIAM	15-11-1852 23- 3-1859	29 36	

RABLAIN, Joseph	63/273	Q.M.	CORNWALLIS	8- 5-1861	21	
RADFORD, Joseph	4,575A	Q.M.	PYLADES	20- 7-1870	20	
RADFORD, William	42/225	Captn Forecastle	CONSTANCE	1-12-1849	21	‡
RADMORE, John	44/349	Admiral's Coxswain	ASIA	17- 5-1851	22	*
RANDALL, William C.	78/502	Ships Stwd 1st Cl	SERAPHIS	18- 4-1872	22	
RAWLINGS, Thomas	6,045	Captn After Guard	CLIO	13- 7-1868	21	*
RAX, William	45/108	Q.M.	FOX	16- 5-1864	27	
RATTENBURY, John	44/26	Carpenter's Mate	PHILOMEL	17-10-1849	24	‡
RAYMOND, Thomas	65/281	Sailmaker	NEPTUNE	11-12-1862	20	
READ/REID, George	48/403	Ropemaker	ATLANTA	2- 5-1860	28	
REARDON, Henry	5,931	Q.M.	DUKE OF WELLINGTON	30- 1-1874	20	
REAY, Thomas	67/493	Q.M.	QUEEN	5-12-1863	21	
REED, Thomas	36/420	Sailmaker	COLLINGWOOD	10- 7-1848	24	*
REED, William	62/355	Sick Berth Stwd	HERO	12-11-1862	24	
REED, Willia,	74/215	Lamptrimmer	MEGAERA	11-12-1867	21	
REES, William	42/374	Q.M.	CALEDONIA	14- 6-1851	21	
REES, William	69/427	Ward Room Cook	ROYAL GEORGE	22- 4-1865	21	
REEVES, John	76/319	Leading Stoker	OCTAVIA	20- 7-1869	22	
REEVES, William	4,693	Ch Gunner's Mate	DURHAM	20- 6-1874	20	
REMMINGTON, George	60/514	Bosun's Mate	AMETHYST	14-12-1860	22	
REMPHRY, William	47/6	Ship's Cook	AURORA	13-12-1867	24	*
REYNOLDS, James	1,195	Ship's Cook	MAGPIE	29- 4-1874	29	
REYNOLDS, Richard	45/474	Captn After Guard	TOPAZE	24-12-1863	33	
RICE, Henry	6,339	Ship's Cook	FLORA	26- 3-1873	27	
RICH, Charles	62/437	Q.M.	HYDRA	20- 8-1862	22	*
RICH, John	8,121	Ship's Corporal	BACCHANTE	27- 7-1864	20	
RICHARDS, Charles	47/515	Bosun's Mate	VENGEANCE	24- 4-1855	23	*
RICHARDS, John	69/411	Admiral's Coxswain	EURYALUS	13- 9-1865	23	
RICHARDSON, John	2,060	Captain of Hold	MEANDER	7- 5-1862	20	
RICHARDSON, Thos.	60/231	Bosun's Mate	CURLEW	6-12-1858	20	
RICHARDSON, Wm.	62/220	Bosun's Mate	SANS PAREIL	4- 7-1861	22	
RICKARD, Henry	44/479	Carpenter's Mate	GROWLER	22- 9-1852	23	
RIDDETT, Charles	82/285	Chief Boatman	H.M.Coast Guard	9- 3-1874	32	
RIDGE, William	84/66	Chief Boatman i/c	H.M.Coast Guard	17- 4-1873	38	
RIDLER, George	12,221	Leading Stoker	PIGMY	17-12-1868	20	
RIGGS, James	61/233	Coxswain of Launch	PEMBROKE	3- 1-1861	24	
RIGGS, Thomas	60/500	Q.M.	CHESAPEAKE	9-10-1861	22	
ROBERTS, George	41/213	Gunner's Mate	SCOURGE	9- 5-1849	21	
ROBERTS, Peter	28/356	A.B.	CALEDONIA	14- 6-1851	27	
ROBERTS, Richard	32/225	A.B.	CRANE	9- 1-1851	24	
ROBINSON, William	6,854	Leading Stoker	SEVERN	2- 6-1866	21	
ROBINSON, William	37,647A	Coxswain of Pinnace	TOPAZE	20- 8-1869	20	
ROBSON, William	37/135	Q.M.	COLLINGWOOD	10- 7-1848	23	
ROGERS, Henry	63/313	Ch Gunner's Mate	EXCELLENT	23-12-1862	22	
ROLLING, William	48/350	Captn Forecastle	HAVANNAH	16-11-1859	24	
ROOK, William	45/303	Ship's Cpl (ex RM)	RATTLESNAKE	11-11-1850	24	‡
ROPER, Henry	2,287	Captain of Hold	SERAPIS	24- 7-1873	20	
ROSE, Henry	71/214	A.B.	EXCELLENT	1- 1-1866	24	
ROSS, John	47/194	Bosun's Mate	RODNEY	23- 1-1856	24	

ROWE, Richard	44/458	Bosun's Mate	GANGES	14- 1-1852	21	
ROWE, William	33,495	M.A.A.	HERO	12-11-1862	21	*
ROWLEY, James	4,203	Leading Stoker	JACKAL	19- 6-1873	20	
ROWLINGS, John	936A	Bosun's Mate	ROYAL ADELAIDE	16- 5-1874	20	*
RULE, Billy	59/425	Chief Boatman i/c	H.M.Coast Guard	18- 2-1874	41	
RUNDLE, John	46/301	Ship's Corporal	WELLESLEY	13- 6-1851	24	
RUSSELL, Ellis	38,061	Carpenter's Mate	VICTORIA & ALBERT	23- 1-1875	20	*
RUSSELL, Richard	58/339	Gunner's Mate	EXCELLENT	14-12-1859	24	
RYDER, Edward	28,170	Caulker	GALATEA	15-12-1870	20	*
SAGE, John	23,030	Q.M.	BEACON	19- 1-1872	20	
SALTER, Henry	(*Vide* : REARDON, Henry)					
SALTER, John H.	81/359	Steward for General Mess	TRAFALGAR	12- 8-1871	20	
SALTER, Johnson	84/32	Ship's Corporal	ST VINCENT	30- 1-1873	20	
SALTER, William	45/22	Q.M.	NIGER	24- 1-1856	25	
SAMMELS, John	13,718	A.B.	INDUS	30-12-1868	20	*
SAMNELS, Richard	58/393	Captain of Hold	CONQUEROR	6-12-1859	22	
SAMPSON, Thomas	3,836	Sailmaker	DASHER	31-12-1869	20	
SANDFORD, Edward	11,430	Leading Stoker	MALABAR	11- 5-1874	20	
SANDS, William H.	21,816	Captn Forecastle	RESERVE	5- 6-1873	20	
SAUNDERS, Edward	61/283	Ch Gunner's Mate	CAESAR	18- 1-1862	23	
SAUNDERS, James	48/371	Q.M.	TIGER	16- 5-1855	23	
SAUNDERS, Robert	37/81	Ship's Cook	FIREBRAND	27-11-1852	26	
SAUNDERS, Samuel	4,742	Bosun's Mate	CALEDONIA	7-11-1873	20	*
SAUNDERS, William	49/155	Q.M.	HANNIBAL	21-12-1861	28	
SAVELL, William	46/525	Q.M.	FROLIC	20-10-1851	21	
SAW, George H.	81/355	Ship's Steward	HECTOR	11- 8-1871	20	
SCALE, John	44/91	Q.M.	BELLEROPHON	1-11-1850	23	‡
SCOBLE, Thomas S.G. on edge	28,643	Bosun's Mate	IRON DUKE	29- 1-1875	20	*
SCOTT, David	39/384	Gunner's Mate	ROLLA	28-12-1847	22	
SCOTT, James	78/307	Ship's Cook	HAVOC	19- 5-1870	24	
SCOTT, Robert	69/221	Captain of Hold	FORMIDABLE	14-12-1864	21	
SCULLY, Cornelius	9,346	Leading Stoker	SERAPIS	9- 1-1874	20	
SEAGAR, Charles	45/166	Ship's Corporal	SUPERB	7- 6-1852	23	
SEAGROVE, Charles	53/293	Sailmaker	DEVASTATION	22- 6-1855	22	
SEAL, Daniel	45/333	Captn Forecastle	FURY	28-11-1850	21	‡
SEANOR, William	1,753	Captn After Guard	FALCON	1-10-1862	22	
SEARLE, John	65/519	Bosun's Mate	HAWKE	16- 4-1864	21	
SEARLE, William	67/30	Q.M.	ALGIERS	9-12-1862	21	
SEER(S), Thomas	61/122	Bosun's Mate	CENTURION	6-12-1859	21	
SELBY, Henry	39,345	Q.M.	RAPID	12- 1-1867	25	
SERGEANT, William	41/421	Captn Forecastle	PHILOMEL	11- 7-1856	25	
SETTON, John	69/549	Ship's Cook	MEDEA	22- 6-1865	30	
SHARP, Henry	70/143	Captain's Steward	JUNO	16- 3-1870	25	
SHEA, James	47/451	Q.M.	PRINCESS ROYAL	28- 7-1856	25	*
SHEEHAN, Douglas	27,829	Ropemaker	VALOROUS	28- 4-1873	20	*
SHEEN, George	68/152	Chief Q.M.	MEEANEE	19- 2-1866	23	
SHEEN, Timothy	40/326	Captn After Guard	DAPHNE	9- 8-1852	25	
SHEET, Joseph	(*Vide* : STREET, Joseph)					
SHEPHARD, James	42/326	Coxswain of Launch	PRESIDENT	26- 1-1849	22	*
SHEPHERD, Joseph	31,657	Leading Stoker	DAUNTLESS	9- 5-1867	20	*
SHERMAN, George F.	64/539	Captain's Cook	DUKE OF WELLINGTON	19- 7-1864	21	
SHERRELL, Richard	59/151	Actg Ship's Cook	SPITFIRE	20- 2-1861	23	

SIDNEY, John	64/482	Q.M.	JAMES WATT	14- 6-1862	20	
SILVER, Francis	11,790	A.B.	SUTLEJ	29- 7-1867	21	*
SIMMONDS, John	21,937	Chief Bosun's Mate	HECTOR	6- 3-1867	20	
SIMMONS, James	65/80	Gunner's Mate	CAMBRIDGE	26- 2-1862	22	
SIMON, John	3,183	Captain's Coxswain	ROYAL OAK	5-12-1867	20	*
SIMPSON, Henry	29,818A	Leading Stoker	ORWELL	10- 7-1874	20	*
SIMPSON, William	19,996	Caulker	STROMBOLI	28- 5-1866	20	
SIMS, James	60/439	Ship's Cook	DUNCAN	14- 6-1867	23	
SKELTON, Nicholas	2,420	Blacksmith	DEVASTATION	29- 7-1866	20	
SKELTON, William	81/257	Leading Stoker	SALAMIS	5- 4-1871	20	
SLADE, William	11,056	Leading Stoker	PRINCE ALBERT	10- 5-1866	20	
SLEE, William	16,088	Q.M.	PHOEBE	20- 6-1866	23	*
SLEEP, John	61/263	Captain's Coxswain	SATELLITE	21- 1-1861	22	
SMALE, James	993	Captain's Coxswain	CONSTANCE	16-12-1868	21	
SMALL, William	5,321	Gunner's Mate	ST VINCENT	17- 4-1874	20	
SMITH, David	24,218	Captn Forecastle	ORESTES	14- 6-1865	20	
SMITH, Francis	62/77	Bosun's Mate	MAGICIENNE	24- 4-1861	26	
SMITH, George	45/276	Q.M.	BELLEROPHON	2-11-1850	21	‡
SMITH, Henry	69/328	A.B.	EXCELLENT	31-12-1865	23	
SMITH, Henry P.	61/421	Leading Stoker	MINOTAUR	9- 6-1870	21	
SMITH, James	45/58	Bosun's Mate	VENGEANCE	4- 7-1850	23	‡
SMITH, James	62/255	Ship's Cook	VALOROUS	10- 8-1861	22	
SMITH, John	65/453	Captain's Coxswain	SURPRISE	17- 4-1866	23	
SMITH, John	39/371	M.A.A.	WELLESLEY	13- 6-1851	24	*
SMITH, John	65/257	Ship's Corporal	HERO	12-11-1862	20	
SMITH, John	67/129	Ship's Cook	SCYLLA	26-12-1862	21	
SMITH, Richard	32,003	Ship's Cook	ENTERPRISE	17- 7-1868	24	*
SMITH, Thomas	35/1038	Bosun's Mate	DUKE OF WELLINGTON	16- 6-1856	21	
SMITH, William	6,235	Bosun's Mate	IMMORTALITE	9- 7-1864	20	
SMITH, William	6,711	Sailmaker	HYDRA	17- 4-1856	21	*
SMITH, William	60/372	Captain's Coxswain	BELLEISLE	26- 7-1859	21	
SMITH, William	64/471	Bosun's Mate	CURACOA	4- 6-1862	25	
SMITH, William	35,968	Q.M.	DEFENCE	29- 5-1866	22	
SMITH, William	6,346	Chief Bosun's Mate	BOSCAWEN	11- 9-1860	20	
SMITH, William T.	75/422	Sick Berth Steward	VICTORY	15- 2-1869	20	
SMITHERS, John	26,701A	Blacksmith	EXCELLENT	6- 2-1875	20	*
SNELL, Thomas	27,717	Q.M.	NILE	15- 4-1864	20	
SNELL, William G.	73/154	M.A.A.	ROYAL ALFRED	27- 8-1869	22	
SNOOK, William	9,645A	Chief Q.M.	DUKE OF WELLINGTON	21- 1-1875	20	
SNOW, William H.	62/441	Q.M.	ALERT	27- 9-1861	22	
SOLE, Philip	60/455	Carpenter's Mate	SERINGPATAM or	26- 4-1867	28	
			SERINGPATAM	1- 8-1870	32	
SOMERVILLE, Fdck.	15,875	Captain of Hold	JASON	29- 3-1870	22	
SOUTHGATE, Rbt.G.	4,873	Captn After Guard	LEOPARD	22- 9-1866	21	
SOWDEN, George	57/520	Carpenter's Mate	BELLEISLE	26- 7-1859	22	
SPAIN, William	62/411	Ship's Cook	CORNWALLIS	8- 5-1861	20	
SPARGO, John	21,793	Gunner's Mate	RESISTANCE	21- 2-1870	20	*
SPARKES, John	40/44	Captn Forecastle	PRINCE REGENT	24- 2-1851	23	
SPARKS, Edward	51/218	Ch Captn Fcsle	VENGEANCE	24- 4-1855	22	

SPARKS, Thomas	5,070	Carpenter's Mate	PELICAN	5- 5-1866	22	*
SPENCE, John	45/57	Captn Forecastle	VENGEANCE	4- 7-1850	23	‡
SPENCE, John	41/339	Ship's Corporal	ALECTO	26- 6-1849	21	‡
SPENCER, William	58/429	Captn After Guard	PRINCESS ROYAL	18-11-1859	23	
SPIERES, John	22/281	Ship's Cook	TARTARUS	1- 5-1860	21	
SPRAGGS, James	83/199	Cmmd Boatman	H.M.Coast Guard	8- 4-1874	33	
SPRATT, Richard	3,825	Stoker	ASIA	15-12-1870	20	
STABB, John D.	41/298	Coxswain of Launch	HOWE	5- 7-1850	21	‡
STAGG, Henry B.	30,678	Leading Stoker	IRRESISTIBLE	23- 4-1868	20	
STANBURY, John	38,960A	Captain's Coxswain	DUNCAN	23- 4-1868	20	
STANTON, James R.	64/235	Captn After Guard	TOPAZE	24-12-1863	23	
STARES, George	63/15	Gunner's Mate	CHESAPEAKE	9-10-1861	20	
STARES, Thomas	45/394	Q.M.	CASTOR	29- 1-1853	25	*
STARLING, James	73/138	Carpenter's Mate	COSSACK	16- 2-1867	22	
STARLING, Stephen	38/407	A.B.	NEPTUNE	7- 3-1854	27	*
STARLING, William	62/356	Bosun's Mate	DIADEM	4- 4-1862	22	
STEDSON, William	62/62	Q.M.	PERSIAN	22- 7-1861	21	*
STEEL, William	46/164	Q.M.	RATTLER	10- 4-1851	20	
STEPHENS, George	47/184	Sailmaker	GANGES	14- 1-1852	21	
STEPHENS, Joseph	47/95	Q.M.	RODNEY	23- 1-1856	24	
STEPHENS, Nicholas	57/438	M.A.A.	PRINCESS ROYAL	18-11-1859	24	
STEPHENS, Robert	10,623	Blacksmith	CONQUEROR	6-12-1859	21	
STEPHENS, William	3,745	Q.M.	ZEALOUS	17- 3-1870	21	
STEVENS, Edward J.	24,767	M.A.A.	LIVERPOOL	28-11-1870	20	*
STEVENS, George	60/192	Chief Bosun's Mate	MARS	31- 1-1863	22	
STEVENS, Henry	(*Vide* : STREVENS, Hy.W.H.)					
STEVENS, John	64/385	Bosun's Mate	CORDELIA	1- 4-1862	21	
STEVENS, John	67/445	A.B.	INDUS	30-12-1868	25	
STEWARD, George	55/62	Sick Berth Steward	EXCELLENT	1- 1-1866	28	
STEWARD, William	42/217	Q.M.	SUPERB	24-11-1848	21	
STEWART, Samuel	45/299	Q.M.	FLYING FISH	8-12-1851	22	
STEWART, William	41/238	Sailmaker's Mate	QUEEN	15- 5-1849	22	*
STIDIVER, John	54/649	Ship's Steward	PYLADES	17-11-1856	21	
STILES, James	4,240	Gunner's Mate	ORLANDO	23-12-1865	21	
STONE, Robert	42/470	Q.M.	VANGUARD	24- 3-1849	21	
STONE, William	65/454	Captain of Mast	PEARL	9- 6-1864	24	
STONEHAM, William	38,311A	Ch Carpenter's Mate	ROYALIST	19-11-1870	20	*
STOWELL, Henry	1,902	Leading Stoker	DRAGON	10- 2-1857	22	
STRAW, Philip	15,637	Leading Stoker	CALEDONIA	11- 5-1874	20	
STREET, Joseph	5,971	Q.M.	BRILLIANT	23-11-1857	21	*
STREVENS, Henry.W.H.	2,765	Gunner's Mate	RETRIBUTION	2- 8-1856	21	*
STROUD, Henry	47/398	Q.M.	PENELOPE	22- 3-1854	23	*
STUBINGTON, Hy.P.	20,559	Gunner's Mate	FAVORITE	1- 5-1875	20	
STUPPLE, George	15,986	Q.M.	ANTELOPE	23- 6-1865	23	
SUBBICK, James	48/19	M.A.A. (ex RM)	GANGES	14- 1-1852	23	
SULLIVAN, Cornelius	37/428	A.B.	WELLINGTON	25-11-1850	25	*
SULLIVAN, John	28,133	Q.M.	TOPAZE	20- 8-1869	22	
SULLIVAN, John	48/417	Blacksmith	CUMBERLAND	6- 4-1854	22	*
SUMMERS, Edwin J.	66/6	M.A.A.	FORTE	2- 9-1864	22	
SUMMERS, Thomas	61/7	Q.M.	TARTAR/FORTE	6- 3-1860	22	

SURGISON, William	40/348	Captn Forecastle	VINDICTIVE	13- 6-1848	24	
SWAIN, William	(Vide : PURSELL, Patrick)					
SWINBORN, George	83/96	Q.M.	EUPHRATES	22- 5-1873	22	
SWANTON, James	4,017A	Caulker	HIMALAYA	2- 4-1874	20	
SWINGARD, John	42/135	Ship's Cook	CLEOPATRA	20- 9-1853	24	
SYLVESTER, William	82/157	Ship's Cook	RINALDO	31- 3-1873	22	
SYMONS, Edward	67/187	Q.M.	QUEEN	5-12-1863	20	
TALLACK, George	67/285	Sailmaker	SERINGAPATAM	26- 4-1867	24	
TANSLEY, Thomas	84/78	Chief Boatman i/c	H.M.Coast Guard	5- 5-1873	38	
TAPPER, Thomas	64/97	Blacksmith	HANNIBAL	21-12-1861	20	
TAPSELL, Frederick	5,382	Bosun's Mate	LEANDER	9-10-1866	21	
TARRANT, John	45/228	Gunner's Mate	EXCELLENT	23- 6-1851	22	
TAYLOR, Christphr.	1,633	Gunner's Mate	BRILLIANT	3- 6-1871	20	
TAYLOR, James	23,008	Gunner's Mate	CUMBERLAND	5-12-1868	22	
TAYLOR, Joseph	40/95	A.B.	BRITANNIA	16- 1-1852	26	
TAYLOR, Thomas	6,127	Ship's Cook	ANTELOPE	11- 2-1874	28	*
TAYLOR, William	45/142	Blacksmith	WASP	2- 1-1855	26	
TAYLOR, William	36,559	Ropemaker	DUNCAN	20-10-1874	20	*
TEAGUE, Samuel	6,419	Q.M.	COLUMBINE	14- 1-1868	21	
TEISEO, Antonio	81/477	Bandmaster	PEMBROKE	26- 2-1872	21	
TERRY, James	5,265	Leading Stoker	INCONSTANT	25- 5-1870	20	
THIER, Alfred	3,699	Chief Gunner's Mate	EXCELLENT	9-12-1870	20	
THOMAS, Henry	21,603	Q.M.	MAJESTIC	28- 3-1862	22	
THOMAS, Henry J.	84/68	Ship's Cook	ZEALOUS	18- 4-1873	21	*
THOMAS, John	36/112	Q.M.	ST GEORGE	27- 3-1856	32	
THOMAS, John	49/297	Leading Stoker	EDINBURGH or EXCELLENT	31- 5-1856	24	
THOMAS, Richard	42/157	A.B.	VERNON	31-10-1848	23	
THOMAS, Robert	84/63	Cmmd Boatman	H.M.Coast Guard	17- 4-1873	33	
THOMPSELL, William	47/533	Captn After Guard	HOGUE	25- 8-1852	21	
THOMPSON, James	11,941	Q.M.	AVON	10- 3-1874	20	
THOMPSON, William	58/273	Captn Forecastle	HOGUE	10- 4-1861	23	
THOMSON, William	63/209	Q.M.	HOGUE	10- 4-1861	20	*
THORN, George	63/414	A.B.	LYRA	27-12-1861	23	
THORNBOROUGH, Jn.	55/190	Sick Berth Attendt (ex RM)	ALBION	28-12-1855	26	
THORNTON, John	27/434	Q.M.	IMPREGNABLE	18-12-1851	27	
THORPE, William W.	64/516	Q.M.	LIFFEY	10- 7-1862	21	
TIPPER, William	69/69	Bosun's Mate	VICTORIA	27- 7-1867	20	*
TIPPETT, Walter	60/433	Gunner's Mate	RANGER	6-11-1863	25	
TODHUNTER, Thomas	3,458	Captain of Hold	PEARL	25-11-1870	20	
TOLFREE, Charles	10,851	Chief Gunner's Mate	CALCUTTA	26- 1-1856	21	*
TOMPKINS, Thomas	36/79	Ship's Cook	FIREBRAND	27-11-1852	26	
TOOMEY, Thomas	64/476	Captain of Mast	SANS PAREIL	7- 6-1862	20	
TOPSFIELD, Henry	34,254A	Captain of Hold	WOLVERENE	9- 5-1874	20	
TOSH, Alexander	12,686	Q.M.	TRAFALGAR	9- 5-1867	20	
TOWNLEY, Matthew	64/327	Sick Berth Steward	WELLESLEY	28- 3-1868	27	*
TRACEY, Joseph	40/491	Bosun's Mate	POWERFUL	4- 3-1851	23	
TRATTLE, John	550	Captain of Hold	DUKE OF WELLINGTON	24- 1-1873	20	*
TRESSIDER, Samuel	653	Sailmaker	ORLANDO	23-12-1865	20	*
TRIST, Stephen F.	723	Carpenter's Mate	CAMBRIDGE	17-12-1866	23	
TROD, James	54/17	Ch Captn Fcsle	AGAMEMNON	5- 7-1856	22	

TUCKER, George	53/280	Gunner's Mate	RUSSELL	16- 5-1856	22	
TUCKER, John	31,116A	Q.M.	PIGEON	2- 4-1874	20	
TUCKER, John C.	141	M.A.A.	JASON	26-11-1864	20	
TUCKER, William	63/274	Captn Fore Top	CORNWALLIS	8- 5-1861	20	
TUGGEY, George	22,614	Q.M.	VICTORY	15- 2-1869	23	
TUGNETT, James	29,837	Q.M.	GROWLER	17- 6-1873	20	
TUKLE, Joseph	38/498	Leading Stoker	DRYAD	28-12-1871	26	
TUNE, Michael B.H.	62/386	Bosun's Mate	CROCODILE	30- 7-1861	21	
TURL, George	20,101	Yeoman of Signals	VICTORIA & ALBERT	28-12-1864	20	*
TURNBULL, John	29/308	Carpenter's Crew	VICTORY	27-11-1847	27	
TURNER, George	35/1104	M.A.A.	HOGUE	15- 5-1856	25	
TURNER, John	62/254	Captn After Guard	ELK	15- 8-1860	21	
TURNER, Joseph	2,586	Chief Boatman i/c	H.M.Coast Guard	21- 4-1874	32	
TURNER, Richard	53/41	Q.M.	VIXEN	22- 4-1861	22	
TWYMAN, Henry	61/77	Sailmaker	CRUISER	23- 4-1861	23	*
UNDERHILL, Samuel	45/385	Carpenter's Mate	VICTORIA & ALBERT	22-12-1853	24	
VALLANCE, John	22,970	Ropemaker	CURACOA	15- 2-1867	21	
VEALE, Bezaleal	731	Chief Gunner's Mate	TRAFALGAR	22- 2-1864	22	
VENNING, John	1,313	Blacksmith	AGINCOURT	12- 8-1873	20	
VENNING, Samuel	65/439	Bosun's Mate	QUEEN	5-12-1863	21	
VINCENT, John	37/129	Bosun's Mate	PHILOMEL	18- 9-1849	22	*
WADE, James	83/86	Chief Boatman	H.M.Coast Guard	23- 4-1873	33	
WAKEHAM, John	11,839	Bosun's Mate	VALIANT	2- 2-1874	22	
WAKEHAM, Thomas	66/276	M.A.A.	CANOPUS	5- 4-1867	21	
WAKELY, Henry	69/22	Ship's Stwd 1st Cl	CURACOA	15- 2-1867	23	
WAKEMAN, James	62/354	Ship's Corporal	DIADEM	4- 4-1862	22	
WAKERLY, Thomas	46/453	Q.M.	CROCODILE	6- 1-1858	27	*
WALKER, Andrew	65/182	Gunner's Mate	HERO	12-11-1862	21	
WALKER, William	33,609	Leading Stoker	ASIA	11- 8-1871	20	
WALKER, William	49/72	Leading Stoker	EXCELLENT	14-12-1859	27	
WALLACE, James	1,078	Ch Gunner's Mate	MARLBOROUGH	22-11-1864	20	*
WALLER, William	72/35	Ship's Cook	VICTORY	15- 2-1869	21	
WALLIS, Thomas	63/272	Ch Captn Fcsle	NEPTUNE	29-12-1861	22	
WALSH, John/James	32/360	Bosun's Mate	PRINCE REGENT	24- 2-1851	26	
WALTERS, Francis	45/524	M.A.A.	RODNEY	23- 1-1856	24	
WALTERS, John	77/62	Ship's Stwd 1st Cl	BRITANNIA	11- 4-1872	21	
WALTON, Joseph	12,204	Captain of Hold	VICTORY	14-12-1866	20	
WANNACOTT, William	14,670A	Q.M.	ZEALOUS	17- 3-1870	20	
WANSTALL, George	42/280	Q.M.	CAMBRIAN	2-11-1850	21	‡
WARD, George	60/452	Carpenter's Crew	CORNWALLIS	8- 5-1861	25	
WARD, James G.	26,223	Chief Gunner's Mate	EXCELLENT	16- 5-1873	20	
WARMINGTON, Frdck.	76/349	Painter 2nd Cl	ST VINCENT	29-10-1870	24	
WARNE, James	56/67	A.B.	INDUS	29-12-1863	27	
WARNES, Peter	61/212	Bosun's Mate	SATELLITE	21- 1-1861	22	
WARREL, William	63/530	Captn After Guard	HOGUE	1- 5-1863	22	
WARREN, Henry C.	83/196	Chief Boatman i/c	H.M.Coast Guard	8- 4-1874	33	
WARREN, John	35/1080	Caulker	GANGES	14- 6-1852	26	
WARREN, Thomas	69/392	Admiral's Coxswain	HASTINGS	28- 3-1865	21	
WATERS, John	63/376	Sailmaker	LEOPARD	13- 7-1861	21	
WATFORD, James	47/40	Sailmaker's Crew	SOUTHAMPTON	17- 7-1861	25	
WATSON, Frank	25,543	Chief Q.M.	BLACK PRINCE	7- 5-1866	21	

WATSON, William	44/463	Gunner's Mate	GRECIAN	22- 4-1856	28	
WATTERS, Thomas M.	20,185	M.A.A.	MERSEY	21- 2-1870	23	
WATTS, George	63/160	Ship's Cpl (ex RM)	DONEGAL	19-12-1860	23	
WEAKLEY, James	31,942A	Stoker	MINOTAUR	9- 6-1870	21	*
WEALE, Robert	522	2nd Capt After Gd	ALERT	26- 5-1868	21	
WEATHERHEAD, John	41/364	Q.M.	PEMBROKE	24- 7-1856	28	
WEBB, James	60/126	Cooper	HANNIBAL	21-12-1861	23	
WEBB, John	39/508	Gunner's Mate	CANOPUS	20- 5-1848	21	*
WEBB, Joseph	37/504	Ropemaker	TERRIBLE	23- 9-1849	24	‡
WEBB, Philip	45/277	Coxswain of Launch	BELLEROPHON	2-11-1850	21	* ‡
WEBB, William	58/473	Bosun's Mate & Channel Pilot	DASHER	1- 1-1863	26	
WEBBER, Thomas J.	3,249	Captain's Coxswain	FISGARD	4-11-1870	20	
WEEKS, Robert	64/387	Ship's Cook	INDUS	29-12-1863	22	
WELCH, William	62/16	2nd Capt After Gd	CAESAR	18- 1-1862	22	
WELLMAN, John	49/64	Ship's Corporal	PENELOPE	22- 3-1854	21	
WELLS, James	61/92	Yeoman of Signals	VICTORY	27-12-1861	22	
WELSH, John	46/326	Ship's Cook	EDINBURGH	31- 5-1856	32	
WEST, Charles	65/487	Captn Forecastle	ST VINCENT	14-12-1866	23	*
WEST, James	47/461	Chief Bosun's Mate	BLENHEIM	21- 5-1856	22	
WEST, John	4,459	Sailmaker	CURACOA	1- 7-1861	20	*
WEST, Thomas	63/301	Captn Forecastle	HORNET	10- 9-1864	23	
WEST, Thomas	2,099	Q.M.	IRRESISTIBLE	23- 4-1868	21	
WESTCOTT, Samuel A.	38,347	Actg Ship's Cook	FLY	3- 7-1873	22	
WESTERMAN, Henry	62/397	Ship's Cook	TERRIBLE	12- 5-1869	27	
WEYMOUTH, John	53/425	Captain of Mast	RODNEY	23- 1-1856	23	
WEYMOUTH, John	54/159	A.B.	INDUS	30-12-1868	29	
WHALES, George	69/266	A.B.	ASIA	12-12-1866	21	
WHITBREAD, Robert	63/251	Captain's Coxswain	RACOON	14- 1-1862	20	*
WHITE, James C.	61/262	Gunner's Mate	CASTOR	22- 4-1865	27	*
WHITE, John	65/294	Q.M.	FISGARD	24-12-1862	20	*
WHITE, Joseph	9,311A	Q.M.	RESERVE	21- 5-1873	20	*
WHITE, Thomas	36,613	Chief Bosun's Mate	RESERVE	2- 4-1873	20	
WHITE, William	68/276	Captn Forecastle	RATTLESNAKE	25- 1-1866	22	
WHITE, William	4,774	Sailmaker	BOSCAWEN	3-12-1866	20	
WHITER, Arthur	66/3	Divisional Carpntr	H.M.Coast Guard	17- 3-1874	33	
WIGLEY, George	65/223	Captain's Coxswain	EXMOUTH	7-10-1862	21	*
WILCOX, John	82/11	Ship's Cook	SUPPLY	3- 5-1873	22	
WILKINS, Henry	57/78	Ship's Cpl (ex RM)	HANNIBAL	21-12-1861	30	
WILKINS, Henry	13,479	Ch Gunner's Mate	CAMBRIDGE	4- 6-1874	20	*
WILKINSON, Samuel	62/350	Leading Stoker	SANS PAREIL	4- 7-1861	21	
WILLCOCKS, William	3,334	Ch Captn Fcsle	CALCUTTA	1- 3-1860	21	*
WILLIAMS, Charles	37,656	Chief Gunner's Mate	CAMBRIDGE	17- 1-1872	20	*

WILLIAMS, Edward	71/530	Actg Ship's Cook	ARCHER	24- 1-1866	21	*
WILLIAMS, John	(*Vide* : JONES, Richard)					
WILLIAMS, John	48,502	Captn Forecastle	PRINCESS ROYAL	18-11-1859	21	
WILLIAMS, Thomas	55/24	Captain's Coxswain	BRITOMART	24-10-1855	21	
WILLIAMS, William	43/496	Q.M.	ARROGANT	18- 9-1852	25	
WILLIAMS, William	53/500	Q.M.	MEDUSA	15- 5-1860	21	*
WILLIS, Philip	20,776A	Leading Stoker	NORTHUMBERLAND	13- 3-1872	20	*
WILSON, George H. Schoolmaster	64/169	Seaman's	WELLESLEY	27-12-1861	26	
WILSON, Charles	(*Vide* : HUSER, John)					
WILSON, Horatio	64/429	Chief Q.M.	VICTOR EMMANUEL	6- 5-1862	20	
WILSON, William	55/199	Coxswain of Launch	WATERLOO	23-10-1856	22	
WINDSLAND, John	808	Caulker	MALACCA	4- 9-1869	20	
WINGATE, Richard	2,834	Ship's Cook	AJAX	5- 4-1864	22	
WINGFIELD, Robert	55/332	Ship's Steward	SCYLLA	27- 7-1867	23	
WINGHAM, John/Geo.	39,231	Sailmaker	ESK	8-10-1867	21	
WINTER, John	57/205	Ship's Cook (ex RM)	MARLBOROUGH	15- 3-1861	26	
WIVLEY, George	(*Vide* : WIGLEY, George)					
WOOD, Charles	27,336	Leading Stoker	JASON	29- 3-1870	20	
WOOD, John	32,060	Q.M.	AURORA	2- 8-1872	20	*
WOOD, Peter	62/241	Captn Forecastle	BOSCAWEN	12- 9-1860	21	
WOODHAMS, Henry	47/282	Carpenter's Mate	MONARCH	22-12-1853	22	
WOODHOUSE, Richard	60/402	Q.M.	INDUS	18- 4-1860	22	
WOODROW, Frederick	43/116	Seaman's Schoolmaster	VOLAGE	6-12-1850	28	‡
WOODS, William	54/15	Captain of Mast	HANNIBAL	21-12-1861	27	
WOOLCOCK, William	65/375	Blacksmith	CORNWALLIS	4- 5-1863	22	
WORRALL, Abijah	68/261	Sick Berth Steward	DAUNTLESS	27- 4-1864	28	
WORSNIP, George	61/383	Bosun's Mate	CORNWALLIS	8- 5-1861	22	
WRIGHT, David	32,593	Q.M.	TORCH	3- 3-1864	20	
WRIGHT, John	46/217	M.A.A. (ex RM)	IMPREGNABLE	2- 5-1851	24	
WRIGHT, John	63/432	Sailmaker	URGENT	22-11-1862	26	
WRIGHT, John	53/77	Q.M.	SPARTAN	7-11-1857	23	*
WRIGHT, John D.	41/229	Purser's Steward	ALARM	14- 5-1849	21	‡
WRIGHT, William	60/373	A.B.	INDUS	29-12-1863	24	
WRIGHT, William	64/528	Admiral's Coxswain	NARCISSUS	5- 8-1864	23	*
WYATT, Edward	19,629	Ch Gunner's Mate	SULTAN	1- 6-1874	20	
WYATT, George	65/141	Bosun's Mate	MERSEY	7- 8-1862	23	
YARRAM, Charles	64/414	Chief Bosun's Mate	ALGIERS	9-12-1862	21	
YEALAND, George	65/350	Bosun's Mate	CLIO	20- 5-1863	22	*
YEO, James	5,518A	Captain of Hold	ROYAL ADELAIDE	12- 6-1874	20	*
YEO, William	6,844	Bosun's Mate	BRITANNIA	16-12-1870	20	
YOUNG, Charles G.	6,895A	Captain's Coxswain	FISGARD	18-12-1867	25	*
YOUNG, George	63/180	Ship's Cook	TRITON	11- 1-1861	21	

Abbreviations and Annotations : —
Column heading   'No' as a number = Continuous Service Number (CS No)
                              as [No] / [No] = ADM 29/ Series – Volume No / Page No
                              as L/ = Letter to Admiralty
                              as 12+/ = ADM 12/ Series
                              as 158/ = ADM 158/ Series (RM)
* = medal known   ‡ = 1848 dated Obverse

VICTORIAN WIDE SUSPENSION LS & GC MEDAL ROLL – ROYAL MARINES 1847 – 1875

Although more than half of the service records of marines (ADM 157/- Series) have been weeded for the period under review, the construction of their long service medal roll proved to be simpler and more complete than expected. The solution to an otherwise impossible task came about because nearly all the original 'shore' recommendations for the medal have survived – especially useful since eight out ten of all awards to marines were earned whilst the men were awaiting their discharge as pensioners at their Divisional Head Quarters. Since no 'sea' letters containing recommendations for the award for either sailors or marines have survived, the following roll is deficient in respect of many names of R.M. recipients whose medals bear the inscription 'H.M.S......'.

Since February 1834, submissions were to be forwarded annually in December by the Colonels Commandant of Port Divisions for their quota of 'shore' LS & GC awards to marines – '.. in order that all the cases which may arise within the [preceding annual] period which the medal is to cover, may be equally admitted to competition and and consideration ..'. Initially the annual quota allowed for 'shore' awards was two 'Gs & Ms' (one NCO & one Private) to each Division if its average strength exceeded 700 men. A more flexible principle was established in January 1849 whereby each Division was allowed an annual sum for 'Gratuities' to be spread more evenly across eligible personnel. When first introduced this quota allowance was £30 for each Division, but by 1870 it had been raised to £50/year when the average strength of a Division was 1,000 men, reduced to £20/year when the number was less than 700 NCOs and men. The size of the gratuity varied according to rank and the length of service within it, *viz* : Sergeant with ten or more years as such – £15, Sergeant, Corporal or Bombadier with seven years – £10, Bugler, Gunner or Private – £5. For men joining the marines after July 1837, eligibility for the reward included the rule that men had to prove that they had served ten years of their pensionable time (21 years) at sea or on foreign service

By a stroke of good fortune, most of these aforementioned 'annual lists' of 'shore based' marines recommended for the long service awards (with gratuities) have survived in the Royal Marine Office (RMO) Letter Books for correspondence to the Admiralty (*Vide* : ADM 191/11-38). Complementary and additional information has also survived in the Letter Books containing correspondence between Divisional Commandants and the RMO for the period 1847-1875 (ADM 56/- to 62/- Series). Complete lists of marines receiving the medal without gratuity for the period 1860-1870 have also survived, but in an unexpected place (ADM 201/21).

Not only do these letter books yield the 'annual lists', but they also give information about the changes made to the rules concerning the eligibility for awards to marines. Towards the end of the time when the Wide Suspension medal was issued – from 1870-1875 – the Royal Marine Office followed the new regulations for awards to sailors, whereby long service rewards could be awarded during a ship's Commission – not at the unique time when the vessel was 'paid off'. Henceforth recommendations for marines were accepted at any time of the year, thus nullifying the need for 'annual lists' each December. Construction of the medal roll still proceeded since all the letters referring to individual marines recommended for the 'shore' award, and/or initiation of their 'Parish Notice' have survived in the various 'Letter Books' (*Vide* : Separate Section 'Parish Notices displayed for Meritorious Conduct').

Generally speaking the 'annual lists' imparted more facts about a man's career, such as the amount of sea-time each marine had served – which accounts for more information being found concerning some of the recipients than others, as shewn on the medal roll which follows.

Award of LS & GC medals 'without gratuity'. Following the precedent set in the Royal Warrant dated 16 January 1860 for Army NCOs and men, a Royal Marine Office Circular dated 24 September 1860 extended these new benevolences to members of their Corps in this manner : —

' With reference to Her Majesty's Order in Council, dated 11th January 1859, the Lords Commissioners of the Admiralty have signified that Her Majesty has been graciously pleased to extend the benefits of such Order in Council to the following effect, *viz* :

1. All marines who shall have fulfilled the regulations relating to the awards of the medals and gratuities for 'Long Service and Good Conduct', but who are precluded from becoming recipients of the medals with a gratuity, in consequence of the aggregate amount to be annually awarded [the quota allowance in pounds sterling] being already appropriated shall be granted the said 'medals without gratuities' to the extent of three for each Division.

2. Non Commissioned Officers, Drummers, Privates and Gunners who may have been qualified before discharge shall be eligible to receive 'medals without gratuity', if recommended by their Commanding Officers within three years after their discharge.

3. Non Commissioned Officers on the permanent Staff of the Militia, or filling corresponding situations in the Naval Services, who were eligible previous to their discharge from the Corps for the medal with gratuity, shall also be eligible to receive 'medals without gratuities', and no limit shall be placed on the grant as regards the date of discharge in the case of such men so scrving.

4. Commandants of Divisions will, therefore, be authorized in future to make annual applications for the limited numbers (three) of 'medals without gratuities' in the same form as that now used [for medals with gratuities], but on a separate form.'

It will be noticed on the 'RM Wide Suspension LS & GC Medal Roll' that some awards without gratuity were approved up to 23 years after the marine was pensioned – explained by the rules mentioned in paragraph 3 quoted above. This factor thus causes particular difficulties when searches are made for the service histories of some of the 'No Gratuity' marine recipients.

Even though most of the Royal Marine Divisional Description Books (ADM 158/- Series) have survived – no notation was ever made of the award of the LS & GC medal within them. These books do however supply the date the marine was pensioned for his length of service, which sometimes proves to be a useful guide to the period when his long service award was approved.

Whilst this 'RM Wide Suspension LS & GC Medal Roll' has proved to be about 95% complete for 'Shore' awards to personnel recommended from R.M. Port Divisions, a concomitantly inclusive Roll of 'Ship' awards to marines has proved impossible to compile – due to the lack of archival sources. Of the 724 'Shore' rewards on the Roll some 126 medals are known to have survived (17%), but the Roll only includes 63 'Ship' awards of which 34 medals are known to have survived (54%) – leading to the conclusion that some 200 'Ship' awards in total were probably made to marines. It therefore assumed that approximately 960 Wide Suspension awards were earned by Royal Marines.

VICTORIAN WIDE SUSPENSION LS & GC MEDAL ROLL – ROYAL MARINES

Name	Rank	Coy No	Div	Years Served Total	At Sea	Awarded	Gratuity	
ABBOTT, Arthur	Pte	65	Cha	21		Apr 1872	£ 5	
ABRAHAMS, Charles	C/Sgt	82	Po	21-109	13-218	Jan 1870	£10	
ADAMSON, John McL.	Pte	37	Cha	23		Oct 1856	£ 5	
ADDYMAN, James	C/Sgt	73	Cha	21- 30	6-111	Jan 1867	No.G	
ADKINS, James	Sgt	67	Ply	26-267	5-186	Jan 1867	£15	
ALBRY, William (MSM)	Sgt Mjr	1	RMA	21		Jun 1873	£ 5	
ALEXANDER, John	C/Sgt	56	Cha	21		Jan 1861	No.G	*
ALLEN, James	Sgt	89	Woo	21 pensioned 1847		Jan 1861	No.G	
ALLINGHAM, Benjamin	C/Sgt	53	Cha	21- 13	11-173	Feb 1863	No.G	
ALLINGHAM, George	Sgt	8	RMA	21		Dec 1874	£ 5	*
ALLISON, William	Sgt	81	Cha	?		Jan 1873	No.G	
AMY, Robert	Pte	95	Ply	22		Jan 1864	£ 5	
				HMS TOPAZE				
ANDREWS, Henry (MSM)	Sgt Mjr	2	Po			Mar 1872	£15	
ANGEL, John	Pte	51	Ply	Not applicable		May 1855	£ 5	
				Special Crimea Gallantry Award (= D.C.M.)				
APPLETON, Richard	Gnr	1	RMA	22- 20	9- 13	Jan 1860	£ 5	
ARNOLD, William	C/Sgt	10	Po	21- 15	7-347	Mar 1865	No.G	
ARSTON, John	Pte	48	Woo	21-109		Apr 1849	£ 5	
ASHTON, James	C/Sgt	86	Po	22		May 1856		*
				HMS HARRIER				
ATHAWES, Robert	C/Sgt	53	Cha	21		Feb 1861	No.G	
ATKINS, George	Sgt Mjr	3	Ply	21- 15	5-331	Jan 1866	£15	*
ATKINSON, John	C/Sgt	8	Woo	21- 26	8-218	Jan 1852	£15	
AUGER, Isaac N.	Sgt	71	Ply	21- 54	9-225	Jan 1862	No.G	
AUSTEN, James	Gnr	11	RMA	21		Feb 1874	£ 5	
AUSTIN, Joseph	C/Sgt	58	Po	21- 32	11-227	Jan 1869	£15	*
AVENSON, Robert	Pte	86	Po	22-270	8-170	Mar 1865	£ 5	
AVERY, William	Sgt	3	Ply	21		May 1873	No.G	
AYERS, William	C/Sgt	74	Po	21- 42	11-142	Jan 1853		
AXE, William	Pte	31	Ply	21		Mar 1874	No.G	
BABAGE, George	C/Sgt	104	Ply	21-328	16-207	Feb 1869	No.G	
BACON, Henry	Pte	62	Po	21- 50	14-303	Jan 1869	£ 5	
BAILEY, Henry	Cpl	86	Po	22- 3	14- 56	Jan 1856	£10	*
BAKER, Humphrey	Pte	39	Ply	21		Apr 1874	£ 5	
BAKER, John	Sgt	4	RMA	21- 48	11-243	Jan 1862	No.G	*
BAKER, Joseph	Bmbdr	13	RMA	21		Jan 1874	£ 5	
BAKER, William	Pte	53	Cha	21- 65	12-216	Jan 1855	£ 5	
BAKER, William	Pte	87	Ply	22- 99	14-123	Feb 1859	£ 5	
BAKER, Young	Pte	72	Woo	21-355	10- 68	Mar 1865	£ 5	*
BANFORD, Thomas	Gnr	1	RMA	21- 94	10-344	Jan 1860	£ 5	
BARKER, John J.	Sgt	4	Cha	21- 12	Nil	Jan 1871	No.G	
BARKHAM, Philip	Sgt	9	RMA	21		Oct 1874	£ 5	
BARNES, Samuel	C/Sgt	51	Ply	21		Oct 1860	No.G	*
BARNETT, John	Q.M.Sgt	4	Cha	?		Oct 1874	£10	
BARRETT, Charles	Cpl	71	Ply	21		Mar 1873	No.G	*
BARTLETT, Robert	Pte	?	Cha	21- 18	16-351	Mar 1850	£ 5	‡

BARTLEY, J.	C/Sgt	89	Cha	21		Jan 1868		*
BASTEN, Isaac	Sgt	43	Ply	21-216	14- 93	Jan 1867	No.G	
BATE, J.J.	Sgt	73	Cha	?		Jan 1873	No.G	
		(Paymaster's 1st Clerk)						
BATSON, David	Pte	42	Po	22-201	7- 99	Jan 1868	£ 5	
BATTEN, Thomas	C/Sgt	90	Po	21-199	11-134	Jan 1862	£15	
BEACHMORE, William	Pte	3	Ply	?		Jan 1872	£ 5	
BEADIAM, James	C/Sgt	5	Cha	?		Feb 1874	£10	
BECKETT, Samuel	C/Sgt	76	Woo	21 pensioned 1838		Jan 1861	No.G	
BEER, John/Henry	C/Sgt	15	Ply	21		Jan 1870	No.G	
BELL, Joseph	Pte	72	Cha	21	16-152	Mar 1848	£ 5	
BENSON, James	Pte	51	Ply	21-261	8-341	Jan 1869	£ 5	*
BENTLEY, George B.	Staff Sgt	4	Cha	?		Nov 1872	£10	
BERELL, William	Pte	?	Po	21- 48	17-235	Jan 1857	£ 5	
BERRY, John.R.	Pte	47	Ply	21		Aug 1873	£ 5	
BEST, George C.	C/Sgt	18	Po	23-130	8-130	Jan 1852	£15	
BIDDINGTON, Joseph	C/Sgt	56	Po	22		Aug 1857	£15	
			HMS FROLIC					
BIGGEN, Thomas	Pte	38	Po	21- 15	8-346	Jan 1867	£ 5	
BIGNELL, George C.	Sgt	19	Ply	21-291	3-351	Jan 1866	No.G	
BILLING, William	Pte	15	Ply	21-153	8-357	Mar 1865	£ 5	*
BIRD, Andrew	Cpl	35	Ply	24- 13	14-333	Jan 1860	£10	
BIRD, William	Pte	11	Ply	21- 67	11-108	Jan 1869	£ 5	
BISHOP, John	C/Sgt	99	Ply	21- 80	13-254	Feb 1863	No.G	
BLACKMAN, John	Cpl	26	Po	21		Apr 1874	£ 7	*
			Ryl Yacht V&A					
BLANCHARD, George	Cpl	32	Po	21		Jan 1872	£ 5	*
BLASTOCK, Frederick	Q.M.Sgt	20	Woo	25-170	4-180	Jan 1861	£15	
BLOW, Arthur	C/Sgt	3	RMA	21- 10	9-177	Jan 1864	No.G	
BLUNDELL, George	Armr Sgt	8	RMA	21		Jun 1874	£ 5	
BOLITHO, William	C/Sgt	55	Ply	21- 42	13- 62	Feb 1869	No.G	*
BOLLIN, William	Sgt	80	Woo	21- 80	11-119	Jan 1867	No.G	
BOND, John	Pte	52	Woo	21		Aug 1861	No.G.	
			HMS MAJESTIC					
BOOTH, Samuel	Pte	77	Cha	?		Jan 1871	£ 5	
BOREHAM, Edward	Pte	45	Cha	22		Feb 1850	£ 5	* ‡
			HMS RALEIGH					
BOSWELL, Thomas	Gnr	9	RMA	21		Mar 1874	£ 5	
BOURLAY, Thomas L.	Pte	9	Cha	?		Apr 1872	£ 5	
BOWERS, Thomas	Sgt	73	Cha	29-113	3- 97	Jan 1862	£15	
BOWLES, David	Pte	34	Po	21		Jly 1874	£ 5	
BOYCE, Thomas	C/Sgt	41	Cha	23		Dec 1860	No.G	
BRADLEY, Thomas	Barck Sgt	9	RMA	22-281	9-229	Jan 1869	£15	
BRADY, James	C/Sgt	?	Po	21-282	9-315	Jan 1853	No.G	*
BRAILEY, William	C/Sgt	72	Ply	21-263	13- 3	Jan 1870	£10	
BRAMBLE, John	C/Sgt	?	Ply	22		Apr 1849	£ 7	*
			HMS VANGUARD					
BRAMBLE, John T.	1st Mskty Sgt Instr	3	Ply	?		Jan 1871	£15	
BRAY, John	Sgt	15	Ply	21		Mar 1874	No.G	
BRETT, William	Sgt	33	Cha	21- 28	9-321	Jan 1862	No.G	
BREWER, Isaac	Sgt	24 ?	RMA	?		Jan 1871	£10	
	Sgt	?	RMA	21		Mar 1863		
BREWER, Thomas	Sgt	4	Woo	21-355	2- 37	Jan 1862	£15	
BRIANT, James	Cpl	42	Po	?		Mar 1873	£ 5	

BRIDGEMAN, Thomas	Pte	63	Ply	21- 19	6-175	Jan 1864	£ 5	
BRIMELOW, Henry	Sgt	10	RMA	21		Jan 1871	£10	
BRISCOE, Henry	Gnr	5	RMA	21- 78	8-210	Jan 1861	£ 5	
BROOKS, John	C/Sgt	29	Cha	21- 63	11- 41	Jan 1855	£15	*
BROOKS, John	Pte	71	Ply	21- 87	15-221	Jan 1856	£ 5	
BROWN, Ephraim	C/Sgt	3	Ply	22		Mar 1857	£15	
				HMS CONFLICT				
BROWN, James	C/Sgt	52	Woo	25		Jun 1853	£15	*
				HMS PERSIAN				
BROWN, John	C/Sgt	7	Ply	21-310	13-288	Jan 1868	No.G	
BROWN, John	Pte	87	Po	21- 38	15- 12	Feb 1848	£ 5	
BROWN, Joseph	Sgt	108	Po	21- 10	13- 5	Jan 1868	No.G	*
BROWN, Richard	Sgt	?	RMA	?		Jan 1871	£15	
BRYAN, Henry	Drummer	22	Po	?		Apr 1873	No.G	
BULLED, William	Pte	7	Ply	21-211	15- 5	Jan 1852	£ 5	
BULPIN, John	Pte	15	Ply	22-259	16- 30	Jan 1864	£ 5	
BUNTON, John	Pte	88	Woo	Not applicable		May 1855	£ 5	*
				Special Crimea Gallantry award (= D.C.M.)				
BURGESS, Daniel (MSM)	C/Sgt	53	Cha	21		Jun 1868	£10	*
				HMS CADMUS				
BURLING, Isaac	Pte	85	Cha	21- 38	8-177	Jan 1864	£ 5	*
BURNETT, Robert	Cpl	90	Po	21- 83	15-229	Feb 1863	No.G	
BUTE, James A. (MSM*)	Sgt	76	Woo	32		Jan 1861	No.G	*
BUTLER, Thomas (MSM)	Sgt	9	RMA	23-143	11-136	Mar 1865	£15	
BYFIELD, Thomas	Pte	5	Cha	21		Jun 1850	£ 5	* ‡
				HMS BULLDOG				
CADDY, Robert	C/Sgt	13	Cha	?		Feb 1872	No.G	
CAFE, Jasper	Pte	87	Ply	21- 73	9-115	Mar 1865	£ 5	
CALWAY, John	Sgt	101	Po	21- 91	1- 78	Jan 1864	No.G	
CAMPBELL, John	C/Sgt	?	Cha	22		Sep 1850		‡
CANN, John	C/Sgt	87	Ply	21- 97	13-321	Jan 1862	£10	
CANTER, J.W.	Drummer	51	Ply	25- 48	16- 16	Jan 1869	£ 5	
CARBINE, James	Pte	35	Ply	22- 55	14-262	Jan 1862	No.G	
CARPENTER, Francis	Pte	46	Po	22-174	13-258	Jan 1868	£ 5	
CARPENTER, John (MSM)	Armr Sgt	4	Cha	?		Nov 1873	£10	
CARSONS, Samuel	Pte	96	Woo	21- 3	14-236	Jan 1869	£ 5	
CARTAIN, Patrick	Pte	40	Woo	21-219	10-217	Feb 1869	£ 5	*
CARTER, Benjamin	Sgt	27	Po	21-257	1- 23	Mar 1865	£15	*
CARTER, William	Pte	13	Cha	21- 44	12- 52	Jan 1856	£ 5	*
CHANDLER, Henry J.	Drummer	78	Po	25-317	4-197	Jan 1866	£ 5	*
CHAPMAN, Michael	Pte	67	Ply	21-261	18-334	Jan 1855	£ 5	
CHAPLIN, John	Pte	74	Po	21-116	15-153	Jan 1862	£ 5	
CHAPPELL, James	Gnr	1	RMA	21		Nov 1860	No.G	
CHARGE, James	Pte	97	Cha	21- 49	15- 8	Feb 1863	£ 5	
CHILES, Arthur	Sgt	22	RMA	21- 27	12-295	Jan 1867	No.G	
CHURCHILL, Charles	Cpl	84	Ply	21		Feb 1872	No.G	
CLACK, Henry	Gnr	7	RMA	21-331	6-180	Jan 1861	£ 5	
CLARINGBOULD, William	Pte	33	Cha	21-257	6-194	Jan 1861	£ 5	
CLARK, George	Sgt	12	Ply	21		Jan 1873	£10	
CLARK, Robert	Sgt	10	RMA	21		Mar 1873	No.G	
CLARKSON, Alexander	Pte	16	Woo	21- 9	11-336	Mar 1865	No.G	
CLIFTON, Samuel	Sgt	6	Po	21-237	14- 58	Jan 1864	£10	
COCHRANE, Henry (MSM)	C/Sgt	37	Cha	?		Jun 1872	£10	*
COCKERTON, Charles	C/Sgt	42	Po	21		Jun 1856		
				HMS FANTOME				
COFFIN, Richard	Cpl	35	Ply	21-102	13- 84	Jan 1853		

Name	Rank	No	Div			Date	Amount	
COLE, James	Pte	98	Po	21- 88	13-210	Jan 1869	£ 5	
COLE, Walter	Pte	23	Ply	21		Sep 1850		‡
HMS THETIS								
COLE, William	C/Sgt	?	Cha	22- 12	10-249	Jan 1860	£15	
COLES, Benjamin	Pte	87	Ply	22-135	8-209	Jan 1861	£ 5	
COLLECK, Henry	Gnr	10	RMA	21- 34	13-149	Mar 1865	£ 5	
COLLINS, John	Pte	40	Woo	21-143	16- 49	Feb 1869	No.G	
COLLINSON, Edwin	Sgt	45	Cha	21-243	Nil	Jan 1864	£15	
COLLIS, Jesse	Sgt	98	Po	21-321	2- 99	Jan 1866	No.G	*
CONGDON, Samuel	C/Sgt	10	RMA	22-151	9-283	Jan 1864	No.G	
COOK, Thomas	C/Sgt	29	Cha	22		May 1861	No.G	*
COOTE, John	Pte	7	Ply	21-336	12-262	Jan 1864	£ 5	
COPE, Daniel	Gnr	8	RMA	22-167	11-134	Jan 1860	£ 5	*
CORBETT, Thomas	Sgt Mjr	?	Woo	21- 0	9-305	Jan 1849	£15	
CORK, George	Sgt	65	Cha	21 Pensioned 1855		Feb 1861	No.G	
CORNISH, John	C/Sgt	27	Ply			Feb 1861	No.G	
Enlisted aged 15 Yrs Oct 1842								
CORNISH, John	Pte	96	Woo	21- 45	9-129	Jan 1868	£ 5	
CORYS, William	Pte	88	Woo	21- 45	9-129	Jan 1868	£ 5	
[COURT ?]								
COURSE, George	Sgt	6	RMA	21		May 1872	£10	
COUSINS, Thomas	C/Sgt	7	RMA	21		Mar 1874	No.G	*
CRANE, Edward	Cpl	74	Po	21- 72	12-236	Jan 1854	£10	
CROSSAN, Henry	Cpl	75	Ply	21		Feb 1872	No.G	
CROW, William C.	Cpl	5	Cha	23-154	NIL	Jan 1864	No.G	
CUNLIFFE, Jonathan	C/Sgt	80	Woo	21-353	10-335	Jan 1852	£15	
CUNNINGHAM, Wm.K (MSM)	Q.M.Sgt	57	Cha	22- 1	7- 16	Jan 1852	£15	
CURRY, William	Cpl	39	Ply	21-221	13-225	Jan 1870	£ 5	
CURTIS, John W.	Pte	20	Po	21		Feb 1872	No.G	*
DALLEY, Edward	C/Sgt	21	RMA	21- 8	9-212	Jan 1867	£10	*
DALLIMER, William	Gnr	8	RMA	21-139	6-200	Jan 1870	£ 5	
DAVEY, Charles	Sgt	1	RMA	21-248	10-334	Jan 1870	£10	
DAVEY, William	1st Mskty Sgt Instr	55	Ply	21		Jan 1872	£10	
DAVIES, Robert	Sgt	34	Po	21		Jan 1874	£10	
DAVIS, John	Bmbdr	12	RMA	21		Jun 1873	£ 7	*
HMS JUNO								
DAWKINS, Charles	Cpl	2	Po	21- 69	17- 24	Jan 1855	£10	
DAWSON, Adam	Gnr	7	RMA	21		Nov 1860	No.G	
DAWSON, John	Prvst Sgt	13	RMA	21		Jun 1874	£ 5	
DAY, George	Pte	69	Cha	?		Jly 1874	No.G	
DEAN, John (MSM*)	Sgt	7	RMA	21-217	6- 67	Jan 1862	£15	*
DEARING, William	1st Msktry Sgt Instr	3	RMA	22-205	6-299	Feb 1869	No.G	
DEEKS, Joseph (MSM)	C/Sgt	33	Cha	21- 48	13-313	Feb 1869	No.G	
DELBRIDGE, Lewis	C/Sgt	31	Ply	21- 28	12-267	Feb 1863	£15	*
DELLER, William	Gnr	21	RMA	21-300	7-128	Jan 1860	£ 5	
DERRY, Henry	Pte	2	Po	21		Apr 1873	No.G	
DIBBIN, George	Q.M.Sgt	2	Po	21		Jan 1871	£15	
DIBBINS, W.G.F.	C/Sgt	83	Ply	21		Dec 1860	No.G	
DIMENT, Francis	C/Sgt	19	RMA	21- 2	8-120	Jan 1866	No.G	
DIX, Simon	Cpl	40	Woo	21- 17	14-245	Feb 1863	No.G	*
DIXON, John	Sgt	57	Cha	22		Nov 1865	£15	*
HMS HIMALAYA								
DOD, George	Pte	?	Woo	?		Oct 1860	No.G	

Name	Rank		Div			Date		
DORE, Isaac	Gnr	8	RMA	21		Feb 1873	£ 5	
DORE, William	C/Sgt	5	RMA	21-161	10-214	Jan 1866	No.G	
DOWNER, John	Sgt	8	RMA	21-268	8- 73	Feb 1863	£10	
DOWSETT, Daniel	Sgt	57	Cha	21- 39	2-153	Feb 1863	No.G	
DRAKE, John (MSM)	Sgt	54	Po	21- 11	12-247	Mar 1865	No.G	*
DRAPER, Edward	Sgt	43	Ply	22-151	9-283	Jan 1864	No.G	
DREDGE, Thomas	C/Sgt	32	Woo	21		Jly 1861	£15	*
				HMS ATHOLL				
DRESDALE, David	Sgt Mjr	4	Woo	22-292	7- 90	Jan 1861	£15	
DRUMMOND, Samuel	Pte	61	Cha	21- 55	8-210	Jan 1870	£ 5	
DRYSDALE, Charles	C/Sgt	32	Woo	26- 51	12- 27	Jan 1869	£15	
DUNGEY, George	Pte	25	Cha	21		Feb 1861	No.G	
DUTTON, John	C/Sgt	78	Po	21		May 1873	£10	
				HMS SERAPIS				
DYER, Joseph	Sgt	83	Ply	21		Jan 1849	£ 7	*
				HMS CALLIOPE				
DYMOND, William	Sgt	23	Ply	21		May 1874	No.G	
EADES, George	Drum Mjr	5	Cha	21 Joined aged 12		Jan 1873	No.G	
EAGLE, Thomas	Gnr	7	RMA	21- 56	7- 83	Feb 1863	No.G	
EARL, John	Sgt	86	Po	27- 95	Nil	Jan 1862	£15	
EARL(E), William	Sgt	44	Woo	22-353	8-177	Feb 1863	No.G	
EASTON, Henry	C/Sgt	22	Po	21		Nov 1860	No.G	
EDWARDS, John	C/Sgt	76	Woo	22-209	7-340	Jan 1862	£15	*
EDWARDS, Thomas	Sgt	8	Woo	32-282	3-357	Jan 1866	£15	
ELDRIDGE, Moses	C/Sgt	1	RMA	23- 54	9-249	Jan 1858	£15	
ELLIOTT, Charles	Cpl	27	Ply	21- 20	14-228	Mar 1865	No.G	
ELLIOTT, John	Sgt	97	Cha	21- 13	14-223	Jan 1869	No.G	
ELLIOTT, Richard	Q.M.Sgt	14	RMA	21		May 1873	£ 5	
ELLIOTT, William	C/Sgt	25	Cha	21- 55	9- 43	Mar 1865	£15	
ELLIS, John	Sgt	12	Cha	21-255	NIL	Jan 1864	£15	
ELSWORTHY, James	Pte					Feb 1848		
ELTON, Allan	C/Sgt	87	Ply	21- 44	10-149	Jan 1868	£15	
EMERSON, George	C/Sgt	5	Cha	21	13	May 1848	£15	
ENDACOTT, John	Pte	39	Ply	21		Jan 1861	No.G	*
ESSERY, William	Gnr	11	RMA	21		May 1873	£ 5	
				HMS St J.D'ACRE				
EVANS, William	C/Sgt	16	Cha	21- 77	7- 67	Jan 1870	£10	
EVANS, William	Gnr	11	RMA	21		Mar 1872	£ 5	
				HMS D of WELLGTON				
EVANS, William L.	Sgt	78	Po	23- 82	12-140	Jan 1856	£15	
EWING, James	C/Sgt	5	Cha	25		Aug 1856	£15	
				HMS MODESTE				
EYRE, Robert	Pte	4	Woo	21- 21	14- 2	Jan 1855	£ 5	
FACEY, Robert	Cpl	83	Ply	23- 72	14-272	Jan 1856	£10	
FANDLEY, Frederick	Sgt	80	Ply	?		Feb 1872	No.G	
FARMER, Samuel	Pte	46	Po	21		Apr 1874	£ 5	
FARRANT, Charles	Pte	57	Cha	24		Feb 1861	No.G	
FAULKNER, William	Cpl	5	RMA	21- 5	8-176	Feb 1863	£10	
FAWKES, John	Cpl	55	Ply	21-148	12-330	Jan 1849	£ 5	
FEBRY, Thomas	Pte	54	Po	22		Jan 1871	£ 5	
FERGUSON, John	Sgt	44	Po	21		Jun 1873	£10	
FERRETT, James	C/Sgt	90	Po	21- 2	13-297	Jan 1870	No.G	
FIDLER, James (MSM)	C/Sgt	3	Ply	21		Jly 1874	No.G	
FINCH, Charles	C/Sgt	35	Ply	21		Nov 1860	No.G	
FLETCHER, John	Drummer	32	Woo	21 Pensioned 1847		Feb 1861	No.G	
				Enlisted aged 12 years in 1819				

FLOWER, Edwin	Cpl	66	Po	23-322	14- 95	Jan 1854	£10	
FLOWER, George	Cpl	14	Po	21- 7	11-280	Jan 1860	£10	*
FLOYDE, James	Pte	35	Ply	21-159	10-347	Jan 1866	£ 5	*
				24 Yrs on medal				
FLY, John	Drummer	71	Ply	22-240	13-325	Jan 1853	?	
FORD, James	Sgt	32	Po	24		Feb 1872	No.G	
FORD, Joseph (MSM*)	Prvst Sgt	23	Ply	27-288	12-143	Jan 1852	£15	
FORD, Nicholas G.	Q.M.Sgt	12	RMA	21		Feb 1872	£10	*
FORREST, William	Q.M.Sgt	46	Po	21		Dec 1873	£10	
FORWARD, James	C/Sgt		Po	21		Sep 1850		‡
FOSBERRY, Frederick	Sgt	28	Cha	21		Jly 1874	No.G	
FOX, George	C/Sgt	9	Cha	21- 15	7-360	Jan 1857	£15	
FRANCIS, Thomas	C/Sgt	89	Woo	23- 87	9-112	Jan 1860	£15	
FRANDLEY, Frederick	Sgt	80	Ply	?		Feb 1872	No.G	
FREEGUARD, Charles	C/Sgt	96	Po	?		Feb 1872	No.G	
FRESHWATER, Thomas	Pte	9	Cha	23		Mar 1872	£ 5	
				HMS FORTE				
FRIEND, John	Pte	77	Cha	21-284	5-341	Feb 1863	No.G	
FROHOCK, John	C/Sgt	21	Cha	21		Jan 1851	£15	
FRYER, James	C/Sgt	26	Po	22- 92	12-284	Jan 1860	£15	
GARDNER, Eli	Pte	32	Po	21- 63	15-203	Jan 1870	£ 5	
GARDNER, Elijah	Gnr	9	RMA	22-257	9- 16	Jan 1870	£ 5	
GARLAND, J.	Pte	79	Ply	21- 23	12-321	Jan 1868	£ 5	
GEDDS, George	Pte		Woo	21- 71	13- 70	Mar 1850	£ 5	‡
GIBBS, John	Sgt	68	Woo	21		Nov 1861	No.G	
GIBBONS, George	Pte	23	Ply	21		Jly 1874	£ 5	
GIDDY, John	Sgt	71	Ply	21- 13	9-329	Jan 1871	No.G	
GILBERT, Robert	Pte	34	Po	21- 40	17- 67	Feb 1863	£ 5	
GILBERT, William	Sgt	14	Po	?		Apr 1874	No.G	
GILKS, James	Pte	73	Cha	21		Jan 1863		*
				HMS TERMAGENT				
GILL, John	Pte	79	Ply			Dec 1872	£ 5	
GILLETT, William	Gnr	2	RMA	21- 24	11-178	Jan 1860	£ 5	
GINGELL, Stephen	Pte	55	Ply	22		Feb 1851	£ 5	
				HMS VOLAGE				
GLASS, James	Pte	48	Woo	21- 21	10-205	Jan 1857	£ 5	
GLASS, Joseph	Pte	18	Po	21-132	12-282	Jan 1870	No.G	*
GLOVER, William	1st Sgt	4	RMA	21		Feb 1872	No.G	*
	Instr of Gunnery							
GODDARD, James	Pte	?	Cha	22- 43	13- 96	Jan 1853		
GODFREY, Charles	Pte	65	Cha	21- 56	9-172	Jan 1871	No.G	
GODFREY, Joseph	C/Sgt	80	Woo	21-164	6-193	Feb 1863	£ 5	
GOLDSBY, Cornelius	C/Sgt	64	Woo	21-363	11-357	Jan 1868	£15	
GOODCHILD, Edward	Pte	46	Po	22		Feb 1856		*
				HMS RODNEY				
GOODCHILD, Richard	Sgt	13	Cha	21		Apr 1861	No.G	
GOODGER, Thomas	Sgt	1	Cha	23		Apr 1855		*
				HMS TRAFALGAR				
GOODLAND, Jacob	Sgt	28	Woo	21- 9	9-325	Jan 1867	£10	
GOSS, John H.	C/Sgt	87	Ply	23-310	11-107	Jan 1856	£15	
GOSS, William	Pte	11	Ply	21- 87	4-158	Mar 1865	£ 5	*
GOUGH, Daniel	C/Sgt	92	Woo	22		Feb 1861	No.G	
GOUGH, J.	Gnr	15	RMA	21- 86	8-303	Jan 1868	£ 5	
GOULD, Edward	Sgt	10	RMA	22-110	9-221	Jan 1871	No.G	
GOULD, John	Cpl	?	Ply	24-157	13- 68	Jan 1861	£10	
GRAY, John	Sgt	70	Po	21- 14	15-151	Feb 1869	No.G	

Name	Rank	No.	Div			Date	£	
GRAY, John	Pte	74	Po	21- 34	7-254	Jan 1867	No.G	
GREENSLADE, John	Pte	47	Ply	21- 3	16-280	Jan 1857	£ 5	
GREGORY, George	Pte	23	Ply	21- 23	14- 81	Feb 1863	£ 5	
GRIFFITHS, Henry	Sgt	67	Ply	25- 60	2-180	Jan 1864	No.G	
GROUNDSELL, Thomas	Gnr	12	RMA	22		Jun 1874	£ 5	
GUY, William	Sgt	2	RMA	21- 11	11-169	Jan 1866	£10	
HADRILL, James	Sgt Mjr	4	Woo	23		Nov 1860	No.G	
HAINE, Charles	Sgt	5	RMA	21		Jul 1873	£ 5	
HALL, John	C/Sgt					Sep 1860	No.G	
HALL, William	Sgt	1	Cha	21		Jul 1874	No.G	
HALTON, W.	C/Sgt					Oct 1860	No.G	
HAMMETT, Edwin	C/Sgt	11	Ply	?		Oct 1874	£10	
HANCOCK, George (MSM*)	Sgt Mjr	4	Woo	21-158	9-332	Jan 1869	£15	
HANEFORD,William (MSM)	C/Sgt	35	Ply	21		Dec 1872	£10	
HARFLETT, Richard	Sgt		Cha	21		Sep 1850		‡
HARLEY, William	C/Sgt	11	Ply	21- 7	10-295	Feb 1848	£15	
HARRINGTON, William	Sgt	76	Woo	21		Aug 1861	No.G	*
			HMS MAJESTIC					
HARRIS, Edward T. (MSM)	C/Sgt	61	Cha	22-222	11-104	Jan 1860	£15	*
HARRIS, Edwin	Sgt	73	Cha	25- 94	8- 27	Jan 1867	No.G	*
HARRIS, Emanuel	Sgt Mjr	3	Ply	21		Feb 1874	£15	
HARRIS, George H.	Sgt	65	Cha	25- 23	10-123	Jan 1868	£15	
HARRIS, Robert	Bugle Mjr	30	Po	21		Oct 1874	£ 5	
HARRISON, Henry	Sgt	105	Cha	21-137	8-193	Jan 1866	£10	
HARRISON, Horatio	Cpl	3	RMA	21- 18	14- 1	Feb 1863	No.G	
HART, Henry	Sgt	17	Cha	25-264	15-239	Jan 1868	£ 5	
Second LS & GC	Master Shoemaker			41 years		1884		
HART, Henry	Gnr	4	RMA	21-182	4-243	Jan 1867	No.G	
HARVEY, Walter	Gnr	8	RMA	21		Mar 1873	No.G	
HARVEY, William	Pte	6	Po	21-150	9-174	Jan 1866	No.G	
HARVEY, William	Cpl	29	Cha	22		Oct 1856	£10	
			HMS SHARPSHOOTER					
HARWOOD, Thomas	Pte	43	Ply	21		Jly 1874	£ 5	
HATCH, Thomas	Sgt	2	RMA	21- 11	7-265	Jan 1864	No.G	
HAVERFIELD, John	Pte	23	Ply	21		Feb 1873	£ 5	
HAWKES, William	Sgt	87	Ply	21-211	11- 90	Jan 1867	£10	*
HAWKINS, Henry	Pte	56	Po	21		Apr 1873	No.G	
HAY, John	C/Sgt	62	Cha	24		Feb 1848	£15	
			HMS MODESTE					
HAYES, Thomas	Pte	33	Cha	21- 47	14-233	Jan 1853		
HAYNES, Joseph	C/Sgt	101	Po	21- 81	11- 38	Mar 1850	£15	* ‡
HEAD, George	Cpl	54	Po	21- 30	8-72	Mar 1865	£10	
HEAL, James	C/Sgt	79	Ply	21- 20	14-174	Feb 1869	No.G	
HEALEY, William (MSM*)	C/Sgt		Po	21- 12	9-122	Jan 1857	£15	*
HELLEN, John	Sgt	43	Ply	21		Jan 1871	£10	
HENDISON, George	Pte	54	Po	24		Mar 1851	£ 5	
HERRING, Wm.H. (MSM)	Brck Sgt	97	Cha	25-185	13-214	Mar 1865	£15	
HEWLETT, William J.	Sgt	12	RMA	21- 10	3-220	Jan 1871	No.G	
HICKNOTT, James	Sgt	69	Cha	22		Feb 1872	No.G	
HIGGS, John	Pte		Ply	21		Oct 1849		‡
HILL, George	Sgt	1	Cha	21		Nov 1873	No.G	
HILL, John	Pte	39	Ply	24		Jan 1871	£ 5	
HILLARD, Abraham	Sgt	19	Ply	21- 23	11-241	Jan 1864	No.G	
HILLS, Henry W.	Cpl	5	Cha	21		Jan 1871	£ 5	*
HINES, Charles	Drummer	88	Woo	21- 60	NIL	Jan 1866	£ 5	
HOARE, John	Cpl	3	Ply	21- 68	10- 47	Jan 1858	£10	

HOBBINS, Thomas (MSM)	Sgt	54	Po	28- 21	3-288	Jan 1861	£15	
Second LS & GC ? Joined aged 13 years 10-12-1827.				Discharged		Oct 1881		
HOBBS, Benjamin	Sgt	86	Po	22-290	12- 44	Jan 1869	£10	
HOBBS, James	Pte	32	Woo	21-133	5-273	Jan 1856	£ 5	
HODGES, William (MSM)	C/Sgt	7	Ply	?		Nov 1873	£10	*
HOLDER, Jonah	C/Sgt	84	Woo	21- 53	5- 54	Jan 1866	£15	
HOLLAND, James	Pte	87	Ply	21- 68	15-139	Mar 1850	£ 5	* ‡
HOLLAND, Richard	Cpl	88	Woo	21		Jun 1857		*
				HMS EXMOUTH				
HOLLIS, Richard	Sgt	108	Po	21- 34	13- 16	Feb 1863	£10	*
HOLLYER, Thomas	C/Sgt	10	Po	22-243	14-126	Feb 1863	No.G	
HOMEWOOD, George	Sgt	1	Cha	21- 33	13-116	Jan 1866	£10	
HONEY, James	C/Sgt	15	Ply	22		Aug 1849		* ‡
				HMS NIMROD				
HOPPER, William	C/Sgt	81	Cha	22-259	9-345	Feb 1859	£15	
HORTON, John	Pte	24	Ply	?		Mar 1874	No.G	
HORTON, Thomas	Cpl	21	Cha	21-111	10- 10	Jan 1867	£ 5	
HOULT, John	Pte	1	Cha	22		Nov 1862		*
				HMS HERO				
HOWARD, Henry	Sgt	81	Cha	21- 20	13- 53	Jan 1868	No.G	
HOWARD, John	C/Sgt	111	Woo	21- 3	10-218	Jan 1867	£10	
HOW(E), James	Pte	47	Ply	21- 78	7-299	Mar 1865	£ 5	
HOWSE, James	C/Sgt	6	Po	22		Jan 1862	No.G	
HUGHES, William	C/Sgt	88	Woo	22- 0	10-162	Jly 1848	£15	
HUMPHREY, William	Pte	76	Woo	23		Oct 1854		*
				HMS RESOLUTE				
HUNT, Edward	Pte	45	Cha	21- 2	15-253	Jan 1849	£ 5	
HUNT, James	Sgt	7	RMA	21- 96	13- 4	Mar 1865	£10	
HUNT, Thomas	C/Sgt	43	Ply	21- 61	3-230	Jan 1866	No.G	
HUNTLEY, Mark	Sgt	76	Cha	21		Feb 1872	No.G	
HURFORD, James	C/Sgt	23	Ply	21- 16	10-169	Feb 1863	No.G	*
HUTTON, John	Sgt	5	Cha	22- 68	3-169	Jan 1867	£15	
HYATT, William	C/Sgt	63	Ply	21- 0	15-201	Jan 1870	No.G	
IRISH, Isaac	Sgt	4	RMA	21-235	12-306	Mar 1865	£10	
ISAAC, James	Pte	83	Ply	21- 39	14-261	Jan 1866	£ 5	
JACKSON, William	Sgt	88	Woo	21-154	13-212	Mar 1865	£10	
JACKSON, William	Cpl Bandsman	12	Woo	21- 23	Nil	Feb 1859	£10	
JACOBS, Josiah	Cpl	6	Po	21		Mar 1872	£ 5	
				HMS ?				
JAMES, Edward	Cpl	?	Ply	21- 71	13- 56	Jan 1853		
JAMES, John (MSM)	C/Sgt	19	Ply	21- 41	8-162	Jan 1871	No.G	
JAMES, Robert	Cpl	9	RMA	21		Feb 1873	£ 5	
JARRARD, Samuel	Pte	52	Woo	22-247	15-154	Jan 1856	£ 5	
JARVICE, Charles	Pte	44	Woo	21-137	17- 59	Mar 1865	No.G	
JEANS, Thomas	Pte	28	Woo	21- 22	11-244	Jan 1864	£ 5	
JEFFEREY, Isaac	C/Sgt	4	Woo	22		Mar 1861	No.G	*
JEFFERIES, Wm. (MSM*)	Sgt	5	Cha	26		Jan 1861	No.G	*
JEFFERY, John	Pte	51	Ply	21-142	12- 51	Jan 1862	£ 5	
JOHNSON, James	Pte	34	Po	25		Nov 1854		*
				HMS AMPHITRITE				
JOHNSON, Thomas	Q.M.Sgt	9	Cha	21- 28	11-167	Jan 1866	No.G	
JONES, George	C/Sgt	1	Cha	21- 50	15- 13	Jan 1870	No.G	
JONES, James Evan	Drummer	46	Po	25-323	2-202	Jan 1866	No.G	
JONES, John	Drummer	24	Woo	21-323	NIL	Jan 1864	£ 5	
JONES, Paul	Sgt Mjr	3	Ply	22-166	4-288	Jan 1864	£15	

JOY, William	C/Sgt	18	Po	21- 1	14-119	Feb 1869	No.G	
KARM(or N), Henry	C/Sgt	78	Po	21- 14	11-291	Jan 1864	No.G	
KEES, Robert	Gnr	17	RMA	21- 30	8-345	Jan 1868	£ 5	*
KELLY, Edward	Pte	32	Po	21		Aug 1874	£ 5	
KELLY, John	Sgt	25	Cha	21 Joined aged 13		Apr 1872	£ 5	
KEMP, John	Sgt	24	Woo	21-113	7- 33	Jan 1862	£10	*
KENNETT, Henry	Pte	63	Ply	21		Dec 1860	No.G	*
KERRIGAN, John	Pte	46	Po	?		Mar 1872	£ 5	
				HMS GLADIATOR				
KERSHAW, Robert	C/Sgt	28	Cha	21 Joined aged 14		Jly 1872	£10	
KILBY, Henry	Pay Sgt	29	Cha	21-317	4-235	Jan 1869	£ 5	
KING, George	Drummer	57	Cha	21		Jun 1873	No.G	
KING, Henry	Sgt	17	Cha	34-246	10-280	Jan 1862	No.G	
KING, Uriah Henry	Sgt	19	Ply	22-134	2- 42	Jan 1857	£15	
				Joined aged 10 years in 1826				
KINGSELL, William	Pte	2	Po	21- 4	17- 98	Oct 1868	£ 5	*
				HMS FALCON				
KIRK, James	Cpl	34	Po	21		Mar 1874	£ 5	
KITCHENER, Robert	C/Sgt	26	Po	21		Sep 1848	£15	
				HMS ?				
KNIGHT, Charles	Sgt	22	Po	21		Dec 1873	£ 5	
KNIGHT, James	C/Sgt	5	RMA	21		Mar 1874	No.G	
KNIGHT, Joseph	Sgt	90	Po	21	HMS ?	Sep 1848	£ 7	
KNIGHT, Thomas	C/Sgt	2	Po	25-220	13-257	Jan 1868	£15	
LAKE, Henry	C/Sgt	11	Ply	21		Feb 1872	No.G	
LAKER, John	Pte	58	Po	21- 78	15-290	Jan 1858	£ 5	
LAMB, William	Pte	89	Woo	21- 11	13-126	Feb 1848	£ 5	
LAMSBY, L.	Sgt	46	Po	21		Dec 1860	No.G	
LANE, George W. (MSM)	Sgt Mjr	93	Cha	21-225	9-244	Jan 1858	£15	
				Joined aged 9 years				
LANGLEY, James	Pte	66	Po	21-126	16-269	Feb 1863	£ 5	
LANHAM, George	C/Sgt	78	Po	21- 48	8- 87	Jan 1870	£15	
LANHAM, Thomas	Pte	54	Po	21		Jan 1872	£ 5	
LARCOMBE, Samuel	Pte	91	Ply	Not applicable		May 1855	£ 5	
				Special Crimea Gallantry Award (= D.C.M.)				
2nd LS & GC Medal C/Sgt	55		Ply	21-181	10-294	Jan 1870	£10	
LAWRENCE, Thomas	Q.M.Sgt	4	RMA	21		Feb 1872	£10	
LEA, John	Pte	35	Ply	21-136	16-224	Feb 1848	£ 5	*
LEAN, William	Cpl	47	Ply	21-232	12-290	Feb 1859	£10	
LEE, George	Sgt	37	Cha	?		Jly 1874	No.G	
LEECH, William	Pte	23	Ply	21-224	14-151	Feb 1863	£ 5	
LEETE, Samuel	Cpl	21	Cha	21- 37	13-307	Feb 1863	£ 5	
LEITH, Robert	Sgt	69	Cha	21-280	14-180	Jan 1862	£10	
LEPPARD, Richard	C/Sgt	5	RMA	21		Oct 1868		*
				HMS WIVERN				
LEVERTON, George	Sgt	95	Ply	21- 18	1-348	Mar 1865	No.G	
LEVY, Thomas	C/Sgt	89	Cha	21- 21	16-137	Jan 1854	£15	
LEVY, William	Drummer	57	Cha	23		Dec 1860	No.G	*
LEWIS, Augustus	Sgt	9	Cha	22- 78	Nil	Jan 1862	£15	
	Drum Major							
LEWIS, James	Sgt	?	Po	21		Nov 1860	No.G.	
LEWIS, John	Sgt Mjr	29	Cha	21-202	13- 83	Jan 1852	£15	
LEWIS, Robert	Cpl	42	Po	21- 69	10-250	Jan 1858	£10	
LIAS, William	C/Sgt	47	Ply	21- 29	9-161	Jan 1861	£15	
LILLEY, Jonas (MSM)	Sgt	21	Cha	38		Dec 1860	No.G	
LILLEY, Thomas L.	Armr Sgt	49	Cha	21-303	Nil	Jan 1869	£ 5	

LINDSAY, Robert	C/Sgt	112	Woo	21- 24	8-125	Jan 1867	£15	
LITTLE, Richard	C/Sgt	19	RMA	22-205	7-162	Jan 1868	No.G	
LOCK, George	Pvst Sgt	8	Woo	22- 90	9-159	Jan 1860	£15	
LOCK, Samuel	Pte	51	Ply	21- 30	12-321	Jan 1868	£ 5	
LOCKYER, John (MSM*)	Sgt Mjr	25	Cha	21		Oct 1873	£15	
				Joined aged 14 years				
LONG, Daniel	Sgt Mjr	1	RMA	21-361	6-229	Jan 1866	£15	
LONGBOTTOM, John	Cpl	62	Po	21- 16	13-179	Jan 1870	£10	
LOSEBY, Henry	Cpl	29	Cha	21- 77	10-192	Jan 1868	No.G	
LUCAS, William (MSM*)	Sgt	17	Cha	27-238	12- 75	Jan 1864	No.G	*
LYNE, John	C/Sgt	66	Po	21- 0	11-309	Jan 1871	No.G	*
			(M in D L.Gaz. 6-1-1857. HMS WINCHESTER. 2nd China War)					
MACPHERSON, Angus	C/Sgt			21		Jan 1851	£15	
MADGE, John	Pte	79	Ply	21		Dec 1861		*
				ROYAL ADELAIDE				
MAGEE, Richard	C/Sgt	45	Cha	21- 22	?	Feb 1869	No.G	
MAGGS, George (MSM)	Sgt	7	RMA	21-126	6-277	Feb 1863	£15	
MAGUIRE, Edward	Sgt	19	RMA	21-240	11- 71	Jan 1867	£10	*
MANSER, Michael	C/Sgt	41	Cha	21- 5	11-157	Jan 1869	£10	
MARKS, Henry	Gnr	3	RMA	21- 47	12-350	Jan 1867	£ 5	
MARKS, William	Sgt	30	Po	21- 9	2-301	Feb 1863	£15	*
MARSH, William	Pte	66	Po	21		Jan 1872	£ 5	
MARTIN, George A.	Sgt Mskty	44	Po	21		Dec 1872	£15	
	Instructor							
MARTIN, Joseph	C/Sgt	33	Cha	21		Aug 1861	No.G	
				HMS HASTINGS				
MARTIN, Samuel	Pte	19	Ply	21-173	13-323	Jan 1870	£ 5	
MASLAND, William	C/Sgt	32	Woo	21		Mar 1854		*
MASLEN, John	Pte	32	Woo	22		Sep 1858	£ 5	*
MASON, Charles	Pte	65	Cha	21- 59	Nil	Jan 1862	No.G	
MATSON, John	Sgt	89	Cha	21-249	3-332	Jan 1869	£ 5	
MATTHEWS, Benjamin	C/Sgt	93	Cha	22		May 1857		
				HMS BITTERN				
MAUNDER, James	Pte	59	Ply	21- 37	11-132	Feb 1863	£ 5	
MAUNDER, William	Cpl	63	Ply	29-131	8-340	Jan 1857	£10	
MAW, Cornelius (MSM)	C/Sgt	48	Woo	22		Jan 1860	£15	
				HMS VIGILANT				
MAXWELL, James	Sgt	76	Cha	21- 9	8- 13	Jan 1870	£10	*
McCALL, William	Pte	41	Cha	21- 7	13- 18	Jan 1855	£ 5	
McCORMACK, John	Pte	6	Po	21-128	14-232	Jan 1871	No.G	
McCUE, James	Sgt	54	Po	21- 11	13-103	Jan 1871	No.G	
McDONNELL, John	C/Sgt	76	Woo	27-283	13-189	Jan 1870	No.G	
McELROY, John	Pte	64	Woo	7-200		May 1855	£ 5	*
				Special Crimea Gallantry Award (= D.C.M.)				
McGUINNESS, Thomas	Sgt	4	RMA	21- 81	6- 48	Jan 1870	£10	
McLARNON, Samuel	Pte	22	Po	21- 79	7-248	Jan 1868	£ 5	
McNIE, James	C/Sgt	40	Woo	21- 12	11-279	Jan 1853		
McWILLIAMS, Arthur	Drum Mjr	13	RMA	21- 15	Nil	Jan 1871	No.G	*
				ex Rifle Bde 12 years				
MEAD, John	Pte	3	Ply	21- 67	16-258	Jan 1866	£ 5	
MEDLON, William G.	C/Sgt	27	Ply	21		Feb 1874	£10	
MEIGHAM, James	C/Sgt	9	Cha	21		Feb 1872		*
MERRETT, Joseph	Pte	32	Woo	21- 16	13-202	Jan 1867	£ 5	
MIDDLETON, Samuel	Sgt	41	Cha	21-101	12-265	Jan 1867	£10	
MILES, Joseph	C/Sgt	15	RMA	21-331	10-198	Feb 1863	No.G	

Name	Rank	No	Div			Date	Amount	
MILLER, Isaac	Cpl	7	RMA	22		Dec 1863		*
				HMS QUEEN				
MILLER, John	C/Sgt	66	Po	21- 12	7- 44	Jan 1867	No.G	
MILLINGTON, Henry	Pte	19	Ply	21		Nov 1874	No.G	*
MILLS, Frederick J.	C/Sgt	21	Cha	21		Feb 1857	£15	
				HMS DRIVER				
MILLS, Joseph	Pte	38	Po	?		Sep 1874	£ 5	
MILLS, William	Gnr	4	RMA	21-181	9-134	Jan 1856	£ 5	
MOBLEY, Henry	Pte	?	Cha	?		Dec 1850	No.G	
MORCOMBE, G.T.	Drummer	7	Ply	25-311	14- 90	Jan 1868	No.G	
MORCOMBE, Thomas	Pte	71	Ply	21- 25	11-294	Jan 1864	£ 5	
MORDY, Elijah	Sgt	97	Cha	21-271	15-345	Feb 1863	£10	
MORGAN, George (MSM*)	C/Sgt	23	Ply	21		Jan 1871	£15	*
				Joined aged 13 years				
MORGAN, John	Cpl	5	Cha	21		Jan 1871	£ 5	*
MORGAN, Samuel	Cpl	18	Po	22- 83	11-227	Jan 1857	£10	
MORRIS, Thomas	Sgt	30	Po	22		Jan 1871	£15	
MORRISON, John (MSM)	Sgt Mjr	25	Cha	21-147	10-215	Jan 1858	£15	*
				Joined aged 11 years				
MORSE, George	Pte	48	Ply	21		Apr 1874	£ 5	
MORTIMORE, Thomas	C/Sgt	27	Ply	21- 31	10-249	Feb 1863	No.G	*
MORTLOCK, Thomas	C/Sgt	45	Cha	21		Feb 1857	£15	
				HMS ESPEIGLE				
MULLINS, Henry	Cpl	38	Po	21		Feb 1875	£10	*
				Latest known issue of any WS medal 23 Feby 1875				
				Earliest known issue of an NS medal 22 Feby 1875				
MULLINS, James	C/Sgt	6	RMA	21- 13	11-246	Jan 1868	No.G	*
MUNCEY, Joseph	C/Sgt	41	Cha	21- 33	12- 8	Jan 1867	No.G	
MUNCEY, Thomas	Pte	9	Cha	22		Feb 1861	£ 5	
				HMS PEMBROKE				
MUNN, James	Cpl	25	Cha	21- 6	7-185	Jan 1871	No.G	
MUNN, William	Pte	84	Ply	21		Mar 1872	£ 5	
				HMS VANGUARD				
MURRAY, George	Sgt	45	Cha			Jan 1871	£15	
MUSSELWHITE, Francis	Pte	70	Po	21-327	14-188	Jan 1866	£ 5	
NEELS, William	Pvst Sgt	8	Woo	21-108	11-363	Jan 1857	£15	
NELSON, John	Sgt	44	Woo	27-215	9-137	Feb 1863	No.G	
NEVILLE, John	C/Sgt	15	RMA	21- 8	13-157	Feb 1869	No.G	
NEWICK, Samuel	Pte	88	Woo	21		Nov 1861	No.G	
NEWMAN, David	Pte	25	Cha	21		Dec 1860	No.G	
NEWMAN, Jesse	Sgt	14	Po	21		May 1874	£ 5	
NICHOLLS, Frederick	C/Sgt	7	RMA	21		Jun 1873	£ 5	
NICHOLLS, Henry	Cpl	6	Po	?		Apr 1874	No.G	
NICHOLLS, William	Pte	1	Cha	21		Mar 1861	No.G	
NINCE, John	Pte	28	Cha	?		Jun 1873	£ 5	
NORMAN, Daniel	Cpl	13	Cha	21- 30	12-168	Feb 1859	£10	
NORMAN, Samuel	Cpl	11	RMA	21- 51	7-280	Jan 1862	£10	
NORSWORTHY, Samuel (MSM)	Sgt	75	Ply	21		Mar 1872	£10	
				HMS RESISTANCE				
NORTON, James	Sgt	11	Ply	21- 1	16-190	Jan 1866	£10	
NOTT, William	Pte	24	Ply	(Ex 45th Ft 10 Yrs)		Jly 1870		
NOYES, Giles	C/Sgt	14	Po	21- 14	10-249	Jan 1866	No.G	
NURSE, Henry	C/Sgt	4	Woo	21- 46	8- 25	Jan 1868	No.G	
OBORNE, William	Sgt	17	RMA	21		Feb 1872	No.G	
ORCHARD, William	Pte	36	Woo	21		Feb 1861	No.G	
OSBORN, Richard	Staff Sgt	6	RMA	21		Oct 1874	£ 5	*

OSBORNE, John	Pte	68	Woo	Not applicable		May 1855	£5	
				Special Crimea Gallantry Award (= D.C.M.)				
OTTON, Henry	Pte	35	Ply	21-116	16-144	Jan 1861	£5	
OWEN, William	Sgt	?	Woo	?		Jan 1861	No.G	
PAGE, Nathaniel	Brck Sgt	78	Po	21		Apr 1873	£15	
PAICKFORD, John	C/Sgt	92	Po	21-115	11-221	Jan 1849	£15	
PALMER, Jeremiah	C/Sgt	3	RMA	22		Aug 1856	£15	*
				H.M.S. SIDON				
PALMER, Stephen	C/Sgt	12	RMA	21-317	10-310	Jan 1867	£15	
PALMER, Thomas	C/Sgt	47	Ply	21		Feb 1851	£15	
PANKS, William	Pte	21	Cha	21		Jly 1848	£5	
PARDOE, George	Gnr	6	RMA	21- 80	13-199	Feb 1863	£5	
PARDOE, James	Sgt	68	Woo	21- 58	10-267	Jan 1868	No.G	
PARSONS, George	Pte	63	Ply	23- 30	17-105	Jan 1862	No.G	
PARSONS, Joseph	Pte	70	Po	21		Feb 1872	No.G	
PARTRIDGE, J.	C/Sgt	109	Ply	22-295		Feb 1860		*
				HMS ARACHNE				
PAWSEY, Isaac	Gnr	4	RMA	22		Jan 1871	£5	*
PAYNE, John	Pte	3	Ply	22		Aug 1850		* ‡
				HMS TRINCOMALEE				
PEEKS, Joseph	C/Sgt	33	Cha	?		Jan 1869	No.G	
PEEL, Abraham	C/Sgt	10	RMA	20-364	10-162	Jan 1868	£10	*
PENDLE, Richard	Sgt	73	Cha	21		Jun 1872	£10	
				HMS OCEAN				
PENNELL(S), James	Pte	80	Woo	21- 85	9-238	Jan 1867	No.G	
PERKINS, John	Pte	59	Ply	21		Mar 1873	No.G	
PERKINS, John	C/Sgt	49	Cha	21-150		Apr 1849	£15	
PERRY, Thomas	Pte	20	Woo	21- 10	8- 52	Feb 1863	£5	
PETTIT, William	Pvst Sgt	4	RMA	21-110	9-218	Jan 1866	No.G	
PETTMAN, Charles	Sgt	13	Cha	21- 18	8-276	Mar 1865	No.G	
PHILLIPS, James	Pte	70	Po	23- 79	22- 42	Jan 1860	£5	
PHILLIPS, John	Brck Sgt	78	Po	?		Jan 1871	£15	
PHILLIPS, William	Sgt	5	RMA	21		Mar 1873	No.G	
PHIPPIN, Robert	Pte	15	Ply	21- 84	10-217	Feb 1863	£5	
PINE, William	Cpl	74	Po	21-108	15-152	Jan 1864	No.G	
PIPER, Henry	Pte	13	Cha	21		Mar 1872	£5	
PITCHES, William	Pte	9	Cha	21- 62	19-103	Jan 1856	£5	
PITT, Thomas	Gnr	12	RMA	21		Mar 1874	No.G	*
PLATT, George	C/Sgt	2	Po	21- 77	14- 55	Feb 1863	No.G	
PLEASANTS, William	Pte	1	Cha	21- 6	9- 48	Jan 1866	£5	*
PLUM, John	Pte	?	Ply	21- 49	14-247	Mar 1850	£5	* ‡
POINTER, Henry	Cpl	13	Cha	23- 51	12- 17	Jan 1857	£10	
POINTON, William	Sgt	39	Ply	22		Feb 1872	No.G	*
POPE, William	Sgt	72	Ply	21 Joined aged 14		Mar 1873	No.G	
PORTCH, Wm.H. (MSM)	C/Sgt	84	Ply	21 Joined aged 15		Jan 1872	£15	
PORTLETT, Joseph	Pte	37	Cha	21		Dec 1861	No.G	
POTTER, Emanuel L.	Staff Sgt	5	RMA	23		Nov 1874	£5	
POUTER, Charles	Sgt	93	Cha	21- 45	6-352	Jan 1868	£15	*
POVER, Samuel	Sgt Mjr	2	Po	21-169	8-261	Feb 1848	£15	*
PRATT, Thomas	Pte	1	Cha	21-297	15- 55	Jan 1864	£5	
PRESSY, James	Pte	14	Po	21- 29	15- 97	Jan 1869	£5	
PRETTYJOHNS, John (VC)	Cpl	79	Ply	Not applicable		May 1855	£10	*
	(Actg Lance Sgt)			Special Crimea Gallantry Award (= D.C.M.)				
(2nd LS & GC Medal)	C/Sgt	59	Ply	21- 6	16- 94	Jan 1867	No.G	*
PRICE, Charles	C/Sgt	47	Cha	21		Feb 1872	No.G	
PRIVETT, Charles	Cpl	78	Po	21		May 1873	£5	

PROWSE, James	Pte	87	Ply	21- 16	14-313	Jan 1871	No.G	
PRYOR, Henry	Gnr	8	RMA	21- 64	12- 19	Jan 1864	£ 5	
PUGH, John	Pte	32	Woo	21- 32	4-212	Jan 1864	No.G	
PURSE, John	Gnr	3	RMA	22-364	3-161	Jan 1866	£ 5	
QUIRK, David	Pte		Po	21		Dec 1849	£ 5	‡
RADDENBURY, John	Cpl	19	Ply	21		Nov 1860	No.G	
RAMPLIN, Richard	Pvst Sgt	58	Po	21-158	9-227	Feb 1869	No.G	
RAMPLING, Henry (MSM*)	Sgt Mjr		Ply	22-268	11-151	Jan 1858	£15	*
RATCLIFFE, William	Pte	22	Po	21- 24	12-221	Feb 1863	£ 5	
READ, Charles	Pte	8	Woo	21- 73	2-196	Mar 1865	£ 5	
REYNOLDS, Jonathan	C/Sgt	89	Cha	28- 69	15-241	Jan 1864	No.G	
RHODES, William	Gnr	16	RMA	21		Jan 1874	£ 5	
RICHARDS, Benjamin	Pte	84	Woo	21-152	9-266	Jan 1853		
RICHARDS, Charles	Gnr	10	RMA	21		Aug 1874	£ 5	
RICHARDS, Edwin	Pte	3	Ply	21		Jan 1871	£ 5	
RICHARDSON, Samuel	C/Sgt	6	Po	21		Mar 1872	£10	
				HMS ?				
RIX, George	Pte	30	Po	21-284	12-208	Jan 1864	£ 5	
ROACH, James (MSM)	C/Sgt	47	Ply	21		May 1874	No.G	*
ROBERTS, John	C/Sgt	50	Po	21- 3	11- 63	Jan 1864	£15	
ROBINS, Henry	Pvst Sgt	?	RMA	22- 5	6- 72	Jan 1860	£15	
ROBINSON, Charles	Pte	32	Woo	21- 34	12- 59	Mar 1865	£ 5	
ROBINSON, James	Sgt	1	RMA	22-262	2-239	Jan 1868	£15	
ROBINSON, James	Q.M.Sgt	45	Cha	21 Joined aged 12		Jan 1871	£15	*
ROBINSON, William	C/Sgt	48	Woo	21		Nov 1860	No.G	
				Pensioned March 1846				
ROBINSON, William	Sgt	10	RMA	22		Jan 1871	£15	*
ROBSHAW, Robert	Drummer	40	Woo	21- 48	NIL	Jan 1864	No.G	
ROFFEY, Aaron	Pte	1	Cha	22-104	3-150	Mar 1865	£ 5	
ROLES, Thomas	Pte	42	Po	21- 86	15-136	Jan 1868	No.G	*
ROLF, Jeremiah	Sgt	9	RMA	23		Aug 1857	£15	*
				HMS BARRACOUTA				
ROOTE, Charles	Sgt	81	Cha	20-352	12-192	Jan 1870	£ 5	*
				21 Yrs on medal				
ROPER, Henry G.	Drummer	1	Cha	21		Jly 1873	£ 5	
ROSE, William	Drummer	81	Cha	23- 43	11-231	Jan 1869	£ 5	
ROSE, William	C/Sgt	65	Cha	21		Mar 1861	No.G	
ROWE, Thomas	Pte	35	Ply	21-283	8-235	Jan 1867	£ 5	
ROWLANDS, Richard	Sgt	79	Ply	21-113	10- 90	Jan 1849	£15	*
RUMBLE, George	Cpl	1	RMA	23.		Dec 1860	No.G	
RUNDLE, Reuben R.	Sgt	14	RMA	21-157	9-138	Jan 1870	No.G	*
RUSH, Charles	Gnr	14	RMA	21		Feb 1872	No.G	
RUSSELL, William	C/Sgt	71	Ply	21-128	12-271	Mar 1865	No.G	
RYAN, Daniel J. (MSM*)	Q.M.Sgt	36	Woo	28-224	7- 44	Jan 1856	£15	*
RYAN, William	Sgt	35	Ply	21		Sep 1874	£10	
				HMS INVINCIBLE				
SALMON, Job	Pte	53	Cha	21		Jan 1873	No.G	
SALTER, Henry	Cpl	68	Woo	22		May 1856		*
				HMS MERLIN				
SALTER, William	C/Sgt	6	Po	27-175	17- 55	Jan 1870	No.G	
SANDFORD, Daniel	Sgt	31	Ply	21		Dec 1860	No.G	
SARTIN, John	C/Sgt	22	Po	21		Jan 1862	No.G	*
SAUNDERS, James	Pte	77	Cha	21- 0	14-108	Jan 1854	£ 5	
SAUNDERS, Robert (MSM*)	Sgt Mjr	3	Ply	21		Mar 1873	£15	*
SAVING, James						Feb 1849		

151

SAYER, George	Pte	41	Cha	21		Aug 1850	£5	‡
(Later deserted – medal returned ?) HMS HASTINGS								
SCHOFIELD, John	Sgt	?	Cha	?		Feb 1861	No.G	
SCOTT, Henry	Pte	42	Po	23-364	18- 72	Jan 1862	£5	
SCRIVENER, Thomas	Sgt	37	Cha	?		Jun 1873	No.G	
SEARLE, Samuel	C/Sgt	47	Ply	21- 12	9-323	Jan 1867	No.G	*
SENIOR, Joseph	Sgt	45	Cha	21- 1	8-329	Feb 1863	£15	
SHEIN, Thomas	Drummer	46	Po	24-323	15- 3	Mar 1865	£5	
SHERIDAN, Philip	C/Sgt	48	Ply	21- 6	9-328	Jan 1871	No.G	
SHERLOCK, James	Pte	85	Po	21- 2	18-275	Jan 1860	£5	
SHERLOCK, Richard	Sgt	86	Po	22-148	12-162	Jan 1866	£10	*
SHILL, William	Sgt	42	Po	21-224	9- 42	Jan 1860	£5	*
SHORT, William	Pte	19	Ply	21- 2	10-268	Jan 1867	£5	
SIDEBOTTOM, James	Sgt	28	Woo	21- 11	9-164	Jan 1864	No.G	
SIMMONDS, George	Pte	53	Cha	?		Nov 1848	£5	
				HMS VERNON				
SINCLAIR, William	C/Sgt	8	RMA	21-147	7-203	Jan 1869	£10	
SISMEY, John	Sgt	3	RMA	21		Jan 1872	£5	
SLADDEN, Riphath	1st Mskty Sgt Instr	4	RMA	21- 80	3-319	Jan 1871	No.G	*
SLATER, William (MSM*)	Sgt	16	RMA	21		Feb 1872	No.G	*
SLIBBARD, Samuel	Gnr	?	RMA	?		Jun 1872	£5	
SLUGG, William	Cpl	6	Po	21-120	12-289	Jan 1852	£7	
SMALL, John	C/Sgt	9	RMA	21-334	12- 66	Feb 1859	£15	
SMITH, George	Pte	28	Woo	21.		Nov 1860	No.G	*
SMITH, George	Sgt Mjr	4	Woo	22-136	6-278	Feb 1863	£15	*
SMITH, James	Cpl	30	Po	21- 98	11-217	Jan 1871	No.G	
SMITH, James A.	C/Sgt	11	RMA	25/147	14- 49	Jan 1862	£15	*
SMITH, John	C/Sgt	2	RMA	21		Nov 1860	No.G	*
SMITH, Samuel	Pte	84	Ply	?		Jan 1872	£5	*
SMITH, Thomas	Cpl	17	RMA	22-345	11- 82	Jan 1864	£10	
SMITH, William	Q.M.Sgt		RMA	21-165	11-358	Jan 1870	£10	
SMITHSON, Thomas (MSM*)	Sgt	27	Ply	22-358	2-315	Mar 1865	£15	
SNELL, John	C/Sgt	31	Ply	21- 6	13-343	Jan 1870	No.G	
SNELLING, Elijah	Sgt	74	Po	22- 3	8-364	Jan 1864	£10	
SNOOK, Elijah	Sgt	48	Woo	22- 28	7- 94	Jan 1864	£10	*
SOAL, Samuel (MSM)	Q.M.Sgt	11	RMA	21		Jan 1873	£10	
SOLLEY, Charles	Sgt	5	Cha	21-139	9- 99	Jan 1871	No.G	
SOMERSBY, Henry J.	C/Sgt	44	Woo	21- 0	9- 8	Jan 1868	No.G	
SOUTER, James	Sgt	1	RMA	21		Nov 1860	No.G	
SOUTHWELL, Thomas	Cpl	70	Po	21		Mar 1861	No.G	
SOUTHWOOD, John	Sgt	55	Ply	21- 8	11- 13	Jan 1868	No.G	
SPLATT, Frederick	Cpl	11	RMA	21- 40	9-246	Feb 1869	No.G	
SPOONER, John	C/Sgt	17	Cha	21- 14	11- 31	Mar 1865	No.G	
SPOONER, Joseph	Sgt	7	RMA	21		Dec 1872	£10	
				HMS ROYAL ALFRED				
SPRATT, John	Pte & Master Shoemaker	14	Po	55 years. (Enlisted 20-4-1805)		Dec 1860	No.G	
SPURWAY, Robert	Pte	15	Ply	21-268	16-274	Mar 1850	£5	‡
SQUIRE, James	Gnr	15	RMA	22		May 1873	£5	
				HMS ZEALOUS				
STADDEN (*Vide* : SLADDEN)								
STAGG, Walter	Pte	13	Cha	21- 6	11- 88	Jan 1867	£5	
STAITE, Thomas (MSM*)	Staff Sgt (Barrack)	5	RMA	21		Aug 1872	£10	*

Name	Rank	No.	Depot			Date	Amount	
STARES, Thomas	Pte	20	Woo	21		Nov 1860	No.G	
STARLING, John	Pte	84	Ply	21-188	12-355	Jan 1870	£ 5	
STEDMAN, James	C/Sgt	46	Po	23-108	16-325	Mar 1857	£15	*
				HMS ELECTRA				
STEER, Michael	Pte	5	Cha	22-155	19-196	Jan 1867	£ 5	
STEVENS, Thomas	C/Sgt	3	Ply	21- 23	12-302	Jan 1868	£15	*
STEWARD, Samuel	C/Sgt	75	Ply	21-115	11-215	Jan 1869	£15	
STOCK, William	Sgt	32	Woo	21- 26	4-230	Mar 1865	£15	*
STOCKHAM, Thomas	C/Sgt	?	Ply	?		Dec 1860	No.G	
STOKES, John G.	Gnr	1	RMA	21		Aug 1861	No.G	
STONE, George	Pte	3	Ply	21		Nov 1874	£ 5	
STONE, Henry	Pte	3	Ply	21		Nov 1860	No.G	
STRONG, Henry	Sgt	35	Ply	21- 17	9-269	Jan 1866	No.G	
STUBBS, John	C/Sgt	40	Woo	21-206	18-334	Jan 1855	£15	
SUMMERFIELD, James	C/Sgt	24	Woo	21- 61	14-239	Mar 1850	£15	‡
SURMAN, William	C/Sgt	2	Po	25- 25	16- 38	Jan 1867	£10	
SURTIN, William	C/Sgt	98	Po	21-203	9-332	Jan 1867	£15	
SUTTON, John	C/Sgt	3	RMA	21		Nov 1860	No.G	*
SWAIN, William	Sgt	10	RMA	21- 8	3-270	Jan 1864	£10	*
SYMS, John	C/Sgt	95	Po	22-357	13-345	Feb 1859	£15	
TALBOT, James L.	Gnr	13	RMA	21-124	13-113	Jan 1869	£ 5	
TANNER, Joseph	Pte	93	Cha	21- 12	15-239	Jan 1868	£ 5	
TAPLEY, Thomas	Pte	71	Ply	21-129	9-259	Mar 1865	£ 5	
TAYLOR, E.F.	C/Sgt					Oct 1860	No.G	
TAYLOR, John	Cpl	40	Woo	Not applicable		May 1855	£10	
				Special Crimea Gallantry Award (= D.C.M.)				
TAYLOR, John	C/Sgt	104	Woo	22		Dec 1848	£15	
TAYLOR, John	Sgt (Cpl?)	16	Woo	22		Nov 1848	£ 5	
				HMS COMUS				
THAYER, J.	Cpl	39	Ply	21		Oct 1860	No.G	
THOMAS, Robert	Pte	54	Po	21-312	14- 87	Mar 1865	£ 5	
THOMAS, William	C/Sgt	19	Ply	21- 62	10-283	Jan 1855	£15	
THOMPSON, Zachariah J.	Gnr	?	RMA	?		Sep 1848	£ 5	
THORNCROFT, George	Pte	11	Ply	21		Apr 1849	£ 5	
THORNE, Richard	C/Sgt	86	Po	21- 11	12- 30	Jan 1867	No.G	
THORNTON, William	Brck Sgt	12	RMA	21		Feb 1873	£ 5	
THORPE, Samuel	Sgt	45	Cha	21-108	8- 28	Mar 1865	£ 5	
THYNNE, William	Pte	3	Ply	22-127		Jan 1861	£ 5	
TILLEY, James	Pte	72	Ply	?		Dec 1872	£ 5	
TIMEWELL, Thomas	Pte	79	Ply	21- 11	11- 36	Jan 1870	£ 5	
TINSON, George	Sgt	17	Cha	21-170	6-197	Jan 1870	£ 5	*
TODD, David	C/Sgt	36	Woo	21- 2	8- 68	Feb 1869	No.G	
TONTHON, William	Pte	89	Cha	21- 44	10-239	Feb 1863	£ 5	
TOWLE, William	Pte	12	Woo	21- 61	13- 24	Mar 1850	£ 5	‡
TOWN, George	Sgt	81	Cha	21- 8	10-317	Jan 1868	No.G	
TRIGG, Joseph	Pte	79	Ply	21- 7	16-174	Jan 1862	£ 5	
TRUEMAN, Thomas M.	Cpl	51	Ply	21-280	11- 0	Jan 1854	£10	
TRUSCOTT, Charles	Pte	?	Ply	21- 79	16-255	Jan 1858	£ 5	
TUCK, John	C/Sgt	45	Cha	21		Apr 1872	£10	*
TUCK, William	Gnr	15	RMA	21		Mar 1874	£ 5	
TUCKER, William	Gnr	9	RMA	22		Jan 1871	£ 5	
TURNER, John	C/Sgt	17	RMA	21-213	10-286	Jan 1867	No.G	
TURNER, John	Sgt			22- 11	8-250	Jan 1861	£15	
TURNER, John	C/Sgt	15	RMA	21- 34	11-117	Jan 1868	No.G	
TURNER, William	Sgt	10	RMA	21		May 1868	No.G	
TYRER, John	Cpl	29	Cha	25		Feb 1861	No.G	*

UPTON, James	C/Sgt	108	Po	21- 56	15-357	Jan 1868	No.G	
URQUHART, Robert	Sgt	72	Woo	21		May 1867		*
				HMS DONEGAL				
URSELL, Frederick	Sgt	67	Ply	21- 40	12- 68	Mar 1850	£15	‡
VANDERKISTE, Frederick	Sgt	49	Cha	32- 61	1-324	Jan 1861	£15	
VINCENT, Job	C/Sgt	70	Po	21-224	6-343	Jan 1867	£10	
VINCENT, John	Cpl	8	RMA	21		Mar 1874	No.G	
VINES, Broom	Sgt	18	Po	21- 83	11-179	Jan 1868	£10	
VINES, Matthew	Pte	38	Po	22- 63	12-139	Jan 1857	£ 5	
VINEY, George	Pte	20	Woo	21-327	10-303	Feb 1863	£ 5	*
WAKEFORD, George	Pte	50	Po	21		Jan 1872	£ 5	
WALKER, George	Pte	59	Ply	21- 28	11-349	Feb 1863	£ 5	
WALL, Mark	Sgt	22	Po	22		Feb 1854		*
				HMS NEPTUNE				
WALLACE, Alexander	Brck Sgt	?	Cha	21 Pensioned 1843		Dec 1860	No.G	
WALLACE, Joseph	C/Sgt	40	Woo	21		Feb 1864	£15	
				HMS GORGON				
WATLING, William	Sgt Mjr	56	Cha	21		Oct 1860	No.G	
WALTER, John	Cpl	7	RMA	21		Mar 1873	No.G	
WALTERS, Nicholas	C/Sgt	24	Woo	22- 24	14- 6	Feb 1859	£15	*
WARREN, William	Sgt	65	Cha	22-143	8-104	Jan 1853		*
WARRICK, John	C/Sgt	28	Woo	21- 11	7-193	Feb 1869	No.G	
WARRY, Samuel	Cpl	59	Ply	23-102	13- 13	Jan 1855	£10	*
WASHBURN, Thomas	C/Sgt	72	Ply	?		Mar 1873	No.G	
WATERS, W.	Sgt					Oct 1860	No.G	
WATSON, Thomas M.	C/Sgt	105	Cha	21- 11	10-178	Mar 1865	No.G	
WATTS, John	Pte	3	Ply	23		Jan 1861	No.G	
WAY, William	Pte	84	Ply	21		Mar 1872	£ 5	
WEBBER, Henry	Cpl	7	Ply	21-197	10- 18	Jan 1854	£10	
WEBSTER, Thomas (MSM*)	Sgt Instr Gunnery	4	Cha	21		Sep 1872	£10	*
WEIGHAM, James	C/Sgt	9	Cha	?		Mar 1872	£15	*
WELLS, William	Drum Mjr	52	Cha	?		Jun 1873	No.G	
WENLOCK, John	Pte	32	Po	21		Apr 1874	No.G	*
WESTAWAY, John	Pte	59	Ply	21- 52	14-240	Jan 1867	£ 5	
WESTELL, William	C/Sgt	20	Woo	22 Pensioned 1847		Feb 1861	No.G	*
WESTON, George T.	Drum Mjr	102	Po	24- 8	4-229	Mar 1865	No.G	
WHEELER, William	Pte	85	Cha	22-213	18-351	Feb 1859	£ 5	
WHITE, Elisha	C/Sgt	82	Po	21		Apr 1860	£15	
WHITE, William	C/Sgt	1	RMA	21- 26	10-242	Jan 1861	£15	
WILLIAMS, Charles	Pte	5	Cha	21- 13	15-105	Jan 1870	No.G	
WILLIAMS, George	C/Sgt	102	Po	21- 3	13-311	Feb 1859	£15	*
WILLIAMS, Thomas	Sgt	9	RMA	21- 31	8-214	Jan 1870	No.G	
WILLIS, John	Pte	93	Cha	21- 52	12-267	Jan 1869	£ 5	*
WILLIS, Robert	C/Sgt	26	Po	21		Feb 1865		*
				HMS RINALDO				
WILLOWBY, Wm.H. (MSM) (WILLOUGHBY)	C/Sgt	52	Woo	27- 94	15- 89	Mar 1865	No.G	*
WILLS, Thomas	Pte	35	Ply	21-243	8-253	Feb 1864	£ 5	
WILLS, Walter	C/Sgt	43	Ply	21- 61	14-103	Jan 1869	£10	
WILSHER, John	C/Sgt	9	RMA	21- 48	8-143	Jan 1864	£15	
WILSON, John	Sgt Mjr	2	Po	21-201	4-162	Jan 1866	£15	
WILSON, Thomas	Gnr	15	RMA	21- 41	10-229	Jan 1870	No.G	
WI(or E)WOOD, Thomas	Sgt	15	RMA	21- 152	8- 11	Mar 1865	No.G	
WISE, Benjamin	C/Sgt	2	RMA	23- 88	12- 55	Jan 1861	£15	
WITHERS, Henry (MSM)	Sgt	65	Cha	21-205	12-191	Jan 1866	£15	

WOLFENDEN, George	Pte	88	Woo	21- 50	14-239	Mar 1850	£ 5	*	‡
WOOD, James	Pte	39	Ply	21.		Nov 1860	No.G	*	
WOOD, Jonathan	Drummer	54	Po	21-164	9-254	Jan 1854	£ 5	*	
				Joined aged 13 years					
WOODFORD, Joseph	Pte	38	Po	21		Apr 1874	No.G		
WOODS, Robert	Pte	20	Woo	23- 88	7- 14	Jan 1858	£ 5		
WORTH, William	C/Sgt	24	RMA	21- 84	8-189	Jan 1866	£10		
WOTTLEY, Thomas	Pte	30	Po	21		Aug 1860			‡
				HMS TRINCOMALEE					
WRIGHT, John	C/Sgt	65	Cha	21-106	12- 6	Jan 1864	£15		
YABELEY, Richard	Pte	23	Ply	21- 32	10-125	Jan 1862	£ 5		
YOUNG, George (MSM*)	C/Sgt	14	RMA	21-135	14- 29	Jan 1869	£10		
				(Gallantry MSM 17-10-1864)					
YOUNG, William	Bmbdr	8	RMA	21 Joined aged 14		Jan 1872	£ 5		
ZEBEDEE, W.	Gnr	7	RMA	21-111	5-216	Jan 1868	£ 5		

Abbreviations :   * = Medal known
                    ‡ = Type with Obverse dated '1848'
                    £15, £10 or £5 = Size of Gratuity awarded.
                    No.G = No Gratuity awarded

PARISH NOTICES DISPLAYED FOR MERITORIOUS CONDUCT

Whilst searching through Royal Marine archives (ADM 56/- to 63/ & 191/- Series) at the Public Record Office in order to aid construction of Medal Rolls of Royal Marine recipients of M.S.Ms. and LS & GC Medals (1830-1875) – the previously unknown expression of 'Parish Notice' was sighted on numerous occasions.

Knowledge concerning this somewhat esoteric part of administrative history is not purely of academic use; for instance, the notation of the issue of this 'Notice' provided the only information on those marines who had been awarded their LS & GC awards whilst serving in Ships. Although 'shore' recommendations can be found by other means, the complementary 'Parish Notice' often provided confirmatory and additional information on the recipient. Irrespective of its present use as a research tool, the reason for its institution and the aid it provided in byegone days to dependable ex-servicemen in the 19th century – needs to be retrieved from oblivion and shewn as one part of the social fabric of military life.

The earliest mention found of the phrase 'Parish Notice' appears in an 'Article' of the old Army Mutiny Act. Perhaps a word or two on that Act would not be amiss. Until the year 1661 the military services for England were met by raising and calling out Militia Levies, but from 7 January 1661 there was to be a permanent military establishment under the Monarchy – a Standing Army. From this moment onwards, the Rules governing the Administration and conduct of the Military Force were enshrined in the Army Mutiny Act – a foreshortened title of the official wording 'ARMY, annual Act for punishing Mutiny and desertion, and for better payment of the Army, and their Quarters'. This Act had to receive Parliamentary assent after the accustomed annual Debate, usually resulting in some changes being made to its content.

In 1830 one such amendment introduced this novel principle of 'Parish Notices', which new idea appeared heading an additional 'Article' to the Army Mutiny Act, thus increasing the ever growing list of constraints and rules imposed upon the Commander-in-Chief at Horse Guards. This supplementary piece of legislation was inserted as Article 70 which received Parliamentary approval on 23 March 1830 (II. GEORGE IV. Cap.7.) – published in these words : —

' Notification to Parishes of good and bad Conduct of Soldiers.

LXX. And be it enacted, That the Churchwardens of every Parish in England and Ireland, and the Constables or other Officers of every Parish or Place in Scotland, on receiving a Notification from the Secretary of War of the names of any Soldiers belonging to the said Parish who have, for meritorious Conduct in the Army, received His Majesty's approbation, or who, in consequence of Misconduct, have been dismissed with Disgrace, shall affix such notification on the outside of the door of the Church or Chapel belonging to such Parish or Place on the SUNDAY next succeeding the Receipt of the said Notification. '.

The sudden appearance of this edict was surely no accident, and one does not have to look far to guess the source from which it stemmed. By an Order in Council dated 14 November 1829 the Army were empowered : —

' With a view to rewarding meritorious Soldiers when discharged, and of encouraging good conduct in others whilst serving – a Gratuity in addition to the Pension may in certain cases be given to one Sergeant or Corporal, and one Private, annually to every Regiment of an Establishment of 700 Rank and File and upwards. '.

The Army Mutiny Act passed in March 1830 was thus the first chance to reflect any changes implicit upon the introduction of this 'Gratuity' (but not yet its concomitant medal) for 'Good Conduct' – available to certain specially selected soldiers at the time of their discharge.

A few months later, in June 1830, the Admiralty sought agreement to follow the Army's '1829 Gratuity' example, but most fortunately also suggested that their scheme might go one stage further. The Navy was about to leap-frog the single benefit of the 'Gratuity' so recently introduced for soldiers. The Admiralty received approval (19 July 1830) to award not only the 'Gratuity' for extensive service and good behaviour to selected sailors and marines, but also that recognition of the bestowal of this 'Gratuity' was a pre-condition to subsequent entitlement for the recipient to receive additionally a 'Silver Medal' – a type of reward which henceforth earned the ubiquitous title of 'Long Service and Good Conduct Medal'.

Eleven days later on 30 July 1830 the institution of the Army's LS & GC Medal was approved by an Order in Council, in which the particular and relevant passage appears as – 'Discharged Soldiers receiving a Gratuity for Meritorious Conduct shall be entitled to wear a silver Medal ..'. Thus at least in theory, these Parish Notices should have been affixed to hallowed doors for soldiers honoured by the 'Gratuity', and subsequently for similarly well behaved men in receipt of the 'Gratuity and Medal'. The story now continues with the Admiralty's connection with 'Parish Notices' through the medium of their overall responsibility for the Royal Corps of Marines.

Shortly after the publication of the initial regulations for the award of the Naval gratuity and 'Silver Medal', it was noticed that the rules referred solely to ships and seamen without any reference whatsoever to Royal Marine participation. This unintentional piece of administrative thoughtlessness was soon to be rectified. The very first recommendation which the Admiralty received for the twin awards of the gratuity and medal ('G & M') was on behalf of a Royal Marine N.C.O. serving ashore at the Woolwich Division, quoting the 12th Article of the Naval Pension Rules as the authority for the submission and awards.

This skilful prod from the Royal Marine Office (RMO) – ever willing to gain from either of her sister services – provoked immediate response from the Admiralty on the same day (22 November 1830) by a demi-official letter, which in essence instituted new rules in the following manner : —

'... the 12th Article of the Navy Regulations is meant to apply only to men in ships afloat, and that Gratuities to Marines on shore, must be regulated by the 50th Article of the Army Regulations for granting Pensions and Gratuities, to which Gratuity fixed by that Army Article, a Medal will also be added by the Admiralty. ...'.

But this Admiralty clarification of separate 'Shore' and 'Sea' rules for the awards of 'G & M' to Royal Marine personnel would not have come as a surprise to senior R.M. officers within the RMO in London. The Deputy Adjutant-General R.M. and his small staff had already included a copy of the Army's Article

70 on 'Parish Notices' in their own Marine Mutiny Act ('Marine Forces' Annual Act for Regulations while on Shore) as a new Article 52. Why else had the RMO ordained this additional rule except for the fact that they expected their men to qualify for the 'G & M' under Army rules ? One has to admire the adroitness by which the Royal Marines organised their own arrangements.

The story now switches from 'Theory' to 'Practice', since so often a different tale emerges when comments are made on the manner in which the Authorities interpreted the rules – or even if they ever abided by them, which seems very doubtful for soldiers of the British Army as regards the issue of these 'Parish Notices' for their discharged men.

For the first eight years (1830-1838) when this 'Notice' should have been issued for discharged Royal Marines the regulation appears to have been generally ignored. The earliest archive found concerning the despatch of such a 'Notice' was dated 12 November 1838 (ADM 56/12/391), in which the Colonel Commandant of the Portsmouth Division was informed that :

' In further reference to the Description of Colour Sergeant Pearcey, I am to explain to you that the original document is usually transmitted from the Admiralty to the Parish, and it is requisite that it should be easily understood in the Country.

I am directed therefore by the D.A.G. Royal Marines to return the Description and to request that something to the following effect may be inserted under the heading 'Remarks' : —

' Discharged 7th November 1838 after a faithful service of – years and he has received a Medal and Gratuity as a Meritorious Soldier, awarded to him by the Lords Commissioners of the Admiralty.'.

The next 'find' on this subject proved that as yet no Brigade Order had been issued on the need to provide information for 'Parish Notices'. The initiative still lay with the Admiralty to seek these 'Descriptions', as and when marines were honoured by the reward of a 'Gratuity' (obtainable by personal application to the Cashier of Greenwich Pensions, Tower Hill) and a 'Silver Medal'. This second reference (13 February 1839 – ADM 56/13/94) was sent from the Admiralty to the Commandant of the Portsmouth Division : —

'.. requesting [that] you will furnish him [the Deputy Adjutant General, Royal Marines] with a Description of Private William Lewis, in order that a notification may be made to his Parish that he has, for his meritorious conduct, received this mark of Her Majesty's special approbation. '.

The Royal Marine Office (RMO) now decided to standardise the format of the 'Parish Notice'. The fact that the RMO did not adopt the simple solution of amending an Army Form to their purpose is suggestive that the Army did not in fact possess such a Form. By now – in 1839 – the War Office should have issued well over a thousand 'Parish Notices' for soldiers pensioned with the 'G & M', and one is left with the thought that the Army Authorities had turned a Nelsonic blind eye to Article 70 of their Mutiny Act.

After the next award of the 'G & M' had been approved to a marine, the RMO sent out a pro-forma hand-written Tabular Form to be completed by the staff of the Colonel-Commandant who had recommended the man; this time it was Woolwich Head Quarters who were to learn some new administrative rules (ADM 56/13/127). The Form was a long horizontal one with many vertical columns, and a heading which read : —

' Description of JOHN SHANNON – Woolwich Division of Royal Marines – discharged after faithful service of 21 years on 20th February 1839, at which time he received a Medal and Gratuity for Meritorious Conduct – as a mark of Her Majesty's special approbation. '

The columns under this worthy testimonial had sub-headings to provide some additional personal details. Any reader of this 'Notice' such as a prospective employer could thus be informed of the man's

['Description'] age, height, colour of eyes, hair and complexion, his parish and county of birth, the period of his service in years, months & days, and finally the date and cause of his discharge. But this aide-memoire was sent to only one of the Royal Marine Divisions – Woolwich – and not as a General Instruction to all Colonels Commandant.

Another 18 months were to pass before the Admiralty – acting through the Royal Marine Office – placed their 'Parish Notice' scheme on an official and formalised basis. All the previous arrangements had been demi-official, made individually by the RMO with each of the four Marine Divisions. Now, in 1840, the pleasantries were to be swept away in favour of binding Regulations issued in a Marine Office Circular (ADM 56/16/68) in this manner : —

> ' CIRCULAR. 3rd November 1840
>
> I have the honour to request that whenever a Private is discharged with disgrace from the Division under your Command, it may be notified to the Division that his name will, according to the 65th Section of the Mutiny Act, be posted on the Church Door of his Parish, agreeably to the form for 'Bad Conduct' herewith transmitted.
>
> I transmit also, for your information, a Form for Non Commissioned Officers and men who for 'Good Conduct' receive the Medal and Gratuity as a mark of Her Majesty's approbation, which is in those cases sent by the Admiralty to the Authorities of the Parishes to which such men belong according to the Act above quoted. '.

It is believed that the 'Form' referred to in the second paragraph of this Circular would have been very similar to the one illustrated on Plate No 13, which although issued in 1855 for Private John McElroy was obviously printed earlier. The clue lies in the printed reference on this document to the 68th Section of the Marine Mutiny Act, and this would date the design of this 'Notice' as 1844 or 1845. The handwritten amendment of 78th Section on McElroy's Form would refer to re-numbering of this part of the Marine Mutiny Act in 1848 – still in force in 1855.

Since the Author has not received a single reply to former publicised requests for information concerning the survival of any of these 'Parish Notices', it appears that the copy of McElroy's Parish Notice in ADM 201/21 might well be the only specimen to have survived. Private McElroy's 'Notice' is printed on a white sheet of paper, 12″ by 8″, with bright red letter printing and the personal details written in black ink – all of which makes a most colourful and compelling document to read. Perhaps the pensioned men themselves sought permission from their local parson to retain these impressive 'Notices' as a form of 'Reference' to obtain work – once their more general purpose of advertisement on the parish door had been satisfied.

By a most fortunate chance, this particular surviving 'Parish Notice' was issued for the award of a most interesting and extremely rare – historic – type of medal. It was a 'Gallantry LS & GC Medal', which stemmed from and equated to the recently instituted Distinguished Conduct Medal for the Army, which was not extended to cover acts of gallantry by marines in the Crimea. (*Vide* : 'Naval Medals 1793-1856' in the Section 'R.M. M.S.Ms & Naval LS & GC Medals used as Gallantry Awards'). McElroy's Gallantry LS & GC Medal (which has survived unaccompanied by other medals) has the special distinguishment of 'CRIMEA' officially engraved on its edge – after 'Woolwich Division'. It will be noticed that the printed words on his 'Parish Notice' [*Vide* : Plate No 13] were suitably amended to meet his special award and circumstances, prior to a copy (?) being sent '.. to the Church wardens of the Parish of Aughalurcher, Town of Lisnaskea, Co. Fermanagh ..' on 29 August 1855. (ADM 191/18/139)

A search of the Royal Marine Office Letter Books in the ADM 191/- Series at the Public Record Office should (ultimately !) reveal the Parish details of most 'Shore' and some 'Ship' awarded' LS & GC medals to marines, as well as similar information covering nearly all recipients of the R.M. Meritorious Service Medal. The practice of issuing 'Parish Notices' ceased in 1865, when the relevant Section in the Marine Mutiny Act was deleted/abolished. A search for such details in the ADM 191/- series can prove time consuming, since the Volumes for this 25 year period do not possess 'Subject Indexes'.

ROYAL MARINE COMPANY NUMBERS AND THEIR DIVISIONS

An aid to researching the career of a marine

There is an initial difficulty when attempting to find personal details of a marine when the only clue is his Company Number. The 'Description Books' in the ADM 158/- Series is the place to start, but since there are four sets covering Chatham, Portsmouth, Plymouth and Woolwich Divisions – time can be saved if the man's Division can be interpreted from his Company Number, which is the aim of the list which follows. There is a fifth set of 'Description Books' for the Royal Marine Artillery (RMA), but the full alphabetical index to them in the ADM 158/- Series has to be sought in two places – under the headings 'Royal Marine Artillery' and within the 'Portsmouth Division' index.

ROYAL MARINE DIVISION – COMPANY NUMBERS

C = Chatham PO = Portsmouth PL = Plymouth W = Woolwich

+ = To year heading next column

Company Number	To 1814	1815 +	1817 +	1838 +	1850 +	1869 +
1	C	C	C	C	C	C
2	PO	PO	PO	PO	PO	PO
3	PL	PL	PL	PL	PL	PL
4	C	W	W	W	W	C
5	PO	C	C	C	C	C
6	PL	PO	PO	PO	PO	PO
7	C	PL	PL	PL	PL	PL
8	PO	W	W	W	W	PO
9	PL	C	C	C	C	C
10	C	PO	PO	PO	PO	PO
11	PO	PL	PL	PL	PL	PL
12	PL	W	W	W	W	PL
13	C	C	C	C	C	C
14	PO	PO	PO	PO	PO	PO
15	PL	PL	PL	PL	PL	PL
16	C	W	W	W	W	C
17	PO	C	C	C	C	C
18	PL	PO	PO	PO	PO	PO
19	C	PL	PL	PL	PL	PL
20	PO	W	W	W	W	PO
21	PL	C	C	C	C	C
22	C	PO	PO	PO	PO	PO
23	PO	PL	PL	PL	PL	PL
24	PL	W	W	W	W	PL
25	C	C	C	C	C	C
26	PO	PO	PO	PO	PO	PO
27	PL	PL	PL	PL	PL	PL
28	C	W	W	W	W	C
29	PO	C	C	C	C	C

Company Number	To 1814	1815 +	1817 +	1838 +	1850 +	1869 +
30	PL	PO	PO	PO	PO	PO
31	C	PL	PL	PL	PL	PL
32	PO	W	W	W	W	PO
33	PL	C	C	C	C	C
34	C	PO	PO	PO	PO	PO
35	PO	PL	PL	PL	PL	PL
36	PL	W	W	W	W	PL
37	C	C	C	C	C	C
38	PO	PO	PO	PO	PO	PO
39	PL	PL	PL	PL	PL	PL
40	C	W	W	W	W	C
41	PO	C	C	C	C	C
42	PL	PO	PO	PO	PO	PO
43	CO	PL	PL	PL	PL	PL
44	PO	W	W	W	W	PO
45	PL	C	C	C	C	C
46	C	PO	PO	PO	PO	PO
47	PO	PL	PL	PL	PL	PL
48	PL	W	W	W	W	PL
49	C	C	C	C	C	C
50	PO	PO	PO	PO	PO	PO
51	PL	PL	PL	PL	PL	PL
52	C	W	W	W	W	C
53	PO	C	C	C	C	C
54	PL	PO	PO	PO	PO	PO
55	C	PL	PL	PL	PL	PL
56	PO	W	C	C	W	PO
57	PL	C	PO	PO	C	C
58	C	PO	PL	PL	PO	PO
59	PO	PL	C	C	PL	PL
60	PL	W	PO	PO	W	PL
61	C	C	PL	PL	C	C
62	PO	PO	C	C	PO	PO
63	PL	PL	PO	PO	PL	PL
64	C	W	PL	PL	W	C
65	PO	C	C	C	C	C
66	PL	PO	PO	PO	PO	PO
67	C	PL	PL	PL	PL	PL
68	PO	W	PO	PO	W	PL
69	PL	C	PL	PL	C	C
70	C	PO	C	C	PO	PO
71	PO	PL	PL	PL	PL	PL
72	PL	W	C	C	W	PL
73	C	C	C	C	C	C
74	PO	PO	PO	PO	PO	PO
75	PL	PL	PL	PL	PL	PL
76	C	W	W	W	W	C
77	PO	C	C	C	C	C
78	PL	PO	PO	PO	PO	PO
79	C	PL	PL	PL	PL	PL
80	PO	W	W	W	W	PO
81	PL	C	C	PO	C	C
82	C	PO	PO	PO	PO	PO

Company Number	To 1814	1815 +	1817 +	1838 +	1850 +	1869 +
83	PO	PL	PL	PL	PL	PL
84	PL	W	C	W	W	PL
85	C	C	PO	PO	C	
86	PO	PO	PO	PO	PO	
87	PL	PL	PO	PO	PL	
88	C	W	PL	W	W	
89	PO	C	W	W	C	
90	PL	PO	PO	PO	PO	
91	C	PL	PL	C	PL	
92	PO	W	PO	PO	W	
93	PL	C	PL	PL	C	
94	C	PO	W	W	PO	
95	PO	PL	C	C	PL	
96	PL	W	PO	W	W	
97	C	C	PL	W	C	
98	C	PO	W	W	PO	
99	C	PL	C	W	PL	
100	C	C	PO	W	W	
101	PO	PO	PO	C	PO	
102	PL	PL	PO	PO	PO	
103	C	C	PL	PL		
104	PO	PO	W	PL		
105	PL	PL	C	C		
106	C	C	PO	C		
107	PO	PO	PL	PO		
108	PL	PL	W	PO		
109	C	C	C	PL		
110	PO	PO	PO	PL		
111	PL	PL	PL	W		
112	C	C	W	W		
113	PO	PL	C			
114	PL	C	PO			
115	C	PL	PL			
116	PO	C	W			
117	PL	C				
118	C	C				
119	PO	C				
120	PL	C				

Company numbers exceeding No. 120 were disbanded in 1814. Prior to the year 1814 these higher Numbers had been allocated to Divisions as follows : —

CHATHAM.	121, 124, 127, 130 133.
PORTSMOUTH.	122, 125, 128, 131, 134, 136, 138, 140. 142.
PLYMOUTH.	123, 126, 129, 132, 135, 137, 139, 141, 143.
WOOLWICH.	144 -183. (Division formed in 1805 was abolished 1869)

Once the man's personal details have been found in a 'Description Book', it is necessary to note his date of discharge if he had served in the Portsmouth, Plymouth or Woolwich Divisions in order to continue the search for his service career. The index for the ADM 157/- Series, in which the service histories might be found, is alphabetical for surname and by year of 'discharge' for the three aforementioned Divisions. However, for Chatham the index year refers to the date the man 'enlisted/attested'. Due to robust weeding of archival documents in the ADM 157/- Series, the chance of finding 'your man's' papers and particulars relating to his career are slender. No documents would appear to have survived for Royal Marine Artillery men. In many of the 'Description Book' – pencil written notations of 'C', 'S', 'C/S' and 'S/M' appear alongside the men's names, providing information of the ultimate rank attained from Corporal to Sergeant Major.

In 1885 a Divisional numbering system was introduced, complemented by the creation of Service Record Books (ADM 159/- Series) for men already in the service at that time and for future entrants. These superb single page records provide all possible details pertaining to a man's career, including all his medallic awards (RM MSMs excepted to pensioners) – but are only easily obtained if the man's Division and 'Register' service number is known. Unfortunately, since no index has survived from which a man's 'Register' service number can be matched to his name, access to any marine's career in this Series usually involves a lengthy search of individual pages.

Victorian Naval LS & GC
Narrow Suspension Medal

The majestic 'Wide Suspension' type of Naval Long Service and Good Conduct medal was superseded in March 1875 by an award which was less illustrious in more ways than one. Not only was the new medal supported by a narrower 1 1/4″ ribbon, but the details engraved on its edge now lacked the number of years served by the recipient except in some rare instances, and even this uncommon practice ceased in October 1878 – by which time the machine impressed style of naming had been introduced. The image engendered by wearers of this less impressive looking new medal was diminished further since it could be awarded for as few as ten years service, whereas the 'Wide Suspension' breast symbol had visibly accorded respect to sailors and marines with its recognised minimum of twenty years 'servitude'.

These coincident changes affecting almost every aspect of this medal occurred quite by chance at the same time. Independently, the Royal Mint and the Admiralty had for several months been working towards certain new procedures, which collectively resulted in the issue of 'Narrow Suspension' medals for what was now a shorter period of service – with the edge details being changed from craftsmens' differing artistic skill of hand to the more mundane machine impressed style.

WIDE TO NARROW SUSPENDER.

In a letter to the Treasury dated 31 January 1874, the Master of the Royal Mint recommended a change in the system of manufacture and assembly of medals. Formerly, all medals supplied to the War Office, Admiralty and the India Office had been struck at the Royal Mint. The suspenders and clasps, however, were made and mounted and the medal inscribed with the recipients' details by contractors, under agreements with and advice of the Master of the Mint. The need for a new procedure was occasioned by a rising number of complaints from various Departments concerning such matters as faulty finishing, errors in naming and lengthy delays in the supply of completed medals. To overcome some of these problems the Royal Mint proposed that many outside contracts should be terminated, and that the work of manufacturing suspenders and bars/clasps as well as the mounting of them on the medal – should be undertaken by its own Department.

The opportunity also presented itself at this time for the Mint to advance another alteration in the name of 'standardisation'; that of reducing the Standard of Fineness of silver used previously for all medals (950 parts per 1,000) to the quality pertaining in the nation's silver coinage, namely, 925 parts parts per 1,000. That medals had hitherto been accorded superior status to coins of the realm was an unexpected historical discovery during this archival search.

The Treasury approved these new arrangements, which were brought into operation from 1st April 1874 :–

> '... whereby not only the production of military medals, but the setting up of them, with clasp, bars and riband will now be performed at the Mint. The lettering of them with each recipient's name being alone left to be elsewhere performed, and this latter work being given, no longer to Contractors, but to the Controller of the Royal Arsenal at Woolwich to execute ...'

Since it had already been agreed that the Admiralty were to retain their civilian contractor (Messrs Hunt and Roskill) for the lettering of awards to sailors and marines, no reference to this aspect was made by the Treasury.

The new manufacturing procedures at the Mint had no immediate effect on the issue of naval LS & GC medals, since there was no need to re-stock these awards until much later in 1874. The medal contractor (who held the stock) continued to supply this award – appropriately named – mounted with their own designed suspender to carry the unusually wide 1 1/2″ ribbon. On 16 December 1874 the Admiralty submitted a request to the Mint for their normal re-stocking order of '... 300 LS & GC medals similar to those supplied previously ...', unaware that in numismatic terms this precise wish would not be met. On 15 January 1875 these 300 'Narrow Suspension' medals were sent by the Mint to Hunt & Roskill, with the strict injunction that they were '... not to be issued until present stock is exhausted ....'

Prior to this order being placed with the Royal Mint, the decision had already been taken to 'standardise' the suspenders, which led to the normal 1 1/4″ ribbon carriage being fitted to this initial batch of naval LS & GC medals to be both made and mounted at the Royal Mint. The method of attaching the suspender was also to be different, whereby the new fabricating authority introduced a 'belt & braces' principle. The medal contractor had previously relied solely on squeezing the claws for permanent securement of suspender to the medal, but now the Mint were to drill through the middle of the claw and add a rivet before compressing together both the claw and rivet head. In many cases this was so handsomely accomplished by the craftsmen at the Mint, that a collector today may need an eye-glass to perceive the rivet heads in the centre of the claw.

Bureaucratic records make no reference to this changeover from 'Wide' to 'Narrow' suspension – only to adoption of new administrative and financial procedures. It is thus left to information forthcoming from the study of extant medals that so much gap-filling history emerges. Research of a large number of surviving naval LS & GC medals has led to the disclosure of the following empirical facts :–

Latest known award date of 'Wide Suspension' medal	23 February 1875
Earliest known award date of 'Narrow Suspension'	22 February 1875

ENGRAVED TO IMPRESSED NAMING.

Not unexpectedly, Hunt & Roskill continued to name these naval 'Narrow Suspension' medals by the hand engraving methods formerly used on their 'Wide Suspension' predecessors, but the standard of craftsmanship was to fall. The reason for this decline lay in the quite separate new 'short service' award rules, and the abolition of the unfair 'quota system' regulations simultaneously introduced by the Admiralty – described in the next part of this text. These changes naturally had the effect of dramatically increasing the number of medals presented to seamen and marines – from a monthly throughput of approximately 20 'Wide Suspension' awards to more than 300 'Narrow Suspension' medals. Within two years (1875-1877) more 'Narrow Suspension' type medals had been issued than 'Wide Suspension' awards over their entire life of 28 years (1847-1875). It was this deluge which led the Admiralty to perceive that the 'hand lettering' process was an outmoded and expensive approach. Consequently, in February 1877, their Lordships sought tenders from private firms for this work to be performed by machine.

Messrs Hunt & Roskill declined to reduce their charge of one shilling for naming each medal, whereas Mr John Pinches (Medallist of 27 Oxenden Street, Haymarket, London S.W.) submitted samples lettered by machine which he priced at sixpence per medal; this sum happened (!) to be the same as that submitted by the Royal Arsenal in 1874 for similar '... punching in ...' on army medals. On 5 March 1877 the new contract for naming naval medals, by the method referred to today as 'impressed', was awarded to Mr Pinches.

Confirmation of this change comes once more from a study of extant medals found to have been awarded at this time :–

Latest known award date of engraved 'Narrow Suspension'	14 March 1877
Earliest known award of impressed 'Narrow Suspension'	23 March 1877

By coincidence, both these particular awards were indented on their edge with details of the time served by the recipient, namely '30 Yrs' (engraved) and '22 Yrs' (impressed) respectively – as 'Years on edge variety'. This story is continued later with the probable reason for such rare exceptions to the general rule which omitted the 'years' served from the edge details of 'Narrow Suspension' medals.

QUALIFICATIONS FOR LONG SERVICE AWARD

The naval LS & GC Medal had always been awarded inequitably since its introduction in 1830. The number of medals allowed for presentation was strictly controlled and limited by a quota system tied not only to the size of the ship's company or Division ashore of the Royal Marines, but also to specific dates when recommendations would be countenanced. For Ships the allowance was one medal per 100 (RN & RM) men borne above a starting point of 50 men (smaller vessels had no entitlement), and such awards could only be awarded when a ship 'paid off' at the end of a Commission of three years (or more) duration. For those marines ashore the awards were constrained by an annual end of year 'Long Service Gratuity allowance' proportional to the size of each Port Division, which resulted in the additional inherent restriction that fewer medals could be presented if Sergeants (£15 gratuity) rather than Privates (£5 gratuity) were chosen to be the recipients. In neither sea nor shore instances was the quota of Long Service medallic awards remotely connected with the number of eligible candidates.

Minor alterations to the criteria for award took place over the next forty years. In 1853, the minimum length of service qualification was reduced from 21 years (over age 20) to 20 years (over age 18) to match revised pension regulations. It has to be remembered that from 1830 until early 1875 the award could only be earned by Pensioners, with the cryptic annotation 'P.M.& G.' (Pension. Medal & Gratuity) sometimes inscribed by the clerk on the man's record of servitude (ADM 29/- or 139/- Series). During 1860 the quota of medals was doubled, but the additional awards carried no attached gratuity ('No G'). From 1870 onwards these same quotas ('G' & 'No G') could be awarded at **any time during** a ship's commission – not solely on the date a ship was 'paid off'. This particular change did at least overcome the previous invidious situation in which :–

      (a) The medal could not be awarded until a man had served pensionable time.

Yet (b) Once a man had reached pensionable time he was to be discharged from the service as soon as possible.

The revised Regulations were however only minor variations on rules still firmly tied to the size of complements in Ships or R.M. Divisions.

A rising number of complaints caused a senior clerk at the Admiralty (Mr E.N. Swainson of P.Branch – himself a medal collector) to place a paper dated 17 April 1874 on this subject before a Member of the Board of Admiralty. Included in his submission the following relevant passage appears :–

'... representations continue to be received that the present system is unsatisfactory in its operation, and tends to exclude many deserving men from the honour of receiving this decoration ... it therefore becomes quite a matter of chance whether a man gets a medal or not, and I know cases in which really first class men have had to be refused ... the remedy appears to be to give medals irrespective of Ships ...'

The Sea Lord (Admiral Sir William Tarleton) sympathised with these views when noting that '... it is evident that the present system of awarding Good Conduct medals and gratuities is out of date and belongs to the state of things which has passed away ...' A new scheme was devised and the views of senior officers sought, from which one telling phrase is worth repetition here from amongst a mountain of opinion engendered :–

'... as these rewards are highly prized as an honourable distinction to be held by men leaving the service on being pensioned, and I may add, that they are of material assistance in obtaining for those deserving men, places of trust and responsibility on shore ...'

(Recorded by the Commanding Officer of H.M.S. *ROYAL ADELAIDE*)

ABOLITION OF QUOTA RULES AND INTRODUCTION OF TEN YEAR RULE.

It took the Admiralty several months to formulate new rules which were to annul all former restrictive and unfair conditions, with their publication ultimately appearing in Admiralty Circular P.78 dated 16 December 1874. Henceforth, all medals and gratuities (the latter unchanged pecuniary awards became derisory and were abolished in 1981) were to be awarded '... entirely irrespective of the complements of Her Majesty's Ships, ... it being the intention ... that there should not be any bar, except a man's own conduct to his obtaining those distinguishing marks of their Lordship's approbation ...' The death knell had been sounded on the 'Quota System' of LS & GC awards.

So far, so good – but there was to be an act of extreme liberalism embodied in this Circular which wholly debased the value of the (new) award. The minimum qualifying period for an award was reduced dramatically from twenty to *TEN* years. This quite extraordinary travesty of rewarding ten years servitude with a so called Long Service medal remained in force for the next decade. However, the LS & GC medal could not be awarded unless the man had 'signed on' to complete his time for pension, with the proviso that during the period of the '10 year' rule (up to 31 December 1884), the medal was to be forfeited to the Crown if the recipient left the service prior to completing fifteen years service. Confirmation of these forfeitures can be found recorded on a fair number of individual service histories of Royal Marines in the ADM 159/- series. It is also perhaps of some historical interest that the 'Gratuity' could still not be claimed before the man was recommended to receive his pension – after serving for 20 years.

'YEARS ON EDGE' VARIETY OF NARROW SUSPENSION TYPE (1875-1878).

Extensive searches have so far failed to reveal any archival records relating to this rare practice of – occasionally – placing the years served on the edge of 'Narrow Suspension' medals during their first three years of issue. Thus yet again it is the surviving medals themselves which provide the background history to this humble yet intriguing variety of the award.

Over the past twenty years, sixty-two surviving narrow suspension medals (engraved and impressed) with this exceptional edge detail have been recorded and researched, with the following collated results of this continuing endeavour.

KNOWN SURVIVING NARROW SUSPENSION LS & GC
MEDALS WITH 'YRS' ON EDGE

EDGE DETAILS ENGRAVED (38 known)

Award Date	Recipient's Name	Rate	Ship/Duty	Yrs
8 March 1875	HILL, Oswald	Master at Arms	DUKE OF WELLINGTON	20
16 March 1875	MILLETT, James	Master at Arms	ACHILLES	22
18 March 1875	BROWN, James	Yeoman of Stores	Ryl Naval Barracks	20
19 March 1875	LEE, George	Boatman	H.M.Coast Guard	33
24 March 1875	PALMER, Henry	Chief Boatman	H.M.Coast Guard	28
9 April 1875	GARD, Edward	Cmmd Boatman	H.M.Coast Guard	24
15 April 1875	SHRIMPTON, Charles	Bosun's Mate	HMS HECTOR	20
4 May 1875	WOOD, Francis	Cmmd Boatman	H.M.Coast Guard	26
4 May 1875	SULLIVAN, John	Sgt R.M.A.	9th Company	21
6 May 1875	BREEN, William	Bosun's Mate	HMS GANGES	20
19 May 1875	BARRON, Peter	Painter	HMS REVENGE	20
1 June 1875	TAMLIN, Henry	Chief Boatman	H.M.Coast Guard	28
11 June 1875	PASSINGHAM, George	Cmmd Boatman	H.M.Coast Guard	20
7 July 1875	WEST, John	Ropemaker	HMS INDUS	20
? July 1875	WARD, Edward J.	Chief Boatman	H.M.Coast Guard	23
3 July 1875	BURTENSHAW, Wm.A.	Gunner's Mate	HMS ARIEL	20
15 July 1875	PAYNE, Thomas	Admiral's Cook	HMS NORTHUMBERLAND	24
20 July 1875	FRASER, William	Cmmd Boatman	H.M.Coast Guard	22
22 July 1875	BOND, Henry C.	Quarter Master	HMS DUNCAN	20
29 July 1875	MURRAY, Andrew	Coxswain Launch	HMS EXCELLENT	20
	(Edge 'COXn Lch' and '20 Ys' – not 'Yrs')			
5 Jany 1876	CHISHOLM, James	E.R.A.	HMS ASSISTANCE	20
19 March 1876	STOWERS, John	Quarter Master	HMS VOLAGE	20
6 June 1876	WILLING, John F.	Blacksmith	HMS INDUS	20
19 July 1876	BOXALL, George	Color Sergeant	46th Coy. RMLI	20
1 Sept 1876	HEDDEN, John	Private	17th Coy. RMLI	21
22 Sept 1876	MOORE, Edwin	Chief Boatman	H.M.Coast Guard	21
29 Sept 1876	OERAM, James	Private	16th Coy. RMLI	21
14 Octr 1876	GINN, Henry	Leading Stoker	HMS DUNCAN	20
1 Decr 1876	BARDENS, Henry	Captain Fore Top	HMS ROYAL ADELAIDE	22
22 Decr 1876	PYNE, Henry	Cmmd Boatman	H.M.Coast Guard	22
11 Jany 1877	MANVELL, James	Cmmd Boatman	H.M.Coast Guard	21
7 Feby 1877	FLOWER, James H.	Able Seaman	HMS INDUS	20
15 Feby 1877	WARD, Thomas	Cmmd Boatman	H.M.Coast Guard	21
19 Feby 1877	CARR, John	Able Seaman	HMS ASIA	27
19 Feby 1877	WEST, William	Able Seaman	HMS ASIA	25
20 Feby 1877	CUNNINGHAM, Patrick	Chief Boatman	H.M.Coast Guard	30
28 Feby 1877	MANVELL, John	Bosun's Mate	DUKE OF WELLINGTON	23
14 March 1877	MILES, Thomas	Cmmd Boatman	H.M.Coast Guard	30

EDGE DETAILS IMPRESSED (24 known)

Award Date	Recipient's Name	Rate	Ship/Duty	Yrs
23 March 1877	COKER, John	Able Seaman	HMS ASIA	33
23 March 1877	HENTY, Edward	A.B.	HMS ASIA	29
31 March 1877	JONES, Eli	Shipwright	HMS ASIA	22
12 April 1877	STRAWBRIDGE, John	Boatman	H.M.Coast Guard	23
12 April 1877	GLOYNE, Joseph	Cmmd Boatman	H.M.Coast Guard	27
? April 1877	NICKERSON, James	Cmmd Boatman	H.M.Coast Guard	24
15 May 1877	LAXS, Carl	Stoker	HMS INDUS	21
? May 1877	DRISCOLL, William T.	Shipwright	HMS INDUS	20
16 May 1877	JONES, Henry	A.B.	HMS ASIA	22
15 June 1877	JARVIS, Samuel	Shipwright	HMS IMPLACABLE	20
6 July 1877	CONNOLLY, John	Chief Boatman	H.M.Coast Guard	31
July 1877	HAWKINS, Charles J.	Sgt R.M.A.	3rd Company	21
24 Sept 1877	TYTHERLEIGH, Richard	Cmmd Boatman	H.M.Coast Guard	22
16 Octr 1877	RAVEN, Frederick	Ch Btmn in Charge	H.M.Coast Guard	37
16 Octr 1877	COLE, Richard	Boatman	H.M.Coast Guard	21
17 Octr 1877	THORROWGOOD, S.I.H.	Gunner's Mate	HMS VERNON	23
8 Decr 1877	RILEY, Daniel	Boatman	H.M.Coast Guard	31
19 Feby 1878	GARNER, Frederick	Able Seaman	HMS ASIA	24
23 April 1878	LEAMAN, Theophilus R.	Quarter Master	HMS CAMBRIDGE	22
3 May 1878	SKINNER, Francis	Cmmd Boatman	H.M.Coast Guard	20
3 July 1878	EVANS, David	Ch Btmn in Charge	H.M.Coast Guard	35
19 July 1878	JEFFARD, William	Able Seaman	HMS ASIA	31
28 Augt 1878	RAWLING, William	Ch Btmn in Charge	H.M.Coast Guard	33
6 Sept 1878	TAYLOR, Thomas	Quarter Master	H.M.Yacht VICTORIA & ALBERT	24
17 Octr 1878	DACEY, Denis	Cmmd Boatman	H.M.Coast Guard	31
Yet Unknown	ELLIS, J. ('Years' in full on edge)	A.B.	HMS ASIA	21

To arrive at the reason for these exceptionally indented awards, it is necessary to examine five different chronologically sequenced periods of time, each containing an interlocking factor on this specialised subject. In the absence of crucial archival records, the following scenario is offered as the possible story behind the advent, fluctuating existence and demise of these rare types of naval LS & GC medals.

16 December 1874 to 23 February 1875.

During this period the 'Wide Suspension' medals were awarded exclusively to seamen and marines with not less than 20 years service – under the old rigid 'Quota' rules – until the elegant stock was exhausted. This continuance of former near normal procedure was achieved by the simple expedient of holding in abeyance the actual issue of medals – to the engraver – to all men approved to receive the award under the new '10 year rule' (Circular dated 16 December 1874); i.e. for those successful applicants with only 10 to 19 years servitude. Proof of this restriction comes from researching a list of seamen stated to have earned the LS & GC medal – published in the *Army and Navy Gazette* dated 20 February 1875 – which included two men whose awards (presumably unissued) were approved on 4th and 5th February but who had only served 11 and 15 years respectively.

The stock of 'Wide Suspension' medals would appear to have become exhausted during the last week of February 1875. The latest date known approving an extant 'Wide Suspension' is 23 February 1875, and the earliest date for a surviving 'Narrow Suspension' – which did not have 'Yrs' on its edge – is 22 February. This latter medal was probably issued a day or two later when the stock of 'Narrow Suspension' medals was first broached. The fact that the Admiralty re-ordered 600 medals for stock on 27 February also suggests that this timely measure coincided with the demise of 'Wide Suspension' types of award, and also with the rapid increase of applications under the new 'ten year minimum' rule.

At some stage prior to the demise of the 'Wide Suspension' medals, the established custom of indenting the 'time served' as so many 'Yrs' on all naval LS & GC medals was seen to be an outmoded custom. This practice had never been introduced on similar army awards, whilst the custom of showing the date of approval on their LS & GC medals had long since been discarded. Henceforth, most sailors and marines earning the reward would still have many years to serve before being pensioned – unlike former days when all recipients of the long service award had to be 'pensioners'.

A perceptive administrator, at that time, would have been well aware that the day was fast approaching when all future issues ('Narrow Suspension') would be distributed to both short (10-19 years) and long (20 to 30+ years) servitude men alike – with possible pangs of legitimately voiced enmity by the latter group of 'old salts/jollies.'

Might not the guiding hand of the considerate and numismatically minded Mr Swainson be detected in the differential changes to be adopted ? He had previously championed justice for all eligible men by propounding the (new) non quota rules. In all probability, in like character, he would have been against the radical reduction of 'good conduct time' to the ridiculously low figure of 10 years – henceforth the minimum criteria for issue of the paradoxically named 'Long Service ... Medal.' In fairness, it should be noted that if any man in receipt of the LS & GC medal left the service before serving for 15 years – he had to surrender his reward. No gratuity was paid until the man reached his pensionable time – 20 years adult service.

To assuage justifiable criticism from 'pensioners' earning rewards in the future, someone had the good sense to propose a palliative; namely that the customary practice of placing years on the edge should continue for future recipients qualifying with 20 or more years (old 'Wide Suspension' rule). But that this additional information concerning servitude would henceforth be omitted from the medal's edge for 'half a dog watch' men – some with as little as the minimum 10 years reckonable adult service.

23 February 1875 to late July 1875

Since the earliest known 'engraved Narrow Suspension' awards do not have years on their edge, it is presumed that priority was initially accorded to the 10-19 year applicants held in abeyance whilst all the remaining 'Wide Suspension' medals in stock were distributed. Even this general theory can be contradicted by the recent sighting and research of a LS & GC narrow suspension medal with '20 Yrs' indented on its edge awarded to George Passingham. His service records show that he became a discharged pensioner with 20 years service on 31 January 1875, but the clerk added a somewhat enigmatic notation which reads : 'Application for special medal 3 March 1875, taken up in its turn 11 June 1875.' – maybe the original application for the man's pension excluded the additional benefits of 'Medal and Gratuity' ?

From 8 March to 29 July 1875, the known number of 'Narrow Suspension' medals with 'Yrs' on the medal edge agrees roughly with the expected survival rate (marines excepted) of applications from 20+ year men. It is this observation which leads one to believe that (for this period) the old indenting (of 'Yrs') practice was continued as a general rule for 'pensioned' sailors – but maybe not for similarly qualified marines.

Late July 1875 to 18 March 1876

As the foregoing Table of surviving medals shows, this lengthy period is totally devoid of any known 'years on edge' awards. The author can only offer the following common sense reason for this temporary departure for pensioner recipients. It seems more than likely that the sheer volume of issues under the new 'ten year' rule swamped the former administrative practice of including the 'Years Served' on the naming lists sent to Messrs Hunt & Roskill – the engravers.

The scale of this flood of applications is well illustrated in the following list which shows the re-ordering details of naval LS & GC medals for stock during the period 1872-1876 :–

August	1872	300	Wide Suspension	
October	1873	300	Wide Suspension	(Final batch)
December	1874	300	Narrow Suspension	(Initial batch)
27 Feb	1875	600	Narrow Suspension	
23 March	1875	1000	Narrow Suspension	
20 July	1875	1500	Narrow Suspension	
January	1876	500	Narrow Suspension	
April	1876	500	Narrow Suspension	
December	1876	500	Narrow Suspension	

March 1876 to January 1877

With the throughput of awards now reduced to manageable proportions, the practice of indenting 'Yrs' was again possible, albeit spasmodically with (as yet) no definable criteria, since an equal number of medals issued to pensioners (20 years +) are known to be 'with' and 'without' years on the edge.

January 1877 to May 1878

By now most men completing 20 years servitude would have already received their long service medals. This would seem to have happened especially in seagoing vessels on three year commissions wherein the Divisional Officers closely watched their men's entitlement. This same strict surveillance was also obviously occurring at each Port Division of Royal Marines. It is perhaps of more than academic interest that all H.M.Ships (except *ARIEL* and *VOLAGE*) on the extant list of known medals were moored in harbour (i.e. the *ASIA & INDUS* etc), positioned to serve as Flag, Guard, Gunnery, Coast Guard and Boy's Training ships, to which may be added the Royal Yacht awaiting regal duty in Portsmouth Dockyard.

Of the five surviving 'narrows with years' known to have been issued after May 1878, it may well be no coincidence that four of these recipients had served for more than thirty years. Perhaps the earlier '20+ year rule' was extended to be a '30+ year rule' for indenting 'Yrs' on the edge (Royal Yachts excepted ?), and that this modified demi-official rule just died a natural death due to infrequent use – albeit up to 1885 some Coast Guard medals are known to have been issued to men with 30 or more years service which do not bear 'Yrs' indented on the edge.

MEDALS IN THE COLLECTION

Years on Edge Engraved

Award Date

19- 3-1875	LEE, George	Boatman	H.M.Coast Guard	33 Yrs

Entitled to   Crimea/Seb.   A.B.   ROYAL ALBERT
Turkish Crimea.

Unlike the majority of Coast Guard men who were recruited from seamen of the Royal Navy, George Lee was received into that hierarchy from the Revenue Cruizer Service – at the time when both organisations were under the control of the Board of Customs. To more readily understand his hybrid career, the reader might appreciate the following short history of the Coast Guard Service relevant to George Lee's service life.

Since 15 January 1822 the whole of the forces for the prevention of smuggling – consisting of Revenue Cruizers, Preventive Waterguard and the Riding Officers – came under the sole direction of the Board of Customs, thereby creating for the first time the generic and appropriate term of distinction – 'Coast Guard'. An establishment aided until 1831 by personnel from the Royal Navy employed on Coast Blockade duties. However, when the Blockade force was dissolved, the Admiralty increased its influence on the Coast Guard by obtaining Treasury approval to be its main recruiting source. By regulations introduced on 13 June 1831, vacancies for 'Boatmen' – the most junior rate in that service – were to be filled by seamen as H.M.Ships were paid off, chosen by their Captains as the best entitled. Additional entrants were occasionally admitted from crews of Revenue Cruizers – the Coast Guard still remaining as a whole under the control of the Board of Customs to protect the revenue (anti-smuggling), with enlarged responsibilities from 1841 to include life-saving at sea.

In 1845 a regulation was introduced which to all intents and purposes turned the Coastguard (this singular name coming into usage in 1839) into a 'Reserve' for the Royal Navy in time of war – since all future recruits to that force had to sign an agreement to serve aboard an H.M.Ship if required. The War with Russia during 1854-1855 was to prove these 'Reservists' too old and out of touch with the latest developments in the Fleet, with the result that the Admiralty gained full control of the Coastguard Service on 1st October 1856. During the parliamentary debate on this subject, Admiral Napier had told of his experience with a number of Coastguard men in his Flagship's company, who, when the chaplain began to read divine service, all pulled off their caps to display a long row of very bald heads, while every one put on spectacles ! However, the Admiral added that 'these old gentlemen, even if they were not fit to go aloft, were the steadiest men in the service and a fine example to the youngsters who have been recruited in a hurry and sent to sea without proper training.'

During his service career, George Lee was intimately connected with most of these changes. He had joined the Revenue Cruizer Service on 2 September 1841 in the rate of 'Ordinary Mariner' aboard the Cruizer *VULCAN* – the first steam vessel introduced into that service in 1835 – remaining aboard her until she was paid off from active duty in 1849, during which time he received advancement to 'Mariner' on 9 June 1845.

The employment of *VULCAN* for this period is well documented in *'Kings Cutters'* by Graham Smith (1983, pp 131-2).

After his time in the Revenue Cruizer Service he opted to transfer to the Coastguard, where after being selected he was entered in the rate of 'Boatman' on 11 October 1849. Later, in accordance with the agreement he had signed as a 'Naval Reservist', he was drafted to H.M.S. *ROYAL ALBERT* on 23 March 1854 to serve as an Able Seaman aboard her until returned to Coast Guard duties on 1st May 1856. During his time aboard the *ROYAL ALBERT* he earned the Crimea medal with Sebastopol clasp and the Turkish Crimea medal – receiving these awards on 29 November 1856.

He remained with the Coastguard as a humble 'Boatman' for another nineteen years, earning his Long Service and Good Conduct medal a month before he was retired on 30 April 1875. But there are two other historical points worth mentioning about his annual emoluments in retirement and long service award. The ultimate notation on his service document (ADM 29/82/344) reads : 'This man retires on superannuation. A Treasury man.' – an unusual entry which deserves clarification. By the regulations introduced on 13 June 1831, all civilians appointed to the Coast Guard were required to contribute to a Superannuation Fund, unlike entrants from Naval Service whose time would be aggregated as if it were sea-time towards the granting of a naval pension, and later towards a medal with or without gratuity for long service. All ex-Revenue Cruizer men like George Lee were civilian entrants whose papers had similar notations at the end of their time – when they were to be treated as Treasury men.

Regarding the award of his LS & GC medal, it was fortunate for George Lee that he had served so long in the Coastguard. Fleetmen in that service, inclusive of those who had entered from the Revenue Cruizer Service, were not entitled to the Naval Long Service and Good Conduct Medal and Gratuity until regulations extended its issue to such men in March 1873 – two years prior to his retirement after 33 years total service.

(ADM 29/82/344)

| 24- 3-1875 | PALMER, Henry | Chief Boatman | H.M.Coast Guard | 28 Yrs |

Entitled to   Crimea/Seb.   Captain of Mizzen Top ALGIERS
Turkish Crimea.

Born on 24 January 1824 in Malling, Kent. First entered the service as an Ordinary Seaman aboard H.M.S. *TRAFALGAR* on 14 January 1846, advanced to Able Seaman in February 1850. Drafted to H.M.S. *MEANDER* in June 1852 prior to joining H.M.S. *ALGIERS* in May 1854 for her participation in the Crimean War, during which time he received advancement on two occasions – to Leading Seaman in June 1854, and to Petty Officer status on 17 July 1855, but reverted to Ship's Cook on 6 April 1856 thereby suggesting that he had suffered some physical hurt. A month after being paid off from *ALGIERS* he became a Boatman in the Coast Guard Service on 11 October 1856, rising to Chief Boatman in September 1859, a rate he retained until pensioned on 31 March 1875.

(CS 15,142)

| 15- 4-1875 | SHRIMPTON, Charles | Bosun's Mate | HECTOR | 20 Yrs |

Gr 4.   Baltic.   Ord   BLENHEIM
        2nd China/-.   Ord   TRIBUNE
        Ashantee/-.   P.O. 1st Cl VICTOR EMMANUEL

Born at Portsmouth on 29 March 1836. He joined the service as Boy 2nd Class aboard H.M.S. *BLENHEIM* on 1st July 1851, and later found himself participating in the Baltic Campaign whilst aboard her until June 1856. He was immediately drafted to H.M.S. *TRIBUNE* which was sailed for Eastern waters and the war in China. On 16 August 1858 he was discharged from the service whilst at Hong Kong – '... having completed his apprenticeship as an Ordinary Seaman ...' – an unusual reason for a sailor's discharge.

Other seamen aboard *TRIBUNE* were similarly noted, including an Able Seaman with six years service – which is even more extraordinary.

Shrimpton rejoined the Navy aboard H.M.S. *TRAFALGAR* in August 1859 as an Able Seaman, subsequently advanced direct to Petty Officer status (Captain Mizzen Top) in April 1860 prior to being paid off in September 1861.

Drafted to H.M.S. *VICTOR EMMANUEL* 27 November 1873 until 29 May 1874 as Bosun's Mate. Joined H.M.S. *HECTOR* on 18 June 1874 from which vessel he was pensioned as P.O. 1st Class on 7 May 1875.

Details of the award of his medal and gratuity, approved on 15 April 1875 when he was serving as a Bosun's Mate aboard H.M.S. *HECTOR*, were only entered on his earlier Continuous Service papers under his Number 5,095.A – not as one might expect, entered on his Official Number documents which detailed his service history from 1st January 1873.   (O.No 41,271)

19- 5-1875	BARRON, Peter	Painter	REVENGE	20 Yrs

Born at Merchant's Quay, Cork on 28 March 1835. First entered the service as an Ordinary Seaman aboard H.M.S. *HOGUE* on 8 July 1856 with advancement to Able Seaman in June 1857. His talents allowed him to be rated 'Painter' – a 2nd Class Petty Officer - when joining his next vessel the *LIFFEY* on 1st May 1860. He retained this duty and rate until pensioned from H.M.S. *REVENGE* on 6 July 1876.

                                                                                     (CS 36,727 & O.No 49,898)

1- 6-1875	TAMPLIN, Henry	Cmmd Boatman	H.M. Coast Guard	28 Yrs

Entitled to : Baltic.   A.B. (as TAMLIN)   CUMBERLAND

Born at Millbrook, Cornwall on 11 April 1827. Joined the service as a Boy 1st Class aboard H.M.S. *INCONSTANT* on 24 October 1846 receiving advancement to Able Seaman in July 1850. After serving a Commission aboard H.M.S. *CUMBERLAND* (1851-1854) with his last few months aboard in Baltic waters, he joined H.M.S. *MONARCH* as Coxswain of Cutter on 28 October 1854. He joined the Coast Guard Service as a Boatman on 13 June 1858, but took twelve years to achieve advancement to Commissioned Boatman. Pensioned with 28 years total service on 30 June 1875.

                                                                                     (CS 20,100 & O.No 77,262)

3- 7-1875	BURTENSHAW, Wm.A.	Gunner's Mate	ARIEL	20 Yrs

Gr 4.	Baltic.	Boy 2nd Class	HASTINGS
	2nd China/CA57.	Ord 2nd Class	NANKIN
	2nd N.Z./1863-64	A.B.	ESK

Born at Birmingham in November 1838. Joined as a Boy 2nd Class aboard H.M.S. *VICTORY* on 9 November 1853. By the recent Admiralty Order dated 14 June 1853, no 'Boy' was to be entered under the age of 14 years, nor under the following minimum heights : – 14 to 15 years 4ft-8", 15-16 4ft-10", 16-17 5ft, 17-18 5ft-2" and over 18 years 5ft-4" Other circumstances being equal, preference for entry was given to those who could read and write.

He was drafted to H.M.S. *HASTINGS* in February 1855, and as an Ordinary Seaman 2nd Class to H.M.S. *NANKIN* on 30 August 1857 – subsequently served aboard H.M.S. *ESK* as an A.B. from May 1863 until October 1867. Pensioned and granted his LS & GC rewards as a Quarter Master aboard H.M.S. *EXCELLENT* on 3 July 1875 with 20 years servitude. (CS 5,017)

15- 7-1875	PAYNE, James	Admiral's Cook	NORTHUMBERLAND 24 Yrs
	Entitled to : Ashantee 1873-74/-. Ship's Cook		TAMAR

Born on 1st January 1833 at Bramwell, Somerset. After ten years service in the Army completed in May 1859, he joined the Royal Navy as Captain's Cook aboard H.M.S. *MERSEY* on 8 March 1860. Transferred to the flagship H.M.S. *NILE* (Rear Admiral Sir Alexander Milne) on 1st November 1862 to remain the Admiral's Cook until April 1864. In a less exalted billet he became 'Ship's Cook for General Mess' aboard H.M.S. *TAMAR* from December 1869 until drafted on 1st June 1874 to more familiar duties aboard H.M.S. *NORTHUMBERLAND* with the rate of 'Domestic 1st Class' (as Rear Admiral Lord John Hay's cook). On 5 July 1877 he received an equally prestigious draft when sent to join H.M.Royal Yacht *OSBORNE* on 5 July 1877 as 'Ship's Cook' – remaining there until at his own request discharged to shore as a pensioner on 30 September 1886 with 35 years service – of which two years under the age of eighteen served with the Army was unusually allowed to count. (ADM 29/84/218 & O.No 42,454)

22- 7-1875	BOND, Henry C.	Q.M.	DUNCAN	20 Yrs
	Gr 4. Baltic.	Ord 2nd Cl	TYNE	
	2nd China/CA57 TF58.	A.B.	HESPER	
	Ashantee 1873-74/-.	P.O. 1st Cl	RATTLESNAKE	

Born in Loose, Kent on 11 June 1836. Joined the service as a Boy 2nd Class aboard H.M.S. *FISGARD* on 24 September 1851, and subsequently drafted to H.M.S. *TYNE* in August 1852 for nearly five years encompassing the Baltic Campaign of 1854 – when *TYNE* was employed as a Store Ship. In his next vessel, the *HECTOR*, he received advancement to Able Seaman in March 1857, to Leading Seaman in April 1860 and to Petty Officer status (Quarter Master) on 13 September 1860 – taking part in the earlier actions of the Second China War.

Joined H.M.S. *RATTLESNAKE* as a Quarter Master on 13 July 1870, becoming entitled to the Ashantee medal before being paid off on 25 March 1874. Pensioned from H.M.S. *DUNCAN* on 30 August 1875. He had joined the Navy when there were no service numbers accorded to personnel, but during the remainder of his time he acquired three different Continuous Service numbers, 4,953, 32,009.A, 12,480.B and ultimately an Official Number 66,695 – from which separate sources his career has had to be constructed.

19- 2-1877	CARR, John	A.B.	ASIA	27 Yrs
	Entitled to : Crimea/Seb.	A.B.	VENGEANCE	
	Turkish Crimea.			

Born at Dunbar, Scotland on 15 January 1824. Having served a considerable time in merchant ships he was entered into the Royal Navy in the prime rate of Able Seaman on board H.M.S. *WANDERER* on 11 January 1848. Served aboard H.M.S. *VENGEANCE* from June 1850 until paid off in April 1855, and whilst aboard H.M.S. *ARROGANT* was made Leading Seaman in February 1856, prior to joining the Coast Guard Service as a Boatman in March 1857, but he had to wait eleven years before advancement to Commissioned Boatman – in which rate he was pensioned on 31 May 1871, prior to the time when Coastguard personnel could earn LS & GC medals. He re-entered the service as an A.B. (Pensioner) on 18 July 1871 to serve aboard H.M.S. *ASIA* until finally discharged to shore on 11 October 1877, but this time with a long service award for his 27 years total service.   (CS 21,659 & O.No 48,569)

20- 2-1877	CUNNINGHAM, Patrick	Chief Boatman	H.M. Coast Guard	30 Yrs

Entitled to :	Crimea/Seb. (1854)	A.B.	ARETHUSA
	Baltic.(1855)	A.B.	CRESSY
	Turkish Crimea.		

Born on 8 November 1824 at Headford, Galway. Joined the service as a Landsman aboard H.M.S. *ANDROMACHE* on 16 February 1847. Drafted to H.M.S. *ARETHUSA* in March 1851 receiving advancement to Able Seaman in June 1852 and subsequently seeing service in the Black Sea during 1854. Transferred to H.M.S. *CRESSY* on 15 January 1855 to participate in the war with Russia upon Baltic waters, earning rapid advancement to Leading Seaman in March 1855 and to Petty Officer status as Coxswain of Cutter in May 1856. Upon being paid off he joined the Coast Guard Service as a Boatman on 22 May 1857, being made a Commissioned Boatman in October 1866 and Chief Boatman in April 1874 three years before he was pensioned on 28 February 1877 – eight days after receiving his long service award.   (ADM 29/91/100 & O.No 76,385)

Years on Edge Impressed

Award Date

31- 3-1877	JONES, Eli	Shipwright	ASIA	22 Yrs

Entitled to :	Baltic.	Carp's Crew	NEPTUNE
	2nd China/CA57 TF58.	Carp's Crew	NIMROD

Born in Southampton on 9 September 1833. Joined the service with a craft skill, being entered with the rate of Carpenter's Crew aboard H.M.S. *NEPTUNE* in March 1854 prior to her sailing to Baltic waters at the commencement of the War with Russia. Drafted to H.M.S. *NIMROD* on 24 March 1857 sailing for the Far East, where Eli Jones earned another campaign medal, this time with two clasps – for actions at Canton and Taku Forts, remaining aboard until she was paid off on 1st August 1861.

After serving a Commission aboard H.M.S. *BLACK PRINCE* (1862-1866), he spent most of his remaining time aboard Base vessels at home, receiving advancement to Carpenter's Mate in November 1871, and to Shipwright in March 1876. He was awarded his LS & GC medal in March 1877 prior to his final discharge to shore from H.M.S. *ASIA* on 8 October 1878 with 24 years service.   (CS 18,008 & O.No 41,737)

12- 4-1877	STRAWBRIDGE, John	Boatman	H.M. Coast Guard	23 Yrs

Gr 4.	Crimea/Seb.	Boy 1st Cl	PROMETHEUS
	Canada G.S./F.Rd 1866.	Ldg Seaman	AURORA
	Turkish Crimea.		

Born Tantbury, Devon on 15 March 1837. Entered the service as a Boy 1st Class aboard H.M.S. *PROMETHEUS* on 26 December 1854, where he received advancement to 'Ord' two years later. Served aboard H.M.S. *VICTOR EMMANUEL* (1858-1862) being made an A.B. in June 1861, and subsequently was aboard H.M.S. *AURORA* (1863-1867) where he was advanced to Leading Seaman on 1st July 1866. Joined the Coast Guard Service as a Boatman in November 1870, but received no further promotion before receiving his awards of 'P, M & G' on 12 April 1877. Unusually, but not uniquely, his LS

& GC award was indented with the name of his parent ship for the Coast Guard Service in Southampton Water, H.M.S. *HECTOR*.   (CS 18,060)

| 16-10-1877 | RAVEN, Frederick | Ch Boatman i/c | H.M. Coast Guard | 37 Yrs |

	Entitled to :	Baltic.	A.B. (C.Gd)	PRINCE REGENT	
		Crimea/Seb.	A.B. (C.Gd)	ROYAL ALBERT	
		Turkish Crimea.			

Born in Hornsey, Kent on 25 November 1821. Entered the service as an Ordinary Seaman aboard H.M.S. *DAPHNE* on 10 June 1842, but after more than four years aboard her decided to join the Coast Guard Service as a Boatman in March 1847. Recalled for service in the Fleet for the Russian War – he was drafted to H.M.S. *PRINCE REGENT* in March 1854 as an A.B. to see action in Baltic waters, and subsequently transferred to H.M.S. *ROYAL ALBERT* during November 1854 for duty in the Crimean theatre of war.

Rejoined the Coast Guard on 9 August 1856 for more than twenty years further service, being advanced to Commissioned Boatman in July 1862, to Chief Boatman in August 1865 and Chief Boatman in Charge in August 1869. Finally pensioned on the same day – 16 October 1877 – as receiving his long service rewards. His 37 years reckonable service included one year and 302 days of bonus 'Seaman Gunner' time for the period 1860-1869, a most unusual duty in the Coast Guard Service in which to earn additionally one fifth of time actually served which was allowed to count towards his pension, medal and gratuity.   (ADM 29/80/49 & O.No 75,262)

| 23- 4-1878 | LEAMAN, Theophilus R. | Q.M. | CAMBRIDGE | 22 Yrs |

| | Entitled to : | 2nd China/-. | Boy 1st Cl/Ord | TRIBUNE | |

Born in Newton, Devon on 28 April 1840. Entered the service as a Boy 2nd Class aboard H.M.S. *IMPREGNABLE* on 23 August 1855. Drafted to H.M.S. *RALEIGH* on 24 October 1856 and sailed for Far Eastern waters but his vessel was holed on 20 May 1857 off Macao and subsequently stranded on the beach of a nearby island. He was transferred to H.M.S. *TRIBUNE* for operations during the 2nd China War and paid off from her in August 1860. Advanced to Able Seaman in July 1861, to Leading Seaman in January 1863 and to Petty Officer status (Coxswain of Cutter) in January 1865. Pensioned as a Quarter Master aboard H.M.S. *CAMBRIDGE* on 23 April 1878.

| 19- 7-1878 | JEFFARD, William | A.B. | ASIA | 31 Yrs |

Born at Lyme Regis, Dorset on 15 November 1821. Entered the service as a Boy 1st Class on 2 April 1841 aboard H.M.S. *ANDROMACHE* but left the navy two years later. He re-entered as an Ordinary Seaman when joining H.M.S. *CANOPUS* in March 1845, but it took eight more years before he received advancement to Able Seaman aboard H.M.S. *MEDEA* on the America & West Indies Station, where he achieved direct promotion to Petty Officer status (Captain of the Mast) in September 1855.

For two years (1856-1857) he was employed as a 'Seaman Rigger' in Portsmouth Dockyard, when allowed to count this shore time towards his naval pension – looked upon by the Admiralty as a naval reservist. On 11 January 1858 he joined the Coast Guard Service, rising to Commissioned Boatman in November 1861 prior to his discharge to shore as a pensioner with 23 years adult service on 31 March 1867. He re-entered the service twice more as a pensioner with rates of Ship's Cook and A.B. prior to his final discharge to civil life on 27 June 1878, receiving his long service award nearly a month later.   (CS 5,527 & O.No 70,391)

3- 7-1878	EVANS, David	Chief Boatman in Charge	H.M. Coast Guard	35 Yrs
Pair.	Crimea/Seb Azoff.	Gunner's Mate	VIPER	

Born in Cardiff, Wales on 22 June 1825. Joined the service as a Boy 1st Class aboard H.M.S. *SAN JOSEF* on 15 March 1845. Advanced to Able Seaman in December 1847, and direct to Petty Officer status (Captain of the Mizzen Top) in February 1849 – but for some unknown misdemeanour was disrated to Able Seaman in December 1853. Drafted to H.M.S. *VIPER* as a Gunner's Mate for her Commission commencing September 1854, to participate during the Crimean War in operations upon the waters of the Sea of Azoff. Joined the Coast Guard Service as a Boatman on 27 March 1859, receiving advancement to Commissioned Boatman and Chief Boatman in April and December 1864, and ultimately to Chief Boatman in Charge on 2 August 1869. Pensioned on 31st July 1878 having served a total of 35 years.   (CS 6,432 & O.No 75,639)

THE FIFTEEN YEAR RULE INTRODUCED AND PENSIONABLE TIME INCREASED TO 22 YEARS.

In 1882, Captain Harry Rawson (later Admiral Sir Harry Rawson, GCB, GCMG) – whilst serving as Flag-Captain aboard H.M.S. *ALEXANDRA* – was directed by their Lordships to investigate thoroughly many aspects of 'sailor's' administration such as Ship's Books, Forms and Parchment Certificates, Regulations concerning their Conduct and Character, awards of Good Conduct Badges and '... Good Conduct Medals and Gratuities ...'. After two years work he sought comment from many senior officers on his draft schemes before submitting his final report to a Committee (Chaired by Sir A. Hoskins, KCB) set up to examine all his proposals.

In November 1884 the Committee published their findings, with the following remarks on the matter of the 10 year rule for the long service award :–

'... fully agree with Captain Rawson, and so do all the officers we have consulted, that the good conduct medal is at present too early and too easily gained ... but disagree that it should be extended to 17 years ...'

The new rules for the award of 'Good Conduct Medals and Gratuities' were published in Fleet Circular No 36L dated 21 November 1884 whereby :–

A. A Continuous Service (CS) man had to have served fifteen consecutive years with 'Very Good' character assessments before he became eligible for a Good Conduct Medal.

B. Gratuities to CS men were now to be paid at the same time as the long service medal was approved – not deferred to the time when he was pensioned as previously decreed.

C. Non Continuous Service (NCS) Men were not to be eligible for Gratuities.

D. This change was only to effect men who entered the service after 31 December 1884, inclusive of all boys under training and under the age of 18 years the age at that date. All other men in the service were to remain subject to the existing (10 year rule) regulations.

E. The former character assessment of 'Exemplary', introduced in 1876, '... was admitted on all sides to have proved a failure ...' and was to be abolished with former such classifications corrected to 'Very Good' on men's papers. Annual character assessments were in future to be noted on Parchment Certificates as ' ' : 'V.G.' (Very Good), 'Good', 'Fair', 'Ind' (Indifferent) and 'Bad'.

F. Commanding Officers were to complete a new column on the Parchment Certificate headed with the letters 'RMG' (Recommended for Medal and Gratuity) for those CS men considered eligible after

12 years continuous 'V.G.' conduct until 15 such similar years can be completed. For NCS men the notation was to read 'RM' (Recommended for Medal) under similar rules. Although the heading of the relevant column on the Parchment Certificate was printed 'RMG', the regulations on the subject directed the letters 'MGR' and 'MR' respectively to be used – both alternative arrangements of letters have been sighted on the certificates of individual men !

There was one other major change which took place at the same time affecting the length of time a man had to serve to receive a pension, mentioned here for interest although it had no direct bearing on eligibility for the award of the LS & GC medal. All CS and NCS men joining the service or boys under training already in the service aged less than 18 years on 1st January 1885, had henceforth to serve 22 years (increased from 20 years) from the age of 18 years for CS men or 20 years of age for NCS men. The first engagement for CS men was to be for 12 years, followed by a second engagement (of 10 years) to complete their time for pension. All these new regulations relating to Pension, Medal and Gratuity (the latter abolished in 1981) which became effective on and after 1st January 1885 have – by and large – stood the test of time for more than a century.

In 1885, only the following types/grades of NCS men could earn the LS & GC medal (without gratuity): Bandmaster, Bandsman, Barber, Butcher, Domestics 1st Class (Admiral's Steward, Cook and Domestic, Captain's Steward and Cook, Wardroom Steward and Cook), 1st & 2nd Head Krooman, Krooman, Lamptrimmer, Musician, Seedie, Shoemaker, Tailor, Tindal. Most of these men had however been eligible for some years prior to 1885.

AN AID TO DATING OF LS & GC AWARD FROM DIE DIFFERENCES ON THE MEDAL'S 'REVERSE'.

Since this narrow suspension 'Type' of LS & GC medal was issued over a period of 28 years (1875-1903), it is helpful to any researcher – when trying to find a recipient's career at the Public Record Office – if a far narrower spread of years can be ascribed to the period when the reward was approved, especially in the case of recipients possessing a common set of names (forename and surname). This goal can be achieved – with the aid of an eye glass – by classifying the award in accordance with the following 'Type Table' combined with its illustrations on Plate Nos. 6 & 7.

TYPE TABLE

(*Vide* : Plate No. 14)

Type	Known issued	Mainmast Halyards	Ensign on Stern	Pennant at Peak	Engraved Impressed	Other Die differences
E	2/1875 2/1877	2-2-1	Curled	Flat	Engd	M in exergue
F	3/1877 10/1879	2-2-1	Curled	Flat	Impd	M in exergue
G	6/1880 11/1881	2-2-2	Straight	Flat	Impd	
GG	8/1883 2/1891	1 broken or faint then 2-1	Straight	Edge raised	Impd	Driver Boom gap
H	1/1892 10/1894	2-2-2	Straight	Edge raised	Impd	
J	4/1895 2/1903	1-2-1	Straight	Edge raised	Impd	Driver Boom complete

Whilst it is known that this 'Table' provides a satisfactory answer for most interpretations of the date of award generated from die differences, it has recently come to light that a few medals with 'Type J' features would appear to have been issued during the period 1882-1885.

Medals in the Collection by Rate Alphabetically

VICTORIAN NARROW SUSPENSION ENGRAVED EDGE DETAILS (TYPE E)

Rate	Ship	Recipient	Yrs	Date	
Able Seaman	ASIA	CARR, John	27	2/1877	S
Admiral's Cook	NORTHUMBERLAND	PAYNE, James	24	7/1875	S
Admiral's Coxswain	BELLEROPHON	ISAAC, Charles H.	(22)	7/1875	S
Armourer	THETIS	DINAN, Edward	(16)	1/1876	S
Blacksmith	DUKE OF WELLINGTON	HOWIE, James	(10)	8/1875	S
Bosun's Mate	HECTOR	SHRIMPTON, Charles	20	4/1875	G
Captain Forecastle	NARCISSUS	BURKE, Michael	(13)	6/1875	G
2nd Capt' Forecastle	MONARCH	COOK, James	(10)	9/1875	S
Captain Fore Top	EXCELLENT	KISSICK, Alexander	(12)	5/1875	G
Captain of Hold	CROCODILE	HUDSON, John	(20)	4/1875	G
Captain of Main Top	BLANCHE	WILCOX, Charles	(19)	5/1876	G
Captain Qtr Deck Men	CLYDE	JOHNSON, Samuel	(17)	5/1875	S
Captain Qtr Deck Men	ECLIPSE	MANSHIP, Oliver	(19)	8/1875	S
Carpenter's Crew	CROCODILE	AYLOTT, W.S.	(15)	5/1875	S
Carpenter's Mate	CYGNET	AVENT, John	(15)	9/1876	S
Caulker	LONDON	HENWOOD, John	(13)	6/1878	P
Chief Gunner's Mate	EXCELLENT	ANDREW, John F.	(17)	2/1875	S
Chief Gunner's Mate	EXCELLENT	BAKER, Edward G.	(13)	2/1875	S
Gunner's Mate	ACHILLES	STUBBINGTON, Hy.P.	(19)	5/1875	S
Coxswain of Launch	BELLEROPHON	SNEAD, William J.	(18)	7/1875	S
Domestic	VANGUARD	MUGFORD, William	(10)	6/1875	S
Engine Room Artificer	ASSISTANCE	CHISHOLM, James	20	1/1876	S
	FLORA	CHURCHER, Rchd.J.	(12)	8/1875	S
E.R.Artificer	SULTAN	HARCOURT, Michael	(19)	5/1875	S
Gunner's Mate	ARIEL	BURTENSHAW, Wm.A.	20	7/1875	G
Leading Stoker	DEVASTATION	KINGSFORD, George	(12)	6/1875	S
Leading Stoker	NYMPHE	TAYLOR, William	(17)	8/1875	S
Painter	REVENGE	BARRON, Peter	20	5/1875	S
P.O.1st Cl. QTm	ROVER	LILIENTHAL, F.	Trial piece ?		
Quarter Master	DUNCAN	BOND, Henry C.	20	7/1875	G
Quarter Master	IMPREGNABLE	EDWARDS, James	(19)	8/1875	S
Ropemaker	NEWCASTLE	QUICK, William	(14)	7/1875	S
Ropemaker	CHALLENGER	SHARPLIN, John	(14)	11/1875	S
Ship's Cook	ASIA	COLE, Henry	(11)	5/1875	S
Ship's Corporal	AMETHYST	MOONEY, John	(14)	6/1875	S
Ship's Steward	ROYAL ADELAIDE	BLOWEY, William H.	(12)	7/1875	S
Yeoman of Signals	IRON DUKE	STABLER, Robert	(11)	5/1875	S
Colour Sergeant	RMLI 46th Coy	WESTON, William	(17)	1875	G
Sergeant	RMLI 22nd Coy	BAKER, James	(21)	1875	G
Sergeant	RMLI 2nd Coy	HANSON, Thomas	(20)	1875	S
Chief Boatman i/c	HM COAST GUARD	McKINLEY, George	(20)	6/1875	S
Chief Boatman i/c	HM COAST GUARD	PIERCE, William	(24)	10/1876	S
Chief Boatman i/c	HM COAST GUARD	TICKELL, James	(27)	2/1876	S
Chief Boatman (i/c on his records)	HM COAST GUARD	WHITE, Robert	(30)	5/1875	S
Chief Boatman	HM COAST GUARD	BOND, Henry C.	20	7/1875	G

Chief Boatman	HM COAST GUARD	CUNNINGHAM, Patrick	30	2/1877	S
Chief Boatman	HM COAST GUARD	LARMAN, William	(21)	12/1876	G
Chief Boatman	HM COAST GUARD	PALMER, Henry	28	3/1875	S
Commissioned Boatman	HM COAST GUARD	McKEOWAN, James	(23)	12/1876	S
Commissioned Boatman	HM COAST GUARD	MURPHY, James	(26)	7/1875	S
Commissioned Boatman	HM COAST GUARD	TAMPLIN, Henry	28	6/1875	S
Boatman	HMS HECTOR	BYRNE, John	(19)	3/1876	S
Boatman	HM COAST GUARD	LEE, George	33	3/1875	P

Yrs = Years served when awarded medal – found from career records at PRO
Unbracketed Number = Years engraved on medal's edge
Bracketed Number = Not engraved on medal's edge
G = In a Group P = In a Pair S = Singleton

Medals in the Collection by Rate Alphabetically

VICTORIAN NARROW SUSPENSION IMPRESSED EDGE DETAILS
(TYPES F TO J)

Rate	Ship	Recipient	Yrs	Date		
A.B.	REVENGE	HARRINGTON, D.	(11)	9/1877	F	S
A.B.	HIBERNIA	BORG, John	(13)	9/1894	H	S
A.B.	ASIA	JEFFARD, William	31	7/1878	F	S
A.B. (Pensioner)	INDUS	PICKLES, Jacob	(25)	5/1881	G	S
A.B. (Rigger)	HM Yacht V & A	TEEL, William	(10)	7/1885	J	S
A.B. (Rigger)	HM Yacht V & A	WILSON, Alexander	(20)	9/1896	J	S
Actg Chief Armourer	VERNON	WATERS, William	?	?	J	S
Actg Chief Armourer	SIRIUS	ANDREWS, Frederick	?	?	H	G
Actg C.P.O.	EXCELLENT	THOMPSON, Richard	(18)	5/1893	H	G
Actg Chief Stoker	WILDFIRE	MILLEN, Thomas	(11)	3/1895	J	S
Armourer	BLAKE	HARRISON, John	?	?	H	S
Armourer	EXCELLENT	MILLS, Alfred	(10)	5/1890	GG	G
Bandmaster	SULTAN	COSTER, Charles M.H.	(25)	7/1885	GG	G
Bandsman	BLACK PRINCE	DAVIS, R.	?	?	F	S
Bandsman	WILDFIRE	STREETING, William	(10)	1/1894	G	S
Bosun's Mate	HECTOR	CHANDLER, Frederick	(25)	3/1878	F	S
Captain of Hold	HIMALAYA	NEILL, Thomas	(11)	11/1880	G	P
Captn Quarter Dk Men	TOPAZE	LONG, J.	?	?	F	S
Carpenter's Mate	SAPPHIRE	BONNEY, James	(11)	6/1877	F	G
Caulker	ASIA	RADMORE, William	(13)	8/1880	G	S
Chief Armourer	VIVID	BAILEY, W.	?	?	J	S
Chief Bosun's Mate	SPHINX	CHAPMAN, Charles	(13)	5/1886	GG	G
Ch Carpenter's Mate	THUNDERER	LANDER, Richard H.	(13)	11/1881	G	S
C.E.R.A. 2nd Class	POWERFUL	BARRETT, John T.	(15)	8/1900	J	P
Chief Petty Officer	ANDROMEDA	SILK, E.A.	(15)	3/1901	J	S
Chief Quartermaster	PENELOPE	EVANS, David W.	(16)	8/1879	H	S
Chief Quartermaster (& Pilot 1st Cl)	DASHER	LE HUGUET, John	(15)	10/1877	F	S
Chief Quartermaster	EUPHRATES	LUCAS, John J.	(14)	4/1881	G	S
Chief Stoker	ORION	PIGEON, H.E.	(15)	7/1902	J	S
Chief Stoker	PRINCE GEORGE	BROCKWAY, Robert	(20)	6/1897	J	P

Chief Stoker	DUKE OF WELLINGTON	BROWN, John	(13)	1/1901	J	G
Chief Writer	HIBERNIA	POPE, Edward T.	(15)	5/1901	J	S
Chief Yeoman Signals	COLLINGWOOD	COUGHLAN, P.	(19)	3/1897	J	S
Cooper	ASIA	MAHONEY, David	(12)	7/1890	GG	S
Domestic 1st Cl (Asst Ship's Stwd for General Mess)	TYNE	CARNON, Douglas S. (Flat Ensign, 2 Narrow-2-2)	(15)	9/1884 ?		P
Engine Room Artificer	PEMBROKE	LITTLEJOHN, Alxdr.	(12)	7/1890	GG	S
Engine Room Artificer	ASIA	OAKSHOTT, Willis	(10)	2/1886	GG	G
E.R.A. 2nd Cl	BOOMERANG	BLAGDON, S.J.T.	(10)	9/1894	H	S
E.R.A. 2nd Cl	VICTORY	WILLIAMS, John R.	(11)	11/1894	H	G
Gunner's Mate	PALLAS	McDONNELL, Richard	(10)	3/1877	F	S
Leading Stoker	VICTORY	BENNETT, Fdck.C.	(19)	3/1902	J	G
Leading Stoker	VICTORY	BENNETT, Tom	(13)	7/1892	H	G
Leading Stoker	VIVID	DOWNE, Apollo	(10)	8/1894	H	S
Leading Stoker	HIBERNIA	REDWOOD, Ebenezer	(14)	3/1890	GG	S
Ldg Stoker 1st Cl	SWALLOW	EDWARDS, David	(13)	9/1896	J	G
Ldg Stoker 1st Cl	EXCELLENT	GOFF, Charles	(10)	11/1895	J	S
Ldg Stoker 1st Cl	PEMBROKE (Chatham Torpedo Store)	LAMIE, Wm.J.R.	(13)	4/1896	J	G
Master at Arms	ENDYMION	SNOOK, James H.	(25)	1/1879	F	S
Master at Arms	CAESAR	CROUGHAN, Peter	(15)	4/1902	J	S
Musician	NORTHAMPTON	RILEY, Charles J.	(12)	11/1884	J	S
Musician	DRUID	ZARB, Charlie	(14)	12/1876	F	P
Naval Schoolmaster	LION	GILBERT, William	(10)	2/1890	GG	S
Naval Schoolmaster	IMPREGNABLE	HUTCHINGS, Samuel S.	(11)	9/1889	GG	P
Painter 1st Class	PHAETON	STAUNTON, J.H.	(12)	10/1889	GG	S
Plumber	ASIA	VEYSEY, Charles H.	(18)	3/1881	G	S
P.O. 1st Cl (Capt's Coxswain)	EDINBURGH	BOWLES, Fdck.H.	(13)	8/1890	G	P
P.O. 1st Cl	EXCELLENT	BRYANT, Wm.S.F.	(10)	3/1884	GG	G
P.O. 1st Cl	IMPERIEUSE	CHOAT, Charles A.	(14)	5/1893	H	P
P.O. 1st Cl	VIVID	CLARK, Harry	(10)	7/1892	H	P
P.O. 1st Cl	IMMORTALITE	CROWN, Arthur	(11)	4/1893	H	G
P.O. 1st Cl	VIVID	ELLIS, William H.	(10)	1/1892	H	S
P.O. 1st Cl	SUPERB	FUTCHER, Edward	(10)	2/1884	J	G
P.O. 1st Cl	VERNON	MOCKFORD, T.E.	(12)	2/1891	GG	S
P.O. 1st Cl	DREADNOUGHT	MOORE, William A.	(17)	8/1895	J	G
P.O. 1st Cl	IMPREGNABLE (HMS KINSHA)	PARSONS, Henry	(15)	2/1903	J	G
P.O. 1st Cl	MALABAR	REED, George	(10)	9/1894	H	G
P.O. 2nd Cl	VIVID	WATSON, Thomas	(10)	6/1892	H	G
Quarter Master	CAMBRIDGE	LEAMAN, Theophls.R.	22	4/1878	F	S
Quarter Master	CRUISER	STEWART, Henry	(19)	4/1877	F	S
2nd Capt' Main Top	FAWN	DELL, Henry W.	(10)	9/1878	F	S
2nd Yeoman of Signals	BRITANNIA	GRIMSHAW, Joseph	(10)	9/1894	H	S
Ship's Cook 2nd Cl	DANAE	CAMPBELL, William ex Army			G	S
Ship's Corp 1st Cl	RL NL BARRACKS Issued from old stock ?	BRUNGER, Seamon	(10)	2/1881	F	S
Ship's Corp 1st Cl	URGENT	VINES, George A.	(12)	4/1895	J	S
Ship's Steward	ANTELOPE	ORLEY, Henry	(11)	3/1877	F	S
Ship's Steward	EUPHRATES	BRUMHAM, William	(10)	1/1891	GG	G
Ship's Steward for Cadet's Mess	BRITANNIA	OLIVER, James	?	?	J	S

Ship's Steward for General Mess	TAMAR	WOODLAND, Edwin	(10)	3/1882	J1	G
Ship's Stwd 3rd Cl	ORWELL	WALE, William H.	(10)	12/1887	GG	G
Shipwright	ASIA	JONES, Eli	22	3/1877	F	S
	'Years' in full on edge					
Shoemaker	EXCELLENT	HALL, John E.	(10)	4/1879	F	S
Sick Berth Steward	ST VINCENT	COHEN, Joseph	(10)	5/1884	J	S
Signalman	HIBERNIA	DOMENICO, M.	(13)	2/1890	GG	S
Skilled Shipwright	HECLA	FABIAN, John	(12)	2/1891	GG	S
Skilled Carp's Mate	GOSHAWK	MOUNCHER, John	(10)	4/1889	GG	S
Stoker	HM Yacht V' & A'	STEVENS, H.E.	(12)	4/1895	J	S
Stoker	HM Yacht OSBORNE	STEVENSON, Thomas	(25)	2/1888	GG	S
Stoker	HM Yacht V' & A'	WARN, George	(10)	10/1879	H	S
Tailor	IMPREGNABLE	LEONARD, Charles B.	(11)	11/1877	F	S
Torpedo Artificer	VERNON	CARTER, James F.	(18)	9/1892	H	S
Torpedo Artificer	HECLA	CLEMENTS, William S.	(10)	2/1890	GG	S
Ward Room Steward	ST VINCENT	MAY, William	?	?	G	S
Ward Room Steward (Domestic 1st Cl)	RALEIGH	SCHEMBRI, Antonio	(19)	3/1878	F	S
Writer 1st Class	BOSCAWEN	POINTING, Henry	(10)	1/1889	GG	S
Writer 1st Class	ROYAL ADELAIDE	TAYLOR, Charles	(12)	4/1879	F	S
Writer 2nd Class	IMPREGNABLE	DEACON, Henry	(10)	2/1879	F	S

ROYAL MARINES

Clr Sergeant	RMA 3339	EVANS, Hugh	(10)	2/1902	J	G
Clr Sergeant	PLY 623 RMLI	RIGGS, Charles	(17)	4/1889	GG	G
Clr Sergeant	RMA 2602	SADDON, Frederick E.	(15)	2/1901	J	G
Sergeant	CH 1369 RMLI	BOTTING, Alfred	(10)	7/1888	GG	P
Sergeant	CH 3165 RMLI	HARRISON, Francis D.	(10)	9/1894	H	P
Sergeant	Depot 183 [Deal]	OWEN, William	(15)	9/1901	J	G
Sergeant	42 Coy RMLI	PARSLOW, Thomas	(19)	4/1885	J	G
Sergeant	13th Coy RMA	WHITE, Benjamin	(12)	11/1878	F	G
Private	CH 992 RMLI	GRIFFIN, Thomas	(15)	6/1891	GG	P
Pte RMLI	RL NL BARRACKS	HICKS, Edward	?	?	G	S
Private	PO 2538	LONG, John K.	(10)	5/1894	H	S
Private	PO 336 RMLI	WEST, Richard	(17)	5/1888	GG	G
Musician	CH 926 RMLI	MULFORD, Edwin	(11)	4/1888	GG	S

COAST GUARD

Ch Boatman in Charge	H.M.COAST GUARD	EVANS, David	35	7/1878	F	G
Ch Boatman in Charge	H.M.COAST GUARD	HANCOCK, John	(27)	3/1881	G	S
Ch Boatman in Charge	H.M.COAST GUARD	RAVEN, Frederick	37	10/1877	F	P
Chief Boatman	H.M.COAST GUARD	COON, William	(26)	2/1897	J	S
Commissioned Boatman	H.M.COAST GUARD	DOBEER, Richard	(14)	4/1893	H	G
Commissioned Boatman	H.M.COAST GUARD	FOX, Thomas	(21)	9/1897	J	S
Commissioned Boatman	H.M.COAST GUARD	MELHUISH, Wm.H.	(28)	3/1902	J	S
Boatman	H.M.COAST GUARD	BURSTOW, William	(19)	6/1901	J	G
Boatman	H.M.COAST GUARD	CALLAND, John	(11)	10/1878	F	S
Boatman	H.M.COAST GUARD	PENGELLEY, Wm.H.	(10)	3/1878	F	S
Boatman	H.M.COAST GUARD	SARGENT, George A.	(10)	7/1892	H	G
Boatman	H.M.COAST GUARD	WESTLAKE, A.C. &	(10)	10/1883	J	S
		'alias J. SMITH.' on edge				
Divisional Carpenter	H.M.COAST GUARD	COX, George	?	?	J	S
Divisional Carpenter	H.M.COAST GUARD	PETTY, Alexander G.	(19)	7/1899	J	S

Yrs Column. Years served when awarded medal – found from career records at PRO
  Unbracketed Number = Years engraved on medal's edge
  Bracketed Number = Not engraved on medal's edge
Type Column. F, G, GG, H, & J
Last Column G = In a Group P = In a Pair S = Singleton

RN & RM LS & GC Medals and Bars

Recognition for extra long service performed by active service personnel serving in the R.N. or R.M. – by means of a 'bar' to the long service award – was not introduced for practicable purposes until 1951. The precedent for the distinction of a 'bar' to LS & GC medals for such a purpose had, however, been set for certain naval reservists more than thirty years earlier in 1919.

However, it was not unknown in the nineteenth century for a second LS & GC medal to be awarded to a seaman or marine for extra long service, although there were no official rules governing such action. These few accidental cases almost certainly occurred due to the lack of an Admiralty medal roll for naval long service medals. The prime example of a pair of such awards became known in 1881 when the group of medals awarded to Quarter Master John Prideaux were auctioned. He had received an Anchor Type LS & GC medal (23 years) in November 1847 followed by a Victorian Wide Suspension award in March 1856 (31 years) in a group which also included medals for NGS/Navarino and China 1842 – but by the turn of the century these awards had become separated. Only one medal (NGS/Navarino) from this group has been sighted in the past 25 years – which is in the author's collection.

To place the modern rules in perspective, whereby a 'bar' is awarded for additional service of sufficient length to earn a second or third medal after 30 or 45 years service, it is worth remembering that between 1830 and 1853 it would have required 42 years to earn the modern day first 'bar', lowered to 40 years between 1853 and 1874. But the rules were then changed dramatically whereby the LS & GC medal could be awarded after only 10 years service – allowing a 'bar', had it existed, to be received after only 20 years. The modern rule of 15 years service for a long service award was introduced in 1885, which meant that the earliest date a 'bar' could have been earned – had rules for its existence been in force at that time – would have been 1915.

In May 1945 the Admiralty extended the regulations to allow issue of a 'bar' to the LS & GC medal already held by members of the R.N. and R.M. – who had completed a further fifteen years service under the same conditions governing their original award. However, their Lordships then stated a rule so contradictory as to make it impossible for any active service rating or marine to become eligible. The ridiculous paragraph stated that :–

'It is to be clearly understood that service as a mobilised pensioner or on a further engagement after having been pensioned will not count towards the award of a bar to the R.N. Medal'.

It took the Admiralty six years to alter this facile rule, whereby the only men eligible for the 'bar' would obviously have had to be pensioners – all of whom were debarred. However, in the subsequent six years four men (Bonnici, Gardiner, Kelly and Tai Sing mentioned on the medal roll which follows) did manage to circumvent these regulations – by administrative default ? – to earn 'bars'.

In June 1951 virtually the same rules for award of a 'bar' were repeated in Admiralty Fleet Order 2174/1951, but this time there was an important 'Note' stating that :–

' Pensioners who are mobilized or who re-enter on a further engagement are no longer debarred from reckoning their additional service for this purpose.'

As the subsequent roll confirms, a number of men awarded 'bars' in 1951/1952 had had to serve longer that the necessary additional 15 years – Adamson by 26 years, Boxall by 22 years and White, H. by 26 years etc – thus proving that the 1945 rules had been generally enforced. The new 1951 rules allowed retrospective award of the 'bar', but only for the men '... who would have qualified previously under these revised regulations and who are still serving ...', and repeated that no additional gratuity or pension was allowed with the award of the 'bar'.

Amongst the few statistics found concerning these awards for the 20th Century, comparative figures show that between 1925 and 1938 an average annual number of 2,500 RN/RM LS & GC medals were awarded, but less than an average of 30 'bars' a year were earned for the medals originally presented during 1920-1947 – with the number of men allowed to serve for a 'sixth five' (30 years) rising markedly during the latter (and even later) years. The ultra specialist collector will find it an extremely difficult task – but not impossible – to obtain a G.V. Admiral of the Fleet 'Obverse' LS & GC medal with a 'bar', as these 'Medal Type' dates confirm :–

Obverse. 6- 5-1931 KGV Admiral of Fleet Uniform design ceased
7- 5-1931 KGV Coinage head commenced
27- 8-1937 KGVI Coinage head commenced

[*Vide* : Plate No. 15 for all 'Obverse' Types 1830–1990]

In 1981 revised conditions for the award of the LS & GC medal were introduced by DCI RN 190/81 (Defence Council Instruction), whereby eligibility was extended to officers of the RN, RM, QARNNS who have previous service as ratings or in the ranks. Qualifying service of 15 years of unblemished service from the recently changed commencement of reckonable age – 18 years reduced to 17 1/2 years – remained, of which a minimum of 12 years must have been served as a rating or in the ranks. The award of the medal, in line with the previous conditions of award for officers of the Army and Royal Air Force, was not to attract a gratuity. Previous service to the date of the DCI could be counted.

Retrospective reckonable service time was fully allowed leading, in one case, to a mass presentation of 'bars' to eight Careers Information (ex-rating) Officers in Derby during March 1982. A further incident in Portsmouth is worth mentioning, when in March 1988 three Chief Petty Officers simultaneously left the service. All three C.P.Os. had received a second 'bar' to their LS & GC medal, the BEM and MSM – each having served for more than 48 years, completing their service as Combined Cadet Force Area Instructors.

PARTIAL ROLL OF NAVAL LS & GC MEDALS WITH BARS
(736)

This roll is incomplete since the earliest Admiralty Roll (ADM 171/140) does not comprehend all awards of the LS & GC medal issued between 1920-1928. Deficiencies also occur because the latest volume to be released (ADM 171/145) only includes awards of the original LS & GC award up to mid 1947 – thus denying knowledge of 'bars' issued after mid 1962.

O.No	Name	Rate	Ship	Medal	Bar
K 44,175	ADAMS, W.J.	S.P.O.	PERSEUS	17- 2-1939	15- 6-1954
236,899	ADAMSON, J.G.	C.P.O. Tel	C in C Po	4- 2-1926	7- 9-1951
J 23,338	ADDY, L.E.	P.O.	PEMBROKE	25- 6-1930	29- 8-1951
—	AH CHAN	A.B.	TAMAR	14- 9-1928	1- 6-1951
—	AH CHIN	Steward	CUMBERLAND	7-11-1932	1- 6-1951
—	AH GOO	Ldg Steward	DRAGON	23- 9-1942	2- 2-1955
—	AH POI	A.B.	C in C H.K.	26- 6-1923	1- 6-1951
			2nd bar to TAMAR		25-11-1953

—	AH TING	P.O. Steward	KENT	10- 4-1934	15- 2-1956
—	AH WING	Steward	TAMAR	1- 1-1941	16- 3-1960
—	AH YUNG	Steward	TAMAR	19-11-1941	16- 3-1960
C/MX 47,191	ALBON, A.S.	C.P.O. Writer	PEMBROKE	4- 6-1943	29- 4-1959
P/JX 127,543	ALDELSON, O.K.	P.O.	NILE	30-12-1944	30- 9-1957
F 55,022	ALLEN R.F.	L.A.F.	DAEDALUS	15-12-1939	9-12-1954
L 11,727	ALLEN, W.C.	Ldg Steward	VICTORY / EXMOUTH	25- 6-1935	10-10-1951
J 102,437	ANDERSON, J.L.	P.O.	COSSACK	3- 2-1939	10- 5-1957
Ch 24,209	ANGELL, R.L.	Sgt R.M.	—	3- 3-1939	23- 8-1954
M 34,696	ANTHONY, C.W.	E.A. 1st Cl	CALEDON	4- 7-1934	23- 9-1952
P/JX 128,204	APPERLEY, H.A.	P.O.	MAIDSTONE / SURF	25- 8-1944	22- 7-1959
Po 18,892	ARNOLD, H.	Cpl R.M.	—	22- 6-1931	17- 3-1952
P/JX 130,293	ARNOLD, N.	P.O.	CORMORANT / VANOC	12- 5-1944	18-10-1960
P/J 113,075	ATKINSON, W.	C.P.O.	CANOPUS	14- 1-1942	30-10-1956
M 33,239	ATRILL, G.W.	E.A. 2nd Cl	KENT	21- 8-1936	15- 3-1955
J 19,272	AUDSLEY, H.V.	Yeo Signals	GANGES	25- 6-1930	16- 9-1951
D/MX 45,114	AUSTIN, C.H.	E.A. 1st Cl	FURIOUS	25-10-1940	18-12-1956
C/JX 129,166	AVERY, J.A.T.	P.O.	TRACKER	5- 7-1944	11- 6-1959
C/M 38,862	AYLWIN, L.G.	E.A. 2nd Cl	RESOLUTION	19- 5-1942	20- 6-1954
P/MX 46,879	BACKMAN, J.E.	P.O. Cook	SCYLLA	6- 1-1943	5- 1-1958
FX 75,862	BAILEY, E.	C.P.O.A.F.	LANDRAIL	4- 1-1943	7-11-1960
P/JX 128,148	BAILEY, J.S.F.	P.O.	EXCELLENT	12- 5-1944	14- 4-1959
P/J 112,915	BAILEY, S.W.	P.O.	MAIDSTONE	4-11-1942	24- 4-1957
D/J 109,226	BAIN, J.	P.O.	GRIFFIN	9- 9-1941	14- 8-1956
C/JX 133,435	BAKER, R.	C.P.O. Tel	SMITER	17- 1-1946	19- 4-1961
J 100,380	BALDWIN, A.L.	Actg P.O.	EXCELLENT	29- 6-1937	13- 5-1953
P/JX 128,058	BALL, F.H.M.	P.O.	PALADIN	16- 8-1943	11- 5-1959
P/MX 47,882	BANGER, D.J.M.	Supply C.P.O.	VERNON	8- 1-1946	12- 3-1962
C/JX 125,265	BANKS, E.	P.O.	EDINBURGH CASTLE	27- 4-1942	31- 5-1960
M 8,393	BARBER, H.H.	O.A. 2nd Cl	EGMONT	31-10-1929	2-11-1953
Ch/X 834	BARKER, L.	C/Sgt R.M.	AJAX	18- 1-1946	6- 2-1961
J 97,056	BARNARD, E.J.	Ldg Seaman	DOLPHIN	9- 4-1937	15- 8-1957
P/MX 47,874	BARRETT, P.E.	C.P.O. Writer	HOWE	1- 4-1947	6- 4-1962
C/J 112,009	BARTLETT, C.F.	P.O.	LONDON	17-10-1941	20- 3-1957
C/JX 129,883	BATES, J.P.	P.O.	CAPETOWN	29- 9-1943	3-11-1959
J 87,262	BEDWELL, T.C.	Ldg Seaman	ANTELOPE / ST ANGELO	26-11-1935	9- 8-1957
D/J 113,883	BELL, R.V.	P.O.	DEFIANCE	20-11-1942	1-11-1957
Po 22,241	BELLGROVE, A.	Sgt R.M.	—	2- 9-1943	4- 9-1958
C/JX 132,959	BELLINGHAM, J.W.	Ch Yeo Sigs	PEMBROKE	4- 6-1946	25- 1-1963
FX 75,114	BENNETT, A.	Ldg Stoker	SUSSEX	5-12-1939	26- 8-1954
M 10,025	BENNETTS, F.R.P.	C.E.A. 2nd Cl	DUNEDIN	23-12-1929	5- 5-1952
P/MX 47,168	BERRYMAN, G.	Supply C.P.O.	WESTON / FERRET	7- 7-1943	20- 6-1958
JX 143383	BESLEY, C.I.	Ldg Seaman	BRIDGEWATER	19-10-1937	10- 5-1957
D/J 106,077	BICKELL, W.C.	P.O.	NEWCASTLE	27- 2-1940	9-12-1958
P/LX 21,082	BICKLEY, C.H.	O.Cook 1st Cl	EMERALD	31-10-1944	28- 1-1960
P/KX 79,487	BIRCH, C.J.	Stoker P.O.	ST ANGELO / RYE	10- 8-1943	9-12-1958
P/KX 79,609	BIRD, F.G.	Stoker P.O.	ROYALIST	17-12-1943	14- 4-1959
C/JX 132,720	BIRD, W.J.	C.P.O. Tel	PEMBROKE	14-12-1945	9-12-1960
C/JX 130,072	BISCOE, F.	P.O.	RESOLUTION	23- 8-1943	19- 8-1958
Po/X 1172	BISHOP F.G.	C/Sgt R.M.	—	26- 2 1946	6-12-1963

P/J 111,847	BISHOP, R.	P.O.	ORLANDO / ST MARTIN	24- 7-1942	1- 8-1957
P/J 113,834	BISSET, A.J.	P.O.	HAWKINS	4- 1-1943	6-12-1957
P/JX 132,430	BLACK, J.C.	C.P.O. Tel	DOLPHIN	12- 2-1946	9-12-1960
Po 22,130	BLACKHAM, A.J.	Sgt R.M.	—	14- 9-1939	22- 9-1954
C/JX 129,424	BLENKINSOPP, A.A.	C.P.O.	PEMBROKE	9-11-1945	30- 7-1958
P/MX 47,178	BOATE, H.B.	Supply C.P.O.	VICTORY	14- 7-1943	6-11-1958
K 60,395	BOLTON, T.	Stoker P.O.	VERITY / TAMAR may have 2 clasps	16- 8-1933	18- 8-1971
M 29,725	BOND, A.H. Duplicate medal & bar	Supply P.O.	ROCHESTER	23- 5-1933 26- 3-1971	29- 9-1953
P/J 111,864	BOND, G.W.C.	C.P.O. Tel	GLASGOW	21- 5-1942	18- 7-1957
L 6,697	BONNICI, J.	O.Stwd 2nd Cl	EGMONT	4-11-1930	12- 4-1946
P/J 115,O76	BONNOR, T.	P.O.	FAULKNOR / TYNE	29- 6-1943	27- 2-1959
J 72,607	BONSALL, H.F.	P.O.	BOADICEA/ ST ANGELO	12-10-1934	28- 3-1951
J 48,673	BORSSEL, E.J.	P.O.	ST VINCENT	16- 6-1933	10-10-1951
P/LX 20,428	BOURNE, A.	A/C.P.O. Stwd	NAIAD	1-11-1941	9-11-1956
J 94,036	BOWLES, W.	Ldg Seaman	HOOD	30-11-1936	9-11-1956
J 19,889	BOXALL, C.	P.O.	EXCELLENT	13- 8-1929	1- 1-1952
P/JX 128,997	BRADBURY, F.J.	P.O.	EXCELLENT	12- 5-1944	14- 4-1959
C/J 108,135	BRADLEY, G.E.	P.O.	SEVERN	11- 3-1940	1- 8-1957
P/JX 125,941	BRAXTON, G.L.	Chief Yeo Sigs	KING ALFRED	21- 8-1944	6-11-1958
P/KX 78,804	BRAY, R.M.	Stoker P.O.	QUEEN ELIZABETH	28- 6-1943	1-11-1957
P/MX 46,491	BRAY, S.	Sick Berth P.O.	LANKA	16-10-1942	14-10-1957
J 25,154	BRETT, W.B.	P.O.	DRAGON	20- 8-1928	22- 2-1952
J 92,548	BRINDLEY, J.	Ldg Seaman	TERROR / HAWKINS	20- 2-1934	?- 7-1952
C/JX 128,429	BRITTON, A.E.	C.P.O.	COCHRANE / WOOLSTON	30-11-1943	6-11-1958
Ply 21,029	BRITTON, W.H.	Musician R.M.	(AGRM)	22- 2-1937	9-11-1955
Ch/X 783	BROOKES, T.H.	Sgt R.M.	DRAKE	18- 9-1940	26-11-1962
C/MX 47,471	BROOKS, T.	E.A. 1st Cl	BADGER	11- 4-1944	9- 9-1960
P/MX 125,604	BROOKSHAW, A.J.	Ordnance Mechn	PHOENICIA	15- 3-1944	27- 2-1959
J 92,453	BROWN, A.W.	P.O.	ALECTO / DOLPHIN	10- 5-1935	7- 8-1951
J 77,766	BROWN, L.E.	P.O.	CAIRO	25- 6-1935	27-11-1951
Ply 22,831	BROWN, L.R.	Cpl R.M.	—	27- 1-1942	11- 1-1957
Po 21,482	BROWN, R.H.	Sgt R.M.	ENTERPRISE	15-11-1939	28-10-1954
M 35,426	BROWN, W.	O.A. 2nd Cl	GREENWICH	12-11-1931	17- 3-1952
KX 77,518	BRYAN, T.W.	Stoker P.O.	HECLA	22-11-1941	26- 1-1966
P/JX 138,810	BRYANT, G.E.	Actg P.O.	VERNON	17-10-1941	1-11-1957
J 95,974	BUCKETT, E.E.	A.B.	AMAZON / VERNON	13- 7-1937	2-11-1953
Depot 626	BUCKLEY, T.H.	Q.M.S.I. R.M.	AGRM	16- 5-1929	22- 2-1952
J 97,779	BUDD, J.F.	Ldg Seaman	WESTON	27- 8-1937	21- 5-1958
Po 22,810	BUICK, S.G.	Musician R.M.	VICTORY	16- 4-1942	20- 3-1957
D/JX 133,489	BUNKIN, S.C.	Ch Yeo Sigs	RALEIGH	6- 9-1946	5-10-1961
J 41,138	BURGESS, O.E.	P.O. Tel	PRESIDENT	23-11-1932	15- 3-1955
P/JX 129,895	BUTLER, J.S.	Ch Yeo Sigs	MERITOR	15-10-1943	15-10-1958
M 39,938	BUXTON, C.E.	R.P.O.	WARSPITE	24- 9-1937	21- 5-1958
M 37,597	CAIN F.G.	Supply P.O.	PEMBROKE	12- 7-1938	27- 2-1959
P/MX 67,762	CAIRNS, R.	M.A.A.	HOWE	31- 8-1945	7-11-1960
C/MX 45,935	CAMPBELL, J.	Sick Berth P.O.	IRON DUKE	29-12-1941	18-12-1956
Po 213,726	CAMPBELL, J.H.	Sgt R.M.	VICTORY	5-12-1928	17- 3-1952
J 13,895	CANNING, M.	P.O.	WATERHEN	27- 3-1929	17- 9-1953

J 79,537	CARMICHAEL, A.	Ldg Tel	MALAYA	23- 5-1933	14- 4-1959
P/J 113,812	CARTER, L.	C.P.O.	EXCELLENT	4-11-1942	12- 3-1962
J 102,516	CARTHEW, R.J.H.	P.O.	ST ANGELO / INGLEFIELD	25- 2-1938	13- 7-1955
P/KX 78,283	CARUTH, T.A.G.	Stoker P.O.	IMPULSIVE	5- 3-1943	18- 7-1957
J 40,769	CASEY, C.	Actg P.O.	FROBISHER	18- 1-1932	1- 1-1952
P/J 111,224	CATT, J.G.	P.O.	COCHRANE / LEEDS	2- 6-1942	14- 4-1959
P/J 113,530	CAUDRON, H.E.A.	P.O.	RAMILLIES	22- 7-1942	14-10-1957
D/MX 66,115	CAVE, W.C.	R.P.O.	PHILOETETES	20- 7-1943	6- 2-1961
D/J 113,557	CHALKLEY, H.Y.	P.O.	EDINBURGH	12- 6-1941	21- 7-1967
K 58,213	CHALLINER, A.	Mechn 2nd Cl	NEPTUNE	7-12-1934	13- 6-1955
K 58,021	CHAMBERS, H.	Stoker 1st Cl	FURIOUS	1- 2-1935	16- 6-1952
—	CHAN BOO	A.B.	CICALA	17- 4-1931	1- 6-1951
—	CHAN CHUNG	A.B.	TERN	29-12-1941	26- 6-1954
C/MX 48,179	CHAPMAN, H.F.	Sick B.C.P.O.	LANKA	13- 9-1945	25- 7-1960
D/K 64,011	CHAPPLE, A.T.	Mechn 1st Cl	EXETER	5- 5-1939	7- 7-1954
M 8,886	CHASE, A.G.	Shipt 1st Cl	VICTORY	31- 5-1932	20-11-1951
C/JX 134,078	CHATFIELD, F.J.	C.P.O. Tel	VENGEANCE	11- 4-1947	8- 4-1963
D/MX 53,292	CHEESEMAN, A.E.	R.P.O.	RALEIGH	4-11-1942	6-12-1957
JX 142552	CHEWTER, W.J.	A.B.	BLANCHE / VICTORY	9-10-1936	25- 3-1955
Ch 18,015	CHOWNE, H.J.	C/Sgt R.M.	(AGRM)	13- 8-1929	17- 3-1952
M 5,080	CHUDLEY, J.V.	C.O.A. 2nd Cl	COMUS	5-12-1927	7- 8-1951
—	CHUNG SING	Mess Boy	TAMAR	4-10-1940	30- 3-1960
Ch 24,004	CLARK, J.C.	Sgt R.M.	(AGRM)	31-12-1931	22- 2-1952
C/JX 130,955	CLARK, R.	P.O.	DIDO	16- 6-1944	11- 6-1959
M 39,347	CLARK, T.C.	R.P.O.	VIVID	19- 8-1931	19- 8-1952
J 58,590	CLIFF, F.G.	A.B.	ROYAL OAK	20- 4-1938	27- 7-1953
J 102,747	CLOETE, G.C.J.	P.O.	GALATEA	26- 4-1938	30-10-1956
P/J 112,885	CLOVER, H.C.	A.B.	QUEEN ELIZABETH	18- 6-1942	1- 8-1957
D/J 102,874	COATS, J.	P.O.	DALHOUSIE	5- 5-1939	22- 3-1954
P/JX 130,298	COCKINGS, A.E.	P.O.	VICTORY	23- 4-1945	8- 4-1960
D/JX 129,047	COCKWELL, R.E.	P.O.	PATROLLER	4- 7-1944	13- 2-1964
J 22,464	CODNER, G.C.	P.O.	VIVID	11- 9-1930	26- 9-1951
P/JX 133,599	COLE, G.M.	P.O.	EXCELLENT	5- 5-1947	6- 4-1962
C/K 64,606	COLLIER, C.H.	Stoker P.O.	ST ANGELO / OSWALD	5-12-1939	26- 8-1954
J 15,371	COLLINS, T.L.H.	P.O.	VERITY	30- 8-1929	8- 1-1959
J 98,335	CONYON, J.J.	Actg P.O.	EXETER	20- 8-1937	28- 6-1956
J 72,639	COOK, A.J.	Ldg Tel	MALCOLM / SCIMITAR	12-12-1933	20- 1-1953
C/J 108,588	COOK, B.S.	Actg P.O.	EAGLET / HURRICANE	23- 7-1941	2- 9-1957
M 39,887	COOK, J.F.	R.P.O.	DRAKE	29- 7-1937	21- 8-1953
J 20,147	COOKE, H.G.	P.O. Tel	CLEMATIS	19-10-1929	25- 3-1955
J 50,187	COOKE, S.C.	P.O.	PEMBROKE	7-11-1932	22- 2-1952
J 11,124	COOP, W.P.	Actg P.O.	HMCS STADACONA 2nd bar to VERNON	21-12-1926	17- 8-1951 22-10-1956
Ply/X 2,444	COOPER, A.E.	M.V.S. ?	—	16-10-1945	9- 9-1960
C/J 109,711	COOPER, A.G.	Ldg Tel	PRESIDENT	26- 2-1941	2- 4-1956
J 10,165	COOPER, K.T.McK.	C.P.O.	VERNON	12- 5-1928	7- 8-1951
M 39,715	CORDELL, A.E.	Ldg S.A.	VERNON	2-11-1937	3-10-1957
P/JX 130,076	CORNELIUS, M.	P.O.	VICTORY	16- 1-1945	3-11-1959
P/JX 128,006	COSENS, W.G.	P.O.	EXCELLENT	28- 3-1944	19- 1-1960
Ply 16,605	COTTER, F.	Pte R.M.	(AGRM)	29- 4-1929	17- 8-1951

P/KX 76,684	COTTRELL, G.H.	A/Stoker P.O.	COCHRANE / WESTMINSTER	19- 8-1941	21- 5-1958
D/MX 46,974	COULSON, W.D.R.	C.E.A.	RALEIGH	18- 9-1945	2- 1-1961
P/M 38,705	COWHARD, J.	P.O. Cook	ARK ROYAL	29- 3-1940	12- 1-1956
J 96,295	CRAGGS, N.D.	A.B.	BARHAM	16-12-1936	3- 2-1953
P/JX 125,484	CRAIG, A.W.	P.O.	ARGONAUT	2-12-1942	19-12-1957
M 37,441	CRANNIS, A.E.	Ldg S.A.	VIVID	7- 1-1930	28- 6-1956
J 27,927	CREASER, C.S.	P.O.	VERNON	8- 6-1931	7-11-1951
P/JX 129,534	CRESSWELL, A.N.	Actg Ldg Seaman	PROSERPINE	23- 8-1944	11- 6-1959
J 62,971	CRICK, A.R.	Ldg Seaman	EXETER	5- 7-1933	22- 2-1952
J 96,737	CRIPPS, H.R.	A/Ldg Seaman	PEMBROKE	14- 9-1937	1-11-1957
P/J 113,126	CROKE, J.W.F.	P.O.	MEDWAY	20- 7-1942	6-12-1957
P/J 106,786	CROOK, A.W.	Actg P.O.	MANCHESTER	13- 7-1940	24- 4-1957
P/JX 125,730	CROOK, R.G.	P.O.	AGGRESSIVE	13- 7-1943	8- 4-1960
K 28,697	CROSLEY, R.	Stoker P.O.	DEVONSHIRE	17-12-1930	1- 1-1952
D/JX 127,307	CROSS, R.T.	P.O.	CAROLINE II	11- 4-1944	9-12-1958
D/J 111,251	CROSSE, W.H.	P.O.	JERVIS / JACKAL	19- 2-1942	7-11-1960
M 40,026	CROUCHER, R.J.	R.P.O.	SUSSEX	17- 3-1939	13-10-1954
C/J 113,595	CROWE, J.S.	P.O.	VERNON	21- 5-1942	22- 7-1959
J 92,109	CUMMINGS, R.	P.O.	VEGA / VICTORY	7- 6-1935	18-11-1957
P/J 110,997	CURTIS, A.W.R.	P.O.	DOLPHIN	2- 9-1943	17-12-1957
D/KX 81,093	CURTIS, E.C.E.	Stoker P.O.	LOCHINVAR	1- 4-1947	27- 1-1965
J 22,230	DAMON, A.G.	C.P.O.	SUFFOLK	29- 4-1929	16- 6-1952
D/J 113,696	DANIEL, W.	P.O.	OSPREY	6- 1-1943	7-11-1960
P/MX 47,908	DANIELS, A.H.T.	Sick B.C.P.O.	SHRAPNEL / MASTODON	9- 1-1945	4-12-1959
K 33,977	DANSKIN, W.	Mechanician	DESPATCH	15- 3-1931	23- 9-1952
J 73,212	DARK, A.C.	A.B.	CRICKET / BEE	21-11-1934	28-11-1951
P/M 39,250	DARLING, G.E.	Supply P.O.	FLEETWOOD	30- 5-1940	5-12-1956
J 12.595	DAVEY, W.J.S.	P.O.	RESOLUTION	18- 3-1929	2- 7-1953
C/M 38,885	DAVIES, E.B.	E.A. 1st Cl	SHROPSHIRE	29- 3-1940	26- 9-1956
D/KX 82,311	DAVIS, S.C.	Chief Stoker	DRAKE	18- 9-1945	9-12-1960
J 14,198	DAW, W.S.C.	P.O.	CENTURION	7- 6-1929	7- 4-1953
J 62,899	DAWSON, F(?).	Ldg Seaman	DESPATCH	20- 2-1934	8- 7-1952
K 67,021	DAY, S.E.	A/Stoker P.O.	VICTORIA & ALBERT	23- 3-1936	10-10-1951
D/JX 129,097	DEADMAN, A.E.	Actg P.O.	EXCELLENT	26- 5-1944	16- 3-1960
C/MX 45,614	DENNEY, J.E.	C.E.A.	MILNE	25- 6-1945	5- 5-1960
P/MX 47,913	DINGWALL, W.J.L.	Sick B.C.P.O.	LANKA	16- 1-1945	17- 1-1960
J 74,033	DIXON, J.W.B.	P.O.	GLORIOUS	8- 6-1934	7- 4-1953
M 7,727	DIXON, R.J.	C.O.A. 2nd Cl	DURBAN	31- 3-1930	10-10-1951
K 28,385	DOBLE, T.	Stoker P.O.	VICTORY / DART	1-12-1930	29- 8-1951
C/JX 127,190	DOBSON, A.J.	P.O.	TYRIAN	5- 7-1944	15-10-1958
P/JX 127,455	DODIMEAD, D.A.	P.O.	VERNON	4- 1-1943	9- 1-1958
P/J 113,820	DOE, A.G.	P.O.Tel	PAKENHAM	4- 3-1943	6-11-1958
C/M 39,917	DONALDSON, N.A.	R.P.O.	SHROPSHIRE	5- 5-1939	13-10-1954
P/M 39,538	DORE, W.H.J.	Painter	VICTORY	20- 9-1940	23- 9-1955
P/M 38,993	DOWLING, A.W.	Supply P.O.	VICTORY	5-12-1940	27- 2-1959
J 19,478	DRAGE, A.E.	P.O.	VICTORY	8- 1-1929	30- 7-1952
K 63,136	DREW, C.H.	Ldg Stoker	MEDWAY	16-12-1938	3- 9-1953
C/JX 128,288	DRURY, N.W.	P.O. Tel	ELFIN	11- 4-1944	23-10-1961
D/JX 128,185	DUFFAY, S.M.H.	P.O.	NILE / AMETHYST	25-10-1944	3-11-1959
D/JX 126,323	DUNN, W.J.	P.O.	DEFIANCE	10- 8-1943	12- 6-1958
J 35,238	DURSTON, S.L.	Actg P.O. Tel	RODNEY	19-10-1932	17- 3-1952

C/MX 45,389	DYER, A.W.	Sick Berth P.O.	LANKA	17- 3-1941	17- 5-1956
Po 19,455	DYETT, O.R.	Sgt R.M.	(AGRM)	2- 4-1932	22- 2-1952
J 22,559	EATON, T.	P.O.	NELSON	21- 6-1929	10-10-1951
Po 217,002	EATWELL, A.G.F.	Sgt R.M.	(AGRM)	11- 5-1937	29-10-1952
J 103,951	ECCLES, E.J.	Ldg Seaman	MALAYA	19-10-1937	29- 9-1953
Ply 22,037	EDMONDSON, J.	Cpl R.M.	—	14- 7-1939	15- 3-1955
C/JX 129,488	EDWARDS, C.	P.O.	PEMBROKE	19- 6-1944	15- 7-1966
P/JX 128,090	EDWARDS, W.E.	P.O.	RAVAGER	19- 1-1944	14- 4-1959
J 98,725	EMERY, L.	P.O.	EXCELLENT	22- 2-1937	5- 4-1954
P/JX 130,053	EMERY, W.H.J.S.	P.O.	EXCELLENT	5- 6-1945	19- 1-1960
J 22,491	ENGLAND, H.P.	P.O.	DAFFODIL	9-11-1930	17- 3-1952
J 99,170	EPSLEY, P.G.	P.O.	SHOREHAM	11-10-1937	23- 9-1952
J 101,355	EUSTICE, T.O.	Ldg Seaman	APOLLO	14- 3-1938	2- 7-1953
M 35,941	EVANS, T.P.	Sick Berth P.O.	CARLISLE	10- 2-1936	16- 6-1952
Po/X 1,143	FARRAR, F.	C/Sgt R.M.	(School of Music)	5- 6-1947	29- 1-1963
D/MX 47,104	FELWICK, A.R.C.	Ch Shipwright	CARADOC	10- 8-1943	11- 5-1959
L 15,136	FERNANDO, G.A.	Ldg Steward	LANKA	2-11-1942	18-12-1956
C/L 14,584	FERNLEY, A.W.	Ldg Steward	SOUTHAMPTON	4- 8-1939	26- 8-1954
D/M 38,458	FERRIS, A.E.	C.E.A.	DEFIANCE	10- 4-1942	18- 7-1956
M 38,142	FILLER, T.W.	R.P.O.	VICTORY	14- 4-1930	17- 3-1952
P/M 38,965	FINLAY, W.J.D.	Supply C.P.O.	VICTORY	30- 5-1940	25- 2-1955
P/J 115,354	FISHER, E.G.	P.O.	ADAMANT	24- 8-1943	9-12-1958
Po/X 729	FLETCHER, H.A.	Sgt R.M.	—	9- 1-1945	19- 1-1960
Po/X 1,399	FLETCHER, P.C.	Pte R.M.	—	2- 7-1947	18- 5-1962
M 40,129	FOAD, W.J.	Actg R.P.O.	DOLPHIN	28- 3-1938	23- 2-1953
M 10,710	FORBES, E.	C.E.A. 2nd Cl	DEFIANCE	23-12-1929	7- 9-1951
Ply/X 762	FOSTER, H.W.	C/Sgt R.M.	—	4- 6-1946	17-10-1962
Ch 24,027	FOSTER, N.	Sgt R.M.	(AGRM)	13- 2-1933	27- 7-1959
D/KX 78,261	FOSTER, S.J.	Stoker P.O.	RODNEY	25- 8-1942	20- 6-1957
J 101,669	FOX, J.B.	P.O. Tel	PEMBROKE	1-11-1938	17- 9-1953
K 60,363	FOY, M.	Chief Stoker	GREENWICH	13-12-1937	4- 5-1953
C/M 39,899	FRANCIS, C.J.	M.A.A.	PEMBROKE	16- 5-1940	18-12-1955
J 40,965	FREEMAN, A.J.B.	Ldg Seaman	VERNON	30-12-1932	20-11-1951
M 39,802	FREEMAN, C.E.	R.P.O.	ST ANGELO	20- 1-1937	19- 8-1952
P/J 113,099	FROST, A.R.P.	Ldg Tel	PRESIDENT	2-12-1942	19-12-1957
Ply 22,542	FROST, H.	Sgt R.M.	—	13- 9-1940	17-11-1955
J 41,502	FROUD, W.	P.O. Tel	ROCHESTER	28- 5-1932	29- 4-1959
—	FUNG KUM SING	A.B.	MOTH	16-10-1931	1- 6-1951
RMA 11497	GARDINER, B.P.	Cpl R.M.A.	(AGRM)	15- 1-1921	20-12-1945
Ply 18,764	GARDNER, T.E.	Sgt R.M.	(AGRM)	9-10-1931	7- 4-1953
D/M 38,712	GARDNER, W.G.J.	Plumber 1st Cl	NORFOLK	27- 2-1940	10- 2-1955
D/MX 46,767	GARLAND, R.	Supply C.P.O.	FERRET	20-11-1942	4-12-1959
D/JX 125,911	GARRETT, J.E.	P.O.	NEWCASTLE	31- 3-1944	7-11-1960
L 13,771	GARRETT, P.	P.O. Steward	YORK	10- 2-1937	22- 2-1952
C/JX 147,193	GASKELL, G.E.	P.O.	OSPREY	21- 1-1944	6- 2-1961
J 42,684	GATENBY, W.V.	P.O. Tel	TITANIA	27- 3-1935	17- 2-1954
C/M 39,342	GIBSON, H.T.	Sick Berth P.O.	OXFORDSHIRE	8- 7-1940	31- 1-1956
P/MX 67,759	GILLMAN, C.C.	R.P.O.	GOSLING	17-11-1943	27- 2-1959
J 86,782	GISSING, J.A.W.	P.O.	MEDWAY	25- 6-1935	13-11-1953
C/J 111,037	GODFREY, F.	P.O. Tel	WARSPITE	4-10-1940	23-10-1961
D/JX 128,431	GOLLOP, E.G.G.	P.O.	ROBERTS	8-10-1943	9-12-1960
J 31,248	GOODMAN, C.G.	P.O.	DUNDALK / VICTORY	14-12-1931	17- 3-1952
D/JX 129,252	GOVEY, J.G.	Yeoman Signals	ST ANGELO / TEASER	14- 7-1944	30- 9-1959
D/JX 129,369	GRAHAM, L.	P.O.	SPHINX	23- 8-1943	3-11-1959

J 44,749	GRAY, A.G.	P.O.	PEMBROKE	29- 5-1933	22- 2-1952
D/JX 125,395	GREEN, A.R.E.	P.O.	KONGONI	16-10-1945	11- 6-1959
P/JX 131,049	GREEN, J.G.	P.O.	EXCELLENT	11- 4-1944	14- 4-1959
M 38,018	GREEN, M.L.	Supply P.O.	RESOLUTION	21- 8-1936	10-10-1951
C/KX 95,485	GREVETT, H.G.	Stoker P.O.	BENBOW	28- 7-1942	15-10-1958
P/J 110,473	GRIFFIN, J.C.	Actg P.O.	ARGUS	17- 2-1941	17-11-1955
C/MX 45,493	GROSS, S.F.	Ldg S.B.A.	PEMBROKE / MAINE	13- 8-1941	28- 6-1956
P/MX 45,888	GUILBERT, C.J.	C.P.O. Writer	COCHRANE	17-10-1941	20- 3-1957
D/J 115,232	GUNN, J.T.	P.O.	DRAKE	5- 8-1942	6-12-1957
M 27,255	GUY, A.E.	C.P.O. Writer	VICTORY	29- 6-1931	26- 9-1951
C/MX 47,261	GWATKIN, A.W.	Ch Shipwright	UGANDA	24- 8-1943	30- 7-1958
P/MX 46,626	HAGAN, W.H.	P.O. Cook	FERRET	24- 7-1942	18- 7-1957
P/MX 803,888	HALFORD, S.	Elect Mechn	COLLINGWOOD	14- 7-1947	23- 2-1961
P/JX 132,762	HALL, W.	P.O.	COCHRANE / WINDSOR	6- 4-1945	26- 4-1960
P/J 112,395	HAMBLIN, F.	C.P.O. Tel	INDOMITABLE	30- 9-1942	30- 9-1957
D/J 114,010	HAMBLY, H.T.	P.O.	NEWFOUNDLAND	4- 3-1943	2- 1-1958
D/J 106,371	HAMMERTON, C.A.	P.O.	DOLPHIN	27- 2-1940	4- 1-1955
D/J 112,753	HAMPSON, A.H.	Yeoman Signals	HELICON	10- 4-1942	7- 2-1957
P/JX 126,610	HANOCK, P.W.	Ldg Seaman	MERCURY	7- 1-1944	27- 2-1959
P/J 113,730	HANSON, L.A.C.	P.O.	VERNON	28- 8-1943	1-11-1957
C/J 108,298	HARBRIDGE, P.G.	P.O. Tel	PEMBROKE	8- 8-1940	26- 2-1960
C/J 113,872	HARDMAN, G.R.	Ldg Tel	PRESIDENT	25- 8-1942	19-12-1957
J 38,564	HARRAD, J.	P.O.	RAMILLIES	19- 8-1931	17- 3-1952
P/J 108,343	HARRIS, E.J.	P.O.	NELSON	12- 6-1941	27- 2-1959
Ch 23,340	HARRIS, H.H.	Sgt R.M.	COLOMBO	10- 5-1935	7-10-1934
C/J 104,931	HARRIS, R.A.	P.O.	WILD FIRE	12- 5-1939	31-12-1954
Ch/X 169	HARRIS, W.W.	Sgt R.M.	ROYAL SOVEREIGN	30- 3-1942	18-10-1957
L 13,562	HARRISON, L.P.	P.O. Steward	COURAGEOUS	17- 9-1937	19- 8-1953
P/J 106,964	HART, E.F.G.	A.B.	DUNEDIN / HAWKINS	23- 6-1939	9- 8-1957
C/JX 127,165	HART, J.H.H.	C.P.O. Tel	SUSSEX	22- 2-1943	8- 1-1959
234,645	HARTLEW, W.A.	Yeo Signals	C in C Po	11- 6-1923	23- 5-1963
C/JX 125,649	HARVEY, A.F.	P.O.	CENTURION	5- 7-1943	9- 1-1958
D/KX 80,007	HASKIN, W.	Actg Stoker P.O.	PEMBROKE / AVONDALE	25- 8-1944	24- 9-1959
C/JX 131,291	HAWES, A.E.V.	C.P.O.	PEMBROKE	17- 1-1946	9-12-1960
P/J 105,891	HAWKINS, D.H.	Seaman Rigger	ST VINCENT	24-11-1939	11-11-1954
C/JX 130,247	HAWKINS, G.	P.O.	VIGILANT	4- 9-1944	8- 4-1960
J 14,376	HAZELL, E.F.	P.O.	VERNON	5-12-1928	1- 8-1951
C/MX 46,149	HEARN, S.	Actg Ch E.A.	PHILOCTETES	27- 7-1942	9- 9-1960
Ply 17,409	HENRY, S.	Pte R.M.	(AGRM)	18-11-1929	17- 8-1951
Po 22,813	HERBERT, W.L.	Musician R.M.	VICTORY	16- 4-1942	18- 7-1957
J 107,279	HEWETT, G.R.E.	A.B.	WARSPITE	30- 8-1933	17- 3-1952
M 37,250	HIBBERD, W.H.	A/Sy.P.O.	RENOWN	18- 1-1927	26- 9-1951
C/JX 125,310	HILL, H.R.	P.O.	PEMBROKE	9- 5-1945	23- 1-1958
J 6,753	HIRST, A.W.	P.O.	EXCELLENT	30- 6-1927	22- 2-1952
D/J 109,468	HODGES, J.R.H.	P.O. Tel	VALKYRIE	10-11-1941	20- 3-1957
M 37,163	HOGBEN, H.E.	C.P.O. Writer	VICTORY	17-12-1937	7- 7-1954
Po/X 742	HOGG, J.	C/Sgt R.M.	—	16-10-1945	11- 3-1960
D/J 109,882	HOLDING, S.L.	Actg P.O.	ORION	13- 8-1941	27- 2-1959
C/J 106,740	HOLMES, G.R.	P.O.	PEMBROKE	20- 6-1940	28- 1-1960
P/MX 60,233	HOLMES, S.	Stoker P.O.	STAG	24- 7-1947	7- 2-1962
P/JX 130,949	HOLT, W.A.F.	P.O.	AURORA	11- 4-1944	18-10-1960

P/MX 48,671	HONEY, C.E.E.	Sick B.C.P.O.	VICTORY	1- 7-1946	5-10-1961
D/J 113,319	HOOKER, C.E.	Ldg Seaman	RODNEY	29-11-1941	3-11-1959
J 56,251	HOOKHAM, E.J.H.	P.O.	DOLHIN	5- 5-1933	17- 8-1951
M 25,766	HOPKINS, F.J.	S.B.P.O.	PEMBROKE	25- 5-1932	22- 2-1952
P/J 110,617	HOPKINS, G.	P.O.	EXCELLENT	16- 9-1941	19- 8-1958
K 62,798	HORABIN, S.	Mechanician	SUSSEX	26- 3-1934	22- 9-1954
J 23,590	HORROCKS, S.E.	P.O.	C in C Dev	19- 3-1926	17- 8-1951
Ply 22,517	HORTON, T.H.	Sgt R.M.	—	8-12-1939	2- 2-1955
D/KX 80,055	HOWELLS, W.J.	Chief Stoker	TYNE / WESSEX	6- 4-1945	28- 1-1960
J 101,871	HUDSON, W.T.	Actg Ldg Tel	SEALION / DOUGLAS	21- 6-1938	31- 5-1960
P/JX 130,388	HUGGINS, E.	P.O.	EXCELLENT	25- 5-1945	22- 9-1960
P/MX 46,815	HUGHES, W.H.	C.P.O. Writer	BOSCAWEN	20-11-1942	19-12-1957
D/JX 132,010	HUMPHREYS, C.E.	Yeoman Signals	DRAKE	25- 6-1945	26- 4-1960
M 35,537	HUNTLEY, E.W.	P.O. Cook	ST VINCENT	3- 8-1935	1- 1-1952
D/J 106,734	HURRING, F.G.	P.O.	NIMROD	17- 2-1941	1- 8-1957
P/J 108,492	HURST, B.	Ldg Seaman	NILE / MOHAWK	26- 6-1941	3-10-1957
D/KX 79,074	HUSBAND, W.J.W.	Stoker P.O.	BOSCAWEN	4- 3-1943	6- 5-1958
D/KX 77,441	HUSTLER, J.	Chief Stoker	DRAKE / CHURCHILL	29-11-1941	19- 1-1960
P/J 108,638	HUXFORD, G.H.	P.O. Tel	VICTORY	3- 8-1940	11- 6-1959
C/MX 47,533	INGLIS, A.M.	Supply C.P.O.	MERLIN	21- 1-1944	27- 2-1959
M 26,645	IRELAND, A.E.	C.P.O. Writer	VIVID	9- 8-1932	11- 6-1959
M 30,316	JAGO, H.D.	E.A. 1st Cl	MEDWAY	12- 7-1933	24-10-1951
D/JX 132,701	JAKES, H.F.	Actg P.O.	WHITE BEAR	4- 6-1946	29- 3-1962
D/JX 127,424	JAMES, G.R.J.	P.O.	DRAKE	23- 8-1944	22- 9-1960
Po 217,004	JAMES, W.J.C.	Sgt R.M.	SUFFOLK	4- 6-1937	20- 1-1953
J 98,933	JAMESON, F.A.	P.O.	VERNON	12-11-1937	28- 6-1956
J 53,191	JARVIS, E.B.	P.O.	CUMBERLAND	31- 3-1933	10-10-1951
D/J 113,790	JEFFERY, H.A.	P.O. Tel	DIOMEDE	17- 9-1942	6- 6-1961
C/MX 47,501	JEFFERY, J.	Supply C.P.O.	CLAVERHOUSE	12- 1-1944	27- 2-1959
D/JX 134,793	JEFFRIES, J.C.	C.P.O.	DRAKE	24-10-1947	3-10-1962
C/MX 39,618	JELLEY, C.E.	Sick Berth P.O.	LYNX	3- 4-1941	16- 4-1956
J 17,219	JENVEY, W.H.	P.O.	EXCELLENT	26- 1-1929	26- 9-1951
D/MX 48,483	JEPSON, W.	Supply C.P.O.	DRAKE	30- 1-1946	21-11-1961
P/JX 158,644	JERRUM, E.F.	P.O.	MAIDSTONE	19-11-1941	11- 1-1957
D/J 107,782	JOHNS, R.H.	P.O.	CERES	21- 3-1941	1- 8-1957
M 34,922	JOHNS, S.J.	E.R.A. 1st Cl	PROTECTOR	9- 4-1937	17- 3-1952
M 35,413	JONES, A.P.	E.A. 1st Cl	VICTORY/ WESTMINSTER	27- 2-1935	10-10-1951 bar in V & A
M 35,461	JONES, A.S.	A/C.E.A. 2nd Cl	PEMBROKE	3- 7-1935	19-12-1957
P/J 104,893	JONES, J.H.	Actg P.O.	EXCELLENT	12- 5-1939	12- 5-1954
J 47,860	JONES, W.J.	P.O.	WARSPITE	13- 2-1933	4- 6-1953
C/J 113,151	KAY, J.A.R.	P.O.	WOOLWICH	25- 8-1942	24- 9-1959
J 43,094	KAY, T.F.	Ldg Seaman	MEDWAY	5- 7-1933	1- 1-1952
Ch 23,999	KELLARD, A.	Sgt R.M.	VALIANT	2- 5-1932	26- 9-1951
Ply 17,847	KELLY, W.J.	Pte R.M.	(AGRM)	10- 2-1930	11- 7-1949
M 5,168	KELSEY, A.G.	C.O.A. 1st Cl	DESPATCH	5-12-1927	2-11-1953
P/JX 127,822	KENNETT, J.J.	C.P.O. Tel	? (illegible)	20-11-1944	11- 6-1965
J 23,569	KENT, C.A.	P.O.	VICTORY / COLNE	17- 2-1931	26- 9-1951
P/JX 129,596	KENT, G.L.	C.P.O.	EXCELLENT / VICTORY	31- 8-1943	20- 7-1958
—	KINDO, W.J.	2nd Hd Krooman	C in C Africa 2nd bar to Simonstown	10-11-1920	4-12-1954 2-12-1954
D/JX 134,124	KING, N.J.	Ldg Tel (SWS)	PRESIDENT	2-12-1946	21-11-1961
J 53,435	KINGSTON, H.G.D.	Ldg Tel	GLORIOUS	23-11-1932	13- 6-1955

D/J 112,841	KIRKPATRICK, A.J.	C.P.O. Tel	DRAKE	2-11-1942	2- 9-1957
P/JX 130,802	KITCHER, G.A.	C.P.O.	QUEEN ELIZABETH	6- 4-1945	5- 5-1960
D/J 109,021	KNIGHT, A.W.	P.O.	BONAVENTURE	27- 9-1940	5-12-1956
Ply/X 471	KNIGHT, E.H.	Cpl R.M.	—	25- 5-1945	29- 3-1962
—	KWOK YIM	A.B.	TAMAR	18- 5-1932	1- 6-1951
D/KX 79,985	LACK, S.T.	Stoker P.O.	FURIOUS	5- 7-1944	11- 6-1959
J 90,801	LAVER, C.	P.O.	MEDWAY / PEMBROKE	18-11-1935	20-12-1955
D/JX 127,972	LAW, D.W.	P.O.	ASBURY renamed ARBITER	22- 5-1944 6- 3-1945	30- 1-1959
P/LX 23,286	LAWRENCE, B.	P.O. Steward	NELSON	29- 8-1946	15- 2-1956
J 93,459	LAWRENCE, C.W.E.	P.O.	PEMBROKE	9- 9-1936	5- 5-1952
J 44,835	LAWRENCE, E.R.	Ldg Seaman	REPULSE	13-12-1937	27-11-1951
C/KX 79,730	LAWRENCE, R.	Stoker P.O.	TYNE	2-10-1942	14- 4-1958
M 37,654	LAYFIELD, J.L.	Sy P.O.	CERES	11-11-1933	4- 5-1953
M 36,957	LEAHY, W.J.	P.O. Cook	MEDWAY / PEMBROKE	9- 4-1937	8- 7-1952
J 26,796	LEDDRA, H.	P.O.	VERNON	30- 4-1930	19- 8-1952
Ply 22,776	LEDGER, T.E.S.	Cpl R.M.	(AGRM)	22- 6-1937	9-11-1955
M 35,124	LEE, A.E.	C.P.O. Writer	VICTORY	18- 7-1933	11- 1-1954
Po 213,812	LEE, J.	Sgt R.M.	(AGRM)	26- 1-1929	22- 2-1952
K 59,746	LEECH, J.	Stoker P.O.	PEMBROKE / VALOROUS	20- 3-1933	17- 9-1953
D/JX 130,509	LEEN, G.A.	P.O.	DRAKE	26- 6-1944	19- 1-1965
Ch/X 213	LEIGHTON, F.	Sgt R.M.	ROYAL SOVEREIGN	18- 6-1941	6- 2-1961
P/J 114,904	LELLIOTT, A.E.	C.P.O.	EMERALD	14- 7-1943	7- 7-1958
P/M 38,913	LENTON, F.M.	Sick Berth P.O.	VICTORY	11- 3-1940	19- 8-1958
J 1,554	LESTER, A.C.	C.P.O.	C in C Nore	30- 4-1925	17- 3-1952
M 25,925	LEUTY, H.	C.P.O. Writer	PEMBROKE	31- 5-1932	22- 2-1952
J 102,792	LEWIS, F.A.W.	Seaman Rigger	VICTORIA & ALBERT	19- 9-1938	11- 1-1954 bar in V & A
M 37,069	LEWIS, J.	R.P.O.	GANGES	21-11-1930	22- 2-1952
Po 215,142	LILLYWHITE, W.	Sgt R.M.	WARSPITE	22-12-1931	29- 8-1951
P/MX 47,876	LIMBURN, A.F.	C.P.O. Writer	VICTORY	5- 5-1947	12- 1-1970
J 39,960	LING, A.	A/P.O.	DRAGON	30-12-1932	22- 5-1953
P/J 104,125	LING, W.	P.O.	VICTORY	14- 7-1939	19- 7-1954
Ch 17,201	LITTLEWOOD, W.T.	Sgt R.M.	HERMES	10- 8-1931	22- 2-1952
Po/X 914	LLEWELLYN, H.J.	Cpl R.M.	—	31-10-1944	29- 9-1959
—	LO CHEW	A.B.	TAMAR	5-11-1927	1- 6-1951
J 22,561	LOCKYER, P.J.	P.O.	VICTORY	15- 8-1930	29- 8-1951
C/MX 61,289	LOGAN, A.	R.P.O.	NABBINGTON	5- 7-1945	9- 5-1962
D/J 109,989	LOVE, J.C.B.	P.O.	EDINBURGH CASTLE	4- 4-1942	18-12-1956
D/KX 77,479	LOWDEN, F.C.	Chief Stoker	EDINBURGH	14-11-1941	11- 6-1959
P/MX 46,553	LYON, A.E.	Actg C.O.A.	HIGHFLYER	23- 4-1945	9-12-1960
Po 215,649	LYONS, F.A.	Sgt R.M.	(AGRM)	15-11-1932	17- 3-1952
Po 18,197	MACAULEY, R.J.	Sgt R.M.	PRESIDENT	18- 3-1936	9-12-1958
D/J 108,776	MADDOCK, B.L.	C.P.O.	DRAKE / COTSWOLD	21- 3-1941	7- 7-1958
D/JX 130,986	MALLETT, A.J.	Actg P.O.	ADAMANT / TERRAPIN	13- 6-1945	25- 7-1960
C/K 66,017	MALONE, W.H.	Ldg Stoker	THANET	2- 5-1940	13- 6-1955

P/JX 126,785	MANDEVILLE, R.E.A.	C.P.O.	VICTORY	17-10-1943	17- 7-1962
J 27,689	MANN, C.H.	Seaman Rigger	VICTORIA & ALBERT	28- 2-1931	7- 8-1951
J 13,905	MANNEL, C.H.	P.O.	EXCELLENT	18- 3-1929	16- 6-1952
P/J 112,296	MANNELL, A.C.	P.O.	VICTORY	27- 7-1942	18- 7-1957
P/JX 132,931	MANSFIELD, E.P.	Ldg Tel	PRESIDENT	16- 5-1946	29- 5-1961
P/JX 130,004	MANTON, L.	P.O.	ST ANGELO / LAUDERDALE	5- 6-1945	26- 4-1960
Ply 15,837	MARRIOTT, C.H.	Sgt R.M.	RODNEY	12-11-1930	17- 3-1952
M 26,949	MARSCHNER, E.A.	E.R.A. 2nd Cl	FURIOUS	31- 8-1934	17- 8-1951
P/MX 47,675	MARSHALL, G.W.	O.A. 1st Cl	NELSON	16-10-1946	7-11-1961
D/JX 125,216	MARTIN, W.H.W.	P.O.	TARTAR	5- 7-1943	21- 5-1958
C/M 37,229	MARTYN, R.J.	E.A. 1st Cl	PEMBROKE	22-11-1940	30-10-1956
C/JX 129,101	MASON, J.R.T.B.	P.O.	WOLSEY	13- 1-1941	8- 2-1965
L 12,679	MATTHEWS, J.G.	O.C. 2nd Cl	NEPTUNE	21- 6-1935	24-10-1951 bar in V & A
J 103,699	MAY, F.	A/P.O.	VICTORY	29- 7-1937	3- 6-1954
J 41,406	McARTHUR, J.H.	P.O.	CARADOC	7-11-1932	7- 8-1951
M 1,512	McBRINN, A.P.	E.R.A. 2nd Cl	PEMBROKE	25- 3-1927	23- 2-1953
Po/X 825	Mc.C.HALLIDAY, A.	C/Sgt R.M.	PEMBROKE	18- 9-1945	5-10-1961
C/MX 45,950	McDOUGAL, N.H.	Chief E.A.	ACHILLES	29-12-1941	3-10-1957
Ch/X 159	McGUIRE, J.P.	Sgt R.M.	—	21- 3-1941	11- 6-1959
Depot X4	McILVEEN, W.D.	Pte R.M.	(AGRM)	11-10-1935	7- 8-1951
P/K 64,445	McKENZIE, H.	Stoker P.O.	VICTORY	11- 8-1939	12- 3-1957
C/JX 128,486	McPHEE, C.S.	Ldg Tel	A.C.R. / PRESIDENT	11- 4-1944	14- 4-1959
P/K 66,594	MECHEN, E.R.	Actg Stoker P.O.	NELSON	9-11-1940	29- 4-1959
C/JX 132,791	MERRETT, J.E.	C.P.O. Tel	PHOEBE	29- 1-1946	10- 8-1959
D/MX 46,031	MERWOOD, A.K.	C.E.R.A.	SPARTIATE	19- 4-1944	22- 7-1959
K 57,419	MILLER, R.D.	Ldg Stoker	DUNOON	28- 7-1931	1- 1-1952
M 33,266	MILLS, C.G.	A/C.E.R.A. 2 Cl	SCARAB / BEE	18-11-1935	31- 8-1951
Po 19,150	MILNE, A.C.E.	Sgt R.M.	DURBAN	15- 6-1934	30- 7-1952
P/M 40,249	MIST C.A.	R.P.O.	GREBE	20- 7-1943	4- 9-1958
C/JX 131,376	MITCHELL, D.	C.P.O.	VERNON	6-11-1945	18-10-1960
D/J 114,341	MITCHELL, D.F.	P.O. Tel	PRESIDENT	3- 2-1943	4- 9-1958
P/JX 132,657	MITCHELL, R.F.A.	C.P.O. Tel	COLOSSUS	4- 6-1946	25- 4-1963
C/J 112,816	MIXER C.A.	P.O.	SHROPSHIRE	10- 3-1941	11-11-1957
K 60,253	MOLE, R.W.	Stoker P.O.	VANQUISHER	30- 8-1933	27- 7-1953
D/J 114,681	MOLLOY, E.	R.P.O.	LOCHINVAR	18- 6-1942	30- 1-1959
M 7,312	MOLYNEUX, J.H.	C.P.O. Writer	VIVID	7- 6-1929	29- 8-1951
P/KX 79,564	MONNEY, R.J.	Stoker P.O.	BOSCAWEN / BEAUMARIS	29- 4-1944	31- 5-1960
P/MX 47,524	MONTAGUE, L.P.	Supply C.P.O.	FORWARD / LIZARD	8-10-1943	9-12-1958
M 28,508	MOON, E.J.	E.A. 1st Cl	MALAYA	6- 1-1933	7- 9-1951
P/LX 21,694	MOORE, A.	Ldg Steward	HOOD	1- 1-1940	9-12-1954
Ply 22,098	MOORE, B.S.	Sgt R.M.	—	27- 2-1940	25- 3-1955
D/J 114,504	MOORE, J.	Ldg Tel	PRESIDENT	20- 7-1943	6- 5-1958
P/J 115,296	MORETON, L.W.V.	P.O.	SPHINX	13- 8-1943	25- 2-1960
L 14,753	MORGAN, H.W.	P.O. Steward	VICTORY	21-11-1938	2- 1-1961
D/MX 47,499	MORRIS, W.F.	Supply P.O.	PHILOCTETES	5-11-1943	17- 3-1965
K 57,910	MORTIMER, E.S.	Stoker P.O.	DRAGON	1-10-1934	13- 7-1954
J 44,997	MORTIMER, H.S.	P.O.	PEMBROKE	16- 7-1933	4- 6-1952
D/M 38,200	MOULDER, C.F.	C.P.O. Writer	WARSPITE	14- 7-1939	23-11-1954
J 30,057	MUCKLOW, H.R.	P.O.	CORNFLOWER	7- 3-1931	21- 8-1953

D/J 107,362	MUNDAY, W.J.	P.O.	STAG	13- 8-1941	7- 7-1961
C/JX 127,738	MUNRO, J.	C.P.O.	CUMBERLAND	5- 7-1944	11- 6-1959
M 37,848	MURPHY, A.	Supply P.O.	NELSON	6- 3-1934	9-11-1955
K 21,015	MURRELL, A.R.	Stoker P.O.	BLUEBELL	8- 1-1929	29-10-1952
J 104,431	MUSTY, W.A.	Ldg Tel	WARSPITE	12- 7-1938	7-11-1961
J 36,063	MYLAM, C.L.	P.O.	VERNON	8- 6-1931	22- 2-1952
P/J 70,165	NARRAWAY, H.A.	Tel	DOLPHIN	5- 5-1939	9- 3-1954
P/M 40,126	NASH, J.L.	R.P.O.	ARK ROYAL	14- 9-1939	22- 7-1959
K 58,006	NASH, W.H.	Stoker 1st Cl	VICTORIA & ALBERT	21-11-1934	10-10-1951 bar in V & A
Ply/X 2,885	NEGUS, L.A.W.	Cpl R.M.	—	13- 6-1945	31- 6-1960
J 33,209	NEILSON, W.	P.O. Tel	RESOLUTION	21-11-1931	20-11-1951
C/JX 128,672	NEWELL, R.C.	P.O. Tel	SAMBUR	23-11-1943	6-11-1958
—	NG MOON	Stoker	ROBIN / TAMAR	18-11-1935	23-11-1954
J 40,429	NICHOLLS, S.C.	A.B.	GLORIOUS	30-12-1932	26- 6-1954
M 36,997	NICHOLS, H.G.	P.O. Cook	PEMBROKE	9- 4-1937	8- 7-1952
J 106,091	NICHOLSON, J.W.	P.O.	DRAKE	16-12-1938	10- 5-1957
D/J 107,169	NICOL, A.	Ldg Tel	RODNEY	13- 9-1940	21-11-1961
J 101,855	NOBLE, A.	Ldg Tel	DRAKE	21- 1-1938	4- 6-1953
M 5,288	NORRIS, J.H.	C.P.O. Writer	PEMBROKE	11- 2-1928	24-10-1951
P/JX 125,647	NORRIS, L.W.	P.O.	EXCELLENT	17- 9-1943	15-10-1958
K 59,544	NORTHEY, G.F.T.	Stoker P.O.	CARLISLE	21- 4-1936	26- 9-1951
J 24,244	NUNN, E.F.G.	P.O.	EXCELLENT	9-12-1930	29- 8-1951
P/MX 46,850	OAKES, G.E.	Supply P.O.	QUEBEC	2-12-1942	1-11-1957
P/JX 129,755	OAR, J.	P.O.	DAUNTLESS	20-12-1944	4-12-1959
J 36,782	O'BRIEN, W.	P.O.	MALAYA	6- 7-1931	27- 7-1953
M 39,257	OLDHAM, D.J.	Supply P.O.	HAVOCK / ST ANGELO	20- 8-1937	8- 7-1952
P/JX 127,276	OLIVER, A.D.	P.O.	ST ANGELO	5-11-1943	9-12-1958
P/KX 77,240	OLIVER, D.A.	Stoker P.O.	EAGLET / LA MALOUINE	1-11-1941	7- 7-1958
P/KX 81,207	OLIVER, F.H.	Ldg Stoker	VICTORY	5- 5-1947	8- 8-1961
M 34,115	ONG, H.	O.A. 1st Cl	DEVONSHIRE	19-12-1933	8- 3-1954
J 34,536	O'SULLIVAN, W.	A/P.O.	VIVID	19- 9-1930	28-12-1951
C/JX 128,557	OWEN, W.	P.O.	SUSSEX	19- 2-1943	10- 3-1958
D/J 114,153	PACKHAM, R.	C.P.O.	CORMORANT	24- 7-1942	18-10-1957
D/JX 130,304	PAGE, D.S.	P.O.	VERNON	8-11-1944	22- 9-1960
M 39,910	PAGE, R.A.	R.P.O.	ST ANGELO	4- 6-1937	22-10-1953
J 70,628	PAGE, W.E.D.	Ldg Seaman	OBERON / LUCIA	2-11-1934	13- 5-1953
L 2,120	PARDY, F.W.	O.S. 1st Cl	COVENTRY	4- 3-1927	24-10-1951 bar in V & A
J 103,848	PARKER, F.W.	P.O.	PEMBROKE / FORTUNE	7-11-1938	27- 9-1956
P/JX 129,740	PARKER, W.A.	P.O.	QUEEN ELIZABETH	4- 9-1944	29- 9-1959
J 86,388	PARKER, W.H.	A.B.	PETEREL / BEE	26- 3-1935	29- 8-1951
P/J 114,864	PARNELL, E.K.	P.O.	TANATSIDE	30- 6-1943	26- 4-1960
C/M 40,025	PARNHAM, J.G.	R.P.O.	PEMBROKE / RESOLUTION	14-11-1941	19-11-1956
J 96,256	PARSONS, G.H.	A.B.	BRAZEN / DRAKE	29- 7-1937	13- 6-1955
P/JX 126,637	PASSELLS, G.E.	P.O.	EXCELLENT	28- 3-1944	15-11-1962
P/KX 79,992	PATCHING, W.J.	Stoker P.O.	QUEEN ELIZABETH	19- 6-1944	22- 7-1959
P/JX 131,516	PATTERSON, J.E.	C.P.O.	EXCELLENT	18-12-1945	25- 7-1960
J 79,445	PAUL, W.H.	Ldg Signalman	AFRIKANDER	15- 2-1935	31- 8-1951
K 56,885	PEAK, W.C.	Stoker P.O.	BERWICK	17- 9-1934	26-11-1960
C/M 40,115	PEARCE, W.C.	R.P.O.	PEMBROKE	26- 2-1941	14- 8-1956
RMA 11847	PENFOLD, J.	Gnr R.M.A.	(AGRM)	30-11-1921	27- 7-1953

P/J 112,155	PERT, G.C.	P.O.	TYNE	13- 5-1942	15- 2-1957
J 45,182	PETT, W.E.	P.O.	SCARBOROUGH	3- 3-1933	22- 2-1952
D/J 106,536	PHELAN, J.J.	Actg Ldg Seaman	GLOUCESTER	14- 6-1940	9-11-1956
M 4,621	PICKETT, E.C.	Ldg Cook	ST VINCENT	27- 7-1927	19- 8-1952
M 38,932	PIKE, E.E.	Ldg S.A.	DRAGON	10- 2-1936	28- 1-1960
M 39,849	PIPKIN, G.W.	R.P.O.	VICTORY/ COURAGEOUS	21- 4-1936	1- 8-1951
RMB 2,445	PLAISTER, W.R.	Musician	EXCELLENT	16- 7-1934	24-11-1952
M 27,019	POLLARD, E.J.	Sy P.O.	BERWICK	12- 9-1932	2- 7-1953
J 35,242	POOLMAN, A.J.	P.O.	VIVID	2- 4-1932	7- 8-1951
D/J 111,763	PORTER, T.P.	A.B.	SULTAN	16- 2-1942	25- 2-1960
D/J 109,341	POTTENGER, C.W.F.	P.O.	CORMORANT / FAULKNOR	22- 9-1941	7- 2-1957
P/M 38,614	POWELL, P.J.	Plumber 1st Cl	COCHRANE	12- 4-1940	8- 8-1961
J 69,358	PRENTICE, J.	P.O. Tel	PEMBROKE	27-10-1933	22- 2-1952
J 99,627	PRESTON, W.G.	P.O.	CUMBERLAND	31- 1-1938	9- 1-1957
D/JX 129,965	PRIOR, G.G.	P.O.	VERNON	8-11-1944	30- 3-1960
D/J 107,704	PROCTER, H.J.J.	P.O.	FORTH / TIGRIS	1- 1-1941	9-12-1958
D/MX 46,042	PROVIS, R.H.	C.O.A.	BERMUDA	19- 1-1944	22- 9-1960
P/KX 79,596	PRYALL, M.F.	Stoker P.O.	ABELIA	30-11-1943	28- 2-1962
C/JX 127,806	PULLEN, L.O.	P.O.	LONDON	13- 8-1943	9- 9-1958
J 32,572	PURLAND, J.R.	A.B.	DORSETSHIRE	9- 5-1931	22-10-1954
272,437	PURNIGER, J.B.	E.R.A. 2nd Cl	C in C Dev	30- 4-1925	22- 2-1952
P/JX 125,107	QUADE, R.S.	Actg P.O.	RAMILLIES	28- 7-1942	10-10-1957
—	QUAI AH	P.O. Steward	TAMAR / TERN	29-12-1941	16- 3-1960
J 23,435	RACE, E.	P.O.	FISGARD	28- 2-1931	7- 4-1953
D/JX 130,447	RAINSBURY, F.J.	Ch Yeo Sigs	VINDICTIVE / ONSLOW	9- 5-1945	8- 4-1960
Ch 24,388	RANDALL, L.G.	C/Sgt R.M.	—	12- 4-1940	27- 9-1956
M 29,743	RANDELL, F.J.	E.A. 1st Cl	OSPREY	5- 5-1933	17- 8-1951
P/KX 77,183	RAVEN, J.R.	Stoker P.O.	VICTORY	17-10-1941	30- 7-1958
M 36,452	RAWLINGS, T.G.	C.E.A. 2nd Cl	DRAKE	11-11-1938	30-11-1956
RMB 3,016	REASEY, F.H.	Musician R.M.	—	16- 7-1943	6- 5-1958
P/K 64,619	REDSHAW, M.	Chief Stoker	VICTORY	21- 7-1939	7- 7-1958
P/JX 130,888	REED, G.W.	P.O.	EXCELLENT	29-12-1943	9-12-1958
C/JX 127,244	REES, L.D.W.	P.O.	RAJAH	14- 8-1944	10- 8-1959
C/JX 149,131	REID, G.J.	Actg Ldg Seaman	PEMBROKE	2- 6-1939	24- 4-1957
347,593	REYNOLDS, E.J.	C.P.O. Writer	C in C Africa	12- 4-1924	24-10-1951
P/M 32,735	RICHARDS, H.	E.A. 1st Cl	DOLPHIN	27- 2-1940	25- ? 1955
P/JX 132,169	RICHARDSON, F.	P.O.	OSPREY	22- 2-1944	27- 2-1959
P/M 40,242	RIDDELL, R.W.	Actg R.P.O.	SCOTIA	30- 3-1942	23- 1-1958
D/J 110,805	RIDGWAY, W.J.D.	Actg Ldg Seaman	NILE / JERVIS	2- 9-1941	8- 2-1957
M 36,751	RIDOUT, G.	C.P.O. Cook	DUNEDIN	16-11-1936	29-10-1952
C/JX 129,409	RILEY, J.H.C.	P.O.	OSPREY	22- 2-1944	27- 2-1959
C/JX 126,344	RILEY, J.T.	P.O.	SPHINX / NILE	24- 2-1943	18- 7-1957
J 97,688	ROBBINS, S.T.	Ldg Seaman	REPULSE	11-10-1937	3- 4-1956
F 55,043	ROBERTS, C.T.	P.O.A.	FORMIDABLE	20-11-1942	22- 9-1960
J 45,233	ROBERTS, H.	Ldg Signalman	DIOMEDE	16- 7-1932	1- 1-1952
P/JX 129,296	ROBERTSON, J.	P.O.	GLENDOWER / NELSON	6- 7-1944	19- 1-1960
M 28,383	ROBINSON, A.W.	E.A. 1st Cl	TAMAR / VETERAN	3- 3-1933	19-12-1957
P/MX 46,877	ROBINSON, D.C.	Sick Berth P.O.	DOLPHIN	20-11-1942	6-12-1957
P/M 39,986	ROBINSON, F.D.C.W.	R.P.O.	DOLPHIN	13- 2-1940	12- 1-1955
J 102,433	RODD, T.H.	Ldg Seaman	HARDY / ST ANGELO	14- 9-1937	3- 9-1953

J 74,748	RODGERS, R.	Ldg Tel	CORMORANT	5- 7-1933	1- 6-1951
Po 213,553	ROGERS, E.	Pte R.M.	(AGRM)	14- 9-1928	24-10-1951
C/JX 130,728	ROSENBERG, A.J.B.	Ch Yeo Sigs	PEMBROKE	9-10-1944	30- 9-1959
J 80, 563	RUFFLES, A.S.G.	A/P.O.	SUSSEX	30- 4-1935	23-11-1955
J 53,104	RUSE, W.C.	P.O.	MEDWAY	2- 5-1934	22- 5-1953
C/JX 767,985	SAMUELS, C.M.	Ch Yeo Sigs	PEMBROKE	1- 7-1946	11- 6-1959
J 50,978	SANDELL, P.C.	Ldg Signalman	RESOLUTION	18- 9-1935	7- 4-1953
P/JX 125,304	SATCHELL, R.E.	P.O.	EAGLET	12-10-1943	25- 7-1960
M 39,638	SCAGELL, R.A.	R.P.O.	EMERALD	26- 5-1930	17- 3-1952
J 95,254	SCHOFIELD, W.N.	P.O.	BRILLIANT / PEMBROKE	8- 1-1937	5- 5-1952
J 52,136	SCOTCHER, A.G.	Ldg Seaman	CORMORANT / SHAMROCK	20-10-1933	22- 2-1952
P/JX 127,913	SCOTT, C.H.	P.O.	NELSON	11- 4-1944	27- 2-1959
P/JX 127,121	SCOTT, E.V.	C.P.O. Tel	RAMILLIES	28- 3-1944	30- 1-1959
P/KX 75,951	SCOTT, J.	Stoker P.O.	EAGLET / HIGHLANDER	12- 6-1941	30- 1-1959
D/JX 125,120	SEDGEBEAR, R.	P.O.	DRAKE	30- 9-1942	2- 9-1957
K 60,780	SENIOR, W.	Chief Stoker	FROBISHER	23- 6-1933	6-12-1957
P/JX 129,145	SEYMOUR, J.H.	P.O.	ADAMANT	15- 3-1944	22- 7-1959
C/J 107,835	SHARP, C.W.	P.O.	SCARBOROUGH	8-12-1939	11-11-1957
P/JX 139,930	SHARPE, J.W.	P.O.	VICTORY	8-11-1944	19- 1-1960
Ply/X 755	SHATTOCK, J.C.	Sgt R.M.	QUEBEC	4- 6-1946	29- 5-1961
J 14,819	SHAW, A.	P.O.	SUFFOLK	29- 4-1929	17- 3-1952
J IOO,137	SHEPPARD, A.L.	A.B.	VICTORY	5- 6-1936	30- 7-1958
P/JX 129,283	SHEVINGTON, J.K.	C.P.O. Tel	HOWE	20-11-1944	19- 4-1961
M 8,391	SHIPTON, A.H.	O.A. 2nd Cl	CAIRO	10-10-1929	17- 8-1951
Po 215,152	SHORT, J.	Sgt R.M.	(AGRM)	6- 5-1932	19- 8-1952
C/JX 129,086	SIMONS, J.P.	P.O.	NEMESIS / NIMROD	11- 3-1943	30-12-1970
Po 21,889	SIMPSON, D.H.	Sgt R.M.	LEANDER	8-12-1939	21- 4-1955
M 22,027	SIMPSON, J.	E.R.A. 2nd Cl	Greenwich	18- 7-1933	1- 1-1954
—	SING CHUNG	Mess Boy	TAMAR	4-10-1940	30- 3-1960
	Original as CHUNG SING – duplicate medal & bar				13- 5-1960
J 96,997	SIZER, F.	Actg Ldg Seaman	MEDWAY	7- 3-1938	21- 8-1953
Ply 22,748	SKINNER, V.	Musician	(AGRM)	10- 2-1936	9-11-1955
J 104,077	SMITH, A.V.	P.O.	ST VINCENT	14- 1-1938	13- 5-1953
J 26,476	SMITH, F.W.	P.O.	VICTORY	6- 7-1931	22- 2-1952
D/JX 126,318	SMITH, H.	P.O.	COPRA	23-11-1943	19- 1-1960
Ply 22,805	SMITH, J.	Musician R.M.	—	28- 7-1941	27- 9-1956
M 30,324	SMITH, L.R.	E.A. 1st Cl	CORNWALL	23- 6-1933	17- 8-1951
J 6,884	SMITH, P.P.	C.P.O.	COLUMBINE	3-10-1925	23- 9-1952
P/JX 129,303	SPARROW, S.A.	P.O.	EXCELLENT	8- 3-1945	24- 9-1947
J 96,701	SPEAKMAN, F.	P.O.	VICTORY	11-10-1937	27- 7-1953
J 47,033	SPRIGGS, E.G.	P.O.	VERNON	30-12-1932	4- 4-1952
D/J 108,759	SQUIRE, E.	P.O.	DRAKE / TYNEDALE	17- 3-1941	25- 7-1960
Ply 22,836	SQUIRES, G.F.	Musician R.M.	—	10- 2-1942	8- 2-1957
M 25,414	STAFFORD, H.E.	C.E.A. 2nd Cl	RESOLUTION	6- 5-1932	7- 9-1951
J 16,151	STAINFIELD, E.	P.O.	CICALA	29- 6-1928	17- 3-1952
P/MX 47,022	STAYMAKER, E.T.	Supply C.P.O.	UKUSSA	21- 9-1945	28- 8-1961
P/M 39,985	STEELE, E.E.	R.P.O.	GRIMSBY	29- 3-1940	22- 2-1955
P/K 67,302	STEER, J.H.	Stoker P.O.	HIGHLANDER / FERRET	2- 7-1942	30- 1-1959
D/M 26,976	STEPHENS, L.C.	E.A. 1st Cl	RODNEY	5- 5-1939	17-11-1955

L 14,571	STEPHENS, S.J.V.	O.Cook 1st Cl	OSPREY	19- 9-1938	15- 3-1954
J 102,195	STOCKMAN, E.C.H.G.	P.O.	DEFIANCE	22- 2-1937	11- 1-1957
J 23,756	STONE, R.	P.O.	QUEEN ELIZABETH	15- 8-1930	17- 3-1952
Ch 22,294	STONEHOUSE, T.C.	Sgt R.M.	(AGRM)	27-10-1933	26- 9-1951
Ch 23,080	STOUT, C.F.	Musician	(AGRM)	11-10-1935	7- 8-1951
D/JX 134,322	STOVELL, R.G.	C.P.O. Tel	DRAKE	12- 8-1947	21- 6-1963
P/MX 45,508	STREEL, R.E.	L.S.B.A.	EAGLET / HIGHLANDER	17- 7-1941	4- 9-1958
M 10,021	STRIKE, F.W.	A/C.E.A. 2nd Cl	EFFINGHAM	23-12-1929	5- 5-1952
P/K 65,963	STUBBINGTON, J.	Stoker P.O.	DRAKE / DOUGLAS	9- 5-1940	11- 6-1959
J 28,559	SUMMERFIELD, C.W.	P.O.	HELITROPE	25- 8-1931	7- 4-1953
J 19,736	SUMNERS, A.N.	P.O.	CASTOR	10- 2-1930	22- 2-1952
—	TAI SING	Ldg Seaman	C in C H.K.	26- 6-1923	24-11-1950
J 77,642	TARRANT, E.	A/P.O. Tel	CAIRO	15- 3-1935	26- 4-1960
M 37,980	TAYLOR, C.A.W.	Sick Berth P.O.	ST ANGELO	27- 1-1939	17- 2-1954
D/MX 45,340	TAYLOR, L.C.	E.A. 1st Cl	VALIANT	10- 3-1941	13-12-1956
D/J 113,479	TAYLOR, S.	C.P.O.	NORMAN	18- 6-1942	12- 3-1957
J 82,376	TAYLOR, T.C.G.	P.O.	ST VINCENT	4- 7-1934	5- 4-1954
J 98,241	TAYLOR, W.F.	P.O.	BARHAM	4-10-1937	23- 9-1952
C/J 115,416	TELFORD, G.H.	Ch Yeo Sigs	DRAKE / ASHANTI	25- 5-1945	3-11-1959
C/MX 59,097	TERRY, V.E.C.	M.A.A.	PEMBROKE	11- 4-1944	29-12-1964
C/M 38,856	THOMAS, C.J.	Actg C.O.A.	PEMBROKE	19- 8-1942	19- 1-1960
J 100,097	THOMAS, G.A.L.	A/P.O.	APOLLO	26-11-1937	18-12-1956
C/MX 45,962	THOMAS, J.H.	C.P.O. Writer	BENBOW	9- 9-1944	3-11-1959
L 14,533	THOMAS, R.	O.Ck 1st Cl	FURIOUS	23- 9-1938	12- 1-1956
C/MX 46,465	THOMAS, W.E.	Shipwright 1 Cl	PEMBROKE	17- 9-1942	9- 8-1957
J 102,086	THOMAS, W.P.	Actg P.O. Tel	BARHAM	14- 3-1938	27- 9-1936
Po 22,793	THOMPSON, F.E.	L/Cpl R.M.	—	10-12-1942	30-11-1961
M 26,650	THOMPSON, G.J.	C.P.O. Writer	VIVID	9- 8-1932	17- 3-1952
C/J 125,449	THOMPSON, R.C.	Actg Ldg Seaman	WATCHMAN / FERRET	31- 8-1943	6-11-1958
M 39,913	THOROGOOD, C.G.	R.P.O.	CUMBERLAND	2-11-1937	26- 5-1954
D/JX 129,480	TILLEY, H.E.	P.O.	ST GEORGE	20-11-1944	3-11-1959
J 105,543	TINSLEY, N.W.	P.O.	EXCELLENT	8- 6-1938	20- 6-1957
K 23,309	TOMS, W.J.	A/Ldg Stoker	DELHI / VIVID	5-12-1929	22- 2-1952
Po 215,041	TONGE, T.W.	Sgt R.M.	(AGRM)	6- 1-1932	17- 3-1952
P/J 111,973	TOWNSEND, A.	P.O.	INDOMITABLE	17-10-1941	15- 2-1957
C/M 38,233	TOWNSEND, W.G.	Sick Berth P.O.	MAINE	4- 8-1939	8-11-1954
J 21,479	TREVETHAN, A.E.	P.O.	NORFOLK	4-10-1930	27- 7-1953
J 104,235	TRUST, T.W.	P.O.	GALATEA	27- 1-1939	8- 3-1954
P/KX 77,340	TURNBULL, T.	Actg Stoker P.O.	VICTORY	27- 7-1943	7- 7-1958
C/M 39,515	TURNBULL, W.F.	Shipwright 2 Cl	DELHI	28- 7-1942	9- 8-1957
P/JX 133,129	TURNER, R.	C.P.O.	TAMAR	4- 6-1946	26-11-1962
C/JX 132,561	TURNER, R.C.	Ldg Tel	PRESIDENT	25- 5-1945	8- 4-1960
P/MX 46,367	TURNER, W.A.	C.P.O. Writer	VICTORY	2- 6-1942	18- 7-1957
Ply 22,291	TWAITES, E.J.	C/Sgt R.M.	—	2- 5-1940	15- 9-1955
P/JX 125,303	TWINE, W.F.J.	C.P.O.	EXCELLENT	2- 6-1942	18- 7-1957
P/JX 133,037	TYLER, R.L.	P.O.	VICTORY	29- 8-1946	4-10-1961
D/JX 139,709	TYSON, E.W.G.	Ldg Seaman	DRAKE	16- 2-1942	15-10-1958
M 39,571	USHER, J.F.	R.P.O.	C in C Po	11- 3-1926	29- 9-1952
Ply/X 476	VEASEY, R.	Pte R.M.	VICTORIOUS	30- 9-1944	22- 7-1959
J 13,081	VECK, H.A.	P.O.	ASSISTANCE	17-12-1928	19- 1-1960

C/KX 80,181	VENUS, J.B.	Stoker P.O.	SUFFOLK	9- 5-1945	4-12-1959
P/J 111,529	VINCENT, C.E.	P.O.	DESPATCH	19-11-1941	14- 1-1963
C/MX 47,532	WALES, A.F.	Sick B.P.O.	PRESIDENT	12-10-1943	9-12-1958
J 38,793	WALKER, T.M.	P.O.	QUEEN ELIZABETH	3-10-1931	20-11-1951
P/MX 46,843	WALTERS, H.C.L.	C.P.O. Writer	LANKA	4- 2-1943	19-12-1957
J 72,602	WARD, A.E.	P.O.	DURBAN	26- 9-1934	22- 5=1953
C/MX 76,394	WARD, S.E.	R.P.O.	LONDON	19- 1-1944	22- 7-1959
Ply 22,613	WARD, S.J.	Pte R.M.	(AGRM)	20- 8-1937	24-10-1951
M 40,060	WARD, W.J.	A/R.P.O.	ST VINCENT	11- 5-1937	22- 2-1952
C/J 109,723	WARD, W.L.	Ldg Seaman	SHROPSHIRE	2- 1-1942	11-11-1957
J 78,289	WARE, A.E.E.	A/P.O.	CARDIFF / VINDICTIVE	28- 6-1935	1-11-1957
C/J 115,141	WARR, G.B.J.	P.O.	DOLPHIN	9- 5-1945	28- 1-1960
P/J 107,947	WARREN, R.F.	P.O. Tel	KIMBERLEY	9- 5-1940	27- 9-1956
J 29,668	WATKINS, A.H.E.	P.O.	PEMBROKE	20- 1-1931	1- 1-1952
C/JX 128,992	WATSON, H.W.	C.P.O.	VICTORY	5- 7-1944	23- 1-1961
P/MX 46,825	WATSON, J.A.	C.P.O. Writer	VICTORY	20-11-1942	6-11-1958
J 100,258	WATTS, D.	Actg Ldg Tel	TAMAR	8- 6-1938	7- 2-1957
J 103,175	WATTS, F.B.	Actg P.O.	VERNON	17- 2-1939	10- 3-1938
P/JX 128,210	WATTS, P.H.	C.P.O.	BELFAST	14- 7-1944	22- 7-1959
C/JX 132,286	WATTS, W.	Ch Yeo Sigs	WOOLLOOMOOLOO	29- 4-1946	19- 4-1961
M 39,719	WEAVEN, R.R.	R.P.O.	PEMBROKE	8- 6-1934	1- 8-1951
M 38,239	WEAVIS, B.A.	Supply P.O.	VICTORY / PENZANCE	26- 8-1937	15- 9-1955
J 72,854	WEBB, E.	Ldg Tel	CALCUTTA	17- 9-1934	4-11-1952
C/J 114,118	WEBB, J.	Ldg Tel	PRESIDENT	28-12-1942	19-12-1957
J 105,029	WEBB, S.C.	P.O.	ST ANGELO / ILEX	13- 1-1939	19- 8-1958
J 81,138	WEBSTER, C.E.	P.O.	VICTORY / ST ANGELO	3- 8-1935	4- 6-1953
P/KX 78,629	WEEKS, R.W.	Stoker P.O.	VICTORY	5- 7-1943	19- 8-1958
P/MX 45,137	WELCH, B.C.	Supply P.O.	DRAKE / GREYHOUND	10- 3-1941	19- 1-1960
J 7,605	WELCH, S.I.	P.O.	EXCELLENT	26- 3-1927	20-11-1951
C/JX 132,335	WELLARD, C.E.	C.P.O. Tel	EUROPA	15- 4-1946	23-10-1961
D/JX 141,434	WEST, C.W.	P.O.	SALSETTE II	23- 8-1944	29- 4-1959
D/KX 80,147	WHEELER, J.J.	Stoker P.O.	ADAMANT	14- 7-1944	24- 9-1959
K 62,145	WHEELER, W.H.	Stoker P.O.	DRAKE	5- 9-1938	13-11-1953
J 31,531	WHITE, A.E.	P.O.	EXCELLENT	24- 3-1937	4- 5-1953
P/JX 129,499	WHITE, A.G.	C.P.O. Tel	FORMIDABLE	25- 8-1944	2-11-1957
M 36,828	WHITE, H.	R.P.O.	CAPT SUBMARINES	26-11-1925	20-11-1951
P/J 112,729	WHITE, P.A.	P.O. Tel	CLYDE / MAIDSTONE	23- 9-1942	1-11-1957
J 96,993	WHITELEY, J.J.	P.O.	BRIDGEWATER	12- 9-1937	8- 7-1952
C/JX 130,595	WHITTA, R.W.	C.P.O.	GOLDEN HIND	5- 6-1945	25- 7-1960
P/J 107,561	WHITTAKER, F.E.	C.P.O. Tel	CONDOR	15- 4-1946	25- 7-1960
K 56,867	WHITWORTH, R.	Stoker P.O.	RAMILLIES	7- 1-1935	7- 8-1951
Ply 22,490	WICKS, P.E.	Musician R.M.	—	8- 2-1940	18-10-1957
P/KX 79,101	WIGGINS, S.	Stoker P.O.	BOSCAWEN / ACUTE	4- 3-1943	7- 7-1958
P/J 111,350	WILKINS, A.E.	Tel	AMBROSE / SEVERN	14-11-1940	22- 9-1960
P/M 39,630	WILLCOCKS, A.L.	Supply P.O.	ST CHRISTOPHER	30- 4-1941	12- 6-1958
C/M 39,319	WILLIAM, J.H.	E.A. 1st Cl	WOOLWICH	6- 6-1940	11- 1-1957
J 94,114	WILLIAMS, E.J.	A.B.	TAMAR / DIAMOND	9- 8-1936	19- 7-1954
D/MX 46,772	WILLIAMS, H.M.	Supply P.O.	VICTORY	10-12-1942	19-12-1957
P/MX 47,126	WILLIAMS, J.R.	Actg C.O.A.	EREBUS	2- 7-1943	9- 2-1959
J 9,588	WILLIAMS, R.	Ldg Seaman	HERMES	7- 1-1928	1- 8-1951
J 31,264	WILLIAMS, S.W.	P.O.	MEDWAY	18- 1-1932	7- 9-1951

J 23,015	WILLIS, A.W.	P.O.	ROYAL OAK / PEMBROKE	27- 3-1929	13-11-1953
P/JX 128,443	WILMHURST, S.	P.O.	NUBIAN	4- 9-1944	29- 9-1959
Ch/X 496	WILSON, A.J.	Cpl R.M.	—	30- 3-1943	19- 4-1961
P/JX 132,176	WILSON, J.	Ch Yeo Sigs	QUEEN ELIZABETH	5- 6-1945	25- 7-1960
—	WING BUK	P.O. Steward	DORSETSHIRE	11-10-1935	7- 4-1953
—	WONG HOP	P.O. Cook	CARDIFF	21-11-1938	15- 3-1954
C/MX 46,445	WOOD, A.E.	Blacksmith 1 Cl	PEMBROKE	19- 8-1942	1- 8-1957
P/J 110,031	WOOD, A.W.T.	C.P.O.	FERRET / BANFF	10-11-1941	11- 1-1957
Po 22,716	WOOD, G.E.P.	Cpl R.M.	COURAGEOUS	12- 7-1938	20- 6-1957
M 40,164	WOOD, H.C.	R.P.O.	PEMBROKE	17- 3-1939	30- 3-1954
J 16,436	WOOD, S.	P.O.	ADAMANT	19- 9-1929	22-10-1953
D/J 112,171	WOODALL, H.	Actg C.P.O.	GRIFFIN	5- 6-1942	25- 7-1960
J 104,067	WOODFORD, E.H.	A.B.	VICTORY / BLANCHE	14-11-1937	14- 8-1956
M 36,431	WOODFORD, G.J.T.	E.A. 1st Cl	VICTORY / BOADICEA	24-10-1938	23-11-1954
C/L 14,695	WOODYARD, S.A.	Ldg Steward	ACHATES	5-12-1939	7-10-1954
M 28,700	WORK, H.J.V.	L.S.B.A.	WOLSEY	20- 3-1933	26- 9-1951
D/KX 80,000	WORLEY, L.	Stoker P.O.	PHILOCTETES	20-11-1944	19- 1-1960
D/JX 127,634	WOTTON, S.	P.O.	DEFIANCE	10-12-1942	18-10-1957
P/J 99,973	WRIGHT, B.	C.P.O.	VICTORY / JACKDAW	26- 3-1946	7- 4-1953
J 44,617	WYATT, G.P.	P.O.	RESOLUTION	4-10-1932	18- 8-1953
—	YONG HING	Stoker	SEAMEW	17- 5-1933	2-11-1953
D/MX 47,492	YOUNG, A.J.W.	Supply C.P.O.	CANNAE	4-11-1943	15-10-1958
C/MX 49,427	YOUNG, J.C.	C.P.O. Writer	WOLFE	31-10-1947	18- 9-1963

Medals with bars in the Collection.

George V Admiral of Fleet (fixed suspension)

say 1926 & 1951 bar	FLEMING, David	Private RMLI		PO 14,005

Since his name does not appear on the earliest LS & GC medal roll, which generally only includes men earning their LS & GC medals during and subsequent to 1928 – the award of his bar cannot be verified. However, the afore published roll includes men of the Portsmouth Division RMLI earning their LS & GC medals with official numbers higher than 14,005, viz : 15,545 (medal awarded 11/1925), 16,486 (1/1928), 13,336 (2/1928), 16,322 (5/1928) and 17,095 (3/1929). Extrapolating from these facts it appears reasonable to assume that the 'bar' to Fleming's medal can be considered valid.

26- 3-1927 20-11-1951 bar	WELCH, S.I.	Petty Officer	EXCELLENT	J 7,605

Gr 6.   WW1. 1914/15 Trio.   Ldg Smn/P.O.
WW2. Def & Vic.

George V Coinage Head.

22-12-1931 29- 8-1951 bar	LILLYWHITE, W. Sgt R.M.			PO 215,142

	Gr 6.	R.M. M.S.M. WW1. BWM, Vic. WW2. Def, War	Q.M.S.I. (28- 2-1951) Gnr R.M.A.	RMA 15,142

10-11-1933 4- 5-1953 bar	LAYFIELD, J.L.	Supply P.O.	CERES	M 37,654

	Gr 7.	WW1. BWM. Boy Tel WW2. 39/45, Atl/F&G, Af, Def, War	J 87,765

23- 6-1933 6-12-1957 bar	SENIOR, William Chief Stoker		FROBISHER	K 60,780

	Gr 8.	DSM. GVI. Chief Stoker. WW1. BWM Stoker 2nd Cl AGS. Som 1920. Stoker 1st Cl. CLIO WW2. 39/45, Atl/F & G, Af/N.Af, War DSM. For Malta Convoy *L.Gaz* 8- 9-1942	C/K 60,780 SS.117,833

George VI Coinage Head Ind Imp.

5- 5-1939 7- 7-1954 bar	CHAPPLE, A.T.	Mechn 1st Cl	EXETER	K 64,011

	Gr 6.	WW2. 39/45, Atl, Af, Burma/Pac, War

Two LS & GC Medals – RN and Cadet Forces – in the Collection

J.F. COPSEY

	Gr 10.	WW1. BWM/Vic. Ord WW2. 39/45, Atl, Pac, Ity, War Coronation 1937. (Engd 'F.COPSEY. A.B.') LSGC GV Coinage A.B. NELSON Cadet Forces Medal. EIIR Ty Lt (S.C.C.) R.N.R.	J 83,738

Naval Reserves' Long Service Decorations and Medals

GENERAL INTRODUCTION

Many methods of manning the Navy in times of its expansion for war have been tried over the past two centuries – some by compulsion and others relying on patriotic fervour. Between the periods of impressment during the 'First' Great World War (1793 -1815) and conscription for World War Two (1939-1945), critical voices forced the formation of much needed reserve units to meet the Royal Navy's seven ocean responsibilities in time of war.

Whilst some lessons were learnt from 'volunteer' bodies of men such as the Sea Fencibles (1798-1810), the Royal Trinity House Volunteer Artillery (1803-1805), the River Fencibles (1803-1813), the Royal Naval Coast Volunteers (1853-1873), the Seaman Pensioner Reserve (1870-1903) and the Royal Naval Artillery Volunteers (1873-1892) – none survived in their original form, mainly because their functions were limited to the coastal defence of the United Kingdom.

As the somewhat complicated story concerning naval reserves unfolds it will be noticed that the Admiralty created formations from three distinctly different sources :–

(A)   Men who had served in the Royal Navy for a minimum of four years.

(B)   Merchant seamen and fishermen whose profession was the 'Trade of the Sea'.

(C)   Civilians from non-seafaring walks of life who had a love of the sea.

A FLEET RESERVE – H.M. COAST GUARD SERVICE.

Towards the end of the 'First' Great War even the Admiralty despised the impressment system for so called recruitment, not least because desertions from the service matched impressments at the cost of employing 3,000 healthy 'sailors' ashore on impress duties to produce such a negative result. Their change of heart is detectable in the Order in Council dated 14 December 1814, which not only introduced pensions for long serving and 'medically fit' (formerly only available to 'worne out') seamen – but also mentioned the subject of 'Naval Reservists' in Article 9. It was stipulated that a Register was to be kept of all healthy naval pensioners (hitherto impossible !), and those not wholly incapable of service whose age did not exceed fifty years. These men were all to be liable to appear at naval sea-ports within a reasonable time after a requisition to such effect, or in time of war at such place of assembly appointed – similar mandates were to apply when the Royal Fleet Reserve was eventually instituted in 1900 ! Since no mention of this '1814 Fleet Reserve' was made when Lord Exmouth scoured the Fleet for men to man his expeditionary force in 1816 for the forthcoming Action at Algiers, it seems that this excellent visionary scheme died a natural death in the peaceful times that followed more than twenty years of war.

However it was not long before the foundation for a Fleet Reserve was laid inadvertently by the Admiralty. This accident stemmed from the Admiralty's decision in 1817 to create – somewhat reluctantly – the Coast Blockade force manned from commissioned ships of the Fleet as an adjunct to the anti-smuggling body, the Preventive Water Guard, which was the responsibility of the Treasury. Over the next fourteen years these Blockaders, operating ashore and off the coast, brought the cancerous growth of smuggling under control with the Navy relinquishing its participation in March 1831 when the Coast Blockade Force was abolished.

During this period, in January 1822, all the various forces for the prevention of smuggling were placed under the Board of Customs with the generic title of 'H.M. Coast Guard', with naval officers as its Comptroller General and Deputy Controller and as Inspecting Commanders of all districts. It is hardly surprising that by 1829 the Admiralty sought support from other Ministries to control the Coast Guard – which duly occurred two years later when the Coast Blockade force was abolished.

On 10 May 1831 the Treasury agreed to the remodelling of the Coast Guard, such that all appointments, promotions and recruitment of officers and boatmen (ratings) within that force were in future to be controlled by the Admiralty – 'thus rendering it in all its branches essentially naval' – but an anomaly remained whereby the Board of Customs was to retain overall responsibility for the Coast Guard !

Amongst the reasons put forward by the First Lord of the Admiralty (Sir James Graham) for the administrative changes to the Coast Guard, two particular paragraphs are relevant to 'Reservists' :–

> ' By the adoption of this system I think the Revenue would be more surely protected and in the event of war this guard round the coast of England, composed as it would be of trustworthy naval officers and seamen would perhaps with the addition of a few small armed steam vessels more effectively protect the whole line of coast against any hostile disembarkation than by any other system.

> Another material and very important advantage which would be consequent on the adoption of this system is the extreme facility it will afford the collection of seamen for H.M. Navy either by voluntary entry or by impressment, though I am happy in anticipating that the latter mode need less frequently be resorted to when the real benefits and solid advantages of the King's service shall be evidently shown in the Service of the Coast Guard composed as I now recommend.'

Although the Admiralty now had a 'standing force' for the defence of the coast of the United Kingdom, it did not have a 'Reserve' for its seagoing Fleet in time of emergency. This deficiency was nearly rectified in 1845 when an Admiralty regulation was brought into force stating that all future recruits to the Coastguard – this singular title had come into usage in 1839 – were to sign an agreement to serve aboard any H.M.Ship if required. There was not, however, any legal validity to this piece of paper which seemed to force a member of the Coastguard to be a 'Fleet Reservist'. This contentious point was overcome when the Naval Enlistment Act, 1853 (16 & 17 Vict.Cap.73) was passed in parliament, allowing the Admiralty to draft Coastguardmen (and pensioners) to ships of the Fleet at times of emergency which rendered – in the Admiralty's opinion – such a course advisable. From this time all members of the Coastguard were in every sense 'Fleet Reservists'. After the War with Russia, when thousands of rather old Coastguardmen had been called to serve with the Fleet, the Admiralty was granted full control of the Coastguard Service on 1st October 1856 – a function it retained for 67 years until 1923.

Although all ratings in the Coastguard – ex-Revenue Cruiser men excepted – could, if they wished, serve long enough to receive naval pensions, they did not become entitled to the Long Service & Good Conduct Medal until 1873. Although Revenue Cruiser men in the Coastguard received the equivalent of pensions – in the form of superannuation directly funded by the Treasury – and thus were not considered to be members of the naval service, they did find themselves part of the navy when it came to awards of the LS & GC medal. (*Vide* : 'Earliest L.S. & G.C. Awards to Coast Guard Fleetmen').

Thus the first naval 'Reservists' to receive LS & GC medals were members of the Coastguard, but their award was the normal RN & RM LS & GC medal – a practice which continued until 1923, in parallel for its last few months of issue with the differing long service medal instituted in 1922 for Royal Fleet Reservists.

VOLUNTEER RESERVISTS' LONG SERVICE MEDALS.

The Army were the first to introduce such rewards, both unofficial and official with the latter commencing in 1892 with the 'Volunteer Officers' Decoration' followed by the 'Volunteer Long Service Medal' in 1894. Although the Royal Naval Reserve (RNR) had been instituted in 1859 for ratings and 1861 for officers, and the Royal Fleet Reserve (RFR) in 1900 – the Admiralty made no response to these Army precedents until 1902, when a submission for long service rewards for members of the RNR was presented by Admiral Sir Gerrard E.C. Noel, KCB, KCMG, Admiral Superintendent of Reserves. It failed due the expectation that Sir Edward Grey's Committee on 'Naval Reserves' – which was then sitting – might cover the matter. It did not do so. Nevertheless, the proposals of this Committee did lead directly to the institution of the Royal Naval Volunteer Reserve (RNVR) in 1903.

It was not until two further relevant 'Reservist' types of Army awards had been introduced in December 1904 – 'The Imperial Yeomanry Long Service and Good Conduct Medal' and 'The Militia Long Service and Good Conduct Medal' – that the Admiralty commenced discussions on similar rewards for their 'Reservists'.

In 1906 the Second Sea Lord, Vice Admiral Sir Charles C. Drury, K.C.B., K.C.S.I, put forward proposals for the institution of Long Service and Good Conduct Medals for the Royal Naval Reserve, the Royal Fleet Reserve and the Royal Naval Volunteer Reserve. The Second Sea Lord's case rested on comparability of such awards with those already available to certain Army personnel. Since the Royal Fleet Reserve corresponded to some extent with the Army Reserve, for which no medal existed – this proposal lapsed.

Agreement to introduce LS & GC Medals for the RNR and RNVR was based partly on the fact that the Army Special Reserve (formerly Militia) and Territorial Force (Formerly Volunteers) already had such medals. Proposals were also made to institute long service Decorations for officers of the RNVR and RNR, with assent granted for members of the RNVR but failing at the first attempt for the RNR because Militia Officers were not eligible for a Decoration – nevertheless the Treasury did approve the introduction of Medals and Decorations being extended to Colonial Naval Volunteers and Reserve Forces. The histories concerning the institution of these various 'Reserves', and more details covering the introduction and development of long service rewards for the Royal Naval Reserve, Royal Naval Volunteer Reserve and Royal Fleet Reserve appear in the following Sections.

Royal Naval Reserve

The major contribution made by any person to the creation of the Royal Naval Reserve in 1859 can be traced to the latent visionary qualities of a thirteen year old midshipman, John Hoskins Brown. This stripling had witnessed action aboard H.M.S. *PRINCE* at the Battle of Trafalgar, and later during the 1812 War became a prisoner-of-war of the Americans. Promoted to Lieutenant R.N. in 1814 he was never again to see active service after September 1815 when placed on half-pay – along with 90% of his brother officers of comparable rank.

In 1835 the position of 'Registrar of Seamen' was instituted under the first 'Merchant Shipping Act', an office within the Ministry of the Board of Trade which was to be held from its inception for nearly thirty years by Lieutenant J.H. Brown R.N. Since his department issued 'Numbered Tickets' to all types of British seafarers – who might serve in the Royal Navy, British Merchant Ships both foreign going and home trade, or transfer their services to oft-times better paid billets in foreign vessels – John Brown soon found himself in the most advantageous position of knowing more about the numbers and conditions of service of all British seamen than anyone else in the United Kingdom.

The concept of a Naval Reserve of fully trained seamen from the Merchant Service was first mooted in 1846 by Captain (later Admiral, K.C.B.) B.J. Sulivan R.N., followed in 1847 when Lieutenant Brown put forward a somewhat similar scheme for a voluntary Reserve with less emphasis on the needs of the Royal Navy and more on the practical difficulties to be overcome for its introduction.

The first serious attempt by the Admiralty to address an alternative to 'impressment' in time of war occurred in July 1852, when their Lordships set up 'The Committee for Manning the Navy' under the chairmanship of Rear-Admiral Arthur Fanshaw, C.B. with three experienced Captains R.N. Whilst the recommendations for creating a 'Standing Navy' through the introduction of 'Continuous Service Engagements' and regularising 'Boy Entrants' are its best remembered triumphs, few people today are probably aware that the concepts of future 'Reserves' – the RNR and RFR – feature in the evidence given, stemming from the third principal point to which the attention of the Committee had been directed :

> ' To consider what measures could be put in force, in the event of any sudden armament [mobilisation] being ordered, and a large body of seamen being required for the defence of the country, to secure the services of the requisite number of men; and what regulations or system should now (sic. in italics) be arranged and acted on to ensure the attainment of this important object in time of necessity and danger.
>
> The scheme suggested by Lieutenant [J.H.] Brown, and brought before Parliament in the late session, is to be considered by the Committee.'

Lieutenant Brown, besides being the only person to be called twice for questioning before the Committee, was also directed to forward written answers on three other occasions. A member of the Committee framed one question in this illuminating manner : 'The Board of Admiralty having referred to this Committee a plan for a naval reserve, which it is understood was suggested by you; we have also before us a book, showing the means by which you propose to carry the said plan into effect, with the answers to the several objections which might be raised against the same ... have you any further observations ?'

Lieutenant Brown enlarged on part of his scheme, emphasising the point that amongst the merchant seamen who might form the reserve were thousands 'who have qualified by service in the fleet', who if recommended – would be of enormous benefit as trained fighting men. His proposal in 1852 of a 'Naval Reserve' thus encompassed future entrants to what were to become the RNR (in 1859) and RFR (in 1900).

Except for the creation of 'Royal Naval Coast Volunteers' (16 & 17, Vict, Cap 73.) on 15 August 1853, subsequently disbanded in 1873, no further advance was made towards to the utilisation of merchant seamen in a naval Reserve as a result of this Manning Committee's findings.

In June 1858 a Royal Commission was set up with somewhat similar terms of reference concerning 'Naval Reserves', but with obviously greater power than the Admiralty Committee – thus ensuring that it could reform with zeal those matters left undone previously. Yet again the Registrar-General (J.H. Brown, recently promoted to Commander R.N. on 24 April 1858) was called to give evidence and supply numerous supporting papers. Brown once more put forward his scheme for a 'Naval Reserve' by utilising but not exploiting the latent numbers and talent in the Merchant Service. This time his proposition had overwhelming support from mercantile officials throughout every main port and from many senior naval officers, leading ultimately to the passing of 'Royal Naval Reserve (Volunteer) Act, 1859' (22 & 23 Vict, Cap 40). However, the institution of the Royal Naval Reserve in August 1859 only embraced the recruitment of 'ratings', the Committee with the exception of one voice had been adamantly against the creation of commissioned ranks in the RNR. Not until July 1861, when 'The Royal Naval Reserve Officers Act, 1861' was placed on the Statute Book, did it become possible to raise a force of officers within the RNR.

In 1862 Commander Brown retired from his post as Registrar-General, and at the same time on the recommendation of the Duke of Somerset, First Lord of the Admiralty, he was honoured with the award of a C.B. (Civil Division) on 8 April 1862 – a very rare decoration to be granted to an officer of Commander's rank. On 20 March 1863 Brown was promoted to Captain R.N., but he died soon afterwards on 29 June 1864. Amongst his effects – on display at the Royal Naval Museum, Portsmouth from the Author's Collection [*Vide* : Plate No. 16] – is a beautifully executed illuminated scroll presented in 1862, with such a charming encomium that it deserves publication as part of his obituary :–

'Sir, We the seaman of the Royal Naval Reserve, hearing that you had recently retired from the cares of office after long and arduous service, desire to express to you our warm gratitude for the great benefits which we in common with our brethren throughout the United Kingdom owe to your friendship and unwearied exertions on our behalf.

It is because we deeply feel this that we now intrude for a brief space on your retirement to ask to carry with you these our warm acknowledgements of your service in our cause, and more especially of the crowning service which has linked us, the seaman of the Mercantile Marine with our Brethren in the Royal Navy, in the common defence of our Queen and Country. In obtaining for us this privilege you have gratified our National and Patriotic pride by raising for the protection of our beloved Queen and country a body of men who, in times of need will be found 'ready; aye ready'. [Motto of the Sea Cadet Corps]

Along with this sincere expression of our feelings we beg you to accept the accompanying Testimonial which may serve to perpetuate in your family more effectively than mere words the sentiments and gratitude of those British Merchant seamen who owe to you, amongst other benefits, that of being members of the Royal Naval Reserve. That you may long enjoy in honoured retirement the facts of a public career begun at Trafalgar and worthily closed in organising a new National Bulwark is our heartfelt prayer.

Presented on behalf of the Royal Naval Reserve by the Committee.'

INTRODUCTION OF THE ROYAL NAVAL RESERVE DECORATION AND LS & GC MEDAL.

In 1906 the Second Sea Lord, Vice Admiral Sir Charles C. Drury, K.C.B., K.C.S.I, put forward proposals for the institution of LS & GC Medals for the RNR, RNVR and RFR. The Sea Lord's case rested on comparability of such awards with those already available to certain Army personnel. Since the RFR corresponded to some extent with the Army Reserve, for which no medal existed – this proposal lapsed. The introduction of LS & GC Medals for the RNR and RNVR was based partly on the fact that the Army Special Reserve (formerly Militia) and Territorial Force (formerly Volunteers) already had such medals.

Proposals were also made at this time to institute long service Decorations for officers of the RNR and RNVR, but initially this only proved to be possible for members of the RNVR – that for the RNR failed at the first attempt because comparable officers in the Army – Militia Officers – were not eligible for a Decoration. The Admiralty sought a common denominator of 20 years service before any type of 'Reserve' Decoration and Medal could be awarded. In December 1908 – whilst lengthy discussions were taking place with regard to the designs to be adopted for the naval awards – the service qualifications were altered to correspond with the periods required of the Special Army Reserve and Territorial Force. Also, by the end of 1908, further discussions had led to the approval of an extension of the Officers' Decoration to encompass Royal Naval Reserve Officers – the following periods of service were now required for the award of the Medal and Decoration :–

Royal Naval Reserve LS & GC Medal	15 years
Royal Naval Reserve Officers' Decoration	15 years

Although the general release of the regulations concerning the awards of the RNR Decoration and Medal for long service was not made known until September 1909 – a copy of the Admiralty Memorandum headed 'Decoration for Officers of the Royal Naval Reserve' dated 1st May 1909 was published (leaked !) by a correspondent in the *'Journal of Commerce'* dated 14 July 1909 – with caustic editorial comment. Considerable resentment was voiced subsequently by retired RNR officers due to the restrictions upon eligibility to be found in paragraph 5 of this Memorandum :

'5. The Decoration will not be awarded to any officers whose names are removed from the active list prior to 1st January 1908.'

This offending paragraph did not appear in the Regulations for the award of the Decoration when they were published for the first time in Navy Lists dated September 1909. In fact a large proportion of awards issued between 1909-1911 were made to Retired Officers. The Decoration could be conferred on Commissioned Executive and Engineer Officers of the RNR who had completed 15 years service – inclusive of Acting time – but time served in Honorary rank was not allowed to count. Discretionary awards could be made in special cases to Staff Paymasters and Paymasters RNR after 20 years – inclusive of Honorary time. Unlike the Regulations issued at the same time for RNVR officers allowing the post-nominal letters of 'V.D.' to be used, no submission was made until November 1909 for the use of post-nominal letters of 'R.D.' for RNR officers – approval for which did not feature in published Regulations until September 1913.

The regulations concerning reservists' eligibility for the RNR LS & GC Medal were also issued in September 1909. The Medal could be awarded to all seamen and stokers already enrolled on or after 1st April 1908 upon completion of 15 years RNR service and having satisfactorily completed the training required during that period. The recommendation had initially to receive the approval of the Registrar General of Shipping and Seamen, and finally that of the Admiral Commanding Coast Guard and Resrves.

DESIGN OF RESERVES' LS & GC MEDAL AND RIBBON.

The King had approved the 'general principle' of a Decoration and Medal for officers and men of the RNR and RNVR on 2 January 1908, subject to sight of proposed designs before final Royal Assent would be given. Although the design by Garrards for the Decoration received the Royal Sign Manual on 6 May 1908, that for the medal proved to be contentious and took much longer.

Two sketches of the 'Obverses' with differing legends for the RNR and RNVR LS & GC Medals did not satisfy the First Lord of the Admiralty when he scrutinised them in late January 1908. Since he insisted on introducing the '*DREADNOUGHT*' as the central figure in both cases, the concept of producing dissimilar medals for the two Reserves disappeared – hence the reason for all Naval Reserve LS & GC medals being of the same design, classified only by their differing ribbons (then not perfectly) and from the medal's impressed edge details where the suffix shews the recipient's type of 'Reserve' – RNR or RNVR etc. By October 1908 the King had approved the plain '*DREADNOUGHT*' design – copied from the best available photograph of her on the Starboard bow – devoid of any form of separate legend for the two Reserves. The Royal Mint decided that '... as such – a legend might be omitted altogether ...'

However, even this very plain design for the medal's 'Reverse' did not meet with the approval of the First Lord, who then suggested that the addition of a latin motto would of itself prove a 'measure decorative'. One of five mottos was finally approved – 'DIUTURNE FIDELIS' (Faithful Over Time) – [*Vide* : Plate No. 17] and the Royal Mint so informed on 19 November 1908. The Mint met problems with the preparation of the finished plaster cast for this Naval Reserve Medal, leading to an inability to supply a specimen of the medal until 23 June 1909. Now that the Mint could commence striking the medals, the question concerning the colour of the ribbon(s) was justifiably raised.

Originally in January 1908 it had been proposed to the King that a blue and white design of ribbon should be used. Only now in July 1909 was it officially recalled that the King had 'preferred the green ribbon for the Decoration, and presumably intends it to be used also for the medal.' On 9 September 1909 the King gave final approval '... for the new medal to the RNR and RNVR to be issued with the green ribbon ...'

When these naval Reserve Decorations and Medals were instituted in 1909 the same coloured ribbon as the Army Volunteer Decoration and Medal was used – plain dark green. In October 1941, new coloured ribbons were introduced for the Royal Naval Reserve awards – the Reserve Decoration was to have a white border added to its plain dark green ribbon, and that of the Medal to be the same with an additional white central stripe.

These changes came about because not only were the precedent setting Army awards obsolete, but criticisms to the original colour of the ribbon had been voiced. There were four main objections to the plain dark green ribbon : – '

> (1) It did not show on dark blue cloth [nor had the naval VC blue ribbon until 1918 !] ; (2) It was less distinctive than some less honourable medals ; (3) It was quite unlike Royal Navy Decorations ; (4) The Officers' Decoration and the Men's Medal had the same ribbon. Officers are often entitled to both.' This latter official statement is the only one known to the Author which seems to accept that RNR officers did not have to forfeit their LS & GC medal when gaining the Decoration – but the LS & GC medal roll shews that many officers did ! Similarly placed RNVR officers did not have to forfeit their medal on receipt of the Decoration, but were not initially allowed to wear both rewards – but by regulations issued in December 1919 (AFO 3783/1919) officers of both the RNR and RNVR were allowed to wear the Decoration and the LS & GC medal.

Paragraph 5 of the Admiralty Fleet Order (4354/1941), which publicised approval by the King for the new coloured ribbons, is worth repeating in full for general interest :–

> ' The Ribbons of the Royal Navy are dark blue and white. It is the white which shows on dark blue uniform ; white tells best at the edges. Therefore the first three objections to the old ribbon are removed by the white border , which is the same as that on the dark blue Royal Navy Long Service and Good Conduct Medal Ribbon. The fourth objection is met by the central stripe, which distinguished the RNR Medal ribbon from the Reserve Decoration ribbon in the same way as the DSM ribbon is distinguished from the DSC ribbon. The dark green is the same as that on the old ribbon.'

In December 1957 the various Naval Reserves were amalgamated into one Royal Navy Reserve. The design of the Long Service Medal issued since that date remained unchanged, the ribbon however was altered to five equal stripes of blue/white/green/white/blue – thus embracing the former dominant colours in use for the RNR and RNVR. Men already in possession of the earlier medals were not required to change the ribbon.

DESIGN OF RESERVES' DECORATION AND RIBBON.

In keeping with the decision to use the same design LS & GC medal for both the RNVR and RNR, it was logical that, when at the end of 1909 approval was finally given for a Decoration to be issued to officers of the Royal Naval Reserve, the same designed Decoration and ribbon that had been earlier approved for issue to the RNVR, was selected.

The design proposed by Garrards, and approved by King Edward VII under the Royal Sign Manual dated 6 May 1908, bore a strong resemblance to the Volunteer/Territorial Decoration. Both Decorations are oval in shape with a surrounding silver border encompassing an open central area containing the Royal Cypher surmounted by a Tudor Crown, gilded on the front face. A large silver ring is attached to the top of the crown for ribbon attachment. The main difference between the military and naval designs lies in the border (*Vide* ; Plate No. 17); the oval surround on the military version is wider and consists of a wreath made of oak leaves held in place by three gilded crossed garlands. Befitting on the naval version, the oval surround consists of a length of cable (rope) coming together at the base to form a reef knot. The overall appearance produces a pleasing and unmistakably nautical effect.

Unlike the long service medals where the recipient's name and appropriate Reserve's suffix was impressed on the edge, the officer's Decorations were issued unnamed and, until 1919, when the RNVR ribbon was changed – were identical and indistinguishable. The flat 'reverse' bears only the hallmarking date and manufacturer's initials, ie (SG) for Garrard. In later years, when the Decoration was manufactured by the Royal Mint, these useful date distinguishing marks were to disappear. Decorations are occasionally found which have been privately engraved, normally on the flat surface area found on the 'reverse' of the reef knot. Many of the early issues thus named show the artistic skill of the engraver which prevailed during the early part of this century.

Because of the need for the Decoration to be produced in reasonably economic quantities ie., batches of 100-200 which oftimes exceeded the annual issues of Decorations – it is not uncommon to find groups of medals containing RNR/RNVR Decorations with hallmarks indicating production some two years before the announcement of the award in the *London Gazette (LG)*. Due to the way in which the year is changed in hallmarking it is possible to find a LG award date around the middle of the year with a corresponding hallmark date on the Decoration indicating the immediate following year ie., LG entry May 1929 – London hallmarking lower case 'p' which indicates 1930. The reason for this is that London hallmarks change each year on St Dunstan's day – 19 May, compared with the Birmingham Mint which changes hallmarks annually on 1st July. Thus groups can be correctly found with Reserve Decorations hallmarked two years before or one year later that the *London Gazette* announcement.

During the reign of George VI, the year of issue began to be engraved on the 'reverse' of the reef knot, a practice which continues today in a slightly modified format, and is a useful pointer to the medal collector when trying to locate the *London Gazette* entry. The issue of the RNR Decoration during the Second World War (1939-1945) was interrupted and frequently delayed with many Decorations remaining unissued until well after cessation of hostilities. It would appear that a decision was taken circa 1946/7 that henceforth the date appearing on the 'reverse' of the Decoration would be that of the year in which the receipient became entitled. The year no longer provides a useful pointer when consulting the *London Gazette*, other than to indicate the earliest possible date of *LG* entry. As the Decoration is not issued automatically, but only upon application, it placed the responsibility on the individual officer to apply upon satisfactory completion of training and the required number of years of service. Many officers did not make application until after retirement, frequently being unaware that mobilised war service was allowed to count double time. The Navy List provides a useful reference source for confirmation for both active and retired officers who were awarded the Decoration which is indicated by the post nominal letters R.D.

The concession of 'double time' was granted to mobilised reservists (RFR men excepted) who served during World War One and World War Two, commencing from 4 August 1914 or 2 September 1939 respectively – to the date of demobilisation for officers, or dispersal in the case of men. This bonus time was allowed to count for the purpose of reckoning eligibility for Reserve Long Service Decorations and Medals for officers and men (on Active or Retired Lists) of the RNR, RNVR and RNASBR in both World Wars, and additionally for the RNV(W)R in the Second World War. Permanent RNR and RNVR ratings granted Temporary Commissions during WW2 were eligible to receive the RNR or RNVR LS & GC medal (AFO 5322/1946).

BARS AND ROSETTES TO THE LONG SERVICE MEDAL.

An Admiralty Fleet Order (AFO 3783/1919) of December 1919 introduced new rules applicable to reservists in the RNR, RNVR and RNASBR – whereby they could be awarded a bar to their original medal after serving for a further period which would again have qualified them for a medal. However, more than twenty years were to pass before such men could signify the award of the bar when wearing uniform with medal ribbons only. This deficiency was met in 1942 when the Admiralty introduced new regulations which stated that : 'Rosettes, similar to those worn on the ribbon of the 1914 Star, are to be issued to members of the RNR, RNVR, RNV(W)R and RNASBR who qualify for the award of a bar to their Long Service and Good Conduct Medals ... for serving a further period which would again have qualified them for award of a medal. The Rosette which will be issued at the same time as the bar is to be worn on the ribbon of the LS & GC Medal, when the ribbon is worn without the medal.' These Rosettes were also issued retrospectively to men serving and those who had left the service (AFO 5636/1941 & 3859/1942).

In December 1957 the Naval Volunteer Reserves were re-organized, resulting in the creation of a 'Unified Reserve' (RNR) – with Admiralty Board approval effecting its institution from 1st November 1958 (AFO 2550/1958). The scope of the old Royal Naval Reserve (RNR) was broadened to include the officers and ratings, male and female, previously forming all the various Divisions of the RNVR including the Wireless and Postal Sections. Henceforth eligibility for the 'Royal Naval Reserves Long Service and Good Conduct Medal' required 15 years' service over the age of 18 years (reduced to 17 1/2 years a few years later), after completion of 12 annual periods of training during that time. After 1971 former service in the Regular Forces counted as qualifying service, but a minimum of 7 years of the 15 years for award of the medal must have been served in the RNR, RMR, RNVR, RNV(W)R (W=Wireless), RNV(P)R (P=Postal), RMFVR, WRNVR, WRNR or QARNNSR. All qualifying time served prior to 1st November 1971 counted in full towards a bar to the Decoration or Medal.

BARS AND ROSETTES TO THE LONG SERVICE DECORATION.

It was not until 37 years after the announcement that bars could be awarded to the ratings' medal, that a similar announcement appeared in respect of the officers' Decoration first published in Admiralty Fleet Order P.383/1956 (Item 6) and BR 65 in 1957 – as follows :–

(6) An officer will be eligible for the award of a Bar to the Reserve Decoration after completing ten year's additional service on the Active List. The rules governing the counting of service are the same as for the award of the Decoration itself, except that in no circumstances does any service count double for the assessment of the additional ten years. The award of the Bar is not retrospective, and only officers serving on the Active List on or after 1st June 1954 are eligible for the award.

In the event of a reserve officer failing to claim his RD until 10 years after qualifying date, the time served between becoming eligible for the Decoration, and actually receiving it, may count towards award for the Bar, providing he fulfils all other conditions.

It is unlikely that any delay occurred in the striking and despatch of the Bars, since the design chosen for the Bar was identical to that which was already in use by the Army on Territorial/Efficiency Decorations i.e., a straight slide on silver gilt bar approximately a quarter of an inch wide with a small raised border – and the Monarch's cypher in the centre surmounted by a crown. On the 'reverse' is engraved the year the recipient became eligible for the Bar and not as might be expected, the year that the award was made.

The first list of officers to be awarded bars appeared in the *London Gazette* dated 19 October 1956. The Navy List for 1956 shows however that a number of RNR officers had been awarded bars earlier in 1956. For some inexplicable reason, yet to be resolved, the announcements in the *London Gazette* covering the award of Naval Reserve Decorations ceased in 1954 and did not appear again until October 1956, since which date they have been published without interruption.

An analysis of the awards published in the *London Gazette* for the period 1956-1989 indicates the issue of 1,076 1st bars, 78 2nd bars and the unique award of a 3rd bar to Lieutenant Commander M.J.Hunter, DSC., RNR. The following Roll is a non-exhaustive list of officers who received 2 clasps to their Reserve and Volunteer Reserve Decorations during the period 1956-1989. Some omissions are likely due to the non-publication of awards in the *London Gazette* during the period referred to above. Where the first award was not published in the *London Gazette,* an approximate date is given based on the first year of entry in the Navy List.

Officers who retired subsequent to 1954, although eligible for the award of a bar(s), but had not applied prior to retirement were allowed to apply retrospectively.

ROLL OF THE AWARD OF THE RNR & RNVR DECORATION
WITH TWO CLASPS (79)

Name	Rank	Reserve	Award	1st Bar	2nd Bar
ACKERLEY, G.R.	Lt.Cdr.(Sp)	RNR	R.D.	1956	26- 3-1968
ALLAN, J.N.	Captain	RMZNVR	V.R.D.	11- 2-1958	4- 7-1958
ALLEN, J.R.	Lt.Cdr.	RNVR/RNR	V.R.D	31- 1-1967	17- 4-1973
ALLEN, H.G.	Lt.Cdr.(S)	RMVR/RNR	V.R.D.	17- 9-1965	2- 9-1975
BEATTIE, G.K., CBE	Captain	RNR	R.D.	12- 1-1982	18- 9-1984
CANNING, P.G.	Lt.Cdr.	RNR	R.D.	11- 1-1977	23-12-1985
CHARLES, L.B.	Captain (S)	RNR	R.D.	9- 7-1957	14- 1-1966
CHESTERMAN, H.G. DSC*	Captain	RNR	R.D.	1956	21-10-1966
CHILD, W.H.	Commander	RNVR/RNR	V.R.D.	12- 7-1968	6- 6-1978
CHUBB, P.A.	Commander	RNR	R.D.	16- 6-1964	31- 7-1973
CLARKE, R.S.	Commander	RNR	R.D.	31- 7-1979	5- 7-1988
CLEMENTS, J.W.	Lt.Cdr.	RNVR/RNR	V.R.D.	5- 3-1974	1983
COLLIER, H.M.	Captain	RNR	R.D.	22- 4-1958	17- 6-1966
COLLIER, J.	Captain	RNR	R.D.	1956	2- 3-1965
COLWELL, D.I., MBE	Inst.Lt.Cdr.	RNVR/RNR	V.R.D.	12-11-1974	28- 5-1985
COOPER, E.J.	Commander	RCNR	R.D.	?	18- 2-1975
DILLON, C.B.	Lt.Cdr.	RANVR	V.R.D.	25- 1-1972	25- 1-1972
DOBSON, C.R.C.	Commander	RNVR/RNR	V.R.D.	22- 7-1960	14- 7-1970
DUNCAN, R.F.H.A.	Lt.Cdr.(Sp)	RNR	R.D.	28- 6-1957	31- 1-1967
DUNKLEY, J.L., CBE	Captain	RNR	R.D.	1956	15-11-1963
DUNN, W.E.B. De S.	Lt.Cdr.(Sp)	RNVR/RNR	V.R.D.	10-10-1967	8-10-1974
FLACK, G.W.	Lt.Cdr.	RNVR/RNR	V.R.D.	4- 3-1975	26- 5-1981
FOINETTE, L.T.A.	Lt.Cdr.(Sp)	RNVR/RNR	V.R.D.	16- 6-1970	12- 2-1980
FRANKLIN, A.G.C.	Lt.Cdr.	RNVR/RNR	V.R.D.	?	22-11-1977
GADD, K.A., DSC	Captain	RNR	R.D.	1956	2- 3-1965
GALPIN, J.L.	Commander	RNVR/RNR	V.R.D.	8-10-1974	14- 2-1984
GEDDES, J.G.	Lt.Cdr.	RNVR/RNR	V.R.D.	20- 7-1976	14- 2-1984
GEORGE, W.J.	Lt.Cdr.	RNVR/RNR	V.R.D.	2- 9-1975	21- 4-1985
GIBSON, K.F.	Lt.Cdr.	RNVR/RNR	V.R.D.	?	23- 6-1985
GIBSON, W.J.	Commander	RNR	R.D.	22-11-1977	10- 7-1984
GRIFFITH, A.J. DSC	Lt.Cdr.	RNVR/RNR	V.R.D.	?	17- 4-1973
HAGUE, A.	Lt.Cdr.	RNVR/RNR	V.R.D.	30-12-1958	12-11-1974
HARRADINE, D.V.	Commander	RNR	R.D.	6- 6-1978	5- 7-1988
HARVEY, C.P.T.	Lt.Cdr.	RNVR/RNR	V.R.D.	11- 1-1977	23- 6-1985
HARVEY, W.F.P.	Lt.Cdr.	RNVR/RNR	V.R.D.	8- 4-1969	31-10-1978
HODGES, N.W.	Lt.Cdr.	RNR	R.D.	1- 3-1977	8-12-1987
HOPKINS, E.B.	Commander	RANVR/RNR	V.R.D.	1-12-1970	25- 1-1972
HOWARD, D.	Lt.Cdr.	RNVR/RNR	V.R.D.	22- 7-1975	15-10-1985
HUMPHRIES, H.M.	Cdr. (Sp)	RNVR/RNR	V.R.D.	16- 6-1970	26- 5-1981
HUNTER, M.J., DSC	Lt.Cdr.	RNR	R.D.	29- 1-1963	18- 4-1972
				3rd Bar	22-11-1977
HUNTINGTON- WHITELEY, J.M.	Lt.Cdr.	RNVR/RNR	V.R.D.	18- 2-1975	10- 7-1984
JONES, A.R.E.	Lt.Cdr.	RNVR/RNR	V.R.D.	5- 3-1974	12- 2-1980
JOYCE, D.L.	Lt.Cdr.	RNVR/RNR	V.R.D.	4- 1-1983	15-10-1985
KEAY, T.A.C.	Captain	RNVR/RNR	V.R.D.	10-10-1961	4- 1-1983
MACKAY, K.M.E., MBE	Commander	RNVR/RNR	V.R.D.	1- 3-1977	23- 6-1985
MACKIE, G.	Commander	RNVR/RNR	V.R.D.	12-11-1974	23- 6-1985
MacNAUGHTON, A.R.	Commander	RNR	R.D.	20-12-1977	5- 7-1988

MALBON, J.F.	Lt.Cdr.	RNVR/RNR	V.R.D.	29- 8-1967	11- 1-1977
MARTIN, A.A. DSO,DSC**	Captain	RNR	R.D.	1956	1957
McCATHIE, G.W.	Captain	RNR	R.D.	6- 6-1978	31- 6-1978
MEADE, D.G.	Lt.Cdr.	RNVR/RNR	V.R.D.	30-10-1972	4- 1-1983
NICHOLAS, R.J.M.	Captain	RNR	R.D.	1956	6- 8-1963
NURSEY, K.A.	Lt.Cdr.	RNR	R.D.	25- 3-1956	12-11-1974
O'NEILL, F.C.	Commander	RNR	R.D.	18-12-1962	12- 9-1967
PADDISON, E.F. GM	Lt.Cdr.	RNR	R.D.	29- 1-1963	23- 1-1973
PASCOE, R.H.	Lt.Cdr.	RANVR	V.R.D.	1-12-1970	25- 1-1972
PEARCE, J.S.	Commander	RNR	R.D.	?	27- 8-1968
PELLING, R.W.F.	Commander	RNR	R.D.	?	31-12-1968
PIPER, A.D. DSO, DSC**	Commander	RNR	R.D.	14- 6-1957	11- 2-1966
PIXLEY, N.D., MBE	Cdr (Retd)	RANVR	V.R.D.	30-10-1972	1- 5-1973
PURCHASE, R.G. MBE	Captain	RANVR/RNR	V.R.D.	18- 2-1975	28- 5-1985
RHODES, P.H.H.	Lt.Cdr.	RNVR/RNR	V.R.D.	18- 2-1975	28- 5-1985
RICHARDSON, W.T.	Commander	RNR	R.D.	?	23- 6-1985
ROBERTS, J.R.	Surgn.Capt.	RNVR/RNR	V.R.D.	12-11-1974	18- 2-1975
SEDDON, A.T.	Commander	RNR	R.D.	6- 6-1978	5- 7-1988
SEELEY, A.P., OBE	Commander	RNVR/RNR	V.R.D.	8-10-1974	14- 2-1984
SEWELL, S.A.	Captain	RANR	R.D.	21- 8-1973	21- 8-1973
SMITH, D.J.C.	Lt.Cdr.(Sp)	RNVR/RNR	V.R.D.	1- 7-1969	12- 2-1980
STOREY, F.J.	Captain	RNR	R.D.	1956	2- 3-1965
TETTMAR, D.M.	Commander	RNVR/RNR	V.R.D.	20- 7-1976	23- 6-1985
TURNER, J.B.	Lt.Cdr.	RNVR/RNR	V.R.D.	12- 1-1982	12- 1-1982
VEALE, R.S.	Lt.Cdr.	RANVR	V.R.D.	1- 5-1973	1- 5-1973
WAKEFIELD, D.B.	Lt.Cdr.	RNVR/RNR	V.R.D.	4- 3-1975	28- 5-1985
WEBB, B.M.	Lt.Cdr.(Sp)	RNVR/RNR	V.R.D.	24-10-1967	1- 3-1977
WILFORD, D.J.	Commander	RNR	R.D.	10- 7-1984	8-12-1987
WIMPERIS, P.	Lt.Cdr.	RNR	R.D.	12- 2-1980	21- 4-1987
WOLFENDEN, J.E. DSC	Captain	RNR	R.D.	1956	15-11-1963
WOODWARD, A.P.M.	Commander	RNVR/RNR	V.R.D.	20- 7-1976	21- 4-1987
YATES, A.E.	Lt.Cdr.	RNVR/RNR	V.R.D.	30-10-1972	4- 1-1983

ROLL OF RNR LS & GC MEDALS WITH BARS (234)

Earliest award dates : EDVII 4- 3-1910, GV 10-3-1914 and GV1 27-8-1937

O.No	Name	Rating	Medal	Bar
4968 D	ALDRED, A.J.	Seaman	23-10-1929	5- 1-1943
5533 D	ALEXANDER, W.M.	Ldg Smn	19- 9-1938	16- 2-1948
5346 D	ANDERSON, J.	Seaman	11-11-1931	15- 3-1943
1990 V	ALLEN, C.	Stoker	11- 7-1931	4- 5-1943
1771 V	ALMOND, T.	Ldg Smn	9-10-1930	3- 2-1943
5047 D	ANSELL, A.R.	Ldg Smn	17-12-1929	5- 1-1943
5459 D	ANSELL, P.H.G.	Ldg Smn	3- 9-1937	9-10-1947
137 ED	APPLEBY, T.	E.R.A.	20-11-1929	15- 3-1943
U 1894	AUGUST, J.	Stoker	24- 9-1920	21- 8-1928
2957 C	BARTLETT, A.E.	Seaman	17- 5-1922	8- 2-1935
1934 V	BARTON, G.	Stoker	11- 8-1930	4- 5-1943
138 ED	BARTON, J.	E.R.A.	11- 2-1930	15- 3-1943
7041 C	BARTON, T.C.	P.O.	30- 9-1941	26- 3-1945
1896 V	BATEY, H.	Stoker	20- 4-1934	18- 8-1944
5039 D	BAXTER, J.W.	Ldg Smn	17- 4-1931	3- 2-1943

1941 V	BEATON, L.	Stoker	11- 7-1931	3- 2-1943
175 W	BEGLEY, J.	Ldg Stoker	26- 6-1941	4- 5-1943
1994 V	BELL, J.	Stoker	13- 6-1931	15- 3-1943
1859 V	BENJAMIN, D.J.	Stoker	17- 4-1931	3- 2-1943
5149 D	BENSTEAD, N.J.	Seaman	8- 5-1931	15- 3-1943
5342 D	BETTS, W.P.	Ldg Smn	14-12-1931	26- 7-1943
5805 C	BINNEY, J.	Seaman	24- 1-1934	9- 4-1945
4995 D	BOAK, E.	Seaman	15- 1-1930	5- 1-1943
10 SE	BOCHEL, J.M.	2nd Hand	19- 2-1932	4- 5-1943
1962 V	BOWER, G.M.	Stoker	5-12-1930	4- 5-1943
1909 V	BOWMAN, H.	Stoker	15- 4-1932	26- 7-1943
137 W	BRANNAN. R.	Stoker	3- 9-1935	7- 7-1944
5428 D	BREMNER, A.	Seaman	17- 2-1933	19-11-1943
5426 D	BREMNER, D.	Ldg Smn	5-11-1934	19-11-1943
5343 D	BROOM, G.W.S.	Ldg Smn	29- 8-1931	4- 5-1943
3355 C	BRUCE, R.J.	Seaman	10- 3-1931	26-10-1943
5317 D	BUDGE, J.D.	Seaman	10- 3-1931	3-12-1943
5154 D	BULLARD, W.J	Seaman	17- 2-1933	3- 2-1943
165 ED	BURNETT, H.	E.R.A.	17- 4-1931	4- 5-1943
B 4938	BUTTRESS, W.G.	Seaman	18- 6-1920	5- 3-1929
1803 V	CAHILL, J.	Stoker	23- 6-1930	3- 2-1943
5445 D	CALLAGHAN, W.J.	Seaman	9- 1-1939	9- 4-1945
5187 D	CAMPBELL, A.	Seaman	18- 5-1931	26- 7-1943
C 2350	CAMPBELL, D.	Seaman	8- 5-1920	no date
5477 D	CAMPBELL, M.	Seaman	2- 9-1941	21-10-1947
1310 E	CAMPBELL, R.	Seaman	16- 5-1940	15- 5-1944
1929 V	CARRIBINE, B.	Stoker	11- 6-1930	4- 5-1943
167 EV	CHISHOLM, J.	Engn	5- 4-1930	6- 7-1943
T3/20	CLARK, J.J.	E.R.A. 2 Cl	19- 9-1922	19-11-1935
37 EE	CLARK, R.C.N.	E.R.A.	13- 4-1947	4- 5-1943
1966 V	CLENNAN, W.	Stoker	1- 9-1933	21- 2-1944
D 2690	COLE, W.A.	Seaman	18- 3-1920	11- 3-1931
5437 D	COLEMAN, J.G.	Ldg Smn	26-11-1936	26- 3-1945
1887 V	COLEMAN, P.	Stoker	8- 8-1931	15- 3-1943
5303 D	COLVIN, P.	Seaman	24-11-1933	6- 7-1943
35 SD	COOKSON, J.	2nd Hand	14- 2-1938	11- 2-1947
5092 D	CORSTORPHINE, D.	Ldg Smn	23- 6-1930	4- 5-1943
5100 D	COUTTS, A.	Seaman	14-12-1931	2- 6-1943
2411 WS	CRAIG, D.McB.	Ch Skipper	23- 7-1926	18- 8-1944
5499 D	CREESE, C.H.	Seaman	4-12-1936	4- 5-1945
2463 D	CRELLIN, R.	Seaman	18- 5-1922	no date
5368 B	CULLUM, U or M?	Seaman	16-11-1922	15- 4-1944
1751 V	CUNNINGHAM, T.	Stoker	27- 4-1934	7- 7-1944
1880 V	DAVIDSON, R.W.	Stoker	23- 6-1930	15- 3-1943
983	DAVIE, W.	E.R.A. 3 Cl	8- 9-1944	21- 1-1954
1808 V	DAVIES, J.	Stoker	21-12-1934	20-12-1943
2741 WS	DENNY, R.W.	Skipper	19- 4-1944	19- 4-1944
5449 D	DEWING, H.J.	Ldg Smn	4-10-1937	9-10-1947
5165 D	DONNELLY, B.	Seaman	6- 3-1930	11-11-1942
1826 V	DOWDING, J.	Stoker	23- 6-1930	7- 7-1944
7355 C	DUFFIN, A.E.	Ldg Smn	2- 9-1941	8- 9-1955
1821 V	DUGGAN, M.	Stoker	9-10-1930	4- 5-1943
1413 E	DUNDAS, M.	P.O.	8- 8-1938	15- 3-1943
1755 V	ECCLES, R.	Stoker	22- 5-1933	6- 7-1943
WSC 70	EDEN, J.W.	Ch Skipper	30-11-1922	13- 9-1943
1996 V	EDEN, T.	Stoker	22- 1-1931	4- 5-1943

B 4010	EMERY, J.	Seaman	7- 7-1920	11-11-1931
5200 D	ENNSON, W.J.	Ldg Smn	23- 6-1930	3- 2-1943
1946 V	EVANS, C.W.	Stoker	5-12-1930	15- 3-1943
5444 D	FAHY, J.	Seaman	18- 6-1941	18- 5-1945
1814 V	FAIRNIE, A.	Stoker	5-12-1930	4- 5-1943
1911 V	FERGUSON, F.L.	Stoker	23- 6-1930	4- 5-1943
1932 V	FORSHAW, R.	Stoker	15- 4-1932	11-11-1942
926 V	FORSTER, G.	Stoker	23- 6-1930	15- 3-1943
1735 V	FOY, P.	Ldg Stoker	17-12-1929	5- 1-1943
5056 D	FRENCH, J.H.	Seaman	8- 8-1931	18-12-1942
1993 V	GALL, F.	Stoker	19- 2-1932	4- 5-1943
5248 D	GEORGE, T.E.	Seaman	23- 6-1930	4- 5-1943
5027 D	GERMAN, H.	Ldg Smn	17-12-1929	5- 1-1943
1836 V	GILL, N.	Stoker	8- 9-1933	7- 7-1944
1411 E	GORRY, D.M.	Seaman	6- 3-1936	26- 7-1943
156 ED	GRAHAM, A.	E.R.A.	5- 4-1930	4- 5-1943
5218 D	GRAY, T.	Seaman	11- 6-1930	4- 5-1943
5301 D	GUARD, J.T.	Seaman	25- 2-1932	15- 3-1943
1979 V	HAINES, H.	Stoker	15- 4-1932	4- 5-1943
1872 V	HALL, W.	Stoker	5- 4-1930	5- 1-1943
5045 D	HANSELL, J.W.	Seaman	15- 1-1930	3- 2-1942
5022 D	HANSELL, R.	Seaman	17-12-1929	5- 1-1943
1895 V	HATTON, T.	Stoker	31- 7-1933	7- 7-1944
5753 C	HEARFIELD, W.	P.O.	19- 2-1932	15- 4-1948
5148 D	HEWES, B.S.	Ldg Smn	11- 6-1930	2- 6-1943
1972 V	HEWSON, J.W.	Stoker	16- 9-1930	4- 5-1943
10078 S	HIGGINS, A.	Eng	25- 9-1945	17- 7-1964
1948 V	HOPKINS, D.C.	Stoker	23- 6-1930	4- 5-1943
2002 V	HOWGILL, A.	Stoker	8- 8-1931	15- 3-1943
D 1705	HUNKIN, F.H.	Seaman	16- 4-1920	no date
5264 D	HUNTER, J.	Seaman	11- 7-1931	4- 5-1943
5696 D	HUNTER, J.V.	Ldg Smn	20- 9-1937	18- 9-1946
5521 D	INNES, G.	Ldg Smn	15- 3-1940	24-11-1947
5202 D	JAMIESON, J.T.	P.O.	11- 6-1930	3- 2-1943
1920 V	JEFFCOCK, R.	Stoker	30- 8-1930	4- 5-1943
5322 D	JEFFERY, C.	Seaman	19- 8-1932	15- 3-1943
5483 D	JENKINS, H.W.	Ldg Smn	8-11-1937	9-10-1947
C 2036	JENNINGS, E.W.	Seaman	11- 8-1916	20- 4-1934
1982 V	JOBES, J.	Stoker	21-11-1933	4- 5-1943
19 SD	JOHNSTON, J.G.	2nd Hand	23- 6-1930	4- 5-1943
222 W	KAVANAGH, J.	Stoker	21-10-1941	4- 5-1943
5510 D	KEHOE, J.	Ldg Smn	26- 9-1947	17- 7-1964
5813 C	KEMP, T.H.	P.O.	3- 9-1935	26- 8-1945
3866 C	KENT, A.S.	Ldg Smn	8- 1-1923	15-10-1945
1233 E	KINNON, W.T.	Seaman	21-10-1941	4- 5-1943
20029 A	KILBURN, K.M.	Ldg Smn	26- 9-1947	17- 7-1964
2009 V	KIRTON, G.	Stoker	26- 6-1933	28- 4-1944
5098 D	KLEE, G.T.	P.O.	11- 2-1930	13- 3-1944
5052 D	KNOX, J.	Seaman	5- 4-1930	3- 2-1943
5289 D	LACEY, J.	P.O.	11- 7-1931	15- 3-1943
4734 D	LAWLESS, J.H.	P.O.	13-10-1928	5- 1-1943
2317 WS	LAWRENCE, G.	Skipper	31- 3-1933	31- 3-1933
5188 D	LAWRENCE, J.	Ldg Smn	10- 3-1931	15- 3-1943
2021 V	LAWSON, C.R.	Stoker	10- 9-1931	15- 3-1943
5283 D	LEASK, J.W.	Seaman	22- 5-1933	6- 7-1943
1902 V	LEIGHTON, W.	Stoker	5-12-1930	11- 5-1943

1943 V	LEMON, W.J.	Stoker	31- 3-1933	19-11-1943
5751 D	LEWIS, T.	Seaman	19- 8-1932	27- 6-1945
M 19397	LEWIS, T.W.	E.R.A. 3 Cl	25- 1-1921	8-11-1935
333 EC	LONG J.T.	E.R.A.	14- 1-1938	21-10-1947
5284 C	LORD, J.	Ldg Smn	15- 1-1930	29- 9-1942
5256 D	LOUGH, P.P.	Seaman	23- 6-1930	4- 5-1943
5103 D	LUCK, W.H.	Seaman	9-10-1930	5- 1-1943
5315 D	LUNDSTROM, W.G.	Seaman	21-11-1933	26-10-1943
5493 D	MacDONALD, J.	Seaman	27- 6-1939	21-10-1947
5527 D	MacINNES, D.	Ldg Smn	7- 7-1941	16- 2-1948
1446 E	MACINTOSH, J.E.	Seaman	29- 3-1938	20-12-1943
5500 D	MacIVER, D.	Seaman	19- 2-1937	12- 4-1946
5770 C	MacIVER, D.	Ldg Smn	15- 3-1935	18- 5-1945
5528 D	MacIVER, J.	Seaman	26- 6-1941	16- 2-1948
5541 D	MacIVER, K.	Seaman	11- 6-1937	10- 3-1948
1437 E	MACKAY, J.J.	Seaman	17- 9-1941	26-10-1943
5302 D	MACKAY, R.	Ldg Smn	20- 7-1934	15- 3-1943
5440 D	MacKENZIE, J.	Seaman	20- 1-1942	15-10-1945
5474 D	MacKINLAY, J.	Ldg Smn	19- 2-1937	9-10-1947
5530 D	MACLEAN, D.	Seaman	14- 5-1941	16- 2-1948
5464 D	MACLEAN, M.	Seaman	4- 6-1941	26- 3-1945
1344 E	MacLEOD, A.	Seaman	19- 5-1941	13- 9-1943
1395 E	MACLEOD, D.	Seaman	28- 7-1941	4- 5-1943
1412 E	MACLEOD, D.	Seaman	6- 3-1936	26- 7-1943
5542 D	MACLEOD, D.	Seaman	2- 9-1941	27- 6-1945
1383 E	MACLEOD, N.	Seaman	3- 9-1935	15- 3-1943
5470 D	MAIR, M.	Ldg Smn	13-12-1938	31-12-1947
5368 D	MALCOLMSON, J.A.	Seaman	3- 9-1935	2- 6-1943
378 ?	MARSDEN, W.E.	Eng	29-11-1941	26- 3-1945
1820 V	MARSHALL, W.	Stoker	30- 6-1931	19- 1-1945
218 W	MARTIN, A.	Stoker	24- 5-1935	7- 1-1944
5392 D	MATHESON, J.	Seaman	11- 8-1933	13-11-1946
5189 D	MATHEWS, J.	Seaman	6- 3-1930	2- 6-1943
1831 V	MATTHEWS, E.S.	Ldg Stoker	5- 4-1930	5- 1-1943
1426 E	McDONALD, A.	Seaman	1- 5-1941	15- 3-1943
5423 D	McDONALD, D.McK.	Seaman	19- 2-1937	9-10-1947
1974 QB	McDONALD, N.	Qualfd Smn	21- 8-1924	21- 8-1924
5506 D	McDOUGALL, K.	Seaman	9- 9-1941	15-10-1945
1971 V	McFENTON, W.R.	Ldg Stoker	30- 8-1930	2- 6-1943
5350 D	McGILLIVRAY, A.	Seaman	3- 9-1935	3-12-1943
1427 E	McIVER, A.	Seaman	20- 1-1942	15- 3-1943
257 W	McKAY, J.	Stoker	27- 7-1937	18- 5-1945
1381 E	McKENZIE, J.M.	Seaman	8- 5-1941	15- 3-1943
5383 D	McKINNON, A.	Ldg Smn	21-12-1934	2- 6-1943
5021 D	McLEAN, J.	Ldg Smn	11- 6-1930	5- 1-1943
5535 D	McLEAN, J.	Seaman	7- 7-1941	26- 3-1945
5446 D	McLEMAN, J.	Seaman	4-12-1936	27- 6-1945
2258 E	McLEOD, M.	Seaman	14- 5-1941	3- 2-1943
5462 D	McLEOD, R.	Seaman	26-10-1942	6- 6-1945
1319 E	McMILLAN, A.	Seaman	29-11-1941	11-11-1942
5257 D	MILLAR, R.	Seaman	29- 3-1935	4- 5-1943
5254 D	MILLER, A.	Seaman	23- 6-1930	6- 7-1943
1287 E	MOBBS, E.F.	Ldg Smn	23- 9-1941	15- 3-1943
2698 V	MORGAN, W.J.D.	Ldg Trimmer	22- 3-1923	29- 7-1930
187 W	MORRELL, W.	Stoker	8-10-1941	28- 4-1944
343 E	MORRISON, D.	Seaman	11- 6-1930	11- 6-1930

5261 D	MOUAT, W.	Seaman	19- 2-1932	15- 3-1943
5443 D	MURRAY, M.	Ldg Smn	2- 8-1940	9- 4-1945
1951 V	NESS, G.C.	Stoker	11- 7-1931	15- 3-1943
249 W	NEWCOMBE, C.	Eng	14- 5-1941	7- 7-1944
1792 V	NICHOL, J.	Stoker	5- 2-1934	18- 8-1944
5487 D	NICOLSON, A.A.	Ldg Smn	17-10-1939	9- 4-1945
1424 E	NICOLSON, N.	Seaman	14- 5-1941	4- 5-1943
5279 D	NIVEN, J.H.	Seaman	3-12-1934	4- 5-1943
5298 D	NIXON, J.H.	C.P.O.	11- 8-1930	15- 3-1943
1717 V	NORRIS, W.G.	Stoker	20-11-1929	3- 2-1943
1935 V	O'HANLON, M.	Stoker	27- 4-1934	7- 7-1944
1857 V	O'HARA, J.	Stoker	6- 3-1930	3- 2-1943
1976 V	PARIS, E.	Stoker	5-12-1930	15- 3-1943
1709 V	PARRY, H.A.	Stoker	18- 5-1934	18- 8-1944
5883 D	PATCHITT, T.F.	Ldg Smn	8- 8-1938	16- 2-1948
5355 D	PATIENCE, J.W.	Seaman	5- 2-1934	15- 3-1943
5447 D	PATON, J.C.	C.P.O.	4- 2-1938	5-10-1945
5034 D	PEACOCK, A.	Seaman	11- 6-1930	18-12-1942
5501 D	PEEL, R.M.	Seaman	27- 3-1940	9- 4-1945
5485 D	PERRETT, E.	Ldg Smn	16-11-1936	21-10-1947
5101 D	PETERSON, R.	Seaman	11- 2-1930	4- 5-1943
5116 D	PETERSON, T.J.P.	Seaman	10- 9-1931	4- 5-1943
5704 D	PITT, E.R.	Seaman	8-11-1937	30-12-1946
1335 E	POLESON, J.	Ldg Smn	19- 1-1937	4- 5-1943
5130 D	POLSON, A.J.	Ldg Smn	21- 1-1931	5- 1-1943
181 ED	POOLEY, J.B.	E.R.A.	22-11-1935	27- 6-1946
1397 E	POPE, H.G.	Seaman	16-10-1941	4- 5-1943
166 EV	POTTER, T.	Engn	6- 3-1930	15- 3-1943
5108 D	PRIMMER, W.C.E.	Seaman	30- 8-1930	13- 9-1943
1964 V	PRIOR, J.	Stoker	5-11-1931	6- 7-1943
1874 V	PROFITT, W.	Stoker	6- 3-1930	4- 5-1943
5091 D	PURVIS, W.	Seaman	15- 1-1930	15- 3-1943
224 EC	REDPATH, J.O.	E.R.A.	8- 9-1927	4- 5-1943
1879 V	REGAN, J.	Stoker	30- 8-1930	4- 5-1943
1410 E	REID, G.	Ldg Smn	8- 5-1936	4- 5-1943
5209 D	RITCHIE, J.	Seaman	18- 5-1934	4- 5-1943
5210 D	RITCHIE, N.	Seaman	18- 5-1934	4- 5-1943
141 ED	ROBINS, G.W.	C.E.R.A.	11- 6-1930	4- 5-1943
1975 V	ROBINSON, A.J.	Stoker	13- 6-1931	4- 5-1943
210 ED	ROBINSON, A.P.	E.R.A.	14- 2-1938	9- 8-1948
5486 D	ROSS, H.	Seaman	1- 5-1941	21-10-1947
73 WSB	ROWE, E.C.	Skipper	13- 4-1927	15-10-1945
1961 V	ROWNTREE, H.	Stoker	22- 1-1931	15- 3-1943
1925 V	ROXLEY, J.	Stoker	11- 6-1930	4- 5-1943
5516 D	RUSH, G.	Seaman	10- 5-1939	10-11-1947
1912 V	RUTHERFORD, T.W.	Stoker	11- 7-1931	4- 5-1943
5531 D	SEARLE, A.	Seaman	24- 7-1941	26- 3-1945
5113 D	SEAWARD, A.	Ldg Smn	11- 2-1930	3- 2-1943
1983 V	SHARP, R.	Stoker	24- 6-1932	6- 7-1943
1918 V	SHAW, J.W.F.	Ldg Stoker	11- 6-1930	4- 5-1943
5458 D	SHEPHERD, T.E.	P.O.	11- 9-1936	9-10-1947
1883 V	SHIELDS, A.	Stoker	5-12-1930	4- 5-1943
1832 V	SIMPSON, J.	Stoker	13- 6-1931	3- 2-1943
5084 D	SIMPSON, W.	Ldg Smn	11- 6-1930	26-10-1943
10337 SD	SINDEN, W.	2nd Hand	5- 7-1948	25-10-1963
1955 V	SMITH, E.	Stoker	9-10-1930	15- 3-1943

2011 V	SMITH, E.B.	Stoker	18- 5-1931	3- 2-1943
5514 D	SMITH, H.J.	Ldg Smn	19- 1-1937	10-11-1947
1965 V	SMITH, J.	Stoker	30- 6-1931	4- 5-1943
5082 D	SMITH, P.	Ldg Smn	6- 3-1930	3- 2-1943
2014 V	SMITH, S.C.	Ldg Stoker	18- 5-1934	18- 8-1944
1869 V	SMITH, W.	Stoker	10- 3-1931	15- 3-1943
5258 D	SPENCE, T.	Seaman	23- 6-1930	15- 3-1943
1914 V	SPENCE, T.W.	Stoker	11- 6-1930	15- 3-1943
4971 D	SPICER, F.S.	Ldg Smn	13-12-1930	5- 1-1943
1915 V	STAFFORD, B.B.N.	Stoker	23- 6-1930	15- 3-1943
5143 D	STOREY, A.D.	P.O.	5- 4-1930	3- 2-1943
5243 D	STRACHAN, J.	Seaman	23- 6-1930	3- 2-1943
5547 D	SUTHERLAND, A.	Seaman	24- 7-1941	16- 2-1948
5518 D	SUTHERLAND, A.G.	Seaman	17-10-1939	24-11-1947
5335 D	SUTHERLAND, D.	Seaman	3- 9-1935	2- 6-1943
5168 D	SYMONDS, H.A.J.	Seaman	11- 6-1930	4- 5-1943
4378 B	TAYLOR, D.O.	Seaman	23- 2-1922	24- 6-1932
WSA 2166	TAYLOR, G.B.	Wrt Skipper	22- 1-1918	18- 4-1932
2024 V	TEASDALE, G.	Stoker	26- 2-1934	7- 7-1944
218 ED	THOMPSON, C.H.	C.E.R.A.	29-10-1937	13- 1-1947
4948 D	THOMPSON, J.	Ldg Smn	13-12-1930	3- 2-1943
5054 D	THOMSON, W.	Seaman	11- 2-1930	3- 2-1943
5161 D	THORBURN, W.	Ldg Smn	10- 3-1931	4- 5-1943
5551 D	TUBBS, E.J.C.	P.O.	19- 2-1937	18- 6-1946
5490 D	TURRELL, G.	Seaman	27- 8-1937	26- 3-1945
5128 D	WALKER, A.W.	Seaman	9-10-1930	3- 2-1943
4469 C	WALKER, G.R.	Seaman	17- 5-1922	10- 7-1941
1811 V	WALLACE, G.L.	Stoker	15- 4-1932	5- 1-1943
268 OU	WAPPETT, T.	Stoker	19-12-1924	15- 4-1941
1407 E	WATSON, D.	Seaman	10- 8-1936	15- 3-1943
1967 V	WATSON, J.	Stoker	13- 6-1931	6- 7-1943
15 SD	WATT, A.	2nd Hand	23- 6-1930	12-12-1942
5083 D	WATT, J.	Ldg Smn	6- 3-1930	5- 1-1943
5268 D	WEBSTER, J.	Seaman	23- 6-1930	4- 5-1943
4455 D	WEBSTER, W.E.	Ldg Smn	9- 5-1927	12-12-1942
10030 S	WESTICOTT, G.H.	Engineman	22-10-1946	12-10-1961
8 SD	WHATLING, A.W.	2nd Hand	9-10-1930	29- 9-1942
10071 S	WHYMAN, A.	Eng	22-10-1946	6- 2-1961
1907 V	WILKINSON, G.	Stoker	11- 6-1930	15- 3-1943
1871 V	WILLGRESS, A.A.	Stoker	11- 8-1930	15- 3-1943
5266 D	WILLIAMS, W.	Ldg Smn	23- 6-1930	3- 2-1943
1294 E	WILLIAMSON, G.	Ldg Smn	29- 8-1940	3- 2-1943
376 E	WILLIAMSON, G.	Seaman	18- 1-1932	18- 1-1932
1406 E	WILLIAMSON, R.	Seaman	15- 3-1940	29- 7-1943
1989 V	WILSON, A.	Stoker	11- 7-1931	4- 5-1943
1888 V	WILSON, E.	Stoker	23- 6-1930	4- 5-1943
5186 D	WOOD, G.	Seaman	11- 6-1930	3- 2-1942
9958 S	WOOD, J.	Stoker	15- 1-1946	30- 3-1960
5062 D	WRIGHT, G.	Seaman	6- 3-1930	3- 2-1943
5536 D	WYLIE, P.	Ldg Smn	19- 2-1937	9- 4-1945

Medals in the Collection

8- 9-1927   REDPATH, J.O.   E.R.A. R.N.R.
4- 5-1943 bar

           Gr 8.   WW1. 1914-15 Trio.   E.R.A.   R.N.R. EA.1722
                        WW2. 39/45,Af/42-43, Def, War.
                        LSGC. GV (A of F). RNR & bar.   '224EC E.R.A. R.N.R.'

16-11-1936   PERRETT, Elliot   Ldg Seaman R.N.R.
21-10-1947 bar

           Gr 6.   DSM. GVI   Ldg Seaman   D.5485
                        WW2. 39/45, Atl-F&G, Def, War.
                        LSGC. GV. (Coinage). RNR & Bar.   Ldg Seaman   5485.D
           DSM. *Vide* : *L.Gaz.* 1- 1-1941, p.25-7. New Year Honours. (ADM 1/11663)

? date   BAIN, J.   Seaman R.N.R.
? date bar

           Gr 6.   WW2. 39/45, Af, Ity, F&G, War.
                        LSGC. GV. (Coinage). RNR & Bar.   Seaman R.N.R.   9,477.B
           LS & GC Roll not yet deposited at the Public Record Office.

Miscellaneous RNR LS & GC Decorations and Medals

Sub Lieut W.E. ALLEN R.N.R.

           Gr 9.   WW1 1914-15 Trio.   Sub Lieut/Lieut R.N.R.
           Mercantile Marine Medal. 'William E. ALLEN'
           WW2. 39/45, Atl, Burma, War
           RD. GV. (Hallmark 1928)

           Sub Lieutenant (Ty) 19 March 1915, Lieutenant (Ty) 2 June 1916, Commission terminated when demobilised in April 1919. Rejoined RNR as Lieutenant (Proby) 31 December 1923, Lieut Commander RNR 31 December 1931, Commander RNR 30 June 1935 and retired in the Spring of 1939. Recalled in rank of Captain (Rtd) in Autumn 1939. In command of French Ship EMILE BAUDOT (1941-1944), demobilised as Captain (Rtd) RNR in late 1945. Although his total eligible time served as an RNR officer inclusive of double war service time amounted to 33 years, he could not receive a bar to his Decoration – which was not introduced until 1956.

Petty Officer George W. HEENEY R.N.R.

           Gr 3.   WW1. BWM.   'George W. HEENEY'
           Mercantile Marine Medal.   'George W. HEENEY'
           LSGC. RNR GV1 (Coinage Ind Imp). '7152.C P.O. R.N.R.'

Skipper Charles Benjamin OLLEY R.N.R.

           Single.   LSGC. RNR GV. (A of F. Fixed Susp). 'Skipper ... 13.W.S.'
           Entitled to World War One 1914-1915 Star Trio.

Skipper (Warrant Rank) 27 February 1911, Chief Skipper 7 November 1924 after award of LS & GC medal on 9 August 1923. Retired as Skipper Lieutenant on 19 October 1932.

RNR Trawler Reserve LS & GC Medal

Leading Deck Hand E.H. RICHARDS R.N.R.T. C.3208

His RNR LS & GC medal was issued on 19 March 1920 to an address in Penzance. The medal roll (ADM 171/71) confirms the 'R.N.R.T.' impressed on the edge of this medal.

Royal Naval Volunteer Reserve

The Royal Naval Volunteer Reserve (RNVR), created in June 1903, was a direct descendant of a former source of naval 'Reserves' – the Royal Naval Artillery Volunteers (RNAV) – which suffered a short life-span of only nineteen years from 1873 to 1892.

The RNAV came into being mainly because of the persistent advocacy of Thomas C. Brassey, M.P. (later Earl Brassey, G.C.B.), a name more usually associated with his patriotic work in the publishing world as the founder of *'Brassey's Naval Annual'*. He was a keen amateur sailor with ministerial experience as Civil Lord of the Admiralty who fervently championed the need for Naval Reserves – resulting in the creation on 21 May 1873 of the RNAV which drew its naval reservists from civilians with a love of the sea – 'yachting seamen' – who were not professional seafarers. The services of this force could be called on in times of emergency but only for defence of the coasts of the United Kingdom and adjacent seas, and therein lay the root cause of its demise.

Once Britain's defence policy moved the frontiers from coastal defence, selecting instead an Imperial strategy of maritime security upon all oceans of the world – the existence of the RNAV was doomed. It was a reserve force which most senior naval officers did not like in any case. At midnight on 31 March 1892 the RNAV was disbanded, but the excommunicated enthusiasts saw it only as a battle lost – not the war. Twelve years later the Royal Naval Volunteer Reserve (RNVR) was instituted by an Act of Parliament due to the loyalty of many ex-members of the RNAV, and the pressures exerted by a number of eminent personages.

The man most deserving the title of being the 'Father' of the RNVR was Charles E.H. Chadwyck-Healey, Q.C – a man dedicated to this cause from the moment he became a Sub-Lieutenant in the RNAV on 11 February 1885 until he relinquished his position as Chairman of the Admiralty Volunteer Committee in 1914 when aged 69 years. Whilst in the RNAV he used his own yacht to provide a training ground for these volunteer enthusiasts, sailing as far as week-end cruises allowed, and within a few years found himself chosen as the most powerful advocate for this reserve force. On 28 June 1889 he presented a paper at the Royal United Service Institution on 'The Royal Naval Artillery Volunteers' to a large audience of navally interested parties, including many senior Admirals – but to no lasting avail since this Reserve was disbanded three years later.

On 9 October 1889 Chadwyck-Healey became an Honorary Lieutenant of the Royal Naval Reserve, rising to Honorary Commander RNR in 1904 and Honorary Captain RNR in 1914 – in which rank he commanded the small H.M. Fishing Fleet Hospital Ship *QUEEN ALEXANDRA* from 1915 to 1918. A somewhat bizarre aspect to the career of a man who had not only been largely responsible for creating the RNVR, but who also continued in a prominent post to mould policy during the formative years of this Reserve Force.

In 1892 the ex-members of the RNAV formed sailing clubs in the ports where their Brigades had formerly operated, with the intention of continuing with their own private navally trained reserve force – operating nationally under a 'Resuscitation Committee' of ex-RNAV officers of whom Chadwyck-Healey was a member. The not unexpected prejudices of Admirals could not detract from the excellent work of these 'amateurs', nor from the widespread attention still being given to Royal Naval matters throughout civil communities in such centres as London, Brighton, Hastings, Yarmouth, Liverpool, Southport,

Llandudno, Camavon, Birkenhead, Bristol, Swansea and the Clyde – where RNAV reservists had worn official uniforms previously.

Interest by the British Government in naval reserve forces waned and so did the morale of the 'Resuscitation Committee' and its private reservists. Revival came only after the Marquis of Graham (later the Duke of Montrose) aroused enthusiasm at an open public meeting on this matter held under the auspices of the Lord Provost of Glasgow on Trafalgar Day, 21 October 1899. Soon afterwards a 'National Committee on Naval Volunteers' was formed with Chadwyck-Healey as its Secretary – at a time when the Natal Naval Volunteers (founded in 1885) demonstrated the use of 'amateurs' at Ladysmith during the South African War (1899-1901), with Australian Naval Volunteers performing similar Imperial service during the Boxer Rebellion in China (1900).

At the turn of the century the Admiralty was forced to turn its attention to the urgent need to increase its naval reserves to match the considerably enhanced ship building programme, which led to the institution of the Royal Fleet Reserve (RFR) with its first voluntary enrolments on 1st March 1901 from fleet trained personnel. The 'Reserves' crisis still continued leading to the setting up of a 'Naval Reserves Committee' under the chairmanship of Sir Edward Grey, Bart, M.P. in early 1902 – with wide terms of reference on the need to provide increased levels of reserve forces because of even greater expansion of the size and quality of the Fleet. Larger seamen complements were required due to the increased size of ships with greater firepower, and of even greater urgency there was a need for more engine-room personnel – especially stokers – due to the increase in the number of boilers (coal-fired) needed to produce the horse-power for higher speeds. The Naval Reserves Committee were also called upon to examine the value and use of Colonial Naval Reserves and decide '... how far can a Naval Volunteer Movement be utilized ?'

Chadwyck-Healey was chosen as the witness to appear before Sir Edward Grey's Committee to declare the findings and suggestions of the 'National Volunteer Committee', and answer questions – only to discover that Sir Edward was not to sit as Chairman on the day (24 February 1902) he was called to give his evidence. The Vice-Chairman was Admiral Sir Edward H. Seymour, GCB, who was known to be less than sympathetic to the idea of Naval Volunteers – a personal opinion already reinforced by even more forcibly expressed antagonastic views expressed by naval witnesses ranging from the Second Sea Lord downwards. Although Chadwyck-Healey immediately conceded the needs for the proposed volunteer force to be subject to the Naval Discipline Act, and that 'some' volunteers would serve at sea and go anywhere, thereby removing the major causes for the disbandment of the RNAV – the caveat of 'some' spelt trouble.

The National Volunteer Committee must have been well aware that their proposal for a second 'Class' of naval volunteers, consisting of men with home ties who would be based on land for Home Defence duties – ran contrary to the Navy's views expressed in the House of Lords in July 1901. In a debate on Naval Reserves the First Lord of the Admiralty, Lord Selborne, had said :

> ' Their Lordships will remember that there was once upon a time a corps called the Royal Naval Artillery Volunteers and that corps was, I have no doubt for good reasons, disbanded. A proposal has been made to revive the corps in a new form; not to create a corps of Artillery Volunteers but of Naval Volunteers ... That proposal is now under examination, and all I can say at present is that we are sincerely desirous of adding to the reserve force quite entirely of volunteers, but one condition is imperative, and that it is thoroughly understood by those gentlemen who are interested in the scheme. No volunteers can be of real service to the Navy who are not prepared in time of war to serve wherever their services may be required and to do any duty which the Captain of their ships calls upon them to do.'

After the contentious point of whether or not the new volunteer reserve should have its own officers had been discussed, and agreement reached that the volunteers should wear uniform – even by naval Committee members sceptical about 'landsmen' ever being allowed to form such a reserve force, the final question of the name of the proposed reserve was raised by Admiral Seymour. The answer given by Chadwyck-Healey was – 'The title we venture to suggest is the Royal Naval Volunteer Reserve', which at first was thought to be too long and perhaps should include the word 'Imperial'. Then Admiral Seymour warmed to the original idea which could always be used and written as the initials RNVR, a sentiment obviously dear to Chadwyck-Healey's heart who, when agreeing, stated '... because it has been present to my mind, and to a certain extent it is one's own child.'

On 9 January 1903 Sir Edward Grey and his 'Naval Reserves' Committee members signed their report which included the following relevant statements :

> ' The experience of the Army has shown that large numbers of civilians take a pride in acquiring knowledge and discipline, and in training themselves for service in war. It seems to be wasteful and unnatural that all the amateur talent in this country should, for want of opportunity, be obliged to turn to Military to the exclusion of Naval training, and in view of the expansion of the Fleet that may be found necessary in a struggle for the supremacy of the British Empire at sea, the Committee but think that a body of Volunteers would be likely to prove a most valuable auxiliary branch to the personnel of the Navy in time of War. .....

> Royal Naval Volunteers. The Committee has refrained from going into details as these are being worked out by Chadwyck-Healey's Committee. From the evidence taken, however, it seems quite clear that the movement would be popular and has every prospect of leading to beneficial results.'

On 30 June 1903 the 'Naval Forces Act, 1903' (3 Edw. 7.Ch 6.) was passed in Parliament – being in effect an amendment to the 'Royal Naval Reserve (Volunteer) Act, 1859' (22 & 23 Vict. Cap 40) – which amongst other authorisations now allowed the Admiralty to '... raise and maintain a force to be called the Royal Naval Volunteer Reserve'. Their Lordships acted with alacrity in issuing a Minute stating that they expected the Naval Volunteers to comply with two essential conditions, namely ; To serve anywhere in time of war where the Admiralty may have need of their services, and to accept liability of serving under the provisions of the Naval Discipline Act.

Meanwhile the quasi-official 'Chadwick-Healey's Committee', set up by Sir Edward Grey's 'Naval Reserves Committee', developed into the 'Central Organizing Committee' working out the details for the introduction of the RNVR and earning considerable respect for its work. To differentiate between the source for recruits as between the RNR and RNVR, the Admiralty – acting on advice tendered – wisely made the position very plain on the eligibility of personnel wishing to enter the RNVR :

> ' As regards the man, neither previous knowledge in gunnery nor previous service at sea will be regarded as a necessary condition for entering the force, although every branch of technical knowledge will be welcomed and utilised. The only tests for entry will be in respect of character and physique.'

By a bold stroke – for these were the days of bold forward looking admirals – the Admiralty decided to appoint a Committee of civilians interested in the movement to work the scheme with a naval representative (Rear Admiral C.J. Norcock, later Vice Admiral), with its decisions and actions subject to the approval of the Admiral Commanding Coastguard and Reserves (ACR). Chadwyck-Healey's demi-official committee now became the 'Admiralty Volunteer Committee' where he served as the Chairman from 1903 until relinquishing the position in 1914. This unprecedented form of administering a volunteer force was soon to be used as the model upon which the 'Administrative Board' for the new Territorial Forces was to be based. Amongst the various honours bestowed upon Charles E.H. Chadwyck-Healey, K.C. were the C.B.(Civil) in 1905, the K.C.B.(Civil) in 1909 and a Baronetcy in 1919 (His group of awards and those of Vice Admiral Norcock are in the author's Collection). The medallic awards to Chadwyck-Healey include an Edward VII RNVR LS & GC medal named to him with the rank of Sub-Lieutenant RNV – yet no official confirmation that he was ever officially made an Honorary Sub-Lieutenant RNVR has yet come to light. This medal was amongst the first eight to be issued on 14 December 1909, despatched to him through the office of Admiral Commanding Reserves. Perhaps a Chairman's 'perk' !

INTRODUCTION OF THE RNVR DECORATION AND LS & GC MEDAL.

In 1906 the Second Sea Lord, Vice Admiral Sir Charles C. Drury, K.C.B., K.C.S.I, put forward proposals for the institution of LS & GC Medals for the RNR, RNVR and RFR. The Sea Lord's case rested on comparability of such awards with those already available to certain Army personnel. Since the RFR corresponded to some extent with the Army Reserve, for which no medal existed – this proposal lapsed. Agreement to introduce LS & GC Medals for the RNR and RNVR was based partly on the fact that the Army Special Reserve (formerly Militia) and Territorial Force (Formerly Volunteers) already had such medals.

Proposals were also made at this time to institute long service Decorations for officers of the RNR and RNVR, but initially this only proved to be possible for members of the RNVR – the Decorations for the RNR failed at the first attempt in 1906 (but approved in late 1908) because comparable officers in the Army – Militia Officers – were not eligible for a Decoration.

At this time during 1906 the service qualification in all cases – for Decorations and Medals – was set at 20 years by the Admiralty. In December 1908 – whilst lengthy discussions were taking place with regard to the designs to be adopted for the naval awards – the service qualifications were altered to correspond with the periods required of the Special Army Reserve and Territorials. The following periods of service were now required for the award of the RNVR Medal and Decoration :–

Royal Naval Volunteer Reserve LS & GC Medal	12 years
[Increased when Reserves were amalgamate in 1957 to]	15 years
Royal Naval Volunteer Reserve Officers' Decoration	20 years
[Reduced for officers joining RNVR after 3 Sept 1939 to]	15 years

Regulations concerning eligibility for the RNVR Decoration and LS & GC Medal were issued by the Admiralty in September 1909 :–

'Volunteer Officers' Decoration'. For Commissioned Officers in the RNVR possessing 20 years service, aggregated from the age of 17 years as a Midshipman in the RNVR, RNAV, inclusive of any commissioned service in the Army Volunteer or Territorial Force. Time served as a rating in the RNVR or RNAV counted as half-time towards the Decoration. Up to ten years qualifying time for the Colonial Auxiliary Forces Officers' Decoration was allowed to count towards the 20 years in any of the aforementioned forces. The post-nominal letters of 'V.D.' allowed at this time for officers awarded the Decoration remained until August 1947, when the short title for the Royal Naval Volunteer Reserve Officer's Decoration was changed from 'V.D.' to 'V.R.D.' (Admiralty Fleet Order (AFO) 2722/1947). Prior to 1919, those officers who earned the 'V.D.' who had previously received the RNVR LS & GC medal could retain but not wear this latter award, but in December 1919 the regulations were altered to allow RNR and RNVR officers to wear both the Decoration and LS & GC Medal (AFO 3783/1919).

The concession of 'double time' was granted to mobilised reservists (RFR men excepted) serving during World War One and World War Two, commencing from 4 August 1914 or 2 September 1939 respectively – to the date of demobilisation for officers, or dispersal in the case of men. This bonus time was allowed to count for the purpose of reckoning eligibility for Reserve Long Service Decorations and Medals for officers and men of the RNR, RNVR and RNASBR in both World Wars, and additionally for the RNV(W)R in the Second World War. Permanent RNR and RNVR ratings granted Temporary Commissions during WW2 were eligible to receive the RNR or RNVR LS & GC medal (AFO 5322/1946). In effect all service time as a RNVR rating during their mobilised time could thus be counted – not half as in peacetime – towards award of the RNVR Decoration.

RNVR LS & GC MEDAL.

Members of the RNVR (officers and ratings) could be granted a LS & GC medal after 12 years service in the RNVR or RNAV; former time with the Volunteer, Territorial or Auxiliary Colonial Forces was allowed to count provided the last five years (of the twelve) had been in the RNVR or RNAV. The medal was available to ratings who had retired after 12 years service, and to officers who had served in the ranks but were not eligible for the 'V.D.'. All recommendations were to be sent to the Admiral Commanding Coast Guard and Reserves (ACR). The first awards were despatched on 14 December 1909.

DESIGN OF DECORATION, LS & GC MEDAL AND RIBBON.

The historical details exactly match those for the introduction of the Royal Naval Reserve rewards, already written up in the RNR Section – to which the reader is referred.

BARS AND ROSETTES TO THE LS & GC MEDAL.

An Admiralty Fleet Order (AFO 3783/1919) of December 1919 introduced new rules applicable to reservists in the RNR, RNVR or RNASBR – whereby they could be awarded a bar to their original medal after serving for a further period which would again have qualified them for a medal. However, more than twenty years were to pass before such men could signify the award of the bar when wearing uniform with medal ribbons only.

This deficiency was met in 1942 when the Admiralty introduced new regulations which stated that : 'Rosettes, similar to those worn on the ribbon of the 1914 Star, are to be issued to members of the RNR, RNVR, RNV(W)R and RNASBR who qualify for the award of a bar to their Long Service and Good Conduct Medals ... for serving a further period which would again have qualified them for award of a medal. The Rosette which will be issued at the same time as the bar is to be worn on the ribbon of the LS & GC Medal, when the ribbon is worn without the medal.' These Rosettes were also issued retrospectively to men serving and those who had left the service (AFOs 5636/1941 & 3859/1942).

BARS TO R.N.V.R. OFFICERS' DECORATION.

Officers of the Royal Naval Volunteer Reserve, unlike their men, were unable to receive recognition of further service following the award of the Decoration. This contentious point was finally rectified by Admiralty Fleet Order P.383/1956 which announced the award of a bar to the RNVR Decoration to recognise a further 10 years service, additional to the 15 years required for the award of the Decoration. The new Regulations were explicit in stating that no service was allowed to be counted as 'double time', and that the award of a bar could only be made to officers serving on or after 1st June 1954, and would not be made retrospectively to retired officers, irrespective of the length of their qualifying service. A list of RNVR officers who were awarded the VRD with two clasps appears in the RNR Section of this work.

It has already been mentioned that the RNVR medal was first issued with a dark green ribbon, but circa 1919 the colour of the RNVR ribbon was changed. The only reference so far found for this alteration appears in Taprell Dorling's 'Ribbons and Medals' in this manner : '... At the general request of the RNVR for a distinctive ribbon it was altered to its present colouring in about 1919. The ribbon now in use, with that of the RNVR Long Service and Good Good Conduct Medal, was designed by the writer. The blue represents the sea; the red the Royal Crimson; and the green the old volunteer colour.'

In December 1957 the Naval Volunteer Reserves were re-organized, resulting in the creation of a 'Unified Reserve' (RNR) – but Admiralty Board approval effecting this change did not take place until 1st November 1958 (AFO 2550/1958). The scope of the old Royal Naval Reserve (RNR) was broadened to include the officers and ratings, male and female, previously forming all the various Divisions of the RNVR including the Wireless and Postal Sections. Henceforth eligibility for the 'Royal Naval Reserves Long Service and Good Conduct Medal' required 15 years' service over the age of 18 years (17 1/2 years a few years later), after completion of 12 annual periods of training during that time. The design of the all embracing Naval Reserve Long Service Medal remained unchanged. However, a new ribbon of five equal stripes blue/white/green/white blue was introduced and used on all medals issued from 1958 onwards. Those men in possession of the earlier award were not required to change the ribbon.

Although the unified Reserve effectively saw the demise of the separate RNVR, the Volunteer Reserve Decoration (VRD) continued to be issued with its own distinctive ribbon until 1966 when it was finally superceded by the RNR Decoration.

After 1971 former service in the Regular Forces counted as qualifying service, but a minimum of 7 years of the 15 years for award of the medal must have been served in the RNR, RMR, RNVR, RNV(W)R (W=Wireless), RNV(P)R (P=Postal), RMFVR, WRNVR, WRNR or QARNNSR. All qualifying time served prior to 1st November 1971 counted in full towards a bar to the Decoration or Medal.

EDWARD VII LS & GC MEDALS TO RNVR

All 'reservist' (RNR & RNVR) L.S. & G.C. medals with Edward VII's effigy were issued from 14 December 1909 until 10 March 1914, when distribution of the George V, Admiral of Fleet Type commenced.

Name		Rate		O.No	Date award	Division
ADAMS, H.W.	*	Ldg Seaman		42	11- 7-1910	Sussex
					10- 6-1920	bar
AITKEN, C.		P.O. 1st Cl		201	27- 5-1910	Clyde
AMPHLETT, F.S		P.O. 1st Cl		126	1- 3-1910	Bristol
BALLAM, W.H.		P.O. 1st Cl.	RNAV	B3	19- 3-1913	Bristol
BELL, J.R.		Lieut		—	7- 3-1913	Bristol
BLAIR, F.R.		C.P.O.		6	20-12-1910	Clyde
					18- 1-1922	bar
BREWER, C.S.	*	Surgeon		—	19- 2-1912	Mersey
CAMPBELL, J.F.		C.P.O.		308	9- 3-1911	Clyde
CARR, J.		P.O.		50	16- 8-1910	Clyde
CHADWICK-HEALEY, C.E.H.	*	Sub Lt	RNV	-	14-12-1909	A.C.R.
CHARLESSON, R.W.	*	Sub Lt	RNV	-	4- 5-1910	London
CLARK, J.		A.B.		5/79	30- 1-1913	Tyneside
CLARKE, A.G.F.	*	P.O. 1st Cl		2	1- 3-1910	Sussex
COOK, A.J.	*	Seaman		827	13-10-1910	London
COWBURN, A.D.	*	Surgeon		—	9-11-1911	London
COX, R.J.	*	C.P.O.		11/1	17-10-1912	HMS EAGLE
CURZON, Viscount		Commander		—	12- 6-1913	Sussex
DUMBLETON, A.W.		Ldg Seaman		22	1- 3-1910	Bristol
FRAME, R.G.		Bugle Major		901	1- 3-1910	Clyde
					10- 6-1920	bar
FROUDE, S.B.		Lieut		—	19- 1-1911	Bristol
GRAHAM, Marquess of		Commander		—	9- 3-1914	Clyde

GUINNESS, Hon R.E.C.		Commander CMG.		—	14-12-1909	A.C.R.
HANSON, O.H.		Lieut		—	14-12-1909	A.C.R.
HARRIS, A.E.	*	A.B.		180	1- 3-1910	London
HARVEY, W.G.	*	C.P.O.	RNV	—	1- 3-1910	Bristol
HAWKER, F.C.		A.B.		559	21- 2-1912	Bristol
HOLLAMBY, F.F.		C.P.O.		2/3	13- 1-1914	Sussex
HUNTER, J.	*	C.P.O.		1612	9- 9-1913	Clyde
JUPP, C.E.		C.P.O.		199	9- 2-1911	London
KING, H.D.		Lieut (Dup 1926)		—	2- 2-1911	London
KINGSTON, E.F.		A.B.		92	31- 7-1912	Bristol
					9- 7-1920	bar
KIRKPATRICK, W.D.		A.B.		3/40	20- 1-1913	Mersey
LAMB, V.C.		P.O.		675	17- 5-1910	Clyde
LIFTON, G.H.		P.O.		501	1- 3-1910	Mersey
LOCKETT, H.A.	*	C.P.O.		11	5- 1-1912	London
LONG, A.		Ldg Seaman		1063	20- 9-1912	London
LOWER, G.A.		A.B.		73	26-10-1910	Sussex
					6- 5-1922	bar
MACFARLANE, T.L.		C.P.O.		207	6- 2-1913	Clyde
MANLEY, A.H.		A.B.		63	25-11-1910	London
MARDON, E.G.		Paymaster		—	1- 3-1910	Bristol
MASON, W.J.		C.P.O. (Dup 1917)		7/5	4- 4-1913	Mersey
McKEY, F.		P.O. 1st Cl		496	2- 9-1911	Bristol
McLEAN, H.	*	C.P.O.		20	15- 3-1910	Mersey
MILLER, H.		Lieut		—	2- 2-1911	Clyde
MITCHELL, D.C.		P.O 1st Cl		42	1- 3-1911	Bristol
					8- 4-1920	bar
NISBET, P.		Paymaster		—	14-12-1909	A.C.R.
PITCHER, J.	*	C.P.O.	RNV	—	26- 8-1910	Bristol
POPE, W.R.		C.P.O.		18	1- 3-1910	Bristol
					8- 4-1920	bar
PRINGLE, J.K.		P.O.		38	25-10-1910	Clyde
REYNOLDS, W.J.		P.O. 1st Cl		36	1- 3-1910	Bristol.
ROBERTSON, J.Mc.N.		C.P.O.		18	1- 3-1910	Clyde
RUSSELL, J.A.		A.B.		122	28- 3-1912	Clyde
SADLER, P.R.		A.B.		851	14-12-1909	A.C.R.
SEVERN, E.M.		A.B.		52	14-12-1909	A.C.R.
SEWARD, T.F.		Ldg Seaman		525	6- 5-1911	Bristol
					10- 6-1920	bar
SIMONDS, J.W.G.		Lieut		—	25- 6-1910	Tyneside
SIMPSON, J.B.	*	C.P.O.		150	6- 2-1913	Clyde
SMITH, W.F.		C.P.O.		1	1- 3-1910	Sussex
TAYLOR, W.H.		A.B.		5/1998	29- 3-1912	London
WATLING, S.		P.O. 1st Cl		5	1- 3-1910	Sussex
WEBB, H.J.		P.O. 1st Cl		57	14-12-1909	A.C.R.
WIGENS, G.		C.P.O.	RNV	1	6- 4-1910	Bristol
WILDY, E.		Lieut		—	14-12-1909	A.C.R.
WILSON, G.H.		P.O.		830	2- 4-1912	Clyde
WILSON, R		C.P.O.		2/91	12-11-1912	Tyneside

Note : (Dup ....) = Duplicate issued
        * denotes medal known – totalling 15 = 23% survival
        65 medals awarded, of which 8 subsequently had bars.

Medals in the Collection

14-12-1909   CHADWICK-HEALEY, C.E.H. Sub Lt 'R.N.V.'

        Gr 6.   KCB Civil (1909)
                WW1 1914-15 Trio.   'Hon. Commr. Sir C.E. Chadwyck-Healey. RNR'
                Coronation 1911.
                Vide : Previous text for career.

11- 7-1910   ADAMS, H.W.   Ldg Seaman RNVR   (Sussex Div)
10- 6-1920 bar

        Gr 4.   WW1. 1914-15 Trio.   'S-5-42. ... C.P.O. ... R.N.V.R.'
                LSGC Ed VII.   '42. H.W.ADAMS Lg SEAn R.N.V.R.'

5- 1-1912   LOCKETT, H.A.   C.P.O. RNVR   (London Div)

        Gr 7.   O.B.E. 1st Type Military.
                WW1. 1914 Star Trio.   C.P.O./Lt Cdr RNVR 'L1/3319
                                              COLLINGWOOD BTTN R.N.D.'
                Coronation 1911
                Volunteer Reserve Decoration GVR
                LSGC Ed VII.   '11. H.A. LOCKETT R.N.V.R.'

9- 9-1913   HUNTER, J.   C.P.O. RNVR   (Clyde Div)

        Gr 4.   WW1. 1914 Star Trio.   C.P.O. RNVR 'ANSON BTTN R.N.D.'
                LSGC Ed V11.   'C3/1612 J.HUNTER C.P.O. R.N.V.R.'

This is an appropriate place to mention the group of medals in the author's collection awarded to the senior R.N. officer (Rear Admiral Charles J. Norcock, later Vice Admiral) who assisted Chadwyck-Healey during the formative years of the RNVR – as the senior naval representative on the 'Admiralty Volunteer Committee' set up in 1903.

        Gr 4.   Victoria Silver Jubilee 1897. Silver
                Coronation 1902. Silver
                Egypt Dated 1882. Alex, T-El-K, Su84   Lieut RN   HECLA
                Khedive's Star 1882.

Vice Admiral Charles James Norcock died on 13 March 1933 aged 85 years. In his obituary he was referred to as the 'Sea Daddy' of the RNVR, '... entering the R.N. in June 1861. After serving a Commission in China in the *IRON DUKE*, he decided in 1876 to qualify in the Torpedo Branch, then newly started and joined the *VERNON* of which Sir A.K. Wilson was Commander. Later on when Wilson was appointed to the command of the Torpedo Depot Ship *HECLA*, Norcock served with him at the bombardment of Alexandria in 1882 as senior and torpedo Lieutenant. Taking part later ashore and mentioned in despatches, and was present in the Suez Canal during naval occupation and served at Tel-el-Kebir in September 1882. He was in command of a torpedo party on the Sweet Water Canal and attached to the naval flotilla which removed the wounded to Kassassin and Ismailia. Received special promotion to Commander during November 1882 for his actions in Egypt, reappointed to *HECLA* he saw further service aboard her during the Eastern Sudan Operations in 1884.'

His obituary continued '... After commanding *DEFIANCE* (1884-1887) and *CURLEW* (1887-1889) was promoted to Captain in June 1899. For three years from 1899 he held the post of Assistant Superintendent of Naval Reserves but was retired a few days prior to promotion to Rear Admiral, a rank he attained on the retired list in October 1902, and that of Vice Admiral on 1st January 1907. Appointed to the Governing Body of the newly constituted RNVR in 1903 – the Admiralty Volunteer Committee – and largely assisted in drafting the RNVR Regulations ... where his knowledge and experience were indispensable and before he handed over his post to a Commander R.N., he had the satisfaction of seeing the RNVR firmly established in a manner the value of which was abundantly proved during the World War.'

Many adventures ashore of Norcock fighting the Bedouins during August 1882 are recorded in *'The Life of Admiral of the Fleet Sir Arthur Knyvet Wilson, Bart, V.C., G.C.B., O.M., G.C.V.O, D.C.L.'* by Admiral Sir Edward Bradford, K.C.B., C.V.O. Admiral Wilson's most illustrious group of awards, including not only his broken sword with which he earned his V,C. at the Battle of El-Teb in 1884 but his three other presentation swords and other artefacts, are in the author's collection on permanent display at the Royal Naval Museum, Portsmouth.

RNVR LS & GC MEDALS WITH BARS

O.No	Name	Rate	Medal	Bar
TD/X 28	ACKINCLOSE, J.J.	C.P.O.	8- 9-1933	8- 1-1943
5/121	ADAMS, G.J.	P.O.	27- 4-1921	7- 7-1933
42	ADAMS, H.W.	Ldg Seaman	11- 7-1910	10- 6-1920
2/126	AMPHLETT, F.S.	P.O.	24- 3-1920	10- 8-1920
TAD/126	ANDERSON, J.T.C.	E.R.A. 3 Cl	26- 5-1949	15- 2-1957
CD 430	ANDREWS, T.B.	Blk 1 Cl	11- 6-1937	11- 6-1937
TD/X 237	ARMSTRONG, M.B.	E.R.A. 2 Cl	6-11-1933	18- 7-1946
UD/X 345	BALMER, W.J.	Plumber 1 Cl	10-10-1938	12- 7-1950
5/59	BARKER, J.	Blacksmith	30- 4-1920	5-12-1930
UD/ 269	BAYES, A.C.	P.O.	3-12-1937	23- 1-1958
3/138	BAYS, J.	P.O.	30- 4-1920	9-12-1932
ESD 1/12	BELL, J.	A/Ldg Smn	27- 5-1932	17- 5-1944
CO/X 188	BENTLEY, L.	P.O.	20- 1-1944	9- 7-1948
SD/261	BLACKMORE, F.W.	Joiner 4 Cl	14- 1-1938	15-10-1945
6	BLAIR, F.R.	C.P.O.	20-12-1910	18- 1-1922
LD/X 2730	BONNOR, E.T.	E.R.A. 3 Cl	17- 9-1945	15- 2-1956
57	BORRER, W.A.	P.O.	1- 6-1916	22-11-1924
LD/X 1216	BOWELL, C.W.	P.O. Writer	29- 8-1939	15-10-1945
M3/ 146	BOWMAN, J.	A.B.	11- 6-1937	10-10-1944
L/10/21	BOYES, W.S.	Joiner 3 Cl	22- 9-1927	28- 3-1940
L/X 3162	BRADBROOK, R.C.	P.O. (Ty)	10- 1-1945	21-10-1958
1/8	BRADBURY, H.	Yeo Sigs	8- 5-1920	22- 3-1928
SD/ 1210	BROMIGE, E.R.	A.B.	1-11-1949	12-10-1961
4/1297	BROWN, J.McD.	Painter 2 Cl	11- 5-1920	1- 3-1935
LD/X 51	BRYON, J.E.	P.O. Writer	7- 7-1933	12- 7-1950
L6/2121	BUDD, J.A.	P.O.	15- 5-1920	5- 3-1929
LD4/ 192	BUNKER, J.	C.P.O.	31- 8-1934	5- 4-1940
CD/X 764	BURKE, J.	A.B.	27- 7-1943	14- 1-1950
2/663	BURT, W.G.	E.R.A.	24- 3-1920	26- 6-1933
ESD/X 187	CAIRNS, J.	A.B.	17- 5-1939	18- 6-1958
CD/X 203	CAMERON, J.F.	P.O. Writer	17- 1-1939	4- 5-1945
SD/X 491	CARPENTER, G.	A.B.	22- 8-1940	9- 7-1948
ESD/ 295	CHRISTIE, P.G.	Shpt 2 Cl	9- 6-1936	7- 7-1944

1/14	CLARK, D.	P.O.	19- 5-1920	7- 7-1930
TD/ 219	CLARK, Jos.	Ldg Tel	19-11-1935	12- 7-1950
4/144	CLARKE, F.	A/Ldg Smn	19- 7-1920	21-12-1928
MD/ 824	COLLINS, M.	P.O.	26- 4-1948	22- 2-1952
LD1/38	COOPER, E.S.	Writer	27- 5-1932	15- 4-1941
LD/ 2523	COPPENDALE, S.F.	P.O.	25- 3-1949	20-12-1954
			2nd bar	29-11-1967
TD/ 164	CRODDEN, A.J.	Yeo Sigs	19-11-1935	26- 3-1945
UD/X 1200	CROWE, R.B.	Ldg Smn	20- 6-1945	17- 5-1954
BD/X 102	DALTON, L.H.	P.O.	4-12-1933	28- 4-1944
TD/X 267	DAVIDSON, R.	Shpt 1 Cl	11- 5-1934	18- 8-1944
CD/ 155	DAVIE, F.	Lsg Smn	19- 6-1936	28- 4-1944
5/488	DAVIS, A.	A.B.	5-10-1917	13- 6-1925
M 25995	DAWSON, R.	A/E.R.A. 4 Cl	24- 3-1920	13- 5-1932
TD/ 255	DENNISS, G.H.	Painter 2 Cl	19-12-1932	4- 2-1943
MD/X 695	DICK, T.	Actg P.O.	7- 7-1941	17- 3-1952
ESD/X 154	DOUGLAS, G.W.	C.P.O.	14- 3-1939	7- 8-1949
ESD/X 690	DUNN, J.	P.O.	2- 8-1940	14- 1-1950
1/155	DUTTON, W.H.	A/Ldg Smn	16- 6-1920	21- 8-1936
			2nd bar	19- 1-1945
SD/ 1601	DYER, P.A.	Plumber 3 Cl	28- 7-1949	29- 8-1962
CD/ 11	EDMISTON, G.	P.O.	27- 9-1935	26- 4-1945
TD/ 147	EMMERSON, T.G.	Ldg Sig	5- 3-1929	27-11-1942
2/2572	FARRER, J.C.	Ldg Sig	12- 8-1921	13- 8-1933
ESD 13/72	FILSON, A.	Ldg Smn	3- 7-1936	11- 5-1950
			2nd bar	28- 4-1955
LD/ 865	FITCHES, F.G.	A.B.	13- 5-1938	18- 5-1945
			2nd bar	17- 4-1956
TD/X 1019	FLECK, H.H.	A/Shipt 4 Cl	30- 9-1944	23- 4-1954
B 997,253	FORGES, G.	C.P.O.	21-10-1945	2- 8-1958
			2nd bar	27-10-1969
3/1	FORSYTH, T.	Elect	20-12-1918	11-10-1928
901	FRAME, R.G.	Bugle Major	1- 3-1910	10- 6-1920
CD/X 74	FRASER, D.	Joiner 3 Cl	9- 4-1934	14- 1-1944
? 1217	GIBSON, F.	A.B.	3- 7-1945	19- 8-1957
6/104	GIBSON, H.	E.R.A. 2 Cl	23- 2-1922	7- 7-1930
SD/ 92	GOBLE, H.E.J.	P.O.	30-10-1933	15-10-1945
MD/X 559	GOLDWORTHY, W.	Joiner 3 Cl	27- 6-1940	17- 9-1953
UD/ 590	GORE, W.J.	P.O.	26-11-1947	11- 7-1949
ESD/X 407	GOWANS, J.A.	P.O.	19- 9-1938	15-10-1945
			2nd bar	24- 4-1957
3/128	GUSTAFSON, O.	Ldg Smn	30- 4-1920	9-12-1932
LD/X 667	HALE, P.J.	P.O.	11- 5-1934	22- 5-1953
			2nd bar	22- 5-1953
2/17	HARRIS, E.	C.P.O.	18-12-1915	22-11-1924
4/475	HEMSTED, J.R.	Yeo Sigs	21- 1-1916	13- 6-1925
7/45	HEYES, R.	Ldg Smn	7- 2-1920	16-10-1929
UD/ 155	HIGGINSON, F.	P.O.	27- 8-1937	5- 9-1944
4/479	HILL, A.H.	C.P.O.	24- 3-1920	28- 7-1925
T 6/18	HINDESS, T.	Ldg Smn	4- 1-1924	8- 4-1938
LD5/53	HINES, H.M.C.	Ldg Smn	21-10-1932	26-10-1943
? /X 4816	HOLMES, H.G.	P.O. Radar	3-10-1945	16- 3-1960
			2nd bar	10- 7-1969
1/106	HORRIBINE, J.	Sig	12- 8-1921	25-10-1935
CD/ 13	HOSSACK, A.	Ldg Smn	9- 6-1936	9- 7-1948
3/110	HUNTER, J.W.	A.B.	28-10-1920	21- 6-1935

1/1924	JACKSON, D.	E.R.A. 1 Cl	4- 5-1920	13- 5-1932
TD/X 1156	JOHNSON, J.	P.O.	9- 1-1946	18-11-1953
MD/X 1390	JONES, E.	Tel	19- 8-1943	15- 3-1958
BD/ 1496	JONES, W.A.	P.O.	31- 5-1948	7- 4-1953
BD/X 14	JUSTIN, W.P.	P.O.	22- 5-1933	6-12-1948
LD3/ 741	KEEN, F.T.H.	A.B.	4- 9-1936	28- 4-1944
CD/X 853	KELLY, A.L.	Actg P.O. (Ty)	19- 1-1944	1- 8-1951
TD/X 1953	KELLY, J.T.	P.O.	11-12-1945	26- 6-1967
4/82	KENNEDY, J.	Shpt 1 Cl	30- 4-1920	5-12-1930
TD/X 282	KING, R.G.	P.O.	9- 1-1946	4- 2-1946
92	KINGSTON, E.F.	A.B.	31- 7-1912	9- 7-1920
CD9/X 1437	LAMING, E.G.	Ty A/Sub Lt	28- 1-1944	7- 7-1954
ESD/X 671	LAWRIE, J.	Ldg Smn	20- 1-1942	17- 9-1953
S4/174	LELLIOTT, G.	P.O.	18- 6-1923	27- 4-1928
TD/ 250	LIVINGSTONE, A.S.	E.R.A. 3 Cl	3-12-1937	3-12-1937
TD/X 921	LOGAN, M.	Mtr Mech 3 Cl	2- 4-1942	20- 4-1951
			2nd bar	30- 9-1964
73	LOWER, G.A.	A.B.	26-10-1910	6- 5-1922
LD/ 4562	LOVEJOY, W.	Rd Elect (R)	26- 5-1949	27- 2-1959
CD/X 1321	MACDONALD, E.M.M.	Plumber 2 Cl	9-11-1940	11-12-1947
ESD/X 750	MACDONALD, W.	Ldg Smn	16- 6-1942	5- 9-1945
4/33	MACLEAN, E.F.	E.R.A.	15- 8-1919	7-10-1927
CD/ 2727	MADDEN, H.	P.O.	26-11-1947	19- 8-1957
TD/ 47	MAIN, J.W.	Ldg Smn	3-12-1937	11-12-1947
TD/ 16	MARTIN, R.B.	Ldg Smn	13- 6-1928	10-10-1944
LD/X 1250	MASON, R.	Ldg Smn	28- 2-1936	16-10-1950
CD/ 705	McBAIN, J.	P.O.	1- 4-1948	18-11-1953
T2/67	McCARTNEY, T.H.B.	E.R.A. 4 Cl	18- 6-1923	5- 7-1935
UD/X 607	McCOLGAN, E.C.	Actg P.O.	7- 4-1943	29-12-1950
CD/X 148	McELWEE, R.	E.R.A. 4 Cl	1- 3-1935	10-11-1944
? 1038	McFADDEN, R.S.	P.O.	8- 9-1944	15- 7-1952
271	McFARLANE, W.J.B.	A.B.	5-10-1917	1- 7-1925
CD/X 306	McGHIE, M.	E.A. 2 Cl	13-12-1937	11-12-1947
C5/942	McGILL, P.	E.R.A. 1 Cl	27- 8-1919	8- 5-1930
ESD/X 1002	Mc K.D. FORBES, G.	P.O. (Ty)	17- 9-1945	19- 8-1957
ESD/ 2	McLEOD, J.	P.O.	1- 3-1935	15-10-1945
T/DX 252	McLEOD, V.	Shpt 1 Cl	8- 9-1933	11- 6-1945
? /X 317	McMANUS, H.	E.R.A. 4 Cl	31- 5-1944	12- 7-1950
			2nd bar	16- 3-1960
ESD/26	McMANUS, T.	Ldg Smn	29- 3-1935	24-11-1952
ESD/X 1002	MENZIES, W.	A/P.O. (Ty)	20- 6-1945	7- 4-1953
LD/ 3066	MIDDLETON, E.W.	P.O.	3- 8-1945	9- 1-1957
TD/X 290	MILLAR, J.J.	Plumber 2 Cl	3-11-1939	15-10-1945
TD/ 1942	MILLER, J.	Actg P.O.	2- 1-1948	1-10-1968
UD/X 279	MILLS, G.	P.O.	7- 3-1938	11- 6-1945
42	MITCHELL, D.C.	P.O 1st Cl	1- 3-1911	8- 4-1920
ESD/X 438	MITCHELL, J.	Plumber 1 Cl	21- 4-1939	10- 3-1948
3/118	MITCHELMORE, G.E.	A.B.	10- 8-1920	19-12-1930
LD/X 3055	NICE, C.H.	P.O.	6-12-1945	20-12-1954
ESD/X 224	NISBET, J.	Ldg Sig	8- 9-1933	27-11-1942
TD/ 64	OLIVER, J.E.	C.P.O.	21- 6-1935	26-10-1943
ESD/X 687	O'NEILL, J.	Ldg Smn	19- 2-1942	28- 3-1951
SD/ 95	OSBORNE, H.V.	E.R.A.	3-12-1934	18- 8-1944
LD/X 2040	PACKER, J.H.	Sig/Lt Cdr	20- 1-1948	21- 1-1954
BD/X 936	PARSON, L.C.	A.B.	26-10-1942	16-10-1950
SD/X 11	PARSONS, H.W.	Ldg Smn	12- 9-1939	18- 9-1948

TD/X 493	PARSONS, S.H.	Yeo Sigs	16-12-1938	15- 4-1948
2/200	PENNIFOLD, G.A.	A.B.	4- 5-1920	3- 4-1929
LD/X 2014	PERKINS, E.F.	Actg P.O.	29- 6-1944	24- 4-1957
LD 3099	PHILLPOTT, A.J.E.	E.M. 1 Cl	31- 5-1948	17- 5-1956
18	POPE, W.R.	C.P.O.	1- 3-1910	8- 4-1920
MD/X 861	PROCTER, G.D.	P.O.	29- 7-1942	16- 6-1952
SD/X 895	RAMSON, C.S.	A/E.R.A. 4 Cl	31-10-1946	21- 1-1954
LD/X 4677	READ, J.W.	A/Yeo Sigs	28- 7-1949	13- 1-1967
9/3213	REDFEARN, R.V.	E.A.	25-10-1920	14- 1-1935
5/128	REDPATH, E.E.	E.R.A. 2 Cl	20- 4-1920	7- 7-1930
ESD/X 244	REID, J.	Ldg Smn	6-11-1933	11- 3-1943
ESD/X 652	RENNIE, T.G.	A.B.	31- 7-1941	2- 3-1949
LD3/X 69	RICHARDSON, J.	C.P.O. Writer	14- 7-1933	1- 5-1940
LD/X 4503	ROBERTS, H.	Ldg Sig	5-11-1945	25- 2-1960
1/89	ROBINSON, R.W.	E.R.A.	18- 7-1917	20-11-1925
TD/X 338	ROBSON, W.E.	A.B.	10- 1-1945	28- 3-1941
BD/ 197	SAUNDERS, A.G.	Ldg Smn	3-12-1934	11-12-1944
CD/X 10	SAWERS, A.	Joiner 2 Cl	26- 4-1935	13- 9-1943
P/JX 146,198	SCOTT, J.H.	A.B.	5-11-1945	9- 8-1948
? /X 651	SELL, R.C.	Plumber	28- 1-1944	12- 7-1950
525	SEWARD, T.F.	Ldg Seaman	6- 5-1911	10- 6-1920
MD/X 800	SHAKESHAFT, W.H.	Actg P.O.	19- 2-1942	22- 2-1952
MD/ 237	SHARP. T.	Ldg Smn	21- 8-1936	2- 3-1949
MD/X 1145	SHELDON, S.G.	A.B.	7-12-1945	7- 4-1953
SD/X 1009	SHEPPARD, A.	P.O. (Ty)	1- 6-1945	1- 8-1962
TD/X 1546	SHIELD, A.	C.P.O. Writer	22- 2-1944	7- 7-1955
B4/149	SHOPLAND, J.	O.A. 3 Cl	21- 7-1925	25- 5-1936
C5/30	SINCLAIR, J.	Shpt 4 Cl	24- 4-1922	24-10-1933
CD/X 359	SINCLAIR, W.	E.R.A. 1 Cl	20- 4-1934	26-10-1943
LD/X 1039	SMITH, A.E.	Ldg Sig	12-10-1937	20- 2-1947
ESD/X 12	SMITH, J.	Shipt 2 Cl	19- 6-1939	15-10-1945
3/755	SOUTHALL, N.W.	Ldg Smn	24- 3-1920	22-11-1927
UD/ 1578	SPEERS, J.	P.O.	16- 3-1948	23- 2-1961
TD/ 161	SPENDIFF, E.E.	A.B.	21- 6-1935	5- 9-1944
ESD/X 1069	STEWART, G.	C.E.R.A.	12- 7-1943	4- 4-1952
? / 1287	STILL, J.	P.O.	26- 5-1944	22- 2-1952
2/68	STRAKER, J.D.	A/E.R.A. 4 Cl	10-10-1921	15- 8-1934
TD/ 62	SUMMERSIDE, C.W.	A.B.	21- 6-1935	20-12-1945
BD/X 71	SYMONDS, S.G.	E.A. 2 Cl	11- 5-1934	15-10-1945
5/37	THOMS, W.F.	Blk 4 Cl	23-10-1924	23- 4-1937
TD/X 262	THORN, G.	Shpt 1 Cl	20- 4-1934	7- 4-1943
2/194	TICEHURST, A.R.	Ldg Sig	10- 8-1920	19- 2-1934
SD/ 15	TURNER, G.J.	P.O. Writer	20-12-1935	28- 4-1944
			2nd bar	23- 8-1954
TD/X 144	UMPLEBY, S.	Yeo Sigs	16-10-1934	9- 7-1948
UD/X 6	WADE, S.	Joiner 3 Cl	30-10-1936	15-10-1945
LD/ 565	WAKLEY, E.J.	A/Ldg Smn	1-11-1935	3-12-1952
T 1/76	WALKER, S.H.	E.A. 4 Cl	2-11-1923	3-12-1937
? / 1209	WALKER, T.L.	Actg P.O.	3- 8-1945	9- 1-1957
LD/X 5022	WARD, J.	A/Ldg Smn	28- 3-1946	2-12-1966
CD/X 6	WATSON, J.O.M.	P.O.	29- 6-1934	26- 3-1945
L 1/9	WEBB, J.N.	Ldg Sig	20- 1-1922	4- 1-1935
CD/X 2228	WHITE, D.	Actg C.P.O.	5-11-1945	9- 1-1957
MD/ 51	WHITTINGHAM, W.E.L.	Carp 2 Cl	1- 3-1937	25- 2-1963
			2nd bar	?

5/2739	WIGGINS, J.W.	A.B.	23- 6-1920	3- 1-1933
		2nd bar		28- 4-1944
MD/X 921	WILLIAMS, J.C.T.	Tel	9-12-1943	9- 1-1957
SD/X 904	WILLIS, R.G.	P.O.	20- 5-1946	8- 9-1955
TD/ 827	WILLITTS, C.E.L.	P.O. Sto Mech	23- 8-1948	15- 2-1956
ESD/ 20	WILSON, A.	Ldg Smn	24- 5-1935	11- 5-1950
		2nd bar		List 1456
4/1510	WILSON, P.	E.R.A. 1 Cl	4- 3-1921	19-10-1931
L ?	WITHRINGTON, L.	Sub Lieut	22- 2-1918	19- 3-1925
BD/ 1429	WREN, C.D.	Ldg Smn	31- 5-1948	18- 1-1962
? / 946	WYATT, L.C.V.	P.O.	3- 7-1945	9- 1-1957
4/1988	WYLLIE, C.W.	A.B.	12- 6-1920	21-11-1933
6/2118	YELTON, W.J.	P.O.	25- 5-1921	7-12-1931
TD/X 1599	YOUNG, S.	Ldg Smn	2- 1-1948	17- 5-1956
LD/X 2717	YOUNGSON, R.D.M.	Ch Yeo Sigs	4- 4-1941	11- 5-1950

201 medals with one bar and 13 with two bars.

Medals in the Collection

15- 5-1920   BUDD, J.A.   Petty Officer RNVR
5- 3-1929 bar

       Gr 4.   WW1. 1914-15 Trio.   'L.6 – 2121 Ldg Smn/P.O. R.N.V.R.'
              LSGC GV A of F.   '6/121 J.A.BUDD P.O. R.N.V.R. LONDON DIV'
      Awarded bar as Chief Petty Officer

27- 5-1932   COOPER, E.S.   Writer RNVR
15- 4-1941 bar

       Gr 4.   WW1. 1914-15 Trio.   'LZ – 1523 A.B. R.N.V.R.'
              LSGC GV Coinage.   'LD 1 /38 E.S. COOPER WR R.N.V.R.'

Royal Fleet Reserve LS & GC Medal.

Between 1890 and 1900 the increase in the number and size of ships on the Active and Reserve strength of the Royal Navy had outgrown the number of men to man it in peace and upon mobilisation. This rapid building programme was now seen to be in jeopardy since the 'Reserves' of manpower in the event of war had remained stagnant – even though active service personnel had increased from 68,800 to 114,800 during this period. The Admiralty plan put forward to overcome this increasingly difficult problem had the merits of being simple, practical and economical. It was proposed to initiate a new 'Reserve' by utilising those seamen and marines who left the service for civil pursuits after their first 12 year engagement. The Royal Fleet Reserve (RFR) was established by the 'Naval Reserve Act, 1900' with voluntary enrolments commencing on 1st March 1901 from men completing time in the Royal Navy. There were to be two Classes open to seamen, stokers and marines :–

'Class A Reservists' would be drawn from those men under the age of 45 years who were in receipt of life pensions, and personnel already enrolled in the Seaman Pensioner Reserve (SPR) who could transfer irrespective of age. The SPR had been established by Order in Council, dated 29th November 1870, with entrants limited to Petty Officers and men of the seamen branch who held Seaman Gunner (SG) or Trained Man (TM) qualifications, to Signalmen and some Stokers prepared to earn the qualification of TM – henceforth the SPR was 'allowed to die out'.

'Class B Reservists' would be drawn from men who had completed their first 12 year engagement in the R.N., or with a minimum of four years service if of approved character and conduct – this latter category applied to men who had taken early discharge by purchase.

The Royal Fleet Reserve would thus provide a pool of recently trained Petty Officers and men, and N.C.Os. and men of the Royal Marines – slowly inceasing in size over the ensuing years to a maximum of 7,000 Class A and 15,000 Class B – available for immediate service in the Fleet in time of emergency.

The Naval Reserves Committee of 1902 under the chairmanship of Sir Edward Grey, M.P., received evidence that despite the success of the new RFR the most urgent situation was the lack of stokers. Their proposal to enter non continuous service (NCS) men for 5 years with the Fleet to be followed by 7 years with the RFR met with general support – especially since such a shrewd scheme met the twin needs of the Fleet in both peace and war and because '... the Royal Fleet Reserve was quite the best Reserve we have got.' This recommendation was taken up by Parliament and enacted as part of the 'Naval Forces Act, 1903' (3 Edw. 7.Ch 6.) – with time honoured results.

To place the shortage of stokers in historical perspective, it had been caused by the vast increase in coal-fired boilers in the Fleet during the previous 25 years. A measure of this technological expansion can be gauged from the number of stokers required to man complement billets at sea, which grew from 4,200 in 1875 to 8,900 in 1890 – and became 21,400 by 1901.

The wording in the 'Naval Forces Act, 1903' gave flexible and legal effect to the introduction of a 12 year NCS engagement made up of Fleet and RFR time, adding that a man entering the new scheme '... after serving a number of years' service in the Navy was then liable to serve the residue of his term of engagement in the Royal Naval Reserve – of which the Royal Fleet Reserve was a Division under the

'Naval Reserve Act, 1900' ...' An intriguing legal point ! The 'Royal Naval Reserve (Volunteer) Act, 1859' (22 & 23 Vict, Cap 40) was the basic Act upon which all future additional types of 'Reserve Forces' were to be instituted – as new Divisions of the RNR.

A new 'Class C' of the Royal Fleet Reserve was subsequently introduced consisting of seamen entered for 7 years in the RN followed by 5 years in the RFR, for stokers it was the reverse – 'Five years and then Seven in the Reserve', with enrolments for this Class commencing on 1st July 1903 when the prefix of 'SS' (Short Service) to official numbers was introduced. Although legislation had also been concurrently passed for the institution of a separate Royal Marine Reserve, it was never introduced – marines continued to be eligible for the RFR but confined only to Classes A and B.

The recruiting effects stemming from the 'Naval Forces Act, 1903' were outstandingly successful in raising the level of 'Reserves' for the Navy, so much so that they precipitated unintended historic decisions eleven years later. On 16 August 1914 Winston Churchill was minuted as stating 'In order to make the best possible use of the surplus [20 thousand] naval reservists of different classes, it is proposed to constitute permanent cadres of one Marine and two naval brigades [The Royal Naval Division] ...'. By 26 August 1914 the eight naval battalions of the RND included the following numbers of reservists : 3,400 RNVR, 25,000 RFR and 1,300 RNR.

On 1st April 1920 the Admiralty approved the institution of '... a new decoration to be called the Royal Fleet Reserve Long Service and Good Conduct Medal ...', which could be earned after serving 15 years aggregated RN and RFR time conditional on very good character and having carried out the prescribed training. This award – distinctive as a Reserve medal – had been introduced to satisfy the claim of RFR men to equality in this respect with the RNR and RNVR whose LS & GC medals had been instituted in 1908.

DESIGN OF MEDAL AND RIBBON.

Protracted discussions concerning the design of this medallic reward and its ribbon caused considerable delay to its first issue – in July 1922. In April 1921, one year after approval for this medal had been given, the Head of Naval Branch discovered that although the question of its design had previously been raised '... the papers relative to it have long been lost, apparently in the Accountant General's Department ...'

Shortly after discussions had been reopened, the First Lord of the Admiralty specifically asked for opinions on the design of the medal, and the colour of its riband, from Commander H. Taprell Dorling ('Taffrail'), whose writings and definitive book titled *'Ribbons and Medals'* were by now well known and admired. Commander Dorling submitted that :–

' 1. An additional white stripe down the centre of the Navy L.S. and G.C. riband would make it exactly similar to the riband of the King's Police Medal, which itself was altered from blue with white edges on account of its similarity to the L.S. and G.C. riband.

Any other arrangement of blue and white is difficult to design, as the combinations of these colours already in use are innumerable. It therefore seems necessary to introduce another colour, red, and I suggest the design attached [wide blue centre stripe, flanked by narrow red stripes, with white stripes at its edge], which is not in use on any other medal.

2. In regard to the R.F.R. Medal itself, would it be advisable to suspend it from its riband by means of a ring, instead of by a straight bar, which latter is only of real importance in medals with which clasps are awarded.

If the ring were to be adopted some expense would be saved; the new medal would be distinct in appearance from the R.N.R. and R.N.V.R. medal when detached from its riband, a matter of some importance if one or other of them subsequently acquire a greater sentimental value;

while we should be following the precedent of the now extinct Militia, Special Reserve, and Imperial Yeomanry L.S. medals, and the present Territorial Efficiency Medal.

3. All the four Military medals quoted above are oval in shape, and an oval L.S. medal for the R.F.R. bearing the same obverse and reverse as the R.N.R. and R.N.V.R. medal would further enhance the difference between them.'

The Royal Mint was consulted – with the findings that it would not be practicable to fit into the oval shape the picture of H.M.S. *DREADNOUGHT* depicted on the reverse of the RNR and RNVR medal. Additionally, since there was no oval-shaped effigy of the King in naval uniform, the overall cost of the proposed new shape would in every way be more expensive – than adoption of the medal design already being issued to other 'Reservists'. Since no objections were raised to the 'ring' type of suspension or to the colours of the ribbon – approval was sought for the new style of decoration which was sanctioned by the King on 10 April 1921 [*Vide* : Plate No. 17]. Although recommendations and assent for awards of this medal had been made since December 1921, medals complete with ribbons did not become available before July 1922. By curious coincidence, responsibility for the Coast Guard Service – the progenitor of the RFR – was passed from the Admiralty to the Board of Trade on 1st April 1923, thus ending the tradition of awarding active service LS & GC medals to 'Reservists' !

Unlike the RNR, RNVR, RNASBR and later the RNV(W)R, Reserve Fleet Reservists (ex active service RN or RM personnel) were NOT allowed to count double time for their mobilised war service. There was another misapprehension prevalent in the Fleet – brought to the notice of Commanding Officers in October 1941 by Admiralty Fleet Order 4734/1941. It was pointed out that mobilised RFR (for war) personnel were not allowed to count such time either for pension or for the active service (RN) LS & GC medal. Only those RFR men who re-engaged to complete time for pension with the Royal Navy were eligible for the RN LS & GC medal, and those RFR personnel who had already been awarded the RFR LS & GC medal and who subsequently became eligible for the RN LS & GC medal, would have to surrender their RFR award – the medal rolls confirm at least 200 RFR long service medals were surrendered during the period 1939-1951. It should not, however, come as a surprise that some men slipped through this web of complicated regulations to receive both awards – confirmed by a group of medals held in the author's collection.

By the original rules it would have been impossible for any RFR man to earn a 'bar' to his RFR LS & G.C. medal – as foreseen by Commander Dorling in his statements mentioned earlier in this text. Even under revised regulations only one man appears to have succeeded according to the Rolls so far available for public scrutiny. Leading Signalman F.W.C. Macey (J.23,247/CH B 15,387) earned his RFR long service award initially on 19 January 1934, and was presented with his bar on 27 May 1949 – which because of the 'Ring' suspension could only be attached to the ribbon ! It is usual to find both RN and RFR official numbers on the edge of RFR LS & GC medals as prefixes to the recipient's name on the edge of his reward – an example of such numbers are mentioned above for Leading Signalman Macey (CH B = Chatham B Class RFR).

Medals in the Collection

Harold J.A. GADSDEN

Gr 9.	DSM. Geo VI. Impsd Fixed.	Petty Officer		J.102425
	WW2. 39/45, Atl, Af, Pac, Def, War.			
	LSGC GVI Ind Imp RN.	Acting P.O.		H.M.S. HOOD
	LSGC GVI Ind Imp RFR.	A.B.	'J 102425 (PO.B. 19332) R.F.R.'	

D.S.M. *L.Gaz.* 6 Oct 1942 (4351-2). 'For bravery, endurance and sustained devotion to duty in H.M.Ships *AURORA, AVON VALE, LEGION, KINGSTON, PENELOPE*, and at Malta during and after the passsage of an important convoy'

The active service RN LS & GC Regulations specifically disallowed the award of its medal in addition to the RFR LS & GC medal, which can be noted in the RFR Roll (ADM 171/147) against some hundreds of RFR recipients usually with the words – 'RFR medal surrendered on qualifying for naval LS & GC'. Gasden's RFR LS & GC medal was issued to him as an A.B. aboard H.M.S. *HOOD* on 26 May 1939, but that medal roll has no notation about the surrender of his RN LS & GC medal, issued on 4 October 1940 to him as an Acting Petty Officer whilst still serving aboard H.M.S. *HOOD*. It has to be assumed that errors of omission by inexperienced wartime administrators brought about the otherwise impossible combination of LS & GC awards.

Gasden was fortunate to be drafted from H.M.S. *HOOD* prior to 24 May 1941, when she was sunk by *BISMARCK* with the loss of all but three men of her crew numbering 1,421 personnel. The reader may be interested to know that the MBE group of ten medals earned by Lieutenant A.E.P. (Ted) Briggs R.N., one of the three survivors, is on permanent display at the Royal Naval Museum, Portsmouth.

Group with RFR and RMFVR LS & GC Medals in the Collection

Sergeant E. JACKSON RM/RFR/RMFVR

Gr 8.	NGS. GVI. Palestine 1936-1939.	PLX/891		Corporal R.M.
	WW2. 39/45, Af, Ity, Def, War.			
	LSGC. GVI Fid Def. RFR.	'PLY/X.891 PO/B.2540	Sgt(Ty) R.F.R.'	
	LSGC. EIIR DG. RMFVR.	'RMV 201244	Sgt R.M.F.V.R.'	

His RFR LS & GC medal was awarded on 20 January 1949, and his RMFVR LS & GC medal was most probably awarded between 1964 and October 1966 when the title of RMFVR was changed to Royal Marine Reserve (RMR).

Royal Naval Auxiliary Sick Berth Reserve LS & GC Medal

Prior to the commencement of the 20th century very little attention was paid by the Admiralty to 'Manning for Emergency' in branches other than the seaman and stoker specialisations. In a paper on this subject dated June 1885, the Director General of the Medical Department of the Navy, Sir John W.Reid, K.C.B., M.D., stated his intention of placing Sick Berth pensioners upon a 'Reserves' list – complementary to the 'Seaman Pensioner Reserve' established by an Order in Council dated 29 November 1870. He also considered recruiting Temporary Sick Berth Attendants to meet such a reserves contingency – but both these ideas died a natural death in the ensuing peaceful decade. It was the placement of the 1894 Mercantile Shipping Act on the Statute Book combined with the thriving work of the St John Ambulance Brigade since its institution in 1887 – which changed the climate for the eventual creation of the Royal Naval Auxiliary Sick Berth Reserve.

The 1894 Shipping Act required a medical officer to be carried for every '100 souls' aboard any ship, and subsequently the Board of Trade agreed to endorse any Merchant Navy officer's ticket with the notation that he held St John Ambulance First Aid Qualifications. During the 1890s the St J.A.B. Chief Commissioner's reports regularly mentioned the importance of maritime/marine training – but only with reference to the Mercantile Marine.

In 1898 the Admiralty requirement for Sick Berth Reservists stood at one hundred men, but since this was too small a figure for a standing force of such personnel – the practical matter of recruitment never materialised. However, in the following year the needs of the Army caused them to seek large numbers of similar types of recruit due to the casualties suffered during the Boer War. This requirement caused the Army Ambulance Reserve to be formed, with an appeal from the War Office on 3 November 1899 to the St John Ambulance Brigade for volunteers to supplement orderlies of the Army Medical Service – ultimately resulting in 2,046 St J.A.B. men serving in the South African theatre of operations. This Army Reserve scheme was introduced under the personal guidance of Colonel C. Bowdler, the Chief Commissioner of the St J.A.B., who at this same time almost certainly made the suggestion – privately – to someone in the medical department of the Admiralty that a complementary type of naval reserve might prove beneficial.

Due to pressure of work in the Medical Department of the Admiralty, the proposal to pursue '... the formation of a Reserve by the employment for temporary service of men of the St J.A.B. ... considered practicable by the Chief Commissioner, Colonel Bowdler ...' lay moribund until the autumn of 1901. In the meanwhile the Medical Director General, Admiralty, had noticed that the numbers required of Reservist Sick Berth staff had risen to 345 – of whom there were none. It was then decided advisable to appoint a naval medical officer of standing and previous experience with the St John Ambulance Association and Brigade, to undertake the necessary enquiries to set up a scheme to meet this reservist need. A recently retired 'Inspector General of Hospitals and Fleets', Henry C. Woods, C.V.O., M.D., was selected for the duty – commencing work on 1st August 1901.

Woods soon discovered that staffing proportions of Sick Berth personnel in time of war stemmed basically from casualty figures incurred during Napoleonic times ! Fortunately there were some authentic modern statistics available in the carefully prepared report by Baron Sanayoshi on the Battle of Yalu, fought at sea between the Chinese and Japanese in 1894. This new evidence shewed that not only was there a need to increase the ratio of sick berth staff to ship's company in time of war, but also that more

Hospital Ships would be required upon full mobilization. The size of the proposed 'Auxiliary Royal Naval Sick Berth Reserve' (original title) was increased dramatically to a requirement for 1,200 men.

Negotiations for a Royal Naval Reserve of medical personnel comprised of 'Ambulance Men' proceeded apace, with agreed rules for entry, pay, training, pensions, uniform, bounties etc being reached by May 1902 – the Second Sea Lord pronouncing that Dr Woods had worked out a good scheme. Since there was a 'Naval Reserves' Committee, 1902' chaired by Sir Edward Grey deliberating at this time, with part of its agenda concerning; 'How far are the present systems in force for the provision of Reservists satisfactory or capable of extension to ..., Sick Berth Staff' – Dr Woods' scheme was tabled before its members. It received Sir Edward's approval since it did not interfere with any other proposed Royal Navy Reserve rearrangement. On 6 September 1902 the Treasury agreed to an Admiralty inspired application for an Order in Council to bring the naval medical Reserve plan into operation generally.

What none of these prominent people or departments could have known was that although the whole scheme depended on St John Ambulance men – their Chief Commissioner, Colonel C. Bowdler, had never once been asked officially to help the Navy – as this private letter from Bowdler written on 7 November 1902 from his club to Dr Woods so poignantly explains in a somewhat exasperated tone :–

> ' You must not be displeased if I remind you that I am waiting for an official application, request, or enquiry (let it be the last, if you like) as to whether the St J.A.B. will undertake to endeavour to supply the men required for the R.N. Aux S.B. Reserve *[sic]*.
>
> I have been most happy to give you all my assistance in my power, so far unofficially and demi-officially, and I assure you that I fully intend to do all that I possibly can to make the scheme a success. But as I have already plainly said, it is absolutely necessary for my own protection and in the interests of the Order of St John which I represent, so far as the Brigade is concerned, that I should have an official and direct position in the matter.
>
> We have now arrived at a stage when I think it is proper that the Admiralty (that is the counterpart to the Sec of State for War) should favour me with a scheme under which the Brigade could undertake to employ its machinery in order to supply the men required. That scheme we have now completed, so far as the conditions of service are concerned, in the Draft Regulations which you have sent me a copy.
>
> These regulations assume that the Brigade is willing to co-operate, and it seems to me to be absolutely necessary that the official expression of this willingness should be obtained before the Regulations are submitted for sanction of an Order in Council, or whatever it may be. Please clearly understand that I shall reply in the affirmative, but I must be asked.
>
> It is some years since I made the proposal to the Director General Naval Medical Department, quite apart from any action, previous and subsequent, that you may have taken. In the same way it was long before the War in South Africa broke out that I officially offered the services of the Brigade to the Sec of State for War in case of war or threatened invasion, although there was the usual delay in coming to a decision as to accepting them, I was officially approached when it was found that our help was needed. I write this so that you may know my present position before we meet.
>
> *(written in long hand & signed)*   C. Bowdler.
>
> [Chief Commissioner St J.A.B.] '.

[ADM 1/7612. Council Office]

The response was immediate. Dr Woods asked for Bowdler's approval of the draft copy he had enclosed of the proposed Regulations for an Auxiliary Sick Berth Reserve – to which Bowdler responded on official headed notepaper of the Brigade '... in reply thereto I beg to state that I have much pleasure in co-operating to the utmost of my ability in carrying the issue to a successful issue ... in the hope that a satisfactory response will be made to the appeal for patriotism from members of the Brigade.'

The Admiralty Order in Council No 225 received Royal assent on 19 November 1902, its contents and detailed Regulations being communicated to members of the St John Ambulance Brigade by Brigade Order No 77 dated 20 February 1903 – when enrolment commenced. Ambulance-men were informed that the 'Auxiliary Royal Navy Sick Berth Reserve' had been formed for the purpose of supplementing the Royal Naval Sick Berth Staff in hospitals and afloat in time of national emergency and maritime war. In late 1904 the title was changed to 'Royal Naval Auxiliary Sick Berth Reserve' (RNASBR), by which time training afloat and ashore with the Royal Navy was well advanced – one Reservist commenting at this time :–

' We arrived at Portsmouth at 1 a.m., and were met by a naval policeman who took us to the Sailor's Rest (a splendid institution) where we stayed for the night, the Admiral having previously booked our beds. Our quarters on board are excellent. We have new hammocks and bedding. We have had all the sick-berth instruments, etc, explained to us, but we knew practically all of them, having had them at the advanced course class. We could sling our own hammocks, and the doctor and sick-berth steward seemed surprised at the way we made up the sick cot and changed sheets etc. After practice some sick sailors had to be taken to Haslar Hospital and we took entire charge of them – giving us an opportunity for stretcher drill, and travelling to Haslar in the hospital boat. We are having a delightful time and the food etc is of the very best, and all on board are most kind to us – of whom four men wear their South African [Boer War] medals. As I write we are cruising off Torquay ...'

The peace establishment required of this Reserve was 1,200 men, a figure not realised until a few months after the outbreak of World War One – when circumspectly on Friday the 1st of August 1914 at 5:15 p.m., orders were received from the Admiralty to mobilize the RNASBR, the men to report to Chatham, Devonport and Portsmouth. Within 48 hours of despatch of this summons 849 men had reported to their respective Naval Depots. By the end of the 1914-1918 war 3,024 members of the St J.A.B. had served with the Royal Navy in the RNASBR, and a further number of 1,488 ambulance-men saw service with the Royal Naval Division (Medical Unit).

From 1903 until 1921 all volunteer St J.A.B. men entered the RNASBR as Junior Reserve Attendants (J.R.As), receiving advancement to Senior Reserve Attendants (S.R.As) when they passed either the hospital or man-of-war first aid and nursing examinations. Some of these men who showed special aptitude, and were qualified in all respects, could be advanced to the acting rate of '2nd Class Sick Berth Steward' or 'Sick Berth Steward' on a R.N. vacancy arising in a ship or hospital. The most senior Rate in the RNASBR was 'Reserve Wardmaster' ('R.WDMR' on edge of medal) which equated to Chief Petty Officer status in the R.N.

The RNASBR was reorganised in 1921 (AFO 261/1921) to improve retention of its members and enhance recruitment. At this time there were only 477 on the strength to meet a peacetime requirement of 1,275 men. Kit was to be provided directly in lieu of monetary allowances, bounties and retaining fees were introduced and travelling expenses improved. The old titles of J.R.A., S.R.A. and Reserve Wardmaster were abolished. All men still in the Reserve with these titles, who had served in the World War One, were to be regraded as Sick Berth Attendants, Leading S.B.As or Sick Berth C.P.Os. Entrants to the Reserve were henceforth to be made Probationary S.B.As for a year.

In August 1919 the Royal Naval Reserve LS & GC medal was extended to members of the Royal Naval Auxiliary Sick Berth Reserve (AFO 2863/1919). When worn there were no visual differences between these types of award, the design of medal and ribbon were the same – at least until October 1941 when the RNR ribbon was changed from plain green to green with white borders and a central white stripe. Even this difference disappeared in April 1943 when the RNASBR ribbon was changed to match the RNR ribbon (AFO 1800/1943), when the only method of identifying the recipient's type of Reserve once again reverted to sight of the suffix 'RNASBR' to the man's name on the medal's edge – whose prefix was his RNASBR serial number. This number does not appear on any World War One medals the man may have earned, on which a R.N. official number with prefix 'M' will be found.

Although no entry book with names, dates and numbers has yet been found for the RNASBR serial numbers, the following allocation of identification numbers has been constructed as a rough guide to the year in which the man joined the Sick Berth Reserve :–

1903	150	1912	1250	1921	4500	1933	6300
1904	250	1913	1450 *	1922	4700	1934	6450
1905	300	1914	1750	1923	4950	1935	6600
1906	400	1915	2300	1924	5000	1936	6800
1907	650	1916	3500	1925	5350	1937	6900
1908	800	1917	4000	1926	5400 †	1938	7000
1909	900	1918	4300	1927	6000 ‡	1939	7250
1910	1120	1919	4400	1931	6100	1940	7500
1911	1200	1920	4450	1932	6200	1941	8100

Notes. * = Of total entered to date, only 1015 remained in the R.N.A.S.B.R.

† = Numbers 5525 to 5999 unallocated

‡ = No recruits entered for 1928-1930

In December 1919 additional concessions were to apply to the qualifying time for award of Reserve Decorations and Long Service medals of the RNR, RNVR and RNASBR (AFO 3783/1919) – the latter award becoming available after 12 years reckonable service (AFO 2863/1919). The actual time a man served on mobilised war service could now be counted as 'double time' for the period 4 August 1914 to the date of demobilisation. Admiralty Fleet Order No 3783/1919 also allowed reservists (excluding RFR men) already in receipt of a medal, who now found themselves qualified to receive a second (or third) medal – the right to apply for a clasp (or clasps) to attach to their original award.

Similar 'double time' concessions applied during World War Two for mobilised war service for the period 2 September 1939 until the rating's dispersal date.

When World War Two ended – recruiting ceased but the RNASBR was not disbanded until 1949. A certain mystery remains as to how two members of the Reserve received clasps to their medals after 1949, especially the enigmatic 2nd clasp awarded to A.J.Green in 1970.

RNASBR MEDAL ROLL FOR RECIPIENTS OF ONE OR MORE BARS

RNASBR Number	Name	Rate	Medal awarded	1st & 2nd clasps
1365	ADAMS, W.D.	LSBA	13- 5-1920	24- 3-1933
				30- 7-1942
1566	ANDERTON, J.W.	LSBA	20- 8-1924	10- 1-1938
306	ANDREWS, A.	SRA	14- 2-1920	18- 8-1925
3513	APPLETON, J.	SBPO	15- 2-1937	15- 3-1943
3444	ARRAN, H.H.	LSBA	15- 4-1932	9- 5-1945
4782	ASHWORTH, D.H.	LSBA	12- 1-1939	13-11-1946
4393	ASHWORTH, H.	LSBA	9- 6-1933	18- 7-1946
5459	ASHWORTH, H.	LSBA	10- 1-1938	13-11-1946
388	ATKINSON, J.W.	2 SBS	31- 5-1921	13- 5-1927
1951	BAIRD, J.	LSBA	26-10-1921	6-11-1923
160	BALLS, W.H.	Rsve W'dtr	26-11-1919	27-10-1928
3182	BARKER, R.	LSBA	19-12-1932	6-12-1948
4921	BARNES, S.G.	LSBA	15- 2-1937	22-10-1946
3049	BARRICK, H.	LSBA	3-11-1924	? 1937
				6- 4-1949
5090	BATE, A.	LSBA	19- 1-1937	25- 6-1947
5212	BAXENDALE, W.E.	LSBA	7- 2-1936	31-12-1947
5239	BAXTER, J.	LSBA	15- 2-1937	22-10-1946
1741 & 4599	BIRCHALL, J/H.	LSBA	11-10-1921	24-10-1933
				31-12-1947
5201	BIRCHBY, E.E.	LSBA	11-12-1936	31-12-1947
5077	BIRTLE, A.	LSBA	15- 2-1937	9- 5-1945
5129	BLACK, W.T.	LSBA	15- 2-1937	18- 7-1946
5336	BLACKBURN, J.	LSBA	11-12-1936	31-12-1947
6333	BLACKBURN, W.	LSBA	4-10-1946	11- 5-1950
1049	BLACKLEDGE, E.	Rsve W'dtr	16- 5-1920	19-12-1932
1934	BLYTHE, W.G.	LSBA	1- 8-1922	11- 1-1935
1224	BOARDMAN, W.R.	LSBA	10-11-1921	24-10-1933
				15- 3-1943
1245	BODDY, V.	SRA	30-11-1920	15- 2-1937
5523	BOGIE, T.	LSBA	10- 1-1938	16- 2-1948
1876	BOLT, G.J.	SRA	30-11-1920	3- 2-1933
2153	BOWDEN, E.	LSBA	3-11-1922	7- 2-1936
558	BRADSHAW, W.	SRA	14- 2-1920	13- 5-1927
				6- 5-1941
1040	BRINDLE, J.	SRA	10- 8-1920	19-11-1932
749	BROUGHTON, J.D.	SBS 1 Cl	31- 3-1920	24-10-1933
4808	BROWN, N.	SBPO	12- 1-1939	22-10-1946
6193	BUSH, J.A.	LSBA	?	17- 3-1948
1167	BUTTERFIELD, H.	SRA	9- 3-1921	15- 2-1937
				12- 1-1943
3230	BUTTERFIELD, R.	LSBA	22-11-1927	22-11-1947
498	CARLTON, J.E.	LSBA	25- 1-1923	31- 3-1926
1259	CASSON, A.	SRA	16- 4-1920	29-10-1931
1701	CATLIN, A.H.	SRA	28- 7-1921	?
				20-12-1943
5460	CHADWICK, J.	LSBA	10- 1-1938	22-10-1946
1130	CHESHIRE, W.	A/1Cl SBS	30-11-1920	5-11-1934

1673	COFFELL, C.	LSBA	11- 3-1936	6- 5-1941
1672	COFFELL, J.	LSBA	11- 3-1931	13-11-1946
1899	CONLEY, J.R.	LSBA	8- 6-1922	5-11-1934
4506	CONVY, C.	LSBA	24-10-1933	13-11-1946
6247	COOPER, A.E.	LSBA	?	17-10-1946
1039	COOPER, M.	Snr SBS	5- 7-1920	19-12-1932
				5- 1-1943
1972	COOPER, N.H.	LSBA	8- 6-1922	9-11-1934
				30- 5-1947
919	CORNALL, J.L.	SRA	30-11-1920	11- 3-1931
				11- 5-1943
1839	CORNWELL, J.L.	LSBA	29- 8-1921	24-10-1933
				22-10-1946
1783	COULTON, A.	LSBA	10- 4-1924	10- 1-1938
104	CRIDGE, F.	SBS 2 Cl	14- 2-1920	30- 5-1924
5429	CROSSLEY, W.	LSBA	10- 1-1938	31-12-1947
943	CRUMP, B.	LSBA	8- 6-1922	19-12-1930
699	DALE, W.	Rsve W'dtr	22-11-1919	22-11-1927
1260	DANN, J.	Actg SBS	30-11-1920	20- 1-1943
440	DAVENPORT, J.	SRA	14- 2-1920	11- 3-1926
2145	DAVENPORT, T.	LSBA	23- 8-1923	6-11-1934
4942	DAVEY, F.C.	LSBA	15- 2-1937	7- 8-1947
5319	DENNING, B.	LSBA	12- 1-1939	24-11-1950
6388	DEVANNEY, J.	LSBA	?	6-12-1948
1568	DODD, W.	SRA	17- 2-1921	19-12-1932
1372	EDMONDSON, F.	SRA	9- 3-1921	5-11-1934
1136	ELLIS, I.	SBS 2 Cl	16- 4-1920	19-12-1930
987	ELLMER, J.R.	SBS 1 Cl	16- 4-1920	11-11-1931
366	ENGLAND, J.E.	Actg SBS	15- 7-1920	18- 8-1925
1485	ENGLISH, H.	SBPO	?	19-12-1932
2208	ENTWISTLE, J.	LSBA	25- 2-1922	17- 3-1941
361	FERRIER, C.E.	SRA	15- 7-1920	18- 8-1925
2453	FIELDING, E.	LSBA	8- 6-1922	6- 5-1941
M8836	FODDERING, F.	SBS	13- 5-1920	18- 8-1925
1560	FODEN, W.A.	SRA	27- 4-1921	5-11-1934
6305	FOREMAN, S.	SBPO	?	4-12-1946
2051	FOTHERGILL, R.	LSBA	25- 2-1922	?
				8- 2-1943
416	FOWKES, F.	SRA	14- 2-1920	22-11-1927
5399	FREEMAN, F.W.	LSBA	19- 1-1937	22- 1-1948
231	FRENCH, J.	SRA	31- 5-1921	3-11-1924
1268	FRYER, W.	LSBA	2- 8-1927	5- 1-1943
630	GARRATT, F.	SBS 2 Cl	8- 9-1920	22-11-1927
2160	GARRETT, W.G.	LSBA	11- 3-1926	17- 3-1941
1570	GLOVER, T.	SRA	17- 2-1921	19-12-1932
2248	GODDARD, W.W.	LSBA	8- 6-1922	6- 5-1941
879	GRANT, J.	SBS 2 Cl	8- 9-1920	12-12-1930
6977	GREEN, A.J.	SBPO	1-11-1946	27- 6-1963
				9- 6-1970
1870	GREEN, A.J.	LSBA	11-10-1921	6-11-1933
1137	GREENWOOD, J.	SRA	16- 4-1920	24-10-1933
1898	GREY, N.	LSBA	26-10-1921	6-11-1933
958	GRILLS, P.C.	Actg 2 SBS	13- 5-1920	26- 6-1929
697	HALL, I.	SRA	16- 4-1920	22-11-1927
				6- 5-1941
8	HALL, J.	SRA	14- 2-1920	30- 5-1924

5091	HAMMOND, F.	LSBA	19- 1-1937	7- 8-1947
3349	HANLEY, J.	LSBA	19-12-1930	31-12-1947
951	HANSON, F.	SRA	13- 5-1920	31- 1-1929
642	HARDMAN, W.	JRA	26-11-1919	13- 5-1927
50	HARDY, J.	Rsve W'dtr	8- 9-1920	15- 3-1923
4643	HAYNES, S.A.	LSBA	5-11-1934	11-12-1947
90	HEAP, W.	Rsve W'dtr	8-11-1919	16- 5-1923
6297	HENLEY, W.G.	LSBA	26- 2-1943	18- 7-1946
6080	HERD, J.T.	LSBA	13- 1-1939	30- 5-1947
1153	HICKINBOTHAM, J.H.	SRA	23- 3-1921	5-11-1934
				22- 1-1948
1565	HIGHAM, J.	SRA	17- 2-1921	19-12-1932
				30-12-1946
1835	HOGG, W.	LSBA	8- 4-1924	24- 9-1933
				31-12-1947
813	HOLDEN, G.	LSBA	28- 7-1921	19-12-1930
				15- 3-1943
5446	HOLMES, S.C.	LSBA	19- 2-1937	10- 3-1948
1024	HOLT, J.	SRA	16- 4-1920	17- 3-1941
			2nd & 3rd Clasps	20- 2-1947
4501	HOOD, M.W.	SBA	17-11-1943	24- 4-1947
1367	HORN, H.	SRA	13- 5-1920	18-12-1932
				13- 9-1943
5301	HOWARTH, A.C.	SBA	14- 1-1938	31-12-1947
	or HAWARTH			
2136	HOWCROFT, H.	LSBA	27- 9-1922	6-11-1934
1595	HOWKER, W.	SRA	15-10-1920	6- 5-1941
4580	HOWORTH, J.	LSBA	9- 6-1933	14- 1-1944
952	HOYLE, H.	LSBA	28- 7-1921	31- 1-1929
1778	HUGHES, E.	LSBA	15-11-1923	18- 1-1943
5032	HUGHES, W.	LSBA	15- 2-1937	13-11-1946
2038	HULME, H.	LSBA	26- 7-1923	6- 5-1941
4763	HUNTER, A.	LSBA	19- 1-1937	9- 4-1945
4662	HUYTON, G.E.	LSBA	24- 1-1934	28- 4-1944
2069	JACKSON, E.W.	LSBA	5- 2-1923	17- 3-1941
				30-12-1946
4878	JAYNE, G.H.	LSBA	15- 2-1937	13- 1-1947
3191	JENNINGS, F.W.	LSBA	18- 8-1925	6- 5-1941
2509	JOHNSON, W.J.	LSBA	8- 6-1922	6- 5-1941
1371	KENDRICK, G.T.	SRA	10- 8-1920	5-11-1934
5299	KENNEDY, W.N.	LSBA	11-12-1936	31-12-1949
6024	KIPPAX, E.	LSBA	12- 1-1939	31-12-1947
1042	LAMB, G.	LSBA	1- 8-1922	26- 2-1934
957	LANE, R.G.	Rsve W'dtr	13- 5-1920	26- 6-1929
1932	LAW, J.R.	LSBA	28- 7-1921	24- 1-1934
				24- 9-1943
116	LAYCOCK, A.	Rsve W'dtr	16- 4-1920	19-12-1930
1037	LEEMING, E.	SRA	5- 7-1920	19-12-1932
4825	LEES, W.	LSBA	5-11-1934	13- 9-1943
1329	LEWIS, R.E.	LSBA	8- 4-1924	7- 2-1936
5509	LEWIS, S.W.	LSBA	29-11-1941	30- 5-1947
1986	LOGAN, J.R.	LSBA	28- 7-1921	6-11-1933
1197	LORD, J.H.	SRA	30-11-1920	6-11-1934
1050	LOWE, J.W.	SBCPO	10- 7-1922	24-10-1933
1288	LOWE, R.B.	LSBA	29- 8-1921	24-10-1933
				31-12-1947

6335	LUCAS, J.	LSBA	9- 1-1947	13- 1-1947
6299	MACDONALD, J.T.	LSBA	25-11-1947	25-11-1947
1185	MAITLAND, A.	LSBA	24-11-1922	20- 4-1931
1502	MARKEY, G.	SRA	10-11-1921	15- 2-1937
				14- 1-1944
1959	MASON, H.	LSBA	10-11-1921	15- 2-1937
				14- 1-1944
1289	MATHER, W.	SBA	28- 7-1921	24-10-1933
				5- 1-1943
1395	McDUFF, J.W.	SRA	17- 2-1921	5-11-1934
				18- 9-1946
1999	McGEORGE, T.	LSBA	25- 1-1923	15- 2-1937
2179	McNEILL, T.	LSBA	27- 9-1922	5-11-1934
				19-10-1943
1408	MELLISH, C.	SRA	30-11-1920	5-11-1934
				26-10-1943
64	MILLER, C.	SRA	5- 7-1920	19-12-1930
1588	MONTAGUE, A.	SRA	27- 1-1921	17- 2-1933
1657	MOODY, J.E.	LSBA	16-12-1929	15- 3-1943
3447	MOORE, S.	SBA	19-12-1930	13- 1-1947
1928	MORRIS, R.	LSBA	26-10-1921	24- 1-1934
				22- 1-1943
1795	MOSS, J.	SRA	31- 5-1921	15- 2-1937
1580	NEWMAN, L.	SRA	15-10-1920	15- 2-1920
115	NEWNS, J.E.	Rsve W'dtr	6- 6-1920	18- 8-1925
6612	NEWNS, J.H.	SBPO	12- 1-1939	15- 3-1943
2297	NUNN, E.	LSBA	1- 8-1922	5-11-1934
5393	ODELL, F.G.	LSBA	19- 1-1937	22- 1-1948
4849	OLDFIELD, W.G.	SBA	7- 2-1936	28- 4-1944
2503	OWENS, J.	LSBA	8- 6-1922	5- 1-1943
6073	PAGE, H.R.A.	LSBA	12- 1-1939	18- 7-1946
6105	PAVER, P.	LSBA	12- 1-1939	9- 4-1945
1377	PHILLIPS, A.	SRA	28- 7-1921	5-11-1934
396	PILKINGTON, J.	SRA	15- 7-1920	18- 8-1925
4407	PILKINGTON, J.	LSBA	27- 5-1932	3-12-1958
4044	PITKETHLY, J.H.	LSBA	7- 5-1931	13-11-1945
6074	PLEASANT, H.	LSBA	12- 1-1939	11- 2-1947
1074	POTTER, H.	LSBA	8- 6-1922	7- 5-1931
1691	POTTINGER, G.W.	SRA	10- 8-1920	19-12-1932
4767	POTTS, H.	LSBA	9-11-1934	11- 2-1947
1837	POVEY, C.	LSBA	28- 7-1921	24-10-1933
4874	PRICE, O.	LSBA	15- 2-1937	4- 5-1943
6700	RAMSDEN, B.	SBPO	28- 2-1949	28- 2-1949
4944	RANSLEY, H.	LSBA	15- 2-1937	5- 9-1949
1636	RANSLEY, R.	SRA	31- 5-1921	5-11-1934
5413	READ, W.H.	LSBA	10- 1-1938	30- 5-1949
586	RICHARDSON, H.	SBPO	3-11-1934	20- 4-1931
1728	RIDINGS, J.A.	LSBA	26- 7-1923	6- 5-1941
				11- 2-1947
1988	ROBERTS, S.	LSBA	24-11-1922	15- 2-1937
				5- 1-1943
1376	ROLLS, W.	SRA	30-11-1920	5-11-1934
4639	ROUGHLEY, P.	LSBA	24- 1-1934	28- 4-1944
1284	RUDD, W.	SRA	5- 7-1920	29- 4-1932
519	RUSHBROOK, J.W.	SRA	22-11-1919	11- 3-1931
4838	RUST, A.E.	LSBA	5-11-1934	11- 2-1947

1281	SANDERSON, J.	SRA	15-10-1920	15- 2-1937
2007	SEARLE, W.E.N.	LSBA	30- 5-1924	6- 5-1941
1736	SHANKS, W.	LSBA	8- 6-1922	24-10-1933
434	SHORE, J.H.	SRA	31- 3-1920	22-11-1927
1308	SIMON, J.	A/2nd SBS	16- 6-1920	27- 5-1932
1281	SMALLWOOD, J.	SRA	15-10-1920	15- 2-1937
1247	SMITH, A.	SRA	31- 3-1920	15- 2-1937
888	SMITH, S.	LSBA	29- 8-1921	19-12-1930
1455	SMITHSON, H.	LSBA	1- 8-1922	17- 3-1941
1490	SQUIRES, J.	LSBA	8- 6-1922	24-10-1933
7347	STARK, F.E.	LSBA	17- 5-1945	13- 8-1963
1170	STRICKLAND, J.	SRA	9- 3-1921	6-11-1934
4532	SUNDERLAND, J.	LSBA	24- 1-1934	14- 1-1934
5103	SUTTON, H.	LSBA	15- 2-1937	31-12-1947
1893	TAIT, R.	LSBA	26-10-1921	6-11-1933
				22- 1-1943
425	TAYLOR, W.	SRA	15- 7-1920	18- 8-1925
3723	TAYLOR, W.	LSBA	31- 1-1929	6- 5-1941
				30- 5-1947
4854	THOMPSON, P.	LSBA	15- 2-1937	20- 2-1947
1010	TIMPSON, G.W.	LSBA	26-10-1921	15- 3-1943
				15- 3-1943
127	TITTERINGTON, J.	SBS 2 Cl	14-10-1920	30- 5-1924
1446	TONG, W.	SBA	31- 5-1921	15- 2-1937
5473	TROUGHTON, W.	LSBA	10- 1-1938	20- 2-1947
1578	TURNER, C.	SRA	20- 4-1947	24- 4-1947
372	VALENTINE, J.T.	SRA	15- 7-1920	13- 5-1927
4605	VAN, A.W.G.	LSBA	24-10-1933	8- 4-1947
6366	VINCENT, C.E.	SBPO	20- 4-1947	24- 4-1947
1744	WALKER, R.	LSBA	28- 7-1921	5-11-1934
1230	WALSH, C.	LSBA	29- 8-1921	2- 4-1947
				8- 4-1947
5033	WATKINS, W.	LSBA	15- 2-1937	2- 4-1947
2005	WEBB, E.A.	SRA	28- 7-1921	24-10-1933
				5- 1-1943
446	WHITEHALL, J.	SBS	14- 2-1920	11- 3-1926
		2 Cl		15- 3-1943
5474	WHITTAKER, F.	LSBA	10- 1-1938	31-12-1947
5453	WHITTAKER, T.	SBA	10- 1-1938	31-12-1947
1849	WICKENS, F.	SRA	28- 7-1921	24-10-1933
2021	WILDEY, A.H.	LSBA	11-10-1921	24- 1-1934
273	WILDMAN, H.	A/2nd SBS	15-10-1920	25- 9-1925
1824	WINTERBOTTOM, H.	LSBA	26-10-1921	6- 5-1941
2392	WOODHALL, J.T.	LSBA	10- 4-1924	10- 1-1938
269	WOODS, F.	SRA	14- 2-1920	no date
1819	WORMATCH, C.H.	LSBA	26-10-1921	5-11-1934
1203	WRAY, C.W.	SRA	16- 4-1920	29- 4-1932
				24- 4-1947
6227	WRIGHT, G.R.	LSBA	8-10-1943	6- 4-1949
1444	YEABSLEY, F.	SBS 2 Cl	14- 2-1920	7-12-1931

Medals 1443, one clasp 198, 2 clasps 40, three clasps 1. Total medals and clasps 1,682

Medals in the Collection

George V. Admiral of Fleet

Two Bars

RNASBR No

446   WHITEHALL, J.   SBS 2 Cl RNASBR   (swivel)

      Award Dates.   LS & GC Medal 14- 2-1920,   1st bar 11- 3-1926
                                                              2nd bar 15- 3-1943

      Gr 8.   WW1. 1914-15 Trio.   SRA/Actg SBS.2. RN   M.9597
          WW2. Def & Vic
          Coronation 1937.
          St J.A.B Service Medal. 5 Bars
          '1839 Cpl. Foleshill & Longford Div. No 3 Dis 1919'

1835   HOGG, W.   LSBA RNASBR   (fixed)

      Award Dates.   LS & GC Medal 8- 4-1924,   1st bar 24- 9-1933
                                                              2nd bar 31-12-1947 [missing]

      Gr 5.   WW1. 1914-15 Trio.   JRA RN   M.9231
          St J.A.B. Service Medal. One Bar   '6559 Actg/Offr Daubhill Div No 4
                                                                   Dis 1928'

One Bar

1197   LORD, J.H.   'Sen.R.A.' RNASBR   (fixed)

      Award Dates.   LS & GC Medal 30-11-1920,   1st bar 6-11-1934

      Gr 4.   WW1. 1914-15 Trio.   'S.R.A. R.N.'   M.9554

1371   KENDRICK, G.   'Sen.R.A.' RNASBR   (swivel)

      Award Dates.   LS & GC Medal 10- 8-1920,   1st bar 5-11-1934

      Gr 5.   WW1. 1914-15 Trio.   SRA RN   M.9219
          St J.A.B. Service Medal   Two Bars   '5337 Pte Shipley Div No 5 Dis
                                                                   1926'

2392	WOODHALL, J.T.	LSBA RNASBR	(fixed)

Award Dates. LS & GC Medal 10- 4-1924, 1st bar 10- 1-1938

Gr 5. WW1. 1914-15 Trio. JRA RN M.10,644
St J.A.B. Service Medal. One Bar '6581 Cpl Atherton Div No 4 Dis 1928'

George V. Admiral of the Fleet

No Bars

174	LAMBERT, W.G.	Reserve Wardmaster RNASBR (swivel)

Award Date. LS & GC Medal 26-11-1919

1082	MARKHAM, E.C.	SRA RNASBR	(swivel)

Award Date. LS & GC Medal 31- 3-1920

Gr 4. WW1. 1914-15 Trio. SRA/Act SBS RN M.9190

1364	DIX, T.	2nd R.S.B.S. RNASBR	(swivel)

Award Date. LS & GC Medal 13- 5-1920

Gr 4. Serving Brother St John.
WW1. BWM. SBS RN M.8760
St J.A.B. Service Medal. 4 Bars '2918 Cpl Olney Div. No 3 Dis S.J.A.B. 1923'

991	COOPER, J.	Actg SBS RNASBR	(swivel)

Award Date. LS & GC Medal 5- 7-1920

Gr 3. WW1. BWM. '2 S.B.S. R.N.' M.8776
St J.A.B. Service Medal. No Bars. '1391. Sergt C Divn Bristol Corps No 2 Dist. 1918'

220	PUTT, H.	Actg SBS RNASBR	(swivel)

Award Date. LS & GC Medal 23- 3-1921

Gr 7. WW1. 1914-15 Trio. SRA RN M.8167
Coronation St J.A.B. 1902. Bronze. Pte. (engraved)
Coronation St J.A.B. 1911. Silver. Pte. (engraved)
St J.A.B. Service Medal. No Bars. '2002. Pte No 19(Smet Gas Co) Div No 1 Dis. 1920'

1708	ENTWISTLE, W.R.	LSBA RNASBR	(fixed)

Award Date.   LS & GC Medal 8- 6-1922

Gr 4.	1914 Star with Fire Bar.	'Jun.R.A. R.N.A.S.B.R.'	M.9795
	BWM & Vic.	'S.R.A. R.N.'	

Accompanied by a St John Ambulance Association Badge, with upper ring for attachment of service bars. Badge engraved on reverse - '176116 William R. Entwistle'. Additionally, twenty one separate dated bronze service bars for years 1917 – 1921 and 1924 – 1939, all engraved with his number '176116' on reverse, and two long service thinner bars for 20 years & 25 years, the latter engraved on its face the year '1936' as well as '176116' on its reverse.

He was a member of the RNASBR on the books of H.M.S. PEMBROKE (Chatham), and served with the Naval Brigade at Antwerp during the opening phase of World War One.

George VI Ind Imp.

No Bars Two LS & GC Medals – RN & RNASBR

7414	GRAHAM, A.	LSBA RNASBR

Award Date.   LS & GC Medal 5- 6-1946

Gr 7.	WW2. 39/45, Atl, Dcf & Vic		
	CSM EIIR/Borneo – Malay Peninsula.	S.B.P.O.	MX 802,342
	LSGC. EIIR RN	S.B.P.O.	H.M.S. DRAKE

No Bars

6917	VERNON, E.	SBA RNASBR

Award Date.   LS & GC Medal 10- 7-1946

Gr 8.	WW2. 39/45, Atl, Af/42-43, Ity, Def & Vic.	
	St J.A.B. Service Medal. 3 Bars	'Sgt. No 2 Dis. 1941'

7889	STABLER, G.	SBA RNASBR

Award Date.   LS & GC Medal 25- 2-1947

Gr 7.	St John Serving Brother.	
	WW2. 39/45, Atl, Af, Vic.	
	St J.A.B. Service Medal. 1 Bar.	Pte. Yorks. 1953.

Meritorious Service Medal Group

1095   WEBBER, V.A.W.   LSBA RNASBR

   Award Date. LS & GC Medal 1- 8-1922

   Gr 5. WW1. 1914-15 Trio. 'S.B.A., RN'/'S.R.A. R.N.' M.15411
       LSGC. GV RNASBR. LSBA RNASBR   1095
       MSM. GV.   'SBS. MMR. HOSPITAL BARGE 245.
                 DWINA RIVER.'

His medals were accompanied by many personal papers inclusive of a rare citation for his RN MSM.

This group of awards was acquired 'as worn' by the recipient, who would have been unaware of the official order in which they should have been placed on his pinned attachment bar. His personal preference has not been disturbed. The M.S.M. leads, his L.S. & G.C. Medal follows – ahead of his World War One service medals. Few today would argue with his sentiments, and even less in those days when Jubilee and Coronation medals had recently lost their official precedence in 'order of wear' before campaign awards.

Born on 22 September 1886 at Dovercourt, Essex. Webber became a member of the Chichester Division of the St John Ambulance Brigade on 24 February 1906, and three years later became a naval reservist by joining the Royal Naval Auxiliary Sick Berth Reserve with enrolment number 1095. He responded promptly to the mobilization of the RNASBR ordered on the 1st August 1914, being rated Sick Berth Attendant in an R.N. vacancy aboard H.M.S. *THESEUS* on 2 August when he was given the official number M.15411. His next seagoing vessel was the hired Armed Merchant Cruiser *OROPESA* which he joined on 30 December 1914, renamed *CHAMPAGNE* a year later when loaned to the French Navy – from which Webber was discharged in March 1916 – receiving a report that his Staff Surgeon had '... always found him courteous and reliable under difficult and dangerous circumstances ...'. A gifted statement as events later proved.

For the next four months he served at Mullion Naval Airship Station, prior to joining H.M.S. *ALBION* in July 1916 until the Armistice – when he was placed on the books of H.M.S. *VIVID III* for duty aboard the *KALYAN*. During the war this commercial vessel had been used for troop carrying between England and Egypt and Salonika, but by November 1918 had been converted to an Hospital Ship. It is presumed that Webber upon joining her became a member of the Mercantile Marine Reserve (No 99,051), since she was immediately sailed for North Russia – where she remained berthed in the Dwina River estuary until the spring of 1919. The function of *KALYAN* was that of temporary Base Hospital for British, American, French, Italian, Chinese and Russian sick and wounded – transferred to her by barge from the mainland until the Dwina froze solid, when a railway line was laid upon its surface for similar function.

Only because Webber earned the Meritorious Service Medal are we aware of his duty in this theatre of operations, and even more fortunately his citation accompanied his medals into this Collection – since such details never appear with the London Gazette announcements of this type of award. The generalised heading for the thirteen awards of the naval M.S.M. – which included Webber – published in the *London Gazette*, 12 December 1919, reads for : 'Services in Russia 1918-1919.', which is also known to include awards to nine men serving in H.M.S. *GLORY* based at Murmansk. Most unusually citations for these 13 men earning MSMs can be found at the PRO in ADM 137/1704.

The edge details on his award confirm his privately despatched individual citation and that written by the Senior Medical Officer of the North Russia Expeditionary Force on 6 September 1919 (*Vide* : ADM 137/1704, page 38), with the latter additions to the former citation in brackets [ ] as follows :–

' For services with the Dwina River Expedition Force 1918-19 in connection with which he was specially reported [by the Medical Officer in Charge of Barge 245] – as having exhibited devotion to duty and great ingenuity in devising and carrying out improvisations in the method employed in slinging cots for serious cases [which all tended to increase efficiency]. [Was also brought to my notice] for his excellent work regardless of personal danger when in charge of stretcher parties in recovering wounded from awkward positions [on board H.M.S. *GLOWORM* after the recent explosion] and surmounting great difficulties in their removal'.

He opted to receive his Meritorious Service Medal in London on August 14 at one of the regular presentation ceremonies performed for such investitures each Sunday at 9:45 a.m. during 1920. The precedence he gave this award in his group shews that he would never have elected to receive his award by registered mail. On 1st August 1922 he was awarded his RNASBR Long Service & Good Conduct Medal with its plain green ribbon.

Royal Naval Volunteer (Wireless) Reserve LS & GC Medal

In 1932, the Admiralty decided that the offer of many enthusiastic radio amateurs ('hams') to form an Auxiliary Reserve provided an excellent opportunity to augment the RNVR Telegraphist Branch. The offer was accepted, whereby the civilian volunteers were duly entered into a new formation, the Royal Naval Wireless Auxiliary Reserve (RNWAR). These wireless auxiliary reservists provided their own equipment and were taught Naval Operating Procedures, but were not provided with any form of uniform. Since this formation (RNWAR) had no legal foundation, members were told that in time of war they must hold themselves in readiness for service ashore or afloat but that they were not subject to general mobilization – their instructions continued somewhat enigmatically with the statement that '...the Admiralty would only 'call up' such members as may be required ...' !

On 5 January 1939 the Admiralty Board decided that for the foreseeable future there was '... to be one source only of supply of Reserve W/T ratings, apart from pensioners and the Royal Fleet Reserve, namely the Royal Naval Volunteer (Wireless) Reserve ...' – accorded the short title of RNV(W)R.

This new sub-specialised Reserve was to be composed of the existing members of the Royal Naval Wireless Auxiliary Reserve, which had been reconstituted on 1st January 1939 as the Wireless Section of the RNVR and thus henceforth subject to the provisions of the 'Naval Forces Act, 1903'. At the same time the Telegraphist Branch of the RNVR was disbanded, but automatic transfer to the RNV(W)R of the men affected did not take place – nevertheless, volunteers from this background were expected to join the new specialist Reserve, which was to be administered directly by the Admiral Commanding Reserves as a self contained organisation.

On the outbreak of the World War Two this Wireless Reserve was mobilized and immediately took its place alongside regular telegraphists in the Fleet. In December 1941, the same LS & GC medal concessions which had been granted to the larger 'Reserves' (RNR, RNVR & RNASBR) were also to apply to members of the RNV(W)R. They were similar to the principle of concessions granted for World War One, allowing the actual time a man served on mobilised war service to be counted as 'double time', for the period 2 September 1939 to the date of demobilisation for officers, or in the case of ratings – their dispersal date. The requisite time to earn the RNV(W)R Long Service and Good Conduct medal was the same as that for the RNVR LS & GC award – namely twelve years. When worn, there were no visible differences between these two types of award, the design of medal and ribbon were identical. Classification was only detectable from the naming details impressed on the medal's edge. On a RNV(W)R award – the official number includes within its prefix the letters 'WRX' usually preceded by the Port Division letter (P/ , C/ , or D/ .), with the suffix to the recipient's name of 'RNV(W)R'. Members of this Wireless Reserve were also eligible for a 'bar' to their LS & GC medal, like their RNVR counterparts had been since December 1919 (AFO 3783/1919) – after completing a further period which would again have qualified them for an award of the medal (i.e. 24 years reckonable service inclusive of the war service 'double time' concession).

Since former members of the RNWAR were not fully qualified 'Reservists' within the meaning of the 'Naval Forces Act, 1903', they were unable to count their 'auxiliary' time towards the RNV(W)R LS & GC medal – but volunteers who were transferred from the Telegraphist Branch of the RNVR were allowed to count their former time towards the medal. Just as the RNVR LS & GC medal had, since its inception, been allowed to be earned by officers (unlike the RN LS & GC medal until 1981), so were

RNV(W)R officers eligible. Amongst the total of 211 men on the roll for this award, twenty three officers feature as recipients of the RNV(W)R LS & GC medal, with such varying titles as Lieutenant, Temporary Electrical Lieutenant and Lieutenant Commander (S) ! These officers could retain their LS & GC medal if at a later date they were awarded the Volunteer Decoration.

The RNV(W)R was reconstituted in March 1947 and again opened to recruits, when many pre-war members were the first to re-enrol, moreover the RNV(W)R was the only Reserve which could guarantee its members Telegraphist ratings in the Royal Navy for their National Service. The dedication of these radio specialists is exampled in the fact that all pre-National Service members of this Reserve rejoined the RNV(W)R on completion of that service.

When the Naval Volunteer Reserves were re-organised in December 1957, the separate identity of the RNV(W)R ceased. The newly formed 'Unified Reserve' (RNR – Group A) encompassed many of the existing members of the RNR (General Service & Patrol Service), RNVR, RNV(W)R and WRNVR. RNR Groups C and D were now to include some men and women who had previously been ineligible for the LS & GC Medal such as the RNV(P)R. (P = Postal) – and Local Rating's Reserve, filling shore billets upon mobilization usually in the vicinity of their homes.

At this time of writing, only those LS & GC medals awarded to members of the RNV(W)R up to November 1949 can be found in the LS & GC medal rolls so far released for public perusal at the Public Record Office. This RNV(W)R Roll contains 211 names, of whom only six men have additional notations shewing the date when a 'bar' was issued. Of minor historical interest, the practice of issuing rosettes – 'similar to those worn on the 1914 Star' – to denote the award of a 'clasp' when the ribbon was worn without the medal, commenced in August 1942 (Admiralty Fleet Order 3859/1942). This supplementary sartorial symbol only applied to members of the RNR, RNVR, RNV(W)R and RNASBR, unlike active service personnel of the RN and RM who were not yet even allowed to earn a 'bar' – which in practical terms was not introduced for them until 1951.

ROLL OF RNV(W)R PERSONNEL WHO EARNED BARS TO LS & GC MEDALS

			Medal	Clasp
C/WRX 82	CLARK, R.G.	Actg P.O. Tel (Ty)	12- 7-1943	29- 8-1951
C/WRX 332	FOZZARD, F.W.	Actg P.O. Tel	2- 3-1940	13- 1-1947
P/WRX 798	HILL, H.P.	P.O. Tel	17- 9-1945	13-11-1958
C/WRX 174	SHIELL, A.F.	Tel	13- 5-1947	17- 7-1956
WRX 42	TEMPLAR, W.A.	Tel	28- 1-1944	7-11-1951
C/WRX 431	TURNBULL, J.I.	Tel	29- 7-1947	18-11-1954

Medal with Bar in the Collection

Acting P.O. Tel F. W. FOZZARD R.N.V.(W).R.

Gr 7.	WW1 1914-15 Trio.	J.13721 Tel R.N.
	WW2. 39/45, Def, War.	
	LSGC. GVI Ind Imp with bar.	'C/WRX 332 Actg P.O.Tel R.N.V.(W).R.'
	Medal awarded 2- 3-1940 Bar 13- 1-1947	

An example of a man who had served eleven years in the Telegraphist Branch of the RNVR before voluntarily transferring to the RNV(W)R when the former Branch was abolished – and the latter instituted.

Medal without bar in the Collection

¡VI. Ind Imp.   '1086 S.C.H. TAYLOR. TEL. R.N.V.(W).R.'   Awarded 5-11-1945

Royal Marine Forces Volunteer Reserve
& Royal Marines Reserve
LS & GC Medal

On 30 June 1903 the 'Naval Forces Act, 1903' (3 Edw. 7.Ch 6.) was passed in Parliament – as an amendment to the 'Royal Naval Reserve (Volunteer) Act, 1859' (22 & 23 Vict. Cap 40) – which amongst other authorisations (such as the introduction of the RNVR) also allowed the Admiralty to raise and maintain a force to be called the Royal Marines Reserve (RMR), but the scheme came to nothing at this time.

The Royal Marines Forces Volunteer Reserve (RMFVR) was formed during 1948 stemming from provisions in the 'Royal Marines Act, 1947'. Recruiting commenced on 1st November 1948 for this new Reserve, which came under the direction and administration of the Commandant General, Royal Marines (AFO 3151/1948). On 1st October 1966 the title of this Volunteer Reserve was changed to 'Royal Marines Reserve', not as a complementary force to the Royal Fleet Reserve (RFR) as originally envisaged in 1903. [Note : Since 1903 marines could become members of the RFR and earn the RFR LS & GC medal].

Members of the RMFVR could earn the Royal Naval Reserve LS & GC Medal after 15 years service, with former time in the RM or RFR being allowed to count provided it had not been used for an award of another type of LS & GC medal. Similar rules applied to members of the RMR. By 1978, clasps could be awarded after completion of a further 10 years service, provided applicants had completed a further 7 annual periods of training. Commencing 1st November 1971 there was an overriding rule that any reservist who was out of date with 'Continuous Training' requirements negated eligibility to any medallic reward irrespective of completion of its necessary 'Qualifying Service'.

Medal in the Collection

Sergeant E. JACKSON RM/RFR/RMFVR

Gr 8.	NGS. GVI. Palestine 1936-1939.	PLX/891 Corporal R.M.
	WW2. 39/45, Af, Ity, Def, War.	
	LSGC. GVI Fid Def. RFR.	'PLY/X.891 PO/B.2540 Sgt(Ty) R.F.R.'
	LSGC. EIIR DG. RMFVR.	'RMV 201244 Sgt R.M.F.V.R.'

His RFR LS & GC medal was awarded on 20 January 1949, and his RMFVR LS & GC medal was most probably awarded between 1964 and October 1966 when the title of RMFVR was changed to Royal Marines Reserve (RMR).

Royal Marines Reserve Decoration

Officers must have 15 years' service over the age of 18 years having completed 12 annual periods of training during that time. All time spent as an other rank or officer in the RMFVR and RMR was allowed to count towards the aforementioned 15 years – with the proviso that any time already served which had earned a long service award could not be included. A clasp to the Decoration – same design as RNR and RNVR – could be granted after completion of a further 10 years service provided 7 annual periods of training had been carried out [Navy List 1978].

During the transitional period after the RMFVR was renamed to RMR, from 1st October 1966 to 31 March 1974, the VRD was available to ex RMFVR officers.

Royal Naval Auxiliary Service
Long Service Medal

The pre-history of Royal Naval Auxiliary Service (RNXS) commences with the announcement on 26 January 1952 in the House of Commons by the Prime Minister, Sir Winston Churchill, of the formation of the Royal Naval Minewatching Service (RNMWS). By 1961 the mining threat to the coastline of the United Kingdom had been surpassed by other dangers, such as the growth of the Russian Navy into a deep water fleet and the more pressing thought of nuclear attack. The duties of 'minewatchers' were widened to take over other tasks at ports and anchorages in a 'Port Party' concept – which soon engulfed the original functions of the Minewatching Service.

A formal announcement in the House of Commons on 5 November 1962 brought the Royal Naval Auxiliary Service into being in lieu of the Minewatching Service. The constitution of the RNXS continued unchanged from that of the RNMWS, remaining also as a uniformed civilian volunteer service operated, trained, administered and financed by the Ministry of Defence – Navy. The role of the new Auxiliary Service was to provide port parties in support of the local naval authority, and to support the Naval Control of Shipping Organisation in particular with the boarding and berthing of ships at Assembly Anchorages – thus allowing regular Naval personnel to be relieved for combat duties in the event of war or emergency. At its peak the strength of the RNMWS had comprised 121 units with 4,600 personnel, by 1988 the RNXS possessed 94 units and a strength of 3,800.

During 1961 a proposal was made to initiate a Service Medal for 'Minewatchers', but pressures of other events and the more important task of introducing the Royal Naval Auxiliary Service – set back this morale boosting and numismatic enterprise for four years – by which time the RNMWS had been disbanded. But in 1965 the dedication and domestic sacrifice of many ex-'minewatchers' and newly created 'auxiliaries' – men and women – received their well earned rewards.

On 27 July 1965 the Queen approved the institution of the 'Royal Naval Auxiliary Service Medal' for long service. The Medal, in cupro-nickel, bears on the obverse the crowned effigy of the Queen and, on the reverse, a Naval Crown and fouled anchor (tilted to the left) surrounded by oak leaves – [*Vide* : Plate No. 17] with a supporting ribbon coloured, white, blue, white, with a green vertical stripe through each of these colours.

This Service Medal was to be awarded upon recommendation to officers and auxiliaries, including women, of the Royal Naval Auxiliary Service who had completed a total of 12 years satisfactory continuous service full-time or part-time. Time with the formerly titled Royal Naval Minewatching Service under Admiralty organisation from 12 January 1952, and Navy Department, Ministry of Defence organisation since 1st April 1964 – could be reckoned towards the period of service requisite for the Service Medal. Broken service if spent with the Armed Forces was allowed, provided the members re-joined the RNXS within six months of leaving the Armed Forces. Members are eligible to receive a clasp to the medal on completion of each additional twelve years of qualifying service after the end of the qualifying period for the grant of the Service Medal. Distribution of these medals commenced in 1966, when the lengthy lists caused delays in delivery to recipients due to the time taken to prepare the named awards.

Bibliography : *'The Royal Naval Auxiliary Service – The first twenty five years'* by John Murray, Maritime Books 1988.

Medals in the Collection

Stanley W. JOHNSON

Gr 7. BEM. GVI. 1st Ty. Mily Div.   Petty Officer   R.N. C/SSX 23110
        WW2. 39/45, Atl/F&G, Af/42-43, Def, War.
        LSGC RN Aux S. EIIR DG. and bar.   'S.W. JOHNSON'

Lieut Leonard C.E. GOULD R.N.V.R.

Gr 6. WW1. BWM.   'Lieut L.C.E. Gould RNVR'
        Mercantile Marine Medal.   'Leonard C.E. Gould'
        WW2. Def, War.
        LSGC RN Aux S. EIIR DG.   'L.C.E. GOULD'

G.N. DURHAM

Gr 5. WW2. 39/45, Pac, War.
        Australian Service Medal.   No prefix. 'R.A.N.V.R.'
        LSGC RN Aux S. EIIR. DG.   'G.N. DURHAM'

Miss F. JOHNSON

Gr 5. WW2. 39/45, Af, Ity, War.
        LSGC RN Aux S. EIIR DG.   'Miss F. JOHNSON'

Royal Naval Dockyard Police, Hong Kong, Long Service Medal

The history of this unique police Long Service award stems from one of the points made in a petition dated 5 September 1919, signed by 94 members of the Indian Contingent of the Hong Kong Royal Naval Dockyard Police, which was addressed to the Commander of the Dockyard – and forwarded to the Admiralty with little or no comment. Not only were these men seeking better conditions such as pensions, free married quarters, longer paid leave and free passages for their families from India – they also sought 'Good Conduct Medals and a small sum of money as a reward to show our good service'. The Admiralty, in reply, then sought the views of the Commodore, Hong Kong, with regard to his proposal to institute a medal and gratuity to the Indian members of the Hong Kong Dockyard Police – the European contingent in this Force were deliberately not included at this stage, nor was it intended '.. to apply the Medal to the Police at other Yards.'

The Commodore's report on the subject dated 28 June 1920 contained the basic reason for the introduction of this new award and its proposed rules. The scheme had the approval of the Dockyard Police Officers because the majority of their men were young and inexperienced, and it was considered that it would benefit the Service if an inducement was given to them, in the form of a medal and allowance. The reasoning was that their men might '.. remain on; since the longer a man remains the more confidence he gets in himself and does his work more satisfactorily in consequence.'

It was submitted that the Indian members of the Dockyard Police should be granted a Good Conduct Medal upon completion of fifteen years service of continuous very good conduct, at the discretion of the Commodore, Hong Kong. Unlike most other Long Service gratuities, it was proposed that approved recipients of the award, after serving 15, 20 & 25 years, should receive additional monthly allowances to their pay amounting to HK$ 2,3,4 for Sergeants and HK$ 1,2,3 for Constables respectively. At that time in 1920 there were two Sergeants who had served over twenty years, and three Sergeants and three Constables who had been in the Force for more than fifteen years. The whole scheme was based on that already pertaining to the Indian Contingent within the local Colonial Police Force, who could earn the long established 'Hong Kong Police Medal For Merit'.

After receiving Treasury sanction to these proposals, the Admiralty initiated the new awards in a letter dated 14 January 1921 to the Commodore, Hong Kong : –

'... it is approved for Good Conduct Medals to be granted to members of the Indian Contingent of the Hong Kong Dockyard Police Force under the following conditions, viz : – (1) The Medals will be awarded, at your discretion, subject to a Very Good character being obtained at the end of fifteen years service in the Police Force, account being taken also of the record throughout the whole period of such service. (2) Men holding Medals will be granted extra allowances as under [as in proposals mentioned above] ...'

On 9 March 1921 seven members of the Dockyard Police were awarded Good Conduct Medals (annotated on the accompanying Roll by *) – which had not yet been designed and would not adorn their uniforms until May 1922, but at least these men received their additional allowances with their pay back-dated to 14 January 1921.

After some discussion – when the proposal to issue the Army LS & GC Medal to these policemen was dismissed ! – it was decided that the Commodore's proposal should be adopted, whereby the Hong Kong Dockyard Police Medal should be similar in design to the Hong Kong Civil Police Medal For Merit. Amongst others in the Admiralty, Commander Taprell Dorling ('Taffrail') concurred with this idea – concluding that '.. no existing naval or military medal would be at all appropriate ..'

On 24 November 1921 the Accountant General of the Navy wrote to the Deputy Master of the Mint in this manner : –

' I have to forward herewith a rubbing of the Hong Kong Civil Police Force Medal [HKCPFM] and to inform you that the same design, except for the lettering on the Reverse, has been adopted for the Hong Kong Royal Naval Dockyard Police Medal. The new medal is to be in bronze [i.e. 4th Class HKCPFM as awarded to Chinese and Indian members] and to bear on the Reverse 'ROYAL NAVAL DOCKYARD POLICE HONG KONG' as arranged [sketch provided] in lieu of the words 'HONG KONG POLICE FORCE FOR MERIT' which appear on the existing Civil Police Medal. ... The return of the rubbing [supplied by the Commodore, Hong Kong] is required [since a specimen of the HKCPFM could not be supplied by the Royal Mint].'

Mr J.W.Hocking at the Mint proposed to use the Obverse of the Board of Trade (Sea Gallantry) Medal, with a rearrangement of the words as shewn on the Admiralty sketch for its Reverse, which otherwise would have resulted in the words 'DOCKYARD POLICE' being in very small letters. On 9 January 1922 the Admiralty informed the Royal Mint that the King had approved the design for the Dockyard Police award [*Vide* : Plate No. 18], and requested fifty of these new medals to be supplied as early as possible. They were delivered on 9 March 1922.

Meanwhile it had been decided to despatch the medals unnamed, since there would be no difficulty (or expense to the British Government !) in engraving the edge details locally in Hong Kong. By November 1921 the wrangling over the colour of the ribbon had been resolved, when an order was given to Kenning & Co to supply fifty yards of 1 1/4" wide ribbon, golden yellow in colour with two centrally placed vertical stripes of royal blue each 3/16" wide set 1/8 " apart.

The strength of the Indian Contingent of the Royal Naval Dockyard Police, Hong Kong, in November 1922 amounted to one Sub Inspector, 5 Sergeants, 2 Lance-Sergeants, 3 Acting Lance-Sergeants and 101 Constables.

Some six months after the rewarded men of Indian Police Contingent began wearing their Long Service Medals, four European members of that Force (annotated on the accompanying Roll by +) signed a Petition dated 9 December 1922 requesting similar treatment. Whilst approval for the medal was granted almost immediately, discussions concerning the proposed increase in size of the allowances for Europeans postponed its general implementation. The Commodore, Hong Kong, was once more approached to shed light on the allowances given to Europeans who earned the Hong Kong Civil Police Force Medal for merit. The details he forwarded on this rare award are possibly of wider interest. The annual additional allowances for the 1st, 2nd, 3rd & 4th Class amounted to HK$ 120, 90, 60 & 30. The 4th Class Medals were normally granted for 'long and faithful service' after 20 years service. The 3rd, 2nd and 1st Class Medals were granted under normal circumstances for 'specially meritorious service' after 25, 30 & 35 years service respectively. Any of the classes of award could be awarded under exceptional circumstances such as bravery or devotion to duty – irrespective of length of service. The allowances were not pensionable.

Since the aforementioned civil scales of allowances applied to all ethnic groups within the Hong Kong Civil Police Force, equating to those already allowed to the Indian Contingent of the Dockyard Police – so too were similar allowances applied by the Admiralty to European Sergeants and Constables. No reference has been found as to the allowance (if any) given to members of the Dockyard Force senior to Sergeant. The Admiralty wrote to the Commodore, Hong Kong, on 1st November 1923 granting approval for extension of the awards of the Dockyard Police Medal to Europeans 'under similar conditions and allowances to those which govern such awards to the Indian Section.' The initial batch of twelve unnamed medals for Europeans was despatched from the Admiralty on 18 February 1924, stating that arrangements should be made locally for the engraving of the medals.

These awards were granted at the approximate rate of three a year until the Japanese occupation of Hong Kong in 1941, recommencing in 1947 until the Dockyard was finally closed down in 1961. But this is not the end of the story of awards of the Royal Naval Dockyard Police Hong Kong medal – its final chapter is somewhat bizarre !

After closure of the Naval Base at Hong Kong some of the Dockyard Police were transferred to other British Government Departments in Hong Kong, retaining on a reserved rights basis their previous conditions of service – which included the issue of the Dockyard Police Medal after 15 years very good service. At least sixteen men were taken on by MOD(Army) and nineteen by MOD(RAF), the latter relocated in GCHQ on 1st January 1964 for duty at various installations in the Colony consisted of one Chief Inspector, 2 Inspectors and 16 Police Officers.

In December 1967 the MOD(Army) and GCHQ informed the Royal Mint that they had 14 and 9 men respectively – formerly transferred from the Hong Kong Dockyard Police who had completed the qualifying service for award of their former Force's long service medal, and in addition a further six men from their Departments were due to become qualified by 1971. Unknown to both these authorities, the Naval Medal Office at Bath already held 44 Dockyard Police Medals from its previous replenishment of stock minted in 1955 – hence the unnecessary application by MOD(Army) and GCHQ in December 1967 to the Royal Mint to strike 25 medals for their immediate respective uses.

It has yet to be confirmed from The National Maritime Museum, who received an unissued reward (the recipient died before its despatch) – struck in 1968 – from GCHQ, that the old Elizabeth II, 'BRITT OMN' long legend die on a 'Sea Gallantry' sized award (1.27 inches diameter) was used for these 25 medals. Those awards which passed through the hands of the Army Medal Office, Droitwich, between 1968 and 1973 were named on the rim with the recipient's surname and forename(s) – *vide* : medal in author's collection on EIIR Roll awarded to J.W. Bellamy in 1962 with impressed naming.

The Royal Mint records reveal a total striking of 281 Dockyard Police Medals with four different 'Types' of Obverse during the period of issue 1922-1971.

George V.	Coinage Head Large 5/8″ ring	1922-1932
	Coinage Head Smaller 1/2″ ring	1932-1937
George VI.	Coinage Head 'IND.IMP'	1937-1941
		1947-1948
George VI	Coinage Head 'FID.DEF'	1949-1953
Elizabeth II.	'BRITT : OMN : REGINA F : D :'	1953-1973

INCOMPLETE ROLL OF RN DOCKYARD POLICE, HONG KONG, LONG SERVICE MEDALS AWARDED 1922-1961

(No rolls exist for period 1938-1941 inclusive)

Name	Rank	No.	Year	
AHMED, Fateh	Corporal	117	1952	
AHMED, Noor	Corporal	118	1952	
ALAM, Mir	Sergeant	110	1922	*
ALAM, Mir	?	90	1947	
ALI, Hadayat	Const.1	179	1956	
ALI, Mahomed	Constable	144	1929	
ALI, Mohammed	Sub-Inspr	–	1954	
ALLAN, A.B.	Sergeant	5	1923	+
ALLEN, W.	Sergeant	2	1923	
ASHIQ, Mahommed	Sergeant	84	1949	‡
AZIZ, Abdul	Constable	55	1927	
BAKSH, Kharim	Constable	66	1934	
BAQ, Mahomed Shariff	Sergeant	116	1922	*
BELLAMY, E.	A.P.O.1	–	1947	
BHADU, Sher	Sergeant	113	1947	
BUCKINGHAM, W.A.	?	–	1947	
BUX, Nabi	Constable	97	1922	
CHOOKOR	Constable	63	1931	
CHURCHER, N.	Inspector	–	1926	
CHUTUGA	Constable	99	1922	
COTON, W.H.	Superintdt	–	1953	
CURRY, D.	A.P.O.1	–	1952	
DAB, Jhan	Sergeant	99	1952	
DAD, Allah	Sergeant	82	1949	‡
DAD, Mir	Sgt 2nd Cl	211	1954	
DAD, Noor	?	98	1947	
DEEN, Aziz	Constable	136	1925	
DEEN, Charag	Constable	129	1922	
DEEN, Fazal	Constable	58	1922	*
DEEN, Fazal	Constable	91	1922	
DEEN, Fazal	Constable	57	1933	
DEEN, Froz	Constble	141	1937	
DEEN, Hassam	Constable	75	1933	
DEEN, Imam	Lance Sgt	47	1922	
DEEN, Khair	Sub-Inspr	–	1922	*
DEEN, Nawal	Constable	80	1931	
DEMPSTER, H.	A.P.O.1	–	1953	
DICKIN, W.A.	A.P.O.1	–	1952	
DIN, Ahmed	Sergeant	92	1947	
DIN, Karam	Sergeant	102	1947	
DIN, Seraj	Corporal	146	1958	
DITTA, Alla	Constable	138	1931	
DITTA, Alla	Constable	157	1932	
FARLOW, S.R.	A/Sub Inspr	3	1937	

GEORGE, A.	Sergeant	10	1923	+
GHAFOOR, Abdul	?	87	1953	
GORMAN, J.H.	A.P.O.1	–	1947	
GULL, Rahmat	Constable	107	1923	
HASSAN, Ghulam	Sgt 2nd Cl	205	1955	
HUDSON, R.W.	Euro-Sgt	1	1933	
ISMAIL	Const.1	202	1956	
ISMAIL	Const.	203	1958	
KARIM, Abdul	Corporal	187	1956	
KEMP, I.A.	A.P.O.	–	1950	
KHAN, Ahmed	Constable	126	1932	
KHAN, Allah Dad	Constable	94	1922	
KHAN, Abdul Karim	Constable	112	1929	
KHAN, Ali Mahomed	Constable	89	1929	
KHAN, Awal	Constable	126	1932	
KHAN, Blandah	Constable	88	1927	
KHAN, Fazal	Const.1	141	1954	
KHAN, Ghasni	Sergeant	79	1949	‡
KHAN, Gurma	Constable	123	1934	
KHAN, Haider	Lance Sgt	54	1922	
KHAN, Hassim	Constable	62	1927	
KHAN, Ismail	Constable	100	1934	
KHAN, Jaffer	Const.1	135	1954	
KHAN, Lal	Sergeant	85	1949	‡
KHAN, Maher	?	120	1947	
KHAN, Malam	?	109	1947	
KHAN, Mazor	Sergeant	123	1947	
KHAN, Meme	Constable	71	1923	
KHAN, Mozam	?	97	1947	
KHAN, Muzaffer	Sgt 1st Cl	100	1953	
KHAN, Nab Baksh	Constable	150	1930	
KHAN, Natta	Constable	72	1922	
KHAN, Neyat	Constable	134	1925	
KHAN, Nirdi	Constable	101	1923	
KHAN, Niswaz	Sergeant	103	1947	
[Edge 'Sgt Mowaz Khan 103']				
KHAN, Rait	Sgt 1st Cl	181	1954	
KHAN, Rasham	?	88	1947	
KHAN, Saidulli	Const.	245	1960	
KHAN, Sarsa	?	95	1947	
KHAN, Shamroz	Const.1	214	1957	
KHAN, Sharka	Constable	60	1932	
KHAN, Sher	Sgt 2nd Cl	96	1955	
KHAN, Sherwar	Const.1	136	1957	
KHAN, Zabta	Lance Sgt	85	1922	*
KHAN, Zabta	Sergeant	71	1952	
LAMAN, Shere	Constable	135	1936	
LONG, A.G.	?	–	1947	
LURKHU, Sultan	?	89	1947	
MAHAMMED, Ali	Sgt 2nd Cl	104	1957	
MAHOMED, Don	Constable	106	1923	
MAHOMED, Ghulam	Sergeant	43	1922	*
MAHOMED, Ghulam	Lance Sgt	76	1922	
MAHOMED, Gul	Sub-Inspr	–	1949	‡
MAHOMED, Guul	Constable	146	1937	
MAHOMMED, Mian	Sgt 2nd Cl	208	1954	

MANWARING, A.E.	?	–	1947	
MARRIOTT, H.	Sergeant	14	1923	+
MATTHEWS, W.	Sub-Inspr	–	1923	+
McDONALD, J.	A.P.O.1	–	1947	
MEHARDIN	Const.	269	1961	
MOHAMMED, Atta	Corporal	145	1955	
MUSTAFA	Constable	64	1931	
PINNAR	Sergeant	117	1922	*
REHMAN, Abdul	Corporal	132	1955	
SARGUL	Sergeant	137	1929	
SAWAN	Constable	73	1922	
SELUNDER	Constable	98	1932	
SHAR, Mobarik	Const.1	138	1955	
STEPHENS, L.	?	–	1947	
TOWNSEND, J.	Sergeant	11	1923	
WHELAN, J.F.	A.P.O.1	–	1952	

* = First batch of medals awarded in 1922   ‡ = Free replacements
\+ = Europeans who petitioned for the awards

Although the service numbers have been entered from the official Rolls, it may be noted that in a few cases the same number applies to different men. It is suspected that some numbers from retired personnel were reissued to new recruits. Not unusually the spelling of Indian names on medals may well be found to differ from those on the Medal Roll. The medal (G.VI.Fid Def) in this collection is rather crudely engraved 'I.P.C. 92 Ghazni Khan', which does not appear on the Roll but may well feature on the missing Rolls for 1938-1941. The abbreviation is assumed to represent Indian Police Constable, and it should be noted that the medal to Sergeant Abmed Din is known to have survived – also with the number 92 on its edge !

ROLL FOR MEDALS KNOWN TO HAVE BEEN ISSUED 1968-1973 TO RE-EMPLOYED EX-MEMBERS OF HONG KONG DOCKYARD POLICE FORCE

Name	Grade	Date qualified or medal
BELLAMY, J.W. (Medal in author's collection)	Retired	1- 3-1962
CURRY, L.C.	Retired	2- 9-1962
DEVAL, M.V.	Police Officer	13- 9-1964
EVANS, T.G.	Police Inspector	14- 6-1961
FERRY, L.J.	Retired	23- 7-1970
GALLAGHER, J.	Chief Inspector	28-10-1961
GREENSFIELD, G.R.	Retired	15- 7-1961
GREENWOOD, R.P.	Retired	11-1973
JONES, P.R.	Police Inspector	4- 1-1967
KELLEHER, J.J.	Retired	1- 1-1962
O'REILLY, J.	Police Officer	3- 2-1968
PERRIE, P.	Police Officer	27- 5-1964
SLOW, R.	Retired	10- 8-1971

The Board of Trade Rocket Apparatus Volunteer Long Service Medal

This medal was instituted in 1911, but it was not included in the 'Order of Wear' list published by the Central Chancery until October 1922, when the above quoted title was used in its place of precedence.

The pre-history to this award is somewhat complicated, demanding an understanding of the responsibilities accepted by the Admiralty when it took over the Coastguard Service in 1856 – obligations which hardly altered until 1923 when control of this Service was passed to the Board of Trade, who reorganized it into a Coast Watching Service (with its old Coastguard title) and the Coast Preventive Corps.

The first official reference connecting the Coastguard with life-saving duties appear in Coastguard Instructions dated 1841, when this force was administered by the Board of Customs, but manned almost exclusively by men drawn from active service in the Royal Navy.

'It is the duty of the officers and crews of Cruisers and Coastguard Stations to render all possible assistance to vessels in distress; and in cases of shipwreck, to use their utmost endeavours to save the lives of the persons on board, and to save and protect from plunder and embezzlement the rigging, sails, stores and cargo.'

Under the 'Coastguard Act,1856' (19/20 Vict, Ch. 83) control of the Coastguard was transferred from the Board of Customs to the Admiralty in order to make better provision for : (1) Defence of the Coasts of the Realm. (2) The more ready manning of Her Majesty's Navy in case of War or in Emergency (3) The protection of the Revenue. The Act made no reference whatsoever to 'Life-Saving', nor did the Admiralty show signs of accepting such a function during subsequent decades. Basically, from 1856 onwards, the Admiralty looked upon their Coastguard Service solely as a naval and gunnery trained source of reservists, a continuing attitude well exampled in Article 654 of the Admiralty Coastguard Instructions of 1911 in this manner : –

'It is to be noted that the Admiralty does not accept responsibility for any inadequacy of the system of life-saving arrangements that may exist in any portion of the coasts of the United Kingdom, but at places where Coastguardsmen are stationed, such Coastguardsmen are to render every possible assistance to the local life-saving services, as far as is compatible with their proper duties.'

There were however a number of private life-saving corps in existence well before 1856, which companies, under the provisions of the 'Merchant Shipping Act, 1854', were taken over by the Board of Trade who provided further Life-Saving Apparatus Companies all round the coast. To be fully effective these volunteer life-savers needed the assistance of the Admiralty's Coastguard, and thus problems of efficiency and provisions of equipment came about under such dual control.

The invention of a device to deliver a line between shore and a vessel in distress dates back to the year 1791, followed by other innovative but crude systems. It was not until 1857 that the Board of Trade sanctioned the general use of the 'Boxer' rocket life saving apparatus which remained in use for eighty years.

In 1865 a precedent was set when the Tynemouth Volunteer Life Brigade was formed, followed by a number of other Brigades in subsequent years – all officially sanctioned by the Board of Trade and Admiralty. Instruction, drills and training of these Rocket Life-Saving Apparatus Companies and Brigades were henceforth carried out by teams of naval uniformed coastguardsmen and civilian volunteer life-saving personnel.

INITIATION OF THE ROCKET APPARATUS VOLUNTEER LONG SERVICE MEDAL

The Tynemouth Volunteer Life Brigade at their annual meeting held on 4 April 1906, expressed the hope that the Board of Trade would see their way to grant long service medals to men who had been members of the Brigade for twenty years. The proposal was not entertained at that time due to the expense (a rather normal response !), but also for the curious reason that they would detract from the value of 'gallantry' medals – the Albert Medal and the new Sea Gallantry Medal in its smaller wearable form.

Five years later the Board of Trade responded more positively to Tynemouth's earlier suggestion – receiving Treasury approval in March 1911. On 1st June 1911 Lord Knollys conveyed the King's approval to the President of the Board of Trade for this new long service medal to be instituted. Nine days later '.. the King approved of his effigy and royal legend being reproduced on the obverse of the new medal for long service with the Volunteer Life Saving (Rocket Apparatus) Service ..' The reverse of this award was to possess the circumferential legend of 'Presented by the Board of Trade', with its face struck with the words 'To .. [space for recipient's forename(s) & surname] .. For Long Service With The Rocket Life Saving Apparatus' [*Vide* : Plate No. 18]. The general public were informed of the introduction of this new award by articles in newspapers commencing 21 June 1911. The statistics for the Rocket Apparatus Corps at that time were impressive : 9,407 lives had been saved since 1870 and there were currently 4,400 enrolled volunteers in 251 companies and 6 brigades, of whom 950 had served in excess of 20 years each.

Printed instructions regarding the institution of the award to enrolled volunteers were made known to members by Board of Trade Marine Department Circular 1507, Life Saving Apparatus No 10, issued in August 1911. The rules stated that : 'To entitle a man to a medal – he must have served at least 20 years, been of uniformly good character and prompt and regular in rendering service when called out on wreck duty and at quarterly drills, and be recommended.' It was suggested that after receipt of the medal it should '.. desirably be presented at the next quarterly drill – inviting some local personages to be present – or in other cases a local lady to present them.'

In 1922 a Government Committee on National Expenditure reported that of the 419 Coastguard Stations remaining – 288 were no longer required by the Navy for their own purposes, thus calling into doubt the continuing need of Admiralty responsibility for the Coastguard Service – especially since its reservist function had been more effectively met from RFR and RNVR resources since 1903. On 1st April 1923 control of the Coastguard Service passed to the Board of Trade who set up an organisation based on the recommendations of the Government Committee's Report. A Coast Preventive Force was formed to supplement the Waterguard staff, and a Coast Watching Force was instituted '.. to perform duties in connection with the saving of life, the salvage of wreck ... and other miscellaneous duties' – retaining by Royal sanction the title of His Majesty's Coastguard. This fundamental change of control had no effect on the issue or form of the Rocket Apparatus Long Service medal, which had always been under the patronage of the Board of Trade.

In 1932 the 'Coast Watching Service' (H.M. Coastguard) was reorganised and renamed the 'Coast Life Saving Corps' (H.M. Coastguard), consisting of the former volunteers in the Rocket Apparatus Corps under their new title of 'Life Saving Appliance' (LSA) men – with two additional groups, 'Auxiliary Watchers' and an 'Intelligence Section'.

During November 1933 the Board of Trade proposed that the Long Service Award should be extended to the new 'Auxiliary Watcher' class of the Coast Life Saving Corps, recently created in 1932. The point was made that a 'Watcher' gave a great deal more of his time to the Life Saving Service than the 'Rocket Apparatus' (LSA) man, and that in most cases an enrolled 'Watcher' was also an enrolled 'Life Saving Appliance' (LSA) man at the smaller Auxiliary Stations – and therefore it was logical that the 'Watcher' had similar entitlement to the existing Long Service Medal after 20 years. In 1933 there were 4,712 LSA men, 476 LSA/Watchers and 226 pure Watchers, with 120 Rocket Apparatus Long Service Medals awarded annually. The extension of the award to the 'Watcher' class was estimated to entail – ultimately – the issue of an extra 25 medals each year. The other small class of the Coast Life Saving Corps – the Intelligence Section – was excluded from eligibility for the medal.

Only in August 1934, when preparations were being made to widen the scope of the old 'Rocket Apparatus Volunteer Long Service Medal', was it realised that the the original award had not been instituted in 1911 – as it should have been – by a Royal Warrant ! One contributor to this debate put forward what he thought was a precedent, pointing out that since the Sea Gallantry Medal (SGM) instituted in 1855 did not have a Royal Warrant (RW), then why now was it necessary for a lesser reward ? Although correct in part of his argument (no RW), he failed to mention that the SGM originated from an Act of Parliament – 'The Merchant Shipping Act,1854' – the only Gallantry Medal ever to be so democratically instituted.

At this time the Board of Trade also sought approval to change the inscription on the medal to 'Long and Meritorious Service ..'. The Admiralty were consulted, who pointed out that only three meritorious awards had been awarded by them in the past year. The Board of Trade agreed that they had '.. used the word meritorious in a much easier sense ..' – and retracted their proposition. In theory from this time the Long Service awards should no longer have been made to 'Rocket Apparatus Life Saving' men – as stated in the original legend on the medal – but to LSA men within the 'Coast Life Saving Corps'. Whilst this academic point did not prevail, the requirement did not cease to exist because it could not be met at this time – more than twenty years were to pass before the title on the medal's reverse was altered to : 'For Long Service in the Coast Life Saving Corps'.

The Treasury approved the extension of the award to the 'Watcher Class' in November 1934, recognising that it would be many years before any 'Watcher' became eligible for the reward. The matter was raised again in September 1938, apparently without decision. The file (BT 166/4) in the Public Record Office suggests that it was raised again in 1948/49 – and decisions made on a separate set of papers – not yet lodged at the PRO.

In 1942 the Ministry of Transport took over the responsibilities formerly invested with the Board of Trade for the Coast Watching Service, with an immediate alteration to the circumferential legend on the reverse of the long service award. This legend was now to read 'Rocket Apparatus Volunteer Medal', (RAVM) with the words on its face reduced to 'Presented to [space for recipient's forename(s) and surname] For Long Service' [*Vide* : Plate No. 18].

The rules for issue of the RAVM were abrogated by Royal Warrant dated 27 January 1954 which established the introduction of the 'Coast Life Saving Corps Long Service Medal' (CLSCLSM) [*Vide* : Plate No. 18]. Whilst efforts to sight this Royal Warrant have so far proved unsuccessful, one relevant historical piece of tantalising information has been found in part of an official publication under the heading – 'Coastguard Auxiliary Service Medal' : –

'In 1954 Her Majesty the Queen deemed it expedient that Watchers should be eligible for the medal, and that the conditions for the award of the Medal should be regularised and amended, in the light of present days circumstances, and incorporated in a warrant'.

The award of the CLSCLSM was superceded by Royal Warrant dated 6 July 1966 which established the introduction of the 'Coastguard Auxiliary Service Long Service Medal'(CASLSM) – with minor amendments to its rules and ordinances made by Royal Warrant dated 10 April 1968 (which also has yet to be found). Although the question of a 'Bar' to the Long Service Medal for additional service beyond the twenty years was first raised in 1925, it seems its belated introduction may have come about from an amendment to the Royal Warrant dated 10 April 1968, by which a bar or bars to 'Coastguard Auxiliary

Service Medal' or any earlier form of medal was initiated – for each additional fifteen years served beyond the twenty years to gain the medal originally. Was this – however – the first introduction of 'bars' (clasps) ?

The Royal Warrant dated 11 November 1985 annulled and cancelled all former rules and ordinances for the award of the CASLSM, substituting in their place almost similar regulations. The major change concerned the award of the second bar, which was now to be awarded for a further ten years service – not fifteen years as required under the earlier regulations – thus reducing the time from 50 to 45 years to gain a second bar.

Under the 1986 Rules, members of the Coastguard Auxiliary Service in the Rescue or Lookout Sections, or in both, were eligible to be recommended for the Long Service medal after completing a total of 20 years satisfactory service. Life Saving Apparatus men or 'Watchers', or in both capacities, could count their time in the Coast Life Saving Corps towards the reward. Those even older members (inclusive of Rocket Appartus men and Watchers) who had served in a Volunteer Life Saving Apparatus Company, Brigade, or at a Coastguard or Auxiliary Coastguard Station prior to 1932, could also count that time towards the Long Service Medal – it would appear most likely that this concession was first introduced in the (as yet unseen) Royal Warrant dated 27 January 1954.

To ease this somewhat complicated story, the following synopsis of the types of award to Rocket Apparatus men (& others) might prove useful, inclusive of named medals held in author's collection : –

Medals in the Collection

Circumferential Legend & words on the face of 'Reverse'

'Presented by the Board of Trade'   1911 – 1942
To .... For Long Service with the Rocket Life Saving Apparatus'

GV. (Coinage)	ROBERT WILLIAM McDONALD
GVI. (Ind Imp)	CHARLES WILLIAM RUSSELL

'Rocket Apparatus Volunteer Medal'   1942 – 1954
'Presented to .... For Long Service'

GVI. (Ind Imp)	JAMES A. CRISP
GVI. (Fid Def)	(possibly not issued 1949-1953)

'The Coast Life Saving Corps'   1954 – 1966
'Presented to .... For Long Service'

EIIR. (Brit Omn)	(probably not issued 1953-1954)
EIIR. (Dei Gratia)	JOHN PARRY and bar 'LONG SERVICE'
EIIR. (Dei Gratia)	ALFRED WOOLSTON

'The Coastguard Auxiliary Service'   1966 –
'Presented to .... For Long Service'

EIIR. (Dei Gratia)	THOMAS HUNTER STORRY

The Coast Guard (Coastguard) Service, since it was formed in 1822, has been administered with its differing responsibilities successively by : –

Board of Customs	1822-1856
Admiralty	1856-1923
Board of Trade	1923-1939
Ministry of Shipping	1939-1940
Admiralty	1940-1945
Ministry of (War) Transport	1945-1964
Department of Trade	1964-1984
Department of Transport	1984 to date

Titles of Naval Rates and their Status Applicable 1830-1847

The following list encompasses most of the titles of 'Rates' which will be found engraved on the reverse of Anchor Type LS & GC medals (1830-1847) – recording an encyclopaedic range of 'Rates' officially in force during 1847. A few titles found on men's service papers – on the date they were awarded the medal – do not feature in this list, such as Chief Boatswain's Mate, Boatswain's Yeoman, Gunner's Yeoman and Armourer's Mate. Although there was not at this time a separate group of ratings later nominated as 'Domestics', it is probable that certain men in the accompanying list were ineligible for the LS & GC medal annotated 'Uncl*'.

Rates in order of seniority

1. PO1CL = Working Petty Officer 1st Class (Superior P.O. = S.P.O. on papers)

2. PO2CL = Working Petty Officer 2nd Class (Inferior P.O. = I.P.O. on papers)

3. Uncl = Remainder of Ship's Company

4. Uncl* = Rates probably ineligible for award of LS & GC medal

Able Seaman	Uncl	Coxswain of Pinnace	PO2CL
Acting Cook RN	PO1CL	Flag Officer's Cook	Uncl
Acting 2nd Master RN	PO1CL	Flag Officer's Domestic	Uncl
Admiral's Coxswain	PO1CL	Flag Officer's Steward	Uncl
Armourer	PO2CL	Gunner's Crew	Uncl
Blacksmith	PO1CL	Gunner's Mate	PO1CL
Captain of Afterguard	PO2CL	Gun Room Cook	Uncl*
Captain of Forecastle	PO1CL	Gun Room Steward	Uncl*
Captain of Fore Top	PO1CL	Leading Stoker	PO1CL
Captain of Hold	PO1CL	Master at Arms	PO1CL
Captain of Main Top	PO1CL	Musician	PO2CL
Captain of Mast	PO2CL	Painter	Uncl
Captain of Mizzen Top	PO2CL	Paymaster & Purser's	PO2CL
Captain's Cook	Uncl	Steward (from 1844)	
Captain's Steward	Uncl	Purser's Steward (until 1844)	PO2CL
Captain's Coxswain	PO1CL	Quarter Master	PO1CL
Carpenter's Crew	Uncl	Ropemaker	PO1CL
Carpenter's Mate	PO1CL	Sailmaker	PO1CL
Caulker	PO1CL	Sailmaker's Crew	Uncl
Caulker's Mate	PO2CL	Sailmaker's Mate	PO2CL
Cooper	PO2CL	Seaman's Schoolmaster	PO1CL
Cooper's Crew	Uncl	Ship's Cook	PO1CL
Coxswain of Launch	PO1CL	Ship's Corporal	PO1CL

Sick Berth Attendant	Uncl	Yeoman of Signals	PO2CL
Stoker & Coal Trimmer	Uncl	Yeoman of Store Rooms	Uncl
Subordinate Officer's Cook	Uncl*	Young Gentleman's Cook	Uncl*
Subordinate Officer's Steward	Uncl*	Young Gentleman's Steward	Uncl*
Ward Room Cook	Uncl	(earlier title for Subordinate Officer)	
Ward Room Steward	Uncl		

APPLICABLE 1847-1875

The following list encompasses most of the titles and groups of 'Rates' which will be found engraved on the edge of Victorian Wide Suspension LS & GC medals (1847-1875) – recording an encyclopaedic range of 'Rates' officially in force during 1875. It should be noticed that the status of Chief Petty Officer (CPO) and Leading Seaman/Stoker were introduced during this period, but the title of CPO was rarely used in preference to the man's 'Rate' (e.g. Admiral's Coxswain). Additional sub-specialist suffixes of 'G.I.' (Gunnery Instructor), 'S.G.' (Seaman Gunner), 'T.M.' (Trained Man) or 'Rigger' may occasionally be found engraved on a recipient's award.

There was however one generically titled group – 'Domestics' – to which this broad statement did not apply. In 1875 only Domestics of the First Class were eligible to be considered for award of the LS & GC medal – an exclusive Class limited only to Admiral's Steward, Cook & Domestic as well as Captain's & Ward Room Cook and Steward. This privilege was not extended generally to Domestics 2nd and 3rd Class until the beginning of the 20th century.

Rates in order of Seniority.

1. CPO = Chief Petty Officer

2. PO1Cl = Petty Officer 1st Class

3. PO2Cl = Petty Officer 2nd Class

4. S & S = Seamen & Stokers

5. Art = Artificers who are not P.Os

6. D1Cl = Domestics 1st Class

(*Vide* : additional list for D2 & 3CL)

7. Uncl = Remainder of the Ship's Company

Able Seaman	S & S	Captain of Main Top	PO1Cl
(& A.B. Cadet's Servant)		Captain of Mast	PO2Cl
Admiral's Cook	D1Cl	Captain of Mizzen Top	PO2CL
Admiral's Coxswain	CPO	(Title introduced circa 1870)	
Admiral's Domestic	D1Cl	Captain's Cook	D1CL
Admiral's Steward	D1Cl	(Ship Classes 1st-4th)	
Armourer	PO1Cl	Captain's Coxswain	PO1Cl
Armourer's Crew	Art	Captain's Steward	D1CL
Assistant Sick Berth Attendant	Uncl	(Ship Classes 1st-4th)	
Bandmaster	PO1Cl	Carpenter's Crew	Art
Bandsman	Uncl	Carpenter's Mate	PO1Cl
Barber	Uncl	Caulker	PO1Cl
Blacksmith	PO1Cl	Caulker's Mate	PO2Cl
Blacksmith's Crew	Art	Chief Bandmaster	CPO
Boatswain's Mate	PO1Cl	Chief Boatswain's Mate	CPO
Butcher	Uncl	Chief Captain of Forecastle	CPO
Captain of Afterguard	PO1Cl	Chief Carpenter's Mate	CPO
(by 1870 Quarter Deck Men)		Chief Gunner's Mate	CPO
Captain of Forecastle	PO1Cl	Chief Quartermaster	CPO
Captain of Foretop	PO1Cl	Chief Stoker	CPO
Captain of Hold	PO1Cl	(Title introduced circa 1873)	

Chief Yeoman of Signals	CPO	Seaman's Schoolmaster	CPO
Cook's Mate	Uncl	(title abolished circa 1863)	
Cooper	PO2Cl	2nd Captain of Afterguard	PO2Cl
Cooper's Crew	Art	(by 1870 Quarter Deck Men)	
Coxswain of Barge	PO2Cl	2nd Captain of Forecastle	PO2Cl
Coxswain of Cutter	PO2Cl	2nd Captain of Foretop	PO2Cl
Coxswain of Launch	PO1Cl	2nd Captain of Hold	S & S
Coxswain of Pinnace	PO2Cl	2nd Captain of Maintop	PO2Cl
Domestic (*Vide* : other D1CLs)	D1CL	2nd Captain of Mizzen Top	PO2Cl
Engine Room Artificer	CPO	(Title abolished circa 1870)	
Gunner's Mate	PO1Cl	2nd Head Krooman	Uncl
Head Krooman	PO2Cl	Ship's Cook	CPO
Krooman	Uncl	Ship's Corporal 1st-2nd Class	PO1Cl
Lamptrimmer	Uncl	Ship's Steward 1st-3rd Class	CPO
Leading Seaman	S & S	(& Steward for General Mess)	
Leading Stoker	PO1Cl	(& Cabin Steward)	
Master At Arms	CPO	Ship's Steward's Assistant	Uncl
Musician	PO2Cl	Shipwright	Art
Naval Schoolmaster	CPO	Shoemaker	Uncl
(title introduced circa 1863)		Sick Berth Attendant	PO2Cl
Painter 1st Class	PO1Cl	Sick Berth Steward	PO1Cl
Painter 2nd Class	PO2Cl	Signalman	PO2Cl
Paymaster and Purser's	PO2CL	Stoker & Coal Trimmer	S & S
Steward (Title abolished 1852)		Tailor	Uncl
Plumber	PO1Cl	Tinsmith	Art
Plumber's Crew	Art	Ward Room Cook	D1Cl
Plumber's Mate	PO2Cl	(Ship Classes 1st-2nd)	
Quartermaster	PO1Cl	Ward Room Steward	D1Cl
Ropemaker	PO1Cl	(Ship Classes 1st-2nd)	
Sailmaker	PO1Cl	Writer 1st, 2nd, & 3rd Class	CPO
Sailmaker's Crew	Art	Yeoman of Signals	PO1Cl
Sailmaker's Mate	PO2Cl	Yeoman of Store Room	S & S

Domestics 2nd and 3rd Class in 1875, & 1888

* Ineligible for LS & GC

Captain's Cook *	D2Cl	Gun Room Steward	D2Cl
(Ships below 4th Class)		Secretary's Servant	D2Cl
Captain's Cook's Assistant	D3Cl	Ward Room Cook *	D2Cl
Captain's Servant	D2Cl	(Ships below 2nd Class)	
Captain's Steward *	D2Cl	Ward Room Steward *	D2Cl
(Ships below 4th Class)		(Ships below 2nd Class)	
Commander's Servant	D2Cl	Ward Room Cook's Assistant	D3Cl
Engineer's Cook	D2Cl	Ward Room Officer's Servant	D3Cl
Engineer's Servant	D2Cl	Ward Room Servant	D3Cl
Gun Room Cook	D2Cl	Warrant Officer's Cook	D2Cl
Gun Room Servant	D3Cl	Warrant Officer's Servant	D3Cl

COAST GUARD PERSONNEL

(Eligible for LSGC from March 1873)

Boatman	A.B.	Chief Boatman in Charge	CPO
Commissioned Boatman	PO2CL	Divisional Carpenter	PO1CL
Chief Boatman	PO1CL		

APPLICABLE 1875 – 1900

The following list encompasses most of the titles and groups of 'Rates' entitled to receive the LS & GC medal at the turn of the century. However, during the time the Victorian Narrow Suspension LS & GC medal was awarded (1875-1902) many of the older titles in the previous list (1847-1875) were used on the edge of that award.

Although the substantive rate of Chief Petty Officer was introduced in 1853 as the highest attainable by lower-deck men, it was not used as a title to describe particular grades of men (in official 'Wages Table – Ship's Company') until 1890. Its regular introduction from that year (or earlier) hid each man's duty such as Admiral's Coxswain and all the senior seamen Captains of Tops etc. Similarly the titles of Petty Officers 1st and 2nd Class found frequently on LS & GC medals during this period (1875-1902) also hid their former descriptive 'Rates' such as Quarter Master or Yeoman of Signals etc.

In a few cases additional details to the man's name, rate and ship may be found on the edge of the long service medal. The suffix of 'Pensioner' is known for men not receiving their reward until they became pensioners. Certain sub-specialist qualifications may appear as suffixes, e.g. 'S.G.' = Seaman Gunner, 'S.G.T.' = Seaman Gunner & Torpedo Man, 'T.M.' = Trained Man, 'G.I.' = Gunnery Instructor, 'T.I.' = Torpedo Instructor, 'Diver' or 'Rigger' (Royal Yachts). The title of Ship's Steward may be qualified by additions of (say) '.. for General Mess' or '.. for Cadet's Mess'. The word 'Skilled' may appear for some tradesmen either as a prefix or suffix.

Able Seaman
Armourer
Armourer's Crew
Armourer's Mate
Assistant Sick Berth Attendant
Bandmaster
Band Corporal
Bandsman
Blacksmith
Blacksmith's Crew
Blacksmith's Mate
Butcher
Carpenter's Crew
Carpenter's Mate
Caulker
Caulker's Mate
Chief Armourer
Chief Bandmaster
Chief Carpenter's Mate
Chief Cook
Chief Engine Room Artificer

Chief E.R.A. 2nd Cl
Chief Petty Officer (Seaman Class)
Chief Sick Berth Steward
Chief Stoker
Chief Torpedo Artificer
Chief Writer
Chief Yeoman of Signals
Cook's Mate
Cook's Mate 2nd Cl
Cooper
Cooper 2nd Cl
Cooper's Crew
Domestic 1st Class
Engine Room Artificer
E.R.A. 2nd – 3rd Cl
Head Krooman
2nd Head Krooman
Krooman
Lamp Trimmer
Leading Carpenter's Crew
Leading Seaman

Leading Shipwright
Leading Signalman
Leading Stoker 1st Cl
Leading Stoker 2nd Cl
Leading Torpedo Man
Lithographer
Master at Arms
Musician
Naval Schoolmaster
Painter 1st Cl
Painter 2nd Cl
Petty Officer 1st Cl
Petty Officer 2nd Cl
Plumber
Plumber's Crew
Plumber's Mate
Qualified Signalman
Ropemaker
Sailmaker
Sailmaker's Crew
Sailmaker's Mate
Seedie

Ship's Cook
Ship's Cook 2nd Cl
Ship's Corporal 1st Cl
Ship's Corporal 2nd Cl
Ship's Steward
Ship's Steward's Assistant
Shipwright
Shoemaker
Sick Berth Attendant
Sick Berth Steward
Sick Berth Steward 2nd Cl
Signalman
Stoker
Tailor
Tindal (senior Seedie)
2nd Tindal
Torpedo Artificer
Writer 1st Cl
Writer 2nd Cl
Yeoman of Signals
Yeoman of Signals 2nd Cl
Yeoman of Store Rooms

Official Numbering Systems

ROYAL NAVAL (RN) RATINGS

In general, prior to the year 1853, all ratings of the Royal Navy were casually employed – 'signed on' – for one Commission at a time in an H.M. Ship of their choice, when the country was not at war. An exception occurred in 1832 when 'seamen gunners' were offered renewable 5 or 7 year engagements – unaccompanied by any special numbering system. During 1853, 'Continuous Service Engagements' were introduced by the Admiralty whereby men could 'sign on' for initial and renewable periods of time, which if chosen allowed the rating to complete the number of years service entitling him to a pension. Thus, for the first time, a secure career was open to most men in or wishing to join the Service – and of equal importance, a 'Standing Navy' was created. After 13 June 1853 most of the ratings already in the service and those joining the navy had the option (it was not compulsory) to 'sign on' – when such volunteers were allocated a 'number' – referred to as the man's 'Continuous Service Number' (C.S.No.).

Not every category of rating was allowed to 'sign on' for continuous service. By Circular No 121 dated 14 June 1853, men henceforth (until 1873) with the following (daymen) 'rates' were deemed ineligible to 'sign on' ; Seaman's Schoolmaster, Ship's Cook, Sick-Berth Attendant, Servants, Musicians, Bandmen, Butchers, Barbers, Tailors, Ship's Steward's Assistant, Cook's Mate, Kroomen and Ship's Steward's Boy – some of these types of men were soon to be recategorised under the generic title of 'Domestic' – a group referred to previously in greater detail under the Section 'Naval Rates'.

There were to be three consecutive sets of Continuous Service Numbers : –

(a) Commencing 1853. Numbers 1 to 40,000

(b) Commencing 1859. Numbers 1A to 40,000A

(c) Commencing 1867. Numbers 1B to 21,800B

Care is needed when researching to ensure that due note is taken of these 'suffixes', especially in certain indexes where men appear to be given a plain number but the column heading shows that it refers to numbers with either suffix 'A' or 'B'. A few men are known to have received up to four differing numbers – viz : Quarter Master H.C. Bond with C.S.Nos 4,953, 32,009.A, 14,480.B, and ultimately 'Official Number' (O.No.) 66,695, whose Victorian Narrow Suspension LS & GC medal with years service on its edge is in the author's Collection.

An essential point to remember about this C.S. number is the fact that there was no relationship whatsoever between it and a man's age or his length of service – at the time the 'number' was allocated. A 'boy seaman' joining the navy aged 14 years could be given a C.S. Number with its last digit just one below (or above) that given to an 'old salt', opting at that same time to become a 'continuous service' man when aged 35 years (say) with 17 years adult servitude. A fair number of eligible ratings, already in the navy, saw little advantage in 'signing on' during the early years of continuous service engagements – but the happier experience of others rubbed off on these less adventuress men who then 'signed on' with resultantly high C.S. numbers.

From 1st January 1873 all members of every branch of the Royal Navy who were already in the service – including those formerly disqualified from becoming C.S. men – were allocated an 'Official Number' (O.No.), and subsequently applied to every type of new entrant to the Service. This official numbering system has operated to the present day, albeit with ever increasing complexity, such as the allocation of a block set of numbers or differing prefix and/or suffix letters to denote a man's branch, his specialist duty, his type of entry, his Home Port or geographical area, differing pay scales or length of service in the RN, RNR, RFR, RNVR or RNASBR etc.

To avoid possible administrative confusion, the Admiralty decided that the 'Official Numbers' (O.Nos) should commence from 40,001, thus exceeding any number allocated previously to Continuous Service men. These O.Nos (1873 – 1907) had neither prefix nor suffix letters. Sequential numbers were given to ratings irrespective of their branch – seaman, stoker, artificer or domestic etc – up to O.No 178,000 – prior to introduction of block number allocations for differing branches of ratings in January 1894. At the time of writing this work, only those service records of men with numbers up to O.No 165,000 have been lodged at the Public Record Office, Kew – i.e. research has only been possible for those who joined the Royal Navy prior to 1892, of whom a fair number served during World War One.

Sometimes a man's service career sheet in the ADM 188/- Series ends with the notation 'New Register' – prior to completion of his time in the navy. This does not mean that the man was given a new number, merely that the remaining part of his career was recorded in a small series of 'Continuation Registers' – applicable to relevant men within the boundaries of O.Nos 42,922 to 86,600, whose latter periods of servitude can be gleaned from ADM 188/83-90.

The pieces 1 – 4 within the 'Official Number' ADM 188/- Series refer to the names of men allocated 'Continuous Service' numbers 1-40,000, 1-40,000A and 1-21,800B.

Commencing 1st January 1894 the official numbering (O.No) system for all ratings entering the Service became more sub-specialised. A series of block allocations of numbers were introduced for six differing classes of ratings as shewn in the Table below. Since, by 1907, the overlapping of numbers was seen to be imminent within a 'block system' of proved convenience, a simpler but similar new system was introduced involving the use of four different prefix letters to denote branches, or groups of branches. The revised scheme, applicable to new entrants from 1st January 1908, was promulgated by Admiralty Circular Letter No.82 dated 2 July 1907.

Branches	January 1894 to 31 December 1907 No Prefix (Entrants/Yr)		From 1 January 1908 to 25 October 1925 With prefix
Seamen & Communication ratings	178,001 to 240,500	(4,400/yr)	J. No 1 to115,433
Engine-Room Artificers	268,001 to 273,000	(360/yr)	M. No 1 to 39,555
Stoker ratings	276,001 to 313,000	(2,600/yr)	K. No 1 to 66,973
Artisan & miscellaneous	340,001 to 348,000	(570/yr)	M. No 1 to 39,555
Sick Berth Staff & Ship's Police	350,001 to 352,000	(140/yr)	M. No 1 to 39,555
Officer's Stewards & Officer's Cooks & Boy Servants	353,001 to 366,450	(930/yr)	L. No 1 to 15,101

Although no service records for any rating with a number exceeding O.No. 165,000 have yet been lodged for public scrutiny at the Public Record Office – i.e. for those personnel joining the service after 1892 – it is however possible to gauge roughly when a seaman (with a O.No. exceeding 165,000) entered the navy if the assumption is used that 4,400 seaman recruits joined each year. One must remain mindful that the majority of such entrants joined as 'Boys' aged 15 years, who could not begin to count their time towards a medal or pension until they were 18 years old. A similar pro-rata system can be calculated for the other branches by use of the average annual intake of recruits between 1894 and 1908 mentioned in the former Table.

The miscellany of Branches in the navy with the prefix 'M' post 1908 included : – Engine Room and Electrical Artificers, Armourers, Carpenters, Blacksmiths, Coopers, Painters, Plumbers, Ropemakers, Sailmakers, Shipwrights, Wiremen, Sick Berth Ratings (including Auxiliary Sick Berth Reserve, i.e. Senior and Junior Reserve Attendants), Ships' Police (i.e. Master at Arms and Ships' Corporals), Naval Schoolmasters, Writers, Ships' Cooks & Stewards, Musicians, Bakers, Butchers, Lamptrimmers, Shoemakers & Tailors.

Official Numbers with branch designating prefix letters J,K,L & M were issued to new entrants from 1st January 1908, throughout the period of WW1, until a revised pay code was introduced for new entrant naval ratings and marines in September 1925. This led to a revision of the official numbering system because the Admiralty wished to distinguish all new recruits entering under the new pay code – from those on the old pay scales. All new entrants and re-entrants joining on and after 25 October 1925 were to be allocated the following prefixes with the old continuing numbers – but with a gap of as yet unissued numbers : –

Seamen	J.X. commencing 125,001 & onwards
Stokers	K.X. commencing 75,001 & onwards
Officer's Stewards and Officer's Cooks	L.X. commencing 20,001 & onwards
Miscellaneous	M.X. commencing 45,001 & onwards

At the time of this change from the old official numbers – with single letter prefixes – they had reached the following levels : –

J.115,433	K.66,973	L.15,101	M.39,555

The breaks in the series of numbers for each of these groups (from J. to J.X. etc) were created to leave space for the allocation of new official numbers to old scale ratings transferred from Special Service to Continuous Service, or transfer of a rating from an old – single letter – class to another. Judicious extrapolation of the numbers entered into each of the Classes with single letter J,K,L & M prefixes between 1908 and 1925, should allow a researcher to gauge roughly the year of entry from a man's Official Number – with due allowance for the unique entries of Seamen and Artificer Apprentices who could be recruited below the age of 18 years.

Just as the addition of the letter 'X' to the initial class letters for active service ratings was to denote men who were eligible only for the revised rates of pay introduced in September 1925 (unaltered since 1919), so too was this letter 'X' applied to Short Service 'Royal Fleet Reserve' men (*Vide* : RFR part of this 'Official Numbering Systems' Section).

In 1931 the Admiralty introduced lowered pay scales (AFO 2239/1931) during the national recession when the cost of living was falling – in the belief that this would be acceptable and equitable treatment. It led directly to the historic tragedy termed the 'Invergordon Mutiny'. The consequences of three subsequent Admiralty enquiries led to amelioration of the hardships inflicted on certain ratings, especially some young married men and many ratings then at the point of re-engaging – all still in receipt of 1919 rates of pay with O.Nos. lacking the prefix of 'X'. These men were placed on 1925 rates of pay and had the prefix 'X' added to their their Official Numbers. Others already in possession of this prefix – under similar beneficial rules – did not have their pay reduced from the 1925 level (AFOs 2410/1931 and 2796/1931).

PORT DIVISION AND WELFARE AUTHORITY PREFIX LETTERS. At this point in the chronological allocation of prefix letters and numerals which constituted the man's 'Official Number', it is necessary to go back in time to examine the background to the next change – that of the additional prefix denoting the man's 'Port Division' (known today as his 'Welfare Authority') being combined with his former service style of identification eventually forming part of his 'Official Number'.

In 1894, the Admiralty directed that all men entered from shore, and boys on completing their course of instruction, were to be appropriated to one of the three manning ports, namely Portsmouth, Devonport or Chatham according to the locality in which they may have been recruited. All ratings were to belong to their designated 'Port Division' during the whole of their service, unless specially allowed to transfer to another Division. For administrative reasons the name of this 'Home Port' was henceforth to be noted not only on the first page of the man's parchment certificate in the space provided for the name of the ship on first entry into the Service – but also noted against the man's name in each succeeding Ship's Ledger. The symbols to be used were : –

P. or C. or D.   written immediately over (above) the rating's official number. These letters representing Home Port Divisions of Portsmouth, Chatham and Devonport respectively.

F.   Additional prefix for Fleet Air Arm Ratings introduced on 1st July 1914.

Although these 'Port Division' symbols were intended to form part of each man's official identification, they did not become a universally intimate part of the rating's 'Official Number' until September 1933 – when instructions contained in an amendment to King's Regulations & Admiralty Instructions (KR & AI), Article 1729, Clause 2 stated that : –

' Whenever the official number of a man or boy is quoted, his Port Division is also to be noted in the manner laid down in Article 1705, Clause 2' – which still required the 'Port Division' letter to be noted immediately over (above) the number.

However, within a few months, a revised edition of KR & AI issued in 1934 amended these former instructions in Article 1705, Clause 2 stating that : –

' Port Division. The port division of every man is to be noted against his name, immediately before [not 'over' or 'above'] his official number, and is always to be quoted as part of his official number. ...'.

At the same period in September 1933 two additional 'Port Division' letters were introduced : – 'E' for Maltese ratings 'G' for Goanese ratings. The prefix letter 'G' was amplified as referring to men entered through H.M. Naval Office, Colombo, to serve as native stewards and cooks on the East Indies Station. At some unknown period the letters 'R' for Boom Defence and 'Lt' for RN Patrol Service had been introduced.

For reasons unknown, the use of the additional Port Division symbols (C/ , D/ , P/ .) were not registered in the LS & GC medal roll against each recipient's name prior to 11 April 1939. During the ensuing years some mistakes were made by naval administrators with regards to the proper method of identifying naval ratings, culminating in an admonition on the subject in 1943 (AFO 259/43) when the Admiralty directed : –

' Attention [is required] to the necessity of quoting the Port Division Symbol of rating's official numbers on all documents, as the growing practice of omitting the Port prefix letter is leading to serious inconvenience and delay.'

Commencing on 1st April 1943 a new numbering system was introduced. Prior to this date men from differing branches could possess the same number, with different branch prefix letter(s). There was now to be a common sequential numbering system applicable to all entries into the R.N. commencing with No. 500,000, emulating the original system of Official Numbers which pervaded from 1873 until 1894 – when 'block numbers' for Branches were introduced. A rating was now – post 1943 – to retain his 'number' even if he changed his branch, only his prefix letter(s) changed. When this O.No 500,000 series was introduced the prefix letters J.,K.,L.,M. and F. for normal engagements and SS, SK, SL, SM, SF for Special Service engagements were retained. The 'X' prefix was discontinued for new entries after 1st April 1953 – whose numbers then commenced from 925,000 upwards.

Thus, from January 1908 until April 1953 the following rating class prefix letters were in use for the ratings then serving in the navy : –

J. or J.X.	Seamen and Communication ratings	Active Service
S.S. 1-100,000	as above	Special Service
S.S.X. 12,051+	as above	Special Service
K. or K.X.	Stokers/Engineering Mechanics	Active Service
S.S.100,001+ or	as above	Special Service
S.S.X 126,001+	as above	Special Service
S.K. or S.K.X.	as above	Special Service
L. or L.X.	Officer's Cooks, Officer's Stewards	Active Service
S.L. or S.L.X.	Officer's Cooks	Special Service
	(ex Officer's Cooks (O))	
F. or F.X.	Fleet Air Arm Ratings	Active Service
S.F. or S.F.X.	as above	Special Service
M. or M.X.	Miscellaneous	Active Service
	(E.R.A.s & all other ratings)	
S.M. or S.M.X.	as above	Special Service

The advent of computerised records had its effect upon the next mode of allocating Official Numbers. When the old series of official numbers became exhausted, the next system for new entries was invariably to be a six digit number (commencing 000001) prefaced by three capital letters without spaces or oblique strokes.

The three preface letters were to signify codes for Port Division, Type of Engagement and Branch. The Port Division codes remained practically identical with the former prefixes; P = Portsmouth, D = Devonport, C = Chatham, L = Lee on Solent (FAA), E= Malta, G = Trincomalee. The Engagement codes were to be; C = Continuous Service, S = Special Service, N = National Service, T = Non Continuous or Temporary Service and 'H' held in abeyance for 'Hostilities Only' ratings in time of war. The Branch Codes were to be; A = All Artificers (including Apprentices), B = Sick Berth, C = Cooks (O) & (S), D = Coders, E = Electrical Branch, J = Seaman, Signalman, Telegraphist and Sailmaker, K = Engineering Mechanic and Mechanician, N = Naval Airman and Aircraft Mechanician, Q = Stores (v) and (S), R = Regulating, V= Steward, W = Writer and Z = Artisans. These proposals were promulgated in May 1955 (AFO 1293/1955).

When Centralized Drafting was introduced on 1st April 1957 to supersede individual Port drafting offices, the no longer needed 'Port Division' prefix letters were retained to indicate the rating's 'Selected Depot'.

On 1st April 1959 a new and simplified series was introduced – common to all entries into the service – with the Official Number commencing with the number 050,001 (upwards to 999,999) and prefaced by a single letter to indicate the rating's 'Welfare Authority' (new name for 'Selected Depot').

ROYAL FLEET RESERVE (RFR).

All the former mentioned allocations of letters and numbers within the official numbering system refer to men joining the Royal Navy on the normal engagement term of ten or twelve years active service, to commence from their eighteenth birthday (seaman boy entrants inclusive), with the option later of re-engaging to complete time for pension after 22 years service (increased from 20 years in 1885).

However, in 1903, a new type of engagement was introduced whereby men (seamen and stokers) could enter the Royal Navy on a special 'Short Service' (SS) engagement of either seven or five years in the Royal Navy with the obligation to join the Royal Fleet Reserve (RFR) for 5 or 7 years respectively (*Vide* : Section on 'RFR LS & GC Medal'). The new numbered series for these Short Service men commenced on 1st July 1903 : –

S.S. 1 onwards to 100,000 for Seamen.   S.S.100,001 onwards for Stokers.

There were four classes of men in the RFR, each with a differing prefix :–

Class 'A'   Men in receipt of a life pension from the Royal Navy

Class 'B'   Men who have served in R.N. not in receipt of a pension

Class 'C'   Artisan ratings who have passed through the Dockyards as boy apprentices for the Royal Navy

Class 'IC'   Immediate Class. Men similar to those in Class B, who could be called up for service without a Royal Proclamation.

All Classes of these men were given the initial prefix of their Port Division, Ch (Chatham), Po (Portsmouth) or Dev (Devonport), followed by their Class letter, A, B, C or IC, with each group commencing with the number 1 (one) and the suffix RFR. All members of the Fleet Reserve also retained their RN active service number, which in official reference was to precede their RFR number –

e.g.   John Smith A.B. 200,000 Po.A 236 RFR

(or)   David Brown A.B. J.104,153 Ch.B 19,332 RFR

In 1925, when new pay scales were introduced into the RN and RFR, a revised numbering system was introduced for the wider range of RFR new entrants – embracing the RN policy of allocating prefix letters to denote differing 'Branches' : –

SSX No 12,051 onwards for Seamen   SFX No 1 onwards for Fleet Air Arm

SSX No 126,001 onwards for Stokers   SLX No 1 onwards for Stewards

SMX No 1 onwards for Artificers, Artisans, Cooks etc

It appears possible that in 1925 the prefix SKX commencing from No 1 was introduced for Stokers in lieu of the continuing SSX prefix 126,001+.

ROYAL NAVAL RESERVE (RNR).

Research into the date of introduction of their numbering system and the annual numbers entered into each branch of this Reserve has not been pursued. Nevertheless the following suffix/prefix letters to the mens' official numbers covering the early 20th century period and World War One might prove useful.

Royal Naval Reserve (Ordinary) (Suffix letters)

Ratings in this section are assigned a fresh number on each occasion of commencing a fresh term of enrolment in the Reserve; this number being followed by the distinguishing letter coupled with R.N.R.

A. B. C. D.	Seamen ratings in their 1st – 4th term of enrolment
S. T. U. V.	Stoker ratings in their 1st – 4th term of enrolment
E.A.	Engine room artificers in their 1st term of enrolment
E.B.	Engine room artificers in their 2nd term of enrolment
E.C.	Engine room artificers in their 3rd term of enrolment
M.C.	Mine Clearance Service. Not confined solely to R.N.R.
W.T.S.	Wireless Operators

Royal Naval Reserve (Trawler Section)

D.A.	Deck Hands	S.D. Deck Hands originally in special trawler section – by 1919 amalgamated in D.A.
E.S.	Enginemen	
S.A.	Second Hands	
S.B.	Boys	
S.B.C.	Boy cooks	
T.S.	Trimmers	S.T. Trimmers originally in special trawler section – by 1919 amalgamated in T.S.

Royal Naval Reserve (Trawler Reserve Emergency Section) Fishery Reservists

B.E.	Boys		S.E.	Second Hands
C.E.	Trimmer-Cooks		T.E.	Trimmers
D.E.	Deck Hands		W.S.E.	Skippers
E.X.	Enginemen			

Royal Naval Reserve (Miscellaneous)

A.S.   Ratings in the Australasian section of the R.N.R.

F.   Ratings in Malta section of the R.N.R.

L.   Ratings in the Shetland section of the R.N.R.

M.M.R.   Mercantile Marine ratings engaged under T.124 or kindred agreements.

ROYAL NAVAL VOLUNTEER RESERVE (RNVR).

Prefix letters utilised during World War One

A.A. 1 onwards   Anti-Aircraft Corps (seaman ratings)

B. 1/1 onwards   Bristol Companies 1 to 4. Men entered in the Bristol Division prior to 4 September 1914

B.Z. 1 onwards   Men entered in the Bristol, Birmingham and Leicester Divisions since 31 August 1914

C. 1/1 onwards   Clyde Companies 1 to 6. Men entered in the Clyde Division prior to 5 September 1914

C.Z. 1 onwards   Men entered in the Clyde Division since 7 September 1914

E. 1 onwards   Birmingham Electrical Volunteers. Men specially employed as Wiremen in VERNON, ACTAEON, DEFIANCE. The earlier members of this force were assigned numbers in the London Division of the R.N.V.R. – i.e. L.Z. prefix.

K.P. 1 onwards   Men entered at the Crystal Palace from Kitchener's Army

K.W. 1 onwards   Men entered in 1st Brigade R.N.D. from Kitchener's Army

K.X. 1 onwards   Men entered in 2nd Brigade R.N.D. from Kitchener's Army

L. 1/1 onwards   London Companies 1 to 10. Men entered in the London Division prior to 31 August 1914

L.Z. 1 onwards   Men entered in the London Division since 31 August 1914, also men entered for Magnetophone Mine Stations, Pigeon Service and the earlier members of the Birmingham Electrical Volunteers

M. 1/1 onwards   Mersey Companies 1 to 7. Men entered in the Mersey Division prior to 31 August 1914

M.B. 1 onwards   Motor Boat Section (Motor Mechanics, Motor Boatmen etc).(Includes men recruited in Canada and New Zealand)

M.C. 1 onwards   Mine Clearance Service. Not confined solely to R.N.V.R.

M.Z. 1 onwards   Men entered in the Mersey Division since 5 September 1914

P.Z. 1 – 3,000	Men entered at the Crystal Palace from civil life (followed by entrants prefixed ZP. 1 and onwards)
PZ. 3,001 onwards	Men discharged from the Royal Navy and enrolled in the R.N.V.R. for Special Service ('PRESIDENT III'). A man's service history may appear under either his original active service or R.N.V.R. number – depending on whether the rating returned to the Fleet or not.
R. 1 onwards	Men entered from Army to R.N.D. since May 1916
S. 1/1 onwards	Sussex Companies 1 to 6. Men entered in the Sussex Division
6/1 onwards	prior to 4 September 1914
SZ. 1 onwards	Men entered in the Sussex Division since 4 September 1914
South Africa	South African Royal Naval Volunteer Reserve
A./1 : B./1 onwards	Companies A, B, C etc
T. 1/1 onwards	Tyneside Companies 1 to 6. Men entered in the Tyneside Division prior to 7 September 1914
T.Z. 1 onwards	Men entered in the Tyneside Division since 7 September 1914, and men entered for the Hydrophone service
V.R. 1 onwards	Royal Naval Canadian Volunteer Reserve (all ratings)
W.Z. 1 onwards	Wales Division of R.N.V.R. opened 11 January 1915
Y. 1 onwards	Men enrolled under the deferred scheme for the R.N. and R.N. (Air Service). When called up they signed active service engagements and given active service official numbers.
Z.P. 1 onwards	Men entered at the Crystal Palace from civil life after entrants numbered P.Z. 1-3,000
Z.W. 1 onwards	Men entered in 1st Brigade R.N.D. from civil life
Z.X. 1 onwards	Men entered in 2nd Brigade R.N.D. from civil life

Miscellaneous Forces

A.N.F. 1 onwards	Men entered in Australasia for service in the Imperial Navy.(Not to be confused with prefix R.A.N.)
N.Z. 1 onwards	Men entered by the Colonial Authorities for service in the New Zealand Navy
N.Z.E.F.J.	Irregular Naval Unit. New Zealand Emergency Force – Seamen Class
N.Z.E.F.K.	Irregular Naval Unit. New Zealand Emergency Force – Stoker Class
N.Z.E.F.L.	Irregular Naval Unit. New Zealand Emergency Force – Branches other than seamen or stokers

R.A.N. 1 onwards	Men entered by the Commonwealth authorities for service in the Royal Australian Navy
R.C.N. 1 onwards	Men entered by the Dominion authorities for service in the Royal Canadian Navy
V.J.	Irregular Naval Unit. Hong Kong Special Reserve – Seamen Class
V.K.	Irregular Naval Unit. Hong Kong Special Reserve – Stoker Class

Additional Prefix/Suffix letters used during World War One

F.R. 1 onwards	Fishermen entered for service in commissioned fishing vessels. The men were engaged to serve under Naval discipline, but are paid fishery wages by the owners, and only receive a nominal rate of pay from the Admiralty. Entered under F.124 agreements.
F.1 and onwards	Commencing on 1st July 1914 a new Series was commenced for the Royal Naval Air Service. All men entered into or permanently transferred to that new Service, including skilled and unskilled ratings remaining under Admiralty control (but excluding those R.N. ratings & Marines lent)
M.C. 1 onwards	Mine Clearance Service during World War One. Entrants from shore, R.N., R.N.V.R. and R.N.R. and M.M.R (Mercantile Marine Reserve). Former official numbers retained.
C.M.B. 1 onwards	Coastal Motor Boat Forces. It appears to have been used for men from R.N., R.N.V.R. & R.N.R.

ROYAL MARINES

The general practice of allocating marines individual numbers was officially introduced on 1st July 1885, when the Admiralty directed '.. that every person belonging to the Royal Marines, except Commissioned Officers, shall be described by a Register Number in conjunction with letters indicating the Divisions to which he belongs, instead of his Company and Division as heretofore ..', and that the suffixes 'RMA' and 'RMLI' '.. should be used whenever sufficient from a legal point of view ..'.

Concurrently in earlier years, individual Divisions had begun to allocate register numbers; Chatham in 1842, Portsmouth in 1843, Plymouth in 1856, the Royal Marine Artillery in 1859 and the Depot, Royal Marines Deal in 1866. The official institution of register numbers in 1885 was probably necessary to overcome the administrative muddle which had resulted, at a time when major changes were also taking place concerning seaman's terms of service.

From 1st July 1885 the prefix 'Letters' indicating the Division to which a rank belonged and the suffix 'Letters' denoting his branch of the Corps of Royal Marines were to be as follows : –

CH	Chatham Division Royal Marines Light Infantry	RMLI
PO	Portsmouth Division Royal Marines Light Infantry	RMLI
PLY	Plymouth Division Royal Marines Light Infantry	RMLI
RMA	Royal Marine Artillery	RMA

The registers introduced in 1885 can be found in the ADM 159/- Series at the Public Record Office, but regretfully they are not accompanied by an alphabetical index and thus only of immediate use if the marine's register number is known.

The earliest and latest dates of entry of marines and span of their 'Register Numbers' within the ADM 159/- Series available for public viewing at the P.R.O. are : –

Chatham	1842 – 1905	Nos 1 – 14,872
Plymouth	1856 – 1902	Nos 1 – 11,464
Portsmouth	1843 – 1901	Nos 1 – 11,366
R.M.A.	1859 – 1901	Nos 1 – 9,435

A 'N' or 'S' suffix to any one of the numbers with above quoted prefix letters, CH, PO, PLY or RMA referred to a man who entered any one of these four Divisions for Short Service during World War One.

The prefix 'D' or 'DEPOT' followed by a number of up to three figures, indicates a rank entered on the permanent establishment of the Depot, Royal Marines Deal, between 1866 and February 1947 – when this practice was discontinued, with the ranks transferred to Chatham, Plymouth or Portsmouth and allocated each Division's next available register number.

The prefix 'D' followed by a number of up to four figures with suffix 'N' or 'S' – each from number 1 upwards – indicates a rank entered in the Royal Marines Divisional Engineers, the Royal Marines Divisional Train, the Royal Marines Medical Unit, the Royal Marines Ordnance Company or the Royal Marines Labour Corps for Short Service during World War One.

The prefix 'RME' followed by a number of three or four figures and the suffix 'S' indicates a rank of the Royal Marine Engineers entered for short service during World War One.

On 22 June 1923 the Royal Marine Artillery and the Royal Marines Light Infantry were amalgamated to become a single corps styled 'Royal Marines'. The separate corps titles of R.M.L.I. and R.M.A. were abolished and R.M. introduced in lieu. The Divisional prefix letters of CH, PO, PLY and D or DEPOT were retained. All members of the R.M.A. prior to their amalgamation were placed in one of the three main Port Divisions – all had had five figure R.M.A. official numbers, which were retained on transfer but turned into six figure numbers by the addition of '2' at the beginning to turn their numbers into six figures – with their new Divisions' prefix of CH, PO or PLY. Thus, for example, RMA 33,059 John Smith R.M.A. became PO or CH or PLY 233,059 John Smith R.M.

OTHER PREFIXES

RMB	A man who entered the Royal Naval School of Music between its foundation in 1903 and before October 1925, with numbers up to four figures.
CH/X, PO/X, PLY/X, D/X. CH/RMP/X, PLY/RMP/X, PO/RMP/X each from 1 onwards	From 5 October 1925 all men enlisted and re-entered (with less than 5 years break in service) were allocated former Divisional prefix letters but each with an 'X' added. By the time this system was superseded in 1948, onwards all Divisional sequences (excluding Royal Marine Police) had reached four figure numbers.
RMBX commencing from No 3,400 onwards	Date and entrants as above, but continuing the old numbers after a gap – i.e. not commencing as above with the figure '1'. This system was superseded in August 1955.
EX	Special Reservists entered at Exton Division between October 1939 and July 1940. The men later with 3 or 4 figures transferred to Chatham, Portsmouth or Plymouth Divisions and reallocated numbers as shewn immediately above.
CH/X, PO/X, PLY/X, RMB/X	These prefixes followed by six figures commencing from 100,000 onwards were allocated to men joining for short service during World War 2.
RME	This prefix followed by five figures indicates a rank of Royal Marine Engineers of World War 2
RM	This prefix followed by four or five figures was adopted in 1948, superseding the prefixes CH/X, PO/X, and PLY/X. Allocated without any Divisional prefix letters to all men entering on a Continuous or Short Service engagement between January 1948 and January 1973.
RM	This prefix followed by six figures indicates a National Service man entered between January 1948 and June 1952.
RMV with 5 figures	Commencing in 1952 this prefix was introduced to indicate whether a Reservist was a National Service-man or not. It applied to men becoming Reservists prior to the establishment of National Service, or after his National Service.
RM(V)9	This prefix followed by a five figure number indicates that a man was a Reservist during whole-time National Service.
RMV9	This prefix followed by a five figure number indicates that a man was a Reservist during part-time National Service.

On 1st July 1955, all but one of these prefixes, 'RMV', were abolished, and all Reservists, whether serving on or before that date, were allocated a new number with the 'RMV' prefix – with six figure numbers commencing 200,000.

Printed in the United Kingdom
by Lightning Source UK Ltd.
121663UK00001B/14/A